# THE UNITED NATIONS SERIES

ROBERT J. KERNER, GENERAL EDITOR

SATHER PROFESSOR OF HISTORY IN THE
UNIVERSITY OF CALIFORNIA

❖

## CZECHOSLOVAKIA
EDITED BY ROBERT J. KERNER

## THE NETHERLANDS
EDITED BY BARTHOLOMEW LANDHEER

## POLAND
EDITED BY BERNADOTTE E. SCHMITT

## BELGIUM
EDITED BY JAN-ALBERT GORIS

## CHINA
EDITED BY HARLEY FARNSWORTH MacNAIR

## NEW ZEALAND
EDITED BY HORACE BELSHAW

## BRAZIL
EDITED BY LAWRENCE F. HILL

## AUSTRALIA
EDITED BY C. HARTLEY GRATTAN

## YUGOSLAVIA
EDITED BY ROBERT J. KERNER

❖

*Other volumes in preparation*

# YUGOSLAVIA

# YUGOSLAVIA

*Chapters by* Griffith Taylor, Carleton S. Coon, Robert
J. Kerner, Bernadotte E. Schmitt, John Clinton
Adams, Malbone W. Graham, Joseph S. Roucek,
D. Beatrice McCown, Jozo Tomasevich, Alex N.
Dragnich, Severin K. Turosienski, Matthew Spinka,
Wayne S. Vucinich, George Rapall Noyes,
Harry N. Howard

## EDITED BY ROBERT J. KERNER

SATHER PROFESSOR OF HISTORY IN THE UNIVERSITY OF CALIFORNIA

UNIVERSITY OF CALIFORNIA PRESS
BERKELEY AND LOS ANGELES · 1949

TO

NICHOLAS MIRKOVIĆ

AND TO MANY OTHERS LIKE HIM
WHO GAVE UP THEIR LIVES
THAT THE YUGOSLAV PEOPLE
MIGHT BE FREE

# The United Nations Series

THE UNITED NATIONS SERIES *is dedicated to the task of mutual understanding among the Allies of the Second World War and to the achievement of successful coöperation in the peace. The University of California offered the first volumes of this series as a part of its contribution to the war effort of this state and nation and of the nations united in the greatest conflict known to history; it offers the later volumes, of which this is one, to the peace effort; and it heartily thanks the editors of the respective volumes and their collaborators for their devoted service and for their efforts to present an honest, sincere, and objective appraisal of the United Nations.*

ROBERT J. KERNER
*General Editor*

# Editor's Preface

DR. NICHOLAS MIRKOVIĆ, *after initiating this volume for the Series, volunteered in the struggle for the liberation of the Yugoslavs, and on May 2, 1944, was killed by a low-flying Nazi airplane. He was a young and energetic Yugoslav intellectual with a Western orientation who dreamed of a free and progressive Yugoslavia. To him and to many others like him this volume has been dedicated.*

*Having written three of the chapters for the volume, it became my task to obtain other contributions and to edit it from the beginning to the end. The difficulties of preparing a volume on the Yugoslav people as unique as this one have been almost insurmountable. The background of the Yugoslavs, both physical and historical, is probably more complex than that of any nation in Europe. In addition, since the beginning of the Second World War a complete change of rule has occurred from Bourgeois to Communist.*

*The contributors to the volume have labored to produce a publication which endeavors to tell the many-sided and involved story of this brave people with the scrupulous care for accuracy, impartiality, and understanding expected of responsible scholars. They have achieved a result in line with the lofty objectives of the United Nations Series, which it is hoped will outlast the passions and the whims of the day. For it must not be forgotten that governments may come and governments may go, but nations remain forever.*

*July 14, 1948*                                    ROBERT J. KERNER

# Contents

---

## PART ONE: LAND AND PEOPLE

Professor of Geography, University of Toronto, since 1935; Physiographer, Commonwealth Weather Service, 1910; Senior Geologist, Scott's last expedition, 1910; leader of parties in the Antarctic, 1911–1912; Honorary Lecturer in Meteorology, Commonwealth Flying School, 1914–1918; Lecturer in Physiography, Melbourne University, 1917–1918; Associate Professor of Geography, University of Sydney, 1920–1928; Livingstone Lecturer, Sydney, 1928; Acting Commonwealth Geologist, Canberra; Professor of Geography, University of Chicago, 1929–1935; Messenger Lecturer, Cornell University, 1944; Foundation member, Australian National Research Council, 1919; President, Geography Section, British Association for the Advancement of Science, 1938; President, Association of American Geographers, 1941; awarded King's Polar Medal, 1913; D.Sc. Medal, University of Sydney, 1916; Thomson Gold Medal, Brisbane, 1920; Syme Medal, Melbourne University, 1920; medals of Royal Geographical Society and American Geographic Society; Fellow of the Royal Society of Canada, and of the Royal Geographical Society; co-editor, *Zeitschrift für Rassenkunde; Economic Geography;* co-author of *New South Wales* (1912); author of *Australia in Its Physiographic and Economic Aspects* (1911; 4th ed., 1925); *With Scott: The Silver Lining* (1916); *Australian Environment* (1918); *Australian Meteorology* (1920); *Antarctic Physiography* (1922); *Environment and Race* (1927; Japanese edition, 1931; Chinese edition, 1938); *Antarctic Adventure and Research* (1930); *Australia . . . A Geography Reader* (1931); *Australian Climatology* (1932); *Atlas of Environment and Race* (1933); *Environment and Nation* (1936); *Environment, Race, and Migration* (1937, 1945); *Australia: A Study of Warm Environments and Their Effect on British Settlement* (3d ed., 1945); *Newfoundland* (1946); *Our Evolving Civilization* (1947); *Canada: A University Geography* (1947); *Urban Geography* (1947).

## PART TWO: HISTORICAL BACKGROUND

# Contents

# PART THREE: POLITICAL DEVELOPMENT

Professor of Political Science, University of California at Los Angeles; Faculty Research Lecturer, 1933; lecturer, N. W. Harris Institute, University of Chicago, 1935, 1945; Albert Shaw Lecturer in American Diplomacy, Johns Hopkins University, 1946; member, European Conference of American Professors of International Law and Relations, 1926; member of numerous American learned societies; commander, Order of Gediminas of Lithuania; awarded Vigesimal Medal of Finland, 1939; editor, *International Problems of the Americas* (1928); co-author of *Czechoslovakia* (1940, 1945); *Poland* (1945); author of *The Controversy between the United States and the Allied Governments Respecting Neutral Rights and Commerce . . . 1914–1917* (1923); *New Governments of Central Europe* (1924); *New Governments of Eastern Europe* (1927); *The Soviet Security System* (1929); *The League of Nations and the Recognition of States* (1933); *In Quest of a Law of Recognition* (1933); *The Soviet Union and Peace* (1935); *The Diplomatic Recognition of the Border States* (1935–1941): *Finland* (Part I), *Estonia* (Part II), *Latvia* (Part III); *American Diplomacy in the International Community* (1948); and of numerous articles in learned journals.

Chairman, Department of Political Science and Sociology, Hofstra College, New York; Penfield Fellow, New York University; knight, Star of Rumania, and Order of the Crown of Yugoslavia; editor, *Contemporary Europe* (1941); *A Challenge to Peacemakers* (1944); *Central-Eastern Europe, Crucible of World Wars* (1946); *Twentieth Century Political Thought* (1946); co-editor, *World Affairs Interpreter; New Europe; Introduction to Politics* (1941); co-editor and co-author of *One America . . . Our Racial and National Minorities* (1945); editor and co-author of *Sociological Foundations of Education* (1942); co-author of *Contemporary World Politics* (1939); *Czechoslo-*

*vakia* (1940, 1945); *Poland* (1945); author of *The Working of the Minorities System under the League of Nations* (Prague, 1928); *Contemporary Roumania and Her Problems: A Study in Modern Nationalism* (1932); *The Politics of the Balkans* (1939); and of numerous articles in learned journals.

## PART FOUR: ECONOMIC CONDITIONS

## PART FIVE: SOCIAL CONDITIONS

By ALEX N. DRAGNICH, Ph.D.

Cultural Attaché, Department of State, Washington, D. C., since September, 1947; Assistant Professor of Political Science, Western Reserve University, 1945–1947; A.B., University of Washington, 1938; M.A., University of California, 1939, Ph.D., 1945; Political Analyst, Foreign Agents, Registration Section, Department of Justice, 1942–1944; Research Analyst, Office of Strategic Services, 1944–1945; author of "Eastern Europe: Balkans, Czechoslovakia, Poland, Germany," in *A Foreign Policy for the United States* (1947); and contributor to encyclopedias and learned periodicals.

By SEVERIN K. TUROSIENSKI, M. Philol.

Deceased December 22, 1944; Specialist in Comparative Education, United States Office of Education, 1928–1944; M. Philol., Slavonic Languages, Imperial University, Kharkov, Russia; diploma, postgraduate work in Polish Comparative Philology, Jagiellonian University of Cracow, Poland; Instructor in Comparative Philology, Slavonic Languages, University of Kharkov, 1909–1915; Librarian, University of Kharkov, 1911–1915; officer, Imperial Russian Red Cross, 1915–1918; awarded highest civil honor of Latvia, Order of Three Stars, 1939; commander, Order of St. Sava, Third Class, of Yugoslavia, 1941; author of *Education in Czechoslovakia* (1936); *Poland's Institutions of Higher Education* (1937); *Education in Yugoslavia* (1939); *Education in Cuba* (1943).

By MATTHEW SPINKA, B.D., Ph.D., Th.D. (Prague)

Professor of Church History, Hartford Theological Seminary, since 1943; Associate Professor of Church History, Chicago Theological Seminary and Divinity School of the University of Chicago, 1938–1943; President, American Society of Church History, 1946; co-editor, *Environmental Factors in the History of Christianity* (1939); editor, *Church History* and *Studies in Church History* (monographs, both published by the American Society of Church History); *A History of Illinois Congregational and Christian Churches* (1944); translator of

# Contents

*Chronicle of John Malalas* (1940); *Bequest of the Unity* (1940), and *The Labyrinth of the World and the Paradise of the Heart* (1942), both by Johann Amos Comenius; co-author of *A Bibliographical Guide to the History of Christianity* (1931); *Czechoslovakia* (1940); *A Short History of Christianity* (1940); author of *The Church and the Russian Revolution* (1927); *A History of Christianity in the Balkans* (1933); *Christianity Confronts Communism* (1936, 1938); *John Hus and the Czech Reform* (1941); *John Amos Comenius, That Incomparable Moravian* (1943); and of numerous articles.

CHAPTER XV

By WAYNE S. VUCINICH, Ph.D.

Assistant Professor of History, Stanford University, since 1947; Research Analyst, Coördinator of Information, 1941–1943; Research Analyst, Office of Strategic Services, 1943–1945; attached, as liaison officer and Balkan specialist, to American Contingent, Allied Control Commission, Sofia, 1944–1945; Research Analyst, Division of Research for Europe, Department of State, 1945–1946; author of "American-Serbian Relations in 1903–1904," in *Slavia*, August, 1940; "The Yugoslav Revolutionary Movement," *ibid.*, August, 1941; "Modern Yugoslav Drama," in *American Slavic Review*, May, 1946; "Bulgaria, Consolidation of the Fatherland Front," in *Current History*, November and December, 1947; and a number of other articles.

## PART SIX: CULTURAL DEVELOPMENT

CHAPTER XVI

By GEORGE RAPALL NOYES, Ph.D., Litt.D., LL.D.

Professor of Slavic Languages, Emeritus, University of California; member, School of Slavonic and East European Studies, University of London; foreign corresponding member, Polish Academy of Sciences, Cracow; corresponding member, Slavic Institute of Prague; fellow, American Academy of Arts and Sciences; on board of directors, Polish Institute of Arts and Sciences in America; commander, Order of Polonia Restituta; awarded Golden Laurel of Polish Academy of Literature; American contributing editor, *Slavonic (and East European) Review* (London); editor, *The Poetical Works of John Dryden* (1909); *Selected Dramas of John Dryden* (1910); co-editor (with George R. Potter), *Hymns Attributed to John Dryden* (1937); co-translator or editor of translations of *Heroic Ballads of Servia* (1913); *Poems by Jan Kochanowieski* (1928); *Masterpieces of the*

# Contents

# List of Illustrations

Southeastern Europe

Administrative Divisions of Yugoslavia, 1947

## Part One

### LAND AND PEOPLE

# CHAPTER I

# *The Geographical Scene*

## BY GRIFFITH TAYLOR

THE YUGOSLAV NATION, like most European nations, is primarily the creation of its environment. Not only the present population pattern but also the characteristic culture of the nation are mainly determined by geographical structure. It will therefore be profitable to examine the structure of the regions traversed by the Slav peoples in their migrations southward from the basin of the Vistula to the valleys of the Sava, Morava, and Vardar, and to the Dinaric and Rhodope Mountains.

*Geologic structure.*—The geological formations of Europe may be divided into two basic types: one is "original" Europe (*Ur-Europa*), which forms the widespread plains of Russia; this stable "shield" has altered little throughout the four hundred fifty million years of the later geological record. The other section is "peninsular" Europe, which has been the scene of mountain building, or earth folding, at comparatively regular intervals throughout the earth's history.

About three hundred million years ago a gigantic buckling of the earth produced the Caledonian folds across Britain and Norway. These folds were gradually worn down to low relic stumps. About one hundred fifty million years ago a second period of earth buckling occurred; this produced the Armorican folds, which extended from Spain through Brittany (Armorica) across the

The Library of Congress system of transliteration for Serbo-Croatian has been used throughout this volume, with a number of modifications, especially in regard to words already in common use. The spelling "Yugoslavia" is used officially in English-speaking countries instead of "Jugoslavija."

Ardennes, through Bohemia, and eastward to the Dobrudja and the Crimea. The Armorican folds, in turn, were worn down to relic stumps.

In the Tertiary period, especially in the last fifteen million years, the two parallel ranges which constitute the Alpine folds of southern Europe began to rise. The northern series of these ranges includes the Swiss Alps and is called the Alpides. It extends from

MAIN STRUCTURAL AREAS IN THE BALKANS

| Country | Name of structure | Locality |
|---------|-------------------|----------|
| Yugoslavia.. | Karst limestone mountains........ | Croatia, Bosnia, etc. |
| | Drin basin folds............................ | Montenegro, Albania |
| | Southern Alföld plain.................. | Slavonia, the Banat, etc. (the Vojvodina) |
| | Morava-Vardar corridor.............. | Old Serbia, Macedonia |
| | Eastern Serb Alpides................... | Old Serbia, in east |
| Greece........... | Pindus folds................................. | Epirus, etc. |
| | Morean folds............................... | Peloponnesos |
| | Salonika plain.............................. | Salonika |
| | Rhodope relic............................... | Northeastern coast of Greece |
| Bulgaria....... | Russian shield............................. | Lower Danube plain |
| | Balkan folds................................ | Western and central Bulgaria |
| | Rhodope relic............................... | Southern Bulgaria |

Gibraltar to the Carpathians and Balkans and into Asia. The southern series is called the Dinarides; it extends from Gibraltar through Algeria to Italy, along the Dinarics of Yugoslavia, and into Asia by way of Greece.

Yugoslavia consists essentially of a section of the Dinarides folds in the west and a section of the Alpides folds in the east. Between lies the stable median mass (a resistant, flat block of the crust between folded portions of the crust) of Hungary in the north and of Thrace in the south. These stable areas sometimes appear as plains, as in Hungary, or plateau-like elevations, as in southeastern Serbia. In northeastern Serbia, at the Timok River, the Yugoslav territory barely reaches the prolongation of the Russian shield which underlies the plains of Rumania.

*General topography.*—The major folding which produced the Dinaric Mountains dates presumably from middle Tertiary times, say fifteen million years ago. The last phase of continental evolution was particularly striking in the Balkans. Yugoslavia, in general, was probably much less elevated at first, so that large lakes and inlets of the sea covered the central Morava-Vardar corridor in Pliocene times. This phase suggests that much of the country had been under water. As a consequence, the streams in these calm waters laid down heavy deposits of gravel, sand, and mud which became of great agricultural value in later periods.

The Dinaric folds and the Rhodope mass stood above the lakes in this period. Now began a stage of minor mountain building which was accompanied by frequent cracking of the crust in faults. Much of the Aegean area sank beneath the sea at this time, with volcanic action, as at Santorin Island (Thera). Undoubtedly, the Yugoslav region was soon appreciably elevated. This helped to drain all the lakes, principally into the newly formed depression of the Aegean Sea. The Vardar probably captured some rivers which previously had not belonged to its system. Thus, also, the Maritsa* in Bulgaria acquired large tributaries which formerly reached the Black Sea by independent routes.

The topography within the Dinaric folds is rather unusual. The hills are almost wholly of limestone (either Cretaceous or Triassic), which is readily soluble in water. Hence the surface rocks are honeycombed with hollows and caves. The water gradually dissolves underground passages, the caves tend to fall in, and more limestone is dissolved. Thus oval or elongated hollows are now frequent. Small hollows are known as *doline;* large ones, *polja.* The less soluble part of the rock is left as a deposit of red soil (*terra rossa*) which forms a layer on the floor of the *polje* and is fairly fertile. Elsewhere, much of the surface soil of the steeper slopes has been swept away, exposing the forbidding, gray rocky ridges common in the Dinaric Mountains. The waters deposited in *polja* often drain along caves through the mountain ridges to the west and reach the sea as short surface streams. The latter, however, are not characteristic of Karst topography.

On the inner, eastern slopes of the Dinaric folds are belts of

---

* Bulgarian spelling, Marica; Greek, Evros.

younger Tertiary rocks. These may consist of Eocene shales, called Flysch. They are not permeable like the limestone, and therefore they tend to retain the surface water. On the lower slopes of the Morava corridor and adjacent valleys are thick deposits of silts which were laid down in the Aegean lakes. Thousands of years have elapsed since the uplift which helped to drain the lakes. During this period modern rivers have removed most of the lake deposits and have piled up their own flood silts at lower levels. Farm lands in the hilly regions of Serbia are usually on the upper lake deposits or the lower river silts. Somewhat similar layers of Triassic and Cretaceous rocks occur in northeastern Serbia, but the central and southeastern parts are formed of the older schists and altered rocks of the ancient relic mass.

The plains of northern Yugoslavia are part of the great fold depressions enclosed in the Carpathian arc of the Alpides. This is probably another relic mass, but it is buried under hundreds of feet of alluvial deposited by the Danube and its tributaries. This area was the ancient Pannonian Sea; its floor, built of recent layers of river silts, now bears the grainfields of the Alföld in Hungary and those of Slavonia and other regions of Yugoslavia.

*Topographic control and early migrations.*—A complete picture of the relation between the environment and the evolution of the South Slav peoples should include a discussion of their migrations south from their cradleland in the Vistula basin and the adjacent Carpathians. The difference between the "young" mountains (say, ten million years old) and the relic masses (say, one hundred fifty million years old) is clearly indicated. In the latter (see page 3) the flat plateaus were often occupied by large communities, especially in troubled times. This is particularly true of the southern Carpathian relics, where the Rumanian culture has been preserved in spite of the many invasions of the lands below. The Rhodope and the Bohemian relics have served in a somewhat similar way as refuges at various times.

The young mountains are very different. In essence they are like huge, oval "blisters" in the earth's crust, in which the upper portion has been eroded by rain, rivers, and ice. Thus the cores of young mountains are nearly always composed of much older, harder, and more rugged rocks than are the flanks. The young mountains have formed greater barriers to human migration; this feature obviously enhances the historic importance of the corridors (or gates) which cross them.

It is generally assumed that before A.D. 400 the Slav peoples, united in culture and language, lived somewhere in the region now called Poland. To the south was the Moravian Gate leading into the well-protected lands of Bohemia and Moravia. When the main migrations began, it was natural that the expanding Slavs should press southward through this gate. In Bohemia, protected by the upthrust horsts and relic blocks of the Erz Gebirge and Sudetens, the Czechs have lived since A.D. 450.

The invasions of central Europe by the Avars (akin to the Tatars) about A.D. 560 led to further southward migration of the numerous Slav peoples. Some proceeded as far as Greece and formed a notable stock among the Greeks, though they lost their Slav culture many centuries ago. The exact route of the early southern migrations is not known, but almost certainly the Slavs were, for a time, in the Alföld—that wide expanse of grassland occupying the downfold between the Alpine arcs.

The fierce Avars under Bajan formed an empire in the Alföld region about A.D. 600, but some authorities say that it was destroyed by rebellious Slavs. Migrating Serbs and Croats entered the regions of the Drava and the Sava in the seventh century.[1] It is not unlikely that they were descended from the Sorabs and Chrobati of Poland. It seems probable that about A.D. 630 a leader by the name of Samo united most of the Slavs in one great nation. But that was before the time of accurate historical records for the South Slavs.

The incursion of the ruthless Magyar hordes over the Magyar Pass in the Carpathians took place about A.D. 895. They found the grasslands of the Alföld congenial and gradually displaced the earlier settlers. The Slovaks were driven into the northern Carpathians. The Slovenes took up land on the eastern slopes of the great central Alpine Mountains. The Croats and Serbs made their home on the forest slopes and lowlands to the northeast of the Dinarics. Here, and to the south among the fold arcs of the great corridor, they built an individual culture. By 1350, under Stephen Dušan,

---

[1] For notes to chapter i see page 515.

a large and powerful empire had developed. But Stephen died in the year that the Ottoman Turks gained a foothold in Europe; and, although the Serbs and Magyars gallantly defended the corridors against the Turks, both were overpowered.

The geographical position of the country has proved unfortunate for its people, for Yugoslavia lies across two of the main corridors of Europe. These are, first, the route from the north Adriatic (Peartree Pass) along the Sava and Danube to the Oršova Gate and so to the Black Sea; and, second, the north-south route from the Vienna Gate down to Belgrade and on to the Aegean Sea by the Skoplje Gate. An important Roman road ran from Aquileia (near Venice) up Peartree Pass to Siscia (now Sisak), on to Sirmium (Mitrovica) and Naissus (Niš), and thence to Constantinople. In A.D. 103 Trajan built a road through the narrow granite gorge at Kazan. His inscription is still visible on the southern cliffs, although the road has not been rebuilt since the fall of Rome. Thus the small state of Yugoslavia lies in the path of more powerful countries—Turkey and Austria in the past, Germany and Italy more recently. This, in large part, accounts for its somewhat tragic history.

The present-day topography may be described as follows: on the west is the Adriatic Sea; the Dalmatian coast is marked by many long, parallel islands which are the summits of submerged folds of the Dinaric Mountains. The coast itself is, for the most part, precipitous, although in southern Dalmatia and in Albania marshy coastal plains have developed, with small, wandering streams which reproduce the conditions of the Pontine marshes near Rome. Malaria has, to a great extent, limited the use of such plains.

After the rains, the short rivers dash down the slopes, cutting deep gorges. Occasionally, as with the Neretva and the Drin, the rivers have cut through the limestone ridges. The gorges are of no value for navigation, and most of the valleys are too steep to be accessible by the few rough roads. In one or two places where light railways have been laid, the grade is so steep (e.g., near Sarajevo) that rack-and-pinion haulage is used.

*Climate and vegetation.*—Since Yugoslavia is part of the Balkan Peninsula and projects far southward, one might expect a typical

Mediterranean climate. To geographers the term means a region of hot, dry summers and warm, wet winters. These extremes, however, are not characteristic of Yugoslavia: first, because the Balkans are mountainous; second, the peninsula is so broad that the inland portions are little affected by marine conditions. Only along the Dalmatian coast and in the Vardar Valley are climate and vegetation typically Mediterranean. Most of Yugoslavia has the continental climate of inland Europe, which is marked by

| City | Jan. | Feb. | Mar. | Apr. | May | June | July | Aug. | Sept. | Oct. | Nov. | Dec. | Year |
|---|---|---|---|---|---|---|---|---|---|---|---|---|---|
| TEMPERATURE (degrees F.) | | | | | | | | | | | | | |
| Belgrade | 29 | 34 | 43 | 52 | 62 | 67 | 72 | 71 | 63 | 55 | 43 | 34 | 52 |
| Athens | 48 | 49 | 52 | 59 | 66 | 74 | 80 | 80 | 73 | 60 | 57 | 52 | 63 |
| RAINFALL (inches) | | | | | | | | | | | | | |
| Belgrade | 1.2 | 1.3 | 1.6 | 2.3 | 2.8 | 3.2 | 2.7 | 1.9 | 1.7 | 2.2 | 1.7 | 1.7 | 24 |
| Athens | 2.0 | 1.7 | 1.2 | 0.9 | 0.8 | 0.7 | 0.3 | 0.5 | 0.6 | 1.6 | 2.6 | 2.6 | 16 |

wide range in temperature from January to July, and rainfall which has its maximum in summer, though some rain falls every month in the year. The contrast between continental and Mediterranean climates is illustrated by the figures for Belgrade and Athens, respectively.

On the coast, with its Mediterranean climate, the temperature rises above 32° F. in January and above 72° F. in July. Thus along this isotherm the range of temperature is 40° F. Inland of this section the range becames wider toward the north, where the climate is more continental. In Belgrade, for instance, the range throughout the year is 43° F. whereas at Athens it is only 32° F.

The cooling effect of the mountains on Yugoslavia in summer is indicated by the isotherms. The hottest districts are not in the south, as one might expect, but in the north, in the low Danubian plains and the valley of the lower Morava. In this region the temperature rises above 72° F. in July. Some areas of the elevated country are more than 6,000 feet high. Indeed, the Šar Mountains tower

7,000 feet above Skoplje. Hence their summits are 20° F. cooler than the valley, and their climate and vegetation are alpine in character. On Durmitor, with an altitude of 9,100 feet, patches of snow remain in sheltered places throughout the year. Cirque valleys, formed by glacial erosion in past ice ages, are common on Durmitor, Lovćen, Triglav, and other peaks.

In the cooler months the cold air streams away from the mountains and gives rise to the fierce bora winds from the north. Indeed, most of the winds have a strong northerly component; the so-called etesian winds of this type are the commonest in the Adriatic. These northerly winds are akin to the famous trade winds of the Pacific and are drawn southward by the marked low-pressure areas over the heated tropical lands to the south. In winter the cold European continent also produces winds flowing outward; thus north winds are not uncommon in this season also.

The rainfall on the Balkan Peninsula is, on the whole, rather low, since the area is far removed from the moist westerly winds of the Atlantic Ocean which are the chief rain carriers of Europe. But the high mountains along the western coast of Yugoslavia cause updraft and consequent cooling of all westerly winds. The moist, warm winds blowing from the Mediterranean or the Adriatic deposit heavy rainfall where the topography is favorable. The wettest place in Europe is just behind the Dalmatian coast at Crkvice, with a rainfall of 183 inches yearly. There is a gradual diminution of rainfall to the east, especially in the depressions. The driest area is south of Yugoslavia: Salonika receives only 20 inches a year. The Morava and Vardar valleys receive less than 30 inches, as does most of the area north of Belgrade. However, a rainfall varying from 30 to 60 inches is general throughout the country, and this is sufficient for most crops.

Vegetation, of course, depends upon climate. The inland region, where summer rains fall, was formerly clothed with forests of beech and oak and some conifers. The name Šumadija refers to the early wooded condition of the district south of Belgrade. But most of the forests in Yugoslavia have been cleared at lower levels, as in many other parts of Europe. However, there are large forests in the more rugged parts of the Dinaric Mountains, especially in Bosnia.

In the Bačka district, between the Danube and Tisa* rivers, scanty rainfall has produced a steppe condition similar to the adjacent grasslands of Hungary. The Bačka district is now planted to grain and sugar beets.

Along the Dalmatian coast, with its Mediterranean climate, grows the typical maqui: a covering of shrubs, heaths, and tussocky grass which everywhere borders the Mediterranean Sea. The upper slopes of the Dalmatian mountains are unusually bare, though thin patches of maqui containing thyme, tamarisk, and similar plants occur as high as 1,200 feet. Above this height, juniper is perhaps the commonest plant. Formerly forests grew in the better-watered regions of Dalmatia, but they were cut down by the Venetians for shipbuilding. It has been difficult to reforest these slopes because of the ubiquitous flocks of goats.

*The three main regions of Yugoslavia.*—It is difficult to draw definite boundaries for the subdivisions of the country because of its complex topography. In 1929 the government divided Yugoslavia into nine banovine (counties), which, for the most part, conform to the chief river basins. The land of the Slovenes, west of Zagreb, is now the banovina of Drava. Autonomous Croatia contains two of the original banovine: one is now known as Sava, the other as Primorje (southern Dalmatia and Hercegovina). Bosnia was divided into Vrbas and Drina. Montenegro and the region to the east became Zeta. The Morava and Vardar valleys became two banovine, each retaining the name of the river. The region around Belgrade, including much of the middle Danube and Tisa area, is called Dunav. The relation of these regions to the older provinces is indicated in the table overleaf.

Chataigneau[2] has given a dozen subdivisions in his masterly description, but for this introductory section three main topographic divisions will suffice. They follow naturally from the earlier discussion of geologic structure.

*Region I, the northern lowlands.*—The northern boundary of Yugoslavia, as decreed in 1919, runs from the coast at Fiume and Sušak along the limestone divide to Peartree Pass. Thence it continues north to Mount Triglav (9,400 feet), the highest point

---

* Magyar spelling, Tisza; German, Theiss.

in Yugoslavia. The boundary turns east near the Karavanken Alps, which are about 6,000 feet high, and drops to the Drava River near Maribor. At its confluence with the Danube the Drava becomes the boundary to the marshes. Here the boundary turns northeast and crosses the plain to Subotica, then southeast, reaching the Danube again near Smederevo. Thence it follows the main

REGIONS OF YUGOSLAVIA

| Region | Character | Older provinces | Banovine |
|---|---|---|---|
| I. Northern lowlands. | Mostly below 1,000 ft. Alluvial plains of Sava and middle Danube. | Syrmia (Srem), the Banat, the Bačka, Slavonia, Croatia, etc. | Drava, northern Sava, northern Drina. |
| II. Corridor lands of eastern Serbia. | Mostly between 1,000 and 3,000 ft. Basins of Morava and Vardar. | Šumadija, Kosovo, Macedonia. | Morava, Vardar, upper Sava. |
| III. Highlands of Dinaric folds. | Above 3,000 ft. Karst of Bosnia, tertiary foothills of Drina, etc. | Montenegro, Hercegovina, Bosnia, Dalmatia, western Croatia. | Primorje, southern Drina, Zeta. |

river eastward through the picturesque gorge at Kazan to the mouth of the Timok River above Vidin.

Although the first major division is chiefly lowlands less than 1,000 feet high, it is convenient to include in this section the western hills of Slovenia. Those north of the Sava River are part of the central European Alps. They consist of highly altered crystalline rocks near Maribor and of altered limestones (mainly Triassic) in the Karavanken Alps. Thus the northwestern corner of Yugoslavia at the head of the Sava is protected by lofty, inaccessible ranges.

The natural entrance to this corner of the Balkans is Peartree Pass between Trieste and Ljubljana. Here the limestones at the northern end of the Dinaric folds are low, and the divide is only about 1,900 feet above sea level. The country hereabouts is the typical Karst landscape. The abundant rainfall develops a cover of heathy plants, grass, or forest. But the solution hollows called *doline* and *polja* are common throughout the district. The upper waters of the Sava basin near Postumia flow underground through the limestone, then move normally on the surface where the rocks are less permeable. In the vicinity are the famous Adelsberg Caves. Many of the valleys are deeply filled with alluvium washed down from the mountains. Wheat, oats, potatoes, and flax are the principal crops. Lower in the Sava Valley, where the climate is warmer, vines, hops, and maize are grown on the undulating hills.

Zagreb, the capital of Croatia, has a population of about 400,000. It is an important railway junction for Sušak and Trieste on the Adriatic and for Maribor and Hungary to the north. The Sava is navigable for small steamers as far as Zagreb. The city borders the great plain extending to the Alföld. On its southern margins, outcrops of the ancient underlying median mass appear as rocky hills. North of Zagreb these hills rise to a height of 3,300 feet. The Papuk outcrop is north of Brod. Best known of all is the Fruška Gora between Vinkovci and Belgrade. These outcrops form part of the long divide separating the two parallel tributaries of the Danube—the Sava and the Drava.

The northeastern portion of the lowlands has a much more continental climate, giving rise to steppes. The confluence of the Drava, the Tisa, and the Danube is surrounded by extensive marshes. In the vicinity of Subotica the dry climate has resulted in widespread sand dunes. There are also large areas of wind-blown loam, or loess, which are more fertile and have long been planted to maize and wheat. Novi Sad on the Danube is another large town in the Bačka. It is just north of the Fruška Gora, which is well wooded and bears many vineyards.

Belgrade, with a population estimated at 450,000 in 1941, is by far the most important city in Yugoslavia. The nucleus of the capital city is the great crag of limestone rising 140 feet above the Danube at its junction with the Sava. This crag is the northern end of a long ridge of Cretaceous rocks known as the Avala. It was early crowned with a citadel, and the town was known to the Romans as Singidunum. Few cities have been besieged as often as Belgrade, especially during the Turkish wars of the fifteenth century. It seems, at first sight, to be poorly located for a capital, since it is near the Rumanian border. But it lies at the junction of the three main regions of Yugoslavia and controls the roads to all. About twenty-five miles down the Danube is Smederevo, an interesting walled city which commands the entrance to the Morava Valley.

*Region II, the corridor lands of eastern Serbia.*—This region comprises the Morava basin in the north and the Vardar basin in the south. It agrees fairly closely with the two banovine of the same names. Serbian culture has always centered in the Morava Valley. The southern Vardar portion is inhabited chiefly by Macedonians, whose culture is midway between that of the Serbians and the Bulgarians.

In the northern Morava basin, near Kragujevac, are some inclined formations, mostly of Cretaceous age, which were formerly covered by lakes of the Aegean type. The deposits now appear as widespread terraces, though modern rivers have cut into them deeply and have carried away much of the alluvium. The region south of the junction of the Morava and the Ibar is formed of much older and harder rocks, similar to those which built up the Kopaonik Mountains (6,000 feet). The valleys are generally wide and flat, but are narrowed, in places, by outcrops of older rocks. These constrictions, often approximating gorges, are common along the upper Ibar and at the head of the Morava River north of Skoplje.

The region between the Kopaonik Mountains and the Danube is known as the Šumadija. Today the forests of oak and beech have disappeared from the northern part of the district, but the higher slopes and the southern part are still well wooded. The typical Serbian crops of maize and wheat are grown in the fertile valleys, and plum orchards are almost as abundant as they are farther north. Kragujevac is now a small town of little importance, but a century ago it was a political center and an arsenal.

East of the lower Morava Valley is a complicated series of ancient rocks which forms part of the Balkan Alpides. It contains many eruptives (e.g., andesite). The area is sparsely inhabited, but is interesting because of its valuable minerals, especially copper, which is mined at Majdanpek and Bor. Lignite is abundant between Niš and Majdanpek.

The upper Morava district includes the Ibar Valley. Most of the rocks are ancient, and are predominantly schists belonging to the median mass. Two areas are of special interest: the *polje* of Kosovo and the divide north of Skoplje. The latter is so important in the history of the Mediterranean region that it might well be called the Skoplje Gate.

Throughout southern Serbia the characteristic features are isolated oval valleys containing lacustrine deposits which date from Pliocene times. Half-a-dozen large basins form the most important districts of this region. North of Skoplje are three basins: that of Leskovac, near Niš; of Kosovo, near Priština; and of Metohija, near Prizren. South of Skoplje are the Morihovo and Bitolj basins; Tetovo is just south of the high Šar Mountains. On the Albanian border, at lower levels, are three similar hollows which have not yet been filled with silts. They contain the three large lakes of Ohrid, Prespa, and Scutari. The streams draining these basins tend to run in narrow gorges between level expanses; communication in most areas, therefore, is somewhat difficult.

Just north of Kosovo is Novi Pazar, the chief town of the Raška district. Here the ideals of Serbian nationality were nourished through the long years of Turkish control. The basin of Kosovo forms a natural corridor from the Danube lands to the Aegean and consequently has been the scene of fierce battles, especially against the Turks in 1389 and 1448. Parallel to it and farther east is a similar basin, south of Niš, which is drained by the Morava. The main railway uses this eastern valley, and not the Kosovo Valley, to reach Skoplje to the south. Leskovac is the most important town.

Besides the older lake deposits and the recent river alluvials, some basins contain a black soil which produces abundant crops. Rains are often heavy, especially in August, and, although the winters are long in these elevated basins, the crops are much like those grown in the Morava lowlands. Hemp and peppers flourish, and orchards of apples and pears and groves of chestnuts diversify the landscape. Flocks of sheep graze on the excellent pastures of the more elevated districts. The slopes of the Prokletija Mountains along the northern frontier of Albania are said to be especially suited to grazing.

In the southern portions of the corridor, the somewhat smaller and more elevated basins give a mountainous aspect to the entire region. Bordering them are large fan-shaped deposits which have washed down the steep hillsides. The region is somewhat drier than the area north of Skoplje and the slopes are sparsely forested. Skoplje is in a wide, flat valley that extends almost to the main divide. Thus it is much easier to cross from the Morava to the Vardar basins than to follow the course of the Ibar River north of the Kosovo basin.

Transhumance is much practiced in the pastures of the Vardar area. In winter the shepherds drive their flocks down to the coastal meadows of Musakija on the Adriatic or to the Salonika pastures on the Aegean. The abundance of trout and eel in the lakes of Ohrid and Prespa makes fishing an important occupation. As the Vardar area is somewhat dry, the small streams vanish in summer, and irrigation is necessary near the Greek border. The vegetation is much more Mediterranean than that of other districts. Grapes and tobacco are grown in the southeastern valleys.

The topography between Skoplje and the mouth of the Drin Valley is of great interest not only from a geographic, but also from a migratory, viewpoint. There are three "steps," as it were, in the apparently easy route to the Adriatic. At the top is the *polje* of Kosovo, formed partly by the solution of limestones, partly by infilling from lake and river deposits. Then a fairly easy divide leads west to the Drin basin; the parallel Metohija basin is drained by the White Drin. From Prizren, at its southern end, the Drin descends to the coast by a series of gorges which make it a difficult corridor of communication. However, a narrow-gauge railway is projected to traverse this route. North of the Drin Valley are the high peaks of the Prokletija Range, and to the south are the equally high peaks of the Šar Range. Indeed, the Drin "reëntrant" at this corner of the Adriatic was caused by the marked change in direction of the Dinaric folds. The forbidding nature of the corridor has prevented an influx of Slav peoples, and in the region between Prizren and Leskovac the settlement of Albanians has closed the territory to the Slavs.

*Region III, the highlands of the Dinaric folds.*—The third section of Yugoslavia includes the most mountainous and therefore the least densely populated portion. The whole region consists of folded Triassic and Cretaceous limestones, with narrow formations of younger Flysch near Zara and Sarajevo. The axis of the folds is parallel to the coast; elongated *polja* have been dissolved in the limestone, especially in Hercegovina and the region to the north-west. A number of peaks near the city of Split exceed 6,000 feet in height. Central Bosnia west of Sarajevo consists of an elevated block (or horst) of ancient schists thrust up among the Triassic limestones.

Central Bosnia is, for the most part, still forested. Sarajevo, the chief town, with a population of nearly 80,000, dominates the basin. The crops of the Sarajevo basin are similar to those of the lowlands: tobacco and maize at the lower levels, wheat on the slopes, and oats, flax, and hemp at somewhat higher levels. East of Sarajevo is a grassy plateau on which graze horses, sheep, and cattle. Near Tuzla, north of Sarajevo, important salt deposits have led to the development of the chemical industry in the vicinity. The Krajina district lies west of the Vrbas River. Banjaluka, the largest town, with approximately 24,000 inhabitants, is a noted market for cattle and grain.

In Montenegro, which corresponds roughly to the modern banovina of Zeta, the principal river is the Morača. Its tributary, the Zeta, rising near Nikšić, flows by subterranean passages under a limestone range 1,000 feet high. It crosses a plain and enters Lake Scutari south of Cetinje. The Rijeka River issues from a cave near the same town. The mountains are covered with forests in this region: pines occur as high as 6,000 feet, beeches and oaks grow on the slopes below, and chestnut trees are rarely found higher than 1,000 feet. Small trees, such as wild plum and sumac, are common in the valleys. Agriculture is confined to a few level areas, where some grains, potatoes, and capsicums are produced.

Hercegovina includes the basin of the Neretva with its capital, Mostar. Half of this ancient region is now in Zeta and half in Primorje. Hercegovina is almost wholly in the Karst country; subterranean rivers are therefore common. The Popovo *polje*, about fifteen miles north of Dubrovnik, is drained by a stream which disappears into a solution hollow (*dolina*) and passes under a high range of mountains, to reappear as a gigantic spring near Dubrovnik. Farther north are the rather bare plateaus of Velebit and Lika, which drop abruptly by a steep scarp to the plain of Karlovac behind Zara.

The Dalmatian coast shows the influence of the Mediterranean climate. Olives and figs are common near Zara; farther south, aloes, carobs, and cypress appear. Dalmatia is almost wholly isolated from the rest of Yugoslavia by sparsely wooded, elevated Karst regions. But it has had a remarkable history based almost wholly on sea-borne trade. Kotor (Cattaro), Dubrovnik (Ragusa), Gruž (Gravosa), Split (Spalato), Zara, and Fiume (whose suburb of Sušak is Yugoslav) are well known in European history. Dubrovnik, indeed, remained an independent center of Slav culture when Serbia was submerged by the Turkish invasions.

The Gulf of Kotor consists of a group of deep basins linked together and probably formed by crustal subsidence (graben). The complexity of its structure is scarcely paralleled among the harbors of the world. However, the hinterland is so restricted that Kotor is only a small town. Dubrovnik, chiefly a tourist town today, has been partly replaced by the port of Gruž near by.

Split (Spalato) was an important town even in the early historic period. In A.D. 300 the Roman Emperor Diocletian built a mammoth palace there which covered almost ten acres and was enclosed by thick, high walls. The modern city has spread over the plain in all directions and now contains about 50,000 inhabitants. Exports of wine, fruit, oil, and cement have made it important, especially since it was connected by rail with Zagreb.

Šibenik, a naval port in Austrian days, is situated on the submerged estuary of the Krka River. It exports bauxite and timber. Sušak was assigned to Yugoslavia in 1921, when Fiume (Rijeka) was given to Italy. In the vicinity, the Italian and Slav populations are almost equal in number. Sušak is linked by rail with Zagreb and rivals Split as the chief port of Yugoslavia. The small town of Zara (Zadar), with an Italian population of about 11,000, belonged to Italy up to 1946.

*Agriculture and forestry.*[3]—In 1937 the population of Yugoslavia was estimated at 15,400,000, of whom about 70–80 per cent were engaged in agriculture and forestry and about 12 per cent in mining and transportation. Of the total area of 95,600 square miles, 31 per cent is forested, 30 per cent is arable, and 25 per cent is in pasture. In 1938 about 36,000,000 acres were under cultivation. Thus the Yugoslav is primarily a farmer and a forester, and agricultural production is of outstanding importance to him.

Maize and wheat lead all other crops, for maize occupies 44 per cent of the grain area and wheat 36 per cent. Both are exported by way of the Danube to Austria, Czechoslovakia, and Germany. Maize is the chief food of the nation and often its main export. It is grown chiefly in the warm lowlands of the north near the large rivers, where the soil is better and the climate, with its wet

GRAIN PRODUCTION
(Metric tons)

| Grain | 1931 | 1938 |
|---|---|---|
| Maize | 3,203,000 | 4,407,000 |
| Wheat | 2,689,000 | 3,030,000 |
| Barley | 392,000 | 421,000 |
| Oats | 265,000 | 326,000 |
| Rye | 193,000 | 227,000 |

summers, more favorable than farther south. Wheat has much the same distribution as maize, but it extends farther south and west because the Mediterranean climate is congenial to its cultivation. Other grains are barley, oats, and rye, each of which occupies about 5 per cent of the grain area.

The accompanying table summarizes grain production for two fairly recent years.

About 3 per cent of the country is given over to orchards. Much of the cleared forest lands of central Serbia, especially in the region of the Šumadija, has been set out with plum trees. The short continental spring prevents the trees from flowering too soon and then being nipped by late frost. Large quantities of prunes are exported, especially to Great Britain and Scandinavia.

Nearly 2 per cent of the country is planted to vineyards. Grapes have a wider range than other crops, and are particularly abundant near Zagreb; near Belgrade; at Majdanpek, southeast of Belgrade, and Vršac, northeast of Belgrade; and at Ohrid in the far south. Important areas are found also on the Dalmatian coast, especially around Šibenik and Mostar. Sugar beets, tobacco, hemp, and flax are grown in small quantities, but they are of little commercial importance for export trade.

From the topographic discussion so far presented it is clear that the chief agricultural lands lie to the north and that little can be expected from the large mountainous areas in the west and south. It is believed that perhaps 80 per cent of the Vojvodina (the Bačka, etc.) could be cultivated, 60 per cent of Serbia and northern Croatia, 50 per cent of Bosnia, 40 per cent of Slovenia, 30 per cent of Montenegro, and only 19 per cent of Dalmatia.

| Livestock | Number | Chief regions |
|-----------|--------|---------------|
| Horses............. | 1,216,000 | |
| Cattle.............. | 4,073,000 | Croatia, Slavonia, Bosnia |
| Sheep.............. | 9,568,000 | Belgrade area, southern Serbia, Bosnia |
| Pigs................. | 3,126,000 | The Vojvodina, Croatia, Slavonia |

Forest products are prominent in the export trade. The fir timber of Bosnia and the oaks of Salonika have long been exported as far as Great Britain. Charcoal, wood alcohol, acetone, and allied products, also, are exported from northern Bosnia.

*Animal husbandry.*—Stock raising is of considerable importance. Most of the cattle and sheep are raised in the lowlands, but they also range in hilly regions where there is little or no competition with agricultural crops. In the Dinaric lands transhumance is a prominent feature of sheep raising. In summer the sheep migrate from Dalmatia to the plateaus of Bosnia; in autumn they descend to the maize fields to graze on the stubble.

Hogs are raised where a plentiful maize supply is available, as in the Vojvodina. Bosnia, also, is an important hog-raising region, since its beech and oak forests preclude the growing of other crops. Goats are raised in the poorest parts of the country: the Karst lands of Bosnia and Hercegovina, as well as the relatively bare highlands of southern Serbia.

The accompanying table gives the numbers of livestock in Yugoslavia in 1936.

*Minerals.*—As one would expect from the wide distribution of ancient rocks in the relic masses in Yugoslavia, metallic minerals, also, are widely distributed. Yugoslavia is the chief source of minerals in southeastern Europe, but the annual output is worth only about $20,000,000. Coal supplies of Carboniferous age are very scanty, but there are large deposits of the younger brown coals and lignites. The chief "young" coals occur near Zenica in the Bosna Valley between Brod and Sarajevo. Large deposits occur also in the upper Timok Valley in the extreme east. Some hydroelectric power is being developed on the Krka in Dalmatia and at Fala on the upper Drava.

MINERAL PRODUCTION
(Metric tons)

| Mineral | Amount | Mineral | Amount |
|---|---|---|---|
| Brown coal | 4,024,000 | Lead-zinc ore | 817,000 |
| Lignite | 1,262,000 | Bauxite | 354,000 |
| Iron ore | 629,000 | Chrome | 59,000 |
| Copper ore | 650,000 | Antimony | 8,000 |

Iron ore sufficient for local needs is found at Vareš near Sarajevo and is smelted at Zenica. Another good supply occurs at Ljubljana. Copper is a far more important product, for Serbia produces as much as any European country except Germany. The chief mines are at Bor and Majdanpek. Bauxite is important as a source of aluminum, and a large amount is imported into Germany from Dalmatia.

The accompanying table summarizes Yugoslav mineral production for 1937.

*Foreign trade.*—Percentages of the leading exports in 1936 were as follows: live animals, 14 per cent; cereals (maize and wheat), 12 per cent; timber, 11 per cent; copper, 8 per cent; bauxite, 1 per cent. Austria and Germany rank first as importers, with Czechoslovakia and Great Britain second. Imports into Yugoslavia consist chiefly of manufactured goods such as machinery, iron and steel, and cotton goods.

*Communications.*—During the Austro-Hungarian regime, railways were built to connect the Slav provinces with Budapest and Vienna rather than to benefit the local Slavs. Since 1919 a number of provincial railways have been built. One of the chief of these links Zagreb and Sušak with Split. Another traverses the mountain valleys between Sarajevo and Niš. A third links Skoplje with Bitolj. A fourth passes northward from the Kosovo *polje* to the lowlands and Belgrade. Another is projected up the Drin Valley from Cetinje to Priština and Niš. Western Vrbas has several narrow-gauge lines linking it to Zagreb on the north and to Split on the south. In 1938 there were 4,556 miles of standard-gauge and 2,036 miles of narrow-gauge lines.

In the lowlands north of Belgrade are three fairly important canals. One of these connects the Sava and the Drava near Vin-

| Districts | Density (sq. mi.) | Elevation (ft.) |
|---|---|---|
| Near Zagreb, Belgrade, and Niš...................... | Over 175 | Below 1,000 |
| Northern and eastern slopes of Dinarics........ | 100–175 | 1,000–2,000 |
| Northern Karst, Raška, etc............................ | 60–100 | 2,000–3,500 |
| Lower Alpine meadows.................................. | 40–60 | 3,500–4,500 |
| Higher Alpine areas...................................... | Below 40 | Above 4,500 |

kovci; others cross the marshy country near the mouth of the Tisa River. The Danube, the Sava, and the Drava together supply about 1,200 miles of navigable waterways.

*Population.*—It is not too much to say that the environment virtually controls the population pattern. The accompanying table shows the correlation between density and elevation, except along the narrow Dalmatian coast. The densest settlement is between Zagreb and the Drava, where agricultural facilities are exceptionally good. Much of the Bačka, also, is filled with farms. Almost equally densely populated is the region between Belgrade and Niš, especially along the Morava Valley, where the density exceeds 175 persons per square mile. The next most populous region includes the northern slopes of Croatia, Bosnia, and the Šumadija, as well as the Skoplje Gate in the south. This region has 100–175 persons to the square mile. Much of the remainder consists of pasture land, where the population is about 60 to the square mile. The bare uplands and the alpine summits behind Dubrovnik and Split are the least populous regions of Yugoslavia.

In the 1931 census only seven towns in Yugoslavia exceeded

50,000 in population: Belgrade, 267,000; Zagreb, 186,000; Subotica, 100,000; Ljubljana, 79,000; Sarajevo, 78,000; Skoplje, 65,000; and Novi Sad, 64,000. The total population in 1948 was nearly 15,-000,000, comprising the following cultural groups: Serbs, 7,000,000; Croats, 4,000,000; Slovenes, 1,400,000; Moslem Serbs, Macedonian Slavs, Albanians, Magyars, and Germans, about 500,000 each; and smaller numbers of Turks, Rumanians, Jews, and other Slavs. Religious divisions include approximately 7,000,000 Orthodox, 5,300,000 Roman Catholics, and 1,600,000 Moslems.

# CHAPTER II

# *Racial History*

### BY CARLETON S. COON

THOSE WHO ADMIRE the gallantry and love of freedom of the Yugoslavs may want to know what biological position these brave and admirable people occupy among the races of mankind. They will want to know how closely related they are in physical characteristics to the other peoples who speak Slavic languages and maintain Slavic traditions, as well as to their neighbors in adjacent countries who speak other languages and follow other patterns of behavior.

In these days, to write about any aspect of the concept "race" immediately arouses suspicion because of the political misuses of the term by both Axis propagandists and Allied counterpropagandists. It is a biological term, not a political one. A race is a group of individuals with special genetic characters who breed in isolation. In the case of man, complete isolation rarely occurs. The concept is therefore a relative one only, to be used as a convenient label for combinations of characteristics which occur over and over again. Any attempt to identify a single nation with a certain physique is doomed to failure, for all types of white men are found in all nations. Differences in national types of behavior between European peoples are due to training, not to biological inheritance. Our evaluation of these peoples, moreover, might well be based, not on their material or scientific progress, but on the extent to which they recognize the rights of their neighbors.

The racial history of Yugoslavia has three principal aspects: the composition of its population in pre-Slavic times, the racial char-

acter of the invading Slavs, and the physical results of the amal-
gamation of conquerors with conquered. Unfortunately, none of
these aspects is fully documented, but for each there is enough
evidence to permit the formation of tentative conclusions.[1]

Almost nothing is known about the population of Yugoslavia
before the Iron Age. Županić[2] informs us that early Bronze Age
(Copper Age) inhabitants of this region whose crania have been
preserved in local museums were longheaded, unlike the modern
population, but no further data are available. The rich Iron Age
cemetery of Glasinac in Bosnia, still in use some two millennia
later, contains much skeletal material which indicates that most
of the Illyrians who inhabited the Dinaric highlands at that time
were Nordic in racial type, though a few belonged to the same
Dinaric type which is predominant in that region today, with
round heads, flat behind; wide jaws; and prominent noses. Except
for the Glasinac remains, there is no evidence previous to the
research of the nineteenth and twentieth centuries on skeletal
and living material.

Our knowledge of the racial skeletal structure of the early Slavs
is limited by their custom of cremation. Skulls which escaped the
flames in the pre-Christian period and in the early days of Slavic
Christianity belong, with few exceptions, to the Nordic category,
as do also the early German, Illyrian, Celtic, and Scythian cranial
material. All the Iron Age peoples of central Europe who spoke
Indo-European languages were basically Nordic when they began
their several expansions. All absorbed other peoples as they migrated and settled in new areas. Where these new peoples were
non-Nordic, the invaders lost their identification with the Nordic
racial type. No skeletal evidence from Yugoslavia has been identified with the early Slavs, but, judging by what is known of them
elsewhere, the ethnic ancestors of the Serbs, Croats, and Slovenes
must have been as truly Nordic as the equally exiguous ancestors
of the living Germans or the Irish.

Modern Yugoslavs, like most present-day Europeans who speak
Indo-European languages, resemble the Iron Age Nordics only
slightly. The most distinctive racial fact about Yugoslavia is that
it forms the nucleus of the Dinaric zone of Europe—a zone which

[1] For notes to chapter ii see page 515.

reaches from Switzerland and the Tyrol in the west to Bulgaria in the east, to the Carpathians in the north, and to Epirus in the south. The focal point of this zone might be placed in Bosnia or Montenegro.

The Dinaric race, of which the majority of Yugoslavs are the most numerous and characteristic members, is one of the most easily identified of all white races. The Dinaric is usually tall, long-legged, large-boned but spare, with a head of small to moderate size, noted for its extreme brachycephaly (great width in proportion to length). The Dinaric head is usually short and often flat in the portion behind the ears. The face is usually one of high relief, with a prominent and often convex nose and an equally prominent jaw line. Dinarics usually do not run to fat; they tend to grow thin in old age. Their pigmentation is not distinctive; some are light-skinned, others dark; some have blue eyes, others have brown; and the color of the hair varies.

Not all Yugoslavs are Dinarics, but most of them fit some of these specifications. It is possible to find individuals in every country in Europe who might be called Dinaric, though in the more remote areas, as in Portugal and Finland, they are rare. It is therefore apparent that Dinarics cannot be directly of Slavic origin. The Slavs evidently brought their language and their family system to what is now Yugoslavia, intermarried with the local Illyrians and Thracians, and the colonists settled there by the Roman emperors, and became genetically absorbed. It is possible that the conquered peoples outnumbered the conquerors.

The absorption of the Slavic invaders by the earlier peoples does not explain entirely why Yugoslavia is the center of the Dinaric racial area. The existing evidence indicates that most of the Illyrians and Thracians were not Dinaric. The colonists placed in this region by the Romans came from many parts of the Roman Empire and must have represented a variety of racial types.

Taken by itself, the reason for the predominance of the Dinarics in modern Yugoslavia is a mystery, but when it is considered as a part of European racial history it becomes less difficult to explain. Throughout Europe, since the time of the fall of the Roman Empire and the Völkerwanderung, the tendency has been for some of the genetic characteristics of early types to reëmerge from a minor to a major quantitative position in populations. In Ireland today, for example, a majority of the population shows some of the phenotypical features of Cro-Magnon man, who lived in western Europe during the last Ice Age: large body, large head, heavy brow ridges, wide face, heavy jaw, and long facial length from the nasal septum to the chin. Irish skeletal material of the early Christian period shows little evidence of this combination of characters. As another example, the German-speaking population of Bavaria has gradually changed from the longheaded Nordic type of the eighth century to the predominantly roundheaded Alpine and Dinaric types of the twentieth century.

The food-gathering peoples who inhabited the forests and grasslands of Europe after the Ice Age were the aborigines when Mediterraneans and Nordics came in from the south and east to farm and raise domestic animals. The farmers arrived about 3000 B.C.; from that date until around A.D. 1000 the majority of skeletons found in Europe are Nordic, Mediterranean, or a combination of both. After four millennia of numerical preponderance, some of the physical characteristics of the natives, whom the newcomers drove out in some instances and absorbed in others, are reappearing everywhere on the continent.

In Ireland, Denmark, and southern Sweden the types which reëmerge are tall and large-bodied, with large heads and wide faces. In France, Italy, southern Germany, southern Albania, Greece, and elsewhere they are mostly of moderate stature and head size, thickset, short-legged, roundheaded, and round-faced. In the region centering in Yugoslavia, both of these types are found, but the majority are Dinaric.

The Dinaric head and facial forms are the least primitive found among human beings, and the furthest removed from those of known fossil men. No Dinaric skulls have ever been excavated from sites older than 3000 B.C. The Dinaric combination of features seems to have evolved first in the lands at the northeastern corner of the Mediterranean, including the island of Cyprus. In the third millennium B.C., prospectors from this area went by sea to Spain, Britain, and the continental shores of the North Sea, whence they made their way overland to the metal-rich areas of central Europe, particularly the Dinaric Alps. The Dinarics buried in the Glasinac graveyard were probably descendants of these prospectors.

Roundheadedness, particularly its Dinaric form, is now believed to be genetically dominant. A partly Dinaric population, breeding in the comparative isolation of a remote mountain region, would become increasingly Dinaric as time went on; and that is what seems to have happened in Yugoslavia and northern Albania, since in these countries the degree of isolation has approached that required biologically for race building. The invasions of Slavs, Germanic peoples, and others were too sporadic to interfere with the process. All have been affected by this dominant genetic tendency.*

In surveying the racial characteristics of modern Yugoslavs it is found that the Slovenes, whose ancestors absorbed colonies of Celts as well as of Illyrians, are physically almost indistinguishable from their neighbors, the Austrians of the border provinces. They are, on the average, of moderate to tall stature (168 cm.), with moderately round heads (cephalic index = 83.4), and are predominantly blond, 50 per cent or more having light hair and more than 70 per cent having light or light mixed eyes.

The Croats are taller (170 cm.) and more roundheaded (cephalic index = 85) than the Slovenes, but their pigmentation is similar. Whereas 25 per cent of the Slovenes have concave nasal profiles, this is true of only 15 per cent of the Croats. In this as in other ways the Croats are more frequently Dinaric as individuals and more intensively Dinaric as a population than the Slovenes.

The Serbs proper resemble the Croats in their measurements, but they are much darker—45 per cent with pure brown eyes and only 20 per cent with light. Only 10 per cent have light hair; more than 50 per cent are either black or very dark brown. Morphologically, the Serbs tend to have the facial attributes of the Dinaric race in even greater concentration than do the Croats. The main difference, however, is one of pigmentation; Serbia lies on the outer periphery of the deeply brunet zone which is concentrated in Greece, Bulgaria, and Rumania.

Bosnian and Montenegrin types present another problem. The

---

* Since this chapter was written, evidence has appeared that some of the head-flattening associated with the Dinaric type is due to cradling.—C.S.C.

Bosnians, with regional stature means from 171 to 176 centimeters, are very tall people; the nearer one comes to Montenegro the taller they are found to be. Their brachycephaly (cephalic index = 85) is comparable with that of the Croats and the Serbs, but it varies according to religion. The oldest and most conservative element, the Catholic, has a mean of 86; the Orthodox, of 85; and the Moslem, of 84. Thus the element in the population which is presumably least mixed with outsiders is the most exaggeratedly roundheaded, and extreme brachycephaly is a Dinaric characteristic.

In descending from the Bosnian heights to the narrow Dalmatian coastal strip, a definite change in the appearance of the people is noticed. The Bosnians are intermediate in pigmentation between Croats and Serbs, whereas the Dalmatians are darker. The latter also tend to be shorter (166–171 cm.) and less brachycephalic (cephalic index = 83). Even they, however, are taller as their territory converges on the mountain nucleus of Montenegro.

In this prime refuge area, this eagle rookery of southeastern Europe, is concentrated one of the most distinctive of European populations. The Montenegrins are the tallest people in Europe, with mean statures of 177–178 centimeters. They are also the heaviest people in Europe, with a mean weight of 160 pounds for a man of about forty years of age. Those who have seen Montenegrins in any numbers will recall the massiveness of their frames, the wide shoulders, deep chests, rawboned arms, large, muscular hands, and long, bony legs. They will also remember the huge round or square heads, appropriately capped with round, brimless hats; the large faces thrown into high relief by rugged, bony structure and lean flesh; and the heavy jaws with massive chins. Most distinctive of all are the hawk beaks found in more than half the population. Even the straight noses, and the few that are concave, are large, and there is a tendency for the tip to descend with age.

The pigmentation of the Montenegrins is as unusual as the features described above. With 45 per cent dark-haired and 25 per cent dark-eyed, they are intermediate or mixed, lighter than the Serbs but darker than the Croats. This intermediacy, however, is not unexpected; what is remarkable is a large minority with a reddish tinge to the hair and a tendency to freckle on exposed

skin surfaces. Although little is known about rufosity or its genetic
linkages, it does have a tendency to crop up wherever major sur-
vivals of the large or unreduced paleolithic peoples are found,
as in Ireland and in the mountains of Morocco. In Montenegro,
therefore, rufosity again runs true to form, for the only way in
which the typical Montenegrin physique may be explained is in
terms of such a survival or reëmergence.

Survival and reëmergence form the keynotes to the racial history
of Yugoslavia. But these principles do not apply to race alone;
they are equally valid in the field of human culture. In the mountains of Yugoslavia one finds men using Iron Age tools and agricultural methods. The generous Iron Age hospitality with its
archaic fidelity to clan and religion have likewise survived. Let
us hope that, as the Atomic Age replaces the Iron Age in more
and more sections of Yugoslavia, ways will be found to preserve
these rare and ancient virtues, as well as the freedom for which
the Yugoslavs have so tenaciously fought three times within the
present half-century.

*Part Two*

# HISTORICAL
# BACKGROUND

# CHAPTER III

# The Yugoslav Movement

## BY ROBERT J. KERNER

THE YUGOSLAVS entered their Balkan home from the direction of the Carpathians in the sixth and seventh centuries. Probably speaking more than one dialect of Slavic even then, they later became divided geographically and politically, in religion and in written language, as well as in economic, social, and cultural life. Historically, they had been forced to live under Magyar, Italian, German, and Turkish overlords, each of whom left a legacy of disunion and chaos in which the guiding principle had been the golden rule of imperialism: divide and rule. It is therefore nothing short of miraculous that the movement for unification was achieved as early as 1918. With the destruction of Yugoslavia in 1941 at the hands of Germans, Italians, Magyars, and Bulgars, Yugoslav unity again became the ideal toward which the nation turned.

The Slovenes settled in the northern end of the west Balkan region, the Croats in the center, and the Serbs in the south. Geographical factors tended to separate the Croats from the Serbs. For the Croats who entered the region of the Sava tributary of the Danube the normal direction of expansion was westward, that is, to the coast of Dalmatia, to the Adriatic Sea, while for the Serbs it was southward, up the Morava and down the Vardar toward the Aegean. The Dinaric ridges which run north and south also invited the Serbs to move southward.

At some time early in their history the Slovenes or their ancestors probably occupied a much more extensive territory (perhaps even a large part of German Austria). Rooted as they both were

[ 33 ]

in the foothills of the Alps, they were not separated from the Croats geographically. But they did become separated politically. The German *Drang nach Osten* moved like a great glacier to the south over the Alps and down the Danube and forced the Slovenes to accept German domination and the religion of Rome. In this region only the Magyars were able to resist the pressure of the Germans to which the Slovenes almost succumbed. The Slovenes were thus left the smallest and weakest of the three elements among the Yugoslavs. Their fate until 1918 was wholly bound up with the German north.

Divided geographically, the Croats and the Serbs became separated politically also. The Kingdom of Croatia, after several centuries of independent rule initiated under Tomislav and Držislav in the tenth century, became associated with the Crown of Hungary in 1102 as a separate and independent political entity, and with the Habsburg dynasty after 1527. Legally, Croatia never lost its character as a distinct political entity. Late in the twelfth century the Serbs began their political expansion under the Nemanja dynasty and became the dominant political power in the Balkans under Stephen Dušan in the fourteenth century.

Whereas the Slovenes and Croats had become Roman Christians, the Serbs cast their lot after 1219 with the Orthodox Church of Constantinople. Thus the former accepted the religion and culture of the West and used the Latin alphabet to write Slovene and Croat; the Serbs adopted the religion and culture of the East—Byzantium—and the Cyrillic alphabet for the Serbian language. Had this religious and cultural cleavage not occurred there would not be so basic an internal Yugoslav problem today.

In the Middle Ages the Slovene regions became part of the Habsburg possessions. When the Croats began to lose some of their spirit of independence, a large portion of Croatia fell more and more under the power of the Hungarian Crown; the Dalmatian coast was incorporated in the realm of the Republic of Venice. By the middle of the fifteenth century the Serbs were virtually conquered by the Turks. As was customary, the loss of political independence brought with it the loss of the native nobility either through extermination or through assimilation by the conqueror. With certain minor exceptions, the Yugoslavs, like the Czecho-

CROATIAN HISTORY
A sculpture by Ivan Meštrović

BISHOP GREGORY OF NIN

A bronze statue by Meštrović, presented to the town
of Split by the sculptor

slovaks after the Battle of White Mountain (1620), were gradually reduced to an enserfed peasantry. They lost the political leadership of their wealthiest class, the large landholders. Under such circumstances their religious heads took over the national leadership: the Catholic among the Slovenes and Croats; the Orthodox among the Serbs.

The Yugoslavs remained in this condition for three or four centuries under the rule of German, Magyar, Italian, and Turk, each of whom worked strenuously to prevent union by exaggerating any differences the Yugoslavs might have among themselves, or even to create others in order to perpetuate their rule in this very strategic part of the Balkan Peninsula. During the Second World War, Nazi Germany and Fascist Magyar, Italian, and Bulgar were busy disintegrating the Yugoslavs into a condition similar to that in the fifteenth century.

The Yugoslavs had scarcely reached bottom in their historical evolution when a new course began to develop. The idea of Yugoslav unity germinated first in the imagination, blossomed next in literature and speech, and finally bore fruit in political action. Ragusa (Dubrovnik), famous for its role in medieval commerce, and Montenegro, in large part still unconquered by the Turks, alone kept alive the imagination of the Yugoslav people in the period of their deepest humiliation.

In the sixteenth and seventeenth centuries a few poets in Ragusa, at one end of the Yugoslav regions, and some from the Slovene districts, at the other end, insisted on using the native language in their plaintive themes. The Diets of Croatia continued, though in ever-weakening voice, to resist Magyar and Habsburg pressure. Serb refugees from Turkish Serbia increased in number and in wealth on the cattle ranges of southern Hungary, from which region they would emerge one day to give vigorous aid in the resurrection of Serbia.

Juraj Križanić, a Catholic Croat priest of the seventeenth century, became the first outstanding Pan-Slavist. He had studied in Rome at the College of St. Anastasius for Orthodox converts to the Uniat Church to prepare himself for work among Serbian Orthodox with the intention of winning them over to the Uniat Church. He, it will be remembered, went to Russia and there advocated the regeneration of medieval Russia and its transformation into a progressive, federalized state which would take the leadership in the movement to liberate the Slavs in Europe. He opposed the expansion of an autocratic Russia which might subjugate other Slavs as it had already treated the Ukrainians, and appealed to Tsar Alexis to help save dying Slavdom.

At the end of the seventeenth century and the beginning of the eighteenth, when the Ottoman Empire was beginning to decline and Venice to weaken, Austria and Russia appeared on the scene as heirs to the Balkan and Near Eastern legacy. The advance of these two empires into the Balkans, to the Adriatic, Aegean, and Black seas, contributed to the awakening of the Balkan Slavs. The Habsburgs won back all they had lost to the Turks and in the eighteenth century held a considerable part of Serbia. In anticipation of the time when all Yugoslavs would be included within the confines of the Monarchy, the council of professors of the Royal Academy of Sciences at Zagreb petitioned, in 1790, that it be raised to the rank of a university. This effort became part of the academic background of the idea of Yugoslav national unity. The Russians were advancing steadily toward the Black Sea until, by the end of the eighteenth century, they held nearly its entire northern coast.

The War of the Austrian Succession, which began with the seizure of Silesia by Frederick II in 1740, had greatly influenced the development of the Yugoslav regions. The loss of Silesia, one of the richest provinces of the Habsburgs, as well as the ever-growing menace of the Hohenzollerns to Habsburg supremacy in Germany, led to a political, economic, and military reorganization of the Monarchy under Maria Theresa and Joseph II. They carried out reforms which eventually led to the emancipation of the serf from personal bondage and to his economic and cultural improvement. Although centralization and Germanization had destroyed the medieval institutions which had guarded the historical rights of the nations, the Habsburg reforms and the threatened loss of nationality served to awaken the slumbering Yugoslavs and shock them into action.

The Habsburg Monarchy now sought to redirect its foreign trade from routes transiting north through Germany to routes running south through Trieste and Fiume, as well as down the Danube to the Black Sea—which meant that the Yugoslavs were to be on the main overseas export route of the Monarchy. This favorable situation encouraged economic development in the Yugoslav districts. However, it also led Austria in Trieste and Hungary in Fiume to insist on complete political domination of these ports to the exclusion of the Yugoslavs.

Among the latter, the Serbs of southern Hungary were the first to develop a relatively wealthy middle class, which thereafter was to replace their national nobility, most of whom had been destroyed by Germans, Magyars, Italians, or Turks. The fertile region occupied by the Serbs made them prosperous, and wealth gave them opportunity to make contacts in western Europe. There they became inspired by the new forces of nationalism and liberalism which were soon to triumph in the French Revolution.

With this background, it is no accident that the southern Hungarian Serb, Dositej Obradović (*ca.* 1742–1811), in his first printed work, *Pismo Haralampiju* (Letter to Haralampije), in 1783, began to advocate the use of the spoken or "common" Serbian language in place of Church Slavic Serbian, which was used chiefly by the clergy and intelligentsia, but not by the masses. Obradović thus elevated spoken Serbian to the status of a literary language. Moreover, he was one of the first evangelists of Yugoslav unity in the modern period. He rose above the religious or confessional conception of nationalism to that of a nationalism which embraced religious toleration. For Yugoslavs this was a matter of vital importance.

The literary activity of Vuk Stefanović Karadžić (1787–1864) gave supremacy among Serbo-Croatian dialects to the Što-dialect. His collection of Serbian national poems was a tremendous contribution to the Serb revival. It was therefore not surprising that Serbian Hungary was the starting point of Karageorge's* revolution, which was to give Serbia temporary freedom from the Ottoman Empire in 1804 and autonomy in 1830. It was this development which became the basis of the "Greater Serbia" idea.

In 1809 Napoleon's creation of the Illyrian Provinces brought

---

* "Karageorge" is the common Anglicized form, a transliteration of the Serbo-Croatian "Karadjordje."

Slovenes and Croats under united political rule for the first time. Although the rule of Marmont, the Duke of Ragusa, was relatively brief, it had great significance for the Yugoslavs. New ideas and reforms, especially in governmental administration and in the school system, caused dissatisfaction with the blundering and backward Habsburg rule reëstablished after the Congress of Vienna.

Valentin Vodnik (1758–1819), a Slovene poet, wrote about Illyria in fervent verse. The Croat, Ljudevit Gaj (1809–1872), turned Illyrianism into a Croat ideal in opposition to the policy of Magyarization after 1825. It was he who reformed Croatian orthography on the basis of the Serbian, as Vitez Bleiweiss and Stanko Vraz were doing simultaneously for the Slovene language. In fact, so much did Illyria mean to the Croats that it became the nucleus of the "Greater Croatia" movement among them.

Greater Serbia and Greater Croatia, both created in the first half of the nineteenth century, continued to exist side by side as good neighbors. The Revolution of 1848 inspired their gradual attachment to something greater, something more fundamental than either, namely, Yugoslav unity. The Revolution of 1848 brought about the first public fraternization of Croats and Serbs on a large scale. In it the Serbo-Croats of the Monarchy, supported by Serbs from Serbia, ostensibly fought for the Habsburgs against the Magyars with the hope of obtaining national concessions: the historical rights of the Triune Kingdom (Croatia, Slavonia, and Dalmatia) and of the Serb Vojvodina. Interpreted from the Yugoslav point of view, it would mean the creation of a third state alongside Austria and Hungary, in other words, Trialism. In this the Ban of Croatia, Josip Jelačić, was supported as dictator by the Croatian Diet at Zagreb and by the Serbian Assembly at Karlovac (Karlowitz), while the Serb Patriarch Josip Rajačić and the Croat Bishop Mirko Ožegović gave their blessing. Although the Habsburg dynasty was saved, its promises to the Yugoslavs were either not carried out or were withdrawn, as in the treatment of the Vojvodina in 1861. The succeeding decade of reaction (1850–1860) tended to separate Croat and Serb once more.

The prevailing depression was relieved only by the consciousness that Serbia, under Alexander Karageorgević and his Foreign Minister, Ilija Garašanin, had stretched out a helping hand to its

JOSIP JELAČIĆ (1801–1859)
Ban of Croatia

VUK KARADŽIĆ (1787–1864)
Father of the modern Serbian literary language

brethren in the north, and that Bishop Joseph George Strossmayer (1815–1905) and the historian Franjo Rački (1828–1894) had become the new evangelists among the Croats proclaiming "Yugoslavism as a substitute for Illyrianism." Both believed that the "Croat Question" and the "Serb Question" could be lastingly solved only by complete national unity in an independent Yugoslav state. Mutual respect between Croats and Serbs alone could overcome the obstacles and lead to a synthesis of their hopes and aspirations, but each element—Slovene, Serb, Croat, and Bulgar—would have to surrender something for the common good.

The promising Yugoslav outlook in Serbia at the beginning of the reign of Michael Obrenović (1860–1868) finally deteriorated into mere Great Serbianism and ended in his assassination. The Magyar rulers of Hungary were soon able to increase the advantages they had obtained under the *Ausgleich* of 1867 with Austria by which the Dual Monarchy was created. The Agreement (*Nagodba*) of 1868 with Croatia, arranged with a minority of Croats, riveted that country more securely to the Hungarian state than ever before. The form of autonomy permitted was better than nothing, but it was far from the trialistic solution demanded by the majority of Croats.

The uprising in Bosnia and Hercegovina in 1875 led to war with Turkey in which Russia, Serbia, Montenegro, and the Bulgars participated. It raised an ugly and almost insoluble problem for Croat and Serb, as well as for German, Magyar, and Turk—a problem which was not to be settled in 1878 or in 1908 or in the period from 1918 to 1939. In many ways Bosnia was *the* problem of Yugoslav unity and its solution was to be the test of Yugoslav political maturity. Stronger and more mature nations than the Yugoslav might have failed and did fail to solve similar problems. The Austro-Hungarian occupation of Bosnia and Hercegovina in 1878 made impossible a Greater Croatia or a Greater Serbia. On the contrary, it made the rise of a Yugoslavia inevitable.

The policy of almost complete subservience to Austria on the part of the Serbian Obrenović dynasty, the morally degenerating rule of Count Khuen-Hedérváry, Ban of Croatia from 1883 to 1903, and the inability of the Slovenes to agree upon a political program with vision characterized the generation before the coming of Peter Karageorgević to the throne of Serbia in 1903. This event, followed by the Serbo-Croat Coalition in 1905, and the annexation of Bosnia and Hercegovina in 1908, showed that a new era had dawned. The fate of the Yugoslavs hung in the balance as one event followed another in rapidly increasing tempo. The Serbo-Croat Coalition survived the crude attempt of Baron Rauch in the Agram (Zagreb) treason trial to destroy it through forgeries concocted within the walls of the Austro-Hungarian legation in Belgrade—forgeries which were designed also to provide a cause for war with Serbia. Whereas Serb, Croat, and Slovene were gradually, and in some ways almost reluctantly, drawn together by the course of events, the German, Austrian, and Magyar overlords, whose common objective was destruction of Serbia and complete subjugation of the Yugoslavs, were held apart by their rival appetites. The reconstruction of the Habsburg Monarchy into Austria-Hungary-Yugoslavia, namely, Trialism in place of Dualism, was blocked by Hungary. The previous German and Magyar domination, already undermined by the Serbo-Croat Coalition, was made still more impossible after Serbia had avenged "Kosovo with Kumanovo" in the war with the Turks in 1911–1912.

Out of the Serbian tragedy in the First World War emerged Yugoslavia—the Kingdom of the Serbs, Croats, and Slovenes—implied in the South Slav Parliamentary Club declaration of May 30, 1917, and specified in the Pact of Corfu of July 20, 1917, which was signed by Nikola Pašić, Premier of Serbia, and Ante Trumbić, the head of the London Yugoslav Committee. After the collapse of Bulgaria in September, 1918, there followed in October the declaration of Croatian independence from Austria-Hungary, and in November the requests for union with Serbia on the part of Montenegro, the Serbian Vojvodina, and the National Assembly of Slovenes, Croats, and Serbs in Austria-Hungary. Prince Regent Alexander, on behalf of King Peter I, thereupon proclaimed the Kingdom of the Serbs, Croats, and Slovenes on December 1, 1918.

# CHAPTER IV

# Serbia, Yugoslavia, and the Habsburg Empire

## BY BERNADOTTE E. SCHMITT

FROM THE TREATY OF BERLIN to the Serbian Revolution of 1903 the rulers of Serbia and their governments were under the domination of Austria-Hungary, even though in the last years of his life King Alexander Obrenović had proved difficult to manage. The cabinet of Vienna evidently did not expect the change of dynasty to affect this situation, for the Emperor Francis Joseph was the first monarch to recognize Peter Karageorgević as King of Serbia; the Austrian government was apparently confident that the commercial treaty of 1893 would continue to provide the means for keeping Serbia in subjection.

This calculation, however, was soon proved wrong. The new king, a democrat by conviction and made wise by the experience of his predecessors, determined to be a constitutional rather than a personal ruler and left the actual government of the country to the Radical party, which was the strongest political factor in Serbia. Traditionally friendly to Russia and resentful of the Austrian economic domination, the Radical government, in which Nikola Pašić was a leading figure, embarked on a policy of emancipation by negotiating a customs union with Bulgaria, concluding a favorable commercial treaty with Germany, and planning to buy artillery for the Serbian army, hitherto obtained from the Škoda factories in Austria, through Schneider-Creusot in France.

The Austrian government, greatly surprised at this display of Serbian independence, tried to meet the challenge by denouncing the commercial treaty of 1893 and making a new treaty dependent on a modification of the Serbo-Bulgarian customs union. It also demanded that Austrian industry be given preference in supplying the Serbian government with arms. When these conditions were rejected, the Hungarian frontier was closed to the importation of Serbian livestock.

Instead of yielding to this pressure, Serbia promptly made arrangements with Turkey for the export of pigs and cattle by way of Salonika, bought guns in France and ammunition in Germany, and refused to grant privileges to Austro-Hungarian industry. The little landlocked state successfully defied its mighty neighbor until 1910, when a new commercial treaty was negotiated as between equals. Although this agreement did, it is true, reduce the imports of Serbian livestock into Austria-Hungary, Austrian imports into Serbia were correspondingly reduced—which was what mattered to a government and a people trying to escape from economic subjection. This "pig war" was a bad blunder on the part of Austria-Hungary, not only because it was defeated on a field of its own choosing, but even more because the Serbian peasantry became convinced that the Habsburg state stood in the way of their prosperity and began to develop a bitter hatred of their northern neighbor. The Austrian and Hungarian statesmen, however, never accepted their defeat and regarded with suspicion the overtures which Serbia made from time to time for better relations.

Long before the economic compromise of 1910, relations between Austria-Hungary and Serbia had been further exacerbated by the annexation of Bosnia-Hercegovina in October, 1908. This highhanded action by Austria-Hungary—a deliberate and unilateral violation of the Treaty of Berlin—was occasioned by considerations of internal as well as external policy. By the Compromise of 1867 the Germans had received a privileged position in Austria, the Magyars in Hungary; whereas the Yugoslavs in the southwestern provinces of the Habsburg Monarchy were left partly under Austrian and partly under Hungarian rule—and were thereby rendered powerless.

At the turn of the century this policy of *divide et impera* began to break down, for Slovenes, Croats, and Serbs were beginning to realize that they were all Yugoslavs and complained of the existing political arrangements. In 1905 the Serbs and Croats in the

Croatian Diet, hitherto played off against each other by the governor appointed by Budapest, formed a coalition against him. Eventually, the Croatian constitution was suspended by the Hungarian government and the country was ruled by martial law. Among the Slovenes the obscurantism of the dominant clerical party was resented and challenged. Above all, in Bosnia-Hercegovina the failure of the Austro-Hungarian "occupation" to reform the feudal land regime, the neglect of higher education, the lack of adequate communication with other parts of the Monarchy, and the monopoly in administration by Germans and Magyars caused much discontent, even though some material progress had been achieved since 1878.

Besides these local rumblings, Serbia provided further worries for Austria-Hungary. Down to 1903 its rotten politics and poor economic situation offered no attraction to the Yugoslavs of the Monarchy, but after the revolution of that year its government was free and democratic and its success in the "pig war" made a deep impression in Croatia and Dalmatia. At the coronation of King Peter, Stjepan Radić, the leader of the Croatian Peasant party, shouted, "Long live the King of Yugoslavia!" In the next few years many contacts were established between the political leaders of the Yugoslav provinces and their kinsmen in Serbia. This caused such concern among conservatives in Vienna and Budapest that in August, 1908, the governor of Croatia arrested fifty-two persons on charges of treason, only to postpone bringing them to trial until the following March. Although thirty-one of the accused were convicted, the trial at Zagreb was conducted with great unfairness and the verdict of guilty was not generally accepted outside the Monarchy. Relations between Austria-Hungary and Serbia were only made worse by the affair.

Since the policy of keeping Serbia economically and politically dependent on Austria-Hungary had signally failed, something had to be done. The Emperor Francis Joseph and the ruling groups in both halves of the Monarchy were opposed to any modification of the existing dualism in order to appease the Yugoslavs. Accordingly, Count Alois Lexa Aehrenthal, the Minister of Foreign Affairs, conceived the plan of solving the problem by an external stroke instead of by internal reforms. He proposed the

annexation of Bosnia-Hercegovina, which would put an end
to long-cherished Serbian hopes of obtaining the two provinces,
would pave the way for their incorporation in the Habsburg state,
and would destroy the prestige of Serbia among the restless Yugoslav subjects of the Monarchy. Incidentally, such a step would
prove (so Aehrenthal reasoned) that Austria-Hungary was still a
Great Power in spite of its internal dissension and could act independently of its ally, the German Empire.

As a first move in this boldly conceived policy, Aehrenthal, in
January, 1908, obtained a concession from the Turkish govern-
ment to build a railway from Mitrovica, in the Sanjak of Novi
Pazar, across Turkish territory to Salonika. The new line was
intended to compete with the existing railway from Belgrade to
Salonika and to make possible the transport of troops into Old
Serbia. Fortunately for Serbia, the Young Turk Revolution of
July, 1908, occurred before the line could be built, but its purpose
was obvious. Russia at once made a counterdemand for a railway
from the Danube across Serbia to the Adriatic; this also was over-
taken by the Turkish Revolution. Neither line has yet been built.

The revolution, however, played into Aehrenthal's hands, because the Young Turks summoned representatives from Bosnia-
Hercegovina, which had been left under the nominal suzerainty
of the sultan, to the new Turkish parliament. This, it was argued
in Vienna, would prevent the introduction of constitutional government in the provinces, on which Austria-Hungary had determined; Aehrenthal, on August 19, persuaded the Council of Ministers to agree to the annexation of the two provinces, asserting that
this would be the best means of "putting an end to the Great Serbian dreams of the future." The annexation was, in fact, proclaimed on October 6, 1908. But the consequences were not what
Austria-Hungary had expected.

Before broaching the matter of annexation to the ministers,
Aehrenthal had opened negotiations with the Russian Foreign
Minister, Izvolsky, for in 1897 the Russian government had made
clear that its consent would be necessary for any change in the
status of Bosnia-Hercegovina. This consent Aehrenthal was willing to purchase by assuming a friendly attitude toward Izvolsky's
plans for opening the Straits at Constantinople to Russian men-

of-war. On September 15 the two ministers met at Buchlau, the chateau of Count Berchtold, the Austro-Hungarian ambassador at St. Petersburg, to arrange the details. Although violent disagreement subsequently arose over certain points—whether Aehrenthal explained that annexation was planned for early October and whether Izvolsky made clear that changes must be ratified by a European conference—there is no doubt that Izvolsky agreed in principle to annexation and, both before and after the meeting with Aehrenthal, gave Serbian diplomatists to understand that Serbia must reconcile itself to the loss of the coveted provinces.

This, however, was just what Serbia refused to do. As soon as the annexation was proclaimed, it not only protested but also began to mobilize its army, thereby precipitating a crisis which nearly ushered in a European war. Aehrenthal was furious and refused to receive the Serbian protest, for Serbia was not a signatory to the Treaty of Berlin and could not properly protest against its violation. Nevertheless, Serbia maintained its attitude for nearly six months, thanks to the support of Russia.

Although Izvolsky had certainly accepted the annexation in principle, he asserted that he had been tricked by Aehrenthal as to the time when it would be proclaimed, so that he had had no opportunity to secure the consent of the other Powers to his plan for opening the Straits; he was, therefore, so he argued, released from his promise not to oppose the annexation. Furthermore, Russian public opinion showed no interest in the opening of the Straits, but it was profoundly moved by the annexation of two Slav provinces by a non-Slavic Power. To save himself from the reproaches of the Russian public, Izvolsky was constrained not only to support Serbia against Austria-Hungary but to demand territorial compensation for Serbia.

The British government, having shown little enthusiasm for Izvolsky's scheme to open the Straits, and annoyed by Aehrenthal's cavalier violation of the Treaty of Berlin, also supported Serbia. Germany, on the contrary, stood resolutely behind Austria-Hungary. Although Aehrenthal bought off Turkey, the nominally injured party, for a substantial sum in cash, he was not able to obtain recognition of the annexation from Russia and Great Britain, let alone Serbia. For months the deadlock continued.

By March, 1909, Aehrenthal, who had anticipated a diplomatic triumph at the expense of Serbia, had become desperate enough to yield to the insistence of the Austrian military party, which had long urged war against Serbia. Preparations were made to present Serbia with an ultimatum and to go to war. The Russians learned enough about these plans to become alarmed and, since they were not strong enough to fight the Central Powers alone and could expect only halfhearted support from France and only diplomatic assistance from Great Britain, they withdrew their backing from Serbia.

Left alone and pressed by the other Powers, Serbia, on March 31, 1909, addressed a note to Austria-Hungary, the text of which had been agreed upon by Aehrenthal and Sir Edward Grey, the British Foreign Secretary. Serbia recognized that "the *fait accompli* regarding Bosnia has not affected its rights" and promised "in deference to the advice of the Great Powers ... to renounce from now onward the attitude of protest and opposition which it has adopted with regard to the annexation since last autumn"; it also undertook "to change the direction of its present policy toward Austria-Hungary in order henceforth to live on terms of good neighborliness with the latter." The Great Powers then recognized the annexation.

Aehrenthal's diplomatic victory was, however, quite meaningless. Russia let Serbia know that its recognition of the annexation was not to be taken seriously and that when Russia was adequately prepared in a military way it would "unroll and solve the Serbian question"—that is, at the expense of Austria-Hungary. Not only that, but the Russian government had become convinced of the aggressive designs of Austria-Hungary against Serbia and, with the object of preventing any new humiliation of Serbia and of erecting a barrier against an Austrian advance on Salonika, set about the creation of an alliance between Serbia and Bulgaria.

Owing to the bitter rivalry of the two small states for the succession in Macedonia, the first attempt was unsuccessful, but in 1912 a treaty was concluded between Serbia and Bulgaria. Although directed primarily against Turkey, the treaty was so worded as to make possible its use against Austria-Hungary also. Even if the alliance became operative only against Turkey, it was expected that

Serbia, having abandoned Macedonia to Bulgaria, would conquer Albanian territory and reach the Adriatic, thereby emancipating itself once for all from the economic pressure of Austria-Hungary. Although the cabinet of Vienna obtained some knowledge of this treaty, it apparently did not take the news seriously and made no plans to deal with the situation.

For years Austria and Russia had struggled diplomatically to control the policy of Bulgaria, whose wily Prince Ferdinand cleverly played them off against each other. Gradually Russia forged ahead. In 1902 a military convention was concluded with Bulgaria; in 1909 it was Russia that conceived and negotiated a settlement of the difficulties raised with Turkey by the proclamation of Bulgarian independence in October, 1908. The pro-Russian sentiment of the Bulgarian peasantry was not affected by the maneuvers of Ferdinand.

War between Turkey and the Balkan League broke out in October, 1912. The Austro-Hungarian government toyed with the idea of preventing Serbia from sending troops into the Sanjak of Novi Pazar (which Austria had evacuated at the time of the Bosnian annexation), but apparently Berchtold, who had succeeded Aehrenthal as Foreign Minister on the latter's death in February, 1912, could not nerve himself to vigorous action and events were allowed to take their course. To the consternation of Vienna, the Serbian armies overwhelmed the Turks, marched across Albania to the Adriatic, and announced their determination to retain a "window" on that sea.

The Austro-Hungarian government was nonplused. In Bohemia and throughout the Yugoslav provinces the Serbian victories were hailed with enthusiasm and both volunteers and material aid streamed over the frontier into Serbia; armed intervention against Serbia would be highly unpopular—if not dangerous—among the Slavs of the Monarchy. Yet to admit the Serbian claims would deprive Austria of the last lever for controlling the little state. Berchtold tried to solve the problem by suggesting that Serbia should seek an outlet through Salonika (which would probably lead to trouble with Bulgaria and the breakup of the Balkan League); he also hinted at the possibility of "a close economic relationship" between Serbia and the Monarchy. When this overture was declined by the Serbian government, Berchtold refused to receive Premier Pašić, who offered "all possible economic concessions" if Serbia were allowed to keep its corridor to the Adriatic.

The Austro-Hungarian government finally demanded, in the name of Albanian nationality, that Serbia withdraw from the Adriatic coast and that Albania be established as an independent state. To support this demand, reservists began to be called up and troops were concentrated in Bosnia. Still more important was the fact that the Austrian attitude was supported by Germany and Italy, in proof whereof the renewal of the Triple Alliance was announced early in December, nearly eighteen months ahead of its expiration. Once again the military party in Austria-Hungary hoped to take advantage of the opportunity to bring on war and smash Serbia once for all.

War was, in fact, narrowly averted, for the Serbs were quite willing to risk it. But Russia, although it had been reorganizing its army ever since the Bosnian crisis, was not yet ready and informed Serbia that it would not go to war on the issue of an Adriatic port. As in 1908–1909, Russia was sure of only diplomatic support from Great Britain, though the attitude of France was more resolute. Serbia therefore had to accept the promise of an economic outlet to be secured by a railway across Albania, consoling itself with the hope of a better future held out by the Russian government, for "time was working for Serbia and for the ruin of its enemies."

Because Serbia's submission removed the excuse for war so ardently desired by General Conrad von Hötzendorf, the Austrian chief of staff, Austrian diplomacy attempted to bring about the humiliation of Serbia in another way. Having been excluded from the Adriatic by the fiat of Vienna, Serbia instinctively sought compensation for the loss of the Adriatic "window" by advancing claims to Macedonia, although by the treaty of alliance it had renounced most of this region in favor of Bulgaria. Austria therefore supported the claims of Bulgaria and even discreetly urged Bulgaria to fight Serbia. This calculation also misfired. When Bulgaria treacherously attacked Serbia and Greece at the end of June, 1913, it was defeated and forced to surrender Macedonia. Furthermore, when Berchtold, alarmed by the defeat of Bulgaria, sounded the German and Italian governments on the possibility of Austrian intervention against Serbia, he met with sharp rebuffs and consequently was not able to take any action in behalf of Bulgaria.

Thus Serbia emerged victorious from both Balkan wars: it had doubled its territory as well as its population; perhaps even more important, it had greatly increased its prestige among the Yugoslav population of Austria-Hungary. The rage of Vienna and Budapest was exceeded only by their pessimistic view of the future. Pašić is reported to have declared, "The first round is won; now we must prepare for the second round against Austria." That an open clash was inevitable was now accepted by both sides.

It almost came in October, 1913, when the Serbs, annoyed by raids, occupied some territory which had been awarded to Albania by the Great Powers. Berchtold promptly launched an ultimatum, which this time had the support of Germany, and the Serbian troops were withdrawn. Henceforth the Serbs knew what to expect, especially since Berchtold, two weeks before, had a second time declined to negotiate with Pašić, who had made a special trip to Vienna to see him. Evidently the Serbs were not greatly upset, however, for they decided to bide their time. In February, 1914, Pašić went to Russia to beg for munitions, as the Serbian supply had been exhausted in the Balkan wars, and to ask the tsar to give the hand of one of his daughters to the Serbian Crown Prince Alexander. Without making a definite promise on either matter Nicholas II instructed Nikola Pašić to tell King Peter, in Russian, that "for Serbia we shall do everything." Actually, up to July, 1914, the "everything" had not materialized; on the contrary, Russia was constantly advising Serbia not to provoke Austria-Hungary.

Thus, in the eleven years following the fall of the Obrenović dynasty, Serbia had passed out of the Austrian orbit and had become the protégé of Russia. It was now economically independent and had built up its military prestige. Serbian achievements were cheered by the restless Yugoslav peoples of the Monarchy. The Austro-Hungarian government had rejected both the policy of military conquest advocated by Conrad von Hötzendorf and the offer of compromise put forward by Pašić.

By the spring of 1914 it was evident that Vienna would have to devise a new policy, all the more so because Rumania, the ally of the Habsburg Monarchy since 1883, had been alienated in the course of the Balkan war by Berchtold's pro-Bulgarian policy, had entered into an entente with Serbia, and was even playing up to Russia. Count Tisza, the Hungarian Premier, drew up a memorandum in March, urging that an effort should be made to reconcile Bulgaria and Rumania as a preliminary to the formation of a new Balkan League which should include, besides these two states, Greece and Turkey. In other words, Serbia should be isolated and forced to surrender Macedonia to Bulgaria. The Foreign Office, in June, elaborated Tisza's ideas in another memorandum, which was to be transmitted to the German government, adding the proposal that Bulgaria should be admitted to the Triple Alliance, a move which, it was hoped, would bring Rumania to terms and separate it from both Serbia and Russia.

Just before the memorandum received its final form, the German emperor visited the Archduke Francis Ferdinand at the latter's castle in Konopište, Bohemia. Many stories, some of them ridiculous, have been circulated about this famous meeting, but one thing seems clear: the archduke asked his visitor whether Austria-Hungary could count on the support of Germany in the event of war. There is other evidence, also, which suggests that in the spring of 1914 war against Serbia was being considered in high Austrian circles. As it happened, the excuse for such a course was provided just two weeks after the meeting at Konopište by the assassination of Francis Ferdinand and his wife which took place at Sarajevo on Sunday, June 28, 1914.

Besides the formal relations between Austria-Hungary and Serbia the Yugoslav revolutionary movement must be considered. It was rapidly developing as a result of the political and economic conditions in Croatia, Dalmatia, and Bosnia. Its membership was recruited in large measure from the restless younger generation, who were influenced by the works of Russian revolutionaries. Sometimes they made contacts with Russian terrorists and eagerly imitated their methods.

When the Emperor Francis Joseph came to Sarajevo in 1910 to open the Bosnian Diet that was intended to mark the inauguration of constitutional government in the annexed provinces, a student from southern Bosnia, Bogdan Žerajić, shot at the governor, General Varašanin. The attempt at assassination failed and Žerajić committed suicide on the spot. Two years later, Vladimir Gaćinović, son of an Orthodox priest from Hercegovina, glorified the exploit of Žerajić in "The Death of a Hero," a pamphlet that circulated widely and made Žerajić a martyr in the eyes of many students. Gaćinović became the intellectual leader of the revolutionary movement and helped to organize many terrorist groups and secret societies, one of which, in Sarajevo, is said to have had about a hundred members. These groups undermined discipline in the schools and impelled Austro-Hungarian officials to take drastic measures. Apprehension was increased by the repeated attempts, between 1912 and 1914, to assassinate the governor of Croatia.

The exact connection between the revolutionary organization, the Mlada Bosna (Young Bosnia), and Serbia—whether in official circles or through secret societies—is not known. But there can be no doubt that the agitation in the Yugoslav provinces was stimulated from Serbia, and for that reason many persons in Austria-Hungary sincerely believed that the Monarchy must either crush Serbia or be destroyed by it. Unrest, however, had existed long before Serbian propaganda got to work, for the mass of the population, which was preponderantly Serb, had never reconciled itself to the "occupation" and therefore objected even more to the annexation.

In July, 1914, the Austro-Hungarian government ascribed the unrest to the machinations of a society known as the Narodna Odbrana (National Defense), which had been organized in October, 1908, on the eve of the Bosnian annexation, by a group of Serbian notables to "protect and promote our interests in the annexed provinces." It began to enlist *komitadjis* (guerrillas) for the war which was expected with Austria and to arouse public opinion in both Serbia and Bosnia-Hercegovina. Even after the annexation had been recognized by the Serbian government, the Narodna Odbrana, to which soldiers and politicians as well as private persons belonged, continued to carry on its activity unofficially and to organize the people intellectually and spiritually for a future struggle between Serbia and Austria-Hungary. In 1910 the society had twenty-three branches in Bosnia, of which the most notable were the Prosvjeta (Culture), the Pobratimstvo (Brotherhood), and the Sokols (Falcons), a gymnastic organization copied from the Czechoslovaks. Outwardly, the Narodna Odbrana continued to represent itself as a purely cultural society; its connection with the revolutionary movement was so well concealed that it was not discovered by the Austro-Hungarian government, which incorrectly charged the Narodna Odbrana with activity emanating from another organization, the Ujedinjenje ili Smrt (Union or Death).

The latter had been formed in 1911 by ten men, most of them army officers, as a secret revolutionary society with the object of bringing about "the union of all Serbs" under the aegis of the Kingdom of Serbia. This task it proposed to accomplish by "terrorist action in all the territories inhabited by Serbs,"—that is, in Macedonia and Bosnia. Several hundred members were enlisted, including many important army officers. They were initiated by a melodramatic ceremony and were known to each other only by number. Discipline was rigid and the Central Executive Committee possessed absolute authority over all members, who expected no personal gain. The flag of the society bore a death's head and its other emblems were a dagger, a bomb, and a bottle of poison. Altogether, the society seems to have combined the loyalty of the Jesuits, the ruthlessness of Russian nihilists, and the mystery of the Ku Klux Klan.

Leadership of the organization was soon assumed by Colonel Dragutin Dimitrijević, who had been deeply involved in the Revolution of 1903. A man of great charm, utterly selfless, and possessed of a passionate patriotism, he won the devotion of the members of the society and made it a strong political factor in the state. According to one account, Dimitrijević was an inveterate conspirator. But, although he was executed in 1917 for an alleged attempt to assassinate Crown Prince Alexander, he was almost certainly innocent of the charge.

Other members of the society were Major Vojislav Tankosić, who had been associated with Dimitrijević in the Revolution of 1903; Milan Ciganović, a Bosnian émigré employed by the Serbian state railways; Vladimir Gaćinović, the leader of the Mlada Bosna; and, apparently, a number of people from official circles, although no one of cabinet rank or high political station is known to have belonged. The organization consisted mainly of army officers who distrusted politicians and wished to see the army control the state.

When the Ujedinjenje ili Smrt was first organized, it devoted itself, with the approval of the Ministry of Foreign Affairs, to Serbian propaganda in Macedonia, where the Bulgarians had hitherto not been effectively challenged, and its activity undoubtedly strengthened the Serbian position in that contested area. In the course of the Balkan wars its members opposed concessions to Bulgaria; after the war, when Macedonia had been won, it expected its reward. But a sharp struggle developed in Macedonia between army and civilian administration. The Ujedinjenje ili Smrt supported the army against the Radical party.

In June, 1914, a cabinet crisis was precipitated by the resignation of the war minister. Although Pašić was able, with the help of the Russian Minister, Nicholas von Hartvig, who had great influence in Belgrade, to reconstitute his cabinet and remain in power, he was forced to appeal to the country in a new election. His position was strengthened by the abdication of King Peter, who was supposed to favor the army, and by the appointment of Crown Prince Alexander as regent, but the prime minister faced a bitter fight in which the whole strength of the Ujedinjenje ili Smrt would be thrown against him. Thus a critical situation existed when the murder at Sarajevo occurred.

The quarrel between the army and the Radical party apparently did not affect the activity of the Ujedinjenje ili Smrt outside the frontiers of Serbia, which, after all, was the reason for its existence. In 1911 the Serbian General Staff, of which Dimitrijević was a member, had appointed "frontier officers" along the Turkish and Bosnian borders to obtain military intelligence. When the Ujedinjenje ili Smrt was founded, the officers were taken into the society. On the Bosnian frontier they established contacts with the Narodna Odbrana, which had kept up its activity in Bosnia.

Major Milan Vasić, a member of the Ujedinjenje ili Smrt, became secretary of the Narodna Odbrana. Thus the new, secret revolutionary society took over the older, nominally cultural organization. The Ujedinjenje ili Smrt carried on propaganda and revolutionary agitation in Bosnia-Hercegovina, but allowed it to be done in the name of the Narodna Odbrana. From the Austro-

Hungarian point of view it made no difference which organization carried on subversive activity; but Vienna failed to ferret out the connection between the two, and its indictment of Serbia in July, 1914, did not mention the real authors of the agitation in Bosnia.

According to the testimony of one frontier officer, their activity was too successful. "The warlike feeling and extreme excitement among the masses of our people in Bosnia-Hercegovina attained such proportions that they began to become dangerous." The Serbian successes in the Balkan wars "gave perfect confidence and faith in the power of Serbia to the hearts of our people in Bosnia-Hercegovina and simultaneously awakened the hope that their liberation would soon and surely come." The agitation of the Ujedinjenje ili Smrt was directed particularly toward the youth of Bosnia, for "the older generation had lost faith in itself, had become less capable of resistance, and had strayed away to the paths of compromise and haggling." There is no doubt that the rising generation showed itself receptive to this propaganda and became increasingly revolutionary in both sentiment and action. Discipline in the schools was seriously affected and an increasing number of students crossed the border to Belgrade, where they were subjected to the full force of the Serbian national idea.

The Serbian government was none too pleased at the activity of the Ujedinjenje ili Smrt, for it was afraid of giving Austria-Hungary an excuse for action. The Bosnian agitation, moreover, was inspired by the ideal of Yugoslav unity, whereas those in power in Belgrade were partisans of Greater Serbia. In January, 1914, accordingly, the Serbian government stopped the work of the frontier officers and transferred them to regular duty in the interior. But by this time the revolutionary ferment in Bosnia needed no further stimulation; it was, in fact, more active than ever in the spring of 1914.

The Austro-Hungarian authorities were baffled by the situation. The only solution was repression, and this merely added to the discontent. Only a few persons in the Monarchy recognized that the Yugoslav question could not be solved merely by suppressing Serbia, and that what was needed was a revamping of the political system which would both appease the restless Yugoslavs within the Monarchy and appeal to the Serbs outside.

Among the few was the Archduke Francis Ferdinand, the heir to the throne, who wished to abolish dualism and replace it by a trialism which would establish a Yugoslav kingdom having the same status as Austria and Hungary. His plans were resented not only by the ruling group in Austria and Hungary but by the revolutionary elements in Bosnia and Serbia, who were opposed to the achievement of Yugoslav unity *within* the Habsburg Monarchy and feared that realization of Francis Ferdinand's schemes might destroy the appeal of their own program of Yugoslav unity *outside* the Monarchy. From this point of view, his removal from the scene was greatly to be desired and plots for his assassination were apparently being laid before 1914. In some Serbian circles Francis Ferdinand was expected to try to solve the question by an attack on Serbia which, if successful, would mean the end of Serbian independence. Thus from a Serbian point of view, also, the disappearance of the archduke would be welcome.

In March, 1914, it became known that the Austro-Hungarian army would hold maneuvers in Bosnia in June and that Francis Ferdinand would visit Sarajevo, the capital of the province, on the twenty-eighth. This—St. Vitus' Day—was the national holiday of Serbdom, the anniversary of the Battle of Kosovo in 1389, when the medieval Serb state was destroyed by the Turks. The choice of this day for the royal visit to the Bosnian capital was therefore interpreted in revolutionary circles as a gratuitous insult.

Among those who were disgusted by the news were three young Bosnians, hardly out of their teens, Gavrilo Princip, Nedeljko Čabrinović, and Trifko Grabež, who were living in Belgrade. They plotted to assassinate Francis Ferdinand when he came to Sarajevo. Princip, the leader of the group, was not only an ardent revolutionist but, having been rejected for military service in the Serbian army during the Balkan wars, was anxious to justify himself by a conspicuous deed. Čabrinović had had the roving and enigmatic career of a ne'er-do-well. He possessed no strong convictions, but was ready for any desperate adventure. Grabež, also, was not a very positive character, but he had known Princip since boyhood and was asked to join because Princip did not fully trust Čabrinović. All three were in contact with Milan Ciganović, a fellow-Bosnian, a *komitadji,* and a member of the Ujedinjenje ili Smrt.

It is possible that Princip, under the influence of Vladimir Gaćinović, had conceived the idea of killing Francis Ferdinand as early as the autumn of 1913, but the evidence is inconclusive.

Weapons to carry out the plot against the archduke were obtained from Milan Ciganović, who procured them through Major Vojislav Tankosić. The bombs and revolvers apparently came from the Serbian state arsenal at Kragujevac; according to one account, they were paid for by Colonel Dimitrijević. Ciganović instructed the young men in their use and then arranged for the journey to Sarajevo. The three conspirators left Belgrade at the end of May, crossed the frontier by means of "tunnels" (that is, with the connivance of officials on both sides), and, after several narrow escapes from detection by the Austrian police, arrived at Sarajevo early in June, several weeks before the visit of Francis Ferdinand. They hid their weapons in the house of Danilo Ilić, a schoolteacher who was a friend of Princip and an active member of the revolutionary group.

To what extent Dimitrijević, the leader of the Ujedinjenje ili Smrt, was involved in the scheme is uncertain. In 1923 a Belgrade professor, who was a political enemy, circulated the story that in June, 1914, Dimitrijević, at that time chief of the intelligence section of the Serbian General Staff, received information from Russia that, at their meeting in Konopište, William II had promised Francis Ferdinand to support his plan to attack and overpower Serbia. The Austrian maneuvers to be held in Bosnia pointed in the same direction. Dimitrijević thereupon decided that the impending attack on Serbia could be prevented only by the murder of the archduke.

While he was in this mood, his friend Tankosić informed him that two young Bosnians (Princip and Čabrinović) in Belgrade were planning to assassinate Francis Ferdinand. Dimitrijević at once accepted their services and, through Tankosić, supplied them with weapons. Later he informed the Central Committee of the Ujedinjenje ili Smrt of what he had done; they disapproved so strongly that Dimitrijević agreed to stop the intrigue and sent orders to Sarajevo. But either it was too late or the orders were not obeyed.

Other versions of the story were circulated from time to time, chiefly by friends of Dimitrijević. In the welter of conflicting evidence, the author of this chapter inclines to the view that Dimitrijević heard of the plot being hatched by Princip and his two associates, but thought them too young to be taken seriously and was greatly surprised when they succeeded in killing the archduke. Subsequently, he invented the story of receiving a report from Russia about the meeting at Konopište as an excuse for having had any connection with the scheme. Actually, the three conspirators had reached Bosnia at least a week before William II visited Francis Ferdinand.

In 1914 the Austro-Hungarian government did not charge the Serbian government with involvement in the murder at Sarajevo; the general circumstances of Serbia at that time made its connivance seem most unlikely. In June, 1924, however, ten years after the crime, Ljuba Jovanović, who had been Minister of Education in the Pašić cabinet of 1914, published a statement to the effect that Pašić had informed the cabinet "at the end of May or the beginning of June," 1914, that "there were people who were preparing to go to Sarajevo to kill Francis Ferdinand, who was to go there to be solemnly received on St. Vitus' Day." This declaration precipitated a lively controversy. After a long delay, Pašić impugned the veracity of his former colleague, but he did not produce much evidence against Jovanović. The latter made no reply to charges of exaggeration and misrepresentation. Both men died before the matter was cleared up. Until official documents are published it will be impossible to determine whether the Serbian government knew of the plot.

A possible explanation of the enigma is that sometime before Princip and his friends crossed the frontier another group of agitators trying to pass into Bosnia were caught by the Serbian police and the incident was reported to the cabinet. Ljuba Jovanović, writing years later, may have had this in mind when he declared that Pašić had spoken to the cabinet about Princip.

It is sometimes alleged, also, that Russia was involved in the conspiracy, either through Nicholas von Hartvig, the Minister at Belgrade, who was a strong supporter of Serbian national aspirations, or through Colonel Artamanov, the military attaché. The evidence is not very convincing and is further weakened by the fact that both men were absent from Belgrade on June 28; if they had known that Francis Ferdinand was to be assassinated, they would surely have remained in Belgrade to keep in touch with the situation.

In view of the uncertainty concerning the Serbian government's knowledge of the plot, the question whether it sent any warning to Vienna is not altogether pertinent. Both in 1914 and after the war, it was stated that a warning had been sent, but what actually happened was quite different. Jovan Jovanović, the Serbian Minister at Vienna, aware of the resentment in Bosnia over the approaching visit of Francis Ferdinand and fearful of some incident which might disturb the delicate relations between Austria-Hungary and Serbia, decided on his own initiative to speak to Bilinski, the Minister in Charge of Bosnian Affairs. (His own relations with Berchtold, the Foreign Minister, were somewhat strained.) Jovanović explained that army maneuvers would be regarded in Bosnia as a "provocation" and that some Serbian youth "might put a live cartridge in his rifle or revolver instead of a blank one" and shoot at Francis Ferdinand; "it would, therefore, be well and wise for the archduke not to go to Sarajevo." Bilinski promised to inform Francis Ferdinand, but apparently he did not do so; whether he spoke to Berchtold about the visit of the Serbian minister is uncertain.

Equally uncertain is it whether warnings of the scheme were received by the Austro-Hungarian authorities from other sources. The evidence suggests that some kind of warning was given to Francis Ferdinand and that he was reluctant to go to Sarajevo. The stories lack definiteness, but leave one with the uncomfortable impression that not all the facts have come to light.

Whatever the truth, there is no doubt that the measures taken to protect the royal visitors in Sarajevo were inadequate. In the interest of economy, the local police force was not greatly increased; and, since the visit was being made in connection with army maneuvers, the military authorities insisted on controlling the arrangements. When the Emperor Francis Joseph visited Sarajevo in 1910 for the opening of the Bosnian Diet, the streets were lined with a double cordon of troops; but on June 28, 1914, this precaution was not taken, although General Potiorek, the commander of the garrison, was well aware of the restlessness of the population. He may have felt that such a drastic measure would destroy the good effects of the visit, but he must be held responsible for the consequences of his decision.

Francis Ferdinand and his consort arrived at Ilidža, a resort near Sarajevo, in time for the maneuvers and were well received when they drove through the city on the afternoon of June 26. On Sunday morning, the twenty-eighth—the anniversary of Kosovo, of the Austro-Serbian Treaty of 1881, and of their own marriage,— the august pair made their official visit to Sarajevo. As they were driving to the town hall, Čabrinović hurled a bomb at the archduke, but it struck his adjutant riding in the next car.

After the ceremonies at the town hall, Francis Ferdinand insisted on visiting the wounded man at the hospital. Although this involved a change of route, the chauffeurs of the motorcars were not informed, apparently, and therefore adhered to the directions originally given them. The archduke's car, consequently, made a wrong turn and was forced to back up—at the very corner where Princip was standing. He had let the car go past, but now that it was stopped for a moment, he drew his revolver and shot both Francis Ferdinand and his wife, who died before medical aid could be brought. But for this accident or oversight, it seems unlikely that the archduke would have met his death that day, since Grabež took no action, nor did any of the local "reserves" whom Ilić was supposed to have provided.

The news of the murder was received in Belgrade the same day and the government promptly stopped the celebration of the national holiday that was in progress, and condemned the crime in the semiofficial newspaper. But public opinion, in general, rejoiced over the death of a hated enemy and some newspapers indulged in vituperative language. The government made a tactical blunder in failing to institute an investigation and in allowing Ciganović to escape from Belgrade. Its position was difficult, for any concession to Austria-Hungary would have been exploited by the Ujedinjenje ili Smrt in the election; but the promise of Pašić that, when the inquiry at Sarajevo had been completed, his government would coöperate as far as was "compatible with international usage" was hardly adequate to meet the situation.

In Austria-Hungary the reaction to the crime was what might have been expected. The newspapers were cautious at first, as if awaiting a cue from the government; official circles were agreed that the hour of reckoning had come. Conrad von Hötzendorf and Berchtold thought that "Austria must draw the sword," but the emperor and both the Austrian Premier, Count Stürgkh, and the Hungarian Premier, Count Tisza, wished to wait until the crime could be investigated and the attitude of Germany had been defined. Berchtold thereupon sent a special emissary, his *chef de cabinet,* Count Hoyos, to Berlin to explain the Austro-Hungarian position.

Hoyos took with him a memorandum just completed by the Foreign Office, in which the admission of Bulgaria to the Triple Alliance was proposed, and a letter from Francis Joseph to William II stating that the policy of Austria-Hungary "must in future be directed toward the isolation and diminution of Serbia." He was also to explain, verbally, Berchtold's plan for a surprise attack on Serbia without any diplomatic preparation, which would be followed by a partition of the country. These overtures were cordially received by the German emperor and the German chancellor, who agreed that "immediate action" was necessary and promised full support against Russia if that Power chose to intervene.

With these assurances in his pocket, Berchtold was able to overcome the hesitations of Francis Joseph and Stürgkh and, eventually, of Tisza, though the latter held out for an ultimatum to Serbia which, theoretically, it might accept before military action was undertaken. The investigation conducted at Sarajevo revealed that the conspirators had been provided with arms in Belgrade and smuggled across the frontier by Serbian officials, but it failed to incriminate the Serbian government. Nevertheless, the Austro-Hungarian government determined to make the most of its opportunity and framed a note to Serbia with demands so stiff that it was expected—and hoped—that Serbia would reject them. Austria-Hungary would then have an excuse for war, which Conrad had so long urged. The note was presented in Belgrade at 6 P.M. on July 23, with a time limit of forty-eight hours.

The note began by quoting the Serbian Declaration of March 31, 1909 (see p. 46), according to which Serbia promised to "live on good neighborly terms" with Austria-Hungary. This promise, said the note, had not been fulfilled; rather, Serbia had connived at "a subversive movement" which had led to the murder at Sarajevo. The crime had been planned in Belgrade and Serbian officials had assisted in its execution. The Serbian government was therefore required to publish a declaration in its official journal, on July 26, condemning and repudiating all activity directed against Austria-Hungary and to accept ten specific demands:

1. To suppress any publication directed against Austria-Hungary.

2. To dissolve the Narodna Odbrana and to suppress similar societies in future.

3. To eliminate anti-Austrian propaganda from the public schools.

4. To remove army officers and civil functionaries guilty of propaganda against the Monarchy.

5. To accept the collaboration of Austrian representatives for the suppression of the subversive movement.

6. To take judicial proceedings against accessories to the Sarajevo plot, with Austrian delegates participating in the investigation.

7. To arrest Tankosić and Ciganović.

8. To prevent the illicit traffic in arms and to punish the officials who helped the conspirators to cross the frontier.

9. To explain hostile utterances of Serbian officials.

10. To notify the Austro-Hungarian government of the execution of these measures.

The note cannot be considered a demand, on legal and juridical grounds, for the punishment of criminals, but it was essentially a political *démarche* and was regarded as such, particularly because Point 5, in the opinion of the Powers of the Triple Entente, involved interference with the sovereignty of Serbia.

When the note was presented, Premier Pašić, who was also Foreign Minister, was in southern Serbia in the midst of the election campaign. He was, however, summoned to Belgrade and arrived early on the morning of July 24. What happened in the Serbian capital on this and the following day is somewhat obscure, for the Belgrade archives have not been opened. Certain of the Austrian demands were not acceptable, notably those calling for dismissal of army officers and participation of Austrian officials in any investigation. The cabinet was in almost continuous session.

According to one account, Pašić persuaded the cabinet to defer its decisions until an answer could be received to an appeal for assistance which the prince regent had telegraphed to the tsar on July 24; but since by noon of July 25 no reply had come, the cabinet decided to accept the Austrian demands, including "a mixed commission of inquiry, provided that appointment of such commission can be proved to be in accordance with international usage." Early in the afternoon, however, telegrams were received from Russia urging Serbia to resist and promising help. The reply to the Austro-Hungarian note was thereupon hurriedly recast so that participation of Austrian officials was refused and mobilization was ordered at 3 P.M.

In spite of some circumstantial evidence to support it, this version finds no confirmation in such Serbian documents as have been published. Moreover, the collection of Russian documents published in 1934 by the Soviet government contains only two communications from St. Petersburg to Belgrade, one on July 24, advising Serbia not to resist an Austrian invasion, the other on July 25, urging an appeal for British mediation; it is most unlikely that the Soviet editors would have omitted telegrams urging Serbia to resist and face war. Spalajković, the Serbian Minister at St. Petersburg in 1914, denied sending such telegrams. This version rests, in fact, on the *ipse dixits* of several journalists.

Another story, according to which the Serbian reply, at least in its main lines, was formulated by an official of the French Foreign Office, Philippe Berthelot, also lacks documentary foundation. The advice from London was of the most general nature. Evidently the Serbs were left very much to their own devices.

Their reply to the Austro-Hungarian note was handed to Giesl, the Austro-Hungarian Minister, a few minutes before 6 P.M. on July 25. As it did not accept the Austrian demands unreservedly, Giesl, following explicit instructions, broke off diplomatic relations and left Belgrade at 6:30 P.M. From Zemun, across the river, he telephoned to Vienna, whence the news was relayed to Ischl, the summer residence of Francis Joseph. At 9:23 P.M. the emperor ordered that eight corps, or half his army, were to be mobilized on July 28 for operations against Serbia.

The Serbian reply to the Austro-Hungarian note was more submissive than might have been expected. Though the Austrian demands were not accepted *in toto*—for numerous reservations of detail were offered,—on only one point was there definite refusal: the participation of Austrian officials in the judicial inquiry (Point 6). But an offer was made to refer the entire dispute between Austria-Hungary and Serbia to the Great Powers or to the arbitration of the Hague Tribunal.

After studying the document for several days, the Austro-Hungarian government was able to pick out numerous flaws, some of which were not unjustified. The general tone of the note creates an impression that is perhaps unduly favorable. Nevertheless, the verdict of posterity is likely to be, not that of disappointed officials of the Vienna Foreign Office who hoped for out-and-out rejection of the Austrian demands, but of the two highest personages of the German Empire, Austria's ally. Chancellor Bethmann-Hollweg, after pondering the Serbian note for two days, declared to the Prussian Council of Ministers that "the Serbian reply had, in fact, agreed to the Austrian wishes except on unimportant points." The German emperor was even more explicit: "This is more than one could have expected.... With it every reason for war disappears.... I am convinced that, on the whole, the wishes of the Dual Monarchy have been acceded to. The few reservations which Serbia makes in regard to individual points can, in my opinion, be cleared up by negotiation." Unfortunately, Austria-Hungary was not willing to clear up reservations by negotiation, but was determined on a military solution, which both William II and Bethmann-Hollweg had sanctioned early in July.

The plan of the Austro-Hungarian General Staff was to allow mobilization to be completed before making any military moves—which would not be until August 12. But the German government, upset by various proposals for mediation between Austria-Hungary and Serbia which were being advanced by Great Britain and Russia, exerted great pressure on Vienna to declare war and begin military operations at once, in order to stave off unwelcome proposals. Both Berchtold and Conrad von Hötzendorf were annoyed by this pressure, but they yielded to it. On the morning of July 28 Berchtold sent a telegram to Pašić informing him that a state of war existed between Austria-Hungary and Serbia. On July 29 Austrian monitors on the Danube began to bombard Belgrade and war between the two countries became a fact.

The Emperor Francis Joseph was reluctant to take the final plunge. Berchtold obtained his consent to the declaration of war only by including in it a statement that Serbian troops had already attacked Austria-Hungary at Tamiš-Kovin; but this was not true and the charge was deleted from the declaration of war as it was finally published.

As early as July 24 the Russian government had decided in principle that if Austria-Hungary attacked Serbia partial mobilization of the Russian army would be ordered. When the news of the bombardment of Belgrade reached St. Petersburg, the tsar ordered the districts of Moscow, Kazan, Kiev, and Odessa to be mobilized, as well as the Black Sea and Baltic fleets. On the following day, July 30, this partial mobilization was extended to general mobilization of the entire Russian Empire. Germany promptly demanded that Russia cancel this mobilization and, when Russia refused, declared war (August 1, 1914).

Meanwhile the Austro-Hungarian government had been confronted with proposals, first from Germany and then from Great Britain, that Austria should content itself with the occupation of Belgrade and then negotiate with the Powers for a settlement of its quarrel with Serbia. As this represented a reversal of the German attitude, Berchtold postponed a reply for several days; but the equivocal language of the German chancellor may well have convinced the Austrian minister that the German proposal was not meant seriously. Furthermore, General von Moltke, the German chief of staff, bluntly urged Conrad von Hötzendorf to reject such proposals and to go ahead with the war. On July 31 the cabinet of Vienna rejected both German and British overtures and voted to proceed with the war against Serbia as planned. This decision was taken without regard to the Russian general mobilization; it would surely have caused that mobilization if it had not already been ordered.

The Austro-Hungarian case against Serbia was that Serbia, by inciting and supporting subversive action within the Yugoslav provinces, sought to destroy and did actually endanger the territorial integrity of the Habsburg Monarchy. The assassination of the Archduke Francis Ferdinand was the last straw in a long series of provocations. Serbia, therefore, had to be punished, not only for the protection of Austria-Hungary but in the interest of European peace. In order to reassure the other Powers that the punishment of Serbia, as designed in the ultimatum of July 23, would not disturb the European balance of power, the cabinet of Vienna offered assurances to the other governments that from a territorial point of view the Habsburg Monarchy was "saturated" and did not wish "to possess itself of any portion of Serbia"; it also declared that it would respect the sovereignty of Serbia. Consequently, it claimed a free hand in dealing with the little state.

These assurances were received with skepticism by the Entente Powers in 1914, for the acceptance of the Austrian demands by Serbia was not compatible with the sovereignty of Serbia. From the Austro-Hungarian documents published in 1919 and afterward it is clear that the assurances were not honorably intended. The Austro-Hungarian Council of Ministers had passed a resolution reserving the right to make "rectifications" of frontiers; furthermore, a partition of Serbia for the benefit of Albania and Bulgaria was under consideration. General Conrad von Hötzendorf intended to demand the demobilization and disarmament of the Serbian army. The Austrian premier favored the deposition of the Karageorgević dynasty and the conclusion of a military convention which would have made Serbia dependent on the Monarchy. The Austrian assurances were, in fact, valueless, and the cabinet of St. Petersburg was well aware of this.

Thus the bankruptcy of Habsburg policy drove Austria-Hungary into war to save itself. As events turned out, the war thus begun culminated in the destruction of the Habsburg Monarchy.

# CHAPTER V

## Serbia in the First World War

### BY JOHN CLINTON ADAMS

*Men still talk of the miracle of the Marne, where there is
little that is miraculous. There would be more justification
in talking of the miracle of the Kolubara.*

*British Official History of the World War*

THE SERBIAN ARMY IN 1914 was a compact striking force, well trained, well led, and seasoned by its victories in the Balkan wars. Its total numerical strength has been estimated as high as 450,000 effectives, who were grouped in three levies according to age. Men from twenty to thirty-one made up the first *poziv* (levy); those from thirty-two to thirty-nine, the second; those from forty to forty-five, the third. In an emergency every man who could shoot a rifle would be used, regardless of age. Septuagenarian warriors, affectionately known as *čiče* (uncles), were common in Serbia.

Each army division drew its soldiers from one district and bore a name suggestive of that district, usually the name of a river. Each district, except the territories acquired as a result of the Balkan wars, supplied two divisions, one from the first *poziv* and one from the second. Thus there were the divisions Drina I and II, Danube I and II, Timok I and II, Šumadija I and II, and Morava I and II. There were also a Combined Division of miscellaneous recruits of the first *poziv* not placed in their regional units, an independent Cavalry Division of approximately four regiments, the Defense of Belgrade Group, and the so-called Brigade, or Army, of Užice. The human resources of the new territories had not been exploited for military service at the outbreak of the war, but they would be utilized as soon as possible. Even so, as far as man power was concerned, the army was stronger than it had been at the time of the Balkan wars.[1]

With regard to equipment, however, the situation was different. Matériel lost in the course of more than a year of hostilities had not been replaced. About 60,000 rifles were lacking. The number of batteries assigned to a division of the first *poziv* had been cut from nine to six. A division of the second *poziv* had only three. Seven mountain batteries and a few howitzers comprised the rest of the artillery. The total supply of artillery ammunition available in July, 1914, was as follows: 750 rounds per field piece, 650 per mountain piece, 250 per howitzer. The single large Serbian arsenal and munitions factory, at Kragujevac, could not replenish these deficiencies. Munitions from France and England would have to be landed at the Greek port of Salonika and brought by rail up the Vardar Valley. Food and guns from Russia must come by way of the Black Sea, the Danube, and a narrow-gauge railway. If Bulgaria desired to express an unfriendly attitude it would know how to sever both lines of communication without abandoning official neutrality.

On the afternoon of July 25, while still laboring over their reply to the Austrian ultimatum, the Serbian ministers ordered general mobilization. At the same time they decreed the transfer of the government from Belgrade, which was within range of Austrian land and naval guns, to Niš. King Peter, old and ill, had abdicated, a month before, in favor of a regency headed by his son, the deceptively slight and bespectacled Crown Prince Alexander, who assumed nominal command of the army.

The actual commander was the sixty-seven-year-old Vojvoda[2] Radomir Putnik, chief of the Serbian General Staff and a hero of the Balkan wars. The crisis caught Putnik at a summer resort in Austria, trying to improve his damaged health. The Austrians gallantly permitted him to return home in order to head the defense of his country in the war which would bring extinction—or, perhaps, Great Serbia.

The Austrian declaration of war was received in Niš on the morning of July 28. The Serbs immediately blew up the trestle

---

[1] For notes to chapter v see pages 515–516.

connecting Belgrade with the Hungarian port of Zemun (Semlin) on the other side of the Sava. The Austrians bombarded Belgrade and other towns in desultory fashion, and the Serbian guns replied from the heights of Topčider, behind the former capital.

Days passed. Europe went to war. But the anticipated Austrian offensive did not develop. The delay was caused by a conflict between military and political exigencies. Conrad von Hötzendorf, the Austrian chief of staff, had long been ready for the day when the Dual Monarchy would march into Serbia. His plan, known as "Mobilization B(alkan)," was designed speedily to subdue not only Serbia but Montenegro, whose participation in a general war was rightly assumed.

Desirous of synchronizing his offensive with the formal declaration of war, von Hötzendorf recommended to Count Berchtold, the Austrian Foreign Minister, that this declaration be withheld until August 12, when mobilization and concentration would be completed. Unfortunately for von Hötzendorf, the efforts of the Great Powers in the fourth week of July to attain a peaceful solution of the Austro-Serbian crisis caused Count Berchtold to fear that the only policy he had ever pursued energetically might end in anticlimax. It seemed best to prevent this by cutting the ground from under diplomatic negotiations, as Berchtold himself remarked at the time. Accordingly, he declared war on Serbia at once, two weeks before the Austrian army was ready to act.

The news of Russian general mobilization on July 30 necessitated another change in von Hötzendorf's plans. The Second Army, which was concentrating on the Sava, must now be withdrawn for service in Galicia. But von Hötzendorf did not intend to permit even the arrival of the final struggle between Teutonic civilization and Slavic barbarism to delay the chastisement of Serbia. He was confident that the Fifth and Sixth armies, commanded by General Potiorek, could destroy the viper's nest. Potiorek, who as military governor of Bosnia had been in the automobile with the archduke and his wife when Princip shot them, and for whom Princip's second bullet had been intended, shared this confidence. He decided to begin the offensive on August 12, the first day on which his forces would be ready to move.

The Drina was over a hundred yards wide near its confluence

with the Sava, but many small islands could serve as steppingstones for an invader. The Sava was broad enough in places to be navigable by monitors and not too broad for pontoon bridges. The region on the Serbian side, called Mačva, was mostly level except in the north near the Sava, where the Cer, a wooded mountain, rose more than two thousand feet high. The road to Valjevo ran through the valley of the Jadar, a tributary of the Drina, with steep hills on either side. The terrain was admirably suited to operations by a screen of defenders.

Putnik expected an immediate attack on Belgrade from the north, across the Sava and the Danube. Lining the northern and western frontiers with covering troops, he effected his main concentration south of the city. But the blow came, instead, from the west and northwest. On the night of August 11 the Austrian Second Army, under the protection of heavy bombardment, crossed the Sava and occupied Šabac almost unopposed. Early on the morning of the twelfth the Fifth Army poured over the Drina. All that day and the next, in summer heat which Potiorek described as "fearful," the Serbian cordon, with little or no reinforcement, stopped the Austrians.

Putnik moved swiftly to redeem his miscalculation of the enemy plan of campaign. In two days he faced the Serbian armies west instead of north. Holding the First Army in reserve, he dispatched the Second Army (Šumadija I and the Combined Division) to the Cer and the Third Army (Drina I and II) to the Jadar. Since their speedy arrival was of decisive importance, certain units of these formations marched sixty miles in forty-eight hours and, without rest, plunged into the developing battle.

On August 16 the Austrians attacked along both sides of the Jadar. The Serbian division Drina I, holding the river valley, waited until the enemy was within two hundred yards before firing, in order to save ammunition, then shattered the Austrian Thirteenth Army Corps, on the right of the Fifth Army. A sortie from Šabac was driven back into the town. Farther up the Drina the Sixth Army, Potiorek's own, which Francis Ferdinand had visited Bosnia to review, remained inactive. On this day and the next, despite frightening losses, the Austrians failed to gain much ground. Potiorek requested von Hötzendorf repeatedly and with increasing urgency to allow the Second Army to participate in the engagement, intimating that otherwise the situation of the Fifth Army might become critical and the departure of the Second Army for the Russian front might be prevented. Von Hötzendorf consented only to the limited coöperation of one corps of the Second Army. On the Serbian side, Morava I and II and Timok I arrived as reinforcements, giving the Serbs preponderance in rifle strength. After two more days of exhausting struggle the left of the Austrian Fifth Army was routed. Pursuit began, slow upon the heights but gaining momentum in the valleys. The invading columns streamed back across the Drina into Bosnia. The Austrian Second Army made a last thrust south of Šabac on August 20, but the men of the Šumadija repelled it. The sun over the defeated Austrians went into eclipse as Potiorek ordered the Second Army to recross the Sava. By three o'clock on the afternoon of August 24 the enemy had evacuated Serbian territory. Long contemplated as an eventual necessity, finally undertaken with vengeful relish, the far-heralded *Einmarsch in Serbien* had ended in complete, almost instant, failure.

It was obvious to Putnik, however, that the victory could procure only temporary respite. He attempted to lengthen it by a diversion on Austrian soil. General Mišić, perhaps the most capable of the Serbian field commanders, crossed the Sava on September 6 and invaded the Austrian province of Syrmia (Srem). But the next night the Austrian batteries thundered again along the Drina, indicating that Potiorek was returning to the attack. Mišić was recalled after the adventure had lasted a week. Tragedy marked its conclusion. Timok I was attacked while recrossing the Sava and lost 5,000 men.

For the second time the Austrians crossed the rivers. Potiorek's connections at Vienna had succeeded in liberating him almost entirely from von Hötzendorf's supervision so that he could conduct his campaign without inhibition from higher quarters. After a week of struggle his Fifth and Sixth armies were established on the line Šabac–Cer–Krupanj, but in effecting a concentration near the confluence of the Sava and the Drina he had virtually denuded the upper Drina Valley of troops. Putnik exploited the weakness by ordering the hitherto inactive Army of Užice (Šumadija II and a brigade), which was stationed near the village of that name, to turn the Austrian flank and march on Sarajevo. Terrified Austrian officials in the Bosnian capital transferred Princip, Čabrinović, and Grabež to Theresienstadt in Bohemia as the Serbs drew near, supported by a Montenegrin detachment. Austrian reserves were brought up and the invaders were checked after a four-day battle. But Potiorek's offensive had been halted for a month.

The attack was resumed at the end of October. A general assault on November 7 dislodged the Serbs from their positions and threatened to envelop the Serbian Second Army on the right flank near Šabac. The Serbs were already hampered by shortage of ammunition. Risking an equally dangerous decline in morale, Putnik called for a retreat deep into Serbia. Through rain and snow the Serbs fell back behind the Kolubara, a river flowing north into the Sava not far west of Belgrade. That city, held by the Defense of Belgrade Group, became the anchor of the Serbian right flank. To the south were posted, in order, the Second, Third, and First Serbian armies, and the Army of Užice. The Serbs had obtained some respite from fighting and were nearer to their bases of supply.

The pursuer was farther from his base than he perhaps realized. He, too, crossed the Kolubara, which was almost in a state of flood. Nevertheless, even in the opinion of his enemies, Potiorek had thus far played *un jeu classique.* Steady Austrian pressure in the latter half of November compelled Putnik to order another withdrawal, which exposed Belgrade to the enemy. Potiorek immediately commanded the Fifth Army, constituting his left flank, to seize the city. It fell on December 2, Francis Joseph's birthday. The capture of Belgrade required a tactically unsound extension of front by the Austrian Fifth Army, but it enabled Potiorek to present the emperor with a gift which would presumably enhance the general's standing at court.

On the same day Putnik issued orders for a counteroffensive, to be waged, of necessity, without artillery preparation and reserves. King Peter himself came to the trenches carrying a rifle and told the soldiers that anyone who wished to escape the battle might leave, but that he himself intended to stay. On the morning of December 3 the Serbs broke the entire Austrian front. In the next forty-eight hours the Austrian Sixth Army was driven over the Kolubara.

By the evening of December 7 the Austrian left was yielding ground, the center could hardly maintain itself on the right bank of the Kolubara, and the right was reeling. The Serbs gave the enemy no chance to reëstablish himself and the Austrian defeat became a rout which lasted more than a week. At ten o'clock on the morning of December 15 the Serbian cavalry galloped into Belgrade. During the service of thanksgiving held in the Saborna Crkva, sullen explosions could be heard. The Austrians were blowing up their bridges across the Sava. They had lost 50,000 men at the Jadar and more than twice that number at the Kolubara. Serbian losses also were heavy.

An Austrian communiqué stated that troops of the Dual Monarchy had been withdrawn from Serbia, owing to difficulties of provisioning, adding that the emperor had deigned to relieve *Feldzeugmeister* Oskar Potiorek of his command, at the latter's request, for reasons of health. The last reported utterance of *Feldzeugmeister* Potiorek before he withdrew to a sanitarium was the admonition, "If you have to attack Serbia again, do it only by way of Belgrade."

The communiqué of the Serbian High Command said merely, "On the territory of the Kingdom of Serbia there remains not one free enemy soldier."

> *It was generally known that in the event of a war of long duration and in view of the involved international situation, Bulgarian neutrality could be maintained to the end only if Bulgaria received compensation for it.*
> PREMIER RADOSLAVOV of Bulgaria

The dregs of victory lay thick upon northwestern Serbia. Thousands of unburied corpses littered roads and fields, floated on rivers, choked wells. The living were crowded into cities some of which increased more than fivefold in population. That of Niš, for example, had risen from 23,000 to 130,000. The combination bred a new enemy more formidable than the Austrians—typhus. Month after month the epidemic raged. England, France, Russia, and the United States sent medical and sanitary missions to Serbia. Estimates as to the number of deaths are staggering; it would be conservative to put the figure at 150,000. The plague was not conquered until June, 1915.

Meanwhile, efforts were made to replace the losses of the past campaign. Two more divisions, the Vardar and Bregalnica, were assembled around Skoplje (Usküb) and a third at Bitolj (Monastir) in extreme southern Serbia. These Macedonian formations were called the Troops of the New Regions. On the eastern frontier Putnik created the Timok Army out of third-levy troops, stiffened by Šumadija II, which was transferred from the Army of Užice. The entire Second Army was also sent to the east. The new dispositions signified a growing fear on the part of the Serbs that Bulgaria might soon abandon neutrality.

Official Bulgaria was, indeed, resolved to profit from the war either by receiving payment for its neutrality or by active intervention. It intended to recover the so-called "uncontested zone" in Macedonia which had been allocated to Bulgaria by the Serbo-Bulgarian accord of 1912 and, if possible, the "contested zone" the ownership of which had been left by the treaty to arbitrament by the Russian tsar. Bulgaria considered itself robbed of both regions by Serbia and Greece in the Second Balkan War. If Bulgaria could also regain territory lost to Rumania and Turkey in that war, so much the better. One group of contestants in the present struggle must be persuaded that it was worth while to pay the Bulgarian price.

The members of the Entente had already negotiated to obtain the strict and loyal neutrality of Bulgaria, but they would promise it nothing before the end of the war, and then only if Serbia and Greece received compensation elsewhere. The Bulgars displayed dissatisfaction with these offers by interfering with the transportation of munitions to Serbia. They wanted immediate and concrete profit. Above all, they wanted to ally themselves with the winning side. In May, 1915, the Germans achieved a tremendous break-through against the Russians at Gorlice. Four weeks later Bulgaria let the Central Powers know that it was inclined to make their cause its own—if the price were right.

To no one in Berlin and Vienna was the news more welcome than to General von Falkenhayn, chief of the German General Staff. For some time he had been considering the advisability of eliminating Serbia from the war. Destruction of the small kingdom would end the Pan-Serbian menace and remove a military threat from the flank of the hard-pressed Dual Monarchy. Above all, it would permit the restoration of railway communications between Germany and Turkey. The general had concluded that the help of Bulgaria was a prerequisite for a third campaign in Serbia. The powerful influence of the High Command was therefore thrown behind the efforts of German and Austrian diplomacy to obtain an alliance with Bulgaria.

Complete success was registered in three treaties signed on September 6, 1915. The Central Powers agreed that Bulgaria might seize and hold all Serbian Macedonia and eastern Serbia. If Greece or Rumania intervened, Bulgaria was authorized to regain what it had lost to them in the Balkan wars and to secure additional boundary rectifications in its favor. Turkey ceded Bulgaria a strip of land in Thrace. The Central Powers further contracted to make Bulgaria a war loan of Fr. 200,000,000 in monthly installments, the first to be paid on the day it ordered general mobilization. In return, Bulgaria promised to join the Central Powers in a simultaneous attack on Serbia. A military convention provided that Austria and Germany would commence operations in thirty days with at least six divisions each. Bulgaria was to move in thirty-five days with at least four of its large divisions, which were approximately twice the usual size.

General von Mackensen, the hero of Gorlice, was appointed commander of the combined forces, which exceeded the stipulations of the military convention.[3] Conrad von Hötzendorf supplied Mackensen with the Austrian Third Army, numbering more than six divisions and strengthened by the German Twenty-second Reserve Corps. General von Falkenhayn sent to the Danube a new German Eleventh Army of seven divisions, only one of which was a reserve formation. The Bulgarian First Army had four divisions; the Bulgarian Second Army had two. In accordance with the ideas of Falkenhayn, enough artillery was assembled to insure complete superiority in this respect. The total strength of the Mackensen Army Group was 330,000 men and 1,200 guns.[4]

On September 22, 1915, Bulgaria ordered general mobilization. The Serbs immediately suggested to their allies that the new danger be met by a preventive attack on the Bulgars before the latter could defend themselves. Thereafter, the whole remaining power of Serbia, something over 250,000 men, could be employed against the invasion which was seen to be threatening in the north. Britain and France vetoed the plan. They were still negotiating with Sofia for an alliance and were sure that Russian prestige would keep Bulgaria neutral if it did not secure its adherence to the Entente. In any event, a forthcoming Anglo-French offensive in Champagne and Artois was expected to obtain such decisive results that subsidiary theaters of war could be neglected. Britain therefore counseled Serbia to appease Bulgaria with Serbian land.

Sir Edward Grey, the foreign secretary, would do no more than address a warning to Bulgaria in a speech before the House of Commons: "If Bulgaria assumes an aggressive attitude on the side of the enemies of this country, we are prepared to give to our friends in the Balkans all the support in our power, in the manner that would be most welcome to them, in concert with our Allies, without reserve and without qualification."[5]

An opportunity for Britain and France to send effective help to Serbia by way of Greece was already present, had Britain desired to utilize it. Venizelos, the Greek Premier, was well aware that Greece as well as Serbia was directly menaced by Bulgarian mobilization. Greece and Serbia had concluded a defensive alliance against Bulgaria after the First Balkan War. Venizelos desired to fulfill the obligations of this treaty if Bulgaria attacked Serbia, but he was forced to face two arguments propounded by the adherents of the pro-German King Constantine. The first, that the treaty applied only to a localized Balkan war, could be met easily because the wording was sufficiently vague to include the instance of a general conflict. The second, however, was more specific. Article 2 of the Serbo-Greek military convention stated that at the beginning of hostilities Serbia must concentrate 150,000 men in Macedonia to coöperate with the Greek army.[6] Since this was impossible, the treaty could be considered null and void.

Venizelos attempted to circumvent the objection by asking Britain and France to land 150,000 men at Salonika. If they consented, he thought he could bring Greece into the war under the terms of the Serbo-Greek alliance. France accepted the idea heartily and England followed suit with reluctance. This was the historical genesis of the Salonika expedition.

In spite of Bulgaria's protestations that it had mobilized only to preserve its neutrality, by October 4 it was clear even to Sir Edward Grey that Bulgaria was preparing a concerted action with the Central Powers. On that day Sofia was informed that all offers of compensation from the Entente were withdrawn. France and Russia demanded a clarification of its intentions and the dismissal of all Teutonic officers within twenty-four hours. Bulgaria denied that it had compromised its neutrality in any way.

On the evening of October 4 the Greek parliament, at Venizelos' request, voted to stand by the alliance with Serbia. The next morning King Constantine removed Venizelos from office, or, according to another account, Venizelos resigned because his policy was so much at variance with that of the king, the General Staff, and a large part of public opinion as to entail the risk of civil war. As the champion of intervention fell, the first British and French troops disembarked at Salonika. The neutrality of Greece, which had just been reaffirmed, was thereby violated.[7]

Here, then [comments the *British Official History*], was a situation which would have been ludicrous had it been less tragic. Britain was sending troops only to help Greece fulfill her obligations and now it was almost certain that Greece did not intend to fulfill them. It had been agreed that no force which the Allies could spare would suffice without Greek coöperation, and now it appeared that the troops could hope for no more than neutrality and might have to face hostility from the Greek forces. To crown all, it was probable that the landing had in any case been made too late to save Serbia.[8]

News of the landing reached General Mackensen's headquarters just north of the Danube on October 5. Hostility to the Central Powers was reported to be increasing in Rumania. A quick victory over Serbia would be a wholesome lesson for all small states, especially those so foolish as to contemplate entering the war against Germany and Austria. Everything was in readiness for the initial assault, which this time was to be directed at Belgrade, across the Sava and the Danube. The alliance with Bulgaria provided that the campaign must begin in thirty days. The thirtieth day would be October 6, 1915.

> Our geographical position with reference to Serbia enabled us to undertake effective enveloping operations from the outset.          GENERAL VON FALKENHAYN

*Villages and towns shall burn . . . and the living shall cry
unto the dead, "Arise, O dead, that we may lie down in
your graves!"*       The Serbian "Black Prophecy"

Beleaguered on three sides, outnumbered in man power, and
outweighed in artillery, the Serbs stretched their armies into a thin
cordon over six hundred miles long, reaching from the Drina to
the Sava and the Danube and from the Timok to the Vardar Valley. The Defense of Belgrade Group held the former capital, aided
by the British Admiral Troubridge and his improvised Danube
flotilla, some naval guns, and a party of French marines. The First
and Third armies were posted behind the city. The Timok Army,
the Second Army, and the Troops of the New Regions covered
the Bulgarian frontier. The situation afforded no chance of success, but it was hoped that the enemy might be delayed long
enough for help to arrive from Salonika.

The bombardment of Belgrade and the Serbian positions around
it began on the afternoon of October 6. In the early hours of the
morning, obscured by darkness and rain, the passage of the rivers
was commenced, hampered by the *košava*, a fierce, seasonal wind.
The Austrians and Germans crossed at widely separated places on
the Drina, the Sava, and the Danube, but the main effort was made
at Belgrade. The city was taken street by street in a battle lasting
three days. The bravery of the defenders evoked tributes even from
the Austrians. The Vienna *Reichspost* of October declared: "In the
defense of the dethroned royal town one must grant to our enemy
that he performed prodigies of valor. It was perhaps a theatrical,
useless gesture, but they paid for it with fresh, costly blood, and
fought in their desperate position not for a possible success but
only for the honor of their arms."

On October 14, using a frontier skirmish as pretext, Bulgaria
declared war on Serbia. For a week the Timok and Second armies,
motley collection of veterans, old men, and boys as they were,
pinned the Bulgarian First Army to the frontier. But in the south
the Bulgarian Second Army smashed through the Troops of the
New Regions and cut the all-important Belgrade–Salonika railroad at Vranje, Skoplje, and Veles, severing northern Serbia from
Macedonia. A regiment from the Bulgarian Second Army was on
its way to destroy the great bridge over the Vardar at Strumica

Station, in order to prevent the arrival of assistance from Salonika, when it was unexpectedly attacked and driven off by elements from the French 156th Division.

France was resolved that the Salonika expedition should save Serbia, and for several weeks had been rapidly increasing French forces at Salonika. General Maurice Sarrail was sent out to take command. He immediately dispatched troops up the railroad as far as Strumica Station, where they encountered the southernmost Serbian formations. The French and Serbian staffs hoped that the Anglo-French forces might advance as far as Skoplje or even farther north. The Serbs would then retreat slowly upon them, and eventually a joint counteroffensive would be launched. Vigorous action, however, was required.

Such action was frustrated by the attitude of the English. Despite Sir Edward Grey's promise, the British government was ready to desert Serbia on the ground that it was now too late to help it. Only the threat of General Joffre's resignation prevented Britain from abandoning the Salonika venture. British forces in Greece totaled less than two divisions until November, 1915. The inevitable result was that General Sarrail accomplished little. At Krivolak, a village on the railroad twenty miles south of Veles, his advance units were halted by twenty-four Bulgarian battalions and there they stayed. The gate to the arena wherein Serbia was to be slaughtered was shut in the faces of its rescuers.

For over a week after the capture of Belgrade the Austro-German half of the Mackensen Army Group remained virtually inactive while troops, artillery, and supply trains crossed the rivers. The passage of the Danube, which was a thousand yards wide at Belgrade, had been a formidable undertaking, and it might have been expected that Mackensen would allow his soldiers an interval of rest. Instead, he ordered a general advance, which had to be postponed for several days until men and matériel had been transferred to the right bank of the Danube. Mackensen now planned a maneuver which would speedily terminate the campaign by encircling most of the Serbian army near Kragujevac. If the Serbs did not surrender they would be annihilated in a battle of the Cannae model.

Germans, Austrians, and Bulgars moved forward simultaneously. The Austrian Third Army took Arandjelovac and pressed on into the mountainous region of Rudnik, its right wing delayed by the terrain and by Serbian counterattacks. The German Eleventh Army forced the entrances to the Morava Valley and made steady progress. Its left flank established contact with the right of the Bulgarian First Army, welding the segments of the Mackensen Army Group into a steel ring around the Serbs which was open only at its southwestern extremities. With the fortifications of Zaječar and Knjaževac finally in their possession, the Bulgars crashed against the defenses of Pirot, the last Serbian stronghold in the east, about forty miles from Niš. Pirot fell on October 29 and the remnants of the Serbian Second Army retreated to Niš and Leskovac. The civil government was hastily removed from Niš to Kraljevo. The Serbs were being driven into a compact mass whose center of gravity was at Kragujevac, as Mackensen had intended. On October 30 he ordered the Austrian right flank to push through Čačak and Kraljevo, passing behind Kragujevac, to complete the encirclement. The Germans were to make a direct assault on the town the next day.

The Serbs were aware of their dangerous position. They had intended to fight another delaying battle at Kragujevac to give the Allies more time to arrive, but the prospects were unfavorable and Putnik ordered a resumption of their slow retreat. While rear guards held up the enemy, the Serbs evacuated Kragujevac. They destroyed their stores of munitions, fuel, and food—of which they would soon have direst need. On the night of October 31, with the town a roaring pyre, they turned their backs on it and on all northern Serbia and the straggling columns moved away into the darkness. The right wing of the Austrian Third Army did not advance quickly enough to cut them off.

Mackensen's design for encirclement had failed, but the general and his capable chief of staff, Colonel von Seeckt, the creator of the postwar German army, were not tardy in devising a second attempt. This time Mackensen planned to surround the Serbs in the angle of the western and southern Moravas. On November 4 the Serbian First Army abandoned Kraljevo to the Austrians. The government and a host of refugees had already fled down the Ibar Valley to Mitrovica. The Germans advanced irresistibly. On

November 5, after a three-day storm, the Bulgars took Niš. Nevertheless, the Serbs again escaped encirclement. The Austrian right wing could not swing southeast fast enough to intercept the troops retreating from Kragujevac. Moreover, the Bulgarian First Army was temporarily held on the right bank of the Morava in spite of frenzied efforts to cross it.

But Mackensen saw his next move as clearly as a skillful chess player who pursues his adversary's few remaining pieces across the board, already visualizing the final position from which escape will be impossible. Occupation of the line Nova Varoš–Sjenica–Novi Pazar–Mitrovica–Priština would be checkmate to Putnik and Serbia. The Serbs would be caught on Kosovo Field, where, in 1389, their medieval empire had been overthrown by the Turks. They would be cut off from Greece, with the mountains of Montenegro and Albania at their backs. Mackensen ordered the advance to continue with no relaxation of pressure.

The Austrians went forward with difficulty, for the terrain was increasingly mountainous and the weather was growing colder. The Germans took Kruševac, a town commanding the valleys of the three Moravas. The Bulgarian First Army put one division on its left across the Morava at Leskovac, south of Niš. The Serbs repelled it by a desperate counterattack, but obtained no respite. The Bulgarian Second Army was striving to force the pass of Kačanik, the southern entrance to Kosovo Field. The left of this army engaged the Anglo-French forces in Serbia and eventually drove them back into Greece. Mackensen's vise was closing tight about the Serbs. Central Serbia could be held no longer. Only one chance remained. Although the Allies had not been able to break through to them, they might be able to break through to their Allies. On November 11 Putnik issued orders for the final retreat, the retreat to Kosovo Field, whence the counteroffensive would be launched.

Step by step the Serbs fell back from crest to crest of the heights which confronted the enemy in parallel lines like a heavy sea of rock. As they evacuated each region it seemed to liquefy into a human stream which flowed after the retreating defenders. The march of the invaders suddenly accelerated on November 15. Two days later the major part of the Serbian forces were on Kosovo Field. After more than five hundred years Serbia had returned to this natural amphitheater for another death struggle. The narrow, muddy roads to Priština and Prizren were solid with traffic. That day, without warning, a violent snowstorm descended on Kosovo. Leaving unnumbered dead, the fugitives finally reached Priština.

The Austrians, suffering severely from the snow which caught most of them exposed upon the mountains, took Nova Varoš and Sjenica, two of the five points on Mackensen's encircling arc. The attainment of the other three could be only a matter of a few days. On November 19 the Serbs commenced their attempt at a breakthrough to the south. The divisions of the Morava, Vardar, and Bregalnica, with the Combined and Cavalry divisions, operating over snow and ice, assaulted Kačanik and the peaks on either side of it. They fought their way some distance into the passes. But they could not break through the Bulgars.

On November 21 Putnik ordered a withdrawal to the west. The Serbian armies drew together like trapped animals. The Germans and Bulgars came down onto Kosovo. Priština fell to them on November 23. The next day the Austrians occupied Novi Pazar and Mitrovica, the northern gate to Kosovo. Mackensen's third design for encirclement was complete. If the Bulgars could seize Prizren quickly, the Serbs would be surrounded.

In crowded, terrified Prizren across the Šar Planina from Kosovo and across the whirling waters of the White Drin from Albania, the Serbian civil and military leaders met with the old king and the young regent to decide their course of action. There were three possibilities: Serbia could surrender and conclude a separate peace; it could commit suicide in a last battle, going down gloriously a second time on Kosovo; or it could undertake a retreat through the mountains of Montenegro and Albania to the Adriatic coast in the hope that the Allies would rescue army and civilian survivors. The third course was chosen because it alone contained the possibility of a future for Serbia. A proclamation of the Serbian High Command, dated November 25, announced to the army and the people what lay before them:

> The moment has come when under the pressure of circumstances we must retreat through Montenegro and Albania. . . . A capitulation would be the worst solution. The nation would be lost and our Allies would abandon us entirely. . . . The only way out of this grave situation is a retreat to the Adriatic

coast. There our army will be reorganized, supplied with food, arms, munitions, clothing, and all other necessities which our Allies will send us, and we shall again be a fact with which the Allies must reckon. The nation has not lost its being; it will continue to exist even though on foreign soil. . . . Convince everyone that our retreat is a national necessity, the salvation of the state, and that in these grave days our redemption lies in the fortitude, endurance, and extreme self-sacrifice of us all. With faith in the final triumph of our Allies we must hold out to the end.[9]

The Serbian armies formed a curve extending from Mitrovica to Kačanik. There were, from north to south, the First Army, the Defense of Belgrade Group, the Third Army, the Second Army, the Troops of the New Regions, and the Timok Army. The word "army" meant little, for not one contained more than three depleted divisions. The Army of Užice had been absorbed into the other formations. A few units were at large in the south, between the Bulgarian Second Army, Greece, and Albania.

The High Command devised a plan for a retreat in three main bodies. The first and largest, comprising the First, Second, and Third armies, and the Defense of Belgrade Group, would cross Montenegro to Scutari-in-Albania by way of Peć, Andrijevica, and Podgorica. The Troops of the New Regions would fall back on Prizren, traverse the Drin, and cross Albania by way of Puka and Orosi. Their destination was also Scutari and the near-by town of Lješ (Alessio). The Timok Army would march down the Drin Valley to Debar, incorporate the Serbian units in this vicinity, maintain contact with the Allies as long as possible, and then retreat across central Albania through Elbasan to Durazzo. The High Command itself inaugurated the retreat on November 26 by leaving Prizren for Scutari. The government and the diplomatic corps were already in Montenegro. Temporarily panic-stricken at the task ahead of them, the generals in command of the northern army debated whether to reject the plan and launch a counteroffensive. But the absurdity of this was soon perceived. At Peć and Prizren automobiles, trucks, and much of the remaining artillery were destroyed. Then the Serbian army, accompanied and preceded by thousands of refugees, plunged into the mountains.

The Second Army plodded through the gorge of the Pećska Bistrica and over Mount Čakor, a windy, snow-covered peak. The

Defense of Belgrade Group, followed by the Third Army, scaled Mount Žljeb and, marching via Rožaj and Berane, joined the Second Army at Andrijevica. The First Army, acting as rear guard, held the passes against the Austrians, who entered Peć on December 7. Enemy bombing planes attacked the Second Army. Local Albanians occasionally harassed the retreating troops.

But the worst enemy was hunger. The High Command had promised that supplies of food would be collected at Andrijevica and Podgorica. They found none at either place. Soldiers and refugees died of starvation, cold, and disease. The plight of 20,000 Austrian prisoners who were dragged over the mountains by their captors was most pitiful of all. The vanguard of the northern army did not reach Scutari until December 15. The rest arrived a few days later, except the First Army, which was forced to stay in the highlands some time longer as a reinforcement for the Montenegrins.

The Troops of the New Regions (Morava I and II, the Vardar Division, and a Combined Detachment) began their retreat from Prizren and Djakovica. When the Bulgars took Prizren on November 30, the Serbian forces, with the exception of Morava II, which was at Djakovica, fell back along the valley of the White Drin toward its confluence with the main Drin.

The ensuing march across Albania was one of peculiar horror. Shut in by the narrow defiles of mountain streams, the four contingents were isolated from the northern armies and separated from each other. The local Albanians were eager to avenge their sufferings during the Serbian invasions of 1912 and 1913. The Troops of the New Regions found no provisions at Puka and Orosi, as had been promised by the High Command. They were constantly ambushed by the tribesmen, who were armed and encouraged by Austria. The Combined Detachment, indeed, was surrounded in a pass near Bliniste on December 9 and compelled to buy its way out.[10] After nearly two weeks of torture the Troops emerged from the mountains and reached Scutari and Lješ.

The retreat of the Timok Army (the Bregalnica, Combined, and Cavalry divisions) was the longest in duration and in distance traveled. It was also the most complicated. Leaving Prizren on November 26, the Timok Army proceeded down the gorge of the

Black Drin to Debar, where it incorporated the Serbian units in this area. Soon, however, the Bulgarian Eighth Division hurled it over the Drin into Albania. On December 10 and 11 the Bulgars crossed the river and assaulted Serbian positions along the crest of the Jablanica Range. Near Debar they broke through, opening the Mati Valley and imperiling Scutari and Lješ. The Timok Army fell back on Elbasan, Tirana, and Kavaj.

Fortunately for the Serbs, the Bulgars displayed little activity thereafter. Nevertheless, the Timok Army was forced to stay in the mountains until December 21. Thereafter it was concentrated mostly around Durazzo. Food was exceedingly difficult to secure. Another serious problem arose in connection with one of their allies. The Italians had established themselves at Valona and Durazzo. Instead of welcoming the Serbs, they viewed them with suspicion as rival imperialists, prescribed limits to the movement of their forces, gave orders to Serbian officers superior in rank and seniority, and occasionally threatened to fire on their allies if the latter did not submit to control.

The descent of the Timok Army to the Adriatic coast completed the Serbian retreat through Montenegro and Albania. The withdrawal had cost as heavily as a battle and no one at the time could say that the sacrifice had not been in vain. Twenty thousand men and countless refugees lay dead in the mountains.

Two-thirds of the survivors were now concentrated on the damp, unhealthy plain around Scutari. The help promised by the Allies was slow in coming, for the Italians refused to transport across the Adriatic the supplies which Britain and France had sent to Brindisi, alleging that the proximity of the Austrian naval base at Kotor (Cattaro) made the voyage too dangerous. Diplomatic pressure on Italy by Britain, France, and Russia was necessary to save the Serbs from mass starvation.

The Allies also prepared to undertake the reorganization of the Serbian army after it was removed from Albania. It was first thought that Bizerte might be suitable for this, and about 10,000 men were sent there. Subsequently the Allies decided in favor of Corfu, which was occupied by the French, over Greek protests, on January 12. According to the plan of embarkation the northern group would leave from St. John of Medua, a small harbor near

Scutari, and the rest would go from Durazzo. But in the first week of January the Austrians attacked Montenegro and it surrendered on January 16. The barrier which had protected the hapless men at Scutari no longer existed and the region was hastily evacuated. Soldiers and refugees fled down the coast to Durazzo, barely escaping the Austrians, who occupied Scutari on January 22 and Medua a few days later.

Durazzo was the special domain of the notorious Esad Pasha, the self-styled ruler of Albania. He was on friendly terms with the Serbs, but he could do little to help them since he possessed few resources and was dominated by the Italians. Embarkation of Serbian troops at Durazzo began January 6 and continued intermittently. Thousands of boys who had been brought across Albania to save them from internment camps in Serbia were sent to Valona. Two thousand died before the Italian commander at Valona would permit them to enter the town. After the Austrian prisoners, who had been turned over to the Italians by the Serbs, were transported to Italy, the boys were taken to Corfu. Serbo-Italian relations became so strained that the chief of the French Military Mission, General de Mondesir, had to intervene in behalf of the Serbs. There was no food problem at Durazzo, thanks to the splendid work of the British Adriatic Mission. English engineers labored to improve communications along the coast. It seemed as though the worst was over and deliverance was at hand.

But once again, owing primarily to Italy, plans were changed. The Allies demanded that most of the northern army, which had just arrived at Durazzo, march on down the coast 135 miles to Valona. This demand was justified on the grounds that embarkation at Durazzo would be slow because the harbor lacked adequate facilities and that the Austrians were approaching. Alexander, who had just had an operation for appendicitis, was compelled to agree. The older men and invalids were taken off by sea; the others walked. After a successful skirmish with the Austrians, the Serbs speedily evacuated Durazzo, and the last units left on February 10. The Italians were relieved. Shortly thereafter, the Austrians drove them out of the town and occupied it.

By this time, however, the Serbs were safe. What they later called their crucifixion on the cross of Albania was nearly at an end.

No enemy, aside from their allies the Italians, could disturb them at Valona. A fleet of transports shuttled between it and Corfu. By April 15, 1916, the retreat was over. About 10,000 refugees were scattered from Brindisi to Marseille. On Corfu there was an unconquered army of 155,000 men.[11]

> *Serbs, you were the first to open the way; you were the first to see our enemies in flight.*
> GENERAL SARRAIL's proclamation celebrating
> the recapture of Monastir

> *Belgrade somehow!*          Serbian password on Corfu

Albania continued to take toll of the Serbs even after their arrival at Corfu. Thousands survived the ordeal by winter, mountains, and hunger, only to succumb amid sunshine, comfort, and plenty. The strain had been too great and when it was over they could not recover. Approximately 10,000 men died on Corfu and on the island of Vido near by.

The majority, however, regained health with astonishing rapidity. The French Military Mission drilled them intensively, and the Allies sent new uniforms and equipment. By the summer of 1916, incredible as it seemed to friend and foe alike, they were ready to go back to the front. Greece, although technically still their ally, would not permit them to pass through its territory. Running the gantlet of enemy submarines, they reached Salonika by sea.

At the end of July a Serbian army of 125,000 men had joined the Anglo-French forces under General Sarrail. It still retained the divisional names of Danube, Drina, Timok, Vardar, Morava, and Šumadija. But now there was only one division of each name instead of two. Putnik had resigned as chief of staff at Scutari. He was replaced by General Bojović, commander of the Troops of the New Regions, and finally by General Mišić, the "glorious Vojvoda" of the First Army. The Central Powers, after considering and rejecting an offensive against Salonika, had stabilized the Balkan front. It ran from the Adriatic, north of Valona, across Albania, Serbia, and Greece to the Gulf of Kavalla. Austrian, German, and Bulgarian troops, deeply entrenched, faced the Allied Army of the East. The latter was becoming increasingly heterogeneous. Eventually it included not only British, French, and Serbs, but Russians,

Italians, and even Greeks after the Entente had forced the abdication of King Constantine.

With some misgivings on the part of their colleagues, the Serbs were assigned a sector between Albania and the Vardar. They moved up to the front in September, 1916. Behind almost impassable and strongly fortified mountain ranges lay Serbia, enslaved by the military government of the conquerors. The Serbian army was in exile, shut out of its country by the invader, and could go home only over the bodies of its enemies. The men went back into battle like demons. They fought their way up Kajmakčalan, a mountain 8,000 feet high, driving against the Bulgars and Germans. In wind and snow they recaptured Bitolj on November 19, recovering 400 square miles of Serbian soil. It cost them 27,000 casualties and reduced their divisions from twelve to nine battalions each. For almost two years thereafter the front remained virtually without change.

Political conflict, perforce interrupted by the campaign of 1915, now revived. The world was informed in June, 1917, that Colonel Dragutin Dimitrijević, of the Serbian General Staff, and two other persons had been shot by a firing squad after a trial by a court-martial at Salonika. It was officially explained that they had attempted to assassinate the prince regent. The true facts concerning the episode have never been fully elucidated. It would seem to have been a last phase of the struggle for priority between Serbian civil and military leaders which had begun in 1903, when the army murdered Alexander Obrenović and his wife.

Dimitrijević, moreover, controlled the secret organization called the Ujedinjenje ili Smrt (Union or Death), members of which had carried out the murders at Sarajevo. He and his confidants, if allowed to live, might reveal what they had done and thus disprove the assertions of the civil government that Serbia was in no way connected with the crime. Major Vojislav Tankosić, his accomplice in arranging the death of the archduke, had been killed at Kragujevac. The death of Dimitrijević would do much to keep the secret of Sarajevo. It would also facilitate the destruction of the Ujedinjenje ili Smrt and its influence in Serbian politics. It is almost certain that the alleged attempt on Alexander's life did not take place. If so, Dimitrijević and his associates may be regarded as having been murdered by Pašić and the Radical party. The position of Alexander in this affair is not entirely clear.[12]

During the long lull on the front, progress was made toward the creation of a South Slav (Yugoslav) state after the war by the union of Serbia with those territories of Austria-Hungary whose population was predominantly Serbian, Croatian, or Slovene. The Serbian parliament had declared, in a resolution passed unanimously on December 7, 1914, at the height of the battle along the Kolubara, that its primary war aim was "the liberation and unification of all our subjugated brothers: Serbs, Croats, and Slovenes."[13] A Yugoslav Committee was formed in London and was supported by emigrants all over the world, notably in the United States, Canada, Australia, and New Zealand.

Alexander issued a proclamation on April 7, 1916, which contained this statement: "Our mighty allies and friends ... are now ready and willing to give us powerful assistance in this great conflict in order that we may make Serbia great and that she may include all Serbs (in Serbia) and Yugoslavs (in Austria-Hungary)—in a word, that we may make her into a strong and mighty YUGOSLAVIA."[14]

Oppressed and persecuted as inherently suspect throughout the war, the South Slavic elements in the Dual Monarchy asserted with increasing determination their desire for autonomy or independence. On May 30, 1917, the Yugoslav Parliamentary Club put forward a demand in the Austrian *Reichsrat* that "all the provinces of the Monarchy inhabited by Slovenes, Croats, or Serbs should be united under the Habsburg Crown in a single autonomous and democratic state."[15] Actually, the majority of Yugoslavs in Austria-Hungary wanted complete independence and union with Serbia.

Conferences between the Serbian cabinet and the leaders of the Yugoslav Committee resulted in the Pact of Corfu,[16] signed on July 20, 1917, by Pašić and Dr. Ante Trumbić, former head of the Croatian Nationalist party in the Dalmatian Diet and president of the Committee. This document affirmed the unity of Serbs, Croats, and Slovenes and declared that all branches of the South Slavic race, including Montenegro, should form a single kingdom, on a constitutional and democratic basis, under the Karageorgević dynasty. Local autonomies, delimited by "natural, social, and economic conditions," would be provided for in the constitution of the kingdom.

The immediate effect of the pact was to diminish certain hesitations on the part of the Croats. In August, 1917, Stjepan Radić, the leader of the Croatian Peasant party, stated that he favored union with Serbia, although he preferred a republic to a kingdom and would have liked the Bulgars to enter the new state. Italy's refusal to accept the Pact of Corfu made the Croats and Slovenes somewhat dubious about renouncing Habsburg support, but they were encouraged by an agreement reached in the spring of 1918 between Dr. Trumbić and a group of Italian deputies. This agreement, concluded with the approval of Signor Orlando, pledged both nations to settle territorial controversies in a friendly spirit according to the principles of nationality.

The Yugoslav movement eventually supplied the Serbian army with some badly needed troops. A large number of the Austrian prisoners taken by the Russians were South Slavs and many of them were glad to fight against their former masters. A Serbian Military Mission went to Russia in 1916 and organized them into a corps of two divisions. After service on the Rumanian front, 10,000 of them were shipped to Salonika by way of Archangel, Cherbourg, and Orange. Another 6,000 set out across Siberia in January, 1918, sailed from Port Arthur, and reached Salonika in April. Their exploit was similar to that of the Czech Expeditionary Force.

Italy, also, was asked to allow its prisoners of South Slavic extraction to volunteer for action with the Serbian forces. It refused on the pretext that its captives were loyal Austrians. This was not entirely accurate, since the Serbian legation at Rome received thousands of applications from men in Italian prison camps who wished to serve. Moreover, 20,000 of these prisoners, including a number of Bosnians, had been taken originally by the Serbs and turned over to the Italians after the retreat. But Italy was using them for forced labor and only a few hundred were permitted to join the Serbs on the Balkan front. Small groups of Yugoslav patriots arrived from such distant countries as America and Australia. Finally there were enough volunteers to warrant the creation of a separate Yugoslav Division.

The period of military inactivity came to an end in September, 1918. After a series of councils and confused negotiations in which the British again tried to withdraw from Salonika, General Franchet d'Esperey, who was now in command of Allied forces in Greece, was empowered to undertake a "limited offensive." It began on September 15, after a twenty-four-hour bombardment. East of the Vardar the British made no progress against the Bulgars, although the Greeks scored local successes. West of the river the Serbs and French went forward through the mists of early morning.

The Serbs, chosen to be the spearhead of the attack, assaulted the Dobro Polje, a formidable mountain barrier. The battle "may be taken as the only major operation of the Great War in a European theater, leading to a decision, which was carried out at heights of from 5,000 to 7,000 feet."[17] The operation was successful beyond expectation. By the evening of September 17 the enemy's three lines of defenses had been pierced. The unrivaled power and persistence of the Serbian attack may be inferred from the testimony of a British officer who reported to the War Office, "It is probable that if only Western European troops had been available the attack would at this stage have petered out and the whole offensive movement have failed."[18] As it was, a breach thirty miles wide and eighteen miles deep had been made in the enemy front.

During the next few days the pocket was extended. The Bulgars crumbled steadily and German reinforcements could not stop the Allied advance. The battle of rupture became a pursuit. For a time it seemed that the German Eleventh Army, in its turn, must flee across the Šar Planina toward Prizren and Albania. On the morning of September 29 the French took Skoplje. Later that day, but unknown for some time to the combatants, Bulgaria, after vainly offering to desert the Central Powers and ally itself with the Entente, surrendered. Stolidly the Bulgarian army went home.

Thereafter, the Serbs pursued the Austrians and Germans as hounds pursue a fox. They had been in continuous action for two weeks, but they fought like fresh troops. With the Yugoslav Division usually in the van, they pushed back an enemy of equal numerical strength ten miles a day. They outran their communications; units were separated from each other; the assault waves were out of touch with those behind them; generals did not change their clothing for weeks. Rations and supplies were forgotten. Villagers, swarming out of their houses, offered the soldiers any food which had escaped requisition by the enemy. They devoured it and pressed on.

The Serbs recaptured Niš on October 10. The Austrians and Germans fled north to the Danube. From October 25 to November 1, a little more than three years after they had rolled triumphantly over the Sava and the Danube in the great *Einmarsch,* the invaders recrossed the rivers. Vojvoda Bojović entered Belgrade on November 1, and on the same day Serbian patrols reached the Drina.

Three days later Austria-Hungary surrendered. The Dual Monarchy, Serbia's implacable foe, was in the dust, never to rise again. On November 11 the First World War ended. Ravaged, despoiled, with the best of its manhood dead or wounded, Serbia had, by indomitable resolution, survived the ordeal of a four-year battle. It stood beside its Allies, victorious.

## CHAPTER VI

# Yugoslavia and the Peace Conference

## BY ROBERT J. KERNER

A NY THOROUGH ANALYSIS of how Yugoslavia—that is, the Kingdom of the Serbs, Croats, and Slovenes—obtained final boundaries after the First World War must take account, not only of the work at the Peace Conference and later negotiations, but also of the role played by the collapse of Bulgaria and of Austria-Hungary, and the unstable policy of Italy, fluctuating from one extreme to another. A clear perspective and sound judgment on this difficult problem may best be obtained in such an analysis.

By the Secret Treaty of London, in the spring of 1915, Britain, France, and Russia (the last very reluctantly) promised Italy large strips of territory, inhabited preponderantly by Yugoslavs, in return for its entry into the war. The negotiators of the treaty could not or did not want to foresee the future, when the impossible structure of the Habsburg Monarchy would tumble down like a house of cards under the stress of war. Had they understood the true situation they might not have made the treaty as they did. For the time being, they were giving Italy territories inhabited chiefly by Yugoslavs, and strategic control of the east Adriatic shore, but they were leaving intact a smaller Austria-Hungary, with an outlet through Croatia, and a possible Greater Serbia. They were creating a balance of power on the Adriatic in favor of Italy as the price for what they thought was to be Italy's decisive assistance in winning the war. Viewed from that angle, keen disappointment was in store for the Allies, as the first Italian offensive was short-lived.

The effectiveness of Russia in the Trans-Vistula campaign from October, 1914, to January, 1915, in which the Russians decisively defeated the Austrians, led the Germans to entrench in the west (just when Britain and France faced a crucial lack of ammunition) and to hurl themselves upon Russia. The breaking of the Russian line at Gorlice in May, 1915, was followed by a disastrous retreat. Serbia was crushed late in 1915 by German-led troops from the north and by the Bulgarians from the southeast. This really ended the hopes for a Greater Serbia. The Pact of Corfu in July, 1917, was to demand the creation of a Yugoslavia.

Russia was called on by its allies to make several more drives for which it was unprepared: to help the French at Verdun in March, 1916, by a drive from Riga to Baranovichi; to save Italy in June by a drive under General Brusilov on the southwestern front; and to rescue Rumania in the fall of that year. The March (1917) Revolution in Russia began a demoralization which the Kerensky offensive in June could not stop, and which culminated in the seizure of power by the Bolsheviks in November. The gradual disorganization of the Italian army and its internal front in 1916 and 1917 led to the disaster of Caporetto, causing Italy's allies to rush to its rescue.

But this was not the whole story. When knowledge of the contents of the Secret Treaty of London gradually found its way to the Yugoslavs who lived under the Habsburgs, and who were designated as its chief victims, it made them fight against the Italians as they had never fought before, even though they had been opposed to Habsburg rule. Italian victory and hence Allied victory was to be delayed or prevented until the Allies and Italy had time to reconsider their views on the partition of what they had heretofore treated as enemy territory; this they did in the light of the Russian collapse and the threatened dissolution of the Habsburg Monarchy, in which American diplomacy played a major role.

As this development gained momentum (after the Russian Revolution in March, 1917), the Italians realized that they had to share in the changing diplomacy or be unable to control it for their own purposes. Thus it was that the unofficial Pact of Rome emerged from the unofficial Congress of Oppressed Nationalities

(April, 1918). The right of subject nationalities to national unity and independence was recognized. In particular, the national unity and independence of the Yugoslavs and of the Italians were expressly provided for on the basis of self-determination, with protection for minorities. Although this pact was not a treaty and was viewed with skepticism by the Italian government, as represented by Foreign Minister Sonnino, it was greeted in most circles as a great improvement in the relations between Italians and Yugoslavs. It was all too evident that the Italian position, thereafter, could not be based on both the Secret Treaty of London and the Pact of Rome.

While the Czechoslovaks were being formally recognized by France, Britain, and the United States, and the justice of Yugoslav aspirations was acknowledged by the United States on September 3, 1918, the Italian government, under the pressure of events and through the activity of Italian Liberals led by Bissolati, on September 8 issued a statement to the effect that "Italy considers that the movement of the Yugoslav people for independence and for the constitution of a free state corresponds to the principles for which the Allies are fighting and to the aims of a just and lasting peace." If Italians took this cynically as a mere episode in war propaganda, it is certain that the Yugoslavs did not.

The Pact of Rome and Italy's declaration helped materially to disintegrate Austria-Hungary. The September, 1918, break in the line of the Central Powers in Bulgaria precipitated the defection of Turkey in October, as well as the advance of the Serbs into Serbia by November 1. The collapse of Austria-Hungary followed on November 3. Yugoslav unity was proclaimed at Zagreb on November 24 and accepted in the name of the Karageorgević dynasty by Prince Regent Alexander on December 1.

When the war ended, instead of the Great Power, Austria-Hungary, ally and vassal of the mighty Germany, Italy found across the Adriatic a weak, struggling young nation in the throes of painful unification. What was to be Italy's policy? Was it to be that of the unofficial Pact of Rome and the official Declaration of September 8—a policy which foreshadowed agreement and friendship and even alliance; or was it to be that of the Secret Treaty of London—which foreshadowed a fundamental and irreconcilable hostility in future; or, what was even worse, was Italian policy to demand more than the Treaty of London?

It did not take long to find out. To the great surprise of most students of this problem, Italian policy at the Peace Conference was based on getting more than the Treaty of London. In other words, it virtually repudiated not only the Pact of Rome and the Declaration of September 8 but actually the Treaty of London. The Italians revealed that they sought primarily an absolute strategic control of the Adriatic as well as of all the passes from central Europe over the Alps, and the dominant bridgeheads by land for expansionist possibilities into the valley of the Danube and the Balkan Peninsula. At the Peace Conference they opposed recognition of Yugoslavia and recognized only Serbia.

The policy of the Yugoslavs was to be based chiefly on ethnic considerations along the frontiers of Italy, Austria, and Hungary, and mainly on strategic principles along the Rumanian and Bulgarian frontiers. Other claims—geographic, historic, economic, and cultural—were advanced, but they were clearly subordinated to the ideas indicated above. In an account as brief as this must be, it is possible to stress only the most important features of the intricate peace negotiations as these finally came to be centered chiefly on Fiume and the Adriatic, the basin of Klagenfurt, the Bačka, the Banat, and the strategic salients in eastern Macedonia.

The effort to draw the frontiers between Italy and Yugoslavia nearly wrecked the Peace Conference, for the Secret Treaty of London had promised Italy the Trentino and Istria; Dalmatia and the Adriatic islands; and land or spheres of influence in Albania, Asia Minor, and Africa. These territories included at least 200,000 Germans and 500,000 Slavs.

Certain considerations dominated the discussions and virtually dictated the course of events. In the first place, Britain and France (and to a certain extent the United States) found it inconvenient to accede to the Mediterranean, Asiatic, and African (in other words, the Near East) ambitions of Italy and such other "rights" as were promised it in the Secret Treaty, and hence throughout they preferred to offer Italy a better deal in Europe—necessarily at the expense of Yugoslavs and Germans. This attitude was always uppermost in the minds of those who thought in terms of colonies and imperialism. Nor was it limited to members of the British and French delegations. In the American delegation it was represented by such men as George Louis Beer.

Those who derived their views from the colonial or imperialistic world went so far as to maintain that the Italians were a "superior" race and that the Yugoslavs, being an "inferior" people, should be browbeaten, if necessary, and subjected to Italian rule in order that more convenient deals might be made in other regions of the colonial world where Italy would receive relatively less. Fortunately, on the American side such men were in the minority and could, for the most part, work only behind the scenes because of the wide disparity between their views and the ideals of Woodrow Wilson.

Another consideration was the fact that Italy had real nuisance value as a Power which, if dissatisfied, might not sign the peace treaties. It was therefore hoped that generous treatment, especially in Europe, would find Italy ready to coöperate in the peacemaking. If President Wilson in part shared this view, it was only with definite limitations. When he realized that the majority of his academic advisers were opposed to granting certain promises of the Secret Treaty of London in regard to Europe, and also to yielding to any claims beyond its terms, the President set his course firmly and kept it to the end. He believed that Italy would be generously treated if it obtained a strategically defensible frontier in the Alps and in Istria, and naval domination in the Adriatic through the possession of Pola, Valona, and Vis (Lissa), even if this violated, in Italy's favor, Point 9 of the Fourteen Points, which called for "a readjustment of the frontiers of Italy . . . along clearly recognizable lines of nationality." It was this desire which led him to agree early in the negotiations to give the Brenner Pass to Italy, though a line farther to the south might have been just as defensible from a military point of view and would have included a smaller German-speaking population. It will be seen, however, that Italy went beyond the Secret Treaty of London in its claims in regions inhabited by Yugoslavs.

Still another consideration which must not be lost sight of was the fact that the Yugoslav delegation was jockeyed into a position which at first appeared somewhat advantageous, but which may be judged, in the larger perspective, to have been otherwise. Already keenly alive to the fact that Woodrow Wilson had taken issue with Sonnino's imperialistic views (erroneously called nationalistic), Dr. Ante Trumbić early in February, 1919, offered to leave the final decision to the President and to accept his arbitration. This the latter agreed to do if both parties desired it. Italy, however, formally refused.

This left the Yugoslav case mainly in the hands of Woodrow Wilson and the American delegation. Able as they were, there was danger that they might more easily make concessions which could lose the entire case for the Yugoslavs. There was also the danger that if and when the American delegation left the Conference, or found it convenient or necessary to change its policy, things might turn out to the complete detriment of the Yugoslavs because they had leaned too much on the American delegation (all of whom were by no means friendly to them) and because they had confided to it their *minimum* claims.

It was under such conditions that the Italian delegation at the Peace Conference claimed the port of Fiume in addition to what was set down in the Secret Treaty of London. This would mean not only Italy's acquisition of another bridgehead (besides Trieste and Valona) into the Danubian basin or the Balkan Peninsula, but the loss to the Yugoslavs of their only available economic outlet on the Adriatic (since the Italians claimed Trieste under the Secret Treaty), as well as the sacrifice of another block of territory inhabited overwhelmingly by Yugoslavs.

Two reasons, beyond the flimsy Italian ethnic claim to Fiume and its region, were later advanced for this departure from the terms of the Secret Treaty: one to the effect that the Italians must have Fiume if Trieste was to survive as a port in Italian hands, and the other that, since Bissolati or his party friends had publicly demanded the acquisition of Fiume, the tottering cabinet of Orlando and Sonnino had to claim it or fall. Whatever may have been the reason or reasons, clearly none was valid, for the region of Fiume was preponderantly Yugoslav, even though the little town itself had an unstable Italian plurality—artfully fostered for several decades by the Magyars in order to keep it from falling into the hands of the Croats.

The Yugoslavs under pressure had given the American delegation information based on suggested frontiers about midway between the extreme Italian and Yugoslav claims. This meant the
loss of the western half of Istria, which included Trieste and the
naval base of Pola, and a large stretch of territory inhabited by
the Slovenes to the north and west.

When, on February 18, the Yugoslavs formally presented their
proposal for the Italo-Yugoslav frontier, it consisted of the old
frontier of 1914 between Italy and Austria. It was admitted that
east and south of this line there were Italian majorities or plurali-
ties in such cities and towns as Gorizia, Trieste, Lussino, Fiume,
and Zara, but these were virtually isolated in a preponderantly
Slavic countryside. They were not contiguous to Italian territory
and were even discontinuous from one another.

It was argued that the Yugoslav claim to Trieste was too extreme
because two-thirds of its population spoke Italian or claimed to
be Italian. However, it was known that the majority were not
Italian in origin. Trieste is located in a region overwhelmingly
Yugoslav. Italy had no economic relations of importance with
Trieste. Its immediate Yugoslav surroundings and other states
in the hinterland had vital economic interests in Trieste as their
chief access to the sea. Objectivity in peacemaking—there being
no Great Power interests involved—would have awarded a seaport
to its hinterland with adequate safeguards to the majority in the
city, and with free port privileges to the states in the hinterland.

Even more potent in this sense was the argument against giving
Italy the town of Fiume with its Italian plurality. Italy, backed
by France, was able to have the Italo-Yugoslav frontier settlement
reserved to the Council of the Great Powers. (Yugoslavia was not
represented on the Council because the Secret Treaty of London
had been made between the Great Powers.) The remaining frontiers of Yugoslavia were to be dealt with by a committee in which
experts predominated.

Although the British and the French did not relish the fact that
they would have to stand by the Secret Treaty of London for the
reasons indicated above, they preferred to have the struggle undertaken by President Wilson and to remain on good terms with both
sides. His stand—based on the reports of his academic advisers,

and strenuously opposed by the Italians—was that the Italians be granted the Brenner Pass, western Istria, including Trieste and Pola, as well as the island of Lussino, to which it was expected the Albanian port of Valona would be added in order to insure the strategic control of the Adriatic. Fiume and Dalmatia were to go to the Yugoslavs.

Other members of the American delegation, comprising a chiefly nonacademic minority in which George Louis Beer and Sidney Mezes appear to have played roles, behind Colonel Edward M. House, which were entirely beyond their fields of competence, argued that Italy be given more than was called for by the Secret Treaty of London, namely, Fiume and all Dalmatia. A memorandum by Mezes wound up by suggesting that Italy could then give up the Dodecanese and abandon or abate its claims in Asia Minor and Albania! A competent critic, by no means unfriendly to the Italians or to Mezes, indicates that his memorandum "read rather like quotations from the Italian Memorandum of Claims." To think in such original terms was regarded as "realistic," whereas other views were "too academic."

President Wilson rejected these views. He was conscious of the fact that his stand was based on terms very favorable to the Italians. The concessions had been made on strategic grounds and worked injustice on more than 200,000 Germans and 500,000 Yugoslavs. He was convinced that he had compromised enough in favor of the Italians. This seems to have been the point of view also of the American commissioners, Lansing and White, who were opposed to further compromise. Thus the issue was joined by the third week of April, 1919.

As the time approached for signing the treaty with Germany, the Italians threatened to leave the Peace Conference unless their claims on Fiume and Dalmatia were granted. When all attempts at compromise failed, Lansing and White agreed that a statement should be made by President Wilson to the Italian people. Even Colonel House came to that view, subject to the President's consulting Lloyd George and Clemenceau, who, in fact, favored such a stand. Lloyd George continued in vain to seek a compromise. Fiume was the irreconcilable issue.

Late in the afternoon of April 23, President Wilson's statement

to the Italian people appeared in *Le Temps*. Orlando and most
of the Italian delegation left the next day for Rome. But they returned to Paris on May 5. Woodrow Wilson had not won the
Italian people to his point of view and, since the Italian cabinet
fell six weeks later, the victory was not Orlando's either. Italy
signed the Treaty of Versailles, but the Italo-Yugoslav frontier
was not agreed upon at the Peace Conference, in spite of numerous
proposals in regard to Fiume and Dalmatia. These played with the
idea of Fiume as a buffer state and with the concession to Italy
of a few more islands off the Dalmatian coast in lieu of the Dalmatian mainland (except for Zara).

After the Italian-inspired riots of July 2–3 in Fiume, in which
the lives of French soldiers were lost and General Grazioli was
relieved of his command by the Supreme Council, d'Annunzio
staged his *coup d'état* on September 12. Premier Nitti disavowed
d'Annunzio.

In the meantime the Peace Conference began to dissolve into
the Council of Five. On December 9 a joint Franco-British-Amer-
ican Memorandum attempted once more to solve the frontier
problems. This was followed by the "January (6–14) Compromise"
sponsored by Clemenceau and Lloyd George. It yielded still more
to Italy, which now, among other things, was to have "contiguous
access" to the "independent" city of Fiume. Trumbić virtually
rejected the January Compromise, and President Wilson, in his
Memorandum of February 20, 1920, written in "utmost frankness,"
fairly scorched Britain and France for yielding to the country with
"the most endurance" (Italy) instead of to the country "armed with
a just cause" (Yugoslavia). He stood on the basis of the Memorandum of December 9 and threatened to withdraw the treaty with
Germany and the agreement between the United States and France
then before the Senate—that is, the United States would withdraw
from the peace settlement in Europe. This put an end to the January Compromise. Later, the President stated that he had no opposition to a "mutually agreeable" settlement between Italy and
Yugoslavia, "provided it was not made at the expense of a third
Power" (Albania?).

Thus, comments the late Professor H. W. V. Temperley, "President Wilson had failed to convert Orlando, Nitti to convert

d'Annunzio, the three Powers together had failed to convert Italy, Tardieu and Clemenceau had failed to convert the Yugoslavs. The President of the Conference and the President of the United States had failed to solve the problem, and the two principals were at last left to work out their salvation, which they ultimately did without summoning the League of Nations to their aid."

Direct negotiations, initiated with Trumbić by Premier Nitti, were later resumed after his fall by Giolitti. The plebiscite in the Klagenfurt area (October 10, 1920) had gone against the Yugoslavs in spite of the ethnic majority of the Slovenes. The Democratic party, whose leader had been President Wilson, lost the national election in November. On the twelfth of that month the Treaty of Rapallo was signed. It provided for the grant to Italy of a larger portion of Istria than the Wilson line allowed it: a coastal strip from Istria to the "free" state of Fiume and the islands of Cherso, Lussino, Lagosta, and Pelagosa. The city of Zara went to Italy, and the Italian population of Dalmatia was to be guaranteed certain rights. The treaty was speedily ratified by both countries. D'Annunzio was forced out of Fiume as an "unwanted hero" in January, 1921, leaving in Fiume "my dead, my sorrow, and my victory."

Yugoslavia had lost its fight against Italy. And Italy, because its policy had been based on hostility to Yugoslavia, was to fall into the crushing embrace of a revived Germany and thus lose all in vassalage. Italy might have had the friendship of the Yugoslavs and with them resisted successfully the pressure from the north.

The Austro-Yugoslav frontier involved the old Austrian provinces of Carniola, Carinthia, and Styria. Italy received a part of Carniola. The remainder of Carniola and part of Styria were given to Yugoslavia by the Treaty of St. Germain, signed on September 10, 1919. After some fighting in which the Serbs came out on top, the plebiscite provided for in the treaty was ordered in the Klagenfurt area of Carinthia. The population of this region was predominantly Slovene in speech, but the Slovenes here were under the economic and cultural domination of the Germans, many of whom were extremists, namely, Pan-Germans. When the Slovenes were called on to express their views, they did so timidly. If they thought the Germans would not hear about it, they sided with Yugoslavia—as the author can testify from his experiences on the American Mission which examined the region. It was no wonder, then, that the Yugoslavs lost the plebiscite in the Klagenfurt district on October 10, 1920. They had not developed a national consciousness to the same extent as the Germans.

The frontier with Hungary and Rumania, dealt with in the Treaty of Trianon (signed June 4, 1920) involved the former Hungarian districts of the Baranja, the Bačka, and the Banat. In the Yugoslav part of the Bačka some 200,000 Magyars were included. Had the line been drawn farther south, the 100,000 Yugoslavs in the city of Subotica (Szabadka) near the frontier would have gone to Hungary. The Banat, with an ethnic mixture as complex as that of Macedonia, was divided, with approximately two-thirds going to Rumania and one-third to Yugoslavia. The entire boundary here had great strategic significance: to provide a bridgehead to defend Belgrade. It also gave Yugoslavia a rich agricultural region which was highly desirable for its economy. In the Banat, however, the economic outlet of Temišvar (Timişoara) to the Danube was blocked. As a result, the frontier in the Banat caused marked coolness for a while between Yugoslavia and Rumania.

The making of the frontier between Yugoslavia and Bulgaria was dominated by Yugoslavia's insistent demand that Bulgaria should not be left in a position to attack it again as easily as in 1915, with all its subsequent misery and horror for the Serbs. In that light Yugoslavia demanded minor strategic boundary rectifications: the Strumica salient which came within a few miles (five and twelve) of the Salonika–Belgrade railway and thus made it easy for the Bulgarians to cut off Serbia from the port of Salonika; the Caribrod and Bosiljgrad salients, which closed passes from Bulgaria and put the Yugoslav boundary within thirty miles of Sofia; and a rectification in the Timok Valley. Caribrod in Yugoslav hands blocked four of the seven roads by which the vitally important town of Niš is reached.

The Peace Conference, through the Treaty of Neuilly (November 27, 1919), gave the Strumica, Caribrod, and Bosiljgrad salients to Yugoslavia, but not the Dragoman Pass, because that would have put Sofia at the mercy of Belgrade. Nor did it give Yugoslavia the Bulgarian town of Vidin, though it permitted a slight boundary rectification to protect the Timok Valley railroad from rifle fire on the Bulgarian side. The problem of Macedonia, whether wisely or unwisely, was left as in 1913, after Bulgaria's first treacherous assault upon Serbia and Greece. The boundary of 1913 between Albania on one side and Montenegro and Serbia on the other remained the boundary of Yugoslavia by decision of the Peace Conference.*

Thus it has been seen that Yugoslavia was forced to yield important and almost vital districts to Italy, but gained its proper share or more than its share from Hungary, Rumania, and Bulgaria. In the case of Austria, there was a loss—the Klagenfurt area. For Albania the boundary remained the same. Like other new states, Yugoslavia was compelled to sign a treaty guaranteeing protection to minorities.

The answer to the riddle of the future was to be found, primarily, in the foreign policy of Italy as regards Germany and, secondarily, in the will to vengeance of Bulgaria and Hungary. It was also to be found in the manner in which the Yugoslavs would make use of their newly won liberty.

---

* See Appendix, pp. 485–486.

*Part Three*

# POLITICAL
# DEVELOPMENT

# CHAPTER VII

# *Constitutional Development to 1914*

## BY MALBONE W. GRAHAM

THE MILITARY CONQUEST and partition of the Kingdom of Yugoslavia by Germany and its Axis partners in the spring of 1941 was a tragic event for the South Slavs. But in the long perspective of history it can be viewed as an episode far less enduring in the lives of these heroic peoples than the aftermath of the Battle of Kosovo. Although it marked a major dislocation, a hiatus in constitutional development, it was not the end of the juridical pattern created by the Yugoslav people. The fabric woven throughout fifteen hundred years of common historical experience was not so delicate that a break in the thread of its continuity, even the temporary discontinuance of portions of the design, could permanently destroy the intricately woven tapestry.

This is a fitting time to analyze the constitutional evolution of the Yugoslavs. The patterns for collective behavior (which we call constitutions) are complex. Constitutionalism is principally of nineteenth-century origin. Except for a relatively small part of the English-speaking world, whose continuity in legal structure and institutions stretches back into the seventeenth and eighteenth centuries, the great political movement resulting from the convergence of the American and French revolutions was, par excellence, a nineteenth-century phenomenon. It reached its zenith in the second decade of the twentieth century.

Constitutionalism required the political and economic climate of laissez-faire, then of humanitarian liberalism, for its most complete development. It posited that relative freedom from martial breaking of juridical continuity which currently passed for peace.

Conceived as a scheme for the gradual delegation of monarchical authority to increasingly articulate, if not always politically literate, portions of the population, constitutionalism strove to accommodate within the institutionalized framework of peacetime society the periodically measured strength of lethargic, manipulable, or capricious electorates.

When the current of nationalism flowed too fast to be dammed behind the legal dikes and spillways of monarchial authority, as in the self-emancipation of colonies in the Americas, it became necessary to recognize the right of peoples to carve out their own course in the stream bed of history. Thus the accomplished facts of national revolution were legitimated by the acclamation of national sovereignty. Perhaps the best-known examples in the nineteenth-century constitutional history of Europe are those of Greece and Belgium—pioneers in the emergence from galling tutelage to despised sovereigns. These established dynasties for the governance of new national states. In the long procession of constitutional transformations in the early decades of the nineteenth century, the pashalik principality of Serbia was the next to accept the benefits of a liberal regime.

For the Balkan, as for the Iberian, Peninsula, constitutionalism was an exotic novelty. Four hundred years of Turkish rule had effectively blotted out all vestiges of the institutions which, primitive though they were, marked the high point of progress in the rule of Stephen Dušan in the fourteenth century. From Murad I to Abdul-Hamid the Damned, Ottoman imperial authority made few concessions to subject peoples. Except for a small residuum of religious rights, the Turkish regime permitted to its helots no autonomy, no capitulatory legal system, no deliberative assemblies, no share in administration. The intercession of the Western Christian Powers, themselves not subject to the pressure of the Porte, provided the only measure of mitigation of the harshness of Moslem rule. And when the Ottoman Empire gave successive evidences of impending dissolution, it was their intervention which extorted from the unwilling functionaries of the Yildiz Kiosk the belated reforms destined to govern the transition period between submission and enfranchisement.

It is therefore necessary to look to the *firmans* and *hatti-sherifs* of the later sultans of the Ottoman Empire for documentary evidence of the compulsory devolution of authority, at the instance of the Powers, which marks the start of nationalities on the road to constitutional government. Yet, in the absence of dependable traditions, constitutional documents pertaining to the history of independent Serbia must be regarded as standards of legality to be approximated rather than as codes of rules deduced from accomplished facts.

Viewed in this perspective, the charters, first of the Principality, then of the Kingdom, of Serbia assume new importance. They disclose a fairly consistent pattern of constitutional development and outreaching national life. They appear, at the outset, in rather ill-defined and blanket form, as in the guaranties of the Peace of Bucharest of 1812, which succeeded in extorting from the reluctant Porte the first approximations of cultural, religious, or political autonomy for the Serbs under its jurisdiction.[1]

Owing to the Napoleonic upheaval and the continued revolts of Christian subjects of the Ottoman Empire, little effect was given to these promises until the time of Greece's emancipation. By the Treaty of Ackermann of September 25/October 7, 1826, the Sublime Porte confirmed Imperial Russia's desire to effectuate the stipulated guaranties, and the Separate Act of the same date granted religious liberties to the Serbs and established a framework of executive government in the principality.[2] This was implemented by a *hatti-sherif*[3] issued by the Porte to Serbia on October 1, 1829, and elaborated by a *firman* of October, 1830, which, compared to Serbia's previous subjugation, accorded it a limited dominion status.[4]

This document, reflecting even in the Balkans the unsettling effect of the July revolutions in France and Belgium, amplified the guaranties of religious freedom, fixed the line of princely succession in the House of Obrenović, created a separate military establishment, and outlined a plan for a consultative assembly or legislature. Finally, to link Belgrade and Constantinople more effectively, it gave legal status to the informally recognized group of Serb patriots in the Turkish capital by stipulating that there should "always be at Constantinople a Serbian deputation for

---

[1] For notes to chapter vii see pages 516–518.

the management of the affairs of the Serbian nation." What distinguished this stipulation, antedating by eight years the first
formal constitution, is its prospective character: it anticipated the
emergence of a future instrument and invested its provisions with
"inviolability and stability."

When the time was propitious for further extension of internal
autonomy,[5] the Porte, on December 24, 1838, issued to Serbia its
first full-fledged constitution by promulgation from above. The
existing framework of national authority was enlarged to include
a more complete administration and a separate judiciary. The constitution and the accompanying *firman* established certain safeguards and guaranties to be upheld by the newly created courts.
Although still conceived of as an organic statute capable of revision from above rather than as a freely formulated constitution,
this instrument of government was destined to have the longest
period of continuous application (1838–1859) in Serbian history.[6]

This epoch, however, was far from a record of unbroken progress. Much of the Constitution of 1838 remained a promissory note
which successive holders of the Serbian throne failed to redeem.
Yet there was undeniable consolidation and development. Miloš,
unable to share political power with anyone, was soon driven by
events into abdication and exile. The irremovable Senate created
by the constitution became the real power.[7] Composed of seventeen
members, one from each district, the Senate included Liberal
opponents of Miloš, the former partisans of Karageorge, and new
men, such as Ilija Garašanin, who were winning their way to
national prominence through sheer administrative ability.

In the decades which, in the West, witnessed the explosive force
of the revolutions of 1848 and, in the East, the gathering and dissi-
pation of the war clouds of the Crimean War, the Principality of
Serbia, whose rulers were far from thoroughly established, found its
fulcrum in the Senate. The newly formed party of Constitutional-
ists (Ustavobranitelji) carried through the Senate both the organization of the judiciary along western European lines and a land
reform so thorough that the *morbus latifundii* which plagued the
neighboring Austrian Empire was completely stamped out.

Nevertheless, four changes of sovereigns in as many years (1839–
1843) slowed down the momentum of Serbian institutions and left

the country a prey to the divisive counsels of foreign Powers and the Porte. In the succeeding clashes of policy between Russia and Austria, it was the Senate which proved its undeviatingly anti-Austrian character, whereas the *kneževi* proved far more tractable to the demands of the Ballplatz. And when, in 1858, the first Alexander of the Karageorgević dynasty tried to dispense with the Senate, he found aligned against him a curious but momentarily omnipotent coalition of the "Parisians"—liberals educated in western Europe and reared in the ideology of the French Revolution—and peasants in revolt against the Belgrade bureaucracy. This combination of circumstances permitted the return of the long-exiled Miloš—now a venerable personage enjoying a prestige at once so remote, nebulous, and patriarchal that he was able unilaterally to defy the sultan and again proclaim himself hereditary sovereign.

The death of Miloš in 1860 aroused in Serbia the same hope of constitutional government which currently activated Austrian and Italian life. In the tall, handsome Michael Obrenović, whose first rule from 1839 to 1842 had been only superficially influential, Serbia now acquired a ruler of European caliber with intimate knowledge of the international situation gained from long residence abroad. But it was obvious from the outset that the conceded charter of 1838 no longer suited the situation.

Michael's answer was to draw up and promulgate, despite the protests of the Porte, the so-called Constitution of 1861, a bold, princely expedient which, under the pretext of amending laws previously in force, sought to effect internal reform. Michael endeavored to bring about rapid results, with a wholly appointive Senate virtually deprived of any means of enforcing ministerial responsibility. Provision was made also for an elected Skupština, or National Assembly. Bereft of its bureaucratic element, it became, in fact, a peasant "Chamber of Echoes" which, until 1888, contained no organized opposition and, like the Senate, was unable to hold the ministers to account. Thus the return of Michael to the throne of Serbia quickly effected an amazing degree of arbitrary, quasi-dictatorial, royal centralization. Although these measures were abruptly terminated by Michael's assassination in 1868, they are highly indicative of the role which dynastic authority was to play in Yugoslav national development.

The accession of Milan IV, then still a minor, gave the Serbian nation a new opportunity to try out the benefits of constitutionalism. Under the guidance of Jovan Ristić, head of the Regency Council, a Grand National Assembly was convoked to draft a new constitution. Its deliberations resulted in the Constitution of Kragujevac[8] of June 29/July 11, 1869, which was, to a great extent, the work of Ristić. This realistic document sought to provide liberal institutions, but it placed no undue reliance upon the political maturity of the Serbian people or their ability to conform to western European parliamentarism.[9]

The constitution bore indirect evidences of the tactics of Bismarck in forcing legislation through recalcitrant assemblies, even to the right of repromulgating a previous budget; it kept intact the government's monopoly of initiative in legislation and reserved the right to name an influential number of members in the Skupština, meanwhile forbidding the election of bureaucrats or lawyers. Although elections were made indirect and opened the way to government pressure on electors, the constitution established a basic parliamentary system modeled on those prevailing in central Europe. The Skupština, as a representative assembly, reinforced the principle of ministerial responsibility to a degree which, except in Greece, had previously not been known south of the Danube.

Perhaps the most concrete expression of the constitutional innovations laid down by the new instrument was set forth in the address by which the sovereign closed the Constituent Skupština at Kragujevac:

> After a half century of existence our principality today puts the capstone on its internal independence by giving itself for the first time a constitution.... Our constitution is our own national work ... a foundation laid by ourselves, on which we can construct our political edifice in conformity with our situation and our needs.... If in the last thirty years our sovereigns have fallen, one after the other, putting in jeopardy the public peace, partly because their principal organs were not responsible before the people, we hope that with God's help these scenes shall not be renewed, for their final source has been dried up by the consecration of the great principle of ministerial responsibility.... Civil rights are clearly defined and guaranteed by the constitution. Our country has become a constitutional state.
>
> But the greatest and most important reform which the constitution introduces consists in the organization of the legislative power. Its exercise hence-

forth belongs conjointly to the prince and the National Assembly. This change marks a new epoch in our modern history, for it is the first time that the National Assembly has been raised to the height of a legislative body. Hitherto the National Assembly met only once in three years; henceforth it will meet annually. Hitherto the National Assembly could only express its wishes and grievances; henceforth it will have a deliberative voice, through legislation, on the destinies of the country. No law will have force unless it is promulgated by the prince, but no law will be rendered, abrogated, modified, or interpreted without the assent of the National Assembly. At the side of the prince is a Council of State entrusted with drafting the laws and assisting the government and the Assembly in their tasks; and our ancient institution, the Grand National Assembly, remains to settle certain vital questions, as the nation's supreme recourse.

This was excellent as a blueprint, but its execution required that understanding give-and-take between social classes and organized party groups which, in sharp contrast to the England of the Second Reform Bill era, was utterly lacking in Serbia. Without regularly constituted parties it was impossible to operate a truly parliamentary system. Thus Serbia was destined to gravitate, under an Austrophil dynasty, to the merest sham of constitutional life, meanwhile awaiting the day when new political forces, coming to power as European-educated sons of peasants, could express their kinsmen's wishes in Serbian parliamentary life.[10]

That day came when King Milan, after seventeen years of rule, convoked the Skupština to consider a constitutional revision which should bring Serbia closer to the pattern of western European states. The result was the Constitution of 1889, which marked a new milestone in the delegation of authority—this time under no external compulsions or internal pressure—to the people of Serbia. The instrument of 1889 corresponded, in the Balkan Peninsula, to the liberal reforms of 1884 in France, of 1884 and 1885 in England, and of 1882 in Italy, the delayed repercussions of which reached Serbia in this circuitous manner. The new constitution introduced parliamentary responsibility, proportional representation, and broad guaranties of constitutional rights, which were unequivocally and categorically laid down in the text.

The constitution was promulgated by King Milan on January 3, 1889, in a deeply moving Speech from the Throne.[11] Probably drafted by Ristić, the message was, in fact, a formal *ave atque vale*, for within a few months the sovereign renounced the throne and withdrew from political life. King Milan declared that the delegation of authority was voluntary and not a result of external pressure:

> By my own will I have imposed on my people the task of giving themselves, through a new constitution elaborated in common, which should guarantee greater civil and political liberties and safeguard order, an immovable basis for the political ideas of Serbia. . . . The first ten years of my reign were consecrated to the struggle for the acquisition and strengthening of our political independence; the second period of ten years of my reign was devoted to efforts and attempts to make of patriarchal Serbia a modern state. Perhaps I have gone along this course faster than the people may have desired or wished. Whether or not this was a mistake on my part, history will tell; but I have had the profound conviction that I have served the interests of Serbia, of its independence, of its future, even as I serve its interests today in revamping its fundamental law.
>
> You have earned the right to the recognition of your contemporaries and of future generations of the nation who will enjoy new liberties in their political life. . . . Your master has of his own volition given up the enormous and important prerogatives which the old constitution vested in him. Henceforth there will not be in the National Assembly deputies named by the government; there will not be any state of siege in our beautiful country; in our Serbia, so peaceful and tranquil by nature, it will not be possible to suspend, even for the shortest space of time, any of those political and civil liberties which are the pride of every free nation, mature and conscious of its rights and duties.

Seen in the retrospect of more than half a century, the instrument of 1889 may be said to mark the apex of Serbian liberal constitutionalism in its attempt to transfer to a Balkan milieu the best practices of British and French parliamentarism. From a formal standpoint little fault could be found with the new constitution which, even apart from its historical context, exudes the full flavor of nineteenth-century liberalism. Its primary concern, based on implicit assumption of the continued peaceful development of Serbian nationality, was to weaken royal authority. In this respect it ran counter to the whole tradition of the Kingdom of Serbia and the dynastic leadership underlying the patriarchal Serbian state. For that reason alone, if for no other, it was destined to find the constitutional roots of borrowed parliamentarism rather too shallow and the system of civil rights much too exotic to grow successfully in the stubborn Serbian soil. The main objectives of the constitution—to afford the Serbian people an unbroken national development and to operate under enduring peace—were destined not to be fulfilled.

Recession from the high-water mark of Serbian constitutionalism came quickly. Partisanship in the new legislative chamber, so carefully hedged about with parliamentary immunities, was undoubtedly overzealous. When King Alexander Obrenović could not, by dissolution and elections, procure a more docile chamber or a government completely subservient to his will—both ironically attesting the excessive weakening of monarchical authority under the constitution,—he personally assumed the exercise of the royal power[12] and, after new elections, set aside the Constitution of 1889 and all its works,[13] reverting to the Constitution of 1869.

Before Alexander attempted to redeem his pledge, almost eight years elapsed—years in which Serbian constitutionalism became almost wholly formalistic and reached its nadir in camarilla and petticoat politics which angered military circles and eventually brought about the overthrow of the Obrenović dynasty. Nevertheless, as an eleventh-hour concession to an increasingly rancorous public, Alexander, on April 6, 1901, promulgated a new constitution,[14] much shorter than that of 1889, which reintroduced an elective but indissoluble Senate as a brake against a too powerful Skupština.

In the tension developing between dynasty and people, however, minor constitutional retouchings were of little avail. Certainly, what troubled Serbia was not caused by the structure of local government, the functioning of the Ministry of Public Worship, or the rules of procedure of the Court of Accounts. And when, on April 6, 1903, the king himself capriciously suspended the new constitution for twenty-four hours to square accounts with opponents of the dynasty by extra- and unconstitutional measures, it was plain that the days of the House of Obrenović were numbered. Formalistic constitutionalism, when nullified by dynastic caprice, was intolerable.

"In whatever way one looks at the problem," declared an eminent savant a quarter of a century later, "there appears to have been no other solution, at least as regards the king. In any country a government like that of the last two Obrenovićes was bound to end in blood. How could it be otherwise in Serbia, with the Austrians only two paces away? To be humane in the circumstances was to risk civil war and foreign invasion."[15]

The military *coup d'état* of May 29, 1903, which effected the change in dynasties was, outside the palace precincts, relatively bloodless. It was accepted by the country as a truly national revolution to rescue Serbia from the clutches of the Austrophil coterie then in power. With the accession of King Peter I of the Karageorgević dynasty, liberal constitutionalism was rapidly restored. Only the textual alterations needed to legitimate the status of the new monarch were made in the instrument of 1889.

Serbia now entered a period of constitutional normalcy previously unknown in its history. Under the benevolent Peter I, cabinet government, ministerial responsibility, regular elections, and the free play of political parties became realities. "My most fervent hope," declared the sovereign on his first appearance before the Skupština, "is that, in the Balkans, Serbia shall be a model of legality and order, of peaceful development and of prosperity." The decade and a half of his reign did much to bring the country closer to that ideal. To the end of the history of an independent Serbia— in peace, in war, and in exile—the dynasty stood committed to democratic self-government under parliamentary forms, relying for its support on the power of peasant and praetorian nationalism.[16]

As matters stood on July 28, 1914, the Kingdom of Serbia possessed a full-fledged state apparatus, a functioning parliament and ministry, a well-disciplined army, recently exercised in the two Balkan wars, and a system of local government and courts fully operative in the old kingdom but only recently introduced in southern Serbia. No other political group among the widely scattered Yugoslavs of the Balkan Peninsula—least of all the recently defeated Bulgarians—had either the traditions or the institutions to give it primacy or leadership. Yugoslav unity was regarded by Serbs as a mystically satisfying ideal, but it was always conceived of as involving events in the infinitely distant future and never as a proximate, tangible, or realizable goal.

Outside the kingdom was the independent state of Montenegro, whose mountain fastnesses, rather than its political institutions, were the real buttresses of its independence. In Bosnia and Hercegovina, wrenched from the hands of the Osmanli dynasty by the diplomacy of the Great Powers and farmed out to Austria-Hungary by the Congress of Berlin, there existed only a rugged, impoverished, illiterate, landless peasantry. From its meager resources an army of bureaucrats from Vienna drew taxes and filled their own pocketbooks. Not until 1910 were these provinces given even the beginnings of local institutions through the election of a Diet of limited powers. Hence these lands could add nothing to Yugoslav governmental tradition. Only in the provincial Diets of Styria, Carinthia, Carniola, Istria, and Dalmatia, under an electoral system heavily weighted against the Slovene population, did the Yugoslavs in the Austrian half of the Dual Monarchy enjoy even limited self-government; less than twoscore Yugoslav deputies entered the Tower of Babel called the Reichsrat in Vienna.

Finally, in the Kingdom of Croatia-Slavonia, itself a dependency of the Hungarian, not the Austrian, Crown, a degree of regional autonomy, wrested from Budapest at an opportune moment by the so-called *Nagodba,* or Agreement, of 1868, gave the Catholic Croats a strategic position, with a parliamentary representation in Budapest approximating that of the Austrian Yugoslavs in Vienna. In the political vacuum of the Croatian Diet, or Sabor, at Zagreb, the Croats developed all the artifices of obstructionism to which an irresponsible pseudo parliamentarism lent itself. Coalitions in the Diet succeeded in thwarting the will of the governor, or ban, appointed by Budapest, yet kept their hands free. Thus only parliamentary sabotage was developed and none of the finer statecraft of piloting legislation to successful enactment. The Croats, although they were excluded from policy making both in Vienna and in Budapest, became convinced of their indispensability to the Monarchy, and so lived by small-scale political blackmail. Seldom in political history has such genuine talent been focused on such destructive and negative objectives. This psychological inheritance obviously made difficult, if not impossible, a consensual union and submission to majority rule.

## CHAPTER VIII

# Constitutional Development, 1914–1941

## BY MALBONE W. GRAHAM

ON THE EVE of the First World War the situation in the Yugoslav lands revealed distinct cleavages—chiefly psychological and economic—in the romantic ideal of Yugoslav unification which boded ill for the prospects of Yugoslav union if formally achieved. To fuse into a single state the peoples of kindred blood and origin who were historically divided into many political units was a difficult task. It called for an appreciable interval of time in which to integrate the political folkways of the various Yugoslav peoples and imbue them with a common tradition. But this interval was not vouchsafed to the Yugoslavs. Neither the democratic revolutions of 1848, nor the defeat of Austria at Sadowa, nor the Bosnian crisis in the early 'seventies provided the incentive for unification of the Yugoslav peoples. The failure of abortive movements to shake off the Ottoman yoke, the conspiracy of the Great Powers at Berlin to hold the Balkans in a juridical strait jacket, the appeasement of Austria-Hungary by the allocation to it of Bosnia and Hercegovina—all bear tragic witness to the deliberate retardation, on every side, of the process of Yugoslav unification.

In the half century following the flowering of a romantic literary Yugoslav movement, the institutional patterns of the Yugoslavs outside the Kingdom of Serbia perforce hardened in traditional molds. To the proud and warlike people of Montenegro, modern government came with extraordinary belatedness. Not until 1905 was there a genuine constitution for the country, and to the end of the Petrović dynasty its political institutions were rudimentary. This is not to gainsay its stubborn, hardy mountaineer independence and its unwillingness to bow to the yoke of the Turk. But it is obvious that few political contributions could be made by the people of the Black Mountain country. Nothing could be more false than the legend later perpetrated by the émigré representatives of the defunct Petrović regime that Montenegro was the champion of an ancient federalist tradition. Of federalism as a constitutional concept there was not a trace in the Montenegrin background. In the drafting of the Vidovdan Constitution, federalism was clearly a borrowed concept.[1] In fact, it developed more from the fanciful racial cantonalization proposed by Louis Kossuth in the 1840's for the ills of the Baranja, the Bačka, and the Banat than from any pattern of successfully functioning government.

Of far greater significance to a united Yugoslavia was the psychological persistence of dualism (of the Austro-Hungarian Monarchy), of which the Croats and the Slovenes, as residuary legatees, were the principal protagonists. If the purely Serbian political leaders foresaw, in the future Yugoslav state, only a Greater Serbia, with access to the sea, it is not difficult to discover why unification meant little more to the Croats than the creation of a new dualistic structure in which an enlarged Croatia—heir to Dalmatia, Bosnia, Hercegovina, the Bačka and the Baranja, and parts of Istria, Carniola, and Carinthia—would balance an enlarged Serbia, enriched by Montenegro, Macedonia, and the Banat. Certainly, the half century between 1868 and 1918 of sparring with Budapest for privileges had accustomed the Croats to a bargaining cunning which considered the existing partnership as one between hostile and uncompromising factions held in a common "constitutional" matrix, not by consensual union but by the pressure of external forces. Small wonder that dualistic particularism remained defiant and envenomed long after the dissolution of the Monarchy. Yet the major problem in formulating a constitution for the new state was one of choosing between Serbian and Croatian historical patterns, between the principles underlying a unitary state and those based on a ruined dualism.

---

[1] For notes to chapter viii see pages 518–521.

The initial contest between the ideologies of unitarism and dualism came in July, 1917, when the members of the Yugoslav Committee first faced the representatives of the Serbian government. The resulting Pact of Corfu² pledged the creation of a single Yugoslav state under the Karageorgević dynasty and laid down the bases of a democratic, constitutional, and parliamentary regime. This marked the high tide of wartime consensus in an hour of bitter adversity. To the Yugoslav Committee it meant a pact, or compact, from which it could withdraw at any time; to the Serbian government it signified a declaration binding on both groups. The thorniest problems were left to a Constituent Assembly, but the broad outlines were blueprinted in advance. By accepting the Karageorgević dynasty the Yugoslav Committee rejected a republican regime which might have vested the moderative power in a supreme tribunal rather than in the Crown. It therefore stood committed to a monarchical regime, only to be later disavowed by the professional republicanism of the Croatian Democrats and Populists.

The second meeting of the antagonistic constitutional forces came in the hour of revolution. As the foundations of former legality were crumbling, the Yugoslavs from the Dual Monarchy were torn between insistence on historic rights—at the very moment when these were losing all significance—and reliance on self-determination as the eventual solvent of the old legality and the regenerator of the new. From the manifestoes of this period emerged a maze of contradictory ideas: the unity of all Yugoslavs was stressed in the same breath as the continued separateness of their ethnic and political groupings. Hence the acute struggle for primacy or privileged position between Slovenes and Croats, between Croats and Serbs, and between Serbs and Slovenes.

The separatist forces finally prevailed and a triune monarchy came into being, preserving in its very name—the Kingdom of the Serbs, Croats, and Slovenes—the disputatious possibilities of theological trinitarianism. This is not to say that agreement on a name would have exorcised the outmoded mentality of bygone regimes, but retention of the triple name indicated persistence of thought patterns too enduring to be destroyed by an hour of revolution.

Although theories and formulas were still in flux, the first actions of combined authority began pouring into the new molds of the new state. The diplomacy of Serbs, Czechs, and Yugoslavs at Geneva, the appointment of a common cabinet, the assumption of authority by Prince Regent Alexander, and the convocation of a provisional Skupština at Belgrade steadfastly created accomplished facts too substantial to be greatly endangered by the political intrigues inherited from a dead past. Thus, by the time a provisional constitution was adopted, the cause of dualism was irretrievably lost. Thereafter it was too late to plead for an *Ausgleich* or *nagodba* as a legal hyphen between discordant states. The primacy of unitarism as a vehicle for unification assured the victory of the positive Serbian tradition over the particularist mentality of the Croatian Sabor.

In sharp contrast to the neighboring Succession States, Austria and Czechoslovakia, the Yugoslav state at no time adopted a formal provisional constitution. There was no specially earmarked written agreement to mark the ideological crystallization of the unification movement; its documentary basis was purposely kept small. The provisional regime meanwhile tactfully avoided attempts to settle litigious questions. The omission of a provisional instrument prevented the hardening into juridical rigidity of constitutional premises deriving from Croatian leadership. By shrewdly mixing civil and military administration and avoiding extensive texts, the Yugoslav state kept its working regime flexible. Whether this course was, in the long run, wise is debatable, but there can be no doubt as to the factual basis of the provisional system. In the transitional period a centralized military command and a centralized civil authority, emanating from Belgrade, began the process of tightening the institutional framework of the new kingdom.

The third clash between rival constitutional forces occurred in the Constituent Assembly, which was not elected until the frontiers of the new state were defined and the unitary character of the state was established, at least from the international standpoint, by the peace treaties, and thus accepted as part of the public law of Europe.[3] The arguments advanced for the different systems of government[4] contained little that was new, except for the constitutional projects of the Communists.

The Constituent Skupština considered, first, the official government draft, in which Premier Pašić had endeavored to write large for the new state the constitution of his beloved Serbia. Certain minimum changes were necessary: acknowledgment of equal status for the Moslem, Catholic, and Orthodox religions; broadening of the base of the franchise from property ownership and taxpaying to the right of males to vote; inclusion of modern economic and social principles; and, as a safeguard to public order, a strengthening of police power. Beyond this, however, the project did not go. Positing a firm central control over all parts of the kingdom, it sought to preserve Serbian institutions and extend them to new areas, while legally extinguishing rival political institutions which might challenge the authority of Belgrade.

The second major project was that sponsored by Stojan Protić—a modified type of home rule based on Anglo-Saxon conceptions of self-government within fairly large administrative units. Although it was abruptly rejected as perpetuating decentralization, the Protić project deserves mention, for the principle eventually gained acceptance under the Constitution of 1931. What rendered Protić's project dangerous, in the opinion of Pašić and his following, was the extraordinary dilution of governmental authority it involved. To accord so large a share of local autonomy to regions which had been under the rule of a common government for less than three years was to encourage provincial separatism.[5] Protić's draft, giving virtual dominion status to nine dissident Ulsters, was distinguished from other autonomy projects by its conformity to historic areas—an idea of which King Alexander later made use.

The third major project before the Constituent Skupština was prepared by Croatian autonomists who advocated organizing the country into six provinces: (1) Serbia and Macedonia; (2) Croatia-Slavonia, Dalmatia, Istria, and Medjumurje; (3) Montenegro; (4) Bosnia and Hercegovina; (5) the Vojvodina; and (6) Slovenia. Each was to have an independent government and a constitution which could be modified only by unanimous consent. Clearly a rationalization of the prewar status of the Yugoslav lands, it posited the loosest of confederations. In short, it purposed, with only formal lip service to the idea of unification, to perpetuate the preëxisting disunity and paralyze all national action. It seems inconceivable that in the political atmosphere of 1919–1920 an attempt should have been made to reconstruct a second Poland, with a *liberum*

KING ALEXANDER I
(Ruled 1921–1934)

THE PARLIAMENT HOUSE, BELGRADE

CHURCH OF ST. MARK, BELGRADE

*veto* constitution. The project was nevertheless actually put forward under the specious guise of democratic federalism.

A curious draft drawn up by the followers of Dr. Anton Korošeć, the well-known Slovene autonomist leader, followed the Croat project in part, but unblushingly gerrymandered it in the interests of Catholicism—thus aping the provincial clericalism of Chancellor Michael Mayr of Austria. Just as Mayr had sought to strangle socialism in Vienna by adopting a federal regime, so the Slovene autonomists sought to neutralize the influence of Orthodox Serbia by astutely balancing Catholic and Orthodox provinces. It is obvious that those who had served their political apprenticeship in the Austrian Reichsrat still stuck to outmoded models, even as the Croats blindly followed the obsolete patterns of constitutionalism laid down by prewar Budapest.[6]

In the final alignment of forces, none of the federal plans was accepted by a majority, and prospects for agreement on any instrument of government were far from bright. Under the tenacious leadership of Pašić, however, and by dint of extraordinary measures for the purchase of political support, the first definitive instrument of government for the Kingdom of the Serbs, Croats, and Slovenes was eventually passed by a clear majority, though not by a two-thirds majority, of the Constituent Skupština and was signed by the king. Because it was promulgated on St. Vitus' Day, June 28, 1921, the anniversary of the Battle of Kosovo, it is usually called the Vidovdan Constitution.[7]

Viewed in the retrospect of twenty years, the Vidovdan Constitution symbolizes the triumph of the unitary Serbian tradition over the separatist forces that vainly endeavored to turn the buoyant forces of the Yugoslav national movement in another direction, into the outgrown, sterile constitutionalism of Austria-Hungary. It evidenced to the outside world the resurrection of the martyred Serbian nation, ruled for the first time in modern history with the other South Slav populations.

In reality the Vidovdan Constitution made few modifications in the structure of institutions inherited from Serbia.[8] It changed nothing in essential structure or in the principal agencies of government—executive, legislative, and judicial. Even the prevailing scheme of local government passed essentially unaltered into the new state. What the Constitution of 1889 established for Serbia thus came vicariously to operate over the whole of the triune kingdom. Democratic, parliamentary, national self-government under a centralized administration finally came into legal effect.

Maintaining the unity of the triune kingdom in and through the person of the monarch, the Vidovdan Constitution provided a strong dynasty and a plenitude of royal authority which, judged by traditional western European standards, would mean a firmly anchored parliamentarism. Viewed in terms of Serbia's historical experience, however, the monarchy contained also an extraordinary amount of moderative power which the ruler could freely exercise outside the scope of parliamentarism and which was not subject to parliamentary control.

Considering the multiplicity of parties and their irreconcilable elements, the monarch greatly needed this authority, which is almost entirely absent in the British tradition of parliamentarism, based on the agreed alternation in power of His Majesty's Government and His Majesty's Loyal Opposition. What is more, it is clear from the record that Alexander fully exercised it *within* the framework of the parliamentary tradition and the Vidovdan Constitution as long as was feasible (1921–1929) and *without* and *beyond* the formalities of a written instrument of government (1929–1931) when irreconcilable factions threatened national unity.[9]

Within the limits of the Vidovdan Constitution, the parliamentary system of single-chamber national representation—government by an unstable coalition of fortuitous majorities—functioned hesitantly until 1924, when the abstaining Croats, seeing their boycott of Belgrade failing, responded to an overture from the veteran Pašić, went to Belgrade, and had their first taste of power. However flimsy the theoretical foundations of Croatian separatism in the 1918–1924 period, it is certain that the astute maneuvering of Pašić to bring the Croats into the governmental picture was no small achievement; it officially ended abstentive separatism and started a healing process in the national legislative life.

Throughout the four uneasy years of experimental entente preceding the assassination in 1928 of Stjepan Radić, the Croatian Peasant Republican party leader, the Skupština, with a full complement of 313 deputies, functioned formally, ministries rose and fell, laws were ground through the legislative mills, and party mechanisms, save for that of the Communists, operated normally. The courts also, except for occasional difficulties in reconciling conflicting legal systems inherited from Austria, Hungary, Montenegro, and Serbia, performed with little friction.

Local government, which was left amazingly short-handed at the end of the war, operated with crude bureaucratic efficiency, mainly at the behest of higher officials from the Kingdom of Old Serbia. Such administrators doubtless rode roughshod over local susceptibilities, permitted heavy governmental pressure on electorates, and exercised petty tyrannies particularly galling to Roman Catholic citizens who were subject to Orthodox officials, and vice versa. It is not surprising that, in the process, public liberties were occasionally, and individual liberties quite frequently, impaired, notwithstanding the elaborate guaranties carried over from the Serbian Constitution of 1903 to the new charter. The failures and shortcomings of the Vidovdan regime, ironically enough, were found not so much in international relations or national government as in local administration and maintenance of individual freedom.

Perhaps it was too much to expect the wounds of war to heal so quickly. A single generation could hardly have effected the transition from primitive, frontier tribal feuds, as in Montenegro, to the peaceful settlement of disputes by debate and balloting in a legislative body. It took more than a decade of experimentation to lessen the religious tensions and to erase the bitter memories of earlier antagonisms.

The crowning tragedy of these formative years was the assassination of Radić. It was more than personal vengeance: it was symbolic of the failure of parliamentary procedures to assuage the passions of extremist nationalism. With the Skupština no longer a safe forum for the outpourings of national and regional feeling, the time was ripe for royal exercise of the moderative power.

Alexander acted with astuteness and historical precision. Choosing the tenth anniversary of unification as the moment for the bold, decisive stroke, the king set aside the Vidovdan Constitution as having failed to create the consensus required for national unity and undertook, as was permissible to him in the transitional, constitution-forming period, a personal rule of direct royal responsibility to the people. He was assured, as his father before him had been, of the support of the army. For a second time in little more than a quarter of a century, the state passed into the hands of the sovereign with peasant and praetorian support.

By royal proclamation, on January 6, 1929, a new regime was instituted in the Kingdom of the Serbs, Croats, and Slovenes.[10] The decade of the critical period, with its integrative forces,[11] was at an end. There ensued nearly three years of direct royal government, which swept away much of the debris of historic particularism and built up positive factors in the national life.[12]

The constitutional basis of the royal regime which suspended and then superseded the Vidovdan Constitution was the law, or charter, of January 6, 1929, "On the Royal Power and the Supreme Administration of the State." Following essentially the pattern of the former constitution, it fused executive and legislative power, giving the monarch plenary control over the nation's public life, but leaving untouched the judiciary. This streamlining temporarily removed from the scene the quarrelsome Skupština and vested its power almost exclusively in the king. A state tribunal was empowered to try ministers for dereliction of their legal duties. Legislation, though theoretically royal in origin, was in fact entrusted to a Supreme Legislative Council attached to the Ministry of Justice—a sort of royal bill-drafting bureau—and elaborate safeguards attended the promulgation of each law.

With this authority King Alexander might easily have become an autocrat, but he had no such intention. Although provisionally suspending local self-government and dissolving all political parties, thus holding in abeyance, in the interest of national unity, the intemperate expression of partisan opinion, the monarch regarded himself as the holder (*détenteur*) of authority and not as its source, as the prime servitor of his people and not as their master. In this sense Alexander joined the company of the many benevolent *Statthalters* preceding him down the long corridors of history.

Having established the framework of the interim regime, Alexander set about correcting the major evils of his troubled realm. Foremost was the problem of local government. The prefectural system operating from Belgrade, on whose success Pašić had pinned his hopes, was obviously a failure, and some compromise was necessary between the total destruction of local power and the encouragement of separatism through excessive autonomy. By the laws of October 3 and November 7, 1929, Alexander replaced the prefectural system of rigid centralization by a new division of the country into nine banovine, or provinces, thus returning to the plan originally proposed by former Premier Protić. Alexander thus took "the stone which the builders rejected" and made it the cornerstone of the country's reconstruction.[13] But whereas Protić had been hampered by the presence of separatism, Alexander moved in an atmosphere far more favorable to national unity. He renamed his realm the Kingdom of Yugoslavia to emphasize that the work of unification was being completed.

The old provincial names were wiped out and the new areas were designated by prominent geographical features. The advantageous reduction of thirty-three administrative areas to a smaller number greatly increased—at least on paper—the competence of local officials. Thousands of citizens, previously more conscious of provincial loyalties than of the need for national unity, were brought into government service and direct administration of their country. Finally, distinctions were obliterated between Serbs, Croats, and Slovenes. All became uniformly Yugoslavs, both politically and before the law.

The older units of local self-government, the subprefectures in local districts, and the communal organizations were, however, retained. The new provincial system included both national and regional officers, collectively performing all tasks of general administration in the provinces. From 1929 to 1931 they were assisted by appointive councils whose function was to approve provincial budgets and advise the provincial governors, or bans. Under the Constitution of 1931 they became elective bodies with a large juridical competence which the successive efforts of bureaucrats in the capital did not altogether succeed in whittling down. It cannot be said that the banovine were highly successful administratively, but they broke the backbone of all but Croatian particularism and were successful politically in advancing national unity.

Alexander now turned to the drafting of a working constitution. Aided by jurisconsults from the Ministry of Justice, he promulgated on September 3, 1931, a constitution that was destined to last until the occupation of the country by German forces. Far shorter than the Vidovdan Constitution, it omitted the transitional provisions and the stipulations in regard to social reforms and policies which had appeared in the earlier instrument. This was partly because much of the social program had been executed, and Yugoslavia's participation in many international measures worked out by the International Labor Organization made unnecessary any specific constitutional commitments to what the country was achieving by concerted treaty action. At all events, the constitution included no new social credo, no ideological motivations other than those contributing to national unity. It was wholly uninspired and uninspiring.

It discarded as unessential the conception of parliamentary government and sharply reduced the importance of the national representative bodies, the Skupština and the Senate. It established, presumably in the interest of national unity, a police state with strict censorship, serious abridgments of individual liberties, and severe penalties for actions furthering provincial separatism. Creating a regime with vastly increased executive power and few limitations on its use, permitting the citizen little recourse against governmental acts, however arbitrary, and sharply curtailing the exercise of the franchise, the constitution produced a presidential regime with a crowned *Statthalter* and a fairly independent, stable ministerial council, supporting itself not a little by the docile upper house, which was intended to be a counterweight to the Skupština.

The new Senate, half appointed by the king and half elected by provincial electoral colleges for six-year terms, was believed to be a guaranty against the extremes of the single-chambered regime. In practice it did operate to prevent violence, though it also helped to doom Yugoslav politics to an unhealthy sterility from 1931 to 1941. Actually, the Crown did not make full use of its rights and created only twenty-eight senators, whereas forty-six were elected. The Yugoslav Senate—borrowed in large part from the Serbian Constitution of 1903—did not, however, greatly distinguish itself in the nine years of its functioning.

Under the Constitution of 1931 the Skupština was shorn of many privileges, its jurisdiction was halved by the existence of the upper chamber, and theoretically it was no longer able to discard cabinets in swift succession. But the play of political forces was not to be disposed of by omitting the word "parliamentary" from the constitution. Hence there continued, under the new instrument, the factional molds and parliamentary procedures inveterate in both Serbian and Croatian politics.

By far the most serious innovation was the provision of the electoral laws of September 10 and 26, 1931, that a party gaining a plurality in a national election was entitled to two-thirds of the seats in the Skupština. This proviso, in conscious imitation of the procedure by which Italy passed from parliamentarism to fascism, abolished the system of proportional representation that begat deadlock and instituted a system of national lists and oral voting. It was designed to break down the former rigid stratification of political life and to curtail sharply, and eventually to abolish, the representation of minorities. In practice this widened the gap between the governing Serb-Slovene coalition and the Croat-Democratic opposition bloc. However well-intentioned the monarch who devised it, the scheme was fundamentally inequitable and dishonest. Ironically enough, it only accentuated injustice. The entire electoral law was a bird of ill omen and carried no healing in its wings.[14]

Perhaps because of the dark shadow cast by his father's accession, and a fear of his own assassination, Alexander made elaborate provision for a Regency Council of three members to govern during the minority of the heir to the throne,[15] an arrangement which was destined to prove no guaranty against treachery and collaboration with Nazi emissaries.

It is hardly to be wondered at that the constitution, in its quest for internal stability, did not stop short of the judiciary. Normally, except when social revolution is the eventual determinant, the courts pass through political revolutions unscathed; the Yugoslav monarch, however, considered the situation in his kingdom very unusual. The independence of both ordinary and administrative tribunals was therefore sharply reduced for a five-year period, which Alexander did not live to complete. The irremovability of judges was temporarily dispensed with, and the boundaries of their jurisdiction were somewhat altered. Whether this formalistic safeguard against procedural fettering of the king's contemplated reforms was justified must remain an open question, though the presumptions against an affirmative answer are many: judicial authority, once shaken, is difficult to reëstablish, and the gaining of judicial irremovability was, in the Serbian kingdom, the result of a sixty-year-long struggle—too precious a constitutional heritage to be dispensed with.

On the whole, the Constitution of 1931 was hardly a successful experiment. Indeed, its authoritarianism contrasted strangely with the professions of democracy made by political leaders in opposition or in exile. Characterized by an objective scholar within the country as "a compromise between authoritarian government and the demands of the people . . . a centralized authoritarian constitution endeavoring to reconcile authoritarian conceptions and democratic ideas," and creating a regime which "countenanced but a single party formed from above by the force of authority,"[16] the Alexandrine constitution was at best an expedient born of high motive, at worst a harsh compromise with reality. The decade during which it was in force was singularly barren of constitutional development in the orthodox, juridical meaning of the term. With no ideological content around which psychological forces might crystallize, the constitution became a mere control device actuated by a punctilious, if spiritless, formalism for mechanistic governance of the nation.

Yet the Alexandrine constitution, in spite of numerous shortcomings, served the nation at least negatively by stifling the voices of disunion and dissent and thus working for the realization of unity. Certainly that was the intent of the royal author, whose haste to transform the veiled personal dictatorship into a constitutionalized one was due to the pressure of events in Spain.[17] With the republican triumph in Spain as a constant warning and reminder, Alexander bent every effort to promote national unity. And when he lay cold in death at Marseille in the fourth year of this constitutionalization, his work still stood, though the margin of internal security was small. Even the constitutional façade ill concealed the persistence of personal authoritarianism.

Thereafter, from 1934 to 1941, Yugoslavia had to function without a monarch; the regal void was hardly filled by the members of the Regency Council, and political leadership was in the hands of mediocre men with scant regard for democratic liberties. The best that could be said for this Great Interregnum was that local elections went off easily, without excessive governmental pressure, and so reintroduced at the bottom the political ideals and procedures which were not permitted free expression at the top. The healthiness of this local democracy partly compensated for its rarity at higher levels.

The major problem confronting Serbs and Croats after the death of Alexander was that of effecting a peaceful symbiosis without impairing the security of the state. Not until 1937, however, were overtures made by the Yugoslav government. These ended, notwithstanding the earnest desire of Belgrade to heal the breach, in renewed deadlock. The Croats, through their leader, Dr. Vladimir Maček, insisted on rescinding the Alexandrine charter, abolishing the Vidovdan Constitution, and convoking a new Constituent Assembly elected under a different franchise as preliminaries to a clear-cut pronouncement by the whole people in regard to the regime they wished permanently to espouse.

The government at Belgrade, however, could not agree to an arrangement which jeopardized the future of the Yugoslav state, particularly since Maček insisted that adoption of the new constitution should require explicit approval by a majority of the Slovene representatives in the Constituent Assembly, as well as by a majority of the Croats and the Serbs.[18] This imposed conditions so impossible of attainment as to render fruitless every overture from Belgrade.[19] The long ministry of Milan Stojadinović ended, therefore, without effecting the desired compromise—in the eyes of the Croats, a new *nagodba*—and the country drifted ever more openly toward a *Führerstaat,* with Stojadinović as *Führer.*

Meanwhile, as the Croats failed to attain their desires in dealing with the government, Maček approached the combined opposition leaders and, on October 8, 1937, reached an agreement, or *sporazum,* with them on the constitutional future of the Yugoslav state. This raised to a new dignity the inexecutable Croat proposals and apparently postponed to the Greek calends a reconciliation with the government at Belgrade.[20] No negotiations, therefore, were undertaken by Premier Dragiša Cvetković, the immediate successor of Stojadinović. The most that Belgrade could bring itself to promise was that, after the formal accession of King Peter II to the throne on reaching his majority, September 6, 1941, the Regency Council would no longer stand in the way and the problems of Serbo-Croat relations could be objectively reëxamined.

On the eve of the Second World War, the Croats, with well-calculated timing, turned once more to Belgrade to extort its reluctant accession to their proposals. On August 26, 1939, in the wake of the Russo-German agreements, Maček and Cvetković reached a second and even more important, because immediately effective, *sporazum,* by which the two banovine of Sava and Primorje were combined in the autonomous Banat of Croatia, with its virtually independent governor. This was a personal triumph for Maček, as it restored Croatia almost to its privileged position in the last days of the Habsburgs. However, it opened the doors of the Yugoslav household still wider to Axis connivance and conspiracy. Under these far from benign auspices, and with pro-German leadership, Yugoslavia entered the period of the Second World War.[21]

The constitutional evolution of Yugoslavia in wartime moved in opposite directions. Public opinion, though severely regimented, could not fail to find common ground with Poland, France, Britain, and the small countries of western Europe. The country was formally neutral, but the popular orientation dating from the First World War, which tied the destiny of the South Slavs to the victory of the Western Powers, continued to dominate.

Governmental policy, on the contrary, moved away from neutrality toward collaboration with the Axis Powers. To the initial penchant of Stojadinović for the totalitarian states—which caused his internment early in 1939 in central Serbia—were now added the Germanophil tendencies of Minister of Foreign Affairs Cincar-Marković, who had represented Yugoslavia in Berlin during the Nazi regime. In him, as in Prince Regent Paul, the German government found a pliant tool. These two, especially, worked for the entry of Yugoslavia into the orbit of Axis influence. And when the test came, in February, 1941, both men, along with Premier Cvetković, took the long road to Vienna rather than to Berchtesgaden, though the final result was the same.

After much wavering and hectoring, these men brought about the signature of a pact of nonaggression and collaboration with the Axis—a document signed in the presence of Hitler and Ribbentrop. Yugoslavia was formally committed. But the negotiators, in their blindness, could not have foreseen the immediate, sullen reaction of the populace. The government and the people were no longer on common ground.

In the National Revolution of March 26–27, 1941, the democratic forces in Yugoslavia abruptly reasserted themselves. Peasants and soldiers alike, pouring into the national capital from the countryside, rallied, not to the fawning ministers who would have sold the country to the Axis for a piece of paper, or to the unrepresentative Skupština, but to the person of the young monarch, Peter II, who came into power innocent of all connection with the machinations of his immediate predecessors. He came not only with the same peasant and praetorian support that had made possible the redeeming National Revolution of 1903, but also this time with the virtually unanimous support of the nation. The National Revolution of 1941 was deep, genuine, and sincere, but it had, at that historic moment, no ideological program and no institutional foci. In an hour of extremity the person of King Peter served as the sole linchpin of national loyalties. Had the Yugoslav people been vouchsafed a decade of peace, the frail bark of national unity might have been able to navigate the difficult course between the Scylla of praetorianism and the Charybdis of malignant separatism. But in its inexorable march, history did not concede them that privilege. So Yugoslavia entered its great testing time with a population that, however personally attached to the young king, was deeply divided both as to the ends of societal organization and the means for attaining those ends. The pattern of their society, as it had existed since the days of Miloš, Jelačić, and Francis Joseph, was outmoded, and the reordering that lay ahead was more than could be effected merely by royal manifestoes or the empty paper maneuvers of parliamentarians.

It cannot be gainsaid that the formal façade of authority in Yugoslavia had long been maintained by the stifling of dissent. Thus there were present in the kingdom, at the hour when the Axis smote it, intangible underground forces, as yet politically untried, which called for a historic reckoning. So tenuous was the bond of national unity in that critical hour that survival on the basis of the *status quo* was problematic. A solution by way of decentralization would only have given free rein to a separatism roughly coterminous, geographically, with Catholicism, and both inveterate and envenomed. Clearly the surrender of national unity to the dominant religious influence from the West was no solution; its end was partition, and the nation as a whole rejected that alternative. Save for the frantic fringe of Christian nationalism that espoused the Ustaši and the Duke of Spoleto, it found no support.

But Yugoslavia, under both the Vidovdan and the Alexandrine constitutions, had also remained a sealed barrier against the permeation of the "Eastern influence," as the outthrust of the Russian Revolution was euphemistically called from Finland to the Black Sea. No quarter was given to it, and what Western influences existed in Yugoslavia tended to regard themselves as the last rampart between Moscow and Rome. That this could be continued indefinitely while Serb and Croat fought out the long feud over national power and control appears, in the cold light of retrospect, to have been an absolutely untenable position.

It is now obvious that Serbian leadership in the Yugoslav state had, in the two decades between wars, proved itself incapable of providing the technology of modernization that was needed to transform Yugoslavia from a pastoral to an industrial commonwealth. Thus neither Croatian nor Serbian nationalism per se could offer a formula for the future. The only perceptible third choice was frankly to concede the inevitability of a return to colonial status as an appanage of one or the other of the Great Powers, Germany or Russia, then contending politically and economically for the mastery of the Balkans. It was perhaps in bitter and cynical acceptance of the eventual necessity of choosing between these two contenders that the successive ministers, from Stojadinović to Cvetković and Cincar-Marković were driven, however reluctantly, to accept the entry of Yugoslavia into the orbit of the Axis as the lesser of two evils. But when the nation recoiled, only one course remained.

It was the irony of Yugoslavia's fate that for two decades it had avoided change, excluding from the political arena all the forces of societal reform and stoutly resisting the influx of new political ideas. Hence, when the nation rejected affiliation with the Axis, it was placed in the unenviable position of having to make terms with the "Eastern influence" that it had deliberately disdained. It likewise formally rejected this course. Only after the issue was joined militarily did the Yugoslav people awaken to the fact that the constitutional patterns it had followed in the nineteenth century had been weighed in the balance of history and found wanting.

# CHAPTER IX

# *Yugoslavs in America*

## BY JOSEPH S. ROUCEK

LONG BEFORE the discovery of America, ships from Dalmatia navigated all the known sea routes, and Dalmatian sailors were world renowned for seamanship and love of adventure. A seamen's guild in Dalmatia recently celebrated its thousandth anniversary. Sailors from the Dalmatian coast are said to have been among Columbus's crew. The tradition which links Dubrovnik (the medieval Yugoslav republic of Ragusa) with the discovery of America was retraced by an American, Myrtle Hague Robinson. While examining antiques in the shop of Lujo Kraja on the main street of Dubrovnik, she talked with B. Radmili, a scion of one of the city's old patrician families, who told her the following:

"Our people have always been navigators and seafarers. Dalmatian ships, laden with merchandise, traded with the Orient and distant points of the then known world. To India they went and to Egypt, as well as to Italy, France, and England. The old Slav cemetery at Southampton testifies to a colony of Ragusan merchants established at that port. Our ancient republic once led the world in shipbuilding. The word 'argosy' is derived from Ragusa, whose shipyards constructed vessels for Oliver Cromwell.

"According to tradition, two Ragusan sailors were among the crew that sailed with Columbus on his first voyage to America. One of the sailors returned with a fortune in gold and other treasure, and built the palace now known, from the name of its later owners, as the Palace of Bonda. Is it not a strange turn of fate that two of our citizens should have assisted Columbus to discover

[136]

America in 1492, and that 573 years later one of your American citizens, President Woodrow Wilson, should have assisted us and neighboring South Slav states to become a nation?"

An American Yugoslav, Ivan Mladineo, writes the following about the early immigration of Yugoslavs:

This year American history is celebrating the 350th anniversary of the discovery of Roanoke Island, recalling the establishing of the first English settlement in the New World. North Carolina is building a shrine to this first colony within the present confines of the state. The colony was, in fact, twice settled a full score years before Jamestown and thus takes Anglo-American history back to the sixteenth century. Sir Walter Raleigh's second colony (the first was established on July 29, 1585), under John White, arrived on July 22, 1586, intending certainly to be a permanent one, for it consisted of ninety-five men, seventeen women, and nine children. In August the first white child was born in British Colonial America and named Virginia. Nine days later the child's grandfather, Governor White, sailed away to England, and from that day to this there is no certain word of what happened to the company he left behind.

Not until the spring of 1590 was White able to come to Roanoke. "At the place where they were left in sundry houses," he writes, "we found the houses taken down and the place very strongly enclosed with a high palisade of great trees, with curtains and flankers, very fort-like; and one of the chief trees or posts at the entrance had the bark taken off, and five feet from the ground, in fair capital letters, was graven *Croatan,* without any cross or sign of distress."

This is the first recorded history connecting America with Yugoslavs or, rather, with the Croatian branch. It is believed that a Croatian ship, stopping at this first permanent settlement in America, left its imprint on the big tree and consequently gave its name—*Croatan*—to one of the islands of North Carolina.

It is recorded that a Dalmatian ship sailed to America by way of India early in the eighteenth century, when the first movements of Yugoslavs to America began. After the unsuccessful and bloody uprisings of Croatian and Slovenian peasants against their feudal lords in 1573, during the Reformation—ruthlessly crushed by the edict of the Archduke Ferdinand in 1598,—many Yugoslavs had found refuge in Prussia through the invitation of King Frederick William, who favored the Protestants. Their descendants decided to seek a haven in the New World.

Several hundred of them went to Georgia, where they settled on the right bank of the Savannah River at the confluence of a small creek which they named Ebenezer. Pastors Gronau and Bolcius were the leaders of the group. These early immigrants introduced the cultivation of the silkworm in Georgia, an industry in which many had engaged in their native land. Soon after the Civil War the settlement was abandoned; only the cemetery remains as a monument to a once-thriving colony of the first Yugoslav settlers in America.

Among the earliest Yugoslav immigrants in America were seamen and missionaries. Baron Ivan Rataj, a Croatian Jesuit, died in 1683 as a missionary among the Indians of New Mexico. He was followed by many of his countrymen, the most noted of whom was Ferdinand Konščak (better known under the Spanish adaptation of his name, Gonzales), who came to Mexico in 1730. During the many years of his pioneering work he drafted the first known map of Lower California. Another great Croat missionary was Joseph Kundek, who arrived in 1838. He established several towns in the Middle West, among them Ferdinand and Jasper, Indiana.

The Slovenian missionaries concentrated on the Great Lakes region. Bishop F. Baraga, who devoted his life to the spread of civilization and religion among the Indians, was born in 1797 in his father's castle near Ljubljana. After studying law in Vienna, he entered the priesthood. In 1831 he came to America to fulfill a long-cherished desire to do missionary work among the Indian people. In 1853 he was elevated to the bishopric for the newly created see, which then comprised not only the upper peninsula of Michigan but a great part of lower Michigan, northern Wisconsin, eastern Minnesota, and part of Ontario. He published a grammar and dictionary of the language spoken by the Chippewa Indians and issued translations of the Bible for them. He also compiled a book of prayers in the Ottawa language. The state of Michigan honored him by naming one of its counties after him.

The many Slovene followers of Baraga were men of superior ability; no less than four of them achieved the honor of becoming bishops. In 1845 Ignatius Mrak arrived in America, and was named a bishop twenty-four years later. Ivan Vertin came in 1863 and was made a bishop in 1879. Both occupied the see of Baraga at

IVAN MEŠTROVIĆ (1883–)

A self-portrait

TOMB OF THE UNKNOWN SOLDIER, AVALA

Marquette, Michigan. Coming to America in 1864, Jacob Trobec was consecrated bishop of St. Cloud, Minnesota, in 1897. The last of this glorious list was Ivan Stariha, who arrived in 1867 and became a bishop at Lead, South Dakota, in 1902. Except for Bishop Stariha, who died in his native country, they died in America while in active service. Many of the clergy devoted their lives to the same cause and country, notably Francis S. Pirc, who arrived in 1835 and continued in service among the Indians of the Great Lakes region until 1873.

A port of call for most of the Yugoslavs sailing to the New World was New Orleans. Until the middle of the nineteenth century this was the chief settlement of the Yugoslavs in America. They were engaged in the oyster industry, which they controlled for many decades. When gold was discovered in California, many Yugoslavs joined the gold rush. They advised their relatives and friends in the old country of the fortunes to be made, with the result that several ships sailed from their native shores carrying new prospectors to the Golden Gate. California has always had a special attraction for Dalmatian immigrants, for its climate and topography remind them strongly of their own lovely Adriatic coastland. On the Pacific coast they were unusually successful.

Emigrants, especially those from Dalmatia, came in numbers after 1850 to the Middle West and the East. Slovenes founded Kraintown (named after Krain, or Carniola) and Brockway (St. Stephens) in Minnesota. In the latter town was established the first Yugoslav church. Others settled in Iron Range, Minnesota; Omaha, Nebraska; parts of Iowa; and Chicago, Illinois. In 1873 they arrived in Joliet, Illinois, where they are now represented in large numbers. There is a Yugoslav colony in Calumet, Michigan. Yugoslav settlement in New York dates from 1878.

But it was not until 1890 that Yugoslavs began to emigrate in large numbers. Serbia proper and Montenegro contributed very few. Most of the Yugoslavs in America—Serbs, Croatians, and Slovenes—are from provinces formerly belonging to Austria-Hungary.

*Estimates of immigration.*—Although no reliable statistics are available as to the actual number of Yugoslav immigrants, it is probable that close to 1,000,000 Yugoslavs have settled in the United States, and 200–300 in Alaska. Of this total, the Croatian group should be credited with 700,000; the Slovene, with 200,000 or somewhat less; and the Serbian, with about 100,000.

The official statistics of the United States census before the First World War do not isolate this group. Immigrants from the territories now belonging to the Kingdom of Yugoslavia were recorded as Bulgarians, under the general classification of Bulgaria, Serbia, and Montenegro; or as Germans, Austrians, or Hungarians, since many Yugoslavs were citizens of Austria-Hungary at that time. Furthermore, the Yugoslavs tended to classify themselves according

DISTRIBUTION OF YUGOSLAVS IN THE UNITED STATES
(Yugoslav estimates)

| State | Number | State | Number |
|-------|--------|-------|--------|
| Pennsylvania | 172,000 | Indiana | 25,000 |
| Ohio | 102,000 | New Jersey | 17,000 |
| Illinois | 80,000 | Colorado | 15,000 |
| Michigan | 44,000 | Montana | 15,000 |
| New York | 35,000 | Kansas | 14,000 |
| Minnesota | 30,000 | Missouri | 13,000 |
| California | 26,000 | West Virginia | 12,000 |
| Wisconsin | 25,000 | Washington | 10,000 |

to religion, either as Eastern Orthodox (or Greek), Roman Catholic, or Mohammedan. Thus Bulgarians, Serbs, and Montenegrins were grouped in one Orthodox division; Croats and Slovenes as Catholics; Dalmatians, Bosnians, and Hercegovinians as a Mohammedan group; and a rather large number were classed as Austrians. Only since 1908 has the census recorded nationality.

From 1900 to 1930 the number of Yugoslavs, Bulgars, Dalmatians, and Bosnians who entered the United States was 700,127 plus the 78,750 entering the United States up to 1900—a total of 778,877 in 1930. Of this number, 343,935 returned to Yugoslavia, leaving 434,942. According to the census of 1940 there were 222,300 "native white of foreign or mixed parentage," and 161,093 "foreign-born white" Yugoslavs in America, a total of 383,393. But according to Yugoslav estimates there are some 700,000 Yugoslavs in the United States today—345,000 Croatians, 295,000 Slovenes, and 60,000 Serbians.

*Settlements.*—Sixteen states have nine-tenths of the Yugoslav population, as indicated in the table. According to the census of 1930, 73.1 per cent of American Yugoslavs live in urban districts. The Chicago region has the greatest number of Yugoslav immigrants of any urban area, estimated at between 40,000 and 60,000. This distinction is, however, claimed also by Cleveland, Ohio, with its 60,000 Yugoslavs (40,000 Slovenes), and by Pittsburgh, Pennsylvania, which has the most important Serb colony in America. Pittsburgh has 25,000 Croats and some 50,000 Slovenes.

Other main groupings of South Slavs can be found in Buffalo and surroundings; New York City; Hoboken, New Jersey (17,000); the hard-coal district of eastern Pennsylvania and adjacent parts of New York State; western Pennsylvania (especially the steel and coal districts of Pittsburgh and Johnstown), with adjacent parts of West Virginia (Wheeling), and Ohio (Youngstown and Akron); the copper-mining district of northern Michigan; the vicinity of Cheboygan, Michigan; Milwaukee, Wisconsin; the iron-ore district of northern Minnesota; Kansas City and the coal basin of Pittsburg, Kansas; Denver and the Colorado mining districts; the mining districts of Montana, Wyoming, and Arizona; Salt Lake City, Utah; Seattle, Washington; Portland, Oregon; the coast of California, where San Francisco and Oakland have about 17,000 Yugoslavs; Galveston, Texas; New Orleans, Louisiana; the Mississippi delta; and Juneau, Alaska.

*Occupations.*—Yugoslav immigrants were pioneers in the cultivation of apples and grapes in California. It is recorded that one Mark Rabasa, a native of Dalmatia, was the first apple dealer in Watsonville, Pajaro Valley, in the 'seventies. Jack London, in his novel *The Valley of the Moon,* describes at length and with great admiration the result of the "tenderness and love" which transformed the 12,000 acres of the Pajaro Valley into "one of the most wonderful demonstrations of the United States." He calls it "New Dalmatia" and credits "those first ragged Adriatic Slavs" for making it "the Apple Paradise." Today the thriving population of this center is composed, in great majority, of Slavs. In and about Fresno they have contributed much to the success of the grape industry. Only in California, Colorado, and Minnesota, however, are there well-established Yugoslav farm settlements, and the number of Yugoslavs in agriculture is comparatively small.

Large fleets of fishing boats at San Pedro and Monterey, California, and on the Columbia River in the Northwest are manned by Yugoslav fishermen. The two hundred modern fishing boats on the Columbia River alone represent an investment of several million dollars and are owned by Yugoslav immigrants. In Portland, Tacoma, and Seattle, Yugoslav immigrants have their own fishing companies and shipyards. The largest sardine, tuna, and mackerel cannery in California belongs to Yugoslavs. In the southern states, especially around the mouth of the Mississippi, Yugoslav oyster fishermen lead in this business.

About forty per cent of Yugoslavs were formerly employed in mining and industry, but recently the percentage in coal mining has dropped appreciably. The percentage of workers in the automobile industry of Detroit, however, has increased fivefold since 1920 (to about ten per cent).

It was only during and after the First World War that Yugoslav immigrants entered the commercial life of their newly adopted country. Today they are increasingly interested in trade, road construction and various other public works, and some of the smaller industries. This applies, however, mainly to the Yugoslavs who were born in the United States.

*Religious divisions.*—An intense group consciousness developed at the beginning of the century because of religious differences, for the Croats and Slovenes are Roman Catholic and the Serbs are Eastern Orthodox; and because of differences in the spoken language, as Serbo-Croatian differs slightly from Slovene. Each subdivision of Yugoslavs proceeded to form a separate group.

The Roman Catholics, under the jurisdiction of their respective bishops, were separated early into Croatian and Slovene groups. The few remaining mixed parishes are less cohesive. The Serbian Orthodox Church was under the jurisdiction of the Russian bishops in America until after the First World War, when it was organized as a separate diocese with a bishop of its own for the United States and Canada, nominated by the patriarch in Belgrade. The see of the Serbian Orthodox bishop is at Libertyville, Illinois, and is occupied by the Right Reverend Bishop Dionisije.

There are about seventy Roman Catholic and thirty Serbian Orthodox parishes and churches maintained by Yugoslavs in the

United States. Whereas Roman Catholic churches always remain the property of the diocese, Serbian Orthodox churches belong to the incorporated, individual church community. The Slovene group has an estimated amount of $3,500,000 invested in about forty-five churches and the attached buildings for sisters, priests, and schools. Their yearly upkeep costs approximately $250,000. A rough estimate for the yearly upkeep of Serbian churches would be $150,000, and for Croat churches, $200,000.

There are two Catholic churches of the Greek rite (also called Uniat). The rites are the same as in the Orthodox Church, but the Old Slavonic language is used instead of the Latin. Under certain circumstances the priests are allowed to marry. Otherwise the faith and the tenets are Roman Catholic and the supreme head is the pope in Rome.

There are thirty-eight full-time parochial schools, half of them belonging to the Croat and the other half to the Slovene group. Instruction is in English so that their work will be recognized by the public schools, but the respective national languages are also taught. The total number of pupils is about 13,000, of whom 8,000 are Slovenes and 5,000 Croats. Teaching is entrusted mostly to Franciscan sisters, who number nearly 300. In Lemont, Illinois, are convents and preparatory schools for aspirants to the priesthood and to teaching or religious orders. Orthodox churches conduct classes for the teaching of the mother language. Each group has about 100 in its clerical personnel. Only a few nonreligious schools for the teaching of Yugoslav exist; the best of these is the Slovene National Home in Cleveland, Ohio.

*Social organizations.*—Various nonsectarian educational activities are carried on, but they lack coördination and financial strength, with the exception of the Sokols (physical-training societies) and the literary and publishing activities sponsored by fraternal and political organizations. Leaders among them are sixty-five singing societies, with two federations, a Serbian and a Slovene. The oldest is the Croatian singing society Zora in Chicago. About fifty dramatic societies and as many *tamburica* orchestras are active. Education sections of the Yugoslav Socialist Federation, the Yugoslav Federation of the Socialist Labor Party, and the Yugoslav section of the Communist Party of America try to conduct their partisan work after the pattern of the Yugoslav Education Federation of Chicago. Most of the fraternal organizations have sections devoted to sports; physical education is carried on by the Sokol and Orel societies. Today there are twenty Sokol societies with about 3,000 members. Fifteen are independent and the others are under the Yugoslav Sokol Federation of Chicago, consisting of two subdivisions, one for the Chicago region and the other for the Pacific coast area. There are many other organizations, such as the Slovene Women's Union and the Baraga Association.

*Fraternal organizations.*—New Orleans has the oldest existing settlement of Yugoslavs in the United States, but their first fraternal organization, the Slavonian Mutual and Benevolent Society, was formed in San Francisco in 1857. Its purpose was both social and beneficial; it assisted its members in times of illness and distress. The official languages were English and Slavic. In 1874 the New Orleans Yugoslavs organized the United Slavonian Benevolent Association. The first organization on the Atlantic coast was founded in Hoboken, New Jersey, in 1890, under the name of Slavjansko Dobrotvorno Društvo (Slav Benevolent Society). The First Croatian Benefit Society adopted that name only a decade ago; its original name was Austrijansko Dobrotvorno Društvo (Austrian Benevolent Society). In 1882 the Slovenes organized their first association, the Independent Society of St. Joseph, in Calumet, Michigan. These pioneer organizations still exist and can proudly point to some 3,000 groups in all parts of the country.

The largest Yugoslav organization is the Croat Fraternal Union, the owner of a children's home at Des Plaines, Illinois, which is worth nearly $500,000. About 250,000 Yugoslavs are members in fifteen national fraternal and insurance organizations. Of these, about 80,000 are in the junior branches. Several hundred independent benefit societies exist locally. These, with the 2,700 branches of the national organizations, bring the total to nearly 3,000. There are also some 200 national homes, centers of activity in the various colonies.

*The press.*—Many Yugoslav newspapers have been published in the United States. In fact, the *Iseljenički Muzej,* a weekly of Zagreb, reported in 1938 that outside Yugoslavia there are as many newspapers and periodicals published by Yugoslavs as there are days in the year. Of these, 213 were founded in the United States. The first Yugoslav-American periodical, *Slavenska Sloga* (Slav Unity), appeared in San Francisco in 1884. It was followed by *Napredak,* in Hoboken, New Jersey, and *Amerikanski Slovenec,* in Chicago, both in 1891. Since then some 200 publications have been started and discontinued. At present there are twenty-six established Yugoslav publications: six dailies (with about 61,000 subscribers), two semi-weeklies, twelve weeklies (128,000 subscribers), and six monthlies. Circulation varies from 1,000 to 60,000 copies.

*Political activity.*—The American-Yugoslav press was, from the beginning, concerned with political, social, and cultural problems, especially with European Yugoslav politics. A stirring period of political activity took place during the First World War, especially after the entry of the United States. The Yugoslavs rallied under the banners of their leaders in a remarkable fight for the freedom and union of Yugoslavia. Thousands departed to join either the Serbian army or the Yugoslav volunteers in the American army, and many sacrificed their lives for the cause.

Unfortunately, there was a reversion to petty politics after the war. Thus the question of centralism versus regionalism in Yugoslavia complicated the politics of American Yugoslavs; some immigrants were preoccupied with republicanism, socialism, and communism. But an increased amount of interest is now shown in American politics.

*Contributions to America.*—Yugoslav immigrants have contributed in no small measure to American progress, particularly in science, education, and literature. The late Dr. Michael Pupin, of Columbia University, is well known for his inventions in telephony and wireless telegraphy. Nikola Tesla was the inventor of the polyphase induction motor and the alternating power-transmission system developed by the Westinghouse Electric Company. Science accords him seventy-five original discoveries: all electric machinery using or generating alternating current is due to him. Worthy of mention also are the engineering achievements of John Jager; Lazarovich Hrebelianovich; and A. Dilić, a tunnel builder—the kind of "big boss" who gets big jobs done fast. The father of the oil industry in Texas was Captain F. Lucas (Lučić), a native Yugoslav, who was the first to strike oil in that state.

Dr. Victor Vecki, of San Francisco, was considered an eminent specialist on venereal diseases.

The contributions of the Reverend Francis Jager, professor of agriculture in the University of St. Paul, Minnesota, revolutionized the honey industry.

The late Dr. Henry Suzzallo was a leading educator in the United States, president of the University of Washington from 1915 to 1926, and then president of the Carnegie Foundation for the Advancement of Teaching. He was also a trustee of the Carnegie Corporation of New York. Dr. Paul R. Radosavljević, professor of experimental pedagogy in New York University, has written numerous leading works in his field in Serbian, Croatian, Russian, German, and English. He is best known for his book, *Who Are the Slavs?* and his introduction to Lay's *Experimental Education*.

These significant names, however, do not exhaust the contributions of Yugoslavs to American culture. Other men prominent in education are Professor Francis Preveden of the universities of Chicago, DePauw, and Minnesota, in philology; Professor Emil Weiss, formerly of Zagreb University, now of Loyola University, in pathology and bacteriophage; Professor John Zvetina, Jr., of De Paul and Loyola universities, in the history of law; Dr. Hugon Bren, professor of theology, formerly of Ljubljana, later with the Slovene Theological Seminary of Lemont, Illinois, and now in Rome; Professor Živković, of the University of Chicago; Professor Dinko Tomašić; Dr. I. Altarac; and others.

Louis Adamic, recipient of a Guggenheim Traveling Fellowship in 1932–1933, wrote a best seller, *The Native's Return*. Ivan Zorman, M. Sojat, the Reverend Alexander Urankar, and Vinko Ujčić (pseudonym Georges) led in poetry; Dr. A. Biankini and Ivan Mladineo have contributed to knowledge of the American Yugoslavs and their history. Francis A. Bogadek, Dr. F. J. Kern, and the late George Schubert were compilers of dictionaries. Vlaho S. Vlahović edited and published the *Slavonic Monthly*, the only all-Slav publication in the English language, promoting the ideal of a better understanding of the American Slavs and of the Slavs abroad—a thesis also underlying his *Two Hundred Fifty Million and One Slavs* (New York, Slav Publications, Inc., 1945).

In art, Harvey Gregory Perušek (a Slovene); Macanović, with

his yearly exhibits on the Pacific coast and in Chicago; Tanasko Milović; Mr. and Mrs. Gosar; and Vuk Vučinić are painters residing in Chicago. The well-known Ivan Meštrović contributed the two monumental Indian statues at the entrance of Grant Park in Chicago.

As a composer, Alexander Savine Djimić has been widely acclaimed. Artur Rodzinski, of the Cleveland Symphony, is prominent as a conductor. A pioneer organization in presenting chamber music in America, the famous Kneisel Quartet, had as one of its original members the late Louis Svecenski, also a Yugoslav. The noted Milka Ternina, of the Metropolitan Opera, at the beginning of the century created an unexcelled tradition in the rendition of Wagnerian roles. Worthy successors have been Zlatko Baloković, violinist, and Zinka Milanov, of the Metropolitan Opera; J. Naval-Pogačnik, Tino Patiera, J. Marion Vlahović, and M. Nikolić, of the Chicago Opera; and Teodor Lovich (Pasko Alujević) and Mato Čulić-Dragun, of the San Francisco Opera. Director Slavko Vorkapić is a prominent modernizer of moving-picture technique.

Cleveland's mayor during the Second World War was Frank J. Lausche, of Slovene parentage. In 1944 he was elected governor of Ohio. Quite eloquent is the fact that the first gold-star mother of the Second World War was Mrs. Jennie Dobnikar of Cleveland, a Slovenian American, whose son died in action aboard the destroyer *Kearny*. The Congressional Medal of Honor was awarded to Peter Tomich, chief water tender of the U.S.S. *Utah*, who died at Pearl Harbor; and to Lieutenant Mitchell Paige (Milan Pejić), of the United States Marines, who killed 110 of the attacking Japanese on Guadalcanal. Lieutenant Commander Milton Pavlić, a Slovenian immigrant and a graduate of Annapolis, was instrumental in destroying three enemy warships and thirty-two planes, and gave his life for his adopted country on the U.S.S. *South Dakota*. A new destroyer, the U.S.S. *Pavlić*, was named for him, and he was posthumously awarded the Congressional Medal of Honor.

## Part Four

# ECONOMIC
# CONDITIONS

# CHAPTER X

# *Agriculture*

## BY D. BEATRICE MCCOWN

At the end of the First World War, when the Yugoslavs were finally united, one of the most serious problems facing the newly formed state was that of land tenure and agrarian reform. Almost 80 per cent of the population was engaged in agriculture, for industry had been only slightly developed in the sections formerly under foreign domination. Moreover, every degree of land reform or its total absence could be found. In the former Kingdom of Serbia, feudalism had been abolished when freedom from the Ottoman Empire was attained in 1833. Estates of Turkish landlords were confiscated without indemnity, and former Serbian serfs became peasant farmers in their own right. When additional territory was conquered from the Turks in 1878, confiscation of estates again took place, although this time the Turkish landowners were compensated for their loss.

As a result of these reforms, when the Kingdom of Serbia became a part of the new Yugoslav state it was already a land of small peasant holdings, more than half of which were less than 5 hectares (12.4 acres) in extent, and 96.3 per cent under 60 hectares (less than 150 acres). Units exceeding 100 hectares represented the property of peasant family coöperatives.

In southern Serbia, or Macedonia, the Turkish government had ordered the abolition of feudal rights as early as 1838. The law putting this edict into effect was not published, however, until 1858. By that time the Turkish landowners had already transformed their feudal tenure into legal ownership. Consequently, in 1912, when this section of the Balkan Peninsula became part of the

Kingdom of Serbia, the Serbian peasant, though legally free, was in no better position than a serf. He might have to pay as much as a third of his crops to the landowner; he had to render personal services and dues; and he could not move from one part of the country to another.

In Bosnia-Hercegovina the Turkish feudal rights were not abolished in 1858 as they had been in southern Serbia but were actually confirmed a year later. When this territory came under Austrian administration in 1878, it was part of the policy of the new rulers to win the support of the Turkish lords. Therefore the existing situation was given a permanent status by registering the feudal estates of the Turkish holders as their legal property. Peasants continued to be bound to the land, subject to the complete control of the landowner, either as vassals or because of farming contracts. Not until 1912 was it possible for the serfs to win release from their feudal obligations, and then only by paying the redemption price themselves.

In Dalmatia the situation was extremely complicated. A succession of rulers had controlled the whole or parts of the coast from the days of the first Roman colonies, and different systems of land tenure had been in force at various times. Basically, however, it had been feudal in character, even up to the end of the First World War, for Dalmatia had been specifically excepted from the decrees abolishing feudalism in other parts of the Austrian Empire.

The Montenegrins, like the Serbs in Old Serbia, were peasant farmers. The small cultivable area was so barren, however, that in spite of their being landowners the peasants were actually very poor. Thus landownership brought no substantial improvement in their economic position.

In the richer parts of the country the situation was different. Up to 1848 feudalism had been dominant in the Slovene districts, Croatia-Slavonia, and the Vojvodina. In that year there were widespread peasant revolts which resulted in the final abolition of feudalism. The peasants soon learned, however, that freedom from servitude meant little without land of their own to till. In 1853 and 1857 a few of the large estates were divided among them, but the remainder of the land was regarded as the absolute property of its aristocratic owners. Unfortunately, the area subdivided was so small and the number of peasants so large that many families were unable to make a living from the tiny plots assigned to them. In effect, therefore, their condition was not much better than that of their fellows in Dalmatia, Bosnia-Hercegovina, and Serbian Macedonia.

During the First World War the clamor for redistribution of land and freedom from feudal obligations became increasingly loud. With the creation of the new Yugoslav state in 1918 and the liberation of its various parts from Austrian, Hungarian, and Turkish rule, an excellent opportunity arose to introduce agrarian reforms which would both benefit and please the peasants. These ideas were cardinal points in the first proclamation of the prince regent at the end of 1918 and were incorporated in the constitution adopted on June 28, 1921. True to the promises of the prince regent, a decree was issued on February 25, 1919, which abolished feudal rights and privileges in Bosnia-Hercegovina and provided for expropriation and subdivision of large estates. All extensive forest lands were to become the property of the state. At first the execution of these provisions was entrusted to the Ministry for Social Policy, but experience soon showed that economic, even more than social, problems were involved, and the entire administration of agrarian reform was transferred to a separate ministry set up specifically for the purpose, the Ministry of Agrarian Reform.

Since the problems of land tenure varied sharply in different parts of the new Yugoslavia, the same measures of agrarian reform could not be applied to the entire country. In the north, in the Slovene districts, Croatia-Slavonia, and the Vojvodina the situation was one of extreme contrasts. Here were large private estates nearly half of which were owned by aliens, principally Austrians and Hungarians, and peasant farms so small that the peasants usually had to add to their income by working on estates near by.

The solution of the problem was fairly obvious, namely, division of the large estates among the peasantry. The landowner was allowed to retain a fraction of his estate—the size depending on the district in which it was situated—and to retain control of any woodland belonging to him, though certain privileges of cutting wood were to be allowed to neighboring villages on payment of a small fee. Large forests owned by aliens were taken over by the state and administered for the benefit of the peasants. The remainder of the estate set aside for expropriation was not taken over by the state immediately, but was divided gradually among the local peasantry and new settlers. For the land thus taken from him the landowner received compensation in the form of four per cent bonds guaranteed by the state. In turn, all peasants (except war veterans) who obtained land were called upon to repay the state over a period of thirty years at an interest rate of five per cent.

Various groups were eligible to receive the land thus expropriated. First were peasants already living in the vicinity whose holdings were too small to provide a living, and the residents of local villages who had no land. The next most important group was composed of those who had volunteered for army service during the war. A third group was made up of Yugoslavs living in Hungary who elected to return to Yugoslavia under the terms of the agreement between Yugoslavia and Hungary providing for repatriation of their respective citizens. Persons who had been forced to leave Yugoslavia for economic reasons, or who were living in the poorer areas of the state, could now acquire land.

With so large a number eligible to claim land, the area expropriated from the big estates proved insufficient to supply any one group with farms large enough to form economic units. Up to 1938 some 735,000 hectares (1,900,000 acres) had been distributed among approximately 275,000 families. The result was that local residents received on an average only 2 hectares (about 5 acres); war volunteers and new settlers, 8.5 hectares (20 acres); refugees and optants, 6 hectares (15 acres); and settlers from poor areas, 7 hectares (17 acres).

One of the effects of agrarian reform in the northern districts was a rapid deterioration of economic life. Under the old system, in partial return for his labor the peasant had been given the use of the large landowner's draught animals and equipment to cultivate the soil and harvest the crops. The subdivision of extensive holdings destroyed this relationship between peasant and estate owner; the peasant now received payment in cash.

The influx of large numbers of new settlers aggravated the situation. The size of holdings set up under the reform measures was insufficient to support many peasant families; so, as in former days, they had to supplement their income by working elsewhere. Thus the supply of agricultural labor increased greatly just when demand for it was rapidly subsiding. The peasant had to accept work at any wage offered and became the object of extreme exploitation. The situation became so grave that the government considered prohibiting the use of farm machinery to force absorption of surplus hand labor.

Not only did the peasantry fail to benefit by agrarian reform in these areas, but the fertility of the soil also suffered. In the first place, many new settlers either had little or no experience as farmers or were unacquainted with modern agricultural methods. Many were unable to earn a living from their farms, and poor methods of cultivation caused rapid decline in soil productivity. Second, the resident peasant farmers who had depended on the use of draught animals and equipment from the large estates were no longer able to cultivate their small farms. Moreover, they lacked capital or credit to acquire their own equipment. Even if they had been able to do so, their small holdings made the use of modern machinery uneconomic. Third, since much pasture had been put under cultivation to make more land available for distribution, livestock in these districts declined sharply in number, with consequent decrease in fertilizer to maintain soil fertility.

There was a decline, also, in agricultural processing industries, many of which had been established on large estates to handle their produce: flour mills, dairies, factories for the processing of sugar beets, and distilleries for the manufacture of alcoholic spirits from potatoes. Many large estates were economic units in which processing plants represented the final state of production. Although the new land regulations provided that landowners were to retain acreage sufficient to maintain agricultural industries on their estates, the loss of land through expropriation had a deleterious influence on their output. Annual income from the sugar industry declined by about D. 435,000,000 and that from the spirits industry by about D. 15,000,000.* This led to a further drop in the demand for labor in the very areas where the supply of labor was already excessive.

* The exchange rate averaged 45 Yugoslav dinars to one United States dollar in 1936–1939.

Fortunately, in other parts of Yugoslavia the effects of agrarian reform were less disappointing. In Bosnia and Hercegovina they brought about actual improvement in the position of the peasant. Here the problem was not one of dividing large estates among landless workers but rather of securing the land to those who already lived on it. The feudal obligations of the peasantry had been abolished by the decree of February 25, 1919. Ownership of land was effected by the simple expedient of transferring title to the peasant who lived upon it and abolishing the proprietary rights of the former landlord. Compensation was paid to the former owner by the state, half in cash and half in four per cent bonds.

Although there were no large estates to be subdivided, some colonization took place in this area, but on state-owned lands. During the war a number of persons had taken advantage of the general disorder by settling as squatters in forests and meadowlands held by the Austrian government as public property. With the establishment of the Yugoslav state, further "squatting" in state-owned forests and meadows was prohibited. However, some public land was reserved for settlement by former war volunteers, wounded veterans, and local residents who were landless. All servitudes and rights of pasture possessed by villages and communities in these areas were expressly recognized.

Ownership of land and release from feudal obligations had immediate effects on agricultural production in Bosnia and Hercegovina. That of grains showed tremendous expansion. Pasture declined even more sharply, yet livestock production gained in importance. Fodder crops were grown to a greater degree, and there was a marked shift from grazing to stall feeding. There was also a decided increase in labor-intensive crops: hoe crops such as sugar beets and potatoes; and truck and commercial crops, particularly tobacco, oilseeds, flax, and hemp. The tendency was toward the development of a more commercial type of agriculture with concentration on intensification of production and the growing of crops of high market value.

In southern Yugoslavia the situation was rather different from that in other parts of the country. During the war many peasants had refused to pay feudal dues and had laid claim to the land, buildings, and livestock of their former masters. By order of the minister of agrarian reform, on August 12, 1919, the peasants were confirmed in their ownership, but they were obliged to compensate the former owners. At first it was specified that payment should be made annually in the form of one-half, one-third, or one-fourth of the crop. This provision was particularly distasteful to peasants who had just been told that they were free of feudal obligations, and it was little observed. Only the former landlords who had influence with the government succeeded in obtaining any payments under the system. Eventually, in 1931 and 1933, laws were passed freeing the peasants from payment of this form of rent, and the state assumed the responsibility of compensating the former owners, part to be paid in cash from a special fund established in the State Mortgage Bank and part to be paid from the government budget.

Because of the decimation of the population in the First World War, much of the fertile land in southern Serbia, or Serbian Macedonia, was thinly populated. The new Yugoslav state had the task not only of restoring peace and order to this territory but of repeopling uninhabited areas with citizens who might serve as a protection against encroachment from neighboring states. By royal decree of September 24, 1920, provision was made for the colonization of the new southern districts. Land-hungry peasants from Montenegro and Hercegovina poured into these areas.

Colonization was still so poorly organized, however, that many settlers went to districts where there was not even sufficient drinking water. But after 1929 colonization was more systematically planned on the basis of natural resources and means of communication. Great care was taken not to repeat the mistakes of agrarian reform in the northern districts, so that each family of colonists should have sufficient land to provide a living. For this purpose, public lands and those not needed by communities and villages, as well as abandoned private holdings and the parts of large estates subject to redistribution under the provisions for agrarian reform, were opened up, and an extensive program of reclamation was inaugurated to drain marshlands and irrigate arid areas. In all, some 18,000 families were settled in this area up to 1939.

Since most of the settlers were poor, the state had to provide capital, at first distributed through special organizations and later through coöperative societies. Schools and churches were built by the state in the larger communities, and settlers were given substantial aid in building homes. Every effort was made to assure the success of the new settlements in southern Serbia.

In Dalmatia the complexity of the system of land tenure delayed agrarian reform for many years. Finally, a law which laid the basis for agrarian reform in Dalmatia was passed in 1930, amended in 1931, and put into execution in 1933. Although more complex, the basic principle embodied in this law was similar to that adopted in Bosnia-Hercegovina and southern Yugoslavia, namely, that the peasant should become owner of the land which he had tilled as a serf. In some instances, compensation was paid wholly by the state; in others it was divided equally between the state and the peasant beneficiary.

Although it was probably desirable as a social measure and almost unavoidable as a political measure, agrarian reform in Yugoslavia was of doubtful benefit. In the southern part of the country there were no large estates to divide; so the peasant continued to live on the small plot he had always tilled, the only change being that he was no longer required to share the crops with a feudal overlord. In the north, it is true, there were large estates, but these, when subdivided among the land-hungry peasants, gave each family a farm barely large enough to supply its simplest needs—and not always that when the season was bad. Units of 2 to 8 hectares (5 to 20 acres) can scarcely be regarded as sufficient to support the average family of five persons.

Where farm units are small, two methods may be employed to raise living standards. The first is to cultivate intensively and to concentrate on crops which will bring in the largest return per unit of land, labor, and capital. All observers agree that agricultural production in Yugoslavia could have been greatly increased merely through more intensive cultivation. Except in the north, methods of cultivation were extremely primitive when the new state was founded. Prewar feudal conditions had offered the peasants no incentive to increase production. In former Croatia-Slavonia and the Vojvodina, tractors and other modern equipment and artificial fertilizer had been used on large estates to a certain extent. Much of the equipment was destroyed in the war, however, and, through subdivision of estates, the farm units became too small to utilize modern machinery or the peasants were too poor, ignorant, or conservative to purchase it. Farm units were so small that they had to be constantly under cultivation to provide any sort of living. As a result, rotation of crops could not be carried on efficiently and fertility of the soil was impaired. It became difficult to maintain a proper balance between crop and livestock production. Although in the south there was a tendency toward intensification of production, the peasant will always be limited in this region by the scarcity of cultivable land.

The second means by which small farmers may increase their incomes is by renting or buying additional land to obtain the optimum return for each unit of labor and capital where these are excessive in relation to land. The renting or purchasing of land implies, however, that the farmers possess capital or can accumulate it by producing a surplus. Few peasants in newly formed Yugoslavia had any capital at the end of the First World War, nor was it possible to accumulate it on farms which could hardly provide food, clothing, and cash to pay taxes.

It was this lack of capital that gave the impetus to the establishment of a coöperative society at Vranovo in 1894. So successful was it that others were rapidly organized. In 1897 the first Union of Coöperative Societies in Serbia was founded. In the former Austrian and Hungarian provinces the coöperative movement had had an even earlier start, and from them and from Old Serbia it had spread to Bosnia, Slovenia, and Dalmatia. Thus active coöperative organizations were already in existence when the new Kingdom of Serbs, Croats, and Slovenes was founded. In 1919 a Central Coöperative Federation for the kingdom was established, with headquarters at Belgrade.

The importance of coöperation to the Yugoslav peasant is evident from the fact that about half of the farmers are members of coöperative societies. The main function of the coöperatives is to arrange credit for their members, but they also rent farm machinery. The capital invested in equipment is thus gradually paid off, and the small landowner is enabled to use modern machinery which he could not afford to purchase for himself. Besides credit coöperatives there are consumer, health, dairy, vine-growing, and many other types of coöperatives. All local coöperatives belong to the national coöperative system, which reaches its pinnacle in the General Federation of Coöperative Unions.

Although coöperatives have always been extremely important in obtaining credit for their members, up to 1929 the majority of peasant farmers still applied to banks and private individuals for loans. Many loans were granted on usurious terms which could just be met in periods of comparative prosperity. The state had attempted, in 1925, to extend coöperative credit to farmers through an agricultural credit department, but the effort was unsuccessful. In the depression of the 1930's the credit position of the peasants became unbearable and state intervention was imperative.

The Chartered Agricultural Bank was founded in 1929 with a capital of D. 700,000,000. Its main function was to serve as a central agricultural credit institution, offering loans on favorable terms to farmers so that other creditors would be forced to reduce their charges. The position of the Chartered Agricultural Bank was weakened by the law of 1932, which postponed repayment of farmers' debts during the depression. Finally, in 1936, it was provided that all loans which had been transacted by farmers before April 20, 1932, should be transferred to this bank, which, in turn, would reimburse creditors at a reduced rate. Moreover, debts contracted by farmers before April, 1932, which did not exceed D. 25,000 were reduced by 50 per cent, to be repaid within twelve years at 3 per cent interest. In all, debts amounting to D. 3,000,000,000 were transferred to the Chartered Agricultural Bank.

In spite of the activities of coöperatives and government assistance to peasant farmers in the twenty years before the occupation of Yugoslavia by Germany in 1941, the pressure of population on the land became more intense in this period. Yugoslavia has had the highest rate of population increase in Europe, except for Soviet Russia and Rumania, with 29.8 live births per 1,000 inhabitants in 1935. At the end of the First World War the number of live births per 1,000 inhabitants actually was markedly higher. Not until 1935 did it fall below 31 per 1,000. Because the death rate had been declining rapidly at the same time, the net population increase was more than sufficient to compensate for the terrific loss of life from 1914 to 1918.

Unfortunately, the development of industry was much slower and could not relieve the congestion of population in rural areas. The proportion of the population engaged in agriculture declined from 78.9 per cent in 1921 to 76.6 per cent in 1931. However, in absolute numbers, the agricultural population had increased from 9,500,000 in 1921 to 10,700,000 in 1931. The result was a very high density of farm population, since large sections were unsuited to cultivation.

Of a total area of some 62,000,000 acres, only 11,700,000 acres are really good land, although some 36,000,000 acres are actually under cultivation. In other words, 10,700,000 peasants try to wrest their living from soil two-thirds of which is inferior in quality. It has been estimated that under present farming conditions a family needs at least 25 acres of land for subsistence. However, by 1940 only 10 per cent of the holdings were larger than 25 acres; these accounted for 45 per cent of the total agricultural land. The remaining 90 per cent of the rural population had farms averaging only 8 acres in size and these usually contained only 5 acres of arable land. Moreover, many of the farms of more than 100 acres were actually state-owned and were run as experimental stations for livestock breeding and improvement of seeds and other crops.

Not only scarcity of good land but its uneven distribution are responsible for dense farm population and small size of farms. The best soils are concentrated mainly in the level land in the northern and eastern parts of the country. The result is a heavy concentration of population in these regions. In the south and west much of the land is mountainous or forested, and only a small part is fit for cultivation. In relation to natural resources the density of population is very high. With the scarcity of arable land in the mountainous south and the heavy concentration of rural population in the level north, there has been little new land to absorb the rapid increase in population. It is justifiable, therefore, to say that Yugoslavia is overpopulated, that is, the present population is excessive in relation to natural resources and economic development.

In spite of the efforts of the government, various agricultural institutions, and coöperative societies, improvement in cultural techniques was slow in the postwar period. The conservative peasant farmer was reluctant to adopt new methods. An investigation in 1940 revealed that of every 1,000 peasants in the south, only 438 had iron plows, 183 had wooden plows, and 379 owned none. Standards of living were low. If the farmer had enough to eat and sufficient cash for clothing and taxes he was satisfied. Moreover, there were so many holidays that he rarely worked his land more than 160 days in a year, to the detriment of the crops.

The agricultural situation in Yugoslavia is further complicated by the emphasis placed on cereals. Since the primary function of the farm is to supply food for the family, this is not surprising. Each plot will naturally be used to produce the wheat or maize needed for bread. In the north, wheat is commonly used; in the south, maize. However, the use of mixed flour—wheat with barley, maize, oats, or rye—is not uncommon.

Grains are important in foreign trade also. Since production of raw materials dominates the economic life of Yugoslavia, it is to be expected that 55 per cent of the value of all exports should consist of agricultural produce. In fact, 15–20 per cent of the total export trade consists of maize and wheat, and no other crop approaches them in importance in the foreign trade of the nation. In recognition of this fact, the government has made every effort to stimulate cereal production. Improved varieties of wheat and maize have been developed, and the peasant has been encouraged to increase yields through modern methods.

In 1930 the government established the Prizad, or Chartered Corporation for the Export of Agricultural Products, a limited company with shares owned by the state. Its principal functions are to maintain prices of grain to farmers and to dispose of grains on the world market. Although it possesses no substantial funds to subsidize its purchases, the Prizad does buy and sell wheat on its own account, thus influencing in some degree the internal price. It exercises a legal monopoly by undertaking to fill the quotas granted by importing countries. Since the bulk of wheat exports went to Germany before 1941, it was the price paid by Germany which primarily determined the price at which the Prizad purchased wheat in Yugoslavia.

Although production, prices, and exports of grain could be encouraged and controlled to a certain extent, nothing could prevent the wide fluctuations in quantities harvested which were caused by climatic conditions. In 1935 wheat exports were only 1,200,000 bushels; in 1936 they were 11,000,000. In 1938 wheat exports were only a third of their 1937 total. The same rapid changes in annual production occurred with maize. In an economy dependent on grain, such variations in output are unsettling.

Governmental encouragement, combined with the natural tendency of the peasant farmer to grow familiar crops, led to an increase in the production of grains in the 1920's. When the depression years lowered the prices of wheat and maize, the farmer tried to compensate for low returns per bushel by increasing the output With the passing of the more serious phases of the depression, cereal production seemed to have reached a relatively stable level. In 1938, however, 82.2 per cent of the total arable area of 18,500,000 acres was still devoted to grains; in the northern districts the proportion was more than 90 per cent of the area under cultivation.

In spite of the heavy concentration of grains, a wide variety of crops is grown throughout the country. The Dalmatian coast produces cherries, grapes, wine, and pyrethrum; in the south, cotton, tobacco, and opium are grown. The greatest commercial agricultural production, however, takes place in northeastern Yugoslavia. Thence come the famous plums, apples, and table grapes; beans, cabbage, and tomatoes; soybeans for oil and hops for beer; hemp and flax. In the southern and western regions crops are restricted, for the most part, to the river valleys, and it is obvious that cultivable land in these sections will always be limited.

Developments from 1931 to 1941 tended to offset the disadvantages from which southern Yugoslavia suffers. Interestingly enough, it was the crops grown principally in the south which expanded most in that decade. Area and yields of cereals remained relatively stable, but production of cotton, tobacco, and oilseeds made great strides. Hemp and flax also increased steadily. Fruits, however, showed negligible changes: plums and apples declined in importance; peaches and grapes advanced somewhat.

Probably the most significant development was in oilseeds. Production of soybeans and sunflower seeds increased from 1933 to 1938. The government, seeing an opportunity to encourage more intensive agriculture, established an agency to purchase domestic seed at fixed prices. As a result, soybean production increased rapidly. An encouraging aspect of these various changes was the shift from extensive to intensive crops. Emphasis upon crops of comparatively high value increased the monetary returns per acre of land cultivated. Since such crops were grown principally in the poor southern sections of Yugoslavia, it was this region which benefited most from the expanded production.

Although the mountainous character of much of Yugoslavia tends to limit crop production sharply in many areas, the scarcity of arable land is offset to a certain extent by grazing facilities suitable for livestock production, which has always been an integral part of the Yugoslav agricultural system. In regions of limited cultivable land this is an important source of livelihood to the peasant, though he often supplements his farm income by working in the lumber industry. The significance of the livestock industry is indicated by the following facts: in 1937, 18.3 per cent of national income was derived from stockbreeding as compared with 24.6 per cent from all other branches of agriculture. Livestock exports, especially hogs and pork products, have always been important in Yugoslav foreign trade. In fact, the total value of farm exports from 1935 to 1939 was derived in almost equal proportions from vegetable and animal products.

The Yugoslav government has long been interested in improving breeds of cattle and hogs. Although the regions inhabited by the Yugoslavs were heavy producers of livestock before the First World War, the quality of cattle and hogs, particularly in mountainous areas, where stall feeding was little practiced, tended to be very poor. Studies were made in the selective breeding of cattle, and annual fairs and exhibitions were held to encourage the peasant to improve his stock. Sheep raising, too, received attention because of its importance in mountain regions. Experimental breeding stations were set up, and an institute for research on wool was established in Belgrade.

Another obstacle hampering the development of the livestock industry was scarcity of feedstuffs, owing, in part, to the wide variations in annual yields of fodder crops. This meant that cattle could rarely be stall-fed throughout the year, but had to be sent to graze for part of the year. Peasants were therefore encouraged to grow fodder crops rich in moisture, so that they could be stored and used both in winter and in summer.

The efforts to encourage livestock production were not without success. From 1925 to 1938 the number of cattle increased by 13 per cent, hogs by 23 per cent, and sheep by 28 per cent. Expansion would doubtless have been greater had there been stable export outlets for these products. Although exports of live hogs increased slightly in the periods 1928–1932 and 1935–1939, exports of live cattle were halved and exports of fresh meat declined. Since most of these products had always gone to central Europe and Italy, any contraction in their markets had serious repercussions on Yugoslavia. In fact, the partial closing of the Italian market was the cause of the decline in Yugoslav meat exports. Increased production of cattle was not matched by increased consumption in the rural areas of Yugoslavia, since meat is a rare item in the diet, except in cities. Consequently, it was primarily the rapidly expanding urban population which absorbed the increase in meat products in spite of a declining export market.

In the same period the poultry industry developed even more rapidly than the livestock industry. From 1925 to 1939 poultry increased by almost 36 per cent. This gain was important, for many small peasant farmers depended entirely on poultry and eggs for their cash income. Moreover, the value of exported poultry and eggs usually exceeded that of live cattle and hog exports. Unfortunately for the farmer, egg exports declined in 1928–1932 and 1935–1939. However, increased domestic consumption may have compensated somewhat for the drop in exports.

In a country so little industrialized, and dependent on exports of raw materials to obtain the finished goods it required, the quantity and value of agricultural surpluses were of vital importance. Had the national economy been less one-sided the situation would not have been so grave. Even for an agricultural nation not burdened with problems of land tenure and population pressure, the depressed state of agriculture throughout the postwar world would have presented many difficulties. Moreover, the price of cereal, the commodity in which Yugoslavia specialized, was the most rapidly and deeply depressed on the world market.

To protect its foreign-trade position the government controlled

agricultural exports through two institutions: the Prizad, already
mentioned in connection with wheat, which also controlled exports of plums; and the Institute for Promoting Foreign Trade,
which controlled all other agricultural exports. Unlike the Prizad,
the Institute—a department of the Ministry of Commerce and Industry—did not buy or sell on its own account. Its principal functions were to control the quality of the agricultural exports which
the government wished to promote, and to distribute among registered exporters the import quotas granted by other countries.
From time to time it established export prices for particular commodities. If the price obtained for a certain commodity exceeded
the fixed price, the difference was used to subsidize exports which
had not fetched the price set by the Institute. Thus it served to
smooth out price fluctuations and to assist in the export of some
commodities. It also prevented the sale of exports at prices lower
than those charged in the importing country by eliminating competition for import quotas between Yugoslav exporters.

The necessity for export control arose not only from the low
prices obtainable for agricultural commodities but from a serious
contraction of the world market for raw materials. The latter situation was aggravated by the growth of autarky in many European
countries. This political trend made itself felt very early in Yugoslavia, for Italy had long been one of its chief export outlets. When
the fascist regime took over the reins in Italy and inaugurated a
policy of national self-sufficiency, the effects on Yugoslavia were
immediate and extensive.

Indeed, the situation in Yugoslavia in the postwar period cannot
be painted in colors too dark. The vast majority of the population were peasants, most of whom, only recently liberated from
virtual serfdom, were ignorant of modern methods of farming.
The principal agricultural products were low in value in relation
to finished goods. Moreover, trade with other nations tended to
be restricted by their tariff barriers. The obstacles to economic
development in Yugoslavia seemed almost insuperable. Nor was
the situation improved by the constant political unrest within the
country which existed up to the momentous March of 1941.

In spite of the mistakes made by the state in its agrarian reforms,
the development of agriculture was more promising than appears

from a casual survey of statistics. Peasants were gradually educated to use modern techniques, better qualities of seeds, better varieties of fruit trees, improved breeds of livestock. Development of livestock and production of intensive crops such as oilseeds, cotton, and tobacco were encouraged. Moreover, the government was active in protection and stimulation of export outlets for agricultural commodities in spite of a contracting, depressed world market.

With an economy so little diversified, Yugoslavia was at the mercy of any state or group of states willing to accept its agricultural exports. Owing to historical developments and geographical location, central Europe had long been the chief outlet for exports from that part of the Balkan Peninsula occupied by the Yugoslavs. In the section under Austro-Hungarian rule, all produce had tended to flow to Vienna or Budapest. In the regions under Turkish domination, trade flowed naturally toward Constantinople. So dominant was the north-south direction of trade channels that communications from east to west were practically nonexistent when the new Yugoslav state was founded. In fact, wheat was exported to central Europe from northeastern Yugoslavia at a time when Montenegro, Dalmatia, and Slovenia were obliged to import wheat from overseas because of local crop failures.

In the twenty years after the establishment of Yugoslavia much attention was devoted to development of communications. Italy was long the principal outlet for exports; Germany held second place. After 1935, owing primarily to Yugoslavia's participation in imposing economic sanctions against Italy, the Italian share in Yugoslav exports declined sharply and Germany took first place. Greater Germany and Italy together absorbed 56 per cent of Yugoslav exports from 1935 to 1939. Over a Yugoslavia heavily dependent on export trade to obtain manufactured goods, the power thus acquired by the Axis partners was obvious.

It is safe to assume that in the period of the German occupation agricultural problems became of secondary importance in Yugoslavia. Agriculture, as in most occupied countries, probably suffered less severely than other phases of economic life. With the return of peace and freedom, however, many of the old problems—aggravated by the disruptive and destructive effects of German occupation on the entire economy—must be faced anew. Large areas, especially in the Vojvodina, were not planted because of wartime activities. The land now under cultivation must be carefully managed. Government control of agriculture is therefore extensive, determining what crops shall be grown, and in what proportions, as well as when they shall be planted. State ownership of land, especially in the fertile northern areas, has been extended through confiscation of property formerly belonging to Germans and other enemies of the state.

More scientific methods of cultivation and greater diversification of crops will result in higher monetary returns per acre and per man-hour of labor. But to achieve these improved conditions in a country of small farms a high degree of coöperation will be necessary. The question yet to be answered is: Will the coöperative movement continue to be largely voluntary or will it become a government activity amounting to virtual collectivization?

It should not be assumed, however, that the government intends to retain permanent control over agriculture. Several official pronouncements have emphasized the continuance of private enterprise concurrently with widespread governmental activity. But it seems likely that private enterprise will be subordinated to national interests, which will, presumably, be determined by the government. Only the future can tell how far it will feel obliged to go in regulating economic life, particularly in agriculture.

It seemed reasonable to assume that a program of industrialization would be initiated in Yugoslavia. This should benefit the rural economy by attracting its excess population to more lucrative urban pursuits and thus enable the remaining peasantry to earn higher incomes. The reconstruction of Yugoslav agriculture concerns not merely a small proportion of the inhabitants: raising the standard of living in rural areas will prove beneficial to the nation as a whole.

Nor is agricultural improvement purely domestic in its significance. Measures which are successful in Yugoslavia will inevitably have repercussions in neighboring Balkan countries which are faced with similar difficulties. The fundamental policies behind the measures involved cannot fail to be of interest to the entire world, for they will determine the political and economic role that Yugoslavia is to play among the nations of the postwar world.

# CHAPTER XI

# *Foreign Economic Relations, 1918–1941*

## BY JOZO TOMASEVICH

OREIGN ECONOMIC RELATIONS of Yugoslavia in the period between the First World War and the Second World War were determined by (1) the historical background of the country; (2) its economic structure; (3) its geographic location; and (4) the development of political conditions in Europe.

Yugoslavia was established through the consolidation of territories which up to 1918 had been parts of several different political and economic entities, on different levels of economic development, and with various centers of economic gravitation (Belgrade for Serbia; Vienna and Budapest for the Yugoslav areas of the Austro-Hungarian Monarchy). The problem was to weld these various parts politically and economically, to reorient them from their former centers of gravitation, and then to integrate the state as a whole into the new European political and economic framework that was being constructed after the First World War.

The economic structure of Yugoslavia was characterized by predominantly agricultural production, increasing agricultural overpopulation, dearth of capital, and lack of entrepreneurial experience. These determined the composition of exports and imports, increased emigration, fostered industrial protectionism, forced the country to import capital, and to rely on foreign services in insurance, trading, and technical and business management.

The geographic location resulted in intensive trade ties with the central European industrial countries. Besides their mutual

[169]

economic dependence and traditional economic connections, there were important advantages in transportation costs. Trade ties with western European countries were rather weak because of transport disadvantages, the inferior quality of many Yugoslav export commodities, and lack of traditional business ties with the West. The essential link with the western European countries and the United States was through borrowing of capital.

The development of political conditions in Europe played an essential part: Yugoslavia was a pawn and a battleground of the colliding interests of the Great Powers in the Balkans and the Danube basin. The most important aspect of foreign economic relations in all the Balkan and Danubian countries after 1933 was the systematic drive of Germany to achieve a commanding position in their respective economies in order to make this area a part of its *Grossraumwirtschaft*—a step on the road to war.

Keeping all these factors in mind, the chapter will deal with the regional distribution of the foreign trade of Yugoslavia and the structure of its exports and imports, and to some extent with Yugoslav production and its development during this period; then the problem of emigration and emigrants' remittances, reparation receipts during the 1920's, international economic services, and foreign investments in Yugoslavia; and finally, trade policies.

*Regional distribution of foreign trade.*—The essential shortcoming of the diplomatic alignment of Yugoslavia in the interwar period (see chapter xix) was that it had no solid economic basis. Neither the Little Entente with France, the Little Entente itself, nor the Balkan Entente were linked by strong trade ties. On the contrary, the trade ties of Yugoslavia with its diplomatic adversaries—primarily Germany, Italy, and Austria—were intensive. France and Great Britain had large capital investments in Yugoslavia, but in the system of bilateralism which prevailed in most of Europe after 1932 this could not compensate for the weakness in the exchange of goods.

Relative distribution of the foreign trade of Yugoslavia among selected countries from 1921 to 1939 is shown in table 1 (p. 172). Trade with these countries averaged 86.3 per cent of exports and 89.3 per cent of imports throughout the entire period. Taking the nineteen-year average, Yugoslavia's exports to France accounted for only 3 per cent of its total exports; imports from France, for only 3.9 per cent of its total imports. Czechoslovakia took fourth place in exports, with 10 per cent, and third place in imports, with 15.7 per cent, and was an important trade partner and investor in Yugoslavia.

Trade with the Balkan countries, with an estimated population at the end of 1938 of 51,000,000, accounted, on the average, for only 7 per cent of total exports and 4.8 per cent of total imports. Greece alone was represented with 5.3 per cent of exports and 1.9 per cent of imports. With Rumania, except for the importation of crude oil, trade was negligible. The reason for the small amount of trade among the Balkan neighbors lies in their similar economic structure, though the composition of their exports is quite different (Turkey, Greece, and Bulgaria depend largely on the export of tobacco, and Rumania on the export of petroleum).

The share of Great Britain was 3.6 per cent in exports and 7.6 per cent in imports. Its relative share in exports had increased, especially in the later 1930's, as a result of British policy to counterbalance the German trade drive in southeastern Europe. The increase, however, was not nearly sufficient to achieve its political aim or to lessen Yugoslavia's trade predicament. Trade with the United States, which in the period 1921–1939 took 2 per cent of Yugoslav exports and supplied 4.7 per cent of imports, was also on the increase. Owing to the absence of diplomatic relations with Soviet Russia until late in 1939, virtually no trade relations existed between the two countries in the interwar period.

Trade with Austria, Italy, and Germany accounted for 54.3 per cent of total exports and 47.5 per cent of total imports. Changes in the relative importance of these countries, especially Germany, for Yugoslav trade will be discussed later, but a few facts regarding Yugoslavia's commercial relations with them should be stressed at this point. The reasons for the intensive exchange of goods with these three countries lie in the facts that Yugoslav economy complements their economies and that communications are favorable. The Danube River line for the Austrian and German trade and the Adriatic Sea route for the Italian trade gave cheap means of transport, of special importance for Yugoslavia because of the bulky nature of its main exports (timber, ores, grains, livestock).

## TABLE 1

### Yugoslav Trade with Selected Countries, 1921–1939

(Annual averages of percentage distribution of value of trade)

| Country | 1921–1925 | | 1926–1930 | | 1931–1935 | | 1936–1939 | |
|---|---|---|---|---|---|---|---|---|
| | Exports to | Imports from | Exports to | Imports from | Exports to | Imports from | Exports to | Imports from |
| France............ | 3.5 | 3.6 | 3.4 | 4.3 | 2.4 | 4.5 | 2.8 | 2.3 |
| Great Britain...... | 1.4 | 8.4 | 1.3 | 6.0 | 3.3 | 8.6 | 8.4 | 7.5 |
| Czechoslovakia.... | 7.7 | 19.3 | 9.2 | 18.2 | 12.8 | 14.3 | 10.6 | 10.9 |
| Rumania.......... | 0.4 | 2.8 | 0.5 | 3.3 | 0.6 | 2.2 | 0.9 | 2.1 |
| Greece........... | 6.0 | 3.4 | 7.7 | 1.3 | 4.2 | 1.3 | 3.4 | 1.5 |
| Turkey........... | 1.0 | 0.1 | 0.2 | 0.4 | 0.1 | 0.1 | 0.2 | 0.1 |
| Bulgaria.......... | 0.7 | 0.3 | 0.4 | 0.1 | 0.2 | 0.1 | 0.1 | 0.2 |
| Albania........... | 0.3 | 0.1 | 0.2 | 0.0 | 0.3 | 0.0 | 0.5 | 0.0 |
| Poland............ | 0.3 | 0.5 | 0.8 | 1.8 | 1.4 | 1.7 | 1.1 | 1.0* |
| Austria........... | 26.2 | 24.4 | 18.9 | 18.2 | 17.9 | 13.8 | 11.4 | 9.2* |
| Hungary.......... | 4.9 | 2.6 | 7.0 | 5.7 | 4.5 | 4.0 | 4.2 | 3.4 |
| Italy............. | 27.4 | 18.7 | 25.8 | 12.2 | 21.4 | 12.9 | 7.4 | 7.8 |
| Germany.......... | 8.0 | 7.7 | 10.4 | 14.2 | 14.1 | 16.0 | 28.3 | 34.8 |
| United States...... | 0.5 | 3.5 | 1.0 | 4.3 | 2.7 | 5.3 | 4.9 | 5.9 |
| U. S. S. R........ | 0.0 | 0.1 | 0.1 | 0.1 | 0.0 | 0.1 | 0.0 | 0.1 |
| Total........ | 88.3 | 95.5 | 86.9 | 90.1 | 85.9 | 84.9 | 84.2 | 86.8 |

Source: Yugoslavia, Ministère des Finances, Section des Douanes, *Statistique du commerce extérieur* (1921–1939).
* For Poland and for Austria, averages are for the period 1936–1938.

Yugoslavia, as a producer of food and raw materials, exported commodities in which Italy, Austria, and Germany were deficient, and these countries were able to export to Yugoslavia the com-

### TABLE 2

EXPORTS OF PRINCIPAL COMMODITIES, 1921–1939
(Annual averages in percentage of value of total exports)

| Commodity | 1921–1925 | 1926–1930 | 1931–1935 | 1936–1939 |
|---|---|---|---|---|
| Wheat and flour | 8.79 | 9.72 | 4.46 | 7.72 |
| Corn | 10.24 | 7.09 | 8.61 | 6.46 |
| Fresh and dried prunes | 3.48 | 2.41 | 3.14 | 2.23 |
| Hops | 1.48 | 1.98 | 1.53 | 1.40 |
| Tobacco | 0.23 | 0.89 | 3.60 | 2.27 |
| Hemp | 1.63 | 1.34 | 1.83 | 3.76 |
| Fat hogs | 3.90 | 5.09 | 6.22 | 8.05 |
| Cattle | 7.91 | 4.56 | 2.63 | 2.03 |
| Other livestock | 3.53 | 2.99 | 2.50 | 1.88 |
| Meat | 6.21 | 3.89 | 4.77 | 5.66 |
| Eggs | 6.82 | 7.22 | 5.05 | 2.66 |
| Hides | 2.33 | 1.76 | 1.84 | 2.45 |
| Construction timber | 14.45 | 15.35 | 15.83 | 13.62 |
| Other timber | 2.75 | 4.60 | 2.98 | 1.91 |
| Blister copper | 2.79 | 5.00 | 7.93 | 8.04 |
| Lead | 1.33 | 0.87 | 0.54 | 0.41 |
| Bauxite | 0.05 | 0.17 | 0.29 | 0.96 |
| Ores | 0.82 | 1.46 | 2.49 | 2.05 |
| Lead and zinc concentrates | ............ | ............ | ............ | 3.51 |
| Cement | 1.92 | 1.96 | 2.13 | 0.96 |
| Total | 80.66 | 78.35 | 78.37 | 78.03 |
| Av. total exports { Million dinars .... | D. 6,529 | D. 7,073 | D. 3,828 | D. 5,304 |
| Metric tons........ | 3,028,000 | 4,745,000 | 3,112,000 | 3,648,000 |

SOURCE: Yugoslavia, Ministère des Finances, Section des Douanes, *Statistique du commerce extérieur* (1921–1939).

modities it needed: textiles, machinery, rolling stock, motor vehicles, electrical appliances, coke, dyes, medical supplies, paper. Moreover, they were markets for a number of Yugoslav export products for which no other major markets existed: soft timber, wheat, corn, fat hogs, cattle, hides, meat, eggs, fruits, and some metals. Yugoslav trade with Italy always showed a surplus of exports over imports, which before the period of clearing arrangements assured Yugoslavia of a substantial amount of foreign exchange for payments elsewhere. Important factors in trade with Austria, which in 1921–1925 accounted for one-fourth of all exports and imports, were the business ties established before the First World War. Thus, throughout the whole interwar period, trade relations with Austria, Italy, and Germany were of essential importance to Yugoslavia.

*Structure and development of foreign trade.*—Yugoslavia's share in the foreign trade of the world in the 1930's was only 0.4–0.5 per cent of the total. The export and import trade of Yugoslavia reflected its agricultural and raw-material-producing character and the fact that it was industrially underdeveloped. Table 2 (p. 173) shows the relative value of the major exports in the period from 1921 to 1939.

The chief agricultural exports were wheat and flour; corn; dried and fresh prunes, and other fresh fruits; industrial crops like hops, tobacco, hemp, opium, medicinal herbs; livestock (fat hogs, cattle, sheep, horses), meat, and light hides; poultry, feathers, and eggs; cheese. Yugoslavia was self-sufficient in sugar, but at the very low rate of consumption of 5.5 kg. per capita in the period 1934–1938. The chief food imports were rice, green coffee, oilseeds, and tropical fruits. The country relied heavily on imports, also, for industrial fats such as tallow, copra, fish oil, and oilseeds.

Two facts should be stressed with regard to prewar Yugoslav food exports. With the exception of fruits, cheese, eggs, sheep, and cattle, the bulk of the exports came from the commercialized and specialized agriculture of the Vojvodina, Srem, and Slavonia. This area supplied also the domestic food-deficit regions comprising the whole southwestern part of the country, usually referred to as the Karst area. The bread-grains deficit of this area was between 600,000 and 800,000 metric tons annually. The second and a most essential point is that Yugoslav food exports in the interwar period were not a true surplus above and beyond the nutritional needs of the domestic population but a result of the low purchasing power of most of the Yugoslav peasantry, workers, and urban low-income groups.

In a study of food production and utilization in the period 1934–1938, the author established a rather high average per-capita caloric availability in Yugoslavia of about 3,000 calories a day. But about 77 per cent of the caloric supply was derived from cereals and 41 per cent from corn alone. In some large rural areas corn supplied 85–90 per cent of all calories. The daily supply of proteins was about 90 grams per capita, but only 17 grams were of animal origin. The average per-capita availability of fats was about 50 grams a day, but only 15 grams were derived directly from fats and oils, 17 grams from grains and nuts, and the remainder from meat and dairy products. This diet, deficient in protective foods of animal origin and in fats, resulted in widespread malnutrition and contributed to a high incidence of disease (tuberculosis, intestinal diseases, etc.) because it lowered the resistance of the population.[1]

Yugoslavia has a large flour-milling industry in the Vojvodina, but exports of flour, which in 1921–1925 averaged 37,550 tons annually, fell to 13,108, 2,820, and 5,900 tons in 1926–1930, 1931–1935, and 1936–1939, respectively. The relative importance of hops, which is a typical export crop, rose in the second part of the 1920's but could not be maintained. The relative share of tobacco exports increased greatly in the 1930's. Hemp was an important export crop, especially in the latter half of the 1930's, when Yugoslavia was in second place in Europe as exporter. Increased cultivation of hemp in this period was sponsored mainly by the Germans, who also encouraged increased planting of oilseeds, primarily through their minorities in the Vojvodina, Srem, and Slavonia, but they were much less successful than in Rumania and Bulgaria.

Exports of livestock and animal products were important throughout the interwar period. The basic change was a relative increase in the export of fat hogs (to Germany, Czechoslovakia, and Austria) and a reduction in the export of cattle owing to increased tariff protection in importing countries (Italy, Germany, Austria, and the Middle East). From 1934 on, Germany was by far the most important customer for fresh meat, meat products, and lard, as well as poultry and eggs, followed by Austria and Czechoslovakia.

---

[1] For notes to chapter xi see page 521.

Construction timber was the most important single item of export, accounting for about 15 per cent of total exports in the interwar period. Italy, Germany, and Great Britain were the chief markets for Yugoslav timber, but the wide range of types and the high quality of many products (e.g., Slavonian oak) enabled Yugoslavia to distribute its timber exports to many markets on the European continent, in the Mediterranean area, Latin America, and others. An important aspect of the timber industry was that its chief producing areas are those where agricultural production is deficient; it helped to support large numbers of an otherwise agricultural population.

Yugoslavia is abundantly endowed with mineral wealth, but much of it remains undeveloped. It lacks, however, two essential items—coking coal and oil—which must be imported. The deficiency in coking coal is a basic impediment to the development of heavy industry. In the period 1936–1939 Yugoslavia produced on the average 440,000 metric tons of bituminous coal, 3,730,000 tons of brown coal, and 1,150,000 tons of lignite annually. The imports of solid fuels averaged, in the same period: anthracite, 32,200 tons; bituminous coal, 156,300 tons; coke, 207,000 metric tons. The country had to import all its requirements of oil, averaging 140,000 tons annually in this period.

The reserves of iron ore are estimated only in the two Bosnian areas (Ljubija and Vareš) at 300,000,000 tons. More than two-thirds of the 1937–1940 average iron-ore production of 630,000 tons was exported, for the blast-furnace capacity was sufficient to work only 130,000 tons annually. Both from the economic and the military point of view the low steel output was considered to be a serious deficiency, and determined efforts were made, in the latter half of the 1930's, to increase production. When the state consolidated its coal-, iron-, and steel-producing facilities in Bosnia, steel production rose from 91,000 tons in 1931 to 125,000 tons in 1936, 169,000 tons in 1937, and 220,000 tons in 1938.

Yugoslavia made the greatest advances during the interwar period, particularly in the 1930's, in the production of nonferrous ores and metals. Table 3 (p. 177) shows this production for 1921–1939. As a producer of nonferrous ores Yugoslavia had achieved, in 1937, the following position among European countries, excluding Soviet Russia: first place in copper and antimony ores; second place in chromium and lead ores; and fourth place in bauxite and zinc ore.[2] The exploitation of nonferrous minerals was almost exclusively in the hands of foreign investors, especially the French (Compagnie Française de Mines de Bor), who controlled copper production, and the British (Trepča Mines, Ltd.), who

### TABLE 3
PRODUCTION OF NONFERROUS ORES AND METALS, 1921–1939
(Annual averages in metric tons)

| Commodity | 1921–1925 | 1926–1930 | 1931–1935 | 1936–1939 |
|---|---|---|---|---|
| Copper ore | 123,000 | 331,700 | 527,100 | 751,500 |
| Blister copper | 6,300 | 16,600 | 35,600 | 40,600 |
| Lead and zinc ore | 64,800 | 101,400 | 620,800 | 801,400 |
| Lead (metal content) | ......... | ......... | 55,800 | 56,700 |
| Zinc (metal content) | ......... | ......... | 50,800 | 47,800 |
| Lead (smelter production) | 9,000 | 10,100 | 7,700 | 7,300 |
| Zinc and zinc powder | 1,600 | 4,500 | 3,700 | 4,700 |
| Manganese ore | ......... | ......... | 1,000 | 4,100 |
| Chromium ore | 2,500 | 27,700 | 45,100 | 54,300 |
| Antimony ore | ......... | ......... | 600 | 12,600 |
| Bauxite | 34,600 | 96,200 | 102,800 | 342,900 |

SOURCE: Yugoslavia, *Annuaire statistique*, 1931, 1940.

controlled lead and zinc production. The entire industry was typically an export industry, and proceeds from its sales abroad constituted an important part of Yugoslav foreign exchange receipts.

By pressure and the granting of additional concessions—tax exemptions, duty-free import of machinery, easy transfer of dividends—the government induced the foreign companies to build smelting facilities. An electrolytic copper refinery, with a capacity of 12,000 tons annually, was built by Bor in 1938. In 1939 Trepča built a lead smelter with an initial capacity of 20,000 tons annually, and planned to build a zinc smelter. These were to be gradually increased until they could process all domestically derived ore concentrates. In 1937 an aluminum plant was built with an annual capacity of about 3,600 tons, but it was owned by domestic capital.

Other important industrial exports were cement, artificial fertilizer, soda ash and caustic soda, tanning materials, and ferroalloys.

The relative value of major imports over the period 1921–1939 is shown in table 4. The salient feature of the import trade is the

### TABLE 4

IMPORTS OF PRINCIPAL COMMODITIES, 1921–1939
(Annual averages in percentage of value of total imports)

| Commodity | 1921–1925 | 1926–1930 | 1931–1935 | 1936–1939 |
|---|---|---|---|---|
| Raw cotton | 1.54 | 2.34 | 4.50 | 5.64 |
| Cotton yarn | 4.38 | 6.05 | 9.16 | 7.74 |
| Cotton products | 20.90 | 12.29 | 7.00 | 4.19 |
| Other vegetable-fiber products | 2.24 | 2.33 | 2.00 | 2.00 |
| Raw wool | 0.49 | 1.25 | 1.61 | 2.49 |
| Woolen yarn | 0.43 | 1.20 | 2.12 | 2.41 |
| Woolen products | 8.87 | 6.33 | 4.80 | 4.22 |
| Silk and silk products | 1.32 | 2.71 | 4.12 | 2.67 |
| Hides and leather | 3.88 | 3.91 | 3.24 | 2.25 |
| Coffee | 2.57 | 2.74 | 2.09 | 1.25 |
| Rice | 1.44 | 1.55 | 1.50 | 1.25 |
| Petroleum products | 3.36 | 3.04 | 2.25 | 2.24 |
| Coal, anthracite, coke | 2.58 | 2.63 | 2.63 | 2.82 |
| Iron, steel, and products | 9.68 | 10.71 | 10.04 | 11.42 |
| Machinery and tools | 3.96 | 6.06 | 4.99 | 7.92 |
| Electrotechnical products | 1.24 | 2.18 | 3.27 | 3.47 |
| Transportation means | 1.26 | 2.18 | 1.88 | 4.40 |
| Total | 70.14 | 69.50 | 67.20 | 68.38 |
| Av. total imports { Million dinars | D. 7,170 | D. 7,461 | D. 3,563 | D. 4,761 |
| Metric tons | 1,146,000 | 1,465,000 | 932,000 | 1,118,000 |

SOURCE: Yugoslavia, Ministère des Finances, Section des Douanes, *Statistique du commerce extérieur* (1921–1939).

large share of textiles and textile raw materials. These amounted to 40.2 per cent of total imports in the period 1921–1925, but from 1936 to 1939 their share was only 31.4 per cent. The reason for the drop in value was not a smaller import in terms of quantity of textiles and textile raw materials but the shift from the import of far more expensive finished products and piece goods to the import of raw cotton, raw wool, and cotton and woolen yarns.

The textile industry of Yugoslavia has advanced faster than any other, for it required relatively low investments and had a large and well-protected domestic market. Foreign capital played an important part in the development of the textile industry, and a large number of plants were in the hands of Austrian and Czech concerns, which evaded the protective duty on textiles simply by jumping over the custom walls with part of their production facilities. In fact, many textile plants in Yugoslavia were built with old, imported machinery that had been discarded in other countries but could be used in Yugoslavia because of low wages.

As an industrially underdeveloped country, Yugoslavia was dependent on imports of all kinds of iron and steel products: machinery for industrial installations, mining, agriculture, and forestry; machine tools; electrotechnical products; and transportation equipment. The relative share of these products, which was only 16.1 per cent of the total value of imports in 1921–1925, increased to 21.1 per cent in 1926–1930, dropped by about 1 per cent in 1931–1935 because of the depression and lessened investment activity, and then rose to 27.2 per cent in 1936–1939, reflecting the increased pace of industrialization in this period.

Germany had the greatest relative share in supplying Yugoslavia with such commodities. The more rapid development of Yugoslav metallurgy in the latter half of the 1930's and German preponderance in supplying machinery for this industry were partly consequences of difficulties in German-Yugoslav trade relations. To "rescue" a part of Yugoslav blocked export balances, such products as aspirin and typewriters had to be imported in much larger quantities than were required, but a substantial part of these balances was used for the purchase of capital goods. Virtually all machinery used in the smelting and refining of nonferrous metals, as well as in steel production, was of German origin. From the German point of view this meant the development of an area in Germany's backyard, the industrial potential of which was to be utilized by its war machine while rearming and during the war. Most of the industrialization measures in southeastern Europe after 1935 were actually part of the German armament plans.

Roughly 30 per cent of Yugoslav imports consisted of commodities not included in table 4: artificial organic dyes, medical supplies, insecticides, printing paper, rubber and rubber products, ceramics. For most of these Yugoslavia will remain dependent on imports from abroad.

In the period 1936–1939 Yugoslav exports to the United States amounted on the average to about $5,800,000 and Yugoslav imports from the United States to $6,200,000 annually ($1 = D. 45). Essentially it was an exchange of Yugoslav blister copper and hops for American cotton: the first two represented 69 per cent of Yugoslav exports to, and the last, 62 per cent of Yugoslav imports from, the United States in the period noted. Other important exports to the United States in the same period were chromium ore, dry beans, sour cherries, and medicinal herbs. The most important other Yugoslav imports were automobiles, machinery, lubricants, electrotechnical products, and motion-picture films.

*Emigration and emigrants' remittances.*—The basic characteristic of Yugoslav economy in the interwar period was agrarian overpopulation. This is best shown by the fact that agricultural production would not have suffered had the available man power in agriculture been reduced by 35 per cent, since only 65 per cent of it was utilized. Agricultural development did not keep pace with the growth of the rural population; the result was an increasing number of people per unit of arable land and a decreasing number of cattle and horses in relation to both arable land and rural population. The peasants, owing to their negligible or nonexistent capacity to save, could not improve production techniques. A price disparity existed between agricultural and industrial commodities, and taxes were high. A lowering of the standard of living of the peasant masses was inevitable.

The classical remedy for overpopulation is emigration. Substantial emigration from territories now forming Yugoslavia, especially to the United States, began after 1880 and lasted until 1914. Restrictions by the United States and other extra-European countries in the early 1920's made emigration on a pre-1914 scale impossible, but it was still large until 1929, when the depression virtually halted emigration to countries outside Europe. However, seasonal emigration to France and Belgium, and later to Germany, became relatively more important, but it was never considered a satisfactory substitute for emigration beyond Europe.

The emigration from Yugoslavia is given in the accompanying table. The net emigration from 1919 to 1931 was estimated at 250,000, of whom about 60 per cent were farmers. Of the total number of emigrants, 40 per cent were between the ages of eighteen and thirty. Net emigration absorbed about 13 per cent of the total increase in population from 1920 to 1930. In the 1930's the situa-

| Period | To countries ex-Europe | To Europe |
|---|---|---|
| 1921–1925 | 67,742 | n. d. |
| 1926–1930 | 93,744 | 63,932 |
| 1931–1935 | 15,735 | 45,843 |
| 1936–1939 | 18,713 | 60,901 |

Source: Yugoslavia, *Annuaire statistique*, 1931, 1940.

tion was entirely changed. In the period 1931–1939 the number of emigrants to countries beyond Europe amounted to 34,500; the number of returnees, 29,400. The number of emigrants to European countries was 106,700; the number of returnees, 74,900. The net emigration in this period was only 36,900. Thus in the early 1930's emigration ceased to be a security vent for the increasing agrarian overpopulation, eliminating, so to speak, the export of a commodity (labor) in the supply of which Yugoslavia had the greatest comparative advantage.

Besides alleviating the agrarian overpopulation pressure, especially in the food-deficit areas of the Karst region, emigration was making two singularly important contributions to Yugoslav economy: (1) it served as an important source of income for people in the poorest regions of the country (southern Croatia, Dalmatia, Hercegovina, Montenegro), where, as in many areas of Italy, Albania, Greece, and Bulgaria, economy is based partly on emigrants' remittances; and (2) emigrants' remittances were an important favorable item in the Yugoslav balance of payments.

Estimates of emigrants' remittances in the interwar period differ greatly. Arthur Benko Grado, the leading Yugoslav authority on emigration, estimated in 1940 that emigrants' remittances, including savings brought home by the returnees, totaled $244,000,000 from 1919 to 1938.[3] Considering the varying dollar-dinar rate, this represented between D. 14,000,000,000 and D. 15,000,000,000. In annual averages, based on A. Benko Grado's estimates, these remittances, in current dollars, were as indicated in the accompanying table. Remittances reached their highest point, $20,000,000, in 1924, dropped to $13,000,000 in 1930, and to only $2,000,000 in 1935, to rise again to $5,500,000 in 1937. They closely reflected the

EMIGRANTS' REMITTANCES, 1919–1938

| Period | Average annual value | Period | Average annual value |
|---|---|---|---|
| 1919–1923 | $17,600,000 | 1929–1933 | $9,300,000 |
| 1924–1928 | 17,700,000 | 1934–1938 | 3,900,000 |

economic conditions in countries with large groups of Yugoslav emigrants, primarily the United States, but also the fact that the number of the original emigrants abroad was diminishing because of death and small new emigration. Emigrants' remittances contributed greatly toward the maintenance of the exchange rate of the dinar, especially in the first few years after the War of 1914–1918. Their importance in the Yugoslav balance of payments can best be judged by the fact that they more than doubly covered the import surplus of D. 6,850,000,000 in the period 1919–1938.

*Reparation receipts after the First World War.*—Between 1919 and 1931 Yugoslavia participated in the reparation payments from Germany, Hungary, and Bulgaria. German reparations represented the major part of the receipts. The Yugoslav government had great difficulty in securing its share of 5 per cent in German reparations, since the tendency among the Great Powers was to "indemnify" the smaller nations with territorial concessions. Reparation receipts were of vital importance to the new state for the following reasons: the population losses of Serbia in the First World War were relatively much higher than in any other belligerent country; the credit of the new state was very poor at home and abroad; import needs were several times higher than export capacity; and the state was financed mainly by outright monetary inflation.

Yugoslav reparation receipts from Germany until the Hoover

moratorium in June, 1931, amounted to about 550,000,000 to 600,000,000 gold marks, or approximately D. 8,500,000,000 to D. 9,000,000,000. Of this amount 263,000,000 gold marks were received before the inauguration of the Dawes Plan in September, 1924. Roughly half of it was in rolling stock and railway equipment. Under the Dawes Plan Yugoslavia received 275,200,000 gold marks, and the remainder in the first and only year of the Young Plan. With the exception of about 15 per cent of the German reparations and some cash payments from Hungary and Bulgaria, all Yugoslav reparation receipts were in kind, primarily in railway rolling stock and materials, bridging, machinery, scientific instruments, small ships, coal, coke, and cattle. Yugoslavia also received certain deliveries on the account of French reparations from Germany; their value was later consolidated as a government debt toward France.

Yugoslavia was expected to repay the loans received from the Allies during the war and immediately after the war. The war debts to the United States, Great Britain, and France were regulated by special agreements between 1926 and 1930. Servicing of these debts in the first period of the Young Plan (1929–1966) was supposed to require only 21.3 per cent of the Yugoslav receipts from Germany. As a result, the Yugoslav net reparation receipts were to be relatively much higher than those of any other reparation creditor. But up to the time of the Hoover moratorium only small payments were made.

Austria paid no reparations after the First World War because of its economic plight. Hungary delivered to Yugoslavia, between 1921 and 1926, about 1,250,000 tons of coal, 80 locomotives, 1,200 railroad cars, and some livestock. Part of the reparations had to be paid in cash. However, the question of Hungarian reparations to Yugoslavia, Czechoslovakia, and Rumania was linked with the payment of indemnities by these countries to Hungarian landlords for properties expropriated in the course of the agrarian reform. The Yugoslav share in Hungarian cash reparations was thereby greatly reduced. The value of supplies delivered by Hungary to Yugoslavia on the reparation account probably amounted to about D. 800,000,000.

In the first few years Bulgaria delivered small quantities of coal and livestock to Yugoslavia, but started cash payments on only part of its debt. Bulgaria also paid 14,700,000 gold francs—half in cash and half in wheat, corn, and coal—in restitution for goods taken in Serbia during the occupation. The total Bulgarian payments to Yugoslavia for reparations and restitutions may be estimated at D. 200,000,000–D. 250,000,000.

The total value of reparations received by Yugoslavia from Germany, Hungary, and Bulgaria could thus be estimated at between D. 9,500,000,000 and D. 10,000,000,000. Because of the magnitude of the receipts, the nature of goods received (mostly capital goods and industrial raw materials), and the fact that the supplies were received in the years of greatest need for rehabilitation purposes, reparation receipts were of extraordinary importance to the Yugoslav economy. Their fiscal importance can best be judged by the fact that they amounted to about 15 per cent of the total tax receipts of the Yugoslav state between 1919 and March, 1931.

*Services.*—The most important services for Yugoslavia in foreign economic relations were tourist trade; sea, rail, and postal traffic; insurance; and commercial services. In the 1920's Yugoslavia had an unfavorable balance in tourist trade, but in the second half of the 1930's it became favorable. This was to some extent a result of the Yugoslav exchange control which forced foreign creditors to utilize part of their blocked accounts in Yugoslavia, and a special tourism agreement with Germany in 1934. In sea, river, and rail transport accounts the country had a favorable balance, owing to geographical location, which insured a substantial transit of goods over Yugoslav territory, and to the earnings of its tramp shipping. The postal services always gave Yugoslavia a small but favorable balance. International accounts of insurance premiums and trade commissions have always been unfavorable to Yugoslavia, for a rather large part of its imports and exports and an overwhelming proportion of its insurance business was carried on by foreign firms.

S. D. Obradović[4] has estimated the balances for Yugoslav international accounts for services from 1926 to 1936. (See the table.) Yugoslavia had a favorable balance of about D. 983,000,000. If the periods 1919–1925 and 1937–1940 are included, the favorable balance may have been nearly D. 1,300,000,000, which makes the service account in the Yugoslav balance of payments of relatively secondary importance.

*Foreign investments in Yugoslavia.*—Foreign capital and the servicing of foreign loans were essential to Yugoslavia in the inter-war period. The industrial development of the country at the outbreak of the Second World War was in large degree an accomplishment of foreign capital. Owing to structural undersaving and the resulting import of foreign capital, Yugoslavia was and remains a debtor country, a fact influencing its whole economy and its

| Services | Cumulative balances, 1926–1936 |
|---|---|
| Tourist trade | +D.   280,000,000 |
| Sea and river transport | +     1,103,000,000 |
| Rail transport | +     1,819,000,000 |
| Postal service | +       374,000,000 |
| Insurance premiums and trade commissions | —       509,000,000 |
| Other | —     2,084,000,000 |

economic relations with the outside world. The degree of structural undersaving is perhaps best illustrated by the fact that in the middle 1920's even the best industrial and commercial enterprises paid between 16 and 24 per cent interest on their borrowing from commercial banks. After 1932 the nominal interest rates were limited by law to about 10 per cent, depending on the discount rate of the National Bank, but effective rates (interest plus other charges such as commissions and carrying costs) were never below 12 to 15 per cent.

The first two foreign loans were obtained by Serbia in 1867 and 1876 from Russian banks to finance the wars of liberation waged against the Ottoman Empire. From 1880 to 1910 Serbia obtained several loans through French, Austrian, and German banks for railroads, armaments, and financial consolidation. Only after 1904 did the import of foreign capital for private investments begin. Loans from 1910 to 1914 were again for purely military purposes. In the Yugoslav areas belonging to the Austro-Hungarian Monarchy up to 1918, investments in railroads, canals, industry, and so on were financed by Vienna and Budapest concerns, but most of the capital originated in western Europe. In 1918 such investments, so far as they were not taken over by the government as enemy property, formally became foreign investments.

To lessen the economic and financial dominance of Vienna and Budapest, Yugoslavia, after 1918, moved toward the nationalization of Austrian and Hungarian enterprises. This usually consisted in transforming branches of Austrian and Hungarian firms in Yugoslavia into "Yugoslav" companies. This was only a formality, however: capital and management remained in the same hands, though now, as a rule, with visible participation of western European or Czech capital. A substantial degree of foreign control was exercised through stock ownership and crediting of banks in Yugoslavia, which, true to central European practices, were engaged in the establishment, long-term financing, and direct control of industrial and trade enterprises.

The first substantial amounts of foreign capital came into Yugoslavia after 1918 as government loans. From 1922 to 1931 Yugoslavia negotiated the following loans abroad: the 8 per cent loan of $15,000,000 issued in 1922 through the New York banking firm of Blair and Company; the 5 per cent loan from the French government of F. Fr. 300,000,000 in 1923, to buy military supplies in France; the 7 per cent loan of $30,000,000 issued in 1927 through Blair and Company; the 6.25 per cent Kreuger loan of $22,000,000 in 1928, actually financed by New York banks; and the 7 per cent international stabilization loan of F. Fr. 1,015,000,000 in 1931. Besides these loans, the government negotiated several smaller loans in France, between 1929 and 1932, for railroad construction.[5] The state also guaranteed two foreign loans of the State Mortgage Bank.

But only foreign investments in private enterprises are considered here. Influx of foreign capital for private investment began after the *de facto* stabilization of the dinar in 1925, which subsequently, especially in 1927 and 1928, assumed large proportions. This was reflected also in the fact that the import surplus amounted to D. 886,000,000 in 1927 and D. 1,391,000,000 in 1928. The influx of foreign capital in the second half of the 1920's consisted mostly of import surpluses from such big creditors of Yugoslavia as France, Great Britain, the United States, and Czechoslovakia. Import surplus from these four countries totaled D. 3,050,000,000 in 1927 and 1928. But substantial amounts of foreign capital entered by a roundabout way through Czechoslovakia, Austria, and Germany.

Owing to the influx of foreign capital the country's gold reserve increased from D. 835,000,000 at the end of 1925 to D. 1,050,000,000 at the end of 1929; in the same period the foreign-exchange reserve rose from D. 1,095,000,000 to D. 1,760,000,000. Foreign exchange for the servicing of these loans was obtained by utilizing a part of the proceeds from new loans, although since 1925 the country has had a surplus of exports in every year except 1927, 1928, and 1930. It can safely be stated, however, that, as long as multilateral trade based on free exchange was functioning, the flow of foreign capital into Yugoslavia and the servicing of these loans ran smoothly.

The withdrawal of short-term credits from Yugoslavia was in full swing in 1930. In this year the country's foreign-exchange reserve dropped by D. 1,100,000,000. Just at the breaking point in the financial situation of central and southeastern Europe, in June, 1931, Yugoslavia obtained its last big foreign loan for the purpose of legal stabilization of its currency. This loan, in which French banks participated with F. Fr. 675,000,000, had all the earmarks of French diplomatic subsidization of Yugoslavia. It could not stem the course of events, and a serious financial crisis broke out in the summer of 1931.

Temporary relaxation of the exchange control, in force from June to October, 1931, helped both the withdrawal of foreign credits and the flight of domestic funds from the country. The breakdown in the mechanism of international trade and credit and the difficult position of the Yugoslav balance of payments led to more and more stringent exchange controls and to a transfer moratorium for foreign credits and financial service on foreign loans.

The drop in profit expectations during the depression, which in Yugoslavia lasted in a severe form until 1935, and the exchange control, which constituted a special risk for foreign capital, made its import from the middle of 1931 to 1936 virtually impossible. The only exceptions were small loans which the government obtained in France for railroad construction. In the latter half of the 1930's, however, there was a substantial amount of new investment of foreign capital in Yugoslavia. But it seems safe to say that most of it was financed by using a portion of the profits earned in the country itself, as was true of Bor, Trepča, and other foreign concerns.

Difficulties in the statistical coverage of foreign investments in Yugoslavia are extremely great. The following data represent only the best available estimates of foreign investments through corporate enterprises.[6] The total share capital of the 1,522 odd corporations, including banks, in Yugoslavia at the end of 1937 amounted to D. 7,440,000,000 and their debts to D. 11,150,000,000. It is estimated that D. 5,070,000,000, or 45 per cent, of the latter amount was used for long-term investments. Of the total share capital, only D. 4,630,000,000, or 62 per cent, was represented at shareholders' meetings in 1937. Of this amount, D. 2,387,000,000 was foreign-owned. The total foreign participation in share capital, however, was estimated at D. 3,280,000,000, or 44 per cent of the total. The amount of foreign loans to corporations in Yugoslavia was estimated at D. 2,830,000,000, of which about D. 1,290,-000,000 was for long-term investments. Thus the total foreign investments in private corporations in Yugoslavia at the end of 1937 amounted to D. 6,110,000,000, or 33 per cent, of all corporate financial resources. A certain amount of foreign capital was invested in firms owned by individuals and partnerships, but it was not large.

Table 5 (p. 190) shows the participation, in 1937, of various countries in foreign holdings of share capital in Yugoslavia and the distribution of their holdings in certain basic industries. It also shows the total share capital in these industries and the foreign participation as represented in shareholders' meetings. (Actual foreign ownership was estimated to be 27 per cent higher.)

Besides the ownership in industries shown in table 5, foreign investors owned the following percentages of shares of stock (percentage of total stock represented in shareholders' meetings): transport, 40; insurance, 38; sugar industry, 24; hotels, 21; flour milling, 19; trade, 17; banking, 9. Thus there is no major branch of Yugoslav economy in which foreign capital did not play a vital role. It was most heavily engaged in mining, electric power, and chemical and oil industries. Its share in textiles, timber, and food processing was not high, for these industries work with much smaller fixed capital. Small units are suitable for development by domestic investors who have relatively small amounts of capital; they do not require highly skilled technical and commercial management.

In 1937 France owned one-fourth of the total foreign share capital in Yugoslavia, followed by Great Britain, the United States, and Germany (including Austria and Czechoslovakia). The major part of the French share was represented by hydroelectric plants in Dalmatia producing power and heavy chemicals (La Dalmatienne) and copper mines (Compagnie Française des Mines de Bor). Most of the British capital was represented by lead and zinc mines (Trepča Mines, Ltd.) and the Shell Anglo-Yugoslav Petroleum Company. The American property consisted primarily of a subsidiary of the Socony Vacuum Oil Company and a subsidiary of the American-Yugoslav Electric Company.

Owing to the fact that most of the exploitation rights were secured at very low cost, that wages were extremely low, and that many companies were exempted from several types of taxes (import duty on machinery, etc.), production costs, especially in mining, were relatively low, making it possible for most of the producers to compete effectively on the world market and to obtain large profits. For example, the cost of working lead-zinc ore in 1933 was only 14s. 4d. per ton for the Trepča Mines, Ltd., whereas the production costs of the chief Australian lead producer (Broken Hill, New South Wales) were approximately 30s. per ton.

Trepča was actually the cheapest lead producer in the world and its owners had a particularly strong position in the world market. Its output was always sold four or five years in advance. Between 1933 and 1937, the company distributed tax-free dividends of 16, 12, 20, 25, and 30 per cent, respectively, and accumulated substantial surpluses as well. Although its share capital was only £1,125,000, the dividends distributed from 1931 to 1937 amounted to £1,526,000.[7] In 1938 Trepča increased its share capital to £2,000,000.

Bor increased its share capital in 1936 from F. Fr. 15,000,000 to F. Fr. 60,000,000. For years it has been one of the most profitable mining enterprises in the world. The dividends[8] paid by the company for each 100-franc share of common stock are listed in the table on page 192. The market value of Bor shares was, of course, such that these dividends fluctuated between 2 per cent (1931) and 7.3 per cent (1936) of the respective annual average price of the shares, but few shares changed hands. The chief shareholder

## TABLE 5

### Percentage of Foreign Participation in Share Capital of Corporations in All and in Selected Industries, 1937

| Country | Participation in total share capital | Mining | Cement, bauxite, glass | Electric power | Timber | Metallurgy | Chemicals and oil | Textiles |
|---|---|---|---|---|---|---|---|---|
| France | 25.00 | 36.14 | 48.77 | 66.91 | 10.74 | 22.40 | 2.28 | 6.72 |
| Great Britain | 17.38 | 52.42 | 0.16 | ........ | 41.20 | 1.36 | 23.17 | 3.46 |
| United States | 14.95 | 0.02 | ........ | 17.64 | 20.04 | 0.38 | 43.82 | ........ |
| Germany* | 11.13 | 1.13 | 22.46 | 0.05 | ........ | 16.80 | 5.33 | 48.43 |
| Italy | 9.45 | 2.30 | 0.64 | ........ | 14.00 | ........ | ........ | ........ |
| Belgium | 7.41 | 6.00 | 2.64 | ........ | ........ | ........ | 19.07 | ........ |
| Switzerland | 5.91 | 1.34 | 23.56 | 12.66 | 11.70 | 3.14 | 0.47 | 13.52 |
| Monaco† | 3.25 | ........ | ........ | ........ | ........ | 55.84 | ........ | ........ |
| Netherlands | 2.21 | 0.57 | ........ | 2.31 | 1.02 | ........ | 3.03 | 16.74 |
| Sweden | 1.30 | ........ | ........ | ........ | ........ | ........ | 2.77 | ........ |
| Hungary | 1.30 | 0.02 | 1.77 | 0.43 | ........ | 0.04 | 0.06 | 11.13 |
| Luxemburg | 0.59 | 0.06 | ........ | ........ | ........ | ........ | ........ | ........ |
| Rumania | 0.11 | ........ | ........ | ........ | 1.30 | 0.04 | ........ | ........ |
| Other | 0.01 | ........ | ........ | ........ | ........ | ........ | ........ | ........ |
| | 100.00 | 100.00 | 100.00 | 100.00 | 100.00 | 100.00 | 100.00 | 100.00 |

TABLE 5 (*Continued*)

SHARE CAPITAL AND INDEBTEDNESS

(Million dinars)

| | | | | | | | |
|---|---|---|---|---|---|---|---|
| Total share capital | D. 7,441.0 | D. 877.5 | D. 247.7 | D. 669.6 | D. 337.5 | D. 417.4 | D. 571.6 | D. 296.9 |
| Foreign-owned‡ | D. 3,282.3 | D. 607.5 | D. 91.6 | D. 555.9 | D. 94.5 | D. 136.6 | D. 399.3 | D. 67.4 |
| Percentage | 44.1% | 69.2% | 37.0% | 83.0% | 28.8% | 32.7% | 69.9% | 22.7% |
| Total indebtedness | D. 11,150.0 | D. 736.6 | D. 510.3 | D. 485.2 | D. 1,207.2 | D. 918.1 | D. 588.0 | D. 731.1 |
| Foreign indebtedness | D. 2,832.8 | D. 364.0 | D. 213.9 | D. 408.5 | D. 528.5 | D. 256.0 | D. 308.2 | D. 257.0 |
| Percentage | 25.4% | 49.4% | 41.9% | 84.2% | 43.8% | 27.9% | 52.4% | 35.2% |

SOURCE: Based on V. V. Rozenberg and J. Lj. Kostić, *Ko finansira jugoslovensku privredu?* (Belgrade, 1940), pp. 94–231.

* Germany's share includes the Austrian and the Czechoslovak shares.

† Monaco's share represents the bulk of holdings of the Vienna Kreditanstalt in Yugoslavia before 1931. Chief owners of Monaco's share were actually some British and Belgian banks.

‡ Total foreign participation is estimated; participation in various industries as represented in shareholders' meetings.

was the Paris bank, Mirabaud et Cie. At the end of 1937 the company had an accumulated surplus of F. Fr. 149,000,000. By absorbing part of the surplus the share capital was doubled in 1940.

It is impossible to enter into all the financial ramifications of foreign-owned companies working in Yugoslavia, but it is safe to state that many were simply Yugoslav branches of huge international concerns. Perhaps the most important consequence of

| Year | Dividend | Year | Dividend |
|------|----------|------|----------|
| 1928 | F. Fr. 190 | 1933 | F. Fr. 130 |
| 1929 | 300 | 1934 | 130 |
| 1930 | 125 | 1935 | 160 |
| 1931 | 50 | 1936 | 275 |
| 1932 | 60 | 1937 | 135 |

this fact was that the outlets for their Yugoslav production were well secured, which made it easier to transfer dividends abroad, even in years of rampant bilateralism, without having an export surplus in trade with countries which owned these holdings. Thus, for example, the bulk of Trepča's lead and zinc concentrate was exported to Belgium, while most of the Bor copper was exported to the United States, Germany, and Belgium. It was only in 1939 that France bought 10 per cent of the Bor copper production in order to reduce the export of copper to Germany.

Considering the proportion of industry, mining, insurance, and other branches of Yugoslav economy which was controlled by foreign capital, the latter could not fail to exercise political influence in the country. It was known that acquisition of mining concessions, securing of delivery contracts with the state, and tax and exchange controls were often tainted with graft, and it may be assumed that foreign interests were not less active than domestic interests in evading the letter of the law.

Many foreign companies had accumulated large surpluses which for purposes of judging their capital strength should be added to their share capital. Since surpluses in domestically owned corporations were much smaller, the relative capital strength of foreign-owned corporations should be higher than indicated. Moreover, in many corporations foreign investors owned only a part of the capital, but often exercised greater influence than corresponded to their share capital. Thus a part of the domestically owned corporate resources was actually foreign-controlled, increasing the general influence of foreign investors.

The significant change in Yugoslav foreign investments from 1937 to 1940 was the increase in the share actually controlled by Germany (reflected partly in table 5) . With the *Anschluss* of Austria, Germany acquired all Austrian holdings, and with the dismemberment of Czechoslovakia obtained effective control of, if not always title to, the holdings of that country. Finally, after the conquest of France and the Low Countries, Germany acquired from France half of the capital of the Bor mines, and from Belgium a large share in the capital of the Trifail coal mines in Slovenia. The Germans also acquired from these two countries the controlling interest in one of the leading Yugoslav banks, the General Banking Corporation, in which they had previously had a hand through the Vienna Kreditanstalt-Bankverein. The reorganized bank, which after the dismemberment of Yugoslavia was split into a Croatian and a Serbian branch, became the spearhead and focal point of German financial control of Yugoslavia during the occupation.

Foreign interests exercised a large measure of control of Yugoslav economy through cartels. The degree of cartelization was much higher among the firms within the sphere of influence of foreign capital than among firms of purely domestic ownership. Of about eighty cartels operating in Yugoslavia in 1939, perhaps one-fourth to one-third were of an international character. Especially hard on Yugoslav interests were the cartel arrangements forced upon them by German concerns in 1938 and 1939.

The hold of foreign capital on the economy of Yugoslavia in the interwar period was supplemented by several other factors. Yugoslavia had to import all machinery from abroad and was dependent on foreign firms for spare parts, production processes, and patents. Besides, the leading technicians in firms of foreign capital and in many domestically owned firms were foreigners. Foreign ownership, influence, and control gave the economy of prewar Yugoslavia a semicolonial character which, naturally, was resented by many domestic firms.

Yet domestic capital was lacking and foreign investments were indispensable. Indeed, it is hard to imagine what the condition of the Yugoslav economy would have been in 1940 without the foreign investments of the past sixty or seventy years. Foreign capital was perhaps the most dynamic force in the development of Yugoslav transport facilities, mining, and industry. But Yugoslavia has had to pay a high price for the services of foreign capital. All government loans were obtained at very high interest rates, subscription prices were always well below par, and it was necessary to pay substantial commissions. It was also necessary to accept a degree of foreign financial control within the country (e.g., representatives of foreign creditors in the Administration of State Monopolies), but these controls were less rigorous than in some neighboring countries (Greece, Bulgaria, and Rumania).

Large sums are still unpaid, and it is impossible to predict the total burden of these loans on the national economy. It was evident before the war, however, that the state's foreign obligations must be adjusted to the ability of the country to pay. The damage caused by the war has, of course, greatly increased the necessity of adjustment.

Judging from the profits derived by most foreign companies in Yugoslavia, there can be little doubt that the price paid to private foreign investors for their services was too high. Nor can the cost be measured in terms of dividends alone. Part of the toll was taken in unsystematic development of the country's natural resources. Foreign investors pursued the most profitable and least risky enterprises, without respect as to how their exploitation would affect the general development of the nation's economy. The exploitation of forests, for example, was highly uneconomical, and farming in the neighborhood of the Bor mines was impaired. Foreign capital kept the country producing raw materials and semifinished products, and it was difficult to persuade foreign investors to develop facilities for production of finished products. This, of course, reduced the country's possibilities of utilizing its labor.

The import of foreign capital and the price for its services must be related, in the last analysis, to the problem of agrarian overpopulation as the basic economic and social issue in the country. Foreign capital did not and could not solve the problem, but it made an important contribution in reducing the pressure of over-population in the interwar period. Actually, most of the new industrial capacity and a large proportion of railroad building was financed by foreign capital. It not only created new jobs in its own establishments but stimulated the creation of new jobs or the improvement of old jobs throughout the entire national economy. It is true that low wages were an inducement for the influx of foreign capital into Yugoslavia and contributed to its large profits, but had there been no influx of foreign capital, the pressure on the labor market would have been still stronger and the wage level lower. Thus, in spite of the too-high price that Yugoslavia paid for the services of foreign capital, it seems to the author that its influx was not only necessary but advantageous. Nevertheless, it was quite clear before the Second World War that the conditions under which foreign capital is permitted to operate in Yugoslavia should be thoroughly revised.

Estimates of the balance of payments exist only for the period 1926–1936.[9] With the exception of data on foreign trade, movements of gold, postal service accounts, railroad transit accounts, and government receipts from loans and payments of debts and interest, the data are only general estimates, albeit official. To show the composition of the balance of payments, the latest estimate by Obradović is given. (See table 6, overleaf.)

The most important characteristic of the Yugoslav balance of payments is the share represented by foreign trade. With the exception of the first postwar years and the later 1920's, when the country obtained large sums of foreign capital, the balance of trade always showed an export surplus. This surplus, however, was not nearly large enough to cover current foreign obligations of the government and of private trade and industry. Emigrants' remittances were a steady favorable item in the balance of payments. Postal services, railway transit, and shipping accounts have regularly shown favorable balances, and tourist trade began to do so in 1932. But for insurance premiums and trade commissions the balance has always been unfavorable.

The most important unfavorable items in the Yugoslav balance of payments were the debts and interest service, reflecting a relatively large foreign public debt. Foreign investments in private

## TABLE 6
### BALANCE OF PAYMENTS FOR 1936
(Dinars)

| Accounts | Receipts | Payments | Balance |
|---|---|---|---|
| Current items: | | | |
| Merchandise trade | D. 4,376,000,000 | D. 3,983,000,000 | +D. 393,000,000 |
| Smuggling and corrections | 161,000,000 | 186,000,000 | − 25,000,000 |
| Emigrant's remittances | 264,000,000 | 16,000,000 | + 248,000,000 |
| Tourist trade | 342,000,000 | 163,000,000 | + 179,000,000 |
| Shipping | 124,000,000 | 68,000,000 | + 56,000,000 |
| Railroad freight | 184,000,000 | 7,000,000 | + 177,000,000 |
| Insurance and commissions | 45,000,000 | 79,000,000 | − 34,000,000 |
| Postal services | 26,000,000 | 16,000,000 | + 10,000,000 |
| Diplomatic and consular services | 80,000,000 | 67,000,000 | + 13,000,000 |
| Miscellaneous services | 1,000,000 | 27,000,000 | − 26,000,000 |
| State debt and interest payments | | 729,000,000 | − 729,000,000 |
| Interest and dividends | | 131,000,000 | − 131,000,000 |
| Gold movements | | 9,000,000 | − 9,000,000 |
| Capital movements: | | | |
| Short-term credits | 253,000,000 | 232,000,000 | + 21,000,000 |
| Unexplained items | | | − 143,000,000 |

industry necessitated large payments abroad for dividends and interest as well. When the international credit mechanism is functioning normally, unfavorable balances in current accounts are met by foreign credits, as in the latter half of the 1920's. When the international credit mechanism broke down, in 1930 and 1931, the balancing of accounts required, besides the capital imports of those two years, the use of a large portion of the country's foreign-exchange reserves.

But when the release of foreign exchange became impossible because of the exhaustion of reserves, as was true during the Great Depression, the government was forced to invoke a transfer moratorium for foreign debts, interest obligations, and dividend payments. Thus government payments on interest and debts amounted to D. 1,124,000,000 in 1931 and were reduced to D. 234,000,000 in 1933. The payment of interest and dividends by private enterprises was reduced from D. 514,000,000 in 1931 to only D. 50,000,000 in 1933. But this again meant balancing of the accounts by foreign credits, in this instance of a forced nature.

*Predepression trade policies.*—The basic aim of Yugoslav economic policy in the interwar period was to reinforce the newly acquired political independence by strengthening the economy of the country. In order to achieve this, Yugoslavia was to be made less dependent on imports of industrial products; the financial tutelage of former enemy countries was to be curbed; and the role of foreign intermediaries in its economic intercourse with the outside world was to be reduced. The most essential tasks were development of domestic industry with the aid of a protective tariff, conclusion of favorable trade treaties, and attraction of foreign capital from friendly countries.

With a few exceptions (tobacco, salt, wheat since 1931, opium), foreign trade throughout the interwar period was in the hands of private initiative but was subject to increasing government regulation. Since 1918, except for a few months after the legal stabilization of the dinar in June, 1931, Yugoslavia has maintained a more or less strict control of foreign exchange. Exporters were required to bring into the country all the proceeds of their sales abroad and to offer a part of the proceeds (25 per cent in prosperous times and up to 80 per cent during the Great Depression) to the

National Bank at the official exchange rates. After 1932 official rates were never in agreement with the free market rates. The importers had to "justify" their demand for foreign exchange with the National Bank before effecting payments abroad. It is necessary to emphasize, however, that up to 1936 foreign-exchange control and clearing arrangements were considered by Yugoslav authorities exclusively as measures in defense of the currency and not as measures to regulate the composition and direction of foreign trade. Of course these arrangements greatly influenced both the size and the regional distribution of foreign trade.

Between 1918 and 1925 the Serbian tariff of 1904 was in force, but modified to account for the depreciation of the currency, to give greater protection to domestic producers, and to furnish revenue. The prewar tariff rate expressed in gold dinars was adjusted by adding a premium which rose gradually from 40 per cent in April, 1920, to 1,100 per cent in June, 1925. The successive increases in the premium increased the over-all protection of imports (customs revenue as related to the value of total imports) between 1919 and 1924 in the following percentages: 2.3, 4.6, 10.4, 11.8, 13.0, and 14.0.[10]

The new tariff introduced in June, 1925, was an expression of the industrial protectionism on which Yugoslavia had embarked. Technically it was built on dual rates—maximum rates for countries with which no trade agreements existed and minimum or treaty rates for countries with trade agreements. This was a common instrument for bargaining purposes. Again rates were defined in pre-1914 gold dinars, to which was added a premium amounting to 1,000 per cent between 1925 and 1936 and increased to 1,300 per cent in 1937. The principle of the most-favored-nation clause was the basis of the new tariff policy and was guaranteed in all trade agreements. The first trade agreement was concluded with Italy in July, 1924, followed by agreements with Austria, Bulgaria, Germany, Greece, and Great Britain. The pre-1914 Serbian trade agreements with the United States, Switzerland, and Portugal were continued.

The protection of domestic industry on the basis of the new Yugoslav tariff was among the highest in Europe. Relating the customs revenue to the value of all imports, protection fluctuated in the period 1926–1938 from 18.4 to 25.9 per cent, according to the composition and origin of imports and the rate of premium. But what is most significant is the rate of protection of individual industries. The approximate rate of protection of a number of commodities, in percentage of their estimated costs of production in Yugoslavia, is given in the accompanying table.[11]

| Commodity | Up to 1925 | 1925–1938 | |
|---|---|---|---|
| | | Under maximum rates | Under treaty rates |
| Sugar | 80 | 110 | 80 |
| Beer | .... | 208 | 59 |
| Canned meat | 71 | 167 | 57 |
| Calcium cyanamid | 430 | 509 | .... |
| Copper sulfate | 5 | 53 | 51 |
| Gasoline | 14 | 57 | .... |
| Laundry soap | 55 | 134 | .... |
| Men's shoes | 50 | 69 | .... |
| Cotton yarn no. 12 | 20 | 24 | 20 |
| Woolen yarn to no. 16 | 27 | 28 | 19 |
| Stockings | 62 | 117 | 88 |
| Steel | 51 | 91 | 50 |
| Steel constructions | 20 | 50 | .... |
| Plows | .... | 50 | 25 |
| Wire | 45 | 81 | 57 |
| Writing paper | 63 | 171 | 60 |

Such a degree of protection made the importation of most of these products impossible, and the consumer had to buy domestic goods, which, besides being much higher in price than foreign products (without the import duty), were often of inferior quality. For some items (e.g., plows) the difference in quality was so great that farmers were willing to pay the import duty to obtain foreign plows of well-known makes. The 1925 tariff was steadily modified by the binding of individual rates in new trade treaties, changes in definitions of products so that imports could be favored from one country and made more difficult from others, and lowering or increasing of individual rates.

There are two basic issues in respect to Yugoslav industrial protectionism: Was it necessary, and why? Who carried its burden

and reaped its fruits? The answer to the first lies in the economic
and political structure and conditions of the country. Yugoslavia
wanted to increase its military potential, and to achieve this it had
to develop its industry. Its agrarian overpopulation could be
alleviated only by reducing the number of people depending on
agriculture for their livelihood. Industrialization was the principal means of employing surplus labor, and development of
industry was impossible without tariff protection of infant industries. The basic need of the economy was to increase the productivity of labor, which was impossible without developing industry.

The question, indeed, was not whether to industrialize but what
industries to develop, at what speed to push the process of industrialization, and how to distribute its burden and its benefits.
Undoubtedly, too little attention was paid to these problems.
Industry developed in various parts of Yugoslavia under different
economic and political conditions up to 1918 and continued thereafter without sufficient consideration of the changed conditions.
In the textile industry, for example, profit considerations resulted
in a much larger development of weaving mills in relation to
spinning-mill capacity. Production of agricultural machinery and
implements was adversely affected by disparity between agricultural and industrial prices, which was accentuated by cartel
arrangements among producers, though the necessary increase in
the supply of agricultural machinery could have been stimulated
by government subsidy and prohibition of cartels. Cartel arrangements boosted the price of artificial fertilizers to a point where
domestic agriculture was virtually unable to use them, and substantial quantities of fertilizer were exported.

The rate of industrialization in the interwar period was too
slow to relieve markedly the pressure of agricultural overpopulation.[12] This was due not to lack of tariff protection but to dearth
of capital, lack of skilled management and labor, and lack of
effective demand for products of many potential Yugoslav industries. Scarcity of capital for industrial purposes was aggravated by
the fact that residential housing absorbed an altogether dispro-
portionate share of current domestic savings. Whereas investment
by private enterprises in processing industries was estimated for
1938 at D. 42,000,000, the contractors' estimate of the value of

private housing under construction in the same year, in the seventeen most important cities of Yugoslavia,[13] was D. 1,020,000,000. One of the basic reasons for so large an investment in housing was its heavy subsidization through exceptionally low taxation of rental income.

Both industrialization and general economic advancement were seriously retarded in the interwar period by heavy expenditures for military purposes, which sapped the economic strength of the country. There are no reliable estimates of military expenditures in the interwar period, since some items were disguised or secret, but it seems safe to assume that from 1919 to April, 1941, they reached a total of between D. 70,000,000,000 and D. 80,000,000,-000. The significance of this figure can best be appraised if it is compared with the national income of D. 46,800,000,000 in 1938 and the value D. 13,100,000,000 for all existing industrial developments in the same year.

The burden of industrialization was carried by consumers in the form of high prices and by wage earners in the form of low wages. Since most of the protected industries were in the field of mass consumption, the burden fell heaviest on low-income consumers. The cost of tariff protection was increased by cartel agreements among producers (possible only because of the existence of the tariff) which further increased the prices of industrial products. The benefits of industrialization, on the other hand, were reaped in the interwar period essentially by owners of protected industries, a large proportion of whom were foreign investors. Though the burden of industrialization is always carried by consumers and wage earners, a more sensible price and taxation policy could have prevented the one-sided utilization of its benefits.

In view of the structure of the Yugoslav economy and the nature of economic policies throughout the world in the interwar period, industrial protectionism was the only possible policy for Yugoslavia. In spite of the burden that it entailed, the present industrial capacity of the country is primarily a result of this policy and constitutes a basis for further industrialization.

For several years after the First World War there was a great demand in Yugoslavia for manufactured goods and textiles, and both had to be imported. Between 1919 and 1923 its total exports were only D. 16,208,000,000 as against imports of D. 25,322,000,000, leaving an import surplus of D. 9,114,000,000, most of which was covered by emigrants' remittances. The unfavorable Yugoslav balance of payments and the need to finance a large proportion of state expenditures through the issue of bank notes reduced the purchasing power of the currency and its exchange rate.[14] But this stimulated exports, and by 1923 their value almost equaled that of imports. The country experienced intensive industrial activity. However, the policy of deflation and of intervention in support of the dinar abroad increased its value between August, 1923, and August, 1925, by 57 per cent. The consequences were grave for many newly established industrial enterprises and for the competitive power of the country on the world market. Owing to an increase in the export of agricultural products, timber, and ores, and a reduction in the value of textile imports, the balance of trade in 1924 for the first time showed a large export surplus of D. 1,309,000,000. The bumper crops of corn in 1924 and 1925 and of wheat in 1925 had a salutary influence on foreign trade and on the balance of payments in those two years, and helped to strengthen and stabilize the currency. For a number of years favorable terms of trade continued, primarily owing to the fact that the price relationship between Yugoslav exports (agricultural products) and imports (industrial products) was favorable.

It was in 1925 and 1926 that Yugoslavia began to feel the damaging effects of the competition of overseas agricultural products on the markets of the central European industrial countries. In 1927 Yugoslavia and the other Danubian countries began to plead for tariff preferences for their agricultural products, especially grains, in central European importing countries. But these pleas remained unanswered. Large imports of capital and satisfactory industrial activity temporarily overshadowed the development of a great agricultural crisis and the increasingly precarious position of the credit structure of the country. Withdrawal of short-term credits from central and southeastern Europe, beginning in 1929, put great strain on the economy of central and southeastern Europe. The collapse of the Vienna Kreditanstalt in May, 1931, signified a veritable breakdown in the financial and economic structure of the whole area. The crisis was made more acute by the German banking crisis of July, 1931, and the abandonment of the gold standard by Great Britain in September, 1931.

*The Great Depression and foreign economic policies.*—The extent of the economic breakdown in Yugoslavia during the depression and the slow process of recovery after 1935 is shown in table 7. Owing partly to the fall in prices, partly to decreased industrial production, national income fell from an estimated D. 42,000,000,000 in 1931 (already reduced in comparison with previous years, for which no comparable estimates exist) to about D. 30,000,000,000 in 1933, rising in 1938 to D. 46,800,000,000.

Prices began to fall in 1929; the general price index reached bottom in 1934, losing 37 per cent in comparison with 1926 and 1929. The index of agricultural prices rose faster than that of industrial prices between 1926 and 1928, but the former experienced a greater and more rapid decline, especially in 1933 and 1934. The value of foreign trade reached its lowest level in 1932, when it amounted to only 38.7 per cent of the 1929 value. It recuperated slowly thereafter, but never reached the predepression level.

Bank-note circulation fell from D. 5,800,000,000 in 1929 to D. 4,300,000,000 in 1933, but the deflationary pressure was greatly increased by the contraction of the credit volume of commercial banks, reduced velocity of circulation, reduced government spending, cessation of the influx of foreign capital, and flight of domestic capital.

The banking crisis, during which more than half of the banks with 48 per cent of the total share capital were put under a moratorium, is clearly shown by the decline of savings deposits in commercial banks. More than 50 per cent of all remaining deposits were frozen. The extremely important function of commercial banking in crediting industry and trade was lost to the economy. The role of government banks greatly increased, but savings which flowed into them were almost exclusively loaned to the government. The banking crisis was caused partly by a moratorium on peasant debts that made it impossible for agriculture to obtain credit after 1932.

The government tax revenue fell, between 1929 and 1932, by 26 per cent, in spite of the fact that in the meantime a general

# TABLE 7

## Basic Data on Economic Developments in Yugoslavia, 1926–1940
### (Indices: 1926=100; other columns in billions of dinars)

| Year | Estimated national income* | Wholesale price indices† | | | Foreign trade | | Bank-note circulation | Savings deposits in commercial banks | State tax revenue‡ | Indices for government bonds§ |
| --- | --- | --- | --- | --- | --- | --- | --- | --- | --- | --- |
| | | General | Agricultural products | Industrial products | Exports | Imports | | | | |
| 1926......... | ......... | 100.0 | 100.0 | 100.0 | D. 7.8 | D. 7.6 | D. 5.8 | D. 7.5 | D. 8.1 | 100.0 |
| 1927......... | ......... | 102.6 | 112.4 | 99.3 | 6.4 | 7.3 | 5.7 | 7.6 | 7.8 | 117.5 |
| 1928......... | ......... | 106.2 | 130.1 | 98.0 | 6.4 | 7.8 | 5.5 | 8.4 | 7.4 | 142.3 |
| 1929......... | ......... | 100.6 | 118.6 | 92.6 | 7.9 | 7.6 | 5.8 | 9.3 | 8.5 | 136.9 |
| 1930......... | ......... | 86.6 | 89.3 | 80.3 | 6.8 | 7.0 | 5.4 | 10.3 | 8.1 | 143.0 |
| 1931......... | D. 42.0 | 72.9 | 74.3 | 71.4 | 4.8 | 4.8 | 5.2 | 8.8 | 6.9 | 122.8 |
| 1932......... | 30.0 | 65.2 | 67.5 | 66.2 | 3.1 | 2.9 | 4.8 | 6.7 | 6.3 | 67.6 |
| 1933......... | ......... | 64.4 | 57.2 | 70.8 | 3.4 | 2.9 | 4.3 | 6.4 | 6.4 | 72.6 |
| 1934......... | ......... | 63.2 | 57.4 | 67.4 | 3.9 | 3.6 | 4.4 | 5.4 | 6.6 | 104.6 |
| 1935......... | 37.6 | 65.9 | 68.2 | 66.7 | 4.0 | 3.7 | 4.9 | 6.1 | 6.7 | 120.0 |
| 1936......... | 42.2 | 68.4 | 69.7 | 69.7 | 4.4 | 4.1 | 5.4 | 6.1 | 7.2 | 118.7 |
| 1937......... | 44.1 | 74.7 | 74.1 | 77.6 | 6.3 | 5.2 | 5.8 | 6.4 | 8.0 | 132.8 |
| 1938......... | 46.8 | 78.3 | 85.8 | 78.2 | 5.0 | 5.0 | 6.9 | 6.4 | 8.4 | 153.1 |
| 1939......... | ......... | 79.3 | 82.5 | 79.8 | 5.5 | 4.8 | 9.7 | 5.6 | 8.6 | 147.0 |
| 1940......... | ......... | 114.1 | 137.4 | 110.5 | 6.7 | 6.0 | 13.8 | 5.6 | ......... | 141.3 |

Sources: Yugoslavia, *Annuaire statistique*, 1931, 1936, 1938–1939; National Bank of Yugoslavia, *Quarterly Bulletin*, No. 4, 1932; No. 4, 1936; *L'Activité économique en Yougoslavie*, January, 1941.   * Official estimates of the Ministry of Finance.   † Indices of the National Bank of Yugoslavia.
‡ Budget year April 1 to March 31.   § Indices of the most representative state bond, the 2.5 per cent bond for war damages

rise in tax rates took place. The development of state credit during the depression is shown, in the last column of table 7, in the price indices for the most representative state bond. State bonds were for several years refused as collateral for loans even by state banks. Receipts from reparations were stopped in the middle of 1931. The influx of emigrants' remittances was reduced to a fraction of its volume before the depression.

The cumulative effect of these developments was a crisis which enveloped the economic and financial life of the entire country. It lasted in a severe form until 1935, and in some branches—for example, in commercial banking—until 1941.

This course of events had great influence on Yugoslav economic relations with the outside world. Being fully under the domination of French thinking up to 1935, the government maintained a deflationary policy, trying desperately to balance the budget and especially to save the currency. Exchange controls and clearing agreements were at first aimed exclusively at preservation of the currency. But large, more or less concealed budget deficits became common. In spite of strict exchange control and the fact that approximately three-fourths of foreign trade developed under clearing, the dinar depreciated about one-third. This could not be prevented, even by a transfer moratorium on amortization and interest service on foreign public and private debts.

From the point of view of foreign economic relations, the drop in exports and in prices of export products was the most damaging factor. In the Yugoslav economy the maintenance of exports, especially of agricultural products, and a satisfactory level of agricultural prices, which depend mainly on the extent and prospects of exportable surpluses, are basic preconditions of economic prosperity, for they control the purchasing power of a large part of the population. When exports and agricultural prices cannot be maintained at a satisfactory level, all other measures of recovery—public works, housing booms, reduction in interest rates—are without avail, since they affect only a small part of the national economy.

The drive for tariff preferences for grains, which was discussed at several international conferences (Geneva, Stresa), seemed to promise success. In 1931 Yugoslavia succeeded in concluding agreements with Czechoslovakia, Austria, and France on preferential

treatment of its wheat. The French concession could not be utilized, however, and the Czech and Austrian concessions were only
slightly utilized in 1932 and 1933. But the government was bent
on helping the wheat producers, and in 1931 introduced a state
monopoly both for exports and domestic trade in wheat. The latter
feature was soon abolished, but export of wheat remained in government hands. In 1931 the government tried to maintain the
internal price of wheat on the farm at D. 160 per 100 kg., whereas
the Liverpool parity was only D. 60 per 100 kg. The inability
of the government to finance the difference between the fixed and
the world market price and to store the wheat properly, as well
as the extensive corruption involved, soon resulted in the collapse
of the whole scheme and a loss of D. 450,000,000, which was later
shifted to domestic consumers in the form of a special tax on flour
and bread.

The wheat-export monopoly was the only major measure which
the government undertook in support of the export trade. Since
it ended in failure, the government abstained for years from similar
interference with international trade. Licensing of livestock exports in 1932 and thereafter was devised only to prevent bunching
of deliveries to the terminal markets of states—especially Czechoslovakia and Austria—which granted livestock export quotas to
Yugoslavia. In the 1930's Yugoslavia showed little initiative in its
trade policies, which consisted primarily in dancing to the tunes
played by its chief trade partners, particularly Germany.

One of the greatest obstacles to the export of agricultural products from southeastern Europe in the 1930's was the forced re-
agrarization of European industrial countries that reduced their
import needs for grains, meat, dairy products, and fats, and greatly
limited the natural outlets for these products from southeastern
Europe. Ever since the unsuccessful plan for a German-Austrian
customs union in 1931, plans for economic assistance to the Danubian countries have had the character of diplomatic horse trading
among the Great Powers. France was trying to preserve its political
influence in this area without sacrificing its short-run domestic
economic interest. It was willing to help financially, but the Danu
bian countries needed not only credits but, most of all, foreign
markets and better prices for their products. Germany and Italy

also, were trying to increase their political and economic influence in the area. Yugoslavia concluded a far-reaching preference agreement with Germany in May, 1934. In the Italian market Hungary and Austria, until 1937, had preferred positions for timber and livestock in relation to Yugoslavia.

In 1932 and thereafter the trade of central and southeastern Europe was characterized by bilateral arrangements on exchange of goods, exchange rates, and methods of payment. Yugoslavia concluded its first clearing agreement with Austria in January, 1932; and, in the same year, agreements with Belgium, Switzerland, Czechoslovakia, Germany, Italy, and Greece. In 1933 came agreements with France and Brazil; in 1934, with Turkey, Bulgaria, Rumania, Hungary, and Poland; and in 1936, with Spain. In some instances (Greece, France, Switzerland, Spain), payments for Yugoslav exports were made partly in free exchange, usually 20 per cent. The share of Yugoslav exports and imports, under the clearing regime from 1934 to 1939, averaged 75.6 per cent and 73.3 per cent, respectively.

Except for Germany, which developed the clearing mechanism into a fearful weapon of economic aggression, clearing was the factor chiefly responsible for reducing Yugoslav foreign trade with most of its trade partners. Trade between two countries under a clearing regime tends to balance off at the level of imports of the country which imports less. The basic predicament of Yugoslav trade policy, however, was that, although Yugoslavia had great difficulty in importing enough commodities to rescue its favorable balances in clearing accounts with Greece, Italy, Spain, and above all with Germany, it lacked foreign exchange to pay for goods imported from countries with which it had no clearing agreements, but with which it had an import surplus—namely, the Netherlands, Great Britain, British India, and Argentina. These supplied such key imports as industrial fats, raw cotton, wool, hides, and machinery. The export surplus in 1935 to Germany, Italy, and Austria amounted to D. 590,000,000 and the import surplus from Great Britain, India, Japan, Argentina, and Brazil to D. 375,000,000.

The international flow of capital being at a minimum, bilateralism rampant, and the possibilities of multilateral adjustment of accounts extremely limited, Yugoslavia was forced to inaugurate a policy of increasing imports from clearing countries with which it had a favorable balance of trade, and of reducing imports from non-clearing countries with which it had unfavorable balances in trade, and had to pay for them in free exchange.

*Economic strangulation by Germany.*—The chief problem of Yugoslav foreign trade from 1934 to 1941 was the increasing importance of Germany as customer and supplier. Yugoslavia had had a consistently unfavorable trade balance with Germany, amounting to D. 3,150,000,000, from 1923 to 1932. By foreign-exchange control Yugoslavia blocked about D. 500,000,000 of German balances in 1932. To utilize these balances Germany began to buy large amounts of corn, wheat, lard, and meat, part of which it sold on the world market for free exchange. The Yugoslav trade balance with Germany in 1933 became favorable and so continued as a result of deliberate German policy.

In the same year Germany abrogated the existing trade treaty and a new one was concluded in May, 1934, which, with implementations, regulated trade relations for the next six years. Yugoslavia granted most-favored-nation treatment to Germany for medical supplies and chemicals and bound a number of tariff rates, but received in return fixed export quotas for wheat, corn, livestock, meat, prunes, and timber. Since Germany had price controls for most of these products, the Yugoslav Chartered Corporation for the Export of Agricultural Products (Prizad) concluded special price agreements with various German control boards. Germany granted prices that were above those prevailing on the world market. Thereafter the trade position was reviewed every six months by a standing German-Yugoslav committee, which adjusted export and import quotas, exchange rates, and payment procedures.

The trade agreement of 1934 heralded the beginning of a period of greatly intensified trade relations between the two countries. Undoubtedly there was a political affinity between the Nazi regime and the military-fascist dictatorship of Yugoslavia, particularly under Premier Stojadinović, but there can be little doubt that Yugoslavia was forced into the German economic orbit by circumstances beyond its control, namely, by its economic plight and the unwillingness of France and Great Britain to give effective economic support. It is enough to glance at the figures for 1933 and

1934 in table 7—remembering that this was still at the beginning of the German New Plan, before German rapacity became evident—to realize how advantageous, from a purely economic point of view, the large export quotas and guaranteed prices must have seemed to the Yugoslavs. But they soon discovered that the apparent German concessions were only a means of economic warfare, which, in turn, was part of a general plan for total political and military domination of the country.

One of the chief factors which helped to push Yugoslavia completely into the German economic orbit was the application of

| Country | Average, 1933–1935 | | 1936 | | 1937 | |
|---|---|---|---|---|---|---|
| | Exports to | Imports from | Exports to | Imports from | Exports to | Imports from |
| Italy...................... | D. 731.8 | D. 461.5 | D. 137.2 | D. 101.7 | D. 587.1 | D. 429.8 |
| France.................. | 62.8 | 153.1 | 86.2 | 101.3 | 393.3 | 90.8 |
| Great Britain...... | 161.1 | 328.4 | 431.7 | 346.9 | 464.6 | 409.1 |
| Germany.............. | 606.6 | 491.5 | 1,039.1 | 1,087.6 | 1,361.3 | 1,694.4 |

economic sanctions against Italy from November, 1935, to September, 1936, which proved to be a great blow to Yugoslav economy. This development is illustrated in the accompanying table, in millions of dinars.

The value of Yugoslav exports to Italy from 1933 to 1935 averaged D. 731,800,000; the value of imports from Italy averaged D. 461,500,000, showing a substantial balance in favor of Yugoslavia. Exports to Italy in 1936 dropped to a bare D. 137,200,000 and imports from Italy to D. 101,700,000. Besides, Yugoslavia lost the largest market for one of its important export products, soft timber. The special compensatory increase of imports by Great Britain and Czechoslovakia to help Yugoslavia over the difficulties caused by application of sanctions was sizable, but it was not adequate to relieve Yugoslavia's trade difficulties. France offered no help to Yugoslavia. On the other hand, exports to Germany rose from an average of D. 606,600,000 in the period 1933–1935 to D. 1,039,100,000 in 1936, and imports from Germany advanced from D. 491,500,000 to D. 1,087,600,000. In 1937 exports to Italy were, in the main, restored, and there was a temporary large jump in exports to France (wheat valued at D. 250,000,000). Exports to

Great Britain increased very little in 1937. But exports to Germany rose by another 31 per cent and imports from Germany by about 56 per cent. The consequences of sanctions against Italy were felt even in 1938, the chief problem being the realization of favorable clearing balances. By increasing the imports from Italy in 1938 and by deliberately failing to fulfill the agreed export quotas, these balances were eliminated in February, 1939.

In June, 1936, during the period of sanctions against Italy, the government published a list of commodities the import of which was permitted from non-clearing countries only when licensed by the National Bank. It covered about one-third of the imports from non-clearing countries, including rice, coffee, cotton, cotton thread, woolen and silk goods, tires, typewriters, sewing machines, dynamos, electric motors, radios, automobiles, and electric-light bulbs. In 1937 and 1938 the list was enlarged and by the end of 1938 it included commodities representing four-fifths of the imports from non-clearing countries. This brought about a turning point in Yugoslav commercial policy because it introduced a partial control of imports from non-clearing countries and signified entry into still closer economic relations with Nazi Germany. But the move was unavoidable.

There is no need to review the well-known techniques of German trade aggression. It suffices to say that Germany's basic principle was to import from its victims as much as possible, leaving them the worry of how and when to balance trade accounts. To induce its partners to export to Germany in spite of the difficulties of obtaining the countervalue of the exports, the Nazi government was prepared to pay for many products prices higher than those prevailing on the world market. The resulting blocked balances, which actually constituted large commodity credits to Germany, were then used to blackmail the partners into further concessions and into directing their whole economy according to the needs of the German market. Thus, in spite of the fact that the Yugoslavs experienced great difficulties in rescuing blocked balances in Germany, the German share in Yugoslav foreign trade steadily increased. At the end of 1935 Yugoslav blocked balances in Germany amounted to about D. 400,000,000. At that time Yugoslav exporters had to wait exactly ten months to cash their export bills to Ger many. This meant a loss of interest on their capital and great difficulty in financing their own business.

To relieve their predicament, the National Bank began to grant credits, using these clearing balances as collateral. But the scheme did not work, and in January, 1936, the Bank started to issue the so-called "clearing mark checks" against the blocked balances. The large supply of blocked marks on the market resulted in a depreciation of the mark, which at times (e.g., in May, 1936) amounted to 22 per cent. The Germans tolerated the depreciation of the mark on the Yugoslav market, but they did not recognize it officially until 1938.

The mobilization of blocked mark balances through the National Bank had a tendency to increase bank-note circulation and prices, thereby lessening the competitive power of Yugoslav products on other markets. As the boom in trade with Germany advanced, the terms of trade shifted against Yugoslavia: it often had to take goods which it did not particularly need; prices of German products were rising; and quality of goods was steadily deteriorating. Thus the advantages received by Yugoslavia in the form of higher prices for many of its exports to Germany were wiped out.

In spite of the depreciation of the mark, which was an inducement to increase imports from Germany, blocked balances could not be liquidated through the normal processes of trade. Germany lacked many products in which Yugoslav importers were vitally interested, such as textile raw materials, industrial fats, and heavy hides, and made the export of other essential products difficult. To reduce the amount of blocked balances the government had to step into the breach on several occasions by buying war materials and industrial installations for the infant heavy industries.

The French[15] and British policy of appeasing the Axis made economic aggression in southeastern Europe much easier for the Germans: the entire area was at their mercy. The Yugoslavs tried to lessen the German grip on their trade by proclaiming a policy of exporting to Germany only as much as Yugoslavia could profitably import from Germany (about 25 per cent of the total foreign trade), but this principle could not be followed, since for a large number of products the choice was between export to Germany or no export at all. The Yugoslavs succeeded for some time in obtaining from Germany payment in free exchange for copper, railroad ties, hemp, and other products in which the Yugoslav competitive position was strong, but the endeavor to obtain free exchange for other products proved futile: the Germans countered all such moves by asking payment in free exchange for their key exports to Yugoslavia.

The increasing German influence on Yugoslav trade, internal economy, and politics from the beginning of 1938 was closely related to German expansionist moves. The *Anschluss* of Austria in March, 1938, was a great blow to Yugoslavia economically and politically. In 1937 the German share in Yugoslav exports was 36 per cent and in imports 32.5 per cent, but in 1938, with the inclusion of Austria, it advanced to 42 per cent and 39.5 per cent, respectively. Besides acquiring the tariff concessions formerly given to Austria and increasing its own bargaining power, Germany took over all Austrian-controlled investments in Yugoslavia. The *Anschluss* intensified the danger of war, with grave consequences for Yugoslav economic life; new outlays for national defense greatly increased the financial burden of the nation.

The dismemberment of Czechoslovakia in September, 1938, and March, 1939, showed clearly that the days of all small neighbors of Germany were numbered and that war was imminent. It meant the destruction of one of the most efficient of European military machines, to which the Yugoslav army was closely tied. It also meant that the two most important sources of armament for the Yugoslav army, the Škoda and the Brno armament works, were taken over by the Germans.

The economic consequences of the partition of Czechoslovakia were even more serious than those of the Austrian *Anschluss*. First, Germany acquired all the tariff concessions which were formerly granted to Czechoslovakia without giving reciprocal advantages to Yugoslavia. Second, Czechoslovakia was one of the four most important markets for Yugoslav export products, and in turn supplied Yugoslavia with a number of its key imports, especially cotton and woolen yarns and coke. Germany now obtained a priority on all Czechoslovak production. Third, Czechoslovakia was one of the chief foreign investors in Yugoslavia, owning several large banks and some of the largest and most important industrial plants producing textiles, shoes, chemicals, and glass. By acquiring either title to, or virtual control over, Czechoslovak investments in Yugoslavia, the German position in the Yugoslav corporate structure was greatly strengthened. After the annexation of Austria and Czechoslovakia, Germany took more than 50 per cent of Yugoslav exports and supplied about 50 per cent of Yugoslav imports.

The outbreak of war in September, 1939, almost completely paralyzed Yugoslavia's economic life. In October a German-Yugoslav trade agreement granted new concessions to Germany, especially greater export quotas of nonferrous metals and of food. Yugoslav consumption of meat, fats, and other essential foods was curtailed, primarily to free larger amounts for export to Germany and Italy. It became impossible for Yugoslavia to import many essential commodities because of blockade, greater demand by the nations at war, higher prices, or lack of foreign exchange.

These difficulties became still greater after the Italian declaration of war on France and Great Britain in June, 1940. Victories in the west helped Germany to increase its share in foreign investments in Yugoslavia through partial acquisition of French, Belgian, and Dutch holdings. In September, 1940, Germany forced Yugoslavia to devaluate its currency in relation to the mark from D. 14.80 to D. 17.82. In the meantime the Yugoslav economy experienced an inflation caused by the financing of large military outlays through the National Bank, a decreased supply of civilian goods on the market, and loss of confidence in the currency.

From 1933 to 1941 Germany not only conducted a trade war on Yugoslavia but subjected it simultaneously to a skillful propaganda campaign and engaged in systematic penetration of its economic life and undermining of its political structure. When in March, 1941, Germany, at the pinnacle of its power, presented Yugoslavia with an ultimatum for total surrender, the fruits of the long-continued German endeavor became evident. The government accepted the ultimatum and joined the Axis, but was overthrown on March 27, and the new government made the surrender void. The decision of the country to defy Hitler, thus upsetting his time schedule for assault upon Soviet Russia, and thereby gaining precious weeks for that country, will remain a bright page in its history.

But the new regime was unable to ward off disaster. Politically the country was without leadership and the state structure was barely kept together. The fifth column permeated the country from the top to the bottom. The Yugoslav people were divided into those who, by siding with the Axis and acting as its mercenaries, sought to preserve or acquire power and wealth, and those who, in enemy occupation and fascism, saw the end of their personal liberty and their national independence and were resolved to fight for them. The country was surrounded by an iron ring: German troops were already in Hungary, Rumania, and Bulgaria, and Italian troops were in Albania. The Yugoslav armaments and war potential were pitifully weak, the army was disorganized, and the fighting spirit in the armed forces was nonexistent. Virtually the entire higher officer corps favored immediate surrender. Economically the tightening German squeeze put the country at the mercy of Germany. Thus the speedy military collapse of Yugoslavia in April, 1941, was inevitable.

*Part Five*

# SOCIAL
# CONDITIONS

# CHAPTER XII

## *Social Structure*

### BY ALEX N. DRAGNICH

IN ORDER TO GAIN a clear understanding of the social structure of the Yugoslav state, the origins of South Slav society and its subsequent evolution must be examined. Two points should be borne in mind: first, Yugoslav society is now and always has been predominantly rural; second, social relations are based primarily on ancient Slavic traditions as modified by the codes of the medieval kings.

The early Slavs who migrated to the Balkan Peninsula were not conquerors; they were peaceful tribes whose social organization included only primary groups determined by blood relationship and common possession of land. For centuries the family was the center of social life. The family, moreover, was a direct expression of economic activity, with strict division of labor and with all members participating in the struggle for existence.

Supplementary institutions grew up among the South Slavs—the extended family (*društvo, družina,* later called *zadruga*), known to German sociologists as *Hauskommunion.* The individual family and the extended family were interrelated: the former was the family proper (father, mother, and children); the latter included indirect blood relatives. In this primitive familial organization one notes a significant principle of social relations: every member contributed his share. Thus equality among its members was made possible and, as a matter of fact, did exist. The father was *primus inter pares,* which is quite different from the Roman idea of *patria potestas.* Ancient South Slav society was neither a caste nor a class organization. Hence social stratification was unknown to it. To a degree, therefore, the South Slavs produced a pure, although primitive, form of social democracy.

The growth of equality and democracy was arrested, however, as social organization was extended. Blood-related *zadruge* merged into tribes, and territorially united tribes tended to create a larger organization, the *župa*. Although the *župa* never played a predominant role in the life of the ancient Slavs, it had a military basis and, consequently, the military hero was most likely to become its leader, or *Župan*. Although representatives of all *zadruge* met in assemblies, or *sabori,* to decide important questions, and thereby retained a fair degree of political democracy, the seed of social stratification had been sown and was to issue full-blown in the juristic recognition of social stratification in the first Serbian state in the eleventh to the fourteenth centuries.

In order to understand the basic transformation of South Slav society in the Middle Ages, it should be noted that the social structure among all the Slavs in the south was substantially the same until the early medieval period. The ancient Slavic background is a heritage of Croat and Serb alike, although some scholars who observe Yugoslav society too superficially have neglected this common social denominator. By the ninth century, however, differences began to develop, chiefly because of the varying influences of Constantinople and of Rome.

In Serbia the force of Byzantium was clearly uppermost. The entire life of Serbia—social, political, and secular—was subjected to a peculiar Byzantine variation of the feudal order. But in Croatia and Slovenia, and in other regions geographically accessible to Western ideas, the Roman influence predominated, and Catholicism took root. Catholic internationalism was thus a link between this section of South Slavs and Western civilization. Before contrasting the two feudal systems it may be well to consider the period preceding their establishment.

The Serbian state of the Middle Ages (from the eleventh century to the second half of the fourteenth century) underwent a transformation from a nonstratified to a stratified social order. Under the Nemanja dynasty and the medieval kings, social stratification was codified. An examination of Tsar Dušan's Code discloses the extent to which class distinctions were formulated. The Serbian

LAKE BLED

OLD TURKISH FORTRESS, KALIMEGDAN PARK, BELGRADE

BRIDGE RECONSTRUCTED AFTER THE LIBERATION

masses remained faithful to their ethnic heritage, but the rising nobility began to discard ancient Slavic traditions and to imitate Byzantine social life—decadent, aristocratic, ceremonial, unproductive, hypocritical; occupied with intrigue, antifeminism, and contempt for the ordinary man. Militarism accompanied the development of this new type of Serbian society. Thus, at the very time it was losing its democratic base, Serbian society gained unity and national feeling. This change resulted both from the necessity of dealing with its enemies and from the influence of the new, independent Serbian Church. Christianity as embodied in the Orthodox Church was intensely nationalistic. It combined ancient Slavic paganism with Byzantine-Christian dogma. It is significant that throughout Serbian history the church was under state control and always supported state political activities.

This intense feeling of unity and nationalism enabled the Serbs to meet the Turkish invasions with some degree of unity and tended to preserve their national consciousness throughout centuries of Turkish domination. It was this sense of national consciousness that explains, in great part, the rise and expression of Serbian nationality long before the Croats even dreamed of freedom and independence.

It is true that in the Middle Ages a state was created among the Croats earlier than among the Serbs. But nationalism and unity were not firmly established among the Croats. When their society lost its democratic foundation it did not gain a compensatory feeling of oneness as did Serbian society. This lack may easily be explained by the fact that Croatian society lacked certain factors which made for national consciousness among the Serbs. The first factor was the church. The Catholic Church, of course, was international. But the Croats did not have an independent church to give them the impetus to national awareness which the Serbian Orthodox Church gave to the Serbians. The second factor had to do with their respective conquerors. The Croats faced stronger and more ruthless enemies. These two elements were mainly accountable for the fact that, at the height of medieval civilization, when the Serbs had national kings, the Croat state was either in personal union with the Hungarian state through the king or under direct Magyar subjugation.

Toward the end of the Middle Ages the influences of the divergent feudal systems were discernible among the South Slavs. In Slovenia, Croatia, Slavonia, and the Vojvodina the typical western European feudal order, embracing the familiar master-serf relationship, prevailed. The denationalized aristocracy made up the master class; the remainder were serfs. For a time, however, parts of Croatia were under the Ottoman variation of the master-serf idea which the Turks imposed upon the Serbs.

Unlike the feudalism of western Europe, that of Turkey had a national and a religious basis. The Mohammedans became the masters and the others were serfs, for to the Turks all Serbs were alike. Their failure to recognize social distinctions among the Serbs signified the end of Serbian medieval castes, and the Serbs slowly drifted back to ancient Slavic traditions of social equality and democracy. The *zadruga,* which had been virtually abolished in the era of Serbian national kings, was renewed on a democratic basis under, but independent of, the Turkish regime.

At first the Turks granted the Serbian peasants a freedom of movement which they had not enjoyed under their own medieval rulers. According to Turkish law, all the land in countries occupied by the Turks belonged to the sultan, who exacted one-tenth (*ushr*) of the agricultural produce of the Serbs and other fixed taxes in money (*resm*). The sultan gave the land to distinguished military leaders (*sipāhī*), but the peasants did not lose by this transaction, for the taxes remained the same. A plot of land was tilled by the same family for generations. The peasant was allowed to sell "his" land and, being ignorant of Turkish law, felt that he was the sole master of it. This belief was enhanced by the fact that, according to Turkish law, peasant houses belonged neither to the sultan nor to the *sipāhī* but to the peasants.

With the rapid decline of the Ottoman Empire toward the end of the eighteenth century and throughout the nineteenth century, certain military groups imposed their own regimes. In Yugoslav areas the janizaries, inadequately paid by the Turkish government, began to force the peasants to sell their land but to continue working on it. Besides the traditional taxes, the peasant—thenceforth called *kmet* (*çiftçi*)—was forced to give a fourth, a fifth, or a ninth of his produce to the new landlords (*çiftlik sahibi*).

As the janizaries' regime grew ever more cruel, the Serbs, sensing the rapid decay of the Empire and inspired by the French Revolution, organized an open rebellion in 1804. Two decades later, feudalism was completely abolished in Serbia, but it continued in Croatia and Slovenia until near the end of the Austro-Hungarian Empire.

The conditions which enabled the Serbs to free themselves from the feudal yoke were not present in Croatia and Slovenia. Western feudalism was not based on national and religious differences; all Croats and Slovenes were not placed on the same level. Discriminations were clearly preserved. The masters (members of the denationalized aristocracy, for the most part) coöperated with the Austrians and the Hungarians. The growth of the ecclesiastical hierarchy, moreover, brought new burdens to the Catholic peasantry; besides the tribute exacted by the feudal lords, the church took a tenth of the peasant's income.

Summarizing the circumstances that paved the way for open (though unsuccessful) peasant rebellion, a contemporary Croatian historian wrote:

Unjust punishment, irresponsibility of tax-collectors, forced transporting of husbands from one place to another, dishonoring of women and girls, imprisoning innocent individuals, punishing without court trials, crimes of every kind, and other misfortunes were increasingly killing the peasant's belief in justice, in king, and in God. Even the clergy were against the miserable, injured, and insulted.

The Croats and the Slovenes had to pass through a more scorching fire than did the Serbians, for Austrian and Hungarian administration was modern, efficient, and ruthless. Industrialization and improved communications enabled Austria-Hungary to acquire new power and methods to strengthen its authority. The very existence of the Empire depended on suppression of all subject nationalities, and it made every effort to denationalize them. In Slovenia, for example, Germanization began in the Middle Ages. German colonists built churches and monasteries. A German aristocracy developed, and with it a Germanized Slovene aristocracy. The Slovenes became more and more dependent upon the Germans, who guided their destinies right down to 1918.

The Serbs, on the contrary, were subject to a relatively weak empire. Turkish administration was primitive and permeated with laxity and corruption. The era of commercial development further weakened the Turkish state. The Serbs, moreover, were not subjected to a denationalizing education. In the light of the historical development of Yugoslav society, it is easy to see why the ideas of the French Revolution were able to penetrate Serbia long before Croatia could think of opposing Germanization and Magyarization. Democracy found organized support among the Serbs much earlier than it did among the Croats. This, in part, explains why Serbia was able to destroy feudalism a century before the Croats could build up effective opposition, and why the Serbs did not need a nationalistic literature to inspire revolt. The revolt came first and a nationalistic literature followed.

Although open rebellion failed among the Croats, opposition began to express itself through nationalistic literature. The Illyrian movement, for example, was mainly literary. Nationalist writers were far from realistic in the field of politics. Petar Preradović, for example, was satisfied with passive resistance. Others, like Ljudevit Gaj, after the failure of their revolt, even served as political agents of the Austro-Hungarian rulers. Their struggle for political democracy was carried on by political means—debate, persuasion, and compromise. But this is not to say that they were ineffective. On the contrary, the courageous actions of Ante Starčević in his criticism of Austro-Hungarian centralism laid the foundations for an organized democratic movement of Croatian peasantry. The constructive part of Starčević's political ideology was taken over by the brothers Radić, who founded the Croatian Peasant party.

In their national awakening the Serbs tended to be revolutionary; the Croats and Slovenes were more moderate and, on the whole, evolutionary. This was not an inherent difference. Rather it indicates how the varied circumstances of oppression can materially condition the behavior pattern of a people.

A study of social structure must concern itself with the composition of society, its economic status, health and social welfare, education, political activities, and other relevant factors.

Since approximately 80 per cent of Yugoslavia's population is engaged in agricultural pursuits, and since there is no nobility, Yugoslav society gives the impression of being rather homogeneous and nonstratified. The casual American visitor is struck by the absence of what he calls the "middle class." The very small percentage of wealthy people forms an economic and social "upper crust," but the majority of Yugoslavs are peasant and rural. Of the nonrural population, about 10 per cent are engaged in industry and crafts; another 10 per cent are divided almost equally among commerce, banking, and communications, on the one hand, and public services, independent professions, and the army, on the other.

The preponderance of population is not the only factor lending importance to the rural areas. When the Turks occupied great portions of what is now Yugoslavia, most of the natives left the towns. The country districts thereupon became the refuge of national aspirations and activities and the repository of national traditions and national religion. Later, of course, the towns recovered their national character, but rural areas remained the backbone of the nation.

Analysis of the economic status of the rural population is basic to an understanding of Yugoslav society. In the main, Yugoslavia is a nation of small landholdings. On the basis of output, invested capital, and labor supply, rural ownership can be classified in two categories: minimal and insufficient. Landholdings are too small to give the peasant adequate subsistence. Two-thirds of peasant holdings do not exceed three hectares of productive land, and one-fifth of the rural population possesses no productive land. Furthermore, holdings are too small to allow full use of the available labor supply. To every square kilometer of Yugoslav territory there are forty-five peasants, but to every square kilometer of agricultural land there are ninety-eight, and the number per square kilometer of arable land is even higher. Not only are there nearly twice as many persons to the square kilometer of arable land in Yugoslavia as in western European countries, but cultivation is for the most part primitive. Many regions have never been known to break the soil with an implement more modern than a wooden plow.

Yugoslavia ranks first among European nations in net growth in population. As population increases, land division increases with it and the small holdings become even smaller. The peasants are further impoverished, and some of them lose their land. Thus two forces are at work: pauperization and proletarization. The economic status of the peasant deteriorates, for he has less security. As a result his food is less adequate, his health is endangered, and his value to his family and to the community is definitely minimized. There is greater likelihood of his becoming a ward of the state or the community.

Those who become nonowners, or proletarians, move in increasing numbers to the cities to seek employment in industry, trade, and state services. Thus the proportion of rural inhabitants to city dwellers decreases. Yet, owing to the general increase in population, this urban movement does not minimize the problems that beset the rural community and the nation as a whole.

Agrarian reforms are discussed at greater length in chapter x, above. But it may be noted that, although agriculture constitutes at least three-fourths of the nation's total activity, the state did not succeed in establishing any system regulating the status and development of rural ownership, nor did it even discover the facts concerning the problem. Moreover, the disbursements of the Ministry of Agriculture in this predominantly rural state were only one per cent of the entire government budget. But a newly created state which has had to deal with innumerable postwar problems should not be hastily judged. Its first efforts were, of necessity, directed toward extricating itself from chaos after 1918.

Although the peasant struggled to improve his social and economic position through this inadequate government aid, he did not stop there, but organized independent rural coöperative societies as well. The first coöperative society was established in 1894 in the village of Vranovo (county of Smederevo) through the initiative of Mihailo Avramović, the apostle of the Serbian coöperative movement (*zadružni pokret*). Its program in Serbia included progressive taxation and abolition of monopoly, taxes, tariffs, and direct duties; protection of crafts, domestic production, and rural industry; socialization of industry.

Similar organizations were formed in Croatia. In 1935 the Croatian Peasant party, then in the opposition, created an independent economic organization known as Gospodarska Sloga. It had a threefold task: (1) economic organization of the Croatian people, particularly the peasantry; (2) prevention of exploitation of the national wealth by foreign capital; (3) collection of funds to finance its program. Aside from attempting to find markets for rural products and protecting the interests of peasants generally, the Gospodarska Sloga made a scientific survey of rural problems and published such works as *Kako živi narod* (How the People Live), which describes the living conditions, customs, and traditions of the Croatian peasants.

The Yugoslav peasant lacks the material necessities of life. The status of the urban worker is not dissimilar. He is unorganized and receives low wages. Usually he is ill-housed, ill-clothed, and poorly nourished. From the standpoint of economic abundance, therefore, the city worker is no better off than the peasant. But whereas the city worker may experience occasional periods of independence, the peasant is always dependent on others for any marked improvement in his economic status. He sells his produce at the buyer's price and, in turn, buys what he needs at the seller's price. In this respect he differs little from the American farmer except that, on the whole, the latter lives far better. The city worker is in virtually the same position except that, instead of produce, he sells his labor at whatever price he can get. It is arguable, therefore, that the economic position of the peasant is, in the long run, more desirable and secure than that of the urban worker. The real problem, however, centers around the inescapable fact that economic independence has little meaning for either city worker or peasant.

Almost from the beginning of its statehood, Yugoslavia adopted a system of socialized medicine. A special division of the Ministry of Public Health is devoted to the study of social conditions. Its investigations are concerned chiefly with rural problems and aim essentially at placing laboratory results at the disposal of the people. But this is difficult to achieve, for most doctors, nurses, and hospitals are in the cities, and the state program has aided the urban far more than the rural population. One of the greatest handicaps has been the paucity of hospitals and their overcrowded condition, especially in hospitals for mental diseases. At Stenjevec, near Zagreb, there were only 98 beds for 220 mental patients. On the average, there is one hospital to every 80,000 persons, and one hospital bed to every 600. Conditions are much better in the cities, where the majority of hospitals are located, but most peasants have no access to hospital care. In 1932, for example, 270,000 deaths were recorded; only 12,000 of these took place in hospitals. Thus from 90 to 98 per cent of deaths occurred outside hospitals.

In regard to physicians the situation is similar. In view of living conditions and recreational and other advantages, it is quite understandable that they should prefer to practice in cities. Thus in all the peasant areas (*sela*) of Yugoslavia there are only 800 physicians. Yet Zagreb alone has more than 500, and Belgrade about 700. This high concentration of medical men in Zagreb and Belgrade provides one doctor for every 400 residents. But in the peasant areas there is only one doctor to care for about 16,000 persons.

The peasant is again at a disadvantage in regard to disease. Tuberculosis attacks nearly 500,000 annually, of whom about 40,000 die each year. Most of the sufferers are in the peasant areas. The immediate causes of rural tuberculosis are inadequate nutrition, poor housing, and close personal contact. From venereal diseases, also, country districts often suffer more than towns. Civilization has brought to the robust peasant a far greater enemy in venereal disease than he encountered in the Turk. Preventive and curative measures are more accessible to the urban resident; the peasant frequently fails to recognize his ailment.

Malaria is prevalent in certain regions of southern Serbia and Dalmatia, with some 500,000 cases reported each year. This, however, represents a significant decline of 50 per cent since the First World War. As with other major diseases, malaria is less prevalent in towns. Although it is in some degree a territorial disease, it is promoted by malnutrition, lack of sanitation, and certain types of work. Malaria involves not only a hygienic but also an economic and a social loss, especially in agricultural regions.

Rural hygiene demands more careful attention than urban hygiene. The peasant has few foodstuffs and little knowledge of their preparation. In many regions, vegetables are seldom eaten. Fruits are usually reserved for making brandies. The high rate of infant mortality is an index of the inadequate nutrition. The results of adverse social and economic conditions make themselves felt especially at the time of weaning and in the preschool years.

The government has founded domestic-science schools to give

instruction in household management and economy, hygiene, and care and feeding of infants and children. Special nurses and house-wives have been sent to teach peasant women in their own homes, and women's organizations have been encouraged. Model houses were built by means of a grant from the Rockefeller Foundation, and it was hoped that these might encourage peasants to appreciate the advantages of sanitation and better living conditions. But the facts indicate that the peasantry needs further education in order to utilize these improvements, for tradition is a powerful force.

In education, also, the position of the peasant is worse than that of the urban resident. (See chap. xiii, below.) Illiteracy is extremely high, especially in rural areas. The peasant has rarely needed to know how to read and write. The few necessary calculations were mentally performed. History, drama, epic, folklore—all were trans-mitted by word of mouth from generation to generation. The state could spend little on education, and concentrated on the larger towns. Where country schools did exist, it was difficult to find teachers for them; distances between home and school were fre-quently too far to travel. Thus educational facilities have always been better in cities than in rural areas.

Yet the absence of formal education has not been wholly a curse. The peasant has been forced to think things through, relying on his own mind rather than on books. He knows why he holds cer-tain views and can usually present a logical and well-reasoned defense of them. The illiterate peasant is often misled because he lacks information. But, given the facts, he is likely to judge their significance with a fair degree of accuracy. His inability to read and write has not impaired his social status. Although he fre-quently consults his literate neighbor about written matters, he does so on the basis of equality and does not consider himself in-ferior. Much of the "culture" of the formally educated, especially of the city aristocracy, seems to him corrupt and indicative of decline. This is not to say that he has a contempt for formal education. On the contrary, the average peasant seeks educational opportunities for his children when the economic status of the family permits.

The most significant feature of Yugoslav political life is that the majority of the population—the peasantry—has never been governed with its welfare uppermost in the minds of the rulers. Peasant parties have never had full control of the government, but even outside the government there have been divergent views as to the nature of the peasantry and its proper place in Yugoslav society. The development of the social structure in each instance goes far to explain this divergence.

In Serbia the peasantry has long been conscious of itself as a class. But it should be noted that national consciousness preceded class feeling. By the time the Serbian peasantry became aware of itself as a class, it was conscious also of the existence and the importance of other groups and realized the necessity of solving its problems through a recognition of all groups in society. In the latter part of the nineteenth century Svetozar Marković and Adam Bogosavljević, the leaders of the rising Radical party, looked upon the peasantry as a class, but as only one class among others. Although in the twentieth century the Radical party abandoned the principle of peasant social democracy, in fact if not in theory, one of the Serbian peasant parties has perpetuated the principle.

In Croatia the rise of nationalism was accompanied by the rise of the peasantry. Hence there has been a strong and persistent tendency to identify the two. The peasantry was looked upon not as a class but as the whole people. This concept was predominant among the leaders of the Croatian Peasant party, for they concerned themselves solely with the agricultural problem. To be sure, it was the most pressing one, but the party's complete neglect of the industrial problem resulted in driving Croatian industry into Serbia. Thus a particular concept of the peasantry served to promote a distinct change in the structure of Yugoslav society. Unfortunately, the identification of the peasantry with the people may lead to totalitarianism, even though such may not be the intent. The entrance of the Croatian Peasant party into the government in 1939 is an example. Its claim to be the sole representative of the Croatian people implied that opposition would not be tolerated.

This is not to suggest that fascism would necessarily find fertile ground under such conditions, for, as history has demonstrated, the Yugoslav peasantry formed a strong bulwark against fascism. The appeal of the fascists to "save" the peasant had no real meaning for him, as it did for some of the more prosperous peasants of Germany, for example. The fear-psychology of the fascists elicited no response from the Yugoslav peasant, for he did not possess enough wealth to fear its loss. Fascism could not find fertile ground among a people imbued with the democratic spirit—a people to whom no sacrifice has been too great for the sake of freedom and independence.

Throughout their difficulties and struggles the Yugoslavs have succeeded in preserving their Slavic character, their peasant heritage, and their democratic spirit. At the end of the First World War it was hoped that, in spite of the obstacles created by centuries of separate existence, the Yugoslav people would be free to develop in accordance with their own genius and conception of life. That hope was destined to fade, but now it again emerges—awaiting the dawn of a new day.

# CHAPTER XIII

# *Education*

## BY SEVERIN K. TUROSIENSKI

YUGOSLAVIA, young in its present political form but very old in traditions and culture, organized an educational system in 1918 that was free and obligatory for all its youth from infancy to early manhood and womanhood. Education in Yugoslavia has always had a significance beyond mere instruction in dry facts. It has become a national symbol of vital importance to a people who for hundreds of years were repressed as ignorant serfs by Turks, Magyars, Germans, or Italians. The tremendous value of education to the Yugoslavs can be better appreciated when it is remembered that "Black George," the liberator and first ruler of Serbia, was an illiterate who could sign official documents only by making a rude cross.

Even to this day, illiteracy is high in the country. In the southern districts, where the Turks ruled longest, only 27–37 per cent of those over ten years of age could read and write. By way of comparison, in the Slovene districts, where the somewhat more enlightened Austrian rule had permitted education at a much earlier date, more than 94 per cent were literate. But in spite of the higher degree of literacy in the north, only 54.8 per cent of the nation as a whole could read and write. Among women this proportion was only 43 per cent, though men made a better showing (67.3 per cent).

Where ability to obtain an education has long been associated with freedom from the oppressive rule of a foreign tyranny, attending school and learning to read and write have been regarded as privileges to be cherished, not obligations to be endured. Writers, teachers, and professors have enjoyed a prestige not always bestowed on their colleagues in other countries. The universities of Zagreb and Belgrade have been vital centers of influence. Their professors have been leaders in the political and economic life of the country, and it is no coincidence that they were drawn upon heavily to form the government created by the bloodless revolution of March, 1941.

Nor should the power and influence of the politically conscious student bodies be overlooked. It was the students, often sacrificing their freedom and sometimes even their lives, who helped to carry on the long and bitter fight against the dictatorship. It was again the university students who led the open protest against the humiliating treaty signed by Premier Dragiša Cvetković and Foreign Minister Dimitrije Cincar-Marković with Herr Hitler at Berchtesgaden. Little wonder that among the first acts of the invaders were the closing of all educational institutions, particularly in Serbia, and the execution or incarceration in concentration camps of all intellectual leaders who did not show themselves to be pro-Nazi.

Since freedom of education has long stood as a national symbol, it was only natural that the Yugoslav educational system should have been strongly nationalistic. Not only was it under the direct control of the central government, but the Constitution of September 3, 1931, declared: "All schools must give moral education and develop the national spirit in the sense of national unity and religious toleration. All educational establishments are under the control of the state." These aims were specifically repeated in the laws governing each division of the educational system. Thus the law regulating elementary education stated its aim to be "to educate pupils in the spirit of state and national unity and religious tolerance; to make of them moral, faithful, and active members of the nation and of society."

An interesting example of this nationalist philosophy in education was the experimental elementary school founded at Belgrade in September, 1935, and named for King Alexander I. It was intended to be the embryo of a new Yugoslav school which would apply the psychological methods most appropriate for the pupil's growth and patriotic development. The child was to participate in the process of learning, not only through acquisition of information from books and teachers but through his own activities in exercising mind and body and developing emotions based on national unity.

The two points most emphasized in educational policy were national unity and religious tolerance. The latter was very important in a country containing three strong rival faiths, one of which was the state church. The Serbian Orthodox, Roman Catholic, and Moslem religions received support from the national treasury. (The small percentage of Jews in Yugoslavia were mainly of the Sephardic sect, whose mother tongue is Spanish.) Their rights and privileges were established by agreement between the ecclesiastical authorities and the government. Religious education was compulsory in all elementary, secondary, civic, and vocational schools. The curricula were prepared by the respective denominational authorities and approved by the Ministry of Education.

According to the law of June 10, 1935, each class commenced and closed the day's work with prayers, and all students in elementary and secondary schools were required to meet the obligations of their own faith. If more than 60 per cent of the student body was of one denomination, the entire school observed its holidays. If less than 60 per cent of the students belonged to one of the recognized religions, the students of each faith were excused from attendance on their individual holidays, but the school was not closed. A list of holidays for each denomination was approved by the Ministry of Education and published in its journal, *Prosvetni Glasnik.*

The principle of inculcating a spirit of national unity through the educational system was more difficult to achieve, for it had to be reconciled with the rights of national minorities, which were protected by the Treaty of St. Germain. Where the children of any national minority predominated in a school, instruction was given in the language of that group, although the study of Serbo-Croatian or Slovenian was compulsory in all schools. The result was a multilingual system in which Serbo-Croatian, Slovenian, Czech, Russian, Ruthenian, German, Magyar (Hungarian), Rumanian, Italian, and French were media of instruction. Moreover, Germans, Magyars, and Czechs, in particular, maintained their own schools. It should be noted, however, that university instruction was given only in Serbo-Croatian or Slovenian, except in the Higher Islamic School at Sarajevo, where Turkish was added. In spite of this apparently liberal attitude, the recognition of minority rights was sometimes merely nominal.

Probably the most important educational power held by the government was its control of the appointment and supervision of teachers. Teachers in kindergarten, primary, and advanced elementary schools must have completed the equivalent of the American junior high school and must have graduated from a normal school. Permanent status was attained only after teaching for two years and passing an examination. A "temporary" teacher who failed in the examination three times was subject to dismissal.

Secondary and normal schools included three ranks of teachers: instructors, aspirant professors, and professors. An instructor taught only subjects requiring physical or manual skill, such as gymnastics, manual training, and penmanship. He had to be a graduate of a secondary school, complete at least four semesters of highly specialized university courses, and pass a teacher's examination. An aspirant professor (*suplent*) had to have a diploma from the faculty of philosophy of a Yugoslav university. Like the temporary teacher, he served an apprenticeship of not more than five years. If at the end of that time he had not been made a full professor he was subject to dismissal. All permanent teachers or professors in primary and secondary schools were appointed by the minister of education. A commission nominated two candidates for each vacancy, and from these two the minister made his appointment.

University positions were, on the whole, less subject to governmental control. Professors were selected by a faculty council from candidates who had passed a competitive public examination. In exceptional instances a well-known scholar or scientist might be offered a position without taking the examination. If the election of a professor was approved by the university assembly, appointment might be made for life by the king on recommendation of the minister of education.

University docents (similar in rank to assistant professors) were chosen in the same manner as full professors, except that appointment was made by the minister of education and did not give tenure. Private docents (instructors), like all other candidates for university positions, had to hold the degree of doctor and submit a thesis containing original research. They did not take a competitive examination, however, but were elected by a faculty council and approved by the university senate. Appointments for both university and private docentships were for five years only. If not reappointed, docents lost the right to teach.

All members of the administrative and the teaching personnel in public and accredited private institutions had civil-service status. Appointments were made on a competitive basis and, if permanent, were for life or until the age of retirement. Every teacher had to take an oath of loyalty to the king and the state. Teachers were forbidden to engage in any other profession, though university professors were permitted to serve as advisers to commercial or government institutions. The conduct and work of teachers were periodically rated by inspectors or specially assigned officials of the Ministry of Education. If a teacher's record showed a poor rating he was subject to demotion or dismissal. Promotions were earned by passing examinations conducted by the universities under the Ministry of Education.

With the possible exception of university staffs, government control over appointment, promotion, and dismissal of teachers was highly centralized. In the regular lower schools this control lay in the hands of the Ministry of Education. Special schools were under the supervision of the corresponding ministry. Thus, although control of education was divided among various branches of the government, it was still a function of the central government.

The school system resembled that of most central European countries. Kindergartens, which were not compulsory, took children from four to seven years of age. Personal hygiene, medical care, diet, and outdoor games and exercises were emphasized, though counting, speech exercises, and prayers were also taught. Formal education began at the age of seven. Elementary schools were similar to those of America in that they were compulsory and free to all classes; a large majority were coeducational.

Of the 8,585 schools in 1936–1937, only 111 were private and there were but 114 separate schools for boys and 103 for girls. Their

PEASANT GIRLS LEARNING TO READ

PHYSICAL CULTURE CLASS

THE UNIVERSITY OF ZAGREB

THE UNIVERSITY OF BELGRADE

support usually came not from a general state fund but from the organizers of the school, though in both public and private schools the national treasury paid the salaries fixed by law. Sometimes, however, the state helped to erect new buildings, and in some of the poorer banovine, as in Zeta and Vardar, it assumed the entire expense of maintenance.

In sparsely settled areas, particularly in mountain regions, traveling schools moved from one village to another, staying only five months in each. These gave children in remote regions an opportunity to obtain at least an elementary education. As soon as there were enough pupils, permanent schools replaced them.

On completion of four years in the primary school, the child could continue for another four years in an advanced elementary school. Or, if he passed the necessary examinations, he might choose one of three types of secondary schools, depending on his future vocation. The classical gymnasium, as in other countries, stressed the Greek and Roman classics. The real gymnasium paid more attention to modern languages and history; Latin was taught but not Greek. The real school (*realka*) emphasized mathematics and sciences; classical languages were not taught.

Secondary education in Yugoslavia was strongly influenced by Austria and Hungary and closely followed the central European pattern. The first four years of secondary school were called the junior course (roughly equivalent to the American junior high school). If, at the end of this period, the student passed an examination called the "little *matura*," he might then enroll for a second four-year period, the senior course. If he did so, he eventually had to pass a difficult examination, the "great *matura*," which entitled him to enter any institution of higher learning. If he did not elect the senior course he might enter a normal or vocational secondary school.

In the secondary schools a distinction was drawn between general and specialized education. A variety of special secondary schools offered many types of training. The civic schools, in which tuition was free, paralleled advanced elementary instruction and overlapped and paralleled the first four years of the eight-year secondary schools. They were akin to the civic schools of Hungary, the *mellemskolen* of Denmark, and the middle schools of

Germany. Such schools were intended for young people who were capable of more than the ordinary elementary schoolwork but who were not able to benefit by full secondary-school instruction. The curriculum was the same for all students in the first two years. In the last two years, however, the student had to elect one of three fields: trade and industrial, commercial, or agricultural studies.

The Yugoslav educational system was noted for the abundance of special schools. The Ministry of Commerce and Industry supervised the technical and trade schools. Technical secondary schools were open only to those who had completed the junior course in a general secondary school, or four years in a civic or a lower trade school. Technical secondary schools were designed to train artisans who planned to work independently; they offered such courses as architecture, building trades, and engineering. Trade schools for boys trained skilled craftsmen, developed domestic industries already existing in a region, or started new ones where conditions were favorable. Vocational trade schools emphasized practical training in workshops.

The law of March 31, 1932, governing technical secondary and trade schools for boys required that all students be insured against accidents occurring in school workshops or laboratories, as well as during vacation practice. A policy was made out annually for each institution according to its registration, and each student paid a small annual premium.

Special schools of arts and crafts taught wood carving, metalwork, ceramics, and carpet weaving. Trade schools for girls offered courses in dressmaking and other domestic arts. The teachers for girls' trade schools were educated in the vocational normal schools for girls.

Railway craft and maritime schools were also provided. The National Railway Communication School at Belgrade was taught by officials of the Ministry of Communications; schools for noncommissioned officers were maintained by the Ministry of War and Navy.

There were many commercial secondary schools. Some were maintained by the Commercial League of Youth, an organization founded in 1912 by Belgrade merchants. The commercial academies and the Chamber of Commerce of Belgrade offered one-year commercial courses for graduates of the senior course in secondary schools.

The Ministry of Social Welfare and Public Health had charge of the School for Public Health at Zagreb and various others for public health assistants, hospital attendants, nurses, and midwives, as well as some charitable institutions such as the six schools for deaf-mute and blind children.

Of all the specialized secondary schools the agricultural schools were probably most important, for more than 75 per cent of the population depended on agriculture for a living. National and provincial authorities as well as agricultural coöperative societies were continually striving to improve vocational training in agriculture. A number of schools, usually boarding institutions with free tuition, were founded, and the national government offered scholarships to able students. All agricultural schools except those of university rank were under the control of the Ministry of Agriculture, which prescribed the curricula and appointed the teaching personnel.

Many associations promoted agricultural training and protected the legal and social interests of farmers. The oldest of these was the Slovenian Agricultural Association, which was founded in 1767 and recently boasted 18,500 members. The Serbian Agricultural Association, with headquarters in Belgrade, was formed in 1869 and now has a membership of 10,000.

There were three secondary agricultural schools, which were open to graduates of the junior course of the general secondary school who could pass the entrance examination. The object of these schools was to train future owners of moderate-sized farms. Each school had its model farm and experiment station, and the last year of the four-year course was devoted to practical farming. Obviously, these schools were designed to serve only a small group, since the majority of farmers' sons could not afford to take an advanced course.

Two other types of schools were therefore established: the lower and the specialized agricultural schools. The lower agricultural schools have been under the supervision of provincial authorities since 1929. They accepted farmers' sons from fourteen to eighteen years of age who had completed the advanced elementary course of general education. The last two years of the three-year training period stressed the practical application of theoretical subjects. The special agricultural schools had the same entrance requirements as the lower schools, but they specialized in some branch of agriculture, such as dairying, viticulture, or animal husbandry. The course of training took only one or two years and combined academic and agricultural subjects.

The lower agricultural schools offered short extension courses to farmers; the agricultural departments of various provinces likewise organized extension work, which was directed by a specialist from the Ministry of Agriculture. Courses in domestic science were conducted in all villages, under the auspices of the Women's National Organizations, to train girls for their responsibilities as farmers' wives and mothers. Some schools were itinerant and visited villages on request. Their service in helping to raise the standard of living in rural areas was immeasurable.

In regard to institutions of higher rank the law of December 11, 1931, stated that the universities were "the highest educational institutions for professional training, for the development of sciences, and for the fostering of the national Yugoslav culture." The latter clause was almost superfluous, since the universities had always been leaders in the national movement, long before Yugoslavia existed as a state. Nor had their political and nationalist consciousness diminished after the formation of the state. In fact, some internal difficulties between Serbs and Croats in the past two decades have been aggravated rather than diminished by the attitude of university faculties in the two regions.

This was due partly to historical developments. At Zagreb, the capital of Croatia, the present University of the Kingdom of Yugoslavia dates from an old Jesuit school which, in 1776, was transformed by the Empress Maria Theresa into the Royal Academy of Sciences, with faculties of philosophy and law. Out of this academy grew the university, which was formally opened in 1874 as the Royal Francis Joseph University. With the incorporation of Croatia into the Yugoslav state, the name was of course changed.

The University of Belgrade opened as a lyceum at Kragujevac in 1838. Three years later it was moved to Belgrade, where it was housed in a small one-story building of Turkish construction with a heavy thatched roof and few windows. In 1863 the Ministry of Education of the former Kingdom of Serbia reorganized the lyceum as a high school (*velika škola*) with a technical faculty. In 1905 it became the first Serbian university, and faculties of theology and medicine were formed. But its greatest development took place after the First World War, when Belgrade became the capital of the new Yugoslav state, and the university, like the city, assumed first rank in the entire country.

In many respects the rivalry between the universities of Belgrade and Zagreb represented the essence of the conflict which has existed between Serbia and Croatia. Between two peoples who are racially identical and who speak dialects as closely akin as English and American, differences in outlook can be due only to differences in historical background. Here the dissimilarities were predominantly cultural. While Old Serbia was still struggling to throw off the effects of centuries of Turkish tyranny, Croatia was enjoying the cultural wealth of the Austro-Hungarian Empire.

The University of Zagreb was essentially an Austrian institution, whereas the infant University of Belgrade was composed of ardently patriotic Serbs working to restore a native culture which had been almost obliterated by the Turks. Even the religious conflict between Croatia and Serbia was perpetuated in the two principal Yugoslav universities, for the Faculty of Theology at Zagreb was Roman Catholic and that at Belgrade was Serbian Orthodox.

The only other institution with full university status was the King Alexander I University at Ljubljana, the capital of Slovenia. This university is even older than that at Zagreb, for it was founded in 1596 as a Jesuit college. By royal decree, on July 25, 1919, it became a standard public university and was given its present name. The Faculty of Philosophy at Skoplje and the Faculty of Law at Subotica were founded in 1920 as constituent colleges of the University of Belgrade.

Each of the five institutions had eight departments, or faculties, of study: philosophy (similar to an American college of arts and sciences); law, which included economics; medicine; pharmacology; theology; agriculture and forestry; technical science (architecture, civil and electrical engineering, etc.); and veterinary medicine. At the end of the fourth year the student was required to pass a comprehensive examination. The doctoral degree was granted on the basis of an original dissertation publicly defended. The Faculty of Medicine, however, required a five-year period of training for the degree of doctor of general medicine; an additional year was necessary to obtain the degree of doctor of medical sciences.

In 1925 the School of Public Health at Zagreb was founded as the result of a donation from the Rockefeller Foundation. At first it was part of the Hygienic Institute of Zagreb, but since 1930 it has been a separate institution supported by the national treasury. Its primary purpose was to train graduate physicians for public health service, but it also conducted popular courses in hygiene and social medicine. The library of the University of Belgrade, built through the aid of the Carnegie Foundation, was formally opened in 1926. These examples of American generosity have never been forgotten by the Yugoslavs.

Theological training was offered in both secondary schools and universities. The five Serbian Orthodox theological schools of secondary-school rank were sponsored by the state. Their graduates were certified "for the priesthood, to teach religion, and to continue higher religious education at any faculty of Serbian Orthodox theology." Such higher education was available principally at Belgrade.

Roman Catholic theology was not taught in secondary schools but in nine seminaries of quasi-university rank and at the universities of Zagreb and Ljubljana. The seminaries offered practically the same instruction as the universities, but they were not entitled to grant academic degrees.

The Mohammedan sections of the country maintained Islamic schools of secondary rank comparable to the real gymnasium, and the Higher Islamic School of Sheriat Law and Theology at Sarajevo. The latter institution, founded in 1937, was designed to offer members of the Moslem community the same advantages that were open to Serbian Orthodox and Roman Catholics. On the completion of the four-year course, the graduate received a diploma of the same value as that given by other Yugoslav institutions of university rank.

Mention should also be made of the Jewish religious school at Sarajevo, maintained by Jewish organizations, which trained rabbis and instructors of religion in Jewish parochial schools. Its four-year course was of the same rank as the senior course in a general secondary school.

The arts received generous attention in Yugoslavia. Both Belgrade and Zagreb had national academies of fine arts the objectives of which were to train creative artists and prepare teachers for secondary schools. The academies were perpetuating an already glorious tradition. The distinctive national character of Yugoslav art has probably been demonstrated best to western Europeans and Americans through the works of the renowned sculptor Ivan Meštrović.

Like most Slavic peoples the Yugoslavs are highly musical. Their national academies at Zagreb, Belgrade, and Ljubljana are fitting symbols of the agelong love of music which is inherent in the race. The academy at Zagreb was founded in 1829 by the Music Association of Zagreb and was maintained for nearly a century as a private institution. In 1923, however, it was placed under the Ministry of Education and became a public institution. The first year of instruction was devoted to the study of music theory and the next three years to the study of piano, orchestra, and singing. The student concurrently attended elementary or secondary school. At the end of four years he entered secondary school in the Academy of Music, which usually extended over a six-year period, after which he was eligible to enter a university.

Whereas the National Academy of Music at Zagreb covered all phases of musical instruction from elementary to advanced, a different method was used at Belgrade. All elementary and preparatory work was given in the secondary school of music and only advanced instruction in the academy. Both institutions in Belgrade are relatively new, for they first opened their doors in 1937.

The National Conservatory of Music at Ljubljana, like the academy at Zagreb, has had a long history. In 1882 it was opened as a music school by the Ljubljana Philharmonic Society. With the formation of the Yugoslav state in 1919, it patriotically changed its name to the Yugoslav Conservatory of Music. In 1926 it was legally proclaimed a national institution and was given its present title. Like the Zagreb school, it offered elementary and secondary courses as well as instruction of university rank.

The School of Dramatic Arts of the National Theater of Belgrade, operating under the statute of December 30, 1933, was of-advanced secondary rank. Its function was to train professional actors for the national theaters of Yugoslavia. The school was open to anyone under twenty-five years of age who could pass an examination demonstrating his histrionic ability. The first two years emphasized theory; the last was devoted to theatrical practice.

A number of schools trained officers for the army, navy, and air force. All were under the control of the Ministry of War and Navy. The Naval War Academy was located at Dubrovnik and the military and aeronautical schools at Belgrade.

In a country whose rate of illiteracy was still very high, education had to reach not only the youth but the adult population. For this purpose a Department of National Culture was set up in the Ministry of Education in 1937. It supervised adult education, assisted private associations in organizing courses, opened village libraries, and carried on other activities designed to reduce illiteracy and to enrich the spiritual and cultural life of the people. Courses were held for adults in districts where education had previously been neglected. Soldiers from those areas were taught in special schools during their term of military service. In 1936–1937 the Ministry of Education directed 600 special adult courses in which 29,507 persons were taught to read and write. Civic organizations conducted 36 schools, which instructed 1,057 persons.

People's universities, maintained by endowment funds under the control of the Ministry of Education, were established at key cities and towns throughout the country—Zagreb, Osijek, Vukovar, Subotica, Belgrade, Smederevo, Valjevo, Dubrovnik, Skoplje, and Bitolj. One of the most important was the Kolarac People's University at Belgrade, founded in 1878 by a Serbian patriot, Ilija M. Kolarac, who endowed it with a large sum of money. By its most recent statutes (January 11, 1933) it offered courses in natural science, agriculture, law, sociology, history, philology, and philosophy. Any adult was admitted to courses for which he was prepared. In 1935–1936 the institution enrolled 9,247 students.

A number of private organizations, also, helped to extend general and vocational education by establishing special schools for farming, hygiene, home economics, trade, and commerce; providing books and periodicals; and organizing public lectures, circulating libraries, and reading rooms.

The Moslem Yugoslavs had their own organizations, the most important of which was the Gajret, an educational and philanthropic association that enrolled more than 27,000 members. It maintained nine student houses for over 600 secondary-school students of both sexes and about 200 craft apprentices. It gave scholarships to Moslem students either in Yugoslav schools or in Moslem universities abroad. The Gajret also provided courses for illiterates and maintained craft workshops where Moslem women could learn weaving, carpetmaking, and embroidery. A branch in Belgrade maintained a student house in which 200 Moslem students lived while attending the University of Belgrade.

In all countries which aim to establish a modern, more democratic form of government, one of the most important problems is the reduction of illiteracy. It is obvious that a democratic government can operate successfully only when its citizens are able to follow political events through newspapers and other printed matter. Illiteracy was an enormous obstacle to effective democracy in Yugoslavia; in spite of extensive efforts in the past twenty years, the proportion of illiterates was reduced only from 45 to 40 per cent. The magnitude of the problem is apparent when the figures are compared with those for the United States, in which only 4.3 per cent of the population in 1930 was illiterate. Though the situation is admittedly bad in Yugoslavia, it must be remembered that much of this illiteracy was present in the adult population. After the First World War, education reached a larger proportion of the younger generation. With the reëstablishment of Yugoslavia and the reapplication of compulsory education there is good reason to believe that the time will soon come when Yugoslavia may boast of a well-educated population with a fruitful culture of its own.

# CHAPTER XIV

# Modern Ecclesiastical Development

## BY MATTHEW SPINKA

THE AGE-LONG TRAGEDY of the Slavic race—the division of the Slavic peoples caused by the fact that some had been drawn into the orbit of Western, Latin, Roman Catholic civilization, whereas others derived their culture from Eastern, Byzantine, Orthodox sources—was nowhere more keenly felt than in Yugoslavia. This country affords the clearest example of the divisive effects of cultural schism: the Serbians are culturally and religiously Eastern Orthodox; the Croatians and the Slovenes are staunchly Roman Catholic.

With the political unification of the Serbs, the Croatians, and the Slovenes, which was formally proclaimed on December 1, 1918, the formidable task of making a homogeneous nation from these diverse elements, divided by a millennium of separate historical development, was matched by the no less necessary task of adjusting the diversities of their ecclesiastical organizations. For ecclesiastical disunity threatened to prove a serious obstacle to national unity.

In 1931 the proportions of the various confessions[1] in the population of 13,934,038 were as follows: 6,785,501 Serbian Orthodox (about 48 per cent), which means that the Serbian Church had lost the overwhelming majority it possessed in the Kingdom of Old Serbia; 5,217,910 Roman Catholics (about 37 per cent), which places them in a position of minority, whereas formerly they were

[1] For notes to chapter xiv see page 522.

accustomed to the treatment accorded to the majority group; 1,561,166 Moslems (about 11 per cent); and 369,524 Protestants, Jews, and other confessions (about 3 per cent). Since the two largest confessional groups had formerly enjoyed undisputed hegemony in their respective territories and had lost it in the new united kingdom, it is not difficult to understand that their adjustment to a reduced status was likely to produce friction.

The primary task confronting the newly constituted nation was to secure the unification of the six diverse ecclesiastical divisions of the Serbian Orthodox Church: the metropolitanate of Serbia (the old kingdom); the patriarchate of Karlovac, which had exercised spiritual sway over the Serbs in Croatia-Slavonia, the Bačka, and the Banat; the autonomous church of Bosnia-Hercegovina; the autocephalous metropolitanate of Montenegro; the two episcopal dioceses of Dalmatia (Zara and Kotor); and the newly acquired territories of Old Serbia in Macedonia.

Unification of ecclesiastical jurisdiction was discussed at a conference held at Karlovac, December 31, 1918, with Metropolitan Dimitrije of Belgrade presiding. The task of unifying the church was given to a committee headed by Metropolitan Mitrofan, Ban of Montenegro, which gained canonical transfer of the Dalmatian eparchies from Rumanian control in November, 1919. Then negotiations were begun with the ecumenical patriarch for the transfer of the eparchies in Macedonia. An agreement was reached early in 1920, when, for the payment of $60,000, twelve eparchies passed under Serbian jurisdiction.

On June 30, 1920, the unification of the entire church was proclaimed in the patriarchal palace at Karlovac in the presence of the heir to the throne, Prince Alexander, the governmental representatives, all the hierarchs and some émigré Russian high clergy, administrators of the eparchies, rectors of theological schools, and monastic dignitaries. But to match the political aggrandizement of the new state by an equally imposing ecclesiastical rank, the ancient Serbian patriarchate of Peć was reëstablished in the autumn of the same year. This idea was not new; it had been talked about since 1879, when the Serbian Church regained its autocephaly. To obtain a clearer idea of the reëstablished patriarchate, the more recent history of its component parts should be considered.

The modern metropolitanate of Serbia was founded as a result of the Serbian Wars of Independence (1804–1830). Prince Miloš Obrenović was recognized by Sultan Mahmud's *hatti-sherif* of August 3, 1830, as the hereditary prince of an autonomous Serbian territory. Moreover, Article 1 of this document granted the Serbians "complete liberty of worship in the churches belonging to them." Thereupon Prince Miloš negotiated with the ecumenical patriarch, Constantius I, for an independent ecclesiastical organization for his principality. He secured from the patriarch, in January, 1832, a *tomos*[2] granting the Serbians an autonomous but not an autocephalous church. The Serbian metropolitan and the bishops were to be chosen by the prince and the people from the native clergy, but the ecumenical patriarch reserved the right to confirm the election and to consecrate the candidates-elect. The metropolitan was obliged to pay the patriarch three hundred imperial ducats for the ceremony and, moreover, the Serbian Church had to pay him the "customary annual contribution." The metropolitan could not be deposed without the consent of the patriarch, the prince, and the people.

In the Serbian Constitution of 1869 the Serbian Orthodox Church was proclaimed the dominant ecclesiastical body in the realm, and membership in it was made obligatory for the ruling prince. The government pledged itself to support and defend the state church and forbade all proselytism.[3]

Further important changes occurred in 1877, when Serbia, with Russian aid, secured full political independence from Turkey, which was sanctioned by the Treaty of Berlin in 1878. In accordance with the unwritten law that an independent Orthodox state is entitled to a self-governing church, the government began negotiations with the ecumenical patriarch, Joachim III (1878–1884), to obtain full autocephaly for the Serbian metropolitanate on the grounds that, since Serbia had ceased to be part of the Ottoman Empire, its church should no longer remain under the jurisdiction of the ecumenical patriarchate. Joachim could hardly do otherwise than grant the request, and the *tomos* of October 20, 1879, conferred autocephaly upon the Serbian Church. But he limited the grant by imposing certain conditions: the Serbian metropolitanate was obliged to consult the ecumenical patriarch in important matters,[4] to mention him in the liturgy, and to secure the holy chrism from Constantinople (always a symbol of dependence).

After the victorious Balkan wars of 1912–1913, the Kingdom of Serbia was substantially enlarged. Accordingly, the Serbian Church extended its jurisdiction over five additional eparchies. At this time it also secured from the ecumenical patriarchate the right to prepare its own holy chrism, thereby abolishing the last vestige of dependence on Constantinople. The Serbian government, flushed with victory, even instructed its ambassador to deal with the patriarchate about the restoration of the ancient Serbian patriarchate of Peć, but nothing came of it. Thus the church of the Kingdom of Serbia, at the time of the unification of 1920, was in danger of losing its position as a state church and even found itself outranked by the church of Karlovac, which possessed the patriarchal dignity.

The patriarchate of Karlovac had its origin in the settlement of the Serbian people in the southern part of the Habsburg Empire after the defeat of the Austrian imperial armies by the Turks in 1690. Since the Serbians, under the leadership of Patriarch Arsenije III Crnojević (1676–1706), had rebelled against the Turks at this time, the Turkish victory threatened them with merciless revenge. Fearing for their lives, 37,000 Serbian families—estimated at 200,000 individuals—fled across the Sava River into Austrian territories to join thousands of their brethren who had previously settled there. Many of these emigrants expected the eventual defeat of the Turks and hoped to return to their ancient homes. But the Peace of Karlovac in 1699, which abandoned Serbia to the Turks, destroyed these expectations.

The Austrian emperor, Leopold I (1640–1705), desirous of protecting the southern boundary of his dominions, eagerly welcomed the new settlers and made them hereditary guardians of the Turkish boundary line. In recognition of this service he granted them extensive privileges in August, 1690: their territory was to form the autonomous Vojvodina; they were free to elect their *vojvod* (literally, leader of the army) and their patriarch; Arsenije was acknowledged as an independent hierarch of the Serbian Church of the territory; and the people were guaranteed liberty of conscience and free exercise of worship. Besides these privileges, the

Vojvodina was exempted from all regional jurisdiction and was subordinated directly to Leopold. On the basis of these rights to autonomous civil and ecclesiastical administration, Patriarch Arsenije set up his ecclesiastical rule and divided the territory into seven eparchies.[5]

The church of the Vojvodina later lost its patriarchal rank, but regained it in the middle of the nineteenth century. When the Magyars rose in revolt against the Austrian government in 1848, the Serbians willingly aided the armies which Tsar Nicholas I had sent to put down the revolt. Thereupon a National Assembly, held at Karlovac on May 13, 1848, proclaimed the Vojvodina a politically independent entity and restored the rank of patriarchate to its church. The youthful Emperor Francis Joseph I at first approved these measures, but when Serbian aid against the Magyars was no longer needed he revoked (in 1860) the grant of political independence. The net gain at the time was the restoration of patriarchal rank to the Karlovac church.

The jurisdiction of the new patriarchate was gradually delimited: in 1864 the Rumanian Orthodox eparchy of Sibiu (Hermannstadt), hitherto subject to Karlovac, was set up as an independent body with jurisdiction over Transylvania. In 1878, in accordance with the Habsburg maxim *divide et impera,* the Serbian Dalmatian eparchies of Zara and Kotor were transferred from the jurisdiction of Karlovac to that of the metropolitanate of Czernowitz in Bukovina,—obviously, to weaken the Karlovac patriarchate.

The last of the patriarchs of Karlovac was the notorious Magyarophil, Lucian, who disappeared in August, 1913, and whose mangled body was found two months later. Whether he was murdered or met with an accident has never been ascertained. An administrator was appointed to take his place, and the First World War broke out before a successor could be elected. Accordingly, the see of Karlovac was vacant at the time of the unification of the Serbian churches.

The third constituent part of the unified church was the metropolitanate of Bosnia-Hercegovina. The Orthodox Serbs of this territory, which formerly was part of the Serbian Empire but which had been conquered by the Turks, were under the jurisdiction of the ecumenical patriarchate from 1766 to 1880. After the right of occupation and administration had been granted to Austria by the Congress of Berlin, the territory virtually ceased to belong to Turkey.

Since the jurisdiction of the ecumenical patriarchate extended only over Turkish domains, the Austrian government entered into negotiations with it for the purpose of establishing an independent Orthodox ecclesiastical organization in the territory. These resulted in the concordat of 1880 by which the ecumenical patriarch surrendered most of his rights in Bosnia-Hercegovina to the Austrian emperor, Francis Joseph I. The latter agreed to recompense the patriarch with an annual sum equal to the revenue formerly derived from the three metropolitanates. Thus the patriarch still received the income without troubling himself about the duties involved. Yet the emperor could only nominate candidates for the metropolitan and episcopal sees; the patriarch retained the right to approve them. The same control was extended to parishes: priests were now appointed by the bishops instead of being chosen by the parishes. The hierarchy and the priesthood were economically dependent on the government, which paid their salaries. The arrangement was advantageous for Austria, since the amount collected in taxes was about three times that paid in salaries.[6]

The last vestiges of the right of supervision by the ecumenical patriarchate disappeared when the two provinces were annexed by Austria-Hungary in 1908. Thereafter the church was subjected more than ever to a policy of denationalization. Under these circumstances it is not surprising that the Serbian Orthodox Church in Bosnia-Hercegovina, which, strangely enough, was in a minority, gradually diminished in numbers and strength. The Roman Catholic Church, on the contrary, which was assiduously supported and favored by the government, greatly increased. Between 1879 and 1910 Catholic membership more than doubled (increasing from 209,391 to 451,686).[7]

The fourth Serbian ecclesiastical group to be included in the unified body was the metropolitanate of Montenegro. This picturesque mountain state was the first among the Serbian territories to regain its political independence from Turkey—in 1696/1697, under the leadership of Metropolitan Danilo Petrović Njegoš. Danilo then acted as both political and ecclesiastical head of the nation. When he died in 1735 he was succeeded by a relative, Sava Petrović, who likewise held the dual office.[8]

The traditional theocratic form of government by prince-metropolitans continued up to the reign of Danilo I (1851–1860), who abolished it. The young ruler felt no desire for the monastic life— the prerequisite for hierarchical office—but wished to marry as well as to rule. In 1852 he called a National Assembly which proclaimed Montenegro a secular principality and its political rule hereditary in Danilo's male line. The office of the metropolitan was thus separated from that of the secular prince. It was under the administration of the brave Metropolitan Mitrofan (1884– 1921) that the church of Montenegro was reunited with the Serbian patriarchate.

The fifth component part consisted of the Dalmatian bishoprics of Zara and Kotor. The independent ecclesiastical organization of these two sees dates from 1808, when the Emperor Napoleon I created a bishopric for his Illyrian Provinces. Bishop Benedikt Kraljević chose Šibenik as his see, but in 1841 it was transferred to Zara. In 1870 a second eparchy was created, with Kotor as the episcopal see. A new constitution gave the emperor the right to appoint and depose the hierarchs. As previously indicated, in 1878 both Zara and Kotor were incorporated with the metropolitanate of Bukovina, which lay at the easternmost tip of the Empire. By 1910 there were about 90,000 members in these two eparchies. No one need be so naïve as to wonder about the reasons for this apparently strange action: it was not the policy of the Austrian government to strengthen the Serbian element by uniting its forces.

The sixth group entering the unified Serbian Church comprised the Macedonian eparchies. These had been under the jurisdiction of the ecumenical patriarchate since 1766, when the patriarchate of Peć was abolished, although some territory had been transferred to the Bulgarian exarchate in 1872. When, in the course of the Balkan wars and the First World War, the Greek and Bulgarian bishops left the country, Serbia purchased the rights from the ecumenical patriarchate.

After the proclamation of the reëstablished patriarchate of Peć the Hierarchical Council (Sabor) of the Serbian Church was organized. Upon this body fell the duty of nominating three candidates from whom the Electoral Congress was to choose the new patriarch. The Electoral Congress was a representative group consisting of hierarchs, archimandrites, representatives of the monasteries and of the parochial clergy, heads of theological schools, laity, and the government. The last was represented by the ministers, the president and the vice-president of the Skupština (the House of Representatives), the head of the army, presidents of the state councils, and mayors of the larger cities.

The first patriarch chosen by the reorganized Sabor, on November 12, 1920, was Dimitrije, the metropolitan of Belgrade. King Alexander approved the election and enthroned the new patriarch in a solemn ceremony which was intended to indicate the close relation between church and state.[9]

But in reality the ecclesiastical situation was far from encouraging. Now that Yugoslavia had become the dominant Balkan state, the government was too preoccupied to consider the claims of religion. The army received chief consideration, and the needs of the church were neglected. Education of the clergy was less adequately provided for than in the past. Before the consolidation, theological courses could be obtained at the universities of Belgrade, Karlovac, and Czernowitz, and in numerous Russian theological academies where many Serbians had formerly gone to study. After the war these studies could be pursued only at Belgrade, and the program was rather meager. Many Orthodox Serbians complained that their church possessed only one theological faculty, whereas the less numerous Roman Catholics had two—at Zagreb and at Ljubljana.

New organic statutes were published on November 9, 1929, recognizing the Serbian Church as self-governing within certain limits: the state reserved only the right of "supreme supervision" (Article 2). Spiritual authority for disciplinary and judicial cases involving clergy and monks resided in the hierarchy and its legitimate representatives (Article 4), but the state was to carry out the decisions and execute the sentences of the church. Clerical schools and theological institutions were controlled by the church, which was to decide about their establishment, courses of study, and teaching personnel.[10] Financial support of the church was to be derived from church properties, state subsidies, and ecclesiastical taxes imposed with the approval of the state (Article 9). Church properties were declared tax-free.

The hierarchical synod was charged with the task of preparing the constitution. This important document was promulgated on November 16, 1931—eleven years after the consolidation of the Serbian churches. Hitherto each constituent unit had followed its own customs and regulations. The new law placed supreme ecclesiastical authority in the Episcopal Council (Sabor) and, *ad interim,* in the Holy Synod; the patriarch presides at the meetings of both bodies. Associated with the patriarch in the administration of the church are three bodies: the supreme ecclesiastical tribunal for clerical, monastic, and marital litigation, which is also the court of appeal for cases from the diocesan tribunals; the Patriarchal Council, the supreme authority in the external relations of the church; and the Patriarchal Executive Committee, the administrative organ of the Patriarchal Council.

The Yugoslav kingdom was divided into twenty-one Orthodox eparchies, five of which were metropolitanates: Belgrade, Skoplje, Cetinje, Sarajevo, and Zagreb. Subordinated to the Serbian patriarchate were five dioceses outside the boundaries of the country: the Bohemian eparchy, the Sub-Carpathian eparchy, the Zara eparchy, the vicariate of Scutari in Albania, and the Serbian Church of the United States and Canada.

The eparchies were divided into regional ecclesiastical groups which included all the parishes and monasteries in a given area. A parish usually contains from three hundred to five hundred families. The bishop exercises his juridical function through the diocesan tribunal. Parish priests are eligible for appointment after finishing their theological training and serving at least three years as vicars. In spite of a partial financial dependence on the state, the church was independent in religious and ecclesiastical matters and in its educational and charitable work. It had the right to establish schools for religious and clerical instruction.

After the death of Patriarch Dimitrije on April 6, 1930, at the age of eighty-four, Metropolitan Varnava (Barnabas) was selected patriarch. Born at Pljevlja in 1880, he studied at Prizren and later at the theological academy in St. Petersburg. In 1910 he was made auxiliary bishop of Debar and Veles by the ecumenical patriarch,

Joachim III. Ten years later Patriarch Barnabas became metropolitan of Skoplje. Although he was now only forty years of age, he won this highest office in the church because he enjoyed the patronage of the king. Barnabas was known to favor *rapprochement* with the Anglicans and the Protestants—as did also Patriarch Dimitrije—and reconciliation with the Bulgars. Patriarch Barnabas likewise had the reputation of being a supporter of the government; in his Macedonian metropolitan eparchy, which included many Bulgars, he upheld national Serbian policies. The chief event in his term of office was the bitter struggle of the Serbian Church with the Milan Stojadinović government over the provisions of the concordat with the Vatican. It was even rumored that the ratification of this measure by the Skupština caused the death of the patriarch. But the story of his opposition and defeat will be told later, in discussing the controversy between Catholic and Orthodox groups.

Because of the excited state of public opinion, elections for the new patriarch could not be held until February 20, 1938. In the meantime the vacant see was administered by Metropolitan Dositije of Zagreb. When the Sabor convened, it proceeded to elect six candidates and submitted the list to the minister of justice and the cults. Those entitled to participate in the election then assembled in the patriarchal church and elected three of the six. Metropolitan Gavrilo of Montenegro received the highest vote and was proclaimed Patriarch of the Serbian Church by Prince Regent Paul,[11] in the name of King Peter II.

In the latter days of Yugoslav independence, when Prince Regent Paul submitted to the demands of Nazi Germany, it was Patriarch Gavrilo, supported by the Serbian Orthodox Church, who stood in the forefront of popular opposition to the concordat. Thus the Serbian Church remained faithful to its age-long tradition of intimate contact with the soul of the Serbian people and their national life.

When the Germans overran Yugoslavia in May, 1941, Patriarch Gavrilo was accused of having stolen state property. The charge was based on the circumstance that King Peter's crown jewels were in the custody of the same monastery (Ostrog, in Montenegro) to which Gavrilo had withdrawn. The patriarch, sentenced to imprisonment in the monastery of Rakovica, about thirty miles from Belgrade, was forced to make the journey on foot and clad only in a shirt, for the Nazis had stripped him of the rest of his clothing. Early in 1945 he was transferred to a concentration camp in Germany. During his imprisonment the affairs of the church were administered by Metropolitan Josip of Skoplje. Gavrilo has since returned to his office.

During this period the Ante Pavelić government made the most of the hatred of Catholic Croatians for Orthodox Serbs. Orthodox churches were destroyed or were turned over to the Catholic Croatians; some Orthodox priests lost their lives and others were forcibly removed from their posts. Several hundred thousand lay Orthodox suffered imprisonment and loss of property and many were forcibly converted to Catholicism. Government posts were filled exclusively by Roman Catholics. Orthodox students were banned from the University of Zagreb. In 1943 Dr. Kuhar, a Slovene Catholic and a member of the government-in-exile, broadcast the following accusation: "The Pavelić state has committed many hideous crimes. It is now degrading Catholicism by criminal acts that outwardly might have the appearance of benefiting it. . . . The Pavelić soldiery and police, urged on by German agents, are forcing the Orthodox population into Catholicism."[12]

At least some of the Croatian hierarchy—for instance, the Archbishop of Sarajevo—approved the measures against the Orthodox. Aloisius Stepinac, Archbishop of Zagreb and Primate of Croatia, was sentenced in 1946 for having been a member of the committee directing the forcible conversions of the Serbs, but his trial was not fairly conducted and did not prove what part he played in the matter. He denied the charge.

As discussed elsewhere in this volume (chap. xxi), the transfer of Allied support from General Draža Mihailović to the Partisan forces under Marshal Tito had momentous consequences. In 1944 the government-in-exile, under the premiership of Dr. Ivan Šubašić, reached an agreement with Tito by which the latter was recognized as temporary administrator. In March, 1945, a provisional government, under the chairmanship of Tito and dominated by the Committee for National Liberation, was formed. Under its auspices a new era dawned in Yugoslav history. The adoption of the federal principle obliterated the old territorial divisions, and the country was divided into six new units.

This radical change in political orientation had a catastrophic influence on the ecclesiastical structure. As is usual under Communist regimes, the relationship between church and state was radically altered. By May, 1946, separation of church and state was already an accomplished fact: at first, legislation for compulsory civil marriage was introduced; then religious instruction was made optional in schools; finally, all financial support was withdrawn from the church and its property was nationalized. The Communist press steadily attacked the Supreme Council (Sabor) under Metropolitan Josip as antinational and reactionary.

Another factor which weakened the recently unified Serbian Church was the organization of an autonomous Macedonian Church. This was in harmony with the political program of Marshal Tito. As early as March, 1945, some Macedonian clergy had petitioned the Serbian patriarchate for an independent ecclesiastical status. It is understandable that such a request would be refused. Thereupon the group declared the independence of the Macedonian Orthodox Church and elected Father Jovan Jelev, a seventy-one-year-old priest who was friendly to Tito, as the temporary head of the new organization. A General Council was called, which elected him patriarch of the restored ancient Bulgarian patriarchate of Ohrid. The new church consists of the metropolitanates of Ohrid, Bitolj, Strumica, and Skoplje.[13]

The second largest ecclesiastical group in Yugoslavia is the Roman Catholic, which is composed primarily of Croatians and Slovenes. Like the Orthodox group, they were divided into six administrative units, although, unlike the Orthodox, they were never unified under a common constitution. Thus the separate Catholic units continued to be governed by regulations based on their previous history: Croatia and Slavonia were governed in accordance with the Austro-Hungarian concordat of August 18, 1855; Slovenia and Dalmatia by the unilateral law of 1874; the Vojvodina (in southern Hungary) by a special law; Bosnia-Hercegovina by the convention of July 8, 1881; Montenegro by the concordat of August 18, 1886; and Serbia by the concordat[14] of June 24, 1914.

Since the unification of Yugoslavia, the successive governments at Belgrade had vainly attempted to solve the complications of the Roman Catholic ecclesiastical situation. The principal difficulty was the necessity of negotiating a concordat with the Vatican. The method of direct dealing with ecclesiastical units within the country, which was possible with the Orthodox group, could not be used with the Catholics. Obviously, the churches which were not subject to a highly centralized, extraterritorial, supreme authority could be handled more easily.

Political unity between the Serbian and the Croatian-Slovene groups depended in large degree on satisfactory settlement of the ecclesiastical problem. Whereas the nationalism or separatism of the Serbs found religious expression in Orthodoxy, that of the Croatian-Slovene group was traditionally under the leadership of the Catholic priesthood. Catholics, moreover, were complicating the issue by moving in large numbers into formerly Orthodox Serbian communities.

The government was under pressure to take action in the matter. Conversations with the papal curia were begun in 1923, but they led to no positive results. Two years later a delegation was sent to Rome, but the Vatican refused to accept its conditions. The government found that the principle of ecclesiastical "collective bargaining" was highly favorable to the church which practiced it. In 1931 King Alexander himself tried to break the deadlock, but it was not until July 25, 1935, that a concordat was signed by the Yugoslav government and the Vatican authorities.

The greatest difficulty, however, was yet to come, for the concordat was not legally valid until it was ratified by the Skupština and the Senate. The Stojadinović government had only a bare majority in the Skupština and the temper of the Senate was likewise uncertain. Premier Milan Stojadinović preferred to wait for a more favorable opportunity before requesting the parliament for ratification. But when he did so, on November 23, 1936, opposition was so violent that the government was threatened with popular riots. Patriarch Barnabas and most of his clergy became leaders of this opposition movement.

The forces seeking to obstruct the policy of the government were both political and religious: the former seized the opportunity to discredit the Stojadinović cabinet; the latter objected that the concordat granted privileges to the Catholic minority which the Orthodox majority did not enjoy. The Holy Synod of the Orthodox Church published a declaration that "the Serbian Church cannot be indifferent to the fact that another confessional organization secures rights which the Serbian Orthodox Church does not possess."[15] Specifically, the Orthodox group complained that the Jesuits were permitted to resume their work in the country from which they had been expelled in the eighteenth century, and were to recover the churches lost at the time of their expulsion; the Catholic Church was granted the right to establish, at state expense, as many seminaries and catechetical schools as it pleased; teaching of the catechism was made obligatory in Catholic schools.

The government was in a difficult position: to reject the concordat would give strong support to Croatian-Slovene separatist tendencies; to ratify it would deeply offend the Serbian Church and the patriarch, who threatened, it was popularly asserted, to excommunicate all Orthodox deputies who voted for the measure. Finally, after seven months of heated and even violent discussions, the ratification was adopted by the Skupština on July 23, 1937, by a vote of 167 to 129, but with an amendment granting the Council of Ministers the right to bestow on the Orthodox the same privileges accorded the Catholics.

Three hours after the vote was taken, Patriarch Barnabas died. Immediately the cry was raised that it was the passage of the concordat which had killed him. His death, however, had been expected, though it may have been hastened by his deep emotion on hearing the news. In spite of the testimony of physicians as to the natural cause of his death, the government feared public demonstrations at the funeral.

The Holy Synod, without resorting to the extremity of excommunicating Orthodox supporters of the concordat—as the deceased patriarch had threatened—announced in all Orthodox churches of the kingdom that they were to be deprived of certain rights. Nine members of the ministry, the president of the Skupština, and the Orthodox deputies who had voted for ratification were cited to appear before an ecclesiastical tribunal to answer for their conduct. But the government branded this procedure as unconstitutional and therefore illegal. Thereupon the Holy Synod denied the Orthodox members of the government the right to participate in the election of the new patriarch.

In support of Catholic claims, the conference held in October, under the presidency of Monsignor Ivan Šarić, the Archbishop of Sarajevo, protested against the Orthodox attacks and promised "in such circumstances to defend the right of the Catholic Church and of the six million Catholics in the state." But the political leaders of the Croatians, such as Vladimir Maček, did not interfere actively in the quarrel.

Premier Stojadinović decided to delay the submission of the concordat to the Senate until after he had conferred with Pope Pius and Cardinal Pacelli. What happened in Rome or upon his return is by no means clear, but something changed the situation completely. Stojadinović made no attempt to submit the concordat to the Senate and, what is more astounding, on February 1, 1938, he announced to the Holy Synod that he would not seek final ratification of the document. This declaration was later published officially by the minister of the interior. Thereupon the Holy Synod canceled all measures of punishment meted out to Orthodox members of the ministry and the Skupština (including the prohibition to participate in the election of the new patriarch), and the matter was dropped.

The radical political changes introduced by Marshal Tito affected the Roman Catholic Church as profoundly as they did the Orthodox. Faithful to the anti-Communist policy of the Vatican, the Roman Catholic hierarchy of Croatia refused to accept the revolutionary changes introduced by the new regime. Late in 1945 they issued a pastoral letter protesting against religious persecution based on "false accusations" of war crimes. The protest was signed by all the bishops and was read in most of the churches. It stated: "The enemies of the Catholic Church, being also followers of materialistic communism, which the entire Croatian nation with one assent rejects, have in our Croatia exterminated with fire and sword its priests and the more eminent of the faithful."[16]

Several hundred priests were reportedly executed by the new regime. But some Croatian priests had encouraged the persecution of Serbs in Croatia and had participated in the Pavelić government. Archbishop Stepinac was known to be an outspoken opponent of the Tito regime. Marshal Tito therefore charged the hierarchy with being "deeply hostile toward the new federated Yugoslavia." He denied that any religious persecution existed and pointed to the freedom which all the signers of the pastoral letter enjoyed. "So far, no one has hindered them in their destructive work," he declared.

Nevertheless, it was unthinkable that such a state of affairs should be left unchallenged. On September 18, 1946, Archbishop Stepinac was taken into protective custody and was charged with various crimes: support of the Pavelić government and of the Axis Powers, active coöperation with the Ustaši, chairmanship of the committee which directed the forcible conversion of Orthodox Serbs to Catholicism, and eleven other counts. Although the prosecution brought forward all the witnesses it desired, including the Franciscan provincial of Croatia, Martinić, who testified against the archbishop, the defense was not allowed to do so. Stepinac was sentenced to sixteen years at hard labor, loss of his property, and loss of civil rights for five years. His secretary was sentenced to twelve years at forced labor and loss of civil rights for five years. Eight other priests and Franciscan friars received prison sentences ranging from six months to thirteen years.

It is still impossible to feel wholly confident in passing judgment on the merits of the trial. But the available information is sufficient to show clearly that the archbishop did collaborate with the Pavelić regime, although the procedure adopted by the court was not fair according to democratic standards. That, however, does not prove that Stepinac or his fellow defendants were not guilty, either wholly or in part, of the charges.

The largest remaining confessional group in Yugoslavia is the Moslem bloc. (See chap xv, below.) Its origin goes back to the fifteenth century, when Bosnia-Hercegovina lost its independence to the Turks. These territories had been strongly Patarine before the Turkish conquest. In fact, Patarinism—that is, the adaptation of the Bogomil doctrines which had penetrated Bosnia-Hercegovina from Bulgaria—almost became the national faith. But the native rulers, fearful of the Turkish menace, turned for aid to the Roman Catholic West. The price demanded for Western aid always included religious submission to the supremacy of Rome. The native Patarine population so resented the imposition of Roman Catholicism that they—like the Byzantines before the conquest of Constantinople in 1453—preferred "the mufti's turban to a cardinal's hat."[17] After the Turkish conquest of Bosnia-Hercegovina, many Patarine Serbian nobles turned Moslem in order to retain their lands and feudal privileges. Thus in the course of time a large group of native Serbians in Bosnia-Hercegovina accepted Islam; their modern descendants adhere more strictly to the tenets of Islam than do their co-believers in the Turkey of Kemal Atatürk.

The Moslems of Yugoslavia, as well as the Protestants and the Jews, received a definite constitution in the autumn of 1936.

The part which the religious communions of Yugoslavia have taken in the postwar development of the state illustrates, possibly better than any other aspect of Yugoslav life, the difficulty of welding Serbians, Croatians, and Slovenes into one nation, culturally as well as politically united. Undoubtedly, there was not time enough for the task: peoples separated for a millennium cannot overcome their separatist consciousness within the short space of twenty years. But only unification of these two fraternal peoples can cure the political ills which have caused their weakness.

CHAPTER XV

# Yugoslavs of the Moslem Faith

BY WAYNE S. VUCINICH

FOR CENTURIES the territory of the South Slavs was a scene of conflict between the East and the West. Long and bitter religious disputes raged, with the Bogomils, the Eastern Orthodox, and the Roman Catholics struggling for dominance. When the Ottoman Turks succeeded in conquering the entire Balkans by the end of the fifteenth century, the process of Islamization gradually extended over a large part of the Yugoslav lands. The Ottomans did not, for the most part, impose their faith on the newly conquered peoples, with the exception of boys taken into the janizary and spahi corps. The Orthodox and Catholic churches suffered almost no hindrance in the exercise of their beliefs. But members of the Moslem faith were preferred for government positions and were given other favors by the government. As a result, many Yugoslavs went over to Islam. The nobility accepted Islam in order to preserve their privileged social position and wealth, to protect themselves from Turkish and Albanian attacks, and to escape the blood tax.

Islam was transmitted not only directly by the Turks but indirectly by the Albanians who had fallen under Ottoman rule and accepted Islam in the second half of the fifteenth century. Until the seventeenth century these Albanians lived within their original borders; later they began to expand, forcing the Serbs to become Albanized or to vacate their homes and migrate northward. The Albanian expansion proceeded along the line between Prokletija and Jablanica to the north and northeast, where most of the Slavic population became Albanized as it went over to Islam.

Albanians penetrated Kičevo, Gornji Polog, Donji Polog, Kačanik, and Kosovo. In these regions the Slav element was reduced mostly by emigration rather than by Islamization and Albanization. By the second half of the nineteenth century the Albanians had reached Vranje, Pčinja, and Leskovac, but after 1876 they withdrew to Kosovo, where they strengthened the element already existing there.

Some Slavs, even though accepting Islam, never abandoned their customs and language or intermingled with either the Turks or the Albanians. These may be divided into two groups: those inhabiting the regions southwest of the Rogozna Mountains, including Bosnia and Hercegovina; and those south of the Šar Mountains, namely, the Torbeši, the Apovci, and the Pomaci. There are a dozen or more villages of Torbeši in the Skoplje Valley and near the city of Prilep. The Apovci are the Moslem Slavs of Kičevo. The Pomaci are Macedonian Slavs of Moslem faith. They speak Macedonian and inhabit Pomački Meglen, numbering about 45,000. South of Kostur are thirteen Pomaci villages. Kumanovo, Skoplje, and Štip have each a village of that kind. In the district called Gora, located between Šar and Koritnik, are twenty-seven Moslem villages where only Slavic is spoken. The inhabitants adopted the Moslem faith in the sixteenth century and differ from other Moslem Serbs in retaining certain Serbian customs, for example, the wedding ceremony and the yule-log tradition. The Sanjak of Novi Pazar is inhabited by Moslem Serbs who accepted Islam directly from the Turks in the seventeenth century. Here, also, are Muhadžirs* from Bosnia and Hercegovina, Albanian and Arnautaši (Albanized Serbs) Muhadžirs from Serbia who adopted the Serbian language, and some Turkified Serbs (*poturice*) who were driven out of Montenegro in 1707.

When the Turks began their conquest of the Balkans, two opposing political camps existed in Bosnia, one favoring Magyar protection of the Bosnian kingdom and the other hoping to check Magyar influence with the help of the Turks. This disunity enabled the Turks to attain a high degree of success. The late Professor Vladimir Ćorović, an eminent Yugoslav historian, states that,

---

* Arabic *muhājir*, an emigrant, particularly one who joined in the Hegira (*hijrah*) from Mecca to Medina.

just as many Bosnian nobles and rulers had earlier adopted Catholicism to free themselves from Magyar attacks or to secure Magyar
support, so, in the fifteenth century, for similar reasons they went
over to Islam. The Bogomils were the first to adopt the new faith,
but soon after the fall of Bosnia, in 1463, they were followed by
the nobility of other faiths. In the seventeenth century, and with
the appearance of the janizaries, many peasants also adopted Islam.

The majority of Yugoslav Moslems live in Bosnia and Hercegovina, near the capitals of the two provinces, Sarajevo and Mostar.
Moslems inhabit the region along the Neretva River in rather large

| Religion | 1910<br>Austrian census | 1921<br>Yugoslav census | 1939<br>Yugoslav estimate |
|---|---|---|---|
| Moslem | 612,137 (32.7%) | 588,173 (31.1%) | 858,140 (31.2%) |
| Orthodox | 824,557 (43.5%) | 825,390 (43.7%) | 1,226,991 (44.6%) |
| Roman Catholic | 387,707 (20.4%) | 401,262 (21.3%) | 595,974 (21.7%) |

numbers, and throughout the whole of Hercegovina one finds
Moslem oases. North of Sarajevo, between the Bosna and Drina
rivers, many Moslems have settled, intermingled with the Christians. Along the Sava River and west of the Bosna and Neretva
rivers there are few Moslems, though they may be found as far
west as Bihać, Bosanski Novi, and some of the larger villages of that
region. The number of Yugoslav Moslems in Bosnia and Hercegovina steadily increased until they exerted an appreciable influence on the political and cultural life of the Ottoman Empire.

The accompanying table indicates the distribution of the population of Bosnia and Hercegovina according to religious affilia-
tions.

The Albanians who inhabit western Macedonia and parts of
Montenegro and the Sanjak of Novi Pazar and the Turks who are
concentrated in Macedonia form most of the remaining Moslem
population of Yugoslavia. No exact statistics are available on the
Albanians and Turks; the former are estimated at 550,000 and the
latter at 175,000.

The official census of 1931 lists 1,561,166 Moslems in Yugoslavia.
An official estimate in 1939 indicates that 858,140 Moslems lived
in Bosnia and Hercegovina alone, which was 31.2 per cent of the
total population of the two provinces. The table (see overleaf)

shows the distribution of the Moslem population in 1931, according to banovine.

Among the Yugoslav Moslems one finds traces of the original Turkish settlements, especially in Bosnian Krajina, the military zone which was constantly on the alert against the danger of Austrian invasion. These Turkish settlers were soldiers defending the Ottoman Empire from Austria, as well as from the Banija, Kordun, and Lika Serbs. In the region of Pounje, for example, are several hundred families of Moslems from Anatolia. The Turkish settlers north of Cazin differ anthropologically from the native population,

| | | | |
|---|---|---|---|
| Drava . . . . . . . . | 927 | Vardar . . . . . . . | 499,362 |
| Drina* . . . . . . . | 356,469 | Vrbas . . . . . . . . | 250,265 |
| Dunav . . . . . . . | 2,660 | Zeta . . . . . . . . | 315,677 |
| Morava . . . . . . . | 58,802 | Belgrade prefecture . . . | 3,821 |
| Primorje . . . . . . | 69,360 | | |
| Sava . . . . . . . . | 3,823 | Total . . . . . . | 1,561,166 |

* Drina, Vrbas, and parts of Zeta and Primorje correspond roughly to the provinces of Bosnia and Hercegovina. Vardar included southern Serbia and Macedonia.

since they did not freely mix with them. They are, however, linguistically assimilated and speak the Serbo-Croat language. In the regions of Visoko and Fojnica live Moslems who came originally from Asia Minor. Some Bosnian Moslems have come all the way from Arabia and northern Africa. Thus two processes of assimilation took place in Bosnia and Hercegovina: the Islamization of Yugoslavs and the linguistic assimilation of immigrant Turks.

Many Yugoslav Moslems won high administrative and military positions in the Ottoman government: Mehmed Paša Sokolović, Rustem Paša, son-in-law of Suleiman the Magnificent, Pertev Paša, 'Alī Paša Semiz, Hasan Paša Predojević. The Hercegovinian historian Dr. Safvet Beg Bašagić has collected about seven hundred names of famous Bosnians and Hercegovinians who were in the service of the Ottoman Empire. But Yugoslav Orientalists continue to find others not mentioned by either Bašagić or Joseph von Hammer-Purgstall, an authority on Turkish history.

As a favored group in the Ottoman Empire, the Moslems of Bosnia and Hercegovina, unlike the Serbs, were not forced to migrate and therefore retained some of the oldest Slavic traits. Mehmed Hasan Efendi Skopljak, a Moslem writer of the seventeenth century, stressed their Slav origin. Even the Yugoslav Moslems who reached high government offices in the Empire were conscious of their Yugoslav origin. For example, Mehmed Paša Sokolović (1505–1579), the Grand Vizier, came of a Serbian family of Goražde. It was he who reëstablished the patriarchate of Peć in 1557 and put his brother Makarije on its throne.

The language of the Bosnian and Hercegovinian Moslems is Serbo-Croat, which is a partial proof of their Yugoslav consciousness. Their alphabet, until the Austro-Hungarian occupation in 1878, for other than religious writings was Cyrillic, the writing of the beg, or Old Serbian. In the seventeenth and eighteenth centuries they created a local literature in the national tongue but based on Oriental motifs. Some of the earliest Moslem writers and poets expressed their national consciousness in identifying the Serbs and the Croats as their brother Yugoslavs. Particularly prominent in this group was Mehmed Hevaji Tuzlak, a poet of the first half of the seventeenth century. On the other hand, says Hakija Kulenović, there are examples in Moslem poetry of a complete lack of national consciousness: the Lika and Krajina heroic Moslem songs, and those depicting the plunderings and the battles of Mustaj Beg of Lika, Mujo of Kladun, and Hrnjica Halil (Khalīl) in the Ravni Kotari and bordering region, Ismā'īl Aga's raids in Hercegovina and Montenegro, Kulin Kapetan's attacks in Mačva.

The Moslem national epic, with its decorative elements, dramatic conception, and interest in human characterization, holds a high place in Yugoslav poetry. Usually the hero is not a royal child but the son of the *fukara* (Arabic *al-fuqarā,* the poor), whom the Moslem songs elevate to an ideal height. Two such heroes are Djerzeles Alija and Budalina Tale.

The so-called harem songs are full of lyric character. They have a strong dramatic construction and deal with psychological problems. According to Muradbegović, they express the atmosphere of the harem's exotic environment, and are suffused with emotion and beauty. Another type of lyric is the *sevdalinka,** "the product

---

* From Turkish *sevdalī,* melancholy, or madly in love. The Turkish adjective seems to derive its meaning from both the verb *sevmek,* to love, and the noun *sevda,* a corruption of the Arabic *saudā,* used as a noun for black bile or melancholy. The Slavic *sevdalinka* often has a melancholy note and its theme is usually love.

of both sexes as an expression of their joint emotional life. The *sevdalinka* is a song combining Slavic sentimental feeling with a passionate Oriental accent."

Yugoslav Moslems wrote not only in Serbo-Croatian but also in Arabic, Turkish, and Persian. Their works have been found far from the Yugoslav lands, some of them written with the Arabic alphabet in the Serbo-Croatian language. Many of the seventeenth-century songs, according to Hasan Rebac, are religious in character: the *ilahije* (Arabic *ilāhīa*, theological), or didactic narrative, and the *kaside* (Arabic *qasīda*). Among early Moslem poets may be mentioned Muhamed Havari, Kaimija, Mula Mustafa Bašeskija (popularly known as Šefkija), Sejid Vehab Ilhamija, the most productive of the poets, Šek Abdurahman (Shaikh 'Abd al-Rahmān) Sirija (known as Šek Sikirina), and Omer Humo.

Many other Yugoslav Moslems have been widely recognized for their work in literature. Professor Ćorović lists some of these: Judge Širi ('Alī Beg Hercegović), an excellent commentator on the Persian classics, has been called the most popular Bosnian among the Turkish writers; Derviš Paša Bajazidagić, of Mostar, and his son Ahmed Beg, were poets and prose writers of ability; Hasan Djafi Efendi Pruščanin wrote *The Foundations of Wisdom* in Arabic, which was translated into Turkish at the command of Sultan Muhamed III; the well-known Turkish historian Pechevi (Ibrāhīm Paša Alajbegović) was a Yugoslav Moslem; in the nineteenth century Sarajlija Sālih Muvekit (al-Sarāī al-Muwaqqit) composed a chronicle of Bosnia beginning with the advent of the Turks, *Ta'rīkh-i Diār-i Bosna ve Hersek*.

The decorative arts of the Yugoslav Moslems are best exemplified in their embroideries, rug-knitting, and textile industry. The bridges in Mostar and Višegrad and the four finest mosques—the Begova (the mosque of Gazi Husrev Beg) in Sarajevo, the Ferhadija in Banjaluka, the Karadjozbegova in Mostar, the Aladja in Foča—are outstanding examples of Moslem architectural and engineering ability.

The spiritual head of the Moslems in prewar Yugoslavia was a *shaikh al-Islām*, or *ra'īs al-'ulamā*, whose residence was in Belgrade. He was elected by a council composed of *'ulamā*, *muftīs*, the principal of the school of *qādīs*, and delegates from the commission on the *waqs* of the lower chamber. This election was sanctioned by royal decree. The judges appointed by the *ra'īs* were state officials, trained in the sheriat *(shari'a)* of the Hanafite rite, a special institute at Sarajevo. The Moslem religious administration was divided into two regions—Sarajevo and Skoplje—and these were subdivided into *muftīas,* whose leaders were appointed by the Crown on the recommendation of the *ra'īs al-'ulamā.* The latter acted on the advice of his two councils of four members each. Moslem religious teachers were trained in *medreses* (religious schools).

In the early nineteenth century it was obvious that the Turks had become enemies of the Yugoslav Moslems as well as of Christians. This was especially true after the reforms of Sultan Mahmud II, when the Turks, under the screen of Islam, began to emphasize the unity of the Moslem world. The trend, says the Moslem, M. Begović, is amply illustrated by the slaughter of eminent Moslem leaders which was carried out by Džlal Paša (Jalal Pasha) in Travnik; by the uprising in 1831 of Husein Beg Gradaščević, who was in close contact with the Serbian Prince Miloš; by the murder of 'Alī Paša Rizvanbegović, who had maintained relations with Montenegro; and by the persecution and slaughter by Omer Paša ('Umar Pasha) of Bosnian Moslems who had fought against Turkey.

The occupation of Bosnia-Hercegovina by the Austro-Hungarian Monarchy in 1878 caused a social upheaval among the Yugoslav Moslems. Accustomed to live in a state based on the Koran, they were now deprived of leadership and reduced to a secondary position. Embittered by the new conditions, some of them left Bosnia-Hercegovina. Those who remained, took no part in public life, but lived in the hope that another war might restore the two provinces to the Ottoman Empire. With the help of the Christian Yugoslavs, especially the Orthodox Serbs, they resisted the Austro-Hungarian occupation and, in 1899, started a movement to attain religious and educational autonomy in Bosnia-Hercegovina.

The Moslems of Bosnia-Hercegovina were organized in the Jugoslovenska Muslimanska Organizacija (Yugoslav Moslem Organization), which, under Mehmed Spaho, enlisted the support of large numbers of Moslems from all classes of society. The party was basically conservative and was controlled by the well-to-do.

Spaho supported the successive governments in return for concessions to the Moslem population. He was a close ally of the Slovene People's party, which usually supported the same cabinet in Belgrade—hence a popular prewar saying in Belgrade that Moslems and Slovenes governed Yugoslavia because the leaders threw their weight to the party in power. This opportunist policy was characteristic of Moslem leadership before the Second World War.

The annexation of Bosnia-Hercegovina by Austria-Hungary in 1908 was the final blow to the Yugoslav Moslems. Whereas other Yugoslavs in the two provinces had looked to Serbia, Montenegro, and Russia for assistance, the Moslems had expected aid from the Ottoman Empire—a hope which was destroyed when they learned that the Turks had given them up to Austria-Hungary.

The imperial statute of April 15, 1909, marked the end of a decade of bitter struggle. The Dual Monarchy granted autonomous administration for the Islamic religion and *vakuf-mearif* (*waqf-ma'ārif*) affairs in Bosnia-Hercegovina, but it exploited the weakened Moslem resistance by trimming expected concessions before approving the statute. Even though the law regulating their status was a compromise, it satisfied certain religious and educational aims of the Yugoslav Moslems. They could now be sure that their children would not be influenced by "infidel" ways, but would receive proper Moslem upbringing. As a result of the new law, the emigration of Moslems ceased almost immediately.

By the annexation of Bosnia-Hercegovina and through the statute providing religious and educational autonomy for Yugoslav Moslems, the Dual Monarchy was able to discourage the development of Yugoslav nationalism among them. By its traditional policy of "divide and rule," Austria-Hungary "systematically advanced through the press the concept of the 'Serbian people' for the Orthodox element, of the 'Croatian people' for the Catholics, and of the 'Moslem people' for the Moslems." Many Moslem leaders who had once been classed as enemies of the Monarchy and as Serbophils now sided with the government and eventually became strong Serbophobes.

In 1910 the Austro-Hungarian government granted Bosnia and Hercegovina a constitution that provided for a provincial assembly the representation of which was based on the religious affiliation of the natives. The Austro-Hungarian authorities hoped in this way to promote separatism among the Yugoslavs of different faiths in order to undermine the growing Serbian nationalism.

Osman Djikić, in order to counteract the anti-Serb propaganda of the Moslem literary periodical *Behar*[1] (Turkish *bahar*, springtime), which was published in Sarajevo from 1900 to 1910, founded a rival organ, *Gajret* (Arabic *ghaira*, Turkish *gayret*, zeal), as well as a cultural and educational society, known by the same name, to which pro-Serb Moslems rallied. The work of Djikić marked the beginning of a new chapter in the national awakening of the Yugoslav Moslems. His followers were conscious of their Yugoslav nationality, and were in constant conflict with the Austrophil Moslems who called themselves Bošnjaks (Bosnians). The native Serbs grudgingly referred to these Moslems as *mehkiši,* or *prdekteri.* The Austro-Hungarian authorities looked with disfavor on the gradual awakening of Moslem consciousness and eventually forbade the publication of *Gajret.* But the nationalist spirit passed from this journal to the schools, where Serb instructors taught the Moslem youth Serbian literature and history. According to Hakija Kulenović, a Moslem writer, "Serb writings, books, newspapers, and dynastic and other pictures were distributed secretly."

The Balkan wars (1912–1913) retarded the process of national awakening among the Yugoslav Moslems, stirring to life, instead, the long-dormant idea of the division of the world into Moslem and non-Moslem. The Moslems hoped that a Turkish victory might eventually drive the Austro-Hungarians from Bosnia-Hercegovina. The Dual Monarchy took advantage of these wars to sow discord between the Orthodox and the Moslem Yugoslavs. The consequences of its propaganda were very harmful. The persecution of the Serbs by the *prdekteri* was intensified.

The Moslem position was further complicated by internal dissension. Some favored the Croats and some the Serbs. According to Begović, a pro-Serb orientation was long preponderant among the Moslems because it was the Serbs who had led the fight against the common enemy, Austria-Hungary. In the Balkan wars a number of Moslems had joined the Serbs as volunteers to fight the Turks, and in the First World War there were Moslem volunteers

---

[1] For notes to chapter xv see page 522.

in the Serbian army on the Salonika front, in the Yugoslav division in Dobrudja, and in the army of Captain Pivko, which was organized in Italy.

The situation changed, however, when Turkey became the ally of Austria-Hungary during the First World War. The belief was common among the Moslem masses that the sultan had made an arrangement with Francis Joseph that in the event of victory Bosnia and Hercegovina should go to Turkey and again become part of the Moslem state. Many Yugoslav Moslems in Bosnia and Hercegovina declared it to be a sacred war and held prayers in the mosques for the defeat of Serbia. As the Moslem writer Hasan Rebac expressed it, "While the old Moslems prayed for victory, the younger and stronger ones persecuted the Serbs, acting with special severity against the Serb Moslems who had gathered around Osman Djikić."

The pro-Croat Moslems remained relatively inactive throughout the First World War; those representing a broader Yugoslav nationalism worked with the Mlada Bosna (Young Bosnia) group and the Bosnia-Hercegovina revolutionary movement. The former founded a new Moslem society, the Narodna Uzdanica, "to enlighten the high-school youth in the Croatian national spirit and to direct it to university study at Zagreb." To quote again from Kulenović, "So Belgrade and Zagreb have become antipodal centers for the national, cultural, educational, and economic orientation of the new Moslem intelligentsia."

The lives of the Yugoslav Moslems were influenced, also, by the changes in the Republic of Turkey after the First World War. Once the caliphate had been abolished, Turkey's leadership of the Moslem world was at an end. This tended to weaken Moslem isolationism in the family of the Yugoslav nations, though it never completely disappeared. The Moslems continued to maintain their own periodicals, newspapers, schools, and political parties. The Moslems of southern Serbia and Macedonia were organized in a political party called Džemijet (Arabic *al-Jami'a* society), known at the time of its foundation in 1919 as Islam Muhafazaji Hukuk Džemijet (Society for the Protection of Moslem Rights).

After the unification of Yugoslavia the Moslems were placed in the peculiar position of having to choose between separatism—either Croat or Serb—and centralism. Progressive Mohammedans saw the principal source of Yugoslav difficulties in the nationalistic rivalry drummed up by Serb and Croat chauvinists and in the economic and social misery of their own people. In order to avoid Serbo-Croat conflict, they preferred to be known simply as Yugoslavs.

After 1918 the Serb nationalists were less active in Bosnia-Hercegovina. They believed that their highest ideal had been attained and that further development of the cult of Serb nationalism was not urgent, especially since the central government and the dynasty were theirs and the control of Yugoslavia was indisputably Serbian. Activity in the new state, it was felt, should be inspired by the broader Serbian-controlled Yugoslav nationalism which, if necessary, should be imposed on the various peoples of Yugoslavia.

The Croat nationalists, whose hopes had not been fulfilled by the Yugoslav unification, pressed for the development of their separate nationalism. A well-organized propaganda among the Moslems emphasized that the Serbs and the Serb-dominated government were responsible for their plight and that Moslems were, in fact, Croats. On this basis a claim was advanced to all of Bosnia-Hercegovina, not solely by the Ustaši of Pavelić but by a strong faction in Vladimir Maček's Peasant party. Serb-Croat rivalry over Bosnia-Hercegovina, where most of the Yugoslav Moslems live, became less acute after the *sporazum* (agreement) between the Serbs and Croats in 1939 and the creation of an autonomous Croatian banovina, but the fate of the Moslems remained undecided.

According to Šukrija Kurtović, a Moslem, a large bloc of Serbs, including most of the Moslem leaders, opposed the partition of Bosnia-Hercegovina and the inclusion of its Moslem areas in the newly created banovina. They felt that Croatia was western European and Catholic in culture, but that Bosnia and Hercegovina were under Oriental influence and thus were closer to the Serbian part of Yugoslavia. The late Mehmed Spaho, an eminent Moslem leader, remarked, during the preliminaries to the Serb-Croat *sporazum*, "If Bosnia and Hercegovina cannot get autonomy, then we cannot at any price allow the region to be divided, but let the whole of it go to Serbia."

After Yugoslavia's collapse in April, 1941, the Moslems of Bosnia-Hercegovina became citizens of the Croatian Ustaši state, took part in its government,[2] and oriented their religious and other organizations accordingly. In place of Belgrade, Zagreb was now the center of political activity and propaganda, not only for Moslems who lived in Bosnia-Hercegovina but for those in occupied Serbia, Macedonia, and Montenegro. On one occasion a delegation of Moslems from the Sanjak of Novi Pazar came to Zagreb to appeal to the *poglavnik*, Ante Pavelić, for annexation to the so-called independent Croatian state.

Domestic dissatisfaction and the growing Partisan activity forced quisling Pavelić to grant extraordinary concessions to Moslems to retain their support. He promised them full realization of their material and religious aspirations, gave them opportunity to hold high military positions and have Moslem units in the Croat army, subsidized their schools, and began the construction of a mosque in Zagreb. The grand mufti of Jerusalem visited the large Moslem settlements in Croatia and encouraged them to support the Ustaši regime.

Under these conditions, most Moslems became loyal citizens of the puppet Croat state and accepted the government's anti-Serb policy. The fact that the Moslems identified themselves with the Ustaši and became active participants in the slaughter of the Serbs provoked a bloody revenge on the part of the Četnici. In 1941 and even later the Četnici carried out indiscriminate terror raids against Moslem settlements. A large number of Moslems in areas along the Drina and elsewhere in Bosnia were killed. The attitude of the Četnici estranged many Moslems who hitherto had been more sympathetic to the Serbs than to the Croats. As a result, only a handful of Moslems joined the Četnici. The leading Moslem Četnik was Mustafa Mulagić, a member of the National Council of General Draža Mihailović. Mulagić was tried and sentenced to imprisonment by the Partisan government.

The Moslems were forced to choose between the Ustaši and the Partisans. At first poorly represented in Partisan ranks, they increased in number as many deserted the Croat army to join Tito in the autumn of 1943. Among them were Colonel Sulejman Filipović, who became acting Minister of Forests and Mines in the

Partisan Committee for National Liberation and held the same position in the Yugoslav government; and Muhamed Sudžuka, Pavelić's *veliki župan* (governor) of Travnik. Other leading Moslem Partisans were the late Nurija Pozderac, a former Yugoslav senator and school principal; Osman Karabegović, a Banjaluka student; and the writers Avdo Humo and Skender Kulenović.

In 1946 Bosnia-Hercegovina was given an autonomous position in the new federalized Yugoslavia, a status equal to that of the other federal units, and thus put an end to the rivalry of Serb and Croat nationalists. This appears to be the fairest solution of the problem, which was one of the major obstacles to Serbo-Croat union.

The establishment of Bosnia-Hercegovina as a separate federal unit within Yugoslavia has enabled the Moslems to remain under one administrative unit rather than to be subjected to Serbian or Croatian domination and to periodic administrative division in order to satisfy the insatiable claims of either Serb or Croat chauvinists. The Moslems of southern Serbia, most of whom are Albanians, were given an autonomous district within the federal unit of Serbia. They are represented in the Serbian Council and have been given cultural autonomy. The Moslems are represented also in the other federal governments of Yugoslavia, especially in that of Bosnia-Hercegovina.[3] There are two Moslems in the Macedonian government[4] and one in the government of Montenegro.[5] In the new Yugoslavia religious freedom is guaranteed. However, a series of measures have been announced which aim at restricting the political, economic, and cultural powers of organized religion.

Until recently Moslem education was confined mainly to religious institutions and failed to satisfy the needs of everyday life. In spite of the existence of compulsory primary instruction since 1911, Moslems clung to their own *mekteb*. Until the outbreak of the First World War no educational provision was made for Moslem women. In 1912 the illiteracy among them in Bosnia-Hercegovina amounted to 99.68 per cent and still remains very high. But despite the opposition of the older generation, the number of Moslem children of both sexes attending public schools increased rapidly after 1918. The conservatives were forced to give way before the growing liberal and progressive elements, as was clearly apparent from the declaration of the Hodžinska Kurija (the Curia of Khojas, the supreme religious institution), on July 10, 1928, at Sarajevo, that a Moslem woman can, "when needs require, expose her face, attend all types of public schools, work in stores, and occupy all other offices which are not contrary to the principles of Islamic morality."

At the Moslem Congress of 1928 at Sarajevo an agreement was reached between the spiritual and the secular intelligentsia to extend education among Moslems. A resolution asked the state to establish as many schools as possible in Moslem regions, to extend compulsory public-school education to Moslem girls, and to increase social work among Moslems through coöperation of the state with cultural and educational societies. Plans were laid, also, for the establishment of coöperatives, special public schools for coöperative training, and a required course in coöperatives in the *medreses* (religious schools).

Before the Second World War Yugoslavia had hundreds of confessional schools for Moslems, in which the emphasis was on Arabic and Turkish languages, literature, and history; the Koranic exegesis; and jurisprudence. Graduates of secondary schools had their choice of either the Moslem colleges of jurisprudence and religion or the regular universities. In spite of religious and economic obstacles, educational conditions among the Moslems steadily improved.[6]

After the unification of the Serbs, Croats, and Slovenes the magazine *Gajret* began to reappear. A society called the Beogradski Gajret Osman Djikić was founded in 1923 in Belgrade, which was becoming a center of cultural and educational orientation for Yugoslav Moslems. In 1936–1937 the society maintained and sent through secondary school 429 students, and has paid for the higher education of about 150 students.

Until the enactment of agrarian reform[7] in October, 1918, many Yugoslav Moslems were large landowners, agas and begs. The Reform Act radically changed their social status. Of the total number of landowners with *kmets** in Bosnia-Hercegovina, 91.15 per cent

---

* The *kmets* were tenants who gave their landlord the *mak*, which generally consisted of a third of the crop in kind. They possessed the land by hereditary right and could leave it at will.

were Moslems and 8.75 per cent belonged to other faiths. (See chap. x, above.) The Moslems who lost their land did not receive cash payment for it, but government notes which they were forced to sell below face value. This caused widespread speculation, to the advantage of banks and financiers. The well-to-do Moslems, however, benefited in other ways, owing primarily to the political opportunism and manipulations of their political leaders. A law was passed in 1928 providing for allotment of land to former owners who, it was officially explained, had been left without the minimum necessary for existence. But the insatiable demands of the onetime agas and begs did not end here, and they complained that the land allocated to them was uncultivable and of poor quality. The small Moslem landowners who lived off their land suffered as much as the Christians because of the system of inheritance which required partition of landed estates among the members of a family. Large estates were thus subdivided into a number of separate small farms, the working of which provided a bare subsistence.

Only a little more than a third of the Moslem population is agrarian. The remainder engage in small business, trade, and labor in the cities. But lacking specialized training and effective organization, they have been unable to withstand organized competition. The small Moslem merchants, like their Christian brothers, have gradually been reduced to impoverished shopkeepers. Moslem workers, to a large degree illiterate and accustomed to the old patriarchal ways, could not compete for better jobs, and were usually exploited through overwork and underpayment. The number of Moslems in government and official service, however, has steadily increased, though not in proportion to other Yugoslavs.

## Part Six

# CULTURAL
# DEVELOPMENT

# CHAPTER XVI

# *The Serbo-Croatian Language*

## BY GEORGE RAPALL NOYES

THE SERBO-CROATIAN LANGUAGE belongs to a group of languages united by certain common characteristics and called the Slavic languages. The Slavs, be it said at once, are not at present a race or a nation; they are merely a collection of individuals who speak Slavic languages. So the governmental and literary language of the United States is English, but English is the only mother tongue of millions of Negroes and thousands of American Indians and Chinese and Japanese who dwell within our borders. Nor is there any reason to think that the Slavs ever formed a race. Race is a word so difficult to define that some ethnologists have given up the attempt in despair; there are few, if any, unmixed races in the world, and no branch of the Slavs belongs to any one of the possible few. But it is probable that at the opening of the Christian era there was only one Slavic language, which the philologists call for convenience Primitive Slavic, and that, like the ancient Greeks, the speakers of it formed, in a broad sense of the term, a nation: that is, a people united by common customs and beliefs as well as by a common language, and conscious of their own unity.

The territory occupied by this nation cannot be accurately defined. It almost certainly lay northeast of the Carpathian Mountains; on the east it probably extended to the basin of the middle Dnieper; on the west it may have reached the Elbe and may have gone no farther than the basin of the Vistula; on the north it was separated by a region of lakes and marshes from the lands of the Lithuanians in the basins of the Niemen and the Dvina.

Very early, perhaps in the first century of our era, these Slavs, or speakers of the Primitive Slavic language, began to expand in various directions. Their movement was slow and was not primarily dependent on military campaigns. It was rather a gradual infiltration into comparatively unoccupied regions, similar to that of the American people from the Atlantic seaboard to the Pacific, or of the Russian people across eastern Russia and Siberia and even into Alaska. By the end of the fifth century the Slavs had reached the northern borders of the Balkan Peninsula; by the end of the seventh century the regions now occupied by the Slovenians, Croatians, Serbs, and Bulgarians already had a Slavic population. At this time the Slavs held an unbroken stretch of territory extending from the Baltic to the Mediterranean.

Conditions among the Slavs were soon altered. Near the end of the seventh century the Bulgarians, an Asiatic people, invaded the Balkan Peninsula and established themselves in a territory roughly corresponding to modern Bulgaria. They subjugated the Slavs of this region; but, like the Normans in England, they adopted the language of their subjects: their state remained Slavic in language and in culture.

More important was the invasion of the Magyars, a people who, probably coming from somewhere in eastern Russia, at the close of the ninth century occupied considerable areas along the Danube. The Magyars were so numerous that they either exterminated the Slavs in the lands that they conquered, drove them out before them, or assimilated them; they kept their own language and founded a separate Hungarian kingdom which extended on the west as far as the German dominions, and which has endured to this day.

To the east of the Hungarians the speakers of Rumanian, a language derived from Latin, gradually extended their boundaries until they reached the Black Sea. Thus there was created a band of non-Slavic territory that has effectively separated the Slavs of the Balkan Peninsula from their northern neighbors, the Czechs and Slovaks, the Ruthenians and Ukrainians.

Three South Slavic languages are recognized: Serbo-Croatian, Bulgarian, and Slovenian. The territory occupied by these three languages, which approximates that of Yugoslavia and Bulgaria in 1940, forms a rough quadrilateral bounded on the west by the

Adriatic and by Albania, on the east by the Black Sea, on the south by the Aegean and by Greece, on the north by Rumania, Hungary, and a stretch of German territory. The Bulgarian language, with some 5,000,000 speakers, occupies the eastern part of the quadrilateral; the Slovenian language, with about 1,400,000 speakers, fills a much smaller area in the northwest corner of the quadrilateral; and the Serbo-Croatian language, spoken by about 11,000,000 persons, covers the rest of the quadrilateral.

But these statements, though correct enough for ordinary purposes, do not accurately describe the linguistic conditions in this area. Serbo-Croatian is a neighbor of Bulgarian and of Slovenian; it is also a neighbor of Hungarian. Its neighborliness with the third language, however, is of a totally different sort from that with the other two. Hungarian is a language quite unrelated to Serbo-Croatian, with which it was merely brought into geographical juxtaposition by the invasion of the Magyars into Europe in the ninth century. No forms of speech stand halfway between Hungarian and Serbo-Croatian; the relations between the two languages resemble those between English and Spanish in North America.[1]

The Serbo-Croatian, Bulgarian, and Slovenian languages arose from the gradual breakup into several dialects of a single dialect, Primitive Slavic, the form of speech used by the Slavs when they first entered the Balkan Peninsula.[2] These dialectic variations occurred over the whole peninsula. Each small locality, even a single isolated village, might develop its own linguistic peculiarities. So today a man may walk from Varna on the Black Sea west to Sofia, then down to Bitolj in southern Macedonia, northward to Belgrade, thence west through Slavonia and Croatia to Zagreb, still further west to Ljubljana and into the Slovenian districts annexed by Italy after the First World War; and, if he pay heed to the speech of the peasantry rather than to that of the postmasters and the schoolmasters, he will never cross a definite linguistic boundary dividing Bulgarian from Serbo-Croatian or Serbo-Croatian from Slovenian. In western Bulgaria and eastern Serbia he will hear dialects that are intermediate between Bulgarian and Serbo-Croatian; scholars who class them with one or the other are likely to be guided by patriotism rather than by strict linguistic method. In

[1] For notes to chapter xvi see page 523.

Croatia he will find a speech that is intermediate between Serbo-
Croatian and Slovenian.[3]

Why, then, do people say that only three Slavic languages are
spoken in the Balkan Peninsula? The answer is simple: a language
differs from a dialect in that it is the recognized official speech of
an organized state covering a considerable territory, or the organ
of a developed literature read by large numbers of persons and
forming a bond of union among them. According to varying circumstances, languages diverge into dialects or dialects expand
their territory and become languages. Thus the Latin language,
after the Roman conquests had carried it all over western Europe,
broke up into a multitude of small dialects, which, generally speaking, have remained distinct until the present day. So if a tourist
walks from Rome to Paris and, like the Balkan traveler of whom
I have spoken, pays heed to the speech of the peasantry, he will
not step suddenly from Italian into French; he will pass by degrees
from Italian to Provençal (the speech of southern France) and
from Provençal into French. On the other hand, when France was
united, the dialect of Paris became the official language of the new
kingdom, the language of France, which boys and girls study in
Rouen and Toulouse as well as in Paris, and which they write and
speak correctly, even though they may retain some peculiarities of
the local pronunciation. In Italy, through the literary and cultural
predominance of Tuscany, Tuscan Italian became the standard
language of the whole peninsula. Educated people of Venice are
bilingual; they speak both the Venetian dialect of the workingman
and the Tuscan Italian that they have learned in school. This literary and linguistic unification of Italian cultivated society took
place long before Italy was unified politically.

So in the Balkans the dialect of eastern Bulgaria has become the
basis of the governmental and literary language of Bulgaria as a
whole. In Bulgaria, as in France—though the analogy is by no
means exact—political conditions have shaped the development of
the language. In Slovenia, a region that has never had an independent political existence, the dialect of lower Carniola has become the
basis of a language, created more or less artificially, in which there
exists a literature of real power and beauty. Here there is an analogy, though again an imperfect one, with the situation in Italy.

The conditions that have shaped the growth of the Serbo-Croatian literary language have been extremely complicated. Dialectic, cultural, political, and even religious factors have been involved. The language has varied widely at different times and still varies in different localities.

We are all aware that the standards of English literary style are not quite the same as those of even the most cultivated English speech. In articles meant for print, we do not use forms such as "can't" and "'em," though in conversation it is pedantic to avoid them. A Protestant clergyman in a prayer written for publication, or for that matter in an extempore spoken prayer, imitates the language of the Authorized Version of the Bible, archaic even in 1611, when the translation was published. English poets today do not shrink from a vocabulary that is similarly archaic, and still use words such as "thou," "thee," "lovest," "loveth." The speech of Scotland might have been termed a separate language in the fifteenth century, since it was used in the administration of an independent kingdom and was the organ of a fairly important literature. It has now become a local dialect—yet it retains rights of its own in literature. Robert Burns was bilingual, speaking both Scotch and English, and using the two forms of speech in his poems as best accorded with the temper of his work. He was in a different position from James Russell Lowell, who in *The Biglow Papers* employed the "Yankee dialect," which he understood but did not use in his own speech, merely to add spice and humorous local color to his verse.

The ancient Greeks recognized themselves as a people united by language and distinct from the "barbarians," but they spoke many dialects, several of which attained literary standing. A Greek poet might use different dialects in different poems, or he might mingle in a single poem forms taken from more than one dialect. The language of the Homeric poems is to a large degree an artificial creation, not representing the speech of any one region. Analogies to all these phenomena may be found in the history of the Serbo-Croatian language.

The Serbo-Croatian literary language has been much affected in its development by a language now called by philologists either Old Church Slavic or Old Bulgarian. This language is the oldest of the Slavic languages of which we have literary records of any extent. It ceased to be spoken as early as Anglo-Saxon.

In 863 two Greeks from Salonika, Cyril and Methodius, went to Moravia as Christian missionaries. The speech of the Moravians was not the same as that of the Slavic population centered about Salonika, where Cyril and Methodius had grown up, but the resemblance was close enough for the two missionaries to use in their work the Slavic language known to them, presumably from childhood, a language that is, in general, the ancestor of modern Bulgarian. Into this Old Bulgarian they and their successors translated from the Greek the Gospels, the Psalms, and numerous other religious texts. Their procedure had momentous consequences: the language of Salonika in the ninth century has remained to the present, with relatively small alterations, the church language of the Serbs, the Bulgarians, and the Russians, the three Slavic peoples belonging to the Eastern, or Greek Orthodox, Church.

Soon this Old Bulgarian ceased to be a living language. Hence the scribes no longer wrote it correctly; each copyist modified its spelling and even its grammatical forms under the influence of the Serbian, Bulgarian, or Russian language that he actually spoke. Even so, though to a less degree, the fifteenth-century scribes who copied Chaucer's poems misrepresented his spelling and consequently his grammar, owing to the changes in English pronunciation that had taken place since Chaucer wrote. And untrained writers of today who, for rhetorical effect, try to use Biblical English, are likely to stray from the grammatical standards of the Authorized Version.

The earliest extant manuscripts of Old Bulgarian are undated, but it is doubtful whether any one of them was written before the year 1000. The language of the texts written in the Balkan Peninsula before the year 1100 is called Old Church Slavic. Since even the earliest of these texts were probably written at least a hundred years after the period of Cyril and Methodius, they do not represent absolutely without change the language of Salonika in 863, but they enable scholars to reconstruct with certainty the features of that language. And this Old Bulgarian, or Old Church Slavic, of the ninth century differs surprisingly little from what the Primitive Slavic language must have been before it broke up into dialects. It represents well the Primitive Slavic vowel system, less accurately the Primitive Slavic inflections; it differs markedly, however, from Primitive Slavic in its consonantal system. Thus we have reason to suppose that at the end of the seventh century, when the Slavs had already established themselves in the Balkan Peninsula, their language, or languages, had not much diverged from Primitive Slavic. On the other hand, the texts show that in the eleventh century differences of speech were rapidly arising among the Balkan Slavs.

The language of the Church Slavic manuscripts written in the Balkan Peninsula in the twelfth century or later is known, according to its dialectic coloring, as Serbian Church Slavic or Bulgarian Church Slavic; that of the manuscripts written in Russia, the earliest of which goes back to the middle of the eleventh century, is known as Russian Church Slavic. Since in medieval times almost the only educated persons were clerics, these three forms of the Church Slavic language came to be used for literature, original as well as translated, in their respective countries, to the exclusion of the languages spoken by the people: among the Serbs until the eighteenth century; among the Bulgarians and Russians, with important reservations, for about the same length of time. Church Slavic elements are still prominent in the literary languages of the Serbs and the Bulgarians and, to a vastly greater extent, in that of the Russians.

In order to write the Old Bulgarian language, Cyril—or possibly Cyril and a successor—devised two alphabets, the Cyrillic and the Glagolitic. Which of the two is the older cannot be determined with certainty. Cyril's name is attached to one of the two; but the scholars who regard the Glagolitic as the older alphabet think that the name has been misplaced. Nor is the question settled by the fact that the earliest known manuscripts of Old Bulgarian are written in the Glagolitic character. The meaning of the word "Glagolitic" is unknown. It has been suggested that the priests who used the Slavic liturgy were derisively called "Glagolitics" by their Latin-speaking rivals, since the word *glagola*, meaning "he said," occurs often in the service—but that is a mere guess.

The Cyrillic alphabet, based on the Greek capital letters and supplemented by some additional signs, had before it a glorious

future. With minor changes it is still used for all purposes by the
Serbs, the Bulgarians, and the Russians, that is, by the Slavs who
belong to the Eastern Orthodox Church. The Slavs who belong to
the Catholic Church, such as the Croatians, the Poles, and the
Czechs, use the Latin alphabet, supplemented by diacritical marks.
In America, Serbo-Croatian newspapers often employ both the
Cyrillic and the Latin alphabets in order to please both their
Serbian and their Croatian readers.

The Glagolitic alphabet is constructed on the same general plan
as the Cyrillic, but the letters are far more complicated in design
and are not adapted for rapid writing. Few of them have definite
resemblance to any other alphabet. The later history of the alphabet is curious rather than important. It was not used at all in eastern Bulgaria and there are only traces of its use in Russia; it soon
ceased to be employed even in Serbia, Macedonia, and Moravia.
But, oddly enough, the Glagolitic alphabet survived among the
Catholics of western Croatia, of the region between the Kupa
River and the Velebit Mountains. The early missionaries to the
Slavs had labored among the Croatians and had brought with
them Old Church Slavic texts written in Glagolitic characters. In
later times the Croatians of this particular region, though they belonged wholeheartedly to the Catholic Church, clung tenaciously
to their Slavic ritual. After a long struggle that ended in 1248,
Pope Innocent IV allowed them to retain it. From church books
the Glagolitic alphabet spread to government documents written
in the popular language. This use of the Glagolitic character for
secular purposes ceased early in the seventeenth century. No independent literature in Church Slavic ever developed in Croatia, but
the Church Slavic language is still employed in some Croatian
churches. The days of the Glagolitic alphabet, however, seem to
be numbered. A *Missale Romanum Slavonico idiomate,* authorized by Pope Leo XIII, was printed in the Glagolitic alphabet at
Rome in 1893; but a later edition of that missal, in 1927, was in
Latin letters.

Let us now turn our attention from a dead ecclesiastical language to the living speech of the Serbs and the Croatians. The
boundaries of the region in which Serbo-Croatian, in the strict
sense of the term, is spoken at present are as follows. In the east

and south, starting at the point where the Timok enters the Danube, at the northeast corner of Yugoslavia, the line follows up the Timok to Zaječar, thence to Stalać at the junction of the western and the southern Morava, thence southward through Prokuplje and Kuršumlija to Janjevo (somewhat southwest of Priština), thence to the junction of the Black and the White Drin and along the southern boundary of the Montenegro of 1914 to the point where the Bojana flows into the Adriatic. On the west the line follows the Adriatic coast (including the islands) up to Fiume, then proceeds along the Istrian coast to the tip of the peninsula, then in a zigzag line northward through Villa di Rovigno and Montona to Buje. The northern boundary, which is very irregular, runs from Buje through Sočerga and Rakitović to the sources of the Kupa, down that river to its junction with the Sava, down the Sava to Jasenovac, thence northward to Križevci (Kreuz), thence through Virovitica to Bazje on the Drava and down the Drava to its junction with the Danube, thence straight east to Stari Bečej (Óbecse) on the Tisa (Theiss), finally through Veliki Bečkerek (Nagybecskerek) and Bela Crkva (Weisskirchen) to Moldava on the Danube and down the Danube to the mouth of the Timok.

Any reader industrious enough to follow these boundaries on the map will find that they differ in various ways from those of the Yugoslavia of 1940. On the north they exclude parts of Yugoslavia that once belonged to Hungary; in the northwest they include some territory that was given to Italy after the First World War. On the east they exclude parts of Serbia where—and likewise in adjacent regions of Bulgaria—dialects are spoken that form a transition between Serbo-Croatian and Bulgarian. In the south they exclude most of Macedonia, the dialects of which may be classed as Bulgarian. In the northwest, again, they exclude not only all Slovenia but also the portion of Croatia that lies north of the Kupa and west of the Jasenovac–Križevci–Virovitica line, a region that includes Zagreb, the political and literary capital of Croatia. The native speech of this territory is intermediate between Serbo-Croatian and Slovenian. It is called the Kajkavština or Kaj-speech, because in it, as in the Slovenian, the word for "what" is *kaj*. All statements concerning boundaries between the different Slavic languages of the Balkan Peninsula, or between

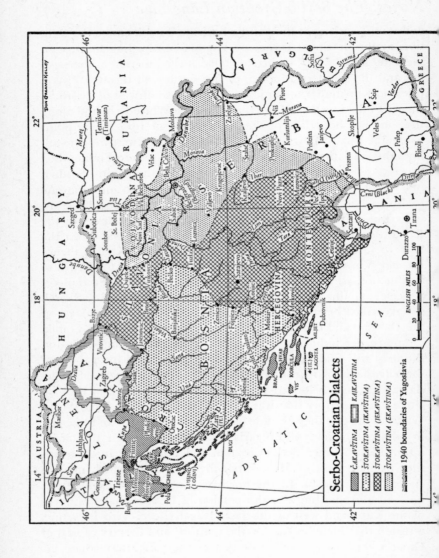

**Serbo-Croatian Dialects**

- ČAKAVŠTINA
- ŠTOKAVŠTINA (IKAVŠTINA)
- KAJKAVŠTINA
- ŠTOKAVŠTINA (JEKAVŠTINA)
- ŠTOKAVŠTINA (EKAVŠTINA)
- 1940 boundaries of Yugoslavia

the different dialects of those languages, be it remembered, are
subject to qualification; the lines of demarcation are not so sharp
and distinct as they are between French and German. Besides this,
scholars may disagree concerning the linguistic peculiarities that
should be regarded as the distinguishing traits of a dialect or even
of a language.[4]

Within the territory occupied by Serbo-Croatian in the strict
sense there are found two main dialects, or rather two groups of
dialects: the Čakavština, or Ča-speech, and the Štokavština, or Što-
speech. Each dialect is named from one of its least essential characteristics. In the Čakavština the word for "what" is *ča* and in the
Štokavština it is *što*. The Čakavština once occupied a fairly large
area, covering the western part of Bosnia and all northern and
central Dalmatia. Its territory has been gradually diminished by
the encroachments of Slovenian and of the Kajkavština in the
north and of the Štokavština in the east. The Čakavština is still
spoken on some of the islands in the Adriatic, in rather small
portions of Dalmatia, and in Istria.

As a consequence of the decline of the Čakavština, the Štokavština now covers nearly all the area occupied by the Serbo-Croatian
language. It is divided into three dialects: the Ekavština, the Jekavština, and the Ikavština. These differ in their development of a
certain Primitive Slavic vowel, an *e*, originally long, which gram-
marians represent by *ě*. This vowel, when shortened, became *e, je,*
and *i* in the three dialects, respectively; when its length was retained it became *ē, ije,* and *ī*. The Ekavština is bounded on the
west by an irregular line running from Stari Bečej to Osijek (Esseg)
on the Drava, thence through Vinkovci to the junction of the Drina
with the Sava, up the Drina to Lešnica (near Loznica), and southeast over the mountains (Cer, Vlašić, Medvednik, Maljen, Suvobor,
Rudnik) to Kraljevo on the Ibar, up the Ibar to Mitrovica, thence
southwest over Mount Mokra Gora to Peć (Ipek), finally to the
junction of the Black and the White Drin. The northern, southern,
and eastern boundaries of the dialect are the same as those of the
Serbo-Croatian language as a whole. The Jekavština lies to the west
of the Ekavština; its western boundary runs from Brčko on the
Sava through Tuzla to Zenica on the Bosna, thence through Fojnica and Konjic to Mostar on the Neretva (Narenta) and down

that river to the Adriatic. The Ikavština covers all the territory west of the Jekavština and south of the Kajkavština that is not occupied by the remnants of the Čakavština. But while broad expanses of territory are occupied almost solidly by the Ekavština or by the Jekavština, most of the regions in which the Ikavština predominates contain also numerous settlements in which one of the other two dialects prevails.

Both political and religious history have influenced the choice of the different dialects of Serbo-Croatian for use in literature, and have affected the general character of the literary language. In the Middle Ages the Balkan Peninsula was the scene of conflict between the Catholic and Greek Orthodox churches. The struggle came to an end in the thirteenth century: Dalmatia, Croatia, and Slavonia had become Catholic, and Serbia, Hercegovina, and Montenegro had become Greek Orthodox. In Bosnia the Bogomil heresy prevailed. The Turks entered Europe in the middle of the fourteenth century; before the end of the fifteenth century they had subjugated Serbia, Bosnia, and Hercegovina. Their rule over these provinces continued until the nineteenth century and thoroughly changed social conditions in them. In Bosnia the Bogomil landowners preserved social leadership by adopting Mohammedanism. In Serbia and Hercegovina the Serbs clung to the Christian religion and were reduced to the common level of peasantry. But the Turks never acquired sovereignty over all Dalmatia, and their comparatively brief rule over Croatia and Slavonia did not transform social conditions among their subjects. Thus one may make the rough general statement that the Orthodox Serbs were the victims of Turkish oppression, while the Catholic Croatians and Dalmatians escaped it.

The Serbs used as their literary language not the speech of the common people but Serbian Church Slavic. In this artificial language they developed a literature of some importance, which, at first exclusively clerical and liturgical, expanded its range in the period just before the Turkish conquest and addressed a wider circle of readers. Under the Turks this progress ceased; written literature lost ground and the Serbs had few books except those intended for use in the church. A new light dawned only in the eighteenth century.

The Catholic speakers of Serbo-Croatian were in a different situation. With an exception noted above, they used Latin as the language of the church and of government: Church Slavic had no influence on their literary development. And among one section of them there arose in Serbo-Croatian the first Slavic literature of a Renaissance type.

Dalmatia, a region whose scanty population lived mainly in a fringe of little seaboard cities, was ruled sometimes by Hungary, sometimes by Venice; its most important city, Dubrovnik (Ragusa), maintained a rather precarious independence. The culture of the cities was Italian; Italian also was the sharp division of the people into a wealthy and cultivated aristocracy and an impoverished plebs. The aristocrats were bilingual, speaking and writing both Italian and Serbo-Croatian. Among them, beginning in the fifteenth century, arose a literature almost entirely in verse, written in Serbo-Croatian but based on Italian models—or even translated from the Italian—which had its centers in Split (Spalato), the island of Hvar (Lesina), and above all in Dubrovnik. Dalmatia was a region in which three dialects, the Čakavština, the Ikavština, and the Jekavština, were in contact and in conflict with one another. Each noble poet wrote as seemed good to his ears. At first the Čakavština prevailed in Dalmatian poetry, then supremacy passed to the Štokavština, of which both the Jekavština and the Ikavština varieties were employed. A poet did not hesitate to use forms from more than one dialect, as suited his rhyme or rhythm. This literature, which died out in the eighteenth century, circulated for the most part in manuscript, rarely finding its way into print before the nineteenth century. It was a plaything of the aristocracy and did not reach the common people. Hence the "Dubrovnik poets," with the exception of the greatest among them, Ivan Gundulić (1589–1638), are little read today, but they have an honored place in history as the first writers to give artistic form to the Serbo-Croatian language.

In Croatia proper the intellectual ferment caused by the Reformation produced, in the sixteenth century, a small amount of literature in the native dialect, the Kajkavština. The suppression of Protestantism checked the growth of this literature, but it lingered on until the nineteenth century.

In Bosnia, from the closing years of the sixteenth century to the beginning of the nineteenth, there was a scanty Catholic religious literature written in Serbo-Croatian. Slavonia produced no literature in the native language until the eighteenth century, when a few religious and secular writers appeared, including a satiric poet of importance, Matija Antun Reljković (1732–1798) .

The regeneration of the language and literature of the Orthodox Serbs began with the eighteenth century. As early as the twelfth century there had begun a northward movement of the Serbs across the Sava and the Danube into lands from which they had been driven by the Hungarians. These migrations were naturally increased by the Turkish invasions. Although the Serbs lost territory in the south, they gained it in the north. The highest point of the movement came in the year 1690, when some 100,000 Serbs, headed by their patriarch, Arsenije III, settled in southern Hungary; their number was increased by later immigrants. These new citizens of Hungary were given the right to retain their own religion and to have a certain amount of self-government. They were a picked community, since the wealthier Serbs—including many priests, tradesmen, and artisans—had emigrated, leaving behind them villagers and mountaineers; and in Hungary they became exposed to the influences of Western civilization. So literature began to develop among them. The first writers used the traditional Serbian Church Slavic. But soon a change came about.

The Serbian settlers had a legal right to retain their Orthodox faith, but they were exposed to a vigorous Catholic propaganda. They naturally turned for help to Russia, the one powerful Orthodox nation. Russia supplied them with church books, schoolbooks, and books of all sorts, written in Russian Church Slavic and in the more or less Slavified literary Russian of the eighteenth century. Hence Russian Church Slavic soon replaced Serbian Church Slavic as the language of the church, and for a time it was used even in secular literature. The change was complete by about 1740; books and manuscripts in Serbian Church Slavic soon became collectors' rarities.

In the last third of the eighteenth century another change took place. Since Serbian authors read mainly books written in literary Russian, they began to imitate in their own compositions this lit-

erary Russian rather than Russian Church Slavic, which came to
be reserved for church use, just as it was in Russia itself. Against
their will they mixed their Russian with Serbisms. Vuk Karadžić
expressed his contempt for their hybrid diction in these words,
using "Slavic" as a term equivalent to either Russian Church Slavic
or Russian, "What you don't know in Serbian, put in Slavic; what
you don't know in Slavic, put in Serbian; and what you don't know
either in Slavic or in Serbian, put as you please, just as it comes into
your head." Educated people used this mixed jargon even in conversation, in order to show their breeding, though their pronunciation of the Russian words by no means conformed to Russian
standards. This hybrid language did not entirely disappear from
literature until nearly the middle of the nineteenth century.

Nevertheless, even learned churchmen recognized that the living
Serbian language could not be disregarded. Gavrilo Venclović
(died about 1747) was probably the best-educated Serbian monk
of his time. Thirteen of his manuscripts remain. When Venclović
wrote for church use or translated from the Russian he employed
Serbian Church Slavic; when he composed homilies for the common people he used a pure, well-turned Serbian. Similarly, Jovan
Rajić (1726–1801), the greatest author of the Russian school, wrote
most of his works either in Russian Church Slavic or in Slavified
Russian, but he used plain Serbian not only in some sermons addressed to the unlearned but in a catechism intended for children
(published in 1776). In the latter instance he bowed to the will of
the Austrian government, which had demanded that Serbian children receive religious instruction in a language that they could
understand. Rajić also composed poems, the majority of them in
Russian Church Slavic but a few in Serbian. The most important
of the latter, *The Combat of the Dragon and the Eagles* (1791),
was occasioned by the war of 1788–1790 between Turkey (the
dragon) and Austria and Russia (the eagles). The use of the popular tongue was meant to heighten the seriocomic tone of the work.

The spoken language of the Serbs, however, was given its rightful place in literature by the labors of two men, very different in
temperament, intellectual tastes, and ideals: Dositej Obradović
(*ca.* 1742–1811) and Vuk Stefanović Karadžić (1787–1864), each
of whom may rightly be called a genius. Both were, in the main,

self-educated; and, curiously enough, each passed a large part of his life outside the lands where Serbian was spoken.

Dositej Obradović, born at Čakovo, a small town in the Banat not far from Temišvar, as a boy had a passion for reading, which he gratified by poring over the only books accessible to him, those of the church, written in Church Slavic. The lives of the saints had the same effect on him that "wild West" stories had on American lads of the 1870's; he ran away from home, headed for Turkey, where he would fain become a saint. But his guardian pursued him and brought him home. In 1757 young Obradović made good his escape to the monastery of Hopovo in Syrmia (Srem), where he was received as a novice. He read more voraciously than ever. Because of his religious zeal he came to be regarded as a saint, and invalids sought his prayers. But despite his sainthood, he tells us, he prayed more fervently for the young girls than for the old women. Then came a revulsion against the absurd legends that had been his daily food. In 1760 he fled from the monastery with as much enthusiasm as he had entered it.

In his remaining years he traveled widely, in Dalmatia, Italy, Greece, Germany, France, England, and Russia. Earning his living as a teacher, he avidly studied languages. He cast off his former clerical point of view and with it his clerical dress, and became an earnest disciple of eighteenth-century enlightenment. In his eyes Joseph II of Austria was almost a divinity. Impressed by the fact that his people the Serbs, capable and intelligent as any that he knew, had no books in their own language, he determined to supply the lack. His works, with only one important exception, are translations, compilations, or adaptations from other languages. Their aim is practical, to impart moral instruction and in particular to combat clericalism and monasticism. The exception, an autobiography published in 1783–1788, *The Life and Adventures of Dimitrij Obradović, Called Dositej as a Monk,* had the same objects: Obradović wished to instruct his countrymen by his own example. That autobiography is the only strictly Serbian book of permanent value published before the nineteenth century. Even today it remains the most important prose work in Serbian literature.

Obradović was a student of languages all his life. He could use with varying skill, French, German, Italian, English, Greek, Latin, Russian, and Rumanian, as well as his native Serbian. But, like the average man or woman, he studied a language simply as a means of acquiring and imparting information. He was not interested in grammar for its own sake. Nor does he defend his procedure by appeals to sentiment or patriotism. "I know that some people may oppose me," he writes, "by saying that if we begin to write in the dialect of the common people, the old language will be neglected and will gradually disappear entirely. I reply: What profit can there be for us from a language which hardly one man in ten thousand in the whole nation understands properly and which is foreign to my mother and my sisters? . . . But the general common dialect everybody knows, and through it everyone who can read can enlighten his mind, improve his heart, and beautify his character. A language is valuable from the benefits it confers."

We may add that the revulsion of Obradović from clericalism may have brought with it a hearty dislike for even the language of the church. And he may have been encouraged by the success of Reljković in Slavonia, not far from his own home. As a disciple of eighteenth-century tolerance he did not share the usual fanatical hatred for everything Catholic.

But in spite of his aspirations Obradović did not and could not write with perfect correctness the language of the Serbian people. His aim was to convey information, not to set up grammatical canons. In general he employed his own Ekavština, but he had no grammar to guide him and, not to speak of his monastic training, which steeped him in Church Slavic, he had lived in the towns, where educated people often used Church Slavic and Russian words in their speech. Hence, though his syntax is fundamentally Serbian, his declensional forms vary and his vocabulary is full of Church Slavic and Russian words, which he probably did not feel to be foreign. However, the effect of his work was far-reaching. Before him almost all literature had been in the hybrid Church Slavic–Russian–Serbian jargon. After him the right of the people's language to be used in serious books was recognized, and the Church Slavic party was on the defensive, seeking to define the conditions under which each language should be employed.

As a follower of eighteenth-century enlightenment, Obradović was a cosmopolitan; he wished the Serbs to assimilate their life and thought to those of western Europe. He cared nothing for the native Serbian village life and customs or for the oral literature of the Serbian people, rich in ballads and folk tales.

Vuk Karadžić resembled Obradović only in the scantiness of his formal school training. He brought into Serbia the ideals of the romantic movement: its cult of national individuality as opposed to cosmopolitanism and of the common village folk as opposed to the educated classes of the city; its almost reverent affection for popular ballads and tales. Finally, though in practical knowledge of foreign languages he was inferior to Obradović—for example, he knew no Greek, though he published a translation of the New Testament—Karadžić had a far keener interest in linguistic problems than his predecessor and an immensely superior acquaintance with the Serbian language.

Karadžić came of a family that in 1739 had migrated from Hercegovina to Serbia, then, of course, still under the Turkish yoke. Born in 1787 in the village of Tršić, he gained his elementary education at a humble country school and in a monastery. Thus his background was of rustic illiteracy rather than of the relatively cultivated town life in which Obradović grew up. In 1804 he went to Karlovac (Karlowitz) in Hungary for further training. Later he was one of the earliest students in the "Great School" (the forerunner of the Serbian University) that Dositej Obradović had organized in Belgrade.

In 1813 Karadžić settled in Vienna, which remained his home for most of his life. Here he came in contact with the Slovene Jernej Kopitar, author of a Slovene grammar and one of the founders of Slavic philology. At this time, scholars were still in doubt whether the speech of the Serbian village folk was nearer to Russian or to the language of the Dalmatian writers. Kopitar, who had described the language of Serbian literature as *"plane barbara, nulla, ficta, stulta, ridicula"* (absolutely barbarous, no good, artificial, stupid, and silly), and had written of the need for a grammar of the contemporary language, found in Karadžić a man who could help him. And promptly in 1814 the latter published his *Grammar of the Serbian Language as Spoken by the Common People,* an immature work, but one that marked progress in the right direction.

Kopitar likewise encouraged Karadžić to collect popular ballads and other folklore materials, and in 1814 Karadžić also published his first songbook. Karadžić continued this work all his life; his collections won fame throughout Europe and lie at the very foundation of the study of Serbian folklore. These collections formed the basis for the *Lexicon Serbico-Germanico-Latinum,* a Serbian dictionary with German and Latin definitions, the first edition of which appeared in 1818. On this book Kopitar coöperated with Karadžić: the latter supplied the words and explained their meaning, and Kopitar supplied the German and Latin definitions. The dictionary, in a much revised and enlarged form (third edition, 1898), is still a standard work. It is more than a dictionary, since it includes some short articles on Serbian folk customs.

The traditional Cyrillic alphabet was not well suited to the living Serbian language. Obradović and others had made minor changes in it; Karadžić reformed it entirely, discarding some symbols and inventing others to serve his purpose. His greatest innovation, the use of the letter *j,* which he borrowed from the Latin, that is, the Catholic alphabet, brought him into ill repute with the clerical party of his own people. After some experiments he produced an alphabet which, he boasted, contained no superfluous letters and no letter with more than one sound, and which lacked no necessary letter. This boast is a bit overdone, but one may say with assurance that no European language has a more strictly phonetic system of writing than Serbian.

Karadžić was not a gentle soul like Obradović, nor was he a scholar who stood aloof from public life. He wished not only to demonstrate to his fellow countrymen the true nature of "the pure and uncorrupted Serbian speech, the language of plowmen and diggers," but to persuade those countrymen to use it in literature. He himself had employed it in learned articles. The beauty of his published folk ballads had shown abundantly that Serbian was adapted to poetry. So in 1815 he started a polemic in its behalf— often conducted on both sides with great acrimony—which continued for more than thirty years and, on the whole, resulted in a victory for his principles.

The opponents of Karadžić had something on their side, however. The present literary language of Russia, though no Russian now feels that it is artificial, developed from Church Slavic almost as much as from the popular speech—perhaps even more than from that speech, for a large part of its vocabulary and some of its inflections have been taken over from Church Slavic. The present active participles of Russian verbs, for instance, are Church Slavic in origin. They are used quite naturally in writing, but are unknown to the Russian peasants and do not often occur in the conversation of the most learned men.

The reforms of Karadžić limited the influence of Church Slavic on Serbo-Croatian merely to vocabulary. But "the language of plowmen and diggers" proved inadequate for the expression of abstract ideas. Karadžić himself, in translating the New Testament into the speech of the people, was forced to borrow some words from Church Slavic and from Russian. Thus he failed to make his practice conform perfectly to his principles and yielded a bit to the point of view of his opponents. These traces of Church Slavic and Russian influence on the modern literary language of the Serbs and the Croatians are, however, a minor matter and do not interfere with the essentially popular character of that language.

Karadžić triumphed, but one must make some important reservations. As we have already seen, "the pure and uncorrupted Serbian speech" is by no means a unit, but consists of numerous dialects. At first Karadžić, though he himself used the Jekavština, conceded that each man had a right to employ his own dialect— a principle that would have resulted in linguistic chaos. Later he put forward the Jekavština as the proper literary language for the following reasons: (1) it was the speech of a large part of the Serbian people; (2) nearly all the popular ballads were composed in it; (3) it had been used by the writers of Dubrovnik (though, as we have seen, other dialects had also been used by them); (4) it was closest to Church Slavic (a statement that lacks foundation); and (5) it was a bond between the Orthodox and the Catholic speakers of Serbo-Croatian. Possibly he was influenced also by the fact that it was the language of Hercegovina, the land of his fathers.

For a time the authority of Karadžić prevailed, while the center of Serbian intellectual life was still in Hungary, first in Budapest and then in Novi Sad (Neusatz). But, with the political and economic progress of Serbia, Belgrade gradually became the intellectual capital of the Serbs; it had gained that position even before 1870 and in later years its predominance has constantly increased. And since Belgrade lay in the territory of the Ekavština, that dialect became the language of the Serbian government and of Serbian literature in general. Nevertheless, the Jekavština was still recognized as a correct form of speech; it was taught in the schools of districts where it was spoken, and students who came to Belgrade from such districts were allowed to continue using it.

Finally, neither the Ekavština nor the Jekavština, as used in literature, is even today as much of a unit as is written English, though English is scattered over four hemispheres. In English authors of varying localities one may find puzzling differences of vocabulary and baffling idiomatic phrases. But the grammar of English is virtually the same everywhere; the usage of London has imposed itself on Edinburgh and has traveled to San Francisco and Melbourne. No similar statement can be made concerning Serbo-Croatian. The lapse of one hundred years has not been sufficient to create a literary norm. For example, some writers avoid the aorist and imperfect tenses of the verb, which in parts of the country have practically died out; others use them freely. The speakers of Serbo-Croatian have attained political unity, but they have never attained full linguistic unity.

Croatia had been annexed to Hungary in 1102. Thereafter its political and intellectual development was separate from that of Dalmatia, with which it had previously formed a unit. As in Hungary, so in Croatia, the language of church and state, literature and education was Latin. The ephemeral literature in the local dialect, the Kajkavština, which began in the sixteenth century and lingered on till the nineteenth, never became a real force in the national life. But a change of sentiment began toward the end of the eighteenth century, the period when national sentiment began to assert itself throughout Europe. Joseph II of Austria (1780–1790) wished to centralize and to Germanize his dominions. As part of this policy, he tried to force upon the Hungarians, and consequently the Croatians, the use of German as the language of government in place of Latin. The Hungarians resisted, asserted the rights of their own Hungarian language in government and education, and tried to force it upon the Croatians. The Croatians,

who had been quite content with Latin as the language of government, rebelled at Hungarian and, supported by the government at
Vienna, which always sought to foster discord among the non-
German minorities of the Empire, began a campaign in favor of
the use of Croatian in government and education.

The Croatian opposition to the Hungarians culminated in the
Illyrian movement of 1835–1849. Political and cultural aspirations
were blended in this movement, which took its name from the
Illyrians of ancient times and from the Illyrian Provinces created
by Napoleon in 1809 and transferred to Austria by the Congress
of Vienna. Ljudevit Gaj (1809–1872), the leader of the movement,
and his comrades, to their great credit, saw clearly that the Kajkavština, the dialect of a small district around Zagreb, with a population of 700,000, was not suitable for a national revolution which
they hoped would eventually embrace all the speakers of Slavic
languages in the Balkan Peninsula. So they shifted the language
of their publications from the Kajkavština to the Jekavština. The
latter was used in parts of Dalmatia—once united politically to
Croatia—and had been given currency among the Serbs by Karadžić, so that it could become a bond between the Croatians and
the Serbs.

The Illyrian movement did not result in a union of the Balkan
Slavs; in fact, a union even of Serbs, Croats, and Slovenes had to
be postponed until 1918. But that movement did secure the right
of the Croatians to use their own language in government and
education, and it made that language the Jekavština. The common
people continue to speak the Kajkavština, but in school they study
the Jekavština. So the latter has become the accepted spoken language of cultivated society, which is thus bilingual. The situation
is similar in Venice, in Prague, in rural Scotland, less exactly so in
rural Kansas. The Croatians, being Catholics, of course write the
Jekavština in Latin letters, but even today their orthography is
not entirely uniform. In the nineteenth century Zagreb became
a center of culture and of literature rivaling and in some ways
surpassing Belgrade.

When in the process of time the Serbs shifted to the Ekavština,
as the speech of the greater part of the Serbian people, the Croatians naturally refused to follow them and clung to the Jekavština.

The differences between the two dialects are comparatively slight and bother the self-conscious natives more than they do foreigners. A foreign student can study both the Ekavština and the Jekavština from one textbook. And the language that he learns, or tries to learn, is generally regarded as the most beautiful of the Slavic tongues. One reason for this opinion is that Serbo-Croatian is the most vocalic of the Slavic languages and eliminates the difficult combinations of consonants that bother foreigners in, for instance, Russian. Thus we have the following pairs of words, in which the first is Russian and the second Serbo-Croatian: *vkus* (pronounced *fkus*), *ukus; lda, leda; mysl', misao*. Another reason given is that the open vowel *a* plays a greater part in Serbo-Croatian than in any other Slavic language: thus *son, san* (Polish and Bohemian *sen*); *den', dan*. These criteria seem to me open to question, and in general I regard disputes concerning the melodiousness of different languages as peculiarly futile. So I do not even offer an opinion, but merely comment that the Serbo-Croatian language has a copious vocabulary and a grammatical system well adapted to express different shades of meaning with grace and precision.

# CHAPTER XVII

# *The Literature of the South Slavs*

## BY GEORGE RAPALL NOYES

MONG THE PEOPLES OF YUGOSLAVIA geography has been a prime factor in shaping the course of history, and history has shaped the course of literature. Leaving out of account, for the moment, the literature of the Slovenes and oral folk literature, there have been at least four distinct written literatures among speakers of the Serbo-Croatian language: the medieval literature of the Serbs, the Renaissance literature of Dubrovnik and other Dalmatian cities, and the modern literatures of the Serbs and of the Croatians. What small literary unity has existed among the different Serbo-Croatian groups has depended on the oral folk literature and on a certain number of modern authors, beginning with the last quarter of the eighteenth century. Among the Serbo-Croatian and Slovene writers few have won international fame. A brief sketch like the present can do no more than define the general characteristics of the different branches of South Slavic literature and mention some of the most important authors.

The literary history of the Slavs begins with their conversion to Christianity. An episode of primary significance in that conversion is the work, in the second half of the ninth century, of Cyril and Methodius, two Greek missionaries who translated, or aided in translating, the Gospels, the Psalms, the liturgy, and other religious texts from Greek into a Slavic language—the speech of the region surrounding their native city of Thessalonica (Salonika)—and devised an alphabet for writing that language. This speech, a dialect of the language that later developed into modern Bulgarian, became the language of the church, and for centuries of all written literature, among all the Slavs who were converted to the Eastern, or Orthodox, Church, thereby separating them intellectually (and usually politically as well) from the Slavs who were converted to the Western, or Catholic, Church and who therefore used Latin as the language of their church service and of most of their written literature. The Orthodox Slavs, the users of the Church Slavic literary language, were in general terms the Serbs of the Vardar and Morava valleys, the Montenegrins, the Bulgarians, and the Russians; the Catholic Slavs were the Poles, the Bohemians, the Croatians, the Slovenes, and some other small groups. As time passed the Church Slavic language became modified by the spoken languages of the peoples using it, so that three types of it arose, Church Slavic of the Serbian, the Bulgarian, and the Russian recension (see also chap. xvi, "The Serbo-Croatian Language").

Church Slavic of the Serbian recension remained the written language of the Serbs until the middle of the eighteenth century. The literature written in it at first consisted exclusively of translations from Greek ecclesiastical texts, including, aside from the liturgy and parts of the Bible, saints' legends, apocryphal stories, sermons, and historical writings. Such productions determined the general character of the literature throughout its history. But works more independent in content, if not in style and intellectual temper, soon developed. Thus St. Sava (1169–1235), the first definitely known Serbian author, wrote a brief biography of St. Simeon, that is, of his father Stephen Nemanja, the founder of the Serbian medieval state, who in his later years resigned his throne and became a monk. In the middle of the fourteenth century there is a notable legal document, the *Zakonik* (Code of Laws) of Tsar Stephen Dušan, the greatest of Nemanja's descendants. Some secular material penetrated to the Serbs: such are versions of the romance of Alexander the Great, of the Tristan story, and of the pseudoscientific *Physiologus*. There is some ecclesiastical poetry in the literature, but scarcely any other verse compositions. The Turkish conquest checked the development of this literature but did not extinguish it. The life of Despot Stephen Lazarević (ruled 1389–1427) by Konstantin of Kostenec, a Bulgarian by birth, is less hagiographic than preceding biographies and shows the beginnings of historical science. Yet the last writer of any account in

Serbian Church Slavic, Djordje Branković (1645–1711), who wrote
a chronicle history of the world (of course with emphasis on the
Serbs) from its creation until 1705 (never printed), is still half
medieval in his methods and his outlook.

The Slavs of the Adriatic seacoast had a totally different cultural
development. Most of them were Catholics and their history was
closely connected with that of Croatia; in fact, the Croatian state
originated in the coastal district, just north of Dalmatia. After the
union of Croatia with Hungary in 1102, Dalmatia was ruled now
by Hungary, now by Venice; its most important city, Dubrovnik
(Ragusa), maintained a precarious independence, protecting itself
from the neighboring Turks more by bribery than by valor. But
whoever their political rulers might be, intellectually the little Dalmatian cities were subject to Italy. In seaboard Croatia and the
neighboring districts of Dalmatia, in Istria and the neighboring
Quarnero islands, Catholic congregations obtained the privilege of
using the Church Slavic language instead of Latin in their church
service; their church books were written in the Glagolitic alphabet
(see chap. xvi). In this region there was also some religious literature—legends, sermons, and kindred productions—written now in
Church Slavic, now in an approximation to the language of the
people. More important, in manuscripts of the fourteenth and fifteenth centuries there are many religious poems, mainly lyrics, in
the popular speech, which spread over all Dalmatia and which are
the first poetry of the South Slavs written on Western models. They
show that religious poetry had been brought from Umbria to the
Croatians by the Franciscans.

But secular Renaissance influences appeared first in southern
Dalmatia, above all in Dubrovnik. The population of that little
city (numbering only about 30,000 in 1587, at its most brilliant
period) consisted of a small, proud, highly educated aristocracy
whose wealth depended on commerce and who had all the political
power, and of an inert, mainly illiterate plebs. The men of the
nobility, and later sometimes the women also, were bilingual or
even trilingual, using Italian and Latin as well as their native
Serbo-Croatian in speech and in writing. Thoroughly familiar with
Italian literature, in the later fifteenth century some of them began
to write, in Serbo-Croatian, lyric poems modeled on the work of

Petrarch, Serafino, and other Italian masters. This Italianate school flourished in the sixteenth century, reached its highest development in the seventeenth, and declined in the eighteenth. The literature that it produced was the plaything of a tiny aristocracy and for the most part remained unpublished until the nineteenth century, when a collection of "old Croatian authors" was printed in a small edition by the South Slavic Academy. Yet this literature is the first of a modern, Renaissance type among the Slavs, beginning earlier than the parallel developments in Bohemia and Poland. At first confined to lyric poetry, it broadened so as to include didactic and humorous verse, drama, and epic. Of prose there was little—some devotional works and a few comedies.

By common consent the greatest of the Dubrovnik poets is Ivan Gundulić (1589–1638), who won fame by his elegiac *Tears of the Prodigal Son,* his pastoral and patriotic drama *Dubravka,* and above all by his stately epic *Osman,* which treats of the war of 1621 between the Poles and the Turks. Gundulić still has readers, though mainly among students of literary history. But when the Italianate school was tottering toward its close a Franciscan friar, Andrija Kačić-Miošić (*ca.* 1702–1760) published about 1756 his "songbook," *Razgovor ugodni naroda slovinskoga* (Pleasant Chat about the Slavic People), which was addressed to the common folk and written in a style influenced by the oral ballad literature. It was greatly enlarged in an edition of 1759. It discourses, mainly in verse, on the history of the Slavs from the time of Alexander the Great, whom it terms a Slavic king, and particularly on their wars with the Turks. Though it has no distinguished literary merit it has appealed to the popular taste by its simplicity and its patriotic tone; it has continued to circulate among Catholic readers up to the present time in repeated cheap editions. This is the oldest Serbo-Croatian book that has remained in general circulation. Some of its poems have passed into the oral ballad literature.

During the period of Turkish rule in the Balkan Peninsula there was a general northward movement of the Serbian population, which took on large proportions toward the end of the seventeenth century. When Austrian armies began a "holy" war against the Turks in 1684, the Serbs rose in support of them; when the Austrians were defeated, the Serbs, fearing Turkish retaliation, moved across the Danube into southern Hungary, which was then partially vacant territory. Here the Austrian government assured them of a privileged position, with free exercise of their own religion. In practice, however, they were exposed to Catholic propaganda, so that they naturally turned for cultural assistance to Russia, the one independent Orthodox nation, which supplied them with books and teachers. Consequently the Russian recension of Church Slavic rapidly replaced the Serbian in the church books of the Serbs of Hungary and in the scanty original literature produced among them. The process was complete by 1750. Educated people in the towns even used Slavicisms and Russicisms in their speech, regarding them as a mark of good breeding.

Among the Serbian writers of Russian Church Slavic the monk Jovan Rajić (1726–1801) was celebrated in his own time. He was a man of industry and of learning, but neither as theologian nor as historian did he leave any work of permanent value. The humbler Zaharija Orfelin (1726–1785) wrote both in Russian Church Slavic and in the language of the Serbian common folk. By his attachment to eighteenth-century rationalism he was a predecessor of Dositej Obradović and by his use of the popular language a predecessor of Vuk Karadžić.

Modern Serbian literature began among the Serbs of Hungary with the work of Dositej Obradović (*ca.* 1742–1811); the center of Serbian literary activity did not shift to Belgrade until the middle of the nineteenth century. Obradović, the orphaned son of a tradesman, as a child had an intense passion for reading; he spent his early years studying languages and reading books. He traveled extensively, from Temišvar to Smyrna, Constantinople, Florence, Paris, London, Riga, Vienna, Leipzig, Halle, earning his living as a teacher of languages. Finding that his countrymen, as intelligent as any people in Europe, had practically no literature in their spoken language, he made it the chief task of his life to supply this lack. His works are mainly translations or adaptations from foreign languages of treatises on practical ethics; they were immensely useful in their own time by combating obscurantism and spreading the ideas of eighteenth-century enlightenment, but today they have lost their savor. A striking exception is his autobiography, published in 1783 and 1788, the first work of any importance by a Ser in his own language, and to this day the most important prose work in Serbian literature. Yet, in spite of his ambitions, Obradović, a townsman by birth and early environment and a cleric by education, did not succeed in writing the unmixed speech of the Serbian common folk; his style, like that of educated city people in his own period, was not free from Slavicisms and Russicisms.

Since Obradović, Serbian literature has developed along the same general lines as other European literatures, but the different movements begin at somewhat later dates than, for instance, in England and France. Eighteenth-century enlightenment, represented by Obradović, and classicism, represented by some third-rate versifiers, were followed by romanticism, the leading figure in which was Vuk Stefanović Karadžić (1787–1864), who, rather curiously, was not a poet or a writer of romances, but a folklorist and a linguistic reformer. His leading achievements were his collection of Serbian popular ballads, his dictionary of the living Serbian language, and his reform of the Serbian written language and of Serbian spelling.

Karadžić was a villager by birth and lacked any systematic higher education. As a child he had listened to Serbian folk ballads; and, when he learned of the importance attached to ballads by European scholars, notably the Slovene Kopitar and the German Jacob Grimm, he devoted himself to collecting the ballads of his own people. The nine volumes that were the result of his labors rank among the best collections of ballads in all Europe. Guided in large measure by the usage of the ballads and of the Dalmatian poets, Karadžić strove to make the western dialect of Serbian, the Jekav-ština (see chap. xvi, "The Serbo-Croatian Language"), the language of Serbian literature. Since the time of Obradović the adherents of Russian Church Slavic or of a highly Slavified Serbian style had, to be sure, been on the defensive; but, as the example of Obradović himself had amply illustrated, the battle was not yet won: Slavicisms still seemed an essential part of a cultivated writer's vocabulary. Karadžić succeeded in almost completely eliminating them, so that today the style of Serbian authors is quite as close to popular speech as is the style of writers in England or America. Of the Serbian village speech Karadžić published an authoritative dictionary, based on his folklore collections, which in a revised edition is still a standard book of reference. He also revised the spelling of that speech on phonetic principles, introducing new characters into the Cyrillic alphabet. His work as a whole has been of decisive and permanent importance.

Among the various elements that show themselves in the romantic literatures of western Europe, enthusiasm for the popular ballads, for the national, patriotic traditions embodied in them, for the old times of which many of them tell, and for the rough life of struggle and warfare that is pictured in nearly all of them, naturally is a leading motif in the romantic literature of the Serbs—but one must make the reservation that chivalric love plays no part in the Serbian popular ballads. Classical influences had been of slight account among the Serbs, so that the romantic school won an easy victory among their writers of the early nineteenth century. And, indeed, the ballads that inspired them are among the most remarkable in the world.

Something had been known of them even before Karadžić, but his collection is the foundation of their fame throughout Europe, a fame wider than that attained by any of the South Slavic men of letters, and of their influence on the literature, art, and general mentality of his own countrymen. They are, for instance, a primary influence in the work of Petar Petrović Njegoš (1813–1851), Prince-Bishop of Montenegro, whose *Gorski vijenac* (Mountain Wreath) is generally regarded as the masterpiece of Serbian poetry. It is a closet drama based on Montenegrin history, full of patriotic eloquence and genuine imagination. It is one of the few works of Orthodox literature that are equally admired by the Croatians. (One may mention, as an illustration of the way in which the most diverse influences affect a single man, that in his religious poem *The Beam of the Microcosm* Njegoš owes much to *Paradise Lost,* which he had read in a Russian version.) Njegoš is a precursor of the romantic school; the first poet who belonged entirely to it was Branko Radičević (1824–1853). And in the work of Radičević and his successors the ideas of Karadžić were a main force.

In the time of Karadžić oral ballad literature still flourished in the South Slavic lands, though it was already losing ground, owing to the spread of education. It thrives even today in the more secluded parts of Yugoslavia, such as the mountainous regions of western Bosnia and of Dalmatia, Hercegovina, and Montenegro; here the ballads are for the population what concerts and the drama are for ourselves. They are sung by both Serbs and Croatians, by Orthodox, Catholics, and Mussulmans. Many collectors have followed in the footsteps of Karadžić; the most important work has been done by the Matica Hrvatska (Croatian Literary Society), particularly in its volume of Mohammedan ballads gathered from Bosnian singers. But, though the ballads are still widely read and though they have greatly influenced, for example, the work of Ivan Meštrović (born 1883), a son of Croatian peasants who has won perhaps the foremost position among contemporary European sculptors, they are now not so much an inspiration to poets as an object of study for folklorists.

Among the Serbs as among other peoples, romanticism was succeeded by realism; the dividing line between the two schools falls about 1870. So far the Serbs have produced no novelists of the first rank. As a writer of short stories Laza Lazarević (1851–1890) attained distinction by work small in extent but notable for its artistic finish, in a technique that owes something both to Turgenev and to French models. Among writers of prose fiction in the present century Borisav Stanković (1876–1927) is perhaps the most notable; his short novel *Impure Blood* (1911) is a powerful, harsh picture of small-town life in Macedonia.

The influence of the popular ballads declined in Serbian literature. So, for entirely different, political reasons, did the influence of German authors. By the Russian prose masters the Serbs were greatly attracted, but they paid less heed to the Russian poets. On the other hand, the Serbian poets, who in general were men of finer talent than the Serbian writers of fiction, fell under the spell of the French poetry of their own time. This is preëminently true of Jovan Dučić (1874–1943) and Milan Rakić (1876–1938), both of them lyric poets of rare talent.

The Serbian drama had the same general development as the rest of the literature. Yet Jovan Popović (1806–1856), the first talented writer for the theater, after unsuccessful experiments in the romantic vein, turned to didactic and satiric comedy and showed himself a true disciple of Molière. Though he was almost forgotten in the years immediately following his death, toward the end of the century he was again recognized as not only the first but the best Serbian writer of comedy. Among more recent writers perhaps the best is the prolific Branislav Nušić (1864–1938), whose *Member of Parliament* (1896) may be mentioned as a genial satire on Serbian political life.

Until the nineteenth century, conditions in Croatia proper, the region about Zagreb, were extremely unfavorable for the development of literature. After 1102 the country was continuously under Hungarian rule and soon became assimilated to Hungary in its social organization and intellectual development. Whereas in Serbia the Turks had crushed or absorbed the aristocracy, so that the people became a nation of peasants, in Croatia the feudal system developed just as in Hungary, with a sharp distinction between a cultivated landed aristocracy, endowed with all political power, and a helpless peasantry. And, as in Hungary, Latin was the language not only of education and of literature but of government as well. Unlike their fellow countrymen in Dubrovnik, the Croatian nobles were not inspired to write in their own language by any familiarity with a great vernacular literature. So there was virtually no Croatian literature in this region until the second half of the sixteenth century, when the Reformation penetrated to the country and caused the printing of catechisms, sermons, and a translation of the New Testament in the language of the common people. Then the Catholic reaction triumphed and the Jesuits checked the development of even these humble beginnings of a national literature.

Besides all this, the language of the region about Zagreb is the Kaj-speech, intermediate between Serbo-Croatian and Slovenian; so the people were more or less separated linguistically from their neighbors. A few poems and a chronicle were written in the seventeenth century and a feeble trickle of utilitarian books flowed on until the end of the eighteenth century, when there were the beginnings of a change. Then the Austrian government made efforts to force German on the Magyars as the language of administration; the Magyars resisted in behalf of their own language and began to introduce Hungarian rather than Latin in the government of Croatia. The Croatian nobles defended their own right to use Latin, but they saw that books in the vernacular must be provided for the common people. Thus even before the Illyrian movement there were symptoms of a literary revival in Croatia.

In Slavonia, where the language is essentially the same as that of Dubrovnik, there were a few writers in the eighteenth century. Matija Antun Reljković (1732–1798), an army officer, gained fame by his poem *The Satyr or Wild Man,* in which a satyr describes both the beauty of the Slavonian land and its wretched condition in comparison with Germany, and indicates the need for reform. The work was printed in the Cyrillic as well as the Latin alphabet, so that it found readers among both Croatians and Serbs. In the nineteenth century this Slavonian literary episode was absorbed into the main current of Croatian literature.

The 1830's saw the beginnings of the so-called Illyrian movement, which ultimately gained intellectual, linguistic, and educational, but not political, independence for Croatia. Its leaders, the foremost of whom was Ljudevit Gaj (1809–1872), were inspired by similar nationalistic movements among the Czechs and the Slovaks and by the Pan-Slavic ideas that were in the air. Their aim was eventual union of all the South Slavs, including the Bulgarians, such as was partially realized after the First World War. In their resistance to the Hungarians they were encouraged by the Austrian government, which consistently played off the different nationalities of the Empire against one another. At first they used in their publications the classical name Illyrian, which had been adopted by Napoleon in 1809 for his newly created Illyrian Provinces, but after 1843 they gradually abandoned it in favor of South Slavs and South Slavic. These terms have continued in favor to the present day, although, quite illogically, as now employed they exclude the Bulgarians.

With sound sense the Illyrian leaders abandoned the use of the Kaj-speech, which was spoken by less than a million persons, in favor of the western dialect of Serbo-Croatian (the Jekavština), as advocated by Karadžić. Henceforth the people of Zagreb and the vicinity, like those of Naples or Venice—or rural Scotland or rural Kansas—spoke one dialect at home and studied another in school. Unfortunately for the cause of future linguistic unity, the Serbs soon thereafter were led by obvious political considerations to adopt as their own language of government the eastern dialect of

Serbo-Croatian (the Ekavština), that spoken in Belgrade and in practically all the Kingdom of Serbia. Since the Croatians are Catholics, they have of course continued to use the Latin alphabet, but they have reformed their spelling on the same principles as those followed by Karadžić, although even today Croatian orthographic usage is not absolutely fixed. And, once having adopted the Jekavština as their literary language, they have steadfastly refused to abandon it. Thus when the Kingdom of the Serbs, Croats, and Slovenes (later Yugoslavia) was organized in 1918, its government of necessity recognized both dialects, the Ekavština and the Jekavština, and both alphabets, the Cyrillic and the Latin, as having equal rights.

Owing to the success of the Illyrian movement, Zagreb soon became a literary center of no less importance than Belgrade. The foundation of the South Slavic Academy in 1867 greatly enhanced its prestige. The Croatians were fewer in number than the Serbs, but they had more material prosperity and a higher level of general education. Several of their earlier writers won permanent fame. The reputation of Ivan Mažuranić (1814–1890), who in his later years held important government posts, including that of Ban of Croatia, depends on his narrative poem, *The Death of Smail-aga Čengijić* (1846), based on a then recent episode in the resistance of the Montenegrins to the Turks. Mažuranić, who writes with a classic concision not at all resembling the style of the folk ballads, is read widely by both Croatians and Serbs. Petar Preradović (1818–1872)—a soldier whose youthful education was so exclusively German that on a visit home he had difficulty in speaking Croatian with his mother; who until 1843 wrote verse only in German; and who reached the rank of general in the Austrian army—became perhaps the most famous of the Croatian poets, noted for his patriotic lyrics. Unlike Serbian literature, Croatian literature is richer in novelists than in poets. In the nineteenth century the two most distinguished—and most prolific—Croatian authors of novels and stories were August Šenoa (1838–1881) and Ljubomir Babić (1854–1935), who wrote under the name of Ksaver Šandor Gjalski. By temperament a romantic and a patriot, Šenoa was the most influential man of letters of his time; he edited the leading magazine in Croatia. A pupil both of Victor Hugo and of Balzac, he wrote romantic poetry, historical romances, dramas, and novels of contemporary life. Gjalski was influenced both by Russian literature, above all by Turgenev, and by French masters such as Zola, Stendhal, Balzac, Flaubert, and Daudet. His works present a panorama of the social life of Croatia, but he treats with special affection of the country gentry. Turning aside from the romanticism of Šenoa, he is a psychologist and a realist, with a tendency toward pessimism.

Perhaps the finest literary talent among Croatian writers is that of Count Ivo Vojnović (1857–1929), a native of Dubrovnik, whose small but highly polished work probably assures him the leading position among dramatists writing in Serbo-Croatian. His masterpiece is *A Trilogy of Dubrovnik,* in which he lends poetic charm to the life of the gentlefolk of the little city with its memories of past glory. A firm champion of union between Croats and Serbs, when friction arose in the new Yugoslavia he became even more popular among the Serbs than with his own people. Among the writers who have become prominent since the First World War the foremost is Miroslav Krleža (born 1893), journalist, essayist, poet, novelist, writer of short stories, and dramatist. In his *Glembay Family* he gives mordant pictures of life among the degenerate Croatian aristocracy.

The literary history of the Slovenes, who live in the northwest corner of Yugoslavia, is a separate story. The Slovenian language is markedly different from Serbo-Croatian, so that the two tongues are mutually unintelligible. The Freising Fragments, religious texts written about the year 1000, are in Slovenian; then the language disappears from view until the fifteenth century, from which a few manuscripts survive, showing strong distinctions of dialect. In the second half of the sixteenth century the Reformation penetrated to the country and caused the printing in the popular language of much religious literature. Primož Trubar (1508–1586), who among other works published a translation of the New Testament into the dialect of lower Carniola that he himself spoke, became the father not only of Slovenian literature but of the Slovenian literary language. From 1551 to 1595 about fifty Protestant works came from the press. But the use of Slovenian as the language of the Protestant churches did not make it the literary language of the country. In their correspondence and for governmental purposes, the Slovenian Protestants still used German, and in general literature either German or Latin. How Slovenian literature might have developed had the Counter Reformation not occurred can only be guessed, for the Protestant pastors were banished from the country in 1598 and the Protestant nobles in 1628. The triumphant Catholics paid small attention to the Slovenian language, issuing from 1574 to 1764 only ninety printed books.

The renaissance of Slovenian literature began in the last third of the eighteenth century and was brought about by the general spirit of the time, in particular by influences coming from Bohemia and Croatia and by a reaction against the efforts of the "enlightened" Austrian government to substitute German for Latin as the language of instruction in the Slovenian gymnasiums. The movement was at first one of amateurs, but it became of serious importance in the first half of the nineteenth century. It followed a somewhat different course from the revival of Croatian literature. The Slovenians were interested in their own local problems and cared nothing for Pan-Slavic aspirations. They did not join in the Illyrian movement and refused to give up the use of their own speech in literature, even though that speech was divided into a multitude of dialects. On the other hand, the Illyrian movement indirectly aided them in creating their own literary language on the basis of the dialect used by Trubar in the sixteenth century. In France Prešeren (1800–1849) they had a lyric poet of true genius and permanent importance. A tiny people—even now there are hardly two million of them—they have cultivated their own garden.

The Revolution of 1848, by extending political rights to broader social circles, furthered the progress of Slovenian literature, but not until the second half of the nineteenth century were the more highly educated classes of the people definitely converted to that literature. In the past hundred years Slovenian literature has been copious both in prose and verse, and has followed the same general trends as the other literatures of Europe. One may mention that Slovenian books have been remarkable for their external beauty of printing and binding.[1] In 1919, with the formation of the Kingdom of the Serbs, Croats, and Slovenes, the Slovenes obtained in

---

[1] For note to chapter xvii see page 523.

Ljubljana a university of their own. Among their recent writers only two need be mentioned. Oton Župančič (born 1878) has won high distinction as a lyric poet and, not to speak of many translations from Shakespeare and other authors, has written a poetic tragedy, *Veronika of Desenice,* the finest of Slovenian dramas. Ivan Cankar (1876–1918), a prolific author, besides writing excellent verse and working as a dramatist in the style of Ibsen, has shown himself the greatest master of the short story among the South Slavs.

From the Slovenians and the Croatians has come a series of scholars each of whom in his own time stood in the very front rank of students of Slavic philology: Jernej Kopitar (1780–1844), Franz Miklosich (1813–1891), Vatroslav Jagić (1838–1923), and Matthias Murko (born 1861). Jagić was a Croatian; the other three were Slovenians. One may say with confidence that these two small peoples, with a combined population of over five million, have advanced the science of Slavic philology more than have the Russians, with twenty times their number.

## Part Seven

# YUGOSLAVIA AMONG THE NATIONS

# CHAPTER XVIII

# Yugoslavia, the Little Entente, and the Balkan Pact

## BY HARRY N. HOWARD

YUGOSLAVIA, like Czechoslovakia and Rumania, was one of the pioneers in building the Little Entente. Moreover, like Greece, Turkey, and Rumania, Yugoslavia played a significant role in constituting the Balkan Pact of February, 1934, and in developing the Balkan Entente, which was constructed on the foundations of the Balkan Pact.[1] Yugoslav statesmen and the people whom they served must be accredited with vision and wisdom in anticipating those institutions on which Danubian and Balkan unity were to be built.

To the peoples of Yugoslavia, the dream of some sort of union was not new, though it took many forms as it moved along the paths of historical evolution. One might turn to the era of Tsar Stephen Dušan the Mighty, in the mid-fourteenth century, or move rapidly into the late eighteenth and early nineteenth centuries and not mistake the dream. Along with Rhigas Pheraios, one remembers Dositej Obradović and Vuk Karadžić, all of whom thought in terms of a union of the South Slavs of the Balkan Peninsula, as did the Croatian, Ljudevit Gaj, the leader of the Illyrian movement and the editor of the *Ilirske Narodne Novine*. Nor could one overestimate the lifework of Bishop Strossmayer, the great Croatian priest-statesman, who also envisioned a Balkan union.

The statesmen, too, had dreamed of union. Though Karageorge Petrović of Serbia found impossible an agreement with Napo-

---

[1] For notes to chapter xviii see pages 523–525.

leon over the latter's Illyrian scheme, Ilija Garašanin in 1844 thought out his *Načertanije* with the idea of bringing about a union of Serbs, Croats, and Bulgarians, the basic South Slavic elements.[2] Finally, in 1860, Prince Michael Obrenović empowered Garašanin to proceed with a federal plan. By 1867–1868 Serbia had reached agreements with Greece and with Rumania. Even with Bulgarian delegates a program of political relations was agreed upon, envisaging a Yugoslav empire allied with both Greece and Rumania. Although Prince Michael's scheme did not look definitely toward federation, it contained the germ of the idea. But Michael's hesitancy in view of Austro-Hungarian policy after the defeat of 1866 and the formation of the *Ausgleich* in 1867, and finally his assassination in June, 1868, put a temporary end to the fulfillment of the dream.[3]

The death of Michael Obrenović did not prevent others from toying with the idea of Balkan unity. Neither did it destroy the belief that a genuine solution of Balkan and Danubian problems could come only through an association of the free and independent peoples of central and southeastern Europe. To the intellectuals, at least, it seemed clear that neither the Ottoman Empire, based on the medieval concepts of the Moslem faith, nor the Austro-Hungarian Empire, based on an utterly false German-Magyar racial superiority and feudal social, economic, and political ideas, could bring real peace and security to the region.[4]

Seemingly, the Balkan communities found their road to liberation in the alliances of 1912–1913, on the eve of the Balkan struggle—a war to end Ottoman authority in Europe. Serbia and Bulgaria signed an alliance on March 13, 1912, Greece and Bulgaria arrived at an understanding on May 29, and Montenegro adhered to the Balkan alliance by verbal understanding in the summer.[5] War followed in October, but by mid-December the Turks were substantially defeated, and a conference was held at London to determine the peace.

Peace did not come, however. Denied an outlet on the Adriatic, primarily by Austria-Hungary and Italy, Serbia sought it through Macedonia at Salonika, only to be opposed by Bulgaria with the backing of the Ballplatz in Vienna. War soon followed among the erstwhile allies, when, without a declaration of war, Bulgaria attacked Greece and Serbia with the encouragement and at the instigation of Austria-Hungary, only to meet an invasion from Rumania and to have to capitulate in the Treaty of Bucharest. Bulgaria lost the Silistria-Balchik district in the Dobrudja and was deprived of its hopes in Macedonia. Turkey, too, was defeated. But Serbia, Rumania, and Greece, as well as Montenegro, were bound together on the basis of the Treaty of Bucharest.

The period of the First World War was significant for the development of Balkan unity, though it could not be realized immediately. On the eve of the great struggle both Entente and Triplice attempted to organize a Balkan League—the Triplice around Bulgaria, including Rumania, Greece, and Turkey, with the object of crushing Serbia; the Entente around Serbia, with Bulgaria, Rumania, Greece, and possibly Turkey in line. Both sides failed. Serbia crumbled in the late fall of 1915 under a combined German-Bulgarian attack; Rumania delayed entry on the Allied side until August, 1916, and was soon crushed; the Greeks entered in 1917, only after revolution; Turkey entered with Germany almost at the beginning.[6]

Though Balkan unity was not achieved, attempts were made to work out a plan embodying not only the Balkans but central Europe as a whole.[7] Men like Thomas G. Masaryk, Eduard Beneš, Take Jonescu, Nikola Pašić, and Ante Trumbić were thinking in terms of union and association. As Masaryk later wrote, "We contemplated a close understanding with the Southern Slavs and the Poles, as well as with the Rumanians and the Greeks, who had made a Treaty of Friendship with Serbia at the time of the Balkan Wars. . . . The idea of the Little Entente was, so to speak, in the air."[8] These sentiments were echoed by Jonescu.

It was not without significance that in President Wilson's address of January 8, 1918, stating the famous Fourteen Points, he not only called for restoration and independence of the Balkan nations but suggested that "international guaranties of the political and economic independence and territorial integrity of the several Balkan states should be entered into." In October, Colonel E. M. House's "Inquiry" declared: "The United States is clearly committed to the program of national unity and independence. It must stipulate, however, for the protection of national minorities, for freedom of access to the Adriatic and the Black Sea, and it supports a program aiming at a confederation of southeastern Europe."

The Paris Conference of 1919–1920 laid the foundation for future collaboration in central and Balkan Europe. Not only did the peacemakers recommend economic collaboration among the states rising from the wreckage of the Habsburg Empire, but Article XXI of the Covenant of the League of Nations, which recognized the principle of the Monroe Doctrine as a "regional understanding," provided for such regional security understandings as the Little Entente and the Balkan Entente.

It was in November, 1919, that Beneš and Trumbić really began alliance negotiations. The discussions between Beneš and Vaida-Voevod of Rumania began in January, 1920. The Czechoslovak-Yugoslav alliance was signed on August 4, 1920; the Rumanian-Czechoslovak, on April 23, 1921; the Yugoslav-Rumanian accord followed on June 7, 1921. The basic purpose of the alliances in the Little Entente was to prevent either a Magyar attempt forcibly to tear up the Treaty of Trianon or a return of the Habsburgs to the Magyar throne—two of which attempts were made in March and October, 1921. In addition, of course, Yugoslavia and Rumania were pledged against any Bulgarian attempt to upset the Treaty of Neuilly. It is noteworthy, however, that there was no obligation to defend Czechoslovakia against Germany, Rumania against Soviet Russia, or Yugoslavia against Italy, so soon to become fascist and aggressive toward Yugoslavia. Common obligations were assumed only toward common problems, and although this was a source of strength in days of relative calm and peace, in the sense that the Little Entente was not venturing too far afield, it was to be a source of weakness in the troubled days which were to come. But basic, also, to the Little Entente was the idea that under such an organization the members could enjoy the peace and security necessary for the achievement of stability, order, and prosperity.[9]

Although Yugoslavia participated realistically and wholeheartedly in the organization of the Little Entente, King Alexander had taken no particular initiative in its organization—that had been the work of Masaryk, Beneš, Jonescu, Titulescu, Pašić, and Trumbić. Nevertheless, Alexander approved of the Little Entente and stood firm against the forces which would destroy it.[10]

The foundations once laid, the Little Entente developed its policy, not without occasional disturbance, though predictions of the collapse of the union always proved premature.[11] In 1920–1922 the Yugoslavs had serious trouble with Italy over Fiume, the Czechs with Poland over Teschen, the Rumanians with the Soviet Union over Bessarabia, and all three with the Hungarian kingdom under the regency of Admiral Nicholas Horthy. By 1922, however, one member of the Little Entente occupied a "permanent" seat on the Council of the League of Nations. Moreover, at the Lausanne Conference the Little Entente acted in unison on the major issues, and Dr. Momčilo Ninčić, the Yugoslav representative, helped to mediate between Bulgaria and Greece in the matter of an Aegean outlet, while rejecting any basic modification of the Treaty of Neuilly. There was reason for congratulations on July 30, 1923, when the Little Entente met at Sinaia to consider the Magyar and Bulgarian problem and the ministers attested "the perfect unity of the Little Entente as a factor of solidarity and peace newly manifested."

By 1924 the Little Entente seemed to be a stable factor in the European balance. On January 25 France, which had not looked with much favor on the organization of the three Succession States, and seemed to be basing its central European policy on royal and feudal Hungary, signed an alliance with Czechoslovakia. This was followed by an alliance with Rumania on June 13, 1926, and one with Yugoslavia on November 11, 1927, although only the first of these alliances was genuinely implemented by a military agreement of apparently binding nature. The agreement with Yugoslavia came after Fascist Italy had refused to make it a tripartite treaty of guaranty in the Adriatic. Il Duce's Balkan and central European policy was revealed more clearly in the agreements with Hungary and Albania in April and November, 1927, which were to foreshadow the plan of encircling and crushing the Kingdom of the Serbs, Croats, and Slovenes.

Interestingly enough, the distinguished Yugoslav diplomatist, Dr. Momčilo Ninčić, Foreign Minister from 1922 to 1926, as well as in Yugoslavia's most tragic hour, played a signal role in the formative years of the Little Entente. Moreover, while Dr. Beneš was chairman of the League of Nations Commission which framed the Geneva Protocol of 1924, and served as president of the Council when Germany was admitted to membership in the League of Nations in 1926 as a result of the Locarno agreements, Dr. Ninčić was president of the Assembly of the League of Nations.

Though the members of the Little Entente, like Poland, were not satisfied with the Locarno treaties, since the eastern frontiers of Germany were not stabilized or guaranteed, there were evidences of a certain consolidation in central Europe. Naturally, all the members participated in the Kellogg-Briand Pact on August 27, 1928, though the Little Entente states felt that real peace could come only through the League of Nations and through regional understandings. Hence it was that on May 21, 1929, Yugoslavia, Czechoslovakia, and Rumania agreed to an automatic renewal of the Little Entente every five years. Finally, the three states signed the Three-Power Pact providing for pacific adjustment of all disputes according to the model treaty of arbitration and conciliation adopted in 1928 by the League of Nations.

But the possibility of a future of peace and prosperity received a rude setback in the autumn of 1929, owing to world-wide political anarchy and policies of economic nationalism. A general economic depression followed the crash on the New York Stock Exchange in October. What would happen to agrarian countries, like Yugoslavia, in central and southeastern Europe, now that the markets of the world were falling about them like so many cards? While political optimism was publicly proclaimed and prosperity was predicted "just around the corner," dark clouds appeared on the horizon and already there were rumblings of thunder when in September, 1931, Japan struck at China.

A year and a half later, on January 30, 1933, Adolf Hitler came to power in Germany, first to occupy that country and destroy the liberties of the German nation, and then to threaten, menace, and destroy the independence and liberties of the neighbors of the Third Reich, one after the other. Eduard Beneš of Czechoslovakia, with the full support of Yugoslavia and Rumania, led the fight for League action against Japan, only to meet the dilatory tactics of Great Britain and France within the League, and confusion in the United States, in spite of the sane attitude of Secretary of State Henry L. Stimson. To the members of the Little Entente it seemed clear that if the League of Nations failed here it would die, and they wondered whether any grouping of small Powers, unsupported by the great Western democracies at Geneva, could possibly stand against a formidable aggressor.

Barely two weeks after Hitler's advent to power the Little Entente became a virtual diplomatic federation and was apparently stronger than ever. At a meeting in Geneva on February 14–15, 1933, with Bogoljub Jevtić, the Foreign Minister of Yugoslavia, presiding, it was definitely decided to sign a "pact of organization of the Little Entente permitting it to act as a unified international organ."[12] The pact was signed on February 16.[13] Under the new "constitution" of the Little Entente, a Permanent Council, composed of the foreign ministers of the three countries, or their delegates, was created; this Council was to meet at least three times a year. Particularly significant was Article VI of its constitution:

> Every political treaty of any one State of the Little Entente, every unilateral act changing the existing political situation of one of the States of the Little Entente in relation to an outside State, and every economic agreement involving important political consequences shall henceforth require the unanimous consent of the Council of the Little Entente. The existing political treaties of each State of the Little Entente with outside States shall be progressively unified as far as possible.

In order to promote and develop "the progressive coördination of the economic interests of the three States," an Economic Council of the Little Entente was established. It was recognized, however, that the problem of economic integration in the Danubian area would be difficult, for both Yugoslavia and Rumania were primarily agricultural communities, whereas Czechoslovakia had a well-balanced economy of both industry and agriculture. Finally, a Permanent Secretariat was set up, one section of which would function permanently at Geneva, the seat of the League of Nations.

Shortly after this momentous gathering came the development of Mussolini's Four-Power Pact in March, 1933, by which Il Duce proposed to set up an international hierarchical system through which Fascist Italy, Nazi Germany, France, and Great Britain—in contradistinction to the more universal and democratic League of Nations and to the exclusion of the smaller states, such as the members of the Little Entente—would manage European affairs. But the members of the Little Entente, together with Poland, succeeded in defeating this threat of domination by their firm opposition to Mussolini's proposal. At a meeting of the Council of the Little Entente on March 25, 1933, that body indicated its refusal to place its fate in the benevolent hands of the four Powers.

On May 29 the states of the Little Entente explicitly declared that they "could not recognize that the cause of good relations between the different countries is served by agreements which aimed to dispose of the rights of third Powers, whether by a concrete decision or by pressure which might be exercised on other states than those which have concluded these agreements."[14] Moreover, by this time formal guaranties had been given by the French government to the members of the Little Entente against any attempt at revision without their consent.[15] At the meeting on May 29, the Little Entente took its stand in favor of "an economic policy of freedom of exchange in contradistinction to the insane and impractical idea of economic autarchy," and set up a well-developed plan to promote commerce among Yugoslavia, Czechoslovakia, and Rumania.

In the summer of 1933 the Little Entente took part in the London Economic Conference. Though apparently little was accomplished in the realm of economic collaboration, on July 4 the Little Entente states and the Soviet Union did sign an important political pact of nonaggression which contained seemingly airtight guaranties of territorial inviolability. Yugoslavia was not to enter into formal diplomatic relations with the Soviet Union until Adolf Hitler unleashed his war in 1939, but Czechoslovakia and Rumania did so in 1934.

By 1934 developments in the troubled Balkans seemed to tend toward establishment of a genuine new order. On February 9, four of the Balkan states—Greece, Turkey, Yugoslavia, and Rumania—signed the Four-Power Balkan Pact at Athens. This pact, in the making of which Yugoslavia played a leading role, had had an interesting background in the Balkan Conferences, from the first meeting at Athens, October, 1930, to the last, at Salonika, November, 1933.[16] The members of the Balkan Conferences were aware that a federation could not be constructed overnight, and, in fact, did not achieve their final aim, but they did lay foundations for a possible solution of the perplexing problems of the Balkan peoples.

The achievements of the Balkan Conferences were not insignificant when measured by the standards of other international gatherings. A Balkan Chamber of Commerce and Industry was set up in Istanbul as early as 1931, a project for a political pact was formulated in 1932, a Balkan Medical Union and an Agricultural Chamber were established and the draft of a Balkan Customs Union was formulated in 1933. Moreover, there was outlined the broad program of social and cultural coöperation which was needed to reënforce political collaboration.

The Greeks and the Turks, under the leadership of Alexander Papanastassiou, had taken the lead in the movement of the Balkan Conferences, though the Yugoslavs and the Rumanians had made significant contributions. From the beginning, however, Yugoslav and Bulgarian delegates were at odds over the problems of minorities and frontiers. Not without justice, one Yugoslav delegate reminded a Bulgarian colleague that he could not forget the period of 1915–1918, when the Bulgars were on the other side of Thermopylae—a fact which was as true in 1941 as it had been during the last great struggle.

But there were other steps along the road yet to be traveled. In September, 1933, Turkey and Greece joined in a pact of mutual guaranty of their Balkan frontiers.[17] Though the Yugoslav government had not always been coöperative in the matter of the Balkan Conferences, and failed to offer the hospitality of Belgrade for the 1933 meeting, it did take the initiative in the development of the Balkan Pact, under the guidance of King Alexander and Bogoljub Jevtić. On September 18 King Alexander met Tsar Boris of Bulgaria at Belgrade, on the latter's return from western Europe; nothing especially significant developed from this first meeting. Alexander was interested in promoting a union among the Balkan peoples which would enable them to resist foreign aggression. Whatever Alexander's limitations, he well knew that no one of the Balkan peoples was capable of defending itself alone and isolated against the Nazi-Fascist menace. Accordingly, he visited Bucharest on September 30 and Varna on October 3. After conversations with President Kemal Atatürk at Istanbul on October 4, he journeyed to Greece. King Alexander's travels on the destroyer *Dubrovnik* were unquestionably important in helping to produce the Four-Power Balkan Pact of February 9, 1934.[18]

The Balkan Pact, which Albania could not, and Bulgaria would not, sign, provided for a mutual guaranty of the Balkan frontiers of Greece, Turkey, Rumania, and Yugoslavia against attack by any other Balkan nation.[19] A "Secret Protocol," soon revealed, stipulated that "the Balkan Pact is not directed against any country. Its direct object is to guarantee the security of Balkan frontiers against aggression on the part of any Balkan state." As in the case of the Little Entente, there were no obligations against any Great Power—Fascist Italy, Nazi Germany, or Soviet Russia. Likewise, when crisis, conflict, war, and brutal invasion descended on the Balkans, the absence of such obligations and of willingness to act together were to prove of grave significance, even to signalize disaster for the Balkan peoples.

Some months after the signing of the Balkan Pact, at a meeting in Ankara, Turkey, from October 20 to November 2, 1934, the four signatories organized the Balkan Entente on the foundations of the Balkan Pact. A Permanent Council and an Advisory Economic Council were established for the purpose of bringing political stability and economic prosperity to the region. The late Nicholas Titulescu, the Foreign Minister of Rumania, sounded a keynote when he remarked that, thanks to the Balkan Entente, the great European Powers would not be able "to pit one of us against the other and thus plunge this part of the world into a war which means a greater conflagration than that of 1914." But that depended on the ability of the members of the Balkan Entente to conciliate both Albania and Bulgaria. Meanwhile the Balkan Entente embarked on a broad program of political, social, and economic collaboration similar to that recommended by the Balkan Conferences and practiced by the Little Entente.

A severe crisis soon tested the foundations of the Balkan Entente and the Little Entente. On September 27, 1934, King Alexander and Queen Marie of Yugoslavia arrived at Sofia to return the visit of the Bulgarian sovereigns the year before. The purpose was to attempt to seal the new friendship through settlement of certain outstanding problems. This was to be followed by a visit of King Alexander to France to discuss France's new policy of close collaboration with Fascist Italy and to report on his conversations with King Boris. But a few minutes after Alexander disembarked from the destroyer *Dubrovnik* to the streets of Marseille both he and Louis Barthou, the Foreign Minister of France, were assassinated.

The murders were committed by a member of the Croatian terrorist Ustaši organization, operating from Hungarian soil, under the orders of Ante Pavelić, the leader of the Croatian terrorists, and at the direction of Count Galeazzo Ciano and Benito Mussolini himself. Years later, in April, 1941, the terrorist Pavelić was fittingly named the chief puppet of "unfree" Croatia after the Nazi-Fascist aggression against Yugoslavia.[20]

Fascist Italy had never accepted as final the frontiers of Yugoslavia and had sought for years to break up Yugoslavia. Through the assassination of King Alexander, Mussolini hoped to achieve two ends: the destruction of Yugoslavia and the dissolution of both the Little Entente and the Balkan Entente. Thereafter, he thought, he would be able to dominate central and southeastern Europe. However, both the Little Entente and the Balkan Entente stood firmly beside Yugoslavia in its hour of trial and prevented any immediate serious trouble. Nevertheless, Mussolini, through the influence of Pierre Laval, the new French Foreign Minister, was able to escape condemnation at the hands of the Council of the League of Nations[21] for his foul deed.

The years which followed the assassination of King Alexander, in spite of misgivings, hesitation, and confusion, were to witness remarkable achievements in both the Little Entente and the Balkan Entente, especially from 1936 to 1938. Certainly the Balkan Entente played a notable role at the Conference of Montreux[22] in July, 1936, when the Lausanne regime of the Straits was revised. The Economic Council of the Balkan Entente rendered excellent service in preparing the ground for fruitful economic collaboration. As early as January, 1936, the Council, in session at Bucharest, proposed a meeting of maritime experts at Istanbul (May–June, 1936). As a result of this meeting, a Permanent Marine Commission was organized at the Piraeus in October. On January 24, 1936, an air convention was signed by Greece, Yugoslavia, Rumania, and Turkey, facilitating inter-Balkan air communications. The Council, meeting at Bled in July, 1936, recommended direct collaboration with the Little Entente in the establishment of a Postal, Telegraphic, and Telephone Union in central Europe. This convention was signed on October 12, 1936, and went into effect on March 1, 1937.

In July, 1936, Czechoslovakia, Rumania, and Yugoslavia approved accords relating to tourists in anticipation of the reciprocal suppression of passports. In November, Rumania and Yugoslavia reached agreement on the erection of a bridge over the Danube between Turnu-Severin and Kladovo, to be built within three years. In the summer of 1937 Greece and Turkey jointly proposed the erection of a bridge over the Danube between Rumania and Bulgaria. A conference of the National Banks of Issue of the Balkan Entente, held at Athens in December, 1936, urged the facilitation of commercial and financial collaboration in the Balkans. Turkey and Yugoslavia signed a new commercial agreement in the latter part of 1936.

The activity of the Little Entente and the Balkan Entente from 1936 to 1938 in social, economic, and cultural coöperation seemed very promising. Indeed, it appeared that the Balkan peoples might have some hope of preserving their peace and freedom.[23] But that was not to be. If the Japanese aggression in Manchuria in 1931 was to have its repercussions in central Europe, trouble was now to come much closer to southeastern Europe—a region in the vortex of possible conflict. Grave consequences were already foreshadowed in the advent of Hitler to power. But Mussolini's invasion of Ethiopia in October, 1935, brought the trouble directly to Yugoslavia and the Balkan region. Soon after the invasion of Ethiopia, the League of Nations, under the leadership of Great Britain, applied economic sanctions to Italy—a sound procedure had it been soundly applied.[24] But it was soon apparent that the aggression of Italy was not to be stopped. France and Britain were not acting together, partly because of the attitude of Pierre Laval, partly because of the rumblings from across the Rhine.

The application of sanctions, in which the states of the Little Entente and the Balkan Entente loyally coöperated, was costly to Yugoslavia, as it was to some of the other Balkan communities, and exposed it to economic domination by Nazi Germany. Yugoslavia saw its exports to Italy drop from the low figure of D. 672,000,000 in 1935 to a mere D. 137,200,000 in 1936, or from 16.68 per cent to only 3.13 per cent of its total exports. Besides this serious curtailment, its commerce with France had been relatively small since 1931.

Nazi Germany now stepped in with tremendous economic activity throughout the Balkans. German imports from Yugoslavia jumped from D. 751,000,000 in 1935 to D. 1,039,100,000 in 1936, though something like D. 470,000,000 was already frozen in Berlin. By 1937 Yugoslavia was sending 21.7 per cent of its exports to Germany and importing 32.4 per cent of its goods from Germany. By 1938 these figures had risen to 41 per cent and 45 per cent, respectively. Almost half of Yugoslavia's total foreign trade thus went to Adolf Hitler's Third Reich. Even so, Yugoslavia provided only 2.6 per cent of Germany's total imports. In the Balkans as a whole, Germany was assuming a dominant role, exploiting its commercial and financial advantages and using for political advantage not only the 500,000 Germans who lived on Yugoslav soil but also the few native fascist elements. The Reich's aim was to convert Yugoslavia and the Balkans into a kind of Nazi colonial hinterland.

Fortunately for Nazi Germany, Milan Stojadinović was Premier of Yugoslavia from June, 1935, to February, 1939, after the fall of Bogoljub Jevtić. Whatever his technical qualifications in the field of finance, Stojadinović was a man of dictatorial tendencies and felt that he could play along with the Axis Powers politically and economically, even at the risk of weakening the ties of the Little Entente and the Balkan Entente, and still maintain some semblance of an independent position in international politics for Yugoslavia. Few have better described the Stojadinović position than Konstantin Fotić, the Yugoslav Minister to the United States:

[Stojadinović] weakened more and more the ties with the former Allies maintained under King Alexander with the French, the Little Entente and the signatories of the Balkan Pact, and he came to depend more and more on coöperation with Yugoslavia's two powerful neighbors, Germany and Italy. He achieved a certain measure of prosperity by means of a cleverly conducted economic policy and a certain amount of prestige and authority by being treated on the part of Germany and Italy as an equally influential factor in international relations. But these "successes" of Mr. Stojadinović's government were not appreciated by the masses of the people.[25]

But if the Stojadinović policy seemed pro-Nazi and pro-Fascist, it is only just to note that the policy of Pierre Laval in 1935 had served to undercut both the Little Entente and the Balkan Entente. Moreover, Stojadinović was encouraged to carry on with his pro-Nazi orientation by the fact that neither Great Britain nor France made a move, beyond protest, when Hitler violated the Locarno Pact and paved the way for the construction of the Siegfried Line by marching his troops into the Rhineland on March 7, 1936.[26] The policy of nonintervention in Spain strengthened the pro–Nazi-Fascist policy. In October, 1936, came the first steps in the formation of the Berlin-Rome Axis, with a possible forecast of a division of central Europe into spheres of influence, with Yugoslavia seemingly falling into the Fascist sphere.

On January 24, 1937, without clearly informing his allies in either the Balkans or the Little Entente of his plans, Stojadinović took a step which, plausible enough in itself, was nevertheless to lead the way toward loosening the ties of the Balkan Entente. For on that date the so-called "pact of eternal friendship" between Yugoslavia and Bulgaria was signed.[27] The treaty proclaimed, with the plaudits of both countries: "There shall be an inviolable peace and a sincere and perpetual friendship between the Kingdom of Yugoslavia and the Kingdom of Bulgaria." All this was well and good, but what of the obligations of Yugoslavia under the Balkan Pact in the event of a Bulgarian attack on another signatory of that pact? Nevertheless, on March 26, 1937, Stojadinović signed a pact of friendship—again without proper consultation with his allies in the Balkan Entente and the Little Entente. While a commercial accord was signed the same day, in the political treaty Yugoslavia opportunely hopped on the European band wagon to recognize the new Italian Empire in Ethiopia, but neglected even to mention the name of the League of Nations in the document.[28]

So grave was the situation in the Little Entente that some thought it had practically ceased to exist. There was evidence of disunity at the Bratislava meeting[29] in September, 1936, and by the spring of 1937 Yugoslavia seemed to be going its separate way with Italy and Bulgaria. There were especially grave fears for the future of the Little Entente when the Council met at Belgrade in April, 1937. This meeting was followed by the visit of President Beneš to the Yugoslav capital.

But outward unity still prevailed among the central European and Balkan allies, and there were even signs that at last it might be possible to make some agreement with certain neighbors—Austria, Hungary, and Bulgaria—in order to produce a united front against the Nazi-Fascist menace from the west and north. Then Austria was seized by the Nazis in March, 1938, and extremely grave fears were felt for Czechoslovakia. In the latter crisis the wavering of France and Britain led to the Munich Pact and eventual catastrophe, but the Little Entente and the Balkan Entente seemed to remain firm.

At a meeting in Salonika on July 31, 1938, the states of the Balkan Entente reached an understanding with Bulgaria to remove the armament restrictions from that country; in return, the government of Boris III reaffirmed its "pacific intentions" in the Balkans. And at the Bled meeting of the Little Entente on August 21—the last fateful meeting of the Council—a futile approach was made to Hungary. Preliminary understandings were arrived at, recognizing equality of rights in the matter of armaments for Hungary, whereas Hungary renounced the use of force in realizing its revisionist aims,[30] but during these very negotiations Budapest was making arrangements with Hitler concerning Hungary's share of the Czechoslovak loot—a portion of Slovakia and all of Sub-Carpathian Ruthenia.

When the Munich crisis finally came, in September, 1938, Yugoslavia and Rumania, owing to popular pressure in both instances, reaffirmed their ties to the Republic and people of Czechoslovakia, warning the Magyars that "in case of an attack of Hungary against Czechoslovakia, they would be obliged to fulfill their engagements as members of the Little Entente."[31] Nevertheless, without French and British support, not to mention that of Soviet Russia, the Czechs were doomed and with them the Little Entente. The Pact of Munich placed Nazi Germany in command of all the great routes leading into the Balkans.

In spite of these adverse events, the Balkan Entente remained—much weakened, of course, by the tragic events of 1938. A small Slavic state was now to be crushed by Nazi Germany, as a lesson, no doubt, to the nations of southeastern Europe, who would, as a Rumanian statesman declared, be blind "to their own ultimate fate" if they did not "make their own peace in time with the new masters of Europe." There was still a slight prospect of some unity of policy with the rest of the Balkan states, despite the "strict neutrality" of the Stojadinović government. The German plan, however, was to convert the Balkan region, Yugoslavia included, into a Nazi *Lebensraum*—which meant the end of the genuine independence of all the Balkan states and an end to the liberties of the Balkan peoples.

Milan Stojadinović was thrown out of office in February, 1939, and was replaced by Dragiša Cvetković as Premier; Dimitrije Cincar-Marković, the Yugoslav Minister at Berlin, became Foreign Minister. Dr. Vladimir Maček, the Croatian leader, entered the cabinet as Vice-Premier, and by late summer a program of Croatian autonomy was achieved. Cincar-Marković immediately announced his adherence to the German ideology of *Geopolitik* and outlined a policy of "friendship with all, alliance with none." In other words, whatever the internal changes, there would be little alteration in Yugoslav foreign policy.

Meanwhile, the Balkan Entente held a meeting[32] at Bucharest from February 20 to 22, 1939, where M. Grégoire Gafencu had taken over the portfolio of the Foreign Ministry. There were the usual expressions of unity. A press communiqué declared that "the members of the Permanent Council were unanimous in stating that they viewed the policy which the Balkan Entente pursues in a perfectly identical manner, profoundly attached to the ideal of peace, which has not ceased to inspire it since its foundation." This, surely, was innocuous enough. But Cincar-Marković, who was attending his first meeting of the Balkan Entente, was more than able to match it. He noted: "With consciousness of the responsibilities which befall us, we have examined the questions which interest the countries of the Balkan Entente and we have searched for the means to contribute to the work of appeasement and understanding. We believe in the triumph of the policy of peace and good neighborhood. We are inspired especially with a desire to avoid antagonisms."[33]

The seventh session of the Economic Council of the Balkan Entente met at Bucharest from May 17 to 27, 1939, with the idea of promoting economic collaboration among the member states.[34] The Council noted a slight increase in inter-Balkan commerce since

1937. It called attention to the creation of a Yugoslav-Rumanian Chamber of Commerce in Bucharest in the spring of 1939. It noted the efforts of Balkan governments to insert a "Balkan clause" in their various commercial agreements. Moreover, it looked toward plans for the improvement of railroad traffic in the Balkans. Progress was also indicated in air and sea traffic.

But the last gathering of any significance of the Balkan Entente was on February 2 to 4, 1940, when the Permanent Council met at Belgrade.[35] Though war had been going on in Europe for six months, it had not yet reached the Balkans. Perhaps it would not come if the unity of the Balkan Entente could be preserved, as Rumania and Turkey and even Greece were urging. Rumania seemed desperate in its demand for firmer guaranties, lest it be forced to capitulate to Nazi Germany.

Cincar-Marković's policy was aptly summed up in the New York *Times*[36] on the eve of the conferences:

1. There is at present no menace in the Balkans and the conference is not expected to produce great surprises.

2. Closer collaboration between the Balkan states, presumably including Bulgaria, which is not an Entente member, may be anticipated.

3. Since Yugoslavia is at the crossroads of the economic interests of the Great Powers, the commercial aspects will be important at the meeting.

4. Yugoslavia will continue to follow a neutral policy, which is parallel to that of Italy, and improved relations between this country, Hungary, and Bulgaria can also be anticipated.

To foreign neutral observers it seemed obvious, at the time, that war could not be kept out of the Balkan region unless a basic unity of policy were pursued by all members of the Balkan Entente. But would the risks of such a policy be assumed—the risks of peaceful collaboration and firm alliance against external enemies? On February 3 Cincar-Marković told his friends something of his hopes:

Three great world Powers, three of the greatest peoples of Europe, who, until now, have led every movement in the political and intellectual life of our continent, are engaged in a grave armed conflict, the development of which cannot be foreseen. . . . We are happy today to be able to declare that our pacific efforts have, up to now, given good results. We consider the future with the same optimism. The Balkans are menaced from no side. The loyal and correct attitude of the Balkan peoples has been justly appreciated and respected by all. I must add with a particular satisfaction that the attitude of the two countries of the Balkan and Danubian regions which are outside the Balkan Pact, Bulgaria and Hungary, has also conformed to the peaceful policy of the states of the Balkan Entente. That justifies the sincere hope that the sentiment of a true solidarity will end by creating durable conditions for a happy future for all the peoples who live in the Balkans and in the Danubian basin.

Moreover, Italy merits special recognition for the precious contribution which it has given to the maintenance of peace in southeastern Europe by the prudent attitude of "nonbelligerance" it took at the beginning of the conflict.

The policy followed by the countries of the Balkan Entente has already surmounted the difficulties of a critical period in the present conflict. Only such a policy permits us in the future, also, to keep the Balkans out of war. Thus the Balkan peoples, in contributing to the localization of the war, work at the same time toward the return of peace in Europe as soon as possible, and facilitate all the noble moves which come from the great statesmen of the world to preserve humanity from an irreparable catastrophe.[37]

When the conference ended, on February 4, 1940, the Balkan Entente contented itself with a vague and general communiqué which merely reaffirmed the "common interest of the four states in the maintenance of peace, order, and security in southeastern Europe." The four states announced a "firm decision to pursue their resolutely pacific policy, in maintaining strictly their positions in relation to the present conflict in order to preserve this part of Europe from the hazards of war." Although they affirmed their "will to remain united" within the Balkan Entente, they also expressed "their sincere desire to enter into and develop their friendly relations with neighbor states, in a conciliating spirit of mutual understanding and peaceful collaboration." They were determined to promote commercial exchanges among themselves. Finally, the Balkan Pact was prolonged for another seven years, beginning with the sixth anniversary of the pact on February 9, 1940, and the ministers decided that they must keep in constant contact. The next formal meeting was scheduled for February, 1941, in Athens—a meeting destined never to be held.

Clearly, the Balkan Entente was passing into history; it made no reaffirmation of common ties or common unity, for neither Yugoslavia nor Turkey seemed prepared to give firm guaranties. It was tacitly recognized that each member of the Balkan Entente would have to look individually to the Great Powers. But if there was any hope that such a policy would keep the Balkan communities out of war it was soon to be disappointed.

Enemies of the Balkan peoples, both within and outside south-eastern Europe, destroyed the great hope of Balkan unity and then overcame the Balkan countries one by one. Magyar feudal lords and the misled Bulgarian government shared in the loot. Mussolini rapaciously laid claim to the Dalmatian coast along the Adriatic.

Yet, if the Balkan peoples failed in their quest for unity and reached only disaster, their failure was the failure of the European peoples as a whole. The mistakes of the Balkan peoples were matched by those of the American people, who, by their determination to avoid "entanglements in Europe's wars," helped to render the organization and development of peace futile from the year 1919. Meanwhile, it is an interesting commentary that, previous to their participation in the looting of their Balkan neighbors, Fascist Italy, feudal Hungary, and peasant Bulgaria had become Nazi-occupied countries and had lost their independence to Berlin.

# CHAPTER XIX

# Foreign Policy in the
# Second World War (1939–1946)

## BY HARRY N. HOWARD

LTHOUGH YUGOSLAVIA was a member of both the Little Entente and the Balkan Entente and had been allied with France since 1927, by the time of the outbreak of the Second World War, in September, 1939, the Yugoslav government—whatever the sentiments of the people—was already oriented in the direction of the Axis. After 1935 especially, commercial relations with Germany had been intensified; in 1937 the political ties with Bulgaria and Italy were strengthened. In spite of this orientation, however, Germany and Italy, especially the latter, seem to have been moving toward a policy of partitioning Yugoslavia when the opportunity arose, although there were reassuring words during the visits of Premier Stojadinović to Berlin and Rome and of von Neurath, the German Foreign Minister, to Belgrade.[1]

The so-called Munich Agreement of September 29–30, 1938, constituted a major landmark in the development of Germany's policy toward southeastern Europe and in the orientation of Yugoslavia itself. After the resignation of Milan Stojadinović on February 4, 1939, and his replacement by Premier Dragiša Cvetković, the close relations with Germany continued. On February 7 the new Yugoslav Foreign Minister, Dimitrije Cincar-Marković, advised von Ribbentrop that he would continue to strengthen German-Yugoslav relations and to examine the problem of Yugoslavia's adherence to the Anti-Comintern Pact. After the destruction of Czechoslovakia

[1] For notes to chapter xix see pages 525–526.

in March, 1939, discussions of Yugoslav-German relations took place. Germany was informed that Yugoslavia was not interested in the British guaranty to Greece and Rumania, which had been communicated also to Turkey. Assured that Germany was both politically and territorially disinterested in Yugoslavia, in spite of its obvious economic interests, Yugoslavia, in turn, professed no interest in extending the obligations of the Balkan Entente, despite the Turkish efforts in that direction.[2] When the Second World War broke out, Yugoslavia, hoping that it would not reach the Balkan region, at once declared neutrality. The last meeting of the Balkan Entente was held in February, 1940, at Belgrade.[3]

*Yugoslavia's adherence to the Axis.*—The Italian attack on Greece[4] on October 28, 1940, which took the German government somewhat by surprise, made the problem of Yugoslavia more acute, especially in view of the successful Greek resistance. In the months which followed, pressure was therefore brought to bear on the Belgrade government to adhere to the Axis pact of September 27, 1940, among Germany, Italy, and Japan. Hungary signed the pact on November 20, 1940, Rumania on November 23, Slovakia on November 24, and Bulgaria on March 1, 1941, while German troops were moving into Bulgaria for the attack on Greece. Yugoslavia and Hungary, it will be recalled, on December 11, 1940, had signed a pact of "perpetual friendship and peace."

The Führer conferred with Premier Cvetković in February, 1941, demanding Yugoslav adherence to the Axis and permission for the transit of German troops and munitions across Yugoslavia, economic collaboration, and acceptance of the German occupation of Bulgaria. The Yugoslav Premier stressed the strong ties between Germany and his country and indicated his understanding of German policy. Moreover, he noted that Yugoslavia was not a democratic country, but was devoted to "order and discipline." He was not yet ready, however, to act positively.

The discussions were continued into the month of March, and on March 25 Premier Cvetković and Foreign Minister Cincar-Marković journeyed to Vienna to sign the Tripartite Pact. It is noteworthy, however, that the agreement included no demand for Yugoslav military assistance, in view of the poor equipment of the Yugoslav army, and no transportation of troops through the Yugoslav state or territory. Both the political independence and the territorial integrity of Yugoslavia were to be preserved. The Germans and Italians hinted at future Yugoslav possession of Salonika.[5]

*The coup d'état of Simović.*—Two days after the signature of the Tripartite Pact at Vienna, on March 27, came the *coup d'état* under General Dušan Simović by which King Peter II was placed on the throne of Yugoslavia. The Germans felt that the Yugoslavs had received much outside encouragement, including that of Great Britain and the United States as well as Soviet influence.

Hitler, who had been very happy over the results of the Vienna meeting, regarded the developments in Belgrade as an open challenge to Germany. The influence on other small countries might be disastrous unless positive action were taken against Yugoslavia. In spite of the efforts of the Simović government to continue negotiations, Hitler decided to attack immediately. In view of the plans for war on the Soviet Union, Hitler could not afford to leave a hostile country on his flank in southeastern Europe. The events in Yugoslavia, therefore, must be considered against the background of the forthcoming German attack on the Soviet Union, for both that attack and the aggression against Greece had already been decided. Had Yugoslavia taken the Bulgarian attitude and permitted the German advance on Greece through Yugoslav territory, there would have been only a minor problem, for Greece might have surrendered more readily to the Germans than to the Italians.[6]

*The partition of Yugoslavia.*—The German attack on Yugoslavia came on April 6, 1941, a few hours after the announcement of the Soviet-Yugoslav treaty of friendship and nonaggression (April 5). Bulgaria and Italy took action the same day and Hungary followed on April 10. On April 17 the Yugoslav army was forced to capitulate.[7] Five days after the surrender, Germany and Italy had reached agreement on the liquidation of Yugoslavia. Croatia was to become an "independent" state under Italian protection, with the Duke of Spoleto as king. Slovenia was to be annexed in part to Italy and in part to Germany. Dalmatia also was to be annexed to Italy, with the status of an Italian "government." Montenegro was to be "independent" once more, but bound in personal union with Italy. Albania, already incorporated into the Italian Empire, was to have an extension of frontiers, especially in the Ohrid region.

Hungary was to receive the Prekomurje, the Bačka, and the Banat; the last, however, was to remain under German military occupation until the end of the war. The Yugoslav portions of Macedonia were to go to Bulgaria, though the latter was not permitted, for the time at least, to occupy Salonika. Serbia itself remained under German military occupation; General Milan Nedić was to establish a puppet government[8] by September, 1941.

Although it was impossible to prevent the defeat of the Yugoslav armies or the partition of Yugoslavia at the hands of the Axis, Mr. Churchill announced that Yugoslavia had "found its soul." On June 4, 1941, the United States government reiterated the indignation of the American people "at the invasion and mutilation of Yugoslavia by various member states of the Tripartite Pact."

*The government in London.*—With the obvious defeat of the Yugoslav armies and the beginnings of guerrilla warfare under General Draža Mihailović, King Peter and his government went into exile, going first to Jerusalem and then to London in the spring of 1941, where the government-in-exile remained until the autumn of 1943, when it moved to Cairo for a time. The Yugoslav government announced, on May 29, 1941, that it had tried to preserve peace through a policy of neutrality and was still holding conversations when the Germans attacked. Now that war and invasion had come, Yugoslavia, in spite of the evil circumstances of the moment, would struggle on to victory with its allies.

The Yugoslav government-in-exile at once began to develop a foreign policy in close association with Great Britain and with the Soviet Union, which was attacked on June 22, 1941, as well as with the United States, which declared war on December 8, 1941, after the Japanese attack on Pearl Harbor. As early as May 12, 1941, the Yugoslav government protested the creation of the so-called independent state of Croatia, although six days later Italy planned the restoration of the Croatian monarchy, and on June 14 Croatia signed an agreement with the Axis. On July 31 Bulgaria formally incorporated parts of Yugoslavia, since the German military authorities had permitted the Bulgarian army "to take possession of certain southern and eastern parts of Yugoslav national territory."

*The Atlantic Charter.*—On June 12, 1941, the Yugoslav government-in-exile, together with thirteen other governments, pledged to fight the war to the end and to work together with other free peoples to achieve victory. The Yugoslav minister at London, in supporting the resolution, protested against Axis violence in his country and the attempt to dismember Yugoslavia, declaring:

> Yugoslavia looks forward with confidence to the outcome of the war, in which she will not cease to take part with all her means, side by side with the Allied states. She feels confident that her Allies will assist her with all the means in their power in this struggle for restoration of right and justice and help free herself from all her enemies and entirely reëstablish her frontiers and the freedom of Balkan nations.[9]

On September 24, 1941,—while General Nedić was taking his place as Premier of the puppet government in Belgrade—the Yugoslav government-in-exile declared its adherence to the Atlantic Charter of August 14, although Foreign Minister Momčilo Ninčić made an important observation concerning general principles:

> The Yugoslav Government is . . . persuaded that in the execution of these principles, which should assure peace, well-being, and prosperity to all peoples, the fact will not be overlooked that this high ideal can be attained only if conditions of international life are established which would give to the peoples a feeling of security and the conviction not only that aggression can never profit the aggressor, but that account will be taken of the damage caused by the aggressor. . . . The inequality of the resultant positions in different nations is very great, and it will be necessary to take account of this, inspired by the conception of justice.[10]

On January 1, 1942, the London government joined the twenty-six governments in the Declaration by the United Nations. Aside from adherence to the general principles of the Atlantic Charter, they agreed to exert every effort toward winning the war and to make no separate armistice or peace with the enemies of the United Nations. On January 14, 1942, the Yugoslav government-in-exile signed the United Nations Declaration on War Crimes.

*The Greek-Yugoslav project for Balkan union.*—Meanwhile, on November 4, 1941, the Yugoslav delegation to the conference of the International Labor Organization in New York City joined with representatives of Czechoslovakia, Poland, and Greece in pledging coöperation in peace, noting that "the countries of central Europe and the Balkans reaffirm their profound devotion to democratic principles and express their solidarity with the great democracies." Indeed, a Central and Eastern European Planning Board was established on January 7, 1942,—though it functioned ineffectively for only a year or so—to further coöperation among these countries.

Thus was foreshadowed the development of a project of Balkan union which was signed by the Greek and Yugoslav governments in London on January 15, 1942. The project was based on two fundamental ideas: (1) lack of close understanding and collaboration had caused the Balkan peoples "to be exploited by the powers of aggression in their aim of achieving political and military penetration and domination of the peninsula," and (2) to assure the independence and peace of the Balkans, their policy must be founded on the principle of "the Balkans for the Balkan peoples."[11]

The project called for the establishment of four permanent institutions: (1) a political organ, composed of the foreign ministers of the member states; (2) an economic and financial organ consisting of two members from each government, who were to have special competence in economic and financial matters; (3) a permanent military organ made up of the chiefs of the general staff or their representatives, to coördinate the military activities and policies of the union and to develop a common plan for defense; (4) a secretariat with political, economic, financial, and military sections.

Aside from the work of the permanent organs of the projected union, the premiers of the member states were to meet whenever necessary to discuss problems of general interest. Moreover, there was to be collaboration among parliaments. The governments of the union were to facilitate regular meetings of parliamentary delegations for exchange of views on questions of common interest. The primary aim of the union was to promote the political stability, economic welfare, and sense of security of the Balkan peoples.

The Greek and Yugoslav governments declared that their agreement represented "the general foundations for the organization of a Balkan union," and looked forward to "the future adhesion to this agreement of other Balkan states ruled by governments freely and legally constituted." The agreement, which was to become binding on Greece and Yugoslavia regardless of the adherence of other Balkan states, was greeted with a pledge of acceptance by the self-constituted Free Bulgarian National Committee in London.

The Greek-Yugoslav project was hailed by the British government; the ceremonies of signature were held in the Foreign Office in the presence of Anthony Eden, the British Foreign Minister. King Peter, in his declaration of January 15, expressed the hope that a central European union, on the basis of the Czechoslovak-Polish agreement, would also be created. The two unions, conceived along similar lines, would create, "together with a single common supreme organ, a great organization which would give serious guaranties for the peace and prosperity of Europe." Four days later, when the Czechoslovak-Polish project was signed, President Beneš declared that the two projects formed "a basis for a wider agreement and complete organization of central and southeastern Europe. . . . In the mutual dependence of all states in this region the Yugoslav-Czechoslovak friendship forms an indispensable link."[12]

Nevertheless, these seeds of union fell on stony ground. Whatever the views of the British government on the matter, the Soviet Union was definitely opposed to any such scheme at the time, and the view was expressed that such projects were premature. After the summer of 1943 little was heard of the Greek-Yugoslav project for Balkan union.

*The United States and mutual assistance.*—On March 18, 1942, a lend-lease agreement was signed between the United States and the Yugoslav government-in-exile; on May 18 a military-service agreement was signed. In reply to a message of Konstantin Fotić, the Yugoslav Minister to the United States, Sumner Welles, the Under Secretary of State, expressed the admiration of the United States government and the American people for the struggle which the Yugoslavs had made against the enemy, and especially hailed the achievements of General Draža Mihailović, who had been made Minister of War on January 13, 1942.

King Peter, together with Foreign Minister Momčilo Ninčić, arrived in the United States on June 21. He addressed Congress and broadcast to the American people. On July 24 President Roosevelt and King Peter announced their complete agreement that all the resources of the two nations should be devoted to the "vigorous prosecution" of the war. Attention was given also to "the principles that should guide our countries in establishing an enduring and prosperous peace under a just application of the Declaration by the United Nations, and the principles of the Atlantic Charter."

An agreement was signed on the principles applying "to mutual aid in the prosecution of the war, pledging their material and spiritual resources to a common victory of the United Nations."[13]

*Beginnings of the United Nations.*—In 1943 the Yugoslav government helped to lay additional foundations for the future United Nations. On January 5, 1943, it joined with other governments in a declaration on the seizure of property by the Nazi-Fascist invaders. It also adhered to the declaration of principles and recommendations of the United Nations Conference on Food and Agriculture at Hot Springs, Virginia (May 18–June 3, 1943). On June 10, 1943, Yugoslavia became a member of the United Nations Relief and Rehabilitation Administration.

*The Četnik-Partisan conflict.*—Meanwhile, by the autumn of 1942, open conflict had broken out between the Četnik forces of General Draža Mihailović, who had led the resistance movement since April 6, 1941, and the Partisan forces of Marshal Tito. From the beginning there had been differences between the two groups in leadership and tactics, and basic conflicts on social, economic, and political points of view. In the autumn of 1941 the two groups had coöperated to some extent and the leaders had met twice to discuss their difficulties. But in the end agreement proved impossible primarily because of the greater conservatism of the Četnici.[14] In view of these differences of opinion on the Četnik-Partisan conflict, it was difficult to bring about agreement among Great Britain, the United States, and the Soviet Union on Yugoslavia.

As early as February, 1943, the Partisans under Tito announced a program looking toward a Yugoslav federation "according full recognition of national rights" to Croatia, Slovenia, and Serbia, as well as to Macedonia and the others. Already, apparently, the Partisans were bearing a large share of the resistance to the Germans and Italians, although there were also reports of the Četnici fighting the Germans. As early as the spring of 1943 Great Britain decided to send a military representative (Brigadier MacLean) to Marshal Tito, a move which was endorsed by the Soviet government. Later in the year Mihailović asked for more Allied assistance, denying charges which had been made against him of collaboration with the enemy. On November 8, 1943, however, General Sir Henry Maitland Wilson, the commander in chief of the Mediterranean

Theater of Operations, warned Četnik collaborators to desert the Nazi cause or be regarded as traitors to the United Nations.

On December 8 the British government announced that more assistance was going to the Partisans than to Mihailović because they were doing most of the fighting against the Germans. Secretary of State Hull announced, on December 9, that the United States intended to furnish war materials to the Partisan forces—or to any other Yugoslav group effectively fighting the Germans. Foreign Minister Eden confirmed British support of the Partisans in the House of Commons on December 14, and two days later it was reported that the United States had a military mission with Marshal Tito, as well as with General Mihailović. At about the same time, while preserving relations with the Yugoslav government-in-exile, the Soviet government refused to sign a treaty of mutual assistance and postwar collaboration with it, and announced its preference for, and support of, the Yugoslav Committee for National Liberation, headed by Marshal Tito.

*The government-in-exile.*—Meanwhile, the Yugoslav government-in-exile, which had been reorganized on August 10, 1943, under Premier Božidar Purić, arrived, with King Peter, at Cairo on September 28. An appeal for the unity of all Yugoslavs was made, but there was no special program to which all elements might be expected to rally. As if in reply to the royal government, the Anti-Fascist Council at Jajce, on November 29, 1943, presented a program for a federal Yugoslavia with equal rights for all and basic rights for minorities—a move which was endorsed on November 30 by the Anti-Fascist Council for the National Liberation of Yugoslavia. The royal government was roundly denounced and deprived of all the rights of a legal government, as also of the right to represent the peoples of Yugoslavia in foreign countries. King Peter was forbidden to return until after the liberation of the entire country, "when the problem of the king as well as the question of the monarchy" could be decided. The Council also recommended that the presidium of the Anti-Fascist Council reëxamine all treaties or obligations undertaken by the Yugoslav government-in-exile, and that no further agreements be recognized.[15]

*Attempts at settlement.*—The long-smoldering conflict between Marshal Tito and the government of King Peter was now com-

PARTISAN GUARD

KING PETER II

pletely in the open and presented grave issues to the British, the Soviet, and the American governments—issues much broader and deeper than the constitutional question involved. Indeed, Anthony Eden announced in the House of Commons, on December 14, 1943, that both parties were agreed that the future form of government was to be decided when Yugoslavia had been liberated. The Great Powers had been in consultation on the matter, attempting to unite all elements for the fight against the common enemy. How difficult was the task may be judged from the mutual recriminations: King Peter denounced the attacks upon him and referred to the Partisans as a movement of "terroristic violence."

In spite of the efforts of the Powers, the rift had become wider by January, 1944. General Mihailović informed a National Congress assembled in the Yugoslav mountains (January 26–28) that he and his forces would remain faithful to King Peter, to the "constitutional and legal order" in Yugoslavia, and would defend its territorial integrity. King Peter, who had returned to London, addressed the Anglo-American Press Association on April 20, 1944:

This war will be won only with the united efforts of the three Great Powers— Great Britain, Russia, and the United States—helped by all the oppressed nations sponsored by that moral foundation on which the present tremendous struggle stands.... The Yugoslav people gave ample proof of vitality and power of resistance through their war effort; and, likewise, we shall spare no effort to win and preserve the peace....

Yugoslavia could be and should be a link connecting and harmonizing the common interests of the Great Powers in that part of Europe. In order, however, to be able to play this historic role, it is necessary that we should have equal and free participation in conversations between the Great Powers when they concern the future and destiny of Yugoslavia and the Balkans.

Owing to strategic and geographic importance, the Balkans constituted, in all the wars in Europe, one of the vital problems.... This fact must not be forgotten nor must it be hushed up. Without free and independent Balkan states, respected by our great Allies, peace in Europe can never be insured. Yugoslavia's mission as an ally of Great Britain, Russia, and the United States, not only in this war but in the last, is, I repeat, to balance and harmonize Allied interests in that part of Europe. The more so as she has always maintained with these Powers the best and the most friendly relations and has never had conflicts with any of them.

Yugoslavia's interests have never conflicted or been opposed to those of Great Britain. Throughout their history the Yugoslav people have not only maintained friendly and allied relations with Russia, but have lived in brotherhood with the Russian people. It is our sincere wish to establish these relations on a permanent and more intimate basis.

In the eyes of Yugoslavs the United States has never stood as merely an arsenal for armaments and gold reserve. To us the United States is a country of lofty idealism and great realism whose conception of freedom, independence, and equality should save our civilization and insure a happier future for mankind.[16]

While King Peter was criticizing the Great Powers because of their failure properly to assist in the struggle of Yugoslavia for freedom, Marshal Tito announced that Yugoslavia was already half freed from the enemy, but help was needed to complete the task.

By June 1, 1944, with Premier Ivan Šubašić heading the government-in-exile, there were signs that British, Soviet, and American influence was about to bring a semblance of unity between the Partisans and the government in London. On June 16 an agreement was signed on Yugoslav territory by Šubašić and Marshal Tito, and a government was formed uniting the conflicting elements.[17] On July 9 Šubašić assured "united" Yugoslavia that Stalin, Roosevelt, and Churchill would do all in their power to restore independence and freedom to the Yugoslav people. Prime Minister Churchill informed the House of Commons on August 2 that there were now good chances of bringing unity out of the Yugoslav chaos. On August 8 the government-in-exile indicated that it was seeking to unify all democratic forces within the country to effect speedy deliverance from the enemy and that it would devote its energies to the development of a democratic and federal Yugoslavia "organized by the free will of the Yugoslav peoples." Tito made a somewhat similar statement on August 17, stressing the agreement of June 16.

How much influence had been brought to bear in order to bring about the agreement of June–August, 1944, may be seen from the fact that Prime Minister Winston Churchill, Under Secretary of War Robert Patterson, and Lieutenant General B. B. Somervell conferred with Premier Šubašić and Marshal Tito in Italy on August 12 and 13. But the difficulties did not end. In Washington the Yugoslav Minister, Konstantin Fotić, rejected the new cabinet and resigned his post as early as July 14. Marshal Tito was clearly to dominate the Yugoslav scene in the months which followed.

*The development of Marshal Tito's policy.*—The struggle between King Peter and Marshal Tito continued in spite of the presumed unity which had been sealed in the agreement of June, 1944, and the pronouncements of August, although it was reported in mid-November that Premier Šubašić and Marshal Tito had reached an agreement on the regency: a plebiscite was to be held after the war to determine whether King Peter could return to his throne. Dr. Šubašić went to Moscow late in November, 1944, where he received the blessing of the Soviet government on his agreement with Tito to establish a unified government at Belgrade.

Meanwhile there were other significant developments. As early as July, Sava Kosanović, who was now a member of the Yugoslav cabinet, urged the formation of a Yugoslav federation which would include Bulgaria, and also Rumania, Greece, and Albania, as a "bridge of harmony" in the Balkan region. There were reports of an agreement between Tito and the Bulgarians, with Russian sanction, in October. Moreover, Premier Stalin was publicly quoted on November 22 as favoring a postwar alliance of "equal Slav states." On November 23 Marshal Tito declared that a federal, democratic government would be established in Yugoslavia and that it would use all its powers to bring about "the closest collaboration and *rapprochement* with its Balkan neighbors," especially with Bulgaria. This sentiment was reëchoed by Premier Kimon Georgiev, of Bulgaria, who stated definitely that Bulgaria would create no difficulties, but "was ready to support the idea of close relations and coöperation between southern Slavs."[18] Premier Enver Hoxha of Albania declared, on November 30, that Albania was seeking a close alliance with Marshal Tito's Yugoslavia, since they were "bound together now with the Yugoslavs by blood ties."

Great Britain, which was none too enamored of the idea of a South Slav bloc under positive Soviet dominance, took steps to limit its application. Prime Minister Churchill, together with Foreign Minister Eden, was in Moscow from October 9 to 18, 1944, to consult with Premier Stalin and Foreign Commissar Molotov on the problem of Yugoslavia. Eventually they reached an agreement "to pursue a joint policy in Yugoslavia designed to concentrate all energies against the retreating Germans and bring about a solution of Yugoslav internal difficulties by a union between the Royal Yugoslav Government and the National Liberation Movement." The right of the Yugoslav people to settle their own future after the war was recognized as inalienable. This meeting took place with the knowledge and approval of the United States government, which was represented in the discussions by Ambassador W. Averell Harriman in the capacity of an observer.

Although the Anglo-Soviet discussions brought about a measure of apparent harmony, no settlement of the complicated issues was, in fact, achieved. Nevertheless, Winston Churchill announced to the House of Commons, on January 18, 1945, that he believed that the Tito-Šubašić agreement was the best which could be made for the immediate future of Yugoslavia, since it preserved the form of monarchy pending a plebiscite. He was unwilling to prophesy as to the future, however, although he was unable to see what else Great Britain and the Soviet Union could have done. Mr. Churchill was aware of King Peter's scruples, but he felt that they could not "in these times indefinitely prevent the march of events."

*The Yugoslav problem at the Yalta Conference.*—The problem of Yugoslavia was discussed at the Yalta Conference in February, 1945. The report of the Conference,[19] on February 11, noted a recommendation to Marshal Tito and Premier Šubašić that "the agreement between them should be put into effect immediately and a new government should be formed on the basis of that agreement." It was recommended also that the new government should declare that: (1) The Anti-Fascist Council for National Liberation (A.V.N.O.J.) should be extended to include members of the last Yugoslav parliament (Skupština) who had not compromised themselves by collaboration with the enemy, thus forming a body to be known as a temporary parliament; and (2) legislative acts passed by the Anti-Fascist Council for National Liberation would be subject to ratification by a Constituent Assembly.

Nevertheless, the Yalta recommendations did not produce their own solutions. Difficulties still lay ahead, especially in regard to the regency problem, in spite of the efforts of Dr. Šubašić to bring about agreement. The form of government was not to be decided until the plebiscite of November 11, 1945, when the National Front of Marshal Tito won some 85 per cent of the votes cast. According to the constitution finally adopted on January 31, 1946, Yugoslavia was to be organized under a Federal Peoples Republic.

*Yugoslavia and the United Nations.*—The royal Yugoslav government was an original signatory to the Declaration by the United Nations of January 1, 1942. The newly formed government under Marshal Tito accepted an invitation to participate in the United Nations Conference at San Francisco on April 6, 1945. The Yugoslav delegation at San Francisco, headed by Dr. Šubašić, Foreign Minister since March, submitted no formal proposals for consideration by the Conference and took little initiative otherwise. Dr. Šubašić, however, declared his hope that the Dumbarton Oaks proposals would be accepted by all the United Nations, and stated his belief in a strong international organization in which the responsibilities of the Great Powers would be matched by their authority. He felt, however, that an effective security organization should rest on a sound moral basis. The Charter of the United Nations was ratified on October 19. Yugoslavia was represented on the Executive Committee and on the Preparatory Commission of the United Nations in the autumn and winter of 1945.

At the first session of the United Nations in London, Edvard Kardelj, the Deputy Prime Minister of Yugoslavia, advised the General Assembly, on January 18, 1946, that the United Nations Charter was clearer than any similar document. He stressed the necessity of continuing to struggle against fascism and of arriving at a basic understanding with the members of the United Nations, founded on a realistic agreement among the Great Powers. Dr. Andrija Štampar, an eminent Yugoslav medical scientist, was elected vice-president of the Economic and Social Council. Dr. Milovan Zoričić was elected to the International Court of Justice (until 1949).

No special problem concerning Yugoslavia arose in connection with the United Nations until, on February 16, 1946, Andrei Vyshinsky, the Soviet delegate, presented a Yugoslav note to the Security Council declaring that 120,000 Polish troops under British command in Italy were moving "steadily toward Yugoslavia and were threatening its frontiers." The Yugoslav delegation, for the most part, followed the lead of the Soviet Union in its voting in the United Nations organs.

*Yugoslav foreign policy.*—On the eve of the San Francisco Conference the Yugoslav government signed a treaty of alliance with the Soviet Union (April 11, 1945),[20] binding the two countries to resist aggression on the part of Germany or its recent allies and to maintain close postwar economic and political collaboration. On September 12, 1945, Marshal Tito reiterated his sentiments in regard to the establishment of "cordial fraternal relations and coöperation with our neighbors, Albania, Bulgaria, and Rumania," constituting a guaranty against outside intrigue "aimed at turning those countries from the road they have taken in their internal organization." In December, 1945, however, Tito told members of the British House of Commons who were visiting Belgrade:

The question of a Balkan federation at present is premature because to create a Balkan federation certain prerequisites are indispensable. In the first place, it is necessary to remove what separated the Balkan peoples in the past and to build friendly relations and realize economic and cultural coöperation. These are the main prerequisites because a federation created without them would be weak. I think that this question cannot be considered now.

Instead, Yugoslavia was then proceeding along rather different lines. On March 18, 1946, a treaty of mutual assistance was signed with Poland, which, like Yugoslavia, was allied with the Soviet Union (April 21, 1945); on May 9, 1946, a similar instrument was signed with Czechoslovakia, after a visit of Marshal Tito to Prague on his return from Warsaw, and a visit of Premier Fierlinger, Vice-Premier Gottwald, and Foreign Minister Masaryk to Belgrade, May 8–10. Czechoslovakia, too, was in alliance with the Soviet Union (December 12, 1943). Thus in east-central Europe there was gradually emerging a pattern not unlike that of the past.

Meanwhile, on December 22, 1945, the American Department of State published the official notes on American recognition of the Federal Peoples Republic of Yugoslavia, pointing out the changes which had taken place in Yugoslav constitutional structure and indicating its opinion in regard to the limitations on basic freedoms in Yugoslavia, including the opportunity of holding free and untrammeled elections. Yugoslavia's claims to Istria, and especially to the city of Trieste, had proved major obstacles in the deliberations of the Council of Foreign Ministers in the autumn of 1945 in London and at the Paris meetings in the spring of 1946, for the United States and Great Britain had failed to accede to the Yugoslav demand for Trieste, and the Soviet Union had refused to move from its position of support to Yugoslavia.[21] Nor did the conduct of the trial of General Draža Mihailović in June, 1946, improve relations between Yugoslavia and the Western democracies.

CHAPTER XX

# The Second World War and Beyond

BY WAYNE S. VUCINICH

O
N FEBRUARY 14, 1941, Hitler summoned to Berchtesgaden the Yugoslav Premier Dragiša Cvetković and Foreign Minister Dimitrije Cincar-Marković and suggested Yugoslavia's adhesion to the Tripartite Pact. After brief negotiations with the Nazis, during which the Yugoslav delegation offered substitutes for outright adherence to the Tripartite Pact which were rejected by Hitler, the cabinet voted, on March 20, to accept his proposal. The cabinet, however, was not unanimous: the first indication of internal disagreement was the resignation of four Serb ministers. The Croat leader, Vladimir Maček, held the scales. When he tipped them in favor of a compact with Germany, the premier and the foreign minister departed for Vienna and, on March 25, signed the Pact. Although the entire content of the Pact with the Axis was not published, it was widely believed that it meant Yugoslavia's full alignment with the fascist Powers. Popular resentment against the government that had signed the Pact grew unchecked and soon reached serious proportions.

Early on the morning of March 27 a bloodless *coup d'état* was effected by a group of officers under the leadership of General Dušan Simović. The premier, the foreign minister, and the regents were arrested. Prince Paul, the principal regent, and his family were sent to Kenya, a few days after Paul had helped to exile to Mauritius the self-styled leader, Milan Stojadinović, who had ruled Yugoslavia with an iron hand from June, 1935, to February,

[353]

1939. The majority of King Peter II was proclaimed, though he was not yet eighteen years old. That the *coup d'état* was completely successful was due primarily to the patriotism of the peasants, workers, students, younger officers, and some members of the hierarchy of the Orthodox Church.

General Dušan Simović, who was entrusted with the formation of a new government, assembled the leading representatives of all political parties except for the quasi-fascist Yugoslav Radical Union (J.R.Z.) of Stojadinović and the very small and uninfluential fascist group of Dimitrije Ljotić. Also not included were the diminutive Slovene Liberal party and the underground Communist party, the existence of which had been forbidden by law. The chief characteristic of the new government was the preponderance of elderly statesmen who formerly had been engrossed in petty political and chauvinist squabbles. The government announced its readiness to accept the published version of the Pact of Vienna, although it had no clearly defined policy and was merely seeking a way out of the existing crisis.

The enraged Führer at once summoned to Berlin his minister at Belgrade and instructed him to demand an apology from Yugoslavia, immediate ratification of the Pact, general demobilization, and compensation for damage done by riotous Yugoslavs to German offices and shops. Foreign Minister Momčilo Ninčić reiterated Yugoslavia's readiness to accept the Pact of Vienna, but expressed a desire for discussions which would safeguard Yugoslav independence. This was too much for Hitler, whose rage increased as Yugoslav popular demonstrations against Germany swept the country. He was especially incensed because the Yugoslav "insult" occurred just at the time of the Japanese foreign minister's visit to Berlin.

The Nazis launched a systematic propaganda offensive against Yugoslavia, accusing its citizens of atrocities and of coöperation with anti-Axis foreign agents. The non-Axis foreign press encouraged the Yugoslav stand against Germany and gave wide publicity to the sympathetic statements of Winston Churchill and Sumner Welles. The Moscow *Pravda* congratulated the people on being worthy of their glorious past. Meanwhile the Yugoslav government urged its people to be calm, to avoid demonstrations, and to refrain from spreading rumors.

Early on Sunday morning, April 6, 1941, German troops invaded Yugoslavia, only a few hours after the announcement of the conclusion of a pact of friendship and nonaggression between Yugoslavia and the Soviet Union. With lightning rapidity the German and satellite columns invaded Yugoslavia from all sides, and wave after wave of low-flying *Luftwaffe* swept over Belgrade, disregarding its status of an "open city." The loss of life was estimated at 15,000–25,000 in Belgrade alone. The *Wehrmacht* easily dealt with the unequal and not yet fully mobilized Yugoslav forces. The Yugoslav government and the High Command at once abandoned the capital. With little chance of establishing itself in Serbia or Bosnia, the government eventually reached Montenegro and thence took off by plane for the Near East.

Almost from the start the High Command lost contact with the army. The main enemy attack came from Bulgaria in the direction of the lower Vardar Valley. The mechanized units of Field Marshal Wilhelm List defeated the Yugoslav Third Army, occupied Skoplje on April 9, and then made contact with the Italian troops advancing from Albania. Another German army crossed the Yugoslav frontier in the direction of Salonika with the object of turning the uncovered Greek flank and taking the city. A column under General Paul von Kleist crossed farther to the north, occupied Niš on April 9, and advanced toward Kragujevac. Elsewhere the situation was even more hopeless for the Yugoslavs. On April 9 the Germans captured Maribor and, on April 10, Zagreb, the Croatian capital. On April 11 Italians occupied Ljubljana, the capital of Slovenia. Entering Yugoslavia from Hungary and Rumania by several routes, German and Hungarian troops easily swept the lowlands of the Vojvodina. On April 12 and 13 the German forces advancing from north and south converged at Belgrade. The Yugoslav High Command, after two days of negotiation, capitulated on April 17.

*The partition.*—The division and partition of Yugoslavia among the Axis Powers and their satellites came immediately after Yugoslavia's military collapse. Each Axis partner received a share of Yugoslav territory; moreover, four quisling regimes were established—Serbia, Croatia, Montenegro, and Slovenia. Germany annexed northern Slovenia, an area of approximately 10,500 square kilometers, with a population of about 900,000. Southern Slovenia, comprising an area of about 4,500 square kilometers and some 300,000 inhabitants, went to Italy. The fertile plains of the Bačka and the Baranja, as well as of Prekomurje and Medjumurje—an area totaling about 12,000 square kilometers with a population of about 1,000,000—were annexed by Hungary.

Besides southern Slovenia, Italy annexed certain areas and islands near Fiume, a portion of the Croatian littoral, and a long strip of the Dalmatian coast.* At one time the Italians extended their occupation of Croatian territory as far inland as a line drawn roughly from Ogulin to Mostar. Moreover, they added to the puppet Albania the Yugoslav districts of Kosovo, Debar, and Struga, a part of the Montenegrin coast around Bar, and the Serbian districts as far inland as Kosovska-Mitrovica and Vranje. Bulgaria for its share in the Axis war effort received most of the former banovina of Vardar (Macedonia) and a portion of the banovina of Morava (section of Serbia) east of Niš. From time to time, however, Bulgaria occupied additional Yugoslav territory and at one time had established military headquarters as far north as Kragujevac.†

*The puppets: Croatia, Serbia, Slovenia, and Montenegro.*—Of the four quisling regimes established by the Axis in the territory of Yugoslavia, the largest and the only "independent" one was the state of Croatia, under a government headed by Ante Pavelić, the well-known organizer of the Ustaši. With years of training for terrorist activity in special Italian and Hungarian camps, Pavelić and his cohorts were well versed in Nazi methods and stood ready to serve fascist interests in Yugoslavia. The puppet Croatia included Srem (Syrmia), Slavonia, part of Dalmatia, Bosnia-Hercegovina, and Croatia proper. At no time was this puppet state "free" and "independent." Territories that were not under Italian or German occupation, or policed by several strong puppet garrisons, eventually fell into the hands of the Četnik and Partisan units advancing to the field of battle. With the growth of these elements, puppet and occupation authorities weakened correspondingly. In spite of German attempts to bolster the Ustaši regime by extensive military operations against the newly created National Liberation

---

*Dalmatia, which included the districts of Zara, Split, and Kotor, was placed under an Italian *governatorato*.

† Bulgaria was assigned approximately 28,500 square kilometers in a population of about 1,300,000.

Army, the Nazis were never able to cope with the internal situation in Croatia, especially after the collapse of Italy. Whereas the Ustaši, Pavelić's most loyal followers, equaled in bravery their Nazi counterpart, Hitler's S.S. troops, the Croat regulars (Domobranstvo) fought half-heartedly.

Pavelić tried to imitate his fascist teachers. *"Za dom spremni"* (Ready for the Fatherland) was the Croat slogan, which meant that there could be no room for the Serbs in Croatia, who were mercilessly persecuted. The objectives were to exterminate the majority of the Serbs and to "Croatianize" the rest. The first was achieved through the mass slaughter of innocent citizens and such concentration camps as that at Jasenovac, and the second through the establishment of the Croatian Orthodox Church under the leadership of Bishop Germogen, a former Russian clergyman. It is important to note that, though many Catholic clergymen resented the regime of the Ustaši and its fascist brutality, some of them not only supported it but engaged in the persecution of the Serbs.[1] The subsequent popular clamor for vengeance recently brought some of these before Marshal Tito's courts, which passed a number of death sentences. Others, among them Ivan Šarić, Archbishop of Sarajevo, are said to have fled Yugoslavia.

Croatia had its Gestapo in the regime of the Ustaši, its *Führer* in *poglavnik* Pavelić, and the *Führer's* assistants in the *doglavniks*. It even had diplomatic representatives in other fascist states and in some neutral countries. Strategic positions in the government and the army were awarded to trustworthy members of the inner circle of the Ustaši. Pavelić reserved for himself the functions of the chief of state and, at first, those of the prime minister. A group of officers of the former Austro-Hungarian Empire, now aged and decrepit, were given high positions in the army. Pavelić had no difficulty in gaining the support of opportunist Moslem leaders such as the brothers Osman and Džafer Kulenović, whose Moslem followers helped to bolster the puppet regime and took part in the slaughter of the Serbs.

In May, 1941, when Croatia was proclaimed a kingdom, Pavelić, probably under German or Italian pressure, hastened to offer the throne to the Duke of Spoleto, a member of the Italian House of Savoy, who was to be known as Tomislav II. Unfortunately for the

---

[1] For notes to chapter xx see pages 526–527.

Italian prince, the unsettled conditions in Croatia prevented him from ever assuming his royal prerogatives. Croatia remained a kingdom without a king.

Puppet Serbia—comprising roughly the territory of Serbia prior to the Balkan wars, and the Banat—was nothing more than a German-occupied territory under the supreme authority of the commander in chief of the German armed forces in Serbia. The Banat, though considered a part of Serbia, was actually administered by the local *Volksdeutsche*. The appeal to the Serbs by General Milan Nedić and his cohorts to rally around their "Government of National Salvation" received sympathetic approval from nationalists, not only at home but abroad. The slogan that too much Serb blood had already been shed seemed convincing to some nationalists whose pride had been injured by the inglorious collapse of the Serb-led Yugoslav army.

Unlike Croatia, which was, at least in name, designated as an "independent state," Serbia was declared merely a *Militärbefehls-haberschaft.** Serbia had no diplomatic representatives in other fascist countries, though it had its own militia (the so-called State Guard), special security battalions (the so-called Volunteers organized by Ljotić), and the Četnici of Kosta Pećanac. Anti-Semitic legislation was passed and stringent measures were enacted against Communists and others opposing the regime. Many a good patriot lost his head in a concentration camp. The Germans promoted anti-Croat sentiment here as they promoted anti-Serb sentiment in Croatia; they played Orthodox elements against Catholic and the Nedić regime against that of Pavelić. Serbia became a haven for thousands of Serbian refugees from Bosnia-Hercegovina who were fleeing from slaughter by the Ustaši. The puppet authorities never fully disavowed their allegiance to King Peter, so that if Germany lost the war they would escape the consequences.

The Italians organized their part of Slovenia into the Provincia di Lubiana under the nominal headship of the former ban (governor) of the banovina of Drava (Slovenia), Natlačen, whose quisling career was soon ended by the gunfire of a Slovene patriot. He was succeeded by General Leo Rupnik, formerly an officer in the Austrian army and later in the Yugoslav army. The majority of the

---

* The full title is *Gebiet des Militärbefehlshabers Serbiens.*

Catholic hierarchy, headed by Bishop Rozman, sided with the enemy, openly or in disguise; the enemy, in turn, left unmolested the local Slovene schools, the university, and the church, which had become centers of fascist indoctrination.

In Montenegro the Italians established a Consulta Tecnica composed of native quislings and so-called nationalists. After the Italian collapse the Germans established a local Montenegrin Council and flirted with the idea of merging Montenegro with Serbia for more efficient resistance to the National Liberation Army. Of all the provinces of Yugoslavia, the resistance to the enemy and the quislings was perhaps strongest in Montenegro. Even today a large percentage of the high-ranking officers in the Yugoslav army are Montenegrins. Local Četnici—such as those commanded by Colonel Bajo Stanišić, General Blažo Djukanović, and Captain Pavle Djurišić, who were in the service of the enemy—were wiped out by Partisan forces.

The persecution of Yugoslavs in the areas occupied by the Axis satellites—Hungary, Bulgaria, and Albania—equaled in ferocity that of the German and Italian occupying forces and the local quisling regimes. The Albanians conducted an indiscriminate slaughter of the Serbs with their fascist-organized Skender Bey Division, composed principally of Albanians living in Yugoslavia. The Hungarian government acknowledged officially that thousands of innocent Serbs were killed by their ill-behaved forces. *Volksdeutsche* made up the Prinz Eugen Division, which was used mostly to fight the National Liberation Army, and which was responsible for the deaths of many thousands of Yugoslavs. Though somewhat better-behaved than the troops of other satellites, the Bulgarian occupation troops also carried on open warfare against the members and followers of the National Liberation Movement. In 1943 they penetrated as far as northern Montenegro.

All this, together with the slaughter of Serbs by the Croat Ustaši and Moslems and the slaughter of the nonconformists, especially the Moslems, by the Četnici (Serbs) in the Sanjak and in Bosnia-Hercegovina, did much to perpetuate national and religious ill feeling among the peoples of Yugoslavia. There was urgent need for a wise leadership that could end this fratricidal bloodshed and unite all patriotic national elements against the common enemy.

*The growth of resistance.*—The combined Axis military forces annihilated the Yugoslav army as an organized force. Only a remnant of soldiers and officers, under the leadership of Colonel Draža Mihailović, remained in the woods and organized the Četnik units on the model of the traditional Serb Četnici whose well-integrated and courageous bands had fought in the past against Turks, Bulgarians, and Germans. On paper the Četnik movement, divided into the usual military subdivisions and army corps, was centralized under the command of Draža Mihailović. In fact, however, it consisted of independent groups functioning in separate provinces—Serbia, Montenegro, Bosnia-Hercegovina, and Dalmatia—and united only ideologically. The best-organized groups were those under the direct supervision of Mihailović, in Serbia proper.

Individual Četnik leaders often acted independently and made "accommodations" with the enemy without the consent of their "supreme command." Loose organization and lack of discipline, together with the brutal excesses perpetrated on nonconformists by a number of Četnik commanders, were the main reasons, according to observers, for Mihailović's failure to produce an efficient army.

In the summer and fall of 1941 individual Četnik units conducted sporadic attacks on the enemy. But in the spring of 1942 Četnik resistance began to lag, owing primarily to the fact that Mihailović himself deprecated such activity. His changed attitude needs elucidation.

Before the Second World War Mihailović was an officer in the regular army and in the 'thirties served at various times as Yugoslav military attaché at Prague and at Sofia. In Bulgaria he was in close contact with the anti-German and pro-Yugoslav liberal circles of the Agrarian party and the Zveno Union.[2] Returning home, he came into conflict with the fascist-minded military leadership, which was gravitating toward an alliance with Germany. Because of this attitude it has been maintained that he was refused the promotions which were due him. His opposition was chiefly on the ground that Yugoslavia was becoming too friendly with Berlin and Rome, and thus he exhibited hatred of both Germans and Italians. There is no reason to believe that he changed his feelings toward them after they invaded his country. If anything, he became more intensely anti-German and anti-Italian. Diaries and official correspondences of prominent Italian and German officers show that although he concluded "accommodations" with the enemy and the quislings, the Axis did not consider him a true friend.

It should be clearly understood that Mihailović was first of all a Serbian nationalist in political outlook. He believed that Serbia should dominate any future Yugoslavia and, because of the great human sacrifices already endured by the Serbs, that no more Serbian blood should be shed through indecisive skirmishes with the enemy. He was convinced that one of the main reasons for Yugoslavia's military collapse was the Croat betrayal of Yugoslavia. To him the Partisan movement was a Communist movement, which advocated a federal Yugoslavia. He did not want a federal Yugoslavia in which Macedonia, Montenegro, and Bosnia-Hercegovina would have autonomy and equal rights with Serbia. Instead, he advocated a triune federation of Serbia, which would include the provinces mentioned, as well as a large part of Croatia proper, and small, powerless, federal units of Croatia and Slovenia.[3] The fact that a Croat led the Partisans bolstered his dislike of them.

Mihailović held that the final defeat of the Axis depended not on him but on the Allied Great Powers, and that the primary aim of his Četnici should be to liquidate the Communists and organize and extend the Četnik movement, which on D-day would be in a position to deliver a final blow to the enemy and seize control of Yugoslavia. And, because he considered communism a greater danger to Yugoslavia than the Axis, whose defeat he believed to be inevitable, he allied his forces with those of the enemy in joint attacks on Tito's forces. This policy committed him to more and much closer collaboration. Eventually Mihailović, who was both anti-German and anti-Croat, found himself in a political and military alliance with the Nazis and the Ustaši.

Mihailović was violently opposed to the Communists on other issues. For one thing, he feared that their eventual objective was to establish communism as a state system for Yugoslavia, and, in spite of numerous declarations of the Communist party to the contrary, he was apprehensive. For him their economic and propagandistic organization, established first on the Serbian territory which they liberated, and administered from Užice, betrayed their real aims. He had associated himself, though belatedly, with the weak Yugoslav Socialist party of Živko Topalović and apparently was willing to accept some socialist legislation in the future Yugoslavia but within the established economic order. Furthermore—and this was the root of his difference with the Communists—he felt that the Communists aimed at a proletarian dictatorship that would definitely mean the end of the monarchy. This loyalty to the king was probably as deeply rooted as his Serbian nationalism. He was, to be sure, cognizant of the steadily declining hold of the king on the Serbian and other Yugoslav peoples, but as Tito's Communists increased in strength and gained popular support, Mihailović's loyalty to the king grew stronger.

In spite of basic antagonisms to the Communists, Mihailović coöperated with them in a common military front in the summer and autumn of 1941. When he failed to unify all the resistance groups under his own command he proposed a division of power in Yugoslavia and a delineation of military and political spheres of operation so that he could strengthen his forces and thus, while awaiting Allied assistance, be ready to challenge any attempt of Tito's forces to seize control of Yugoslavia.[4] But the Communists refused to recognize Mihailović as the supreme commander of the resistance movement in Yugoslavia, especially since their own cause was steadily gaining in popular support. This brief attempt at coöperation with the Communist forces convinced Mihailović that the common front was but a means to achieve Communist domination and that it entailed complete subordination and eventual integration of his followers in the Communist party.

The same plan—the delineation of military and political spheres of operation—was later urged by the British. By that time, however, the fratricidal warfare had reached such proportions that reconciliation between the two resistance movements was impossible. Sporadic clashes between Četnik and Partisan units recurred even after Mihailović and Tito had agreed on a common effort against the enemy.[5] The crisis came during the so-called first enemy offensive against the Partisans, in November, 1941. Mihailović's units not only avoided action but actually threw their support on the side of the enemy in an attempt to expel the Partisans from Serbia. The combined enemy-Četnik forces drove the Partisans from Serbia, and the Mihailović was able to report enthusiastically to his

MARSHAL TITO—JOSIP BROZ

GENERAL DRAŽA MIHAILOVIĆ
Leader of the Četnici, 1942–1945

government abroad that he had delivered a shattering blow to the Communist forces.

The Četnici were the first resistance group to make sporadic forays on the enemy. The Communist leadership, on the other hand, chose at the start a passive policy, engaging only in propaganda while Germany and the Soviet Union were at peace. The German invasion of the Soviet Union on June 22, 1941, and a terrifying wave of Ustaši and Axis terrorism and indiscriminate slaughter of hundreds of thousands of innocent people, especially the Serbs, marked the turning point in the tactics of the Yugoslav Communists. The aroused Slavic sentiments and confidence in Russian military prowess caused uprisings throughout Yugoslavia, especially in Serbia and Montenegro. The Communist party was quick to establish itself as a leader of these uprisings. In Belgrade the executive committee of the Communist party of Yugoslavia laid the foundation for the National Liberation Movement and its first Partisan units.

The leader of the Communist party, Josip Broz—Tito—was an obvious choice for the leadership of the Partisan movement. The details concerning his origin and background are lacking. Born in Croatia, not far from Zagreb, a blacksmith by trade, he served in the Austro-Hungarian army in the First World War and was captured by the Russians. At the time of the Russian Civil War he was in Russia, where he chose the Communist side. After the Communist victory he received thorough training in Communist methods and tactics. In the period between the two wars he played an important part in the Communist underground, eventually heading the Yugoslav Communist party.

The Communists were not slow in making the best of the situation. Their immediate aim was to combine all national forces against the enemy, appealing to the masses with a simple slogan: "Death to Fascism, Freedom to the People!" Political and cultural propaganda accompanied military organization. Local committees (*odbors*) were organized throughout the liberated territories and existed under cover in the occupied territories. Whenever possible, cultural centers and schools were established and papers and magazines were published.

The Communist party was the political factor which gave cohesion to the pro-Allied and Slavophile sentiments of the Yugoslav people, who were united through their common struggle. Of all the political parties, only the Communists succeeded in organizing the masses, regardless of nationality and religion, into a single resistance front. The Partisans, under Communist leadership, took up the Yugoslav banner, adopted a republican platform, and opposed the various brands of Serb and Croat chauvinism, offering an opportunity to Macedonians, Montenegrins, Croats, Slovenes, and others to achieve their national aspirations for equality with the Serbs and autonomous statehood in the new federated Yugoslavia. The Serb nationalist program of the Četnici, with slogans such as "For King and Fatherland!" did not appeal to the masses.

To observers, the military achievements of the Partisans were remarkable. With few arms but with thousands of brave fighting men and women, their Communist leadership organized not merely guerrilla bands but a large army, which at various times pinned down from fifteen to thirty enemy divisions.

*Četnik-Partisan coöperation and the break.*—The general uprising in Serbia after the German invasion of the Soviet Union was led by both Četnici and Partisans, and the forces of the two groups coöperated, with interruptions, until the autumn of 1941. Both had captured large areas of Serbian territory. The Partisans controlled the most important military objectives. The possession of Užice, in which they established their headquarters, gave them an ammunition factory which, under almost insuperable difficulties, manufactured rifles for both Partisans and Četnici.

Četnik-Partisan collaboration virtually ceased when the Četnici decided not to fight the occupation forces and then threw in their lot with the enemy. A few Četnik units, however, continued to work with the Partisans and eventually joined them—as, for example, the unit led by Vlada Zečević, an Orthodox priest. When, on December 3, 1941, Mihailović issued an order for a general Četnik attack on the Partisans, a number of other Četnik adherents went over to the Partisans. The gap between Četnik and Partisan leadership now became unbridgeable.

As a result of combined German-quisling-Četnik offensives in November and December, 1941, the Partisans were forced to withdraw their forces from Serbia into the Sanjak, Bosnia, and Hercegovina. The Partisans consider this the first major Axis offensive against them. It succeeded merely in temporarily reducing them as a military factor in Serbia, and in driving them into neighboring areas, where they continued the struggle against the combined Italian, Četnik, and Croat-quisling forces. They remained the only Yugoslav resistance group actively and effectively engaging the enemy.

Četnik collaboration with the enemy and quisling forces grew closer thereafter. In some areas, particularly in Bosnia-Hercegovina, Dalmatia, and Montenegro, collaboration was open from the very start, but in Serbia an attempt was made to conceal what later became obvious, and an anti-Axis propaganda was conducted for foreign consumption. Agreements between the Četnici and the occupying forces differed from area to area, but usually the enemy, in exchange for Četnik help in fighting the Partisans, offered war matériel as well as medical care in German hospitals, and recognized the autonomous military status of the Četnici.

More and more information on the Yugoslav internal situation came to the attention of the British and the Americans in 1942, although the British in charge of Anglo-American operations in Yugoslavia not only retained but strengthened their mission with Mihailović, in the hope that he might change his policy. Četnik collaboration was first exposed by the British officers attached to individual Četnik corps, and was later substantiated by documentary materials which fell into Allied hands. The collaboration eventually became so obvious that in November, 1943, General Sir Henry Maitland Wilson reprimanded several groups for using the Četnik name to help the enemy. It was now apparent to official circles in Great Britain and the United States that the Partisans were the backbone of the resistance movement in Yugoslavia. In February, 1944, Winston Churchill stated straightforwardly that "The Partisans of Marshal Tito are the only people who are doing any effective fighting against the Germans now."[6] Consequently, the missions with the Partisans grew larger and those with Mihailović shrank until the Allied representatives with Mihailović had been recalled and, early in 1944, all assistance to him ended. In the autumn of that year, however, an American mission was sent to Mihailović, but without military assistance.

Outside Serbia, meanwhile, the ranks of the Partisans rapidly increased. In Montenegro, strengthened by Partisan units driven from Serbia, they were able to recapture a large part of Montenegro. The first to revolt in the so-called independent state of Croatia were the Serbs who had been driven to defend themselves from the Ustaši terror. At the start some joined the Četnici and some the Partisans, but as the Četnik commanders accepted collaboration, especially with the Italian occupying forces, they lost more of their following to the Partisans. In December, 1941, the Partisans operating in Bosnia were reinforced by recently arrived Partisan units from Serbia and became such a menace to the Axis that a combined Ustaši-German offensive was undertaken against them, known in Partisan history as the second enemy offensive. The Partisans successfully resisted the enemy onslaught and captured some of the smaller cities of eastern Bosnia, which they held for several weeks.

In March and May, 1942, a combined Montenegrin Četnik-Italian army, including two strong Alpine divisions, launched the third offensive against the Partisans and succeeded in driving them from Montenegro into Bosnia-Hercegovina. From eastern Bosnia the Partisans undertook several military operations, in May and June, 1942, in the direction of western Bosnia, especially near the Kozara Mountains. Here the enemy tried in vain, though inflicting great losses in men and matériel, to encircle the Partisan forces, which were simultaneously occupied with several military operations in and near Lika. The Partisan success was great. By autumn they had liberated most of Bosanska Krajina, including Bihać, an important city on the Bosnia-Croatia border, which became the administrative and political center of the liberated territory.

*The A.V.N.O.J.*—The Anti-Fascist Council for the National Liberation of Yugoslavia (A.V.N.O.J.), a Partisan-sponsored "parliament" that was convoked at Bihać on November 26, 1942, became the first political organization of the new Yugoslavia. This Council (Veće) represented all Yugoslav areas and, its leaders claimed, all democratic parties. The High Command reported to it on the achievements of the Partisans. It was decided to transform most of the guerrilla detachments into the National Liberation Army, which began to grow with amazing rapidity. The local administrative committees (*odbors*) were given broader functions, but became nominally subordinated to the Council, which coördinated their work. To facilitate the organization of the local committees the Council delegates decided that, while remaining in constant touch with the High Command, they would spend most of their time traveling among the people, organizing the so-called National Liberation committees in villages, communes, districts, and provinces. Their immediate aim was to promote the National Liberation Movement and to coördinate local efforts with the central organization at Bihać. Thus each commune and district in the liberated territory would have its Committee for National Liberation. To supplement these local committees, regional councils were established in Croatia, Slovenia, Bosnia-Hercegovina, Montenegro, and other provinces. The work of this first parliament at Bihać was profoundly significant for the development of the Partisan cause.

*The enemy offensives in 1943.*—The existence of a free territory under the complete control of Partisan troops within a short distance of the Croatian capital and the important railway lines to Split, Fiume, and Belgrade caused the enemy to undertake an offensive against the Partisan forces in Bosanska Krajina, Lika, and Banija. This fourth enemy offensive lasted from January through March, 1943, and included German, Italian, Ustaši, and Četnik units. The forces of Mihailović were so severely beaten that they could no longer seriously obstruct Partisan activity. The Četnici and their leader retreated to Serbia, leaving many documents which revealed their agreements with the enemy. The enemy's failure to crush the resistance movement, although Partisan losses were heavy, enabled the Partisans to regroup their forces and entrench themselves in the mountains of Montenegro, but since they were still a formidable menace to the Axis, a fifth offensive was launched against them in the summer of 1943.

The Partisans were encircled by some 100,000 enemy troops, including German, Italian, Bulgarian, and quisling units.* After great losses in men and matériel, and without any Allied assistance, the Partisans broke the circle and advanced into Bosnia.† The fifth

---

*The major battles were fought in the Zelengora Mountains and near Šavnik, Foča, Kalinovik, and Gacko. The fighting was especially heavy along the Sutjeska River.

† In August, 1943, the Partisan units captured Jajce, an important military objective, and several other small cities in central Bosnia.

offensive was the greatest and most bitter test of Partisan strength and morale. In spite of the difficult terrain and loss of man power through starvation, disease, and repeated enemy attacks, the Partisans not only remained strong but were soon increased by new recruits and were equipped to start offensive action. They recaptured much of their former Bosnian and Dalmatian districts, and were particularly successful in engagements with the Italian armies.

The collapse of Italy in September, 1943, contributed immeasurably to the Partisan cause. The Partisans disarmed several Italian divisions, acquired quantities of arms, increased the number of their troops by 80,000, and by November 1 had liberated large parts of Slovenia, the Croatian littoral, Dalmatia, and Bosnia-Hercegovina. They sent divisions into the Sanjak and Serbia as well. The situation in Macedonia improved appreciably when the local Partisans, whose activity dated from the early autumn of 1941, captured Kičevo and Debar. The Macedonian Partisans became the connecting link between the Yugoslav Partisans and those of Albania, Greece, and Bulgaria. In November, 1943, Tito declared that one of the greatest achievements of the National Liberation Army was the freeing of Istria and the Slovene littoral after Italy's capitulation, and linking them with other liberated territories.

Previously, Partisan operations in Slovenia had been cut off from those elsewhere in Yugoslavia. Here there had been several groups of collaborators besides the outright quislings. The so-called White Guard forces had been organized by the Italian military command and operated as "village guards" under the protection of the Italian army. The political counterpart of the White Guards was the Slovene Alliance (Zveza), composed primarily of clerical groups. The Blue Guards had been organized by former Yugoslav officers and considered themselves a component part of Mihailović's Četnici. The _Landesschutz_ had been organized in that part of Slovenia which was annexed by the Germans. They were used for policing purposes, and worked closely with the German armed forces.

The Slovene Partisans had been sufficiently strong, however, to warrant several Italian punitive expeditions under General Robotti. In July, 1942, seven well-equipped Italian divisions succeeded in dispersing them. But the Slovene Partisans soon retrieved their positions. When Italy collapsed they were able to seize almost

he entire Provincia di Lubiana, except for the capital, Ljubljana.
They liquidated the Slovene White Guard and proclaimed a general mobilization. Most of Venezia Giulia and Istria, with the exception of a few large towns, was liberated. Gradually, however,
he superior German forces succeeded in recapturing the terri-
ories won from the Italians, though the Partisans remained strong
enough to serve as a permanent challenge to the enemy garrisons.

Early in December, 1943, the enemy launched the sixth offensive
gainst the Partisan forces in Bosnia, Croatia, and Dalmatia. The
Partisans were forced to abandon most of Dalmatia and the islands,
and some other territory, including the city of Jajce. Nevertheless,
hey mustered sufficient strength in January, 1944, to attack the
ity of Banjaluka, annihilate the local enemy garrison, and capture
arge quantities of matériel and a number of prisoners. In this
eriod the Partisans achieved marked success in other Yugoslav
reas—Slavonia, the Sanjak, Serbia, and Montenegro. In Monte-
egro the remnants of the Četnik forces and their leaders Djuka-
ović and Stanišić were liquidated.*

*The second session of the A.V.N.O.J.*—Their military and organ-
izational success induced the Partisans to hold a second plenary ses-
ion of the A.V.N.O.J. at Jajce in November, 1943. The A.V.N.O.J.
was then transformed into a legislative and executive body; a pre-
idium of sixty-seven members, with Ivan Ribar as president, was
rganized and invested with executive powers. The Committee
or National Liberation was designated to serve as its executive
rgan. There were appointed thirteen acting ministers (or commis-
ioners), headed by Tito, who also served as Acting Minister of Na-
ional Defense. For the first time Tito's name—Josip Broz—was
made public. The title of marshal was conferred on him. The pro-
isional government included the representatives of all national-
ies, religions, and democratic parties. A resolution was passed
rbidding the government-in-exile and the king to return to Yugo-
avia until the people had decided the form of government they
referred. The Council called for the organization of Yugoslavia
n a federal basis, for the trial of war criminals, and for territorial
aims against Italy.

---

*Blažo Djukanović and Bajo Stanišić were captured at Ostrog on October 18,
943.

The basis for Yugoslav federation had already been laid: the re gional anti-fascist councils became nuclei of the projected separat governments of federal units. The Anti-Fascist Council for Croati (Z.A.V.N.O.H.), formed in Otočac, June 13, 1943, included repre sentatives of the Croat and Serb populations in Croatia. The Slc vene Freedom Front (O.F.), founded in Ljubljana, April 27, 1941 declared the incorporation of Venezia Giulia with Slovenia i September, 1943. In October, at a meeting in Kočevje, there wa formed a Slovene National Committee, which elected one hundre twenty members to the plenum of the Freedom Front and fort delegates to the Anti-Fascist Council of Yugoslavia. In Serbia an Macedonia, where the enemy and quisling forces of occupatio were strong, it was impossible to hold a large congress. Serbian au thority, therefore, was vested in the Supreme Committee for N tional Liberation, and Macedonian authority in the hands of preparatory committee. Toward the end of 1943, at Mrkonjićgrad the Anti-Fascist Council for Bosnia-Hercegovina was formed; o November 15, at Kolašin, the Anti-Fascist Council for Montenegr and for Boka Kotorska; and, a week later, at Pljevlja, the Ant Fascist Council for the Liberation of the Sanjak.

*Government-in-exile.*—Even before the High Command capitu lated to the Axis, the Yugoslav government had departed by a from a Montenegrin airfield to Palestine. From Palestine it move to Egypt and thence to London. In 1943 the Yugoslav governmen moved back to Egypt in anticipation of an early return to Belgrad Throughout the entire period the government was torn by interna conflict between various factions, primarily between representa tives of Serbian and Croatian nationalism. The government, i spite of four cabinet changes, remained so disunited that it was a no time in a position to announce a clear program for Yugoslavi Most of the Serbian representatives advocated the continuance c the Serbian hegemony in the future Yugoslavia. The Croats adv cated a federated Yugoslavia in which Croatia would hold a sem independent status; they were not satisfied with the banovina c Croatia as established in 1939, but demanded territorial expansio and other rights.

Even if he were the most capable of rulers, the young King Pet would have had an almost impossible task. Surrounded by a co servative group of elderly politicians whose party interests transcended those of the people, he continued to tolerate Mihailović's nonactivity in Yugoslavia. His prestige, at the same time, declined because he hesitated for a long time to attack the Serb and Slovene collaborationist groups in Yugoslavia, which were permitted by the Axis to express loyalty to him and even to wear royal insignia.

The cabinet could not agree on any basic issue. Premier Dušan Simović, who was despised by most of his colleagues, began to gather around him military leaders who favored a military government. The Simović cabinet remained in power until January, 1942, when all the ministers submitted their resignations to the king on the grounds that the premier had sought to build a military dictatorship and that he had ordered General Kalafatović to sign Yugoslav capitulation to the Axis without consulting the cabinet.

Slobodan Jovanović, a leading Yugoslav historian and a university professor, was asked to form a new cabinet. Not having engaged in politics, Premier Jovanović was expected to pacify the various factions in the government and to bring about an agreement on policy. Unfortunately, his cabinet included Draža Mihailović, the new War Minister, and as such it condemned the National Liberation Army. Foreign Minister Momčilo Ninčić refused Soviet Foreign Commissar Vyacheslav Molotov's offer to conclude an understanding with Soviet Russia, which was a necessary preliminary to any reconciliation in Yugoslavia between Partisans and Četnici. Moreover, he irritated the Soviet government by branding the Partisans as international criminals and bandits. The followers of Simović, headed by General Bora Mirković, began to cause difficulties to the new cabinet and refused to obey orders. The British authorities were forced to intern almost two hundred officers and men of the royal Yugoslav forces in the Near East.

The military cabinet, an unconstitutional body created by Jovanović, was the force behind the government and the throne. It held levers of power in important military and diplomatic posts and enjoyed the favor of the court. It stirred up trouble in Yugoslavia by sending messages to Mihailović and threatened the Partisan leaders with death after the government came to power.

In January, 1943, Jovanović, in an effort to alleviate internal conflicts, reorganized his cabinet. But the policy of the government remained unchanged and anti-Partisan propaganda was intensified. The "Greater Serbia" program was taken up seriously, and Jovanović himself sought to win Allied support in its favor. According to this program, Serbia would be enlarged at the expense of the Croats and other peoples, and would have a population of approximately 12,000,000. In order to convince the Allies of the merits of the plan, propaganda for Serbian racial superiority was advanced. The relations between the British Broadcasting Company (B.B.C.) and the Yugoslav government deteriorated during this period as the B.B.C. continued to credit the Partisans with their contribution against the common enemy.

In June, 1943, Jovanović resigned and the military cabinet was dissolved, but the harm it had done to the royal government and to Mihailović proved irreparable. A new cabinet was formed by Miloš Trifunović, with essentially the same composition, except for the addition of General Petar Živković, the military dictator of 1929. Trifunović made no change in policy as anti-Partisan propaganda increased in scope and intensity. The cabinet lasted barely two months.

After a delay of several weeks the king, under British advice, entrusted the formation of a new cabinet to Dr. Božidar Purić, a foreign-service man. It was to be nonpolitical and was to comprise officials rather than political leaders, but it turned out to be more politically minded than its predecessors. Partisans were branded as terrorists. Two escapees of doubtful record, Ivo Čičin-Šain and Dr. Nenad Grizogono, were taken into the cabinet as representatives of the underground. Purić thus further alienated the king and the exiled government from the Partisans. Hundreds of officers and men signed allegiance to Tito. The Soviet Union turned down Purić's offer to reach a Yugoslav-Soviet agreement.

The royalist position was further impaired when, in January, 1944, Prime Minister Winston Churchill announced that Tito alone would receive Allied supplies. This statement brought the collapse of the Purić government, after it had steadfastly refused to bring together King Peter and Tito. Royalist exiles, however, did not lose hope, thinking that they might succeed in bringing about the reversal of British policy. They continued to devise various schemes in that direction. One was a proposal by Dr. Miha

Krek—who was appointed in February as the royal Yugoslav delegate on the Allied Commission for Italy—to create a Slovene legion from the Slovenes in Italy and use it as an Allied guard in the invasion of Slovenia.

Tito appreciated the British gesture, coming just when the enemy had launched another large offensive against his forces. At British request he promised not to attack the king, for he fully understood the British position vis-à-vis the exiled government and the king. The British continued to urge a meeting between the king and Tito, while the chauvinist circle led by Purić and Živković urged the king not to negotiate with the Partisans.

The announcement that the Soviet Union had sent its first military mission to Tito in March, 1944, headed by Lieutenant General N. V. Korneyev and Major General A. P. Gorshkov, was of great significance to the Partisan cause. The Soviet Union henceforth became increasingly hostile toward the exiled government.

Meanwhile, to counter Tito's provisional government and the Allied withdrawal of officers and men from his headquarters, Mihailović, early in February, 1944, sponsored the so-called St. Sava Congress, from which emerged the Yugoslav Democratic Popular Committee, with Socialist Živko Topalović as president. Mihailović hoped that the Committee would dispel the accusation that his movement was Greater Serbian, conservative, and unpatriotic. Hence an effort was made to give it a Yugoslav and liberal character by including Slovene, Croat, and Moslem representatives, and by naming Topalović, the chief of the Yugoslav Socialist party, as president of the Committee. All this appeared to be in vain as some of the leading refugees hastened to dissociate themselves from the Četnik movement. These included General Dušan Simović, the leader of the *coup d'état* of 1941; Izidor Cankar, Minister to Canada; and Štanoje Simić, Ambassador to the Soviet Union.

*Relations with the U.S.S.R.*—The government-in-exile was willing to negotiate with Tito, but only if he recognized Mihailović as the leader of the resistance. This situation contributed to the deterioration of the already poor relations between the Yugoslav government and Soviet Russia. Momčilo Ninčić, the Yugoslav Foreign Minister, like most exiled leaders, feared the U.S.S.R. and never gave serious attention to the improvement of relations with it. When it was suggested that King Peter should pay a visit to the Kremlin, the young king was dissuaded by the cabinet on the basis that his visit would be exploited as approval of the Partisans.

On April 1, 1942, after consultation with his military advisers, Prime Minister Jovanović, prompted by Mihailović's complaint against the Partisans, sent a note to the Soviet military attaché in which he condemned the Partisans as international brigands, called their leaders Trotskyites, and urged the Soviets at least to prevent the Partisans from attacking the Četnici, even if the former were not willing to accept the united command.

Repeated complaints from Mihailović induced Jovanović to discuss the possible union of Yugoslav resistance groups with Soviet Minister Aleksandr Bogomolov on May 16, 1942. Bogomolov, interpreting Jovanović's plan as meaning that he wanted the Soviet government to intervene with the Comintern, responded that his government did not accept responsibility for the Comintern and that the matter was one of Yugoslavia's own internal problems in which the Soviets did not wish to mix. He reminded Jovanović that at a recent Pan-Slav Congress an appeal had been made to all Slavs to fight the Germans, that Stalin had thanked all partisans without distinction, and that the Soviet government did not wish to go beyond that. He also pointed out that the Soviet government considered everyone fighting the Germans as partisan.

In mid-1942 the Soviets definitely threw their weight in support of the Partisans. In August the Soviet government protested against Mihailović through the Yugoslav representative at Kuibishev, and quoted series of documents purporting to show Mihailović's collaboration with the Italians throughout 1942. He was also accused of collaborating with the Ustaši in May, 1942, near Nevesinje and Mostar.

The Soviet reply, in the form of an *aide-mémoire* of January 26, 1943, to the Yugoslav memorandum handed to Minister Bogomolov in September, 1942, and to the memorandum of the Yugoslav legation at Kuibishev on August 19, 1942, declared that Yugoslav information was "based on one-sided reports not corresponding to reality." It especially termed incredible the reference to the alleged misbehavior of Partisan detachments, and contained a statement that the Soviets had in their possession documents giving an entirely different picture, namely, that there existed an agreement between Mihailović and the Italians to oppose the Partisans.

*The Tito-Šubašić agreement.*—In March, 1944, the British resumed the discussions with King Peter which had been postponed by his recent marriage to the Greek princess. (The marriage caused dissatisfaction among the Serbian masses; the nationalists accused the king of neglecting the interests of the people at home, who were suffering from fascist rule.) The king promised to coöperate with the British. In mid-May he dismissed Purić and invited Ivan Šubašić, the former Ban of Croatia, who had the reputation of being a sincere Yugoslav and an uncorrupted politician, to form a new government. On June 1 Šubašić succeeded in doing so. On the same day the king called upon the Yugoslav people to join the ranks of the National Liberation Army and agreed not to return to Yugoslavia until a plebiscite had been held, as stipulated by the Anti-Fascist Council at Jajce.

When repeated enemy offensives had failed to annihilate the Partisan forces, the German Command planned to capture Tito. This, they believed, would cause a complete breakdown in Partisan ranks. After long preparation, a crack German airborne battalion swooped down upon Drvar, the Partisan headquarters. Tito and the Allied representatives succeeded in evacuating Drvar, although at considerable cost. The Germans, too, lost heavily, and Drvar was soon recaptured by Partisan troops.

On the basis of the Tito-Šubašić agreement made on the island of Vis on June 16, Šubašić announced, on July 7, the formation of a new Yugoslav cabinet representative of the king, Tito, and the center. Šubašić had failed to induce any of the Greater Serbian politicians to join the cabinet, which included two ministers each of Serb, Croat, and Slovene nationality. The Partisan representatives were Sreten Vukosavljević (Serb) and Drago Marušić (Slovene), neither of whom were Communists.

The policy of the newly formed "unity" government was based on the Tito-Šubašić agreement: Šubašić was to obtain supplies for the National Liberation Army. A joint body of representatives of the Partisans and the royal government was to be established to coördinate matters falling under the competence of the ministries of war, foreign affairs, and reconstruction. It was also specified that the royal government was to recognize the achievements of the Partisans, and the Partisan government as the executive body of the Committee for National Liberation, the Anti-Fascist Council, and the National Liberation Army. The Šubašić government pledged itself to condemn collaborationism. Tito agreed to postpone the question of state organization until after the war, showed Šubašić the documents pertaining to Četnik collaboration, and demanded the release of the Yugoslavs still in Italian concentration camps.

Another meeting between Tito, Šubašić, and General Sir Henry Maitland Wilson, the commander of the Mediterranean Theater of Operations, which was scheduled for July 15 at Caserta, was not held, owing to a sudden reversal by Tito, apparently resulting from disagreement in inner Partisan circles over the wisdom of his participation. However, Tito dispatched to London General Vlatko Velebit and two ministers—Vukosavljević and Marušić. Velebit was to represent Tito near the royal government; the others were to serve as Tito's personal representatives in the Yugoslav government, that is, they were to see that the conditions of the Tito-Šubašić agreement were carried out.

Marshal Tito finally agreed to visit General Wilson at Caserta on August 3, bringing with him two of his aides and advisers, General Arso Jovanović and Lieutenant General Aleksandar Ranković. At this meeting several important matters were considered: military supplies for the National Liberation Army, American airforce assistance to the Yugoslav forces, the formation of a Yugoslav air force, and hospitals and medical care for wounded Partisans. It was agreed to merge the Partisan and royal navies, which would use royal insignia and ply the seas under the commander in chief of the Mediterranean Theater of Operations. British efforts to bring the Partisans and Šubašić closer attained some success. Tito held three discussions with Winston Churchill on the merging of the Committee for National Liberation with the royal government. There was, however, a critical moment in the discussions at Caserta when three Mihailović representatives landed at Bari in American planes and without permission from the Allied Command. Two of them—Adam Pribičević and Živko Topalović—were widely known in Yugoslavia. Mihailović believed that these two would be best qualified to submit his case to the Allied Command, especially since the former was a leading member of the Independent Democratic party and the latter the chief of the Socialist party of Yugoslavia. The arrival of Mihailović's agents caused Tito to suspect the sincerity of the Allies.

In August the three royal ministers—Ivan Šubašić, Izidor Cankar, and Sava Kosanović—who had sympathized with the Partisans and the so-called Yugoslav wing of the exiled government during the war, made a trip to the island of Vis to confer with Tito.

On August 26 King Peter abolished the command of General Mihailović by recognizing Tito as sole leader of the Yugoslav resistance forces. This announcement served as the final blow to the Četnik cause, coming at a time when Partisans and Četnici were jockeying for strategic positions in Serbia in expectation of a sudden German collapse. Another blow to the Četnici came when General Sir Henry Maitland Wilson broadcast a warning "to certain political organizations and individuals in the Balkans who are aiding the German withdrawal and are harming the activities of the patriots."

The advancing Red Army demanded quick political action, and Šubašić urged Tito to assist him in forming a national government. Tito rejected this request on the basis that the principal immediate task was to drive the enemy out of Yugoslavia.

In the meantime the question of Venezia Giulia was gradually coming to the fore. On September 16 Tito announced Yugoslavia's determination to incorporate all the Slav territories given to Italy after the First World War. Tito's Partisans were becoming especially active in Istria, to which the Yugoslavs had already laid claim. A number of American airmen, forced to abandon their craft in this area, were afterward picked up and safely evacuated by the Partisans. That was partial proof of the extent to which the local inhabitants responded to the Partisan cause; it was reported that, should German troops withdraw from the area, Tito's army would be in a position to occupy it before the Allied armies arrived.

Tito's forces had been winning success in every direction, and Mihailović was forced to flee from his headquarters at Ravna Gora. In the political field as well, Tito was gaining ground at the expense of Šubašić: Miha Krek was replaced by Josip Smodlaka on the Allied Council for Italy, and Krek's closest collaborator, Franc

Snoj, caused great surprise by joining the Partisans. Elements hitherto undecided, such as the right wing of the Croatian Peasant party and the Serbian nationalists, began to support the Partisans.

On September 19 Tito left secretly for Serbia and flew thence to Soviet Russia in a Red Army plane. Soon thereafter the Soviets announced an agreement between Tito and the Red Army allowing the latter's temporary entry into Yugoslavia in pursuit of the German and Hungarian armies. The civil authorities in territories occupied by the Red Army were to be in Partisan hands.

Tito's failure to inform the Allied representatives at his headquarters of his departure for Serbia marked the beginning of the deterioration in their relations. It grew worse when the Partisan "Free Yugoslavia" radio announced, on September 28, that the Committee for National Liberation had refused to accept the U.N.R.R.A. proposal for distribution of relief in Yugoslavia unless supplies were distributed by local authorities set up by the Partisans. The latter were willing, however, to accept U.N.R.R.A. controlling delegates to see that supplies were justly handled.

On October 21 Moscow issued a statement on the Stalin-Churchill meeting in that city. The two leaders agreed on a formula for merging the refugee government and the Committee for National Liberation, and reserved the right of the Yugoslav people to determine the form of their government after the liberation. The Partisans were not entirely satisfied with Šubašić and alleged that his government did not live up to its pledges in the Vis agreement. He was accused of supporting Maček and his followers, and was blamed for the failure of the royal navy to support the Partisans and for the failure to remove anti-Partisans from the diplomatic corps.

On October 20 Belgrade was liberated by combined Red Army and Partisan forces, and the Committee for National Liberation (the provisional government) established its headquarters there. Šubašić met with Ivan Ribar, the president of the A.V.N.O.J., on Yugoslav soil on October 25 to discuss the creation of a united Yugoslav government. On November 1 the "Free Yugoslavia" radio announced the Tito-Šubašić agreement for a joint government and a regency, though it was necessary to persuade the king to accept the regency until a plebiscite had been held. In the meantime Prime Minister Churchill announced that the meeting between

Tito and Šubašić had been agreed upon and sponsored by Great Britain and the Soviet Union jointly.

On January 29, 1945, King Peter reappointed Šubašić as Premier. He, in turn, formed a government essentially the same as the one just dissolved. The king also appointed a regency—Dušan Simović (Serb), Juraj Šutej (Croat), and Dušan Sernec (Slovene)—but Tito rejected these appointments. After some delay the king named regents who were acceptable to Tito: Srdjan Budisavljević (Serb), Ante Mandić (Croat), and Dušan Sernec (Slovene). Šubašić left for Belgrade on February 15 to implement the agreement he had made with Tito. There were several questions to be considered, including the recommendation made at Yalta that democratic members of the prewar Skupština be incorporated in the new Yugoslav Assembly.

A provisional government for the newly federated Yugoslavia was inaugurated at Belgrade on March 7. It included members of the Committee for National Liberation and of Šubašić's "unity" government. The new government of twenty-six members was headed by Marshal Tito, who also held the portfolio of Minister of National Defense. Ivan Šubašić was named Foreign Minister. On March 24 an agreement was signed between the provisional government and the U.N.R.R.A. that there should be no restriction on the number of technicians and observers sent to Yugoslavia and that the U.N.R.R.A. would discuss rather than consult with Yugoslav authorities concerning distribution.

Marshal Tito, accompanied by Ivan Šubašić and Milovan Djilas, journeyed to Moscow early in April and was greeted by a group of prominent officials. A Soviet-Yugoslav treaty of friendship, mutual assistance, and postwar coöperation, signed on April 11, listed the conditions under which mutual aid would operate. On April 13 a trade agreement was signed between the two countries.

Concurrently, a Yugoslav delegation, including General Sreten Žujović and Stanoje Simić, Ambassador to the United States, arrived at San Francisco to attend the United Nations Conference. They were joined later by Šubašić, the chief of the delegation.

April was also the month in which provisional regional federal governments were formed: that of Serbia, on April 9; of Croatia, on April 14; of Montenegro and Macedonia, on April 15; of Bosnia-Hercegovina, on April 28; and of Slovenia, on May 5.

The occupation of Trieste and Gorizia by the British Eighth Army, in spite of the fact that the Yugoslav Partisans were the first to enter Trieste, produced a crisis in the relations between Tito and the Allies. The situation was made worse when Allied armies entered Klagenfurt, Trbiž, and Villach on the former Yugoslav-Austrian and Yugoslav-Italian borders. General Jakšić demanded of the British that the Tito-Alexander agreement be put into force: that the demarcation between the Yugoslav and the Allied occupation armies should be drawn along the meeting lines of the two armies. The Partisans resented the facts that there were Polish troops among the British army units and that approximately 20,000 Yugoslav quisling troops had succeeded in entering the British lines. Yugoslav propaganda demanded that the city of Trieste and large sections of Venezia Giulia and Carinthia should be incorporated in Yugoslavia.

The discussions with Yugoslavia ended in an agreement with the Allied Military Government by which the latter was to control the western part of Venezia Giulia (the so-called Zone A) under the command of Marshal Alexander, provided that: Yugoslavia was to be represented in the military government; a token Yugoslav army should remain in the region, but under Alexander's command; and the military government should function through the civil authorities already established in the region. Yugoslav troops evacuated Carinthia, but the Yugoslav authorities launched a vigorous propaganda campaign against the Allied occupying authorities.

On June 9, at Belgrade, an agreement was signed between Yugoslavia and the Allied representatives. It confirmed the previous verbal accord between Tito and Marshal Alexander: the Allies were to assume control

over territory west of a line running north from the Adriatic and including railway and roads to Austria which pass through Trieste, Gorizia, Caporetto, and Tarvisio, as well as Pola and the anchorage on the western coast of the Istrian Peninsula; a token Yugoslav force not to exceed 2,000 men of all ranks to remain in occupation of restricted districts west of the line under Alexander's command; the Yugoslav government to repatriate all nationals of the area west of the line who had been arrested or deported, except Yugoslav nationals as of 1939.

*The National Front.*—The Yugoslav government was no less busy internally than externally. Under its sponsorship the delegates of the National Front, originally organized on the basis of federal territorial units without a nation-wide representation, met at Belgrade on August 3 and formed a central executive committee headed by Marshal Tito. The new program promulgated by the executive committee, and announced on August 8, pledged the National Front to safeguard the integrity of Yugoslavia; to oppose all "chauvinist, hegemonistic, and separatist tendencies, as well as all advocates of national, religious, and racial intolerance"; to work toward the establishment of harmonious relations between Yugoslavia and Bulgaria; to cement the friendly relations with Soviet Russia, other Slavic countries, and Western democracies; to support Yugoslavia's full participation in the United Nations; to seek the destruction of fascism in the country and abroad; to strengthen the republican form of government; to insist that the new Yugoslavia be built up under the sole leadership of the National Front; to defend "the democratic peoples' authorities, the principal achievement of the National Liberation struggle"; to preserve the government by the working people; to extend the participation of the mass of the people in the government; to strive to attain freedom of assembly, freedom of association, freedom of the press, the secret ballot, equal voting privileges for all Yugoslavs, the equality of women, and full social security; to attack all forms of bureaucracy, lawlessness, corruption, and special privilege; to combat the "speculators" and "exploiters" of the people; to demand that public servants be held responsible politically and legally for their acts; to aim at the transformation of the Yugoslav army into a modern military force; to mobilize all national forces for economic reconstruction; to advocate electrification and industrialization of the country, extensive development of coöperatives, and improved sanitation; and to respect private property.

The National Front is not a single political party, but is composed of several groups which are allowed to preserve an independent organization. It is not a coalition of parties, however, for its component groups are expected to sacrifice *in toto* their individual programs. Though the Communist party's organization, statutes, and executive officers continue to be kept secret, it is known that the Communists are the actual force behind the National Front, whose program, though in some respects non-Communist, has been crystallized by the leadership of the Communist party. Yugoslavia's Politburo, also, is secret, but there is no doubt that its members are the architects of the new Yugoslavia.

*The third session of the A.V.N.O.J.*—In compliance with the Yalta declaration, the A.V.N.O.J. was expanded to include thirty-six members of the prewar Yugoslav parliament who did not collaborate with the Axis. Moreover, thirteen members of the Democratic party, twelve of the Agrarian party, thirteen of the Croat Peasant party, eleven of the Independent Democratic party, eleven of the Republican party, eight of the National Peasant party, and thirteen persons without political affiliation were added. The expanded A.V.N.O.J., now called the Provisional Assembly, held its third session in August, 1945. Its principal task was to prepare the legislation necessary for the election of the Constituent Assembly. The electoral law of August 10 gave suffrage rights to all citizens, regardless of sex, and to all soldiers, regardless of age. The same law denied voting rights to former Axis collaborators. Further legislation provided for a bicameral Constituent Assembly, made up of the Federal Council, composed of representatives elected on the basis of one deputy for each 10,000 voters, and of the Council of Nationalities, representing the peoples republics (the federal units). On August 16 the Provisional Assembly passed a law abrogating all mining privileges of private concerns, and, on August 23, a law for agrarian reform and internal colonization, which provided for the confiscation of landed estates of more than fifty acres* in extent, landholdings of institutions (unless they were for the public good), holdings of churches and monasteries in excess of twelve acres, and lands belonging to *Volksdeutsche* and fascists.

The political opposition made itself heard in the Provisional Assembly. It came almost exclusively from Milan Grol, a vigorous champion of democratic parliamentarism, and his supporters in the Democratic party, who criticized the parliamentary procedures, the enacted legislation, and the limited jurisdiction of the Assembly.

---

*According to the agrarian reform law of August 28, 1945, and the amendments of March 19, 1946, the maximum and the minimum landholdings an individual may possess were established at eighty-six acres and fifty acres, respectively.

In the preëlection campaign the government attacked the opposition for its alleged intention of bringing the prewar quasi-fascist regime to power. Internal dissension and government pressure hastened the deterioration of the parties which refused to join the National Front and which finally decided not to participate in the elections, on the ground that "inimical political laws have demonstrated from the first day of their application that the exclusive authority of the regime makes the situation impossible." This naturally intensified government attacks on the opposition. The opposition was joined by the Catholic Church when, at a conference in Zagreb, eighteen Roman Catholic bishops issued their first pastoral letter, charging the government with persecution of the clergy and violation of freedom of worship, freedom of the press, and rights of private property.

The climax in the opposition's activity was reached when Foreign Minister Šubašić resigned in a strongly worded memorandum to Tito. He was followed by two other members of the Croatian Peasant party—Juraj Šutej, Minister without portfolio, and Tomo Jančiković, the vice-governor of the National Bank.

As was expected under the circumstances, the elections held for the Constituent Assembly on November 11, 1945, favored Tito overwhelmingly. On November 29, 1946, the fourth anniversary of the first meeting of A.V.N.O.J., the Constituent Assembly was convoked. Its first act was the abolition of the monarchy and the proclamation of the Republic. The official name of the country became the Federal Peoples Republic of Yugoslavia.

On January 31, 1946, the Constituent Assembly voted unanimously to approve the constitution of the Federal Peoples Republic of Yugoslavia, which sanctioned and legalized the political, social, and economic reforms of the new regime. Patterned after the Soviet constitution of 1936, the new Yugoslav constitution[7] proclaimed Yugoslavia "a federal peoples state, republican in form"; established a bicameral legislature; defined the jurisdiction of the respective peoples republics (Serbia, Croatia, Slovenia, Bosnia and Hercegovina, Macedonia, and Montenegro); set forth the basic provisions concerning the supreme authority of the state in starting and safeguarding a planned economy; and proclaimed an alliance of the government with the workers. In this way Yugoslavs accepted the Soviet principle of federation, according to which the central government is the sole and absolute authority in matters pertaining to foreign affairs, national defense, communications, merchant marine, postal service, and foreign trade.

In matters of finance, internal order, justice, industry, mines, commerce, agriculture, forests, labor, and public works the peoples republics function under the guardianship of the central authorities. The constitution does not define the matters in which the republics will have full independence, but states that they will be set up by the constitution of each individual republic "in conformity with the constitution of the Federal Peoples Republic of Yugoslavia."

Unlike the Soviet model, the Yugoslav constitution does not provide for the abolishment of private property, though it imposes heavy restrictions on it; and does not proclaim the Communist party—or, for that matter, any other political organization—the backbone of the new regime.

The federal government includes, besides the various ministries, the Federal Planning Commission and the Federal Control Commission. The former is entrusted with the task of planning the entire national economy and paving the way for the establishment of state socialism, and the latter has full surveillance over the application of federal laws by the central and provincial governments and their subsidiaries. Both of these all-powerful offices are strongly centralized and exercise their authority through auxiliary offices established in each republic.

Theoretically, the Peoples Assembly, composed of the Federal Council, representing the nation as a unit, and the Council of Nationalities, representing the nation as a federation of republics, autonomous provinces, and autonomous regions, is the highest legislative body in Yugoslavia, "the supreme organ of state authority of the Federal Peoples Republic of Yugoslavia." However, as the Assembly is composed almost entirely of the adherents of the present regime, its function has been relegated to mere sanctioning of the laws promulgated by the federal government.

On February 1, 1946—a day after the proclamation of the new constitution,—the "provisional government" resigned and on the same day Marshal Tito formed the first cabinet of postwar Yugoslavia backed by the necessary legal and constitutional authority. The new cabinet, containing an overwhelming Communist majority, demonstrated its efficiency in organizing the state apparatus, in carrying out the new economic policy, and in improving the economic status of the people. The government moved to stabilize the currency, crush the black market, restore transportation, and increase industrial and mining production. In May, 1946, the government abolished the decision of August, 1945, according to which the peasants were forced to sell the entire surplus of their produce to the government, and issued a new decree allowing them to sell 10–40 per cent of their produce in the free market. This apparently was undertaken to secure for the present regime the political backing of the peasants, who represent about 75 per cent of the Yugoslav population, and who are conservative and skeptical about the sweeping reforms of socialism.

The leaders of the new Yugoslav regime are cognizant of the Marxian axiom that the economic factor is the basis of social structure and political power. They maintain that, although during the war they had crushed the Yugoslav bourgeoisie—their principal internal opponent—as a military factor, and although in the November, 1945, elections they had crushed it politically, the Partisan regime would not achieve internal stability and full guaranty for survival until the bourgeoisie was destroyed economically. Prominent on the agenda of the regime's current activities is establishment of the financial supremacy of the state over private financial resources. Except for agriculture, where private interests are still predominant, the state has already established complete control. The principal industrial and wholesale commercial enterprises, the leading banks, foreign trade, the transportation system, and the mines are already the property of the state. Although Yugoslav Communist leaders insist that state socialism has not yet been established in Yugoslavia, they profess that it is their ideal to emulate the Soviet model of socialist economy.

With economic stabilization the government is trying to consolidate its political forces and expand its following. The capture and execution of General Draža Mihailović eliminated the last bulwark of "Greater Serbia" followers and thus the last formidable political opposition to the regime. Many of the prewar political parties have been absorbed by the Communist-dominated National Front, torn by internal dissension, or prevented by the government from active work. The hierarchy of the Catholic Church, incensed by the execution of the clergymen who actively supported the German order in Yugoslavia, by the sweeping agrarian reform which affected the Church adversely, by restricting the teaching of religion in the schools, and by changing marriage in the Church from a compulsory to an optional status, has continued to oppose the present regime. The Serbian Church, which has no backing abroad, can oppose the present regime only on a much smaller scale.

Whatever its merits and shortcomings, the present Yugoslav government is a going concern. Its leaders are the stolid and unsophisticated sons of Yugoslav peasants, whose school was the Communist underground and who succeeded in organizing effective resistance to the Germans and their satellites. They have given the Yugoslav people a sorely needed ethnic democracy—an equality of the nationalities which make up this ethnically heterogeneous country—but they have not given their people a political democracy. The success or failure of their efforts to raise the standard of living of their countrymen through a socialist economy is still to come, and the present situation provides no ground for conclusive judgment and adequate evaluation.

# CHAPTER XXI

# *Postwar Foreign Economic Relations*

BY JOZO TOMASEVICH

THE SECOND WORLD WAR and its outcome have completely altered the internal political structure of Yugoslavia and have brought about profound changes in the economic institutions and the economic and political thinking of the country. The postwar political shifts in Europe and elsewhere have changed the Yugoslav position in diplomacy. These changes are bound to influence its economic relations with the outer world.

*Wartime developments.*—The objectives of the German invasion of Yugoslavia in April, 1941, were: (1) to secure the right flank for their impending war against Russia; (2) to obtain the Balkan route for their operations in the eastern Mediterranean; and (3) to utilize Yugoslav resources and man power for their war machine. After a two-week campaign the Yugoslav state and army disintegrated and the country was dismembered. (See chap. xx.)

Germany (and Italy in the Italian-occupied parts of Yugoslavia) stripped the country of all accumulated stocks of food and raw materials, took away a large portion of railroad rolling stock and shipping, and later dismantled and carried away a number of factories. To facilitate its command over Yugoslav resources and current production Germany exacted huge occupation costs. The exploitation of the country was divided among a few big German combines which controlled all the important mining, industrial, trade, and banking enterprises. The most important combines were the Hermann Göring Werke (Bor copper mines, Trepča mines, Danube shipping, engineering industry), Krupp (chrome and steel), I. G. Farben (chemicals), and Mannesmann (steel and engineering).

In Serbia economic controls were in the hands of the German economic plenipotentiary, Franz Neuhausen, who had been groomed for this job by eight years in Belgrade as German consul general and representative of the National Socialist party. The German-owned banks, representing the Deutsche Bank, the Dresdner Bank, the Reichskredit-Anstalt, and the Vienna Kreditanstalt-Bankverein, supplemented the controls exercised by the military administration and by the industrial concerns.

In Croatia, where few large enterprises of importance for war economy are located, the same German concerns were in action, but on a smaller scale, and most of the controls over industry were exercised by the German-owned banks. In fact, if not in name, the German Minister in Croatia, S.S. General Kasche, had a position similar to that of Neuhausen in Serbia.

Slovenian industry and banking were simply "annexed" by the German firms. In order to export the greatest possible quantity of supplies from the country and to insure that the small imports from Germany and elsewhere were utilized so as to increase the economic contribution of the area to the German war machine, a host of German trading firms for export and import were created.

To maximize the production, collection, and export of food and industrial crops, Germany assumed direct control of the surplus area of the Banat (officially a part of the puppet state of Serbia), which it managed through the *Volksdeutsche*. In the Hungarian-occupied areas of the Bačka and the Baranja, as well as in Croatian areas with large German minorities (Slavonia and Syrmia, or Srem), the economy was also directed by the *Volksdeutsche*. This minority had a special legal status and was an effective weapon of German economic penetration and exploitation as well as a policing factor. The *Volksdeutsche* had been prepared for this role ever since the advent of the Nazis. In this way Germany fully controlled the granary of Yugoslavia, from which virtually nothing was sent south of the Danube-Sava River line, thus contributing greatly to the starvation in these regions throughout the war. In all areas under effective German control, strict regulations on production, collection, and consumption were imposed with the sole purpose of deriving the largest possible quantity of goods for Germany. Italy imposed similar controls in areas occupied by its army.

Including war prisoners, Germany utilized from 400,000 to 500,000 Yugoslavs as workers outside the Yugoslav borders.

The German military and economic calculations with respect to Yugoslavia proved to be wrong. The collapse in April, 1941, meant the end of the old regime but not the submission of the people. Hostilities against the occupation forces and domestic quislings began as early as July, 1941. As the war advanced, these hostilities, under the leadership of the Yugoslav National Liberation Army— usually referred to as the Partisans—assumed the proportions of a large-scale upheaval. Instead of an occupation job involving only small garrisoning troops, the Germans soon had to fight over most of the Yugoslav territory, employing about fifteen German and many satellite divisions after 1943. One of the important functions of the Yugoslav guerrillas was to sabotage transportation and production facilities in order to impede enemy movements and to make it impossible for the enemy to exploit the economic resources of the country.

There are no definite data on the quantities of food, nonferrous metals, and other raw materials which the Germans obtained from Yugoslavia during the war. Supplies were not so large as the Germans had expected, but it is safe to say that the amounts of grains, livestock products, and especially nonferrous metals were not inconsiderable. Copper and chromium ores, the production of both of which was increased by the Germans, undoubtedly rendered substantial aid to the German war economy: it was estimated that Yugoslav mines supplied about 44 per cent of German copper requirements and 40 per cent of German chromite requirements.

The emergence of the National Liberation Movement (which eventually became and is now the dominant force in the country), its basic political ideas, and its amazing power of resilience have been discussed (see chap. xx, above), but one question of an economic nature is within the scope of this chapter: How did the Liberation Movement solve its wartime economic problems? All available stocks were placed at the disposal of the army in areas controlled by the Partisans. But since they had access to only the poorest and purely agrarian areas until the last months of the war, and the enemy used "scorched earth" tactics intensively against the Movement, supplies were very short, consisting principally of livestock, grains, and vegetables, as well as some clothing and footwear. Thus it was imperative to find other sources of supply.

Throughout the war the principal source of arms and munitions was the enemy. Enemy sources supplied, also, a part of the clothing, food, and medical stores. In fact, some military operations were conducted exclusively to obtain the necessary materials. The Italian collapse in September, 1943, was highly advantageous to the National Liberation Army: captured Italian stores helped it to pull through some of the most critical months of its existence. In the autumn of 1943 and thereafter, supplies came by sea and by air from the western Allies, who also helped with the evacuation of the wounded and the civilian refugees. Late in 1944 and in 1945 some provisions came from Soviet Russia. In the final stages of the war the American and British air forces synchronized their operations in Yugoslavia with those of the National Liberation Army. There is, however, no account of what share of supplies the Yugoslavs derived from various sources, and there may never be one.

*Economic consequences of the war.*—The wartime damages sustained by the Yugoslav economy influence and will, for a number of years, continue to influence the production and export capacity of the country and its import needs. Most of the following data come from the reports of the United Nations Relief and Rehabilitation Administration Mission in Yugoslavia, which obtained them from official Yugoslav sources and, when possible, checked them. Since most of the data were compiled by local liberation committees which were inexperienced in administrative work, and since statistical services in Yugoslavia have always been poor, final computations of damages will necessitate much revision. Nevertheless, the data are sufficient to convey the order of magnitude of the destruction and damage sustained during the war.

The first and most important fact is that Yugoslavia has lost a large part of its population. Yugoslav sources estimate these losses at 1,700,000, which, in relation to the estimated population of 15,970,000 at the end of March, 1941, means a loss of 10.6 per cent. After Poland, this was relatively the largest wartime loss of population in the world. It is not known whether the figure includes the shifts in population across the national boundaries, such as the 500,000 *Volksdeutsche* who left the country in the last months of the war. Nor is it known how this estimate accounts for the loss in population through a lower birth rate resulting from the separation of sexes and fewer marriages; the increased mortality of infants and children from starvation and exposure, and from lack of clothing, medical supplies, and care; a higher death rate among adults from tuberculosis and other diseases. The war left hundreds of thousands of wounded and maimed, and has resulted in much greater morbidity (e.g., tuberculosis, rheumatic fever, malaria), reducing the labor power and increasing the number of consumers who do not produce.

There are several tens of thousands of persons now in Italy, Germany, and Austria who, for political reasons, do not want to return to Yugoslavia. According to a special agreement of January, 1946, between Yugoslavia and Poland, a small colony of Poles in Bosnia—numbering about 25,000—had to be transferred to Poland within six months. It seems that at least part of the Czechoslovak and Hungarian minorities in Yugoslavia will also be transferred. Moreover, the war led to a relatively greater loss of highly skilled workers, farmers, and managers. All these losses and shifts in population (conclusive data on which will be obtainable only after the next census) have reduced the aggregate labor power of the country, both numerically and with regard to skills, and thus its production and export capacities.

One of the greatest wartime losses was in housing. Some areas (e.g., Lika and northwestern and northeastern Bosnia) were completely obliterated. It is estimated that 310,000 buildings in rural areas and 98,000 in towns were destroyed; the number of heavily damaged buildings was estimated at 90,000 in rural areas and 31,000 in cities. Thus about one-sixth of the prewar housing was destroyed or heavily damaged.

The second most staggering loss was in livestock, as may be seen from the table on page 392. The replenishment of pigs, goats, sheep, and poultry can be accomplished within a relatively short time, and the drop in their numbers has unfavorable effects only on food supply and exports. But the replenishment of cattle and horses is a long and tedious process. Their loss affects not only food and export position; the reduction of draft power by 1,000,000 draft-power units will impede agricultural production for years.

Wartime losses of agricultural machinery and implements by destruction and wear and tear were probably as heavy as losses in livestock, that is, 40–50 per cent. The losses of livestock and machinery, the decreased production of manure, and the loss in farming skill have resulted in deterioration of cultivation standards and thus in a reduction of yields which may take years to bring back to prewar levels. Barring natural disasters such as the drought of 1945, the Yugoslavs may not need to import grains in future, but they

| Livestock | Average number, 1934–1938 | Percentage remaining, 1945 |
|---|---|---|
| Horses | 1,230,000 | 40.5 |
| Cattle | 4,100,000 | 46.7 |
| Sheep | 9,540,000 | 50.3 |
| Goats | 1,890,000 | 53.4 |
| Hogs | 3,100,000 | 48.4 |
| Poultry | 21,650,000 | 49.0 |

will long remain dependent on imports of meat, milk, and fats if the population is to be assured of a reasonable supply of protective nutrients. How different from conditions after the First World War! In 1919, 1920, and 1921, 28, 14, and 40 per cent, respectively, of Yugoslav exports consisted of live animals and livestock products.

From a general economic point of view the most crippling losses were sustained in transport. At the time of liberation there was no railroad line of any importance which could operate. Of the total length of railroads of 12,000 km., about 6,100 km. were destroyed or damaged. Destruction of key bridges proved to be a formidable bottleneck in the attempt to reëstablish railroad traffic. By November, 1945, about 75 per cent of railroad lines were open for traffic, but at a greatly reduced rate of turnover. Losses of rolling stock during the war compare as follows with the number existing in 1940: locomotives, 1,190 out of 2,180; passenger cars, 2,920 out of 5,080; freight cars, 30,300 out of 53,600. Besides, the railroads were hard hit by the destruction of signal and servicing facilities and repair shops, which reduced the repair capacity for locomotives by about 40 per cent and for freight cars by 60 per cent.

Although the number of automobiles and trucks was unusually

small in Yugoslavia before the war—in 1940 there were about 15,000 automobiles and 6,000 trucks and buses—the war wiped out virtually all of them. Moreover, about 40 per cent of peasant carts, the chief means of transportation in rural areas, were lost. In 1940 Yugoslavia had a merchant fleet of 410,000 gross register tons, of which 55,000 tons were serving the Adriatic coast. It lost more than half of the ocean-going ships and more than two-thirds of coastal shipping, as well as the bulk of its river fleet. About 45 per cent of all telegraph and telephone equipment was destroyed or damaged.

These losses in communication facilities have manifold consequences for future international economic relations. First, transport difficulties impair the general economic rehabilitation of the country, lessen its production and export capacity, and increase its import needs. Second, since most of the means of transport must be imported, the rehabilitation of transport will burden the Yugoslav economy and foreign-exchange reserve for years. Third, favorable items in the balance of payments which Yugoslavia derived from transport services to foreign countries throughout the interwar period will probably become unfavorable items.

No less detrimental than the losses in transport and even more difficult and costly to repair was the damage, ranging between 20 and 60 per cent, inflicted on Yugoslav industries. They suffered also from four years of insufficient maintenance and from plunder and destruction of key items such as belting, motors, and tools.

The lumber industry, which supplied 17.5 per cent of the value of all exports in the interwar period, was perhaps hardest hit. The prewar processing capacity for construction timber was about 7,000,000 cu. m. annually, of which about 4,200,000 cu. m. were consumed domestically. The annual rate of production in 1946 was less than 1,000,000 cu. m., though the domestic demand has greatly increased. Thus prospects for early export of substantial quantities of timber are poor indeed. One of the most difficult bottlenecks in the timber industry is lack of transport facilities for logs. All the other industries which are closely related to the lumber industry—wood pulp, paper, plywood, and dry distillation—have lost a large part of their production capacity.

The damage in the nonferrous metals industry—the chief export industry in the field of mining—was not extensive. The Trepča mines were flooded and some flotation facilities were impaired. Machinery in the Bor mines was damaged considerably by the retreating Germans. It seems, however, that equipment in both these great enterprises has already been repaired. The antimony mines were not damaged, but flotation facilities for chromium ore were partly destroyed. The aluminum plant at Lozovac in Dalmatia was put out of action by the removal of essential parts. Almost all mining enterprises lack tools, steel cables, and especially transport facilities. The nonferrous-metals industry of Yugoslavia was enlarged by the Idria mercury mines in the Julian March. The inclusion of Istria may enable Yugoslavia to become one of the world's leading producers of bauxite.

Two of the six leading plants for heavy chemicals (at Jajce and Lukavac) were almost completely destroyed. They were producing soda ash, caustic soda, and chlorine derivatives, the lack of which impedes the glass, soap, paper, and textile industries. The productive capacity for fertilizers, insecticides, calcium carbide, and sulfuric acid was not markedly diminished. Since part of the production of soda ash and caustic soda, chlorine derivatives, and fertilizers was formerly exported, damages to the chemical industry will have a direct bearing on export possibilities in the next few years. The cement industry, which also used to export part of its production, was not seriously injured. In spite of greatly increased domestic needs, small quantities have already been exported.

In the textile industry, which in 1940 had about 250,000 cotton spindles, 70,000 wool spindles, 25,000 cotton looms, and 16,000 wool looms, wartime losses amounted to about 40 per cent of capacity in cotton and 20 per cent in wool. A large part of the belting, motors, and various accessories has been pillaged or sabotaged, but much of the damage was made good. Since the liberation of the country the textile industry has been working almost exclusively with raw materials imported by the U.N.R.R.A. Besides the replacement of capacity lost during the war, the most difficult problem of this industry will be the import of raw materials. For the next few years the country will need to import more cotton and woolen yarn than it did in the latter part of the 1930's, thus increasing the costs of textile imports. It will be necessary, also, to import more wool, owing to the halving of domestic herds of sheep.

In the leather-tanning and footwear industries, wartime damage as not large, and present production capacity could probably satfy domestic needs. But imports of more raw materials may be necssary since the domestic supply of hides was reduced by more than o per cent from losses in livestock and reduced rate of slaughter.

Impairment of the sugar, flour-milling, fruit-processing, and oilcessing industries was not excessive, but all produced exclusively r mostly for the home market. The meat-packing industry, which a prewar years exported part of its production and was kept in full peration by the Germans throughout the war, is virtually intact, ut it will lack raw materials, owing to the losses in livestock.

The damage was very heavy in iron-ore mining and pig-iron and eel production. At the time of liberation, iron-ore mining capacy was reduced to 30 per cent of the prewar level. By March, 1946, roduction in the two principal mines had reached 50 per cent of ae prewar tonnage. Steel production both at Jesenice in Slovenia nd at Zenica in Bosnia was for some time at a standstill because f the destruction of key machinery and the lack of coke. The Jeseice mills have been largely restored; so have the Zenica mills, after ame of the essential electric installations were repaired by maanery imported through the U.N.R.R.A. Closely related is damge in the engineering industry, which before the war was engaged a construction, especially the repair of railroad rolling stock. One f the most important plants, at Kraljevo, which was completed in 936, was dismantled and carried away by the Germans; two other arge plants, at Smederevo and at Niš, were almost completely deaolished. The biggest plant in this industry, at Brod, escaped with ainor injury.

Wartime losses in the coal industry amounted to about 60 per ant of the prewar capacity, and in 1945 and 1946 scarcity of coal as one of the greatest difficulties with which the Yugoslav econmy had to contend. Damage was inflicted by flooding, wrecking f power plants serving the mines, wrecking of mine transport, and aunder and destruction of tools and implements. Important addions to the Yugoslav coal industry after the war were the Arsa coal aines in Istria, which in 1940 had an annual capacity of about 000,000 tons. Unfortunately, Arsa coal, though of fairly good uality, is not suitable for coking. Some of the coal and coke deficit in 1946 was covered by U.N.R.R.A. imports and a part, amountin to about 30,000 tons of brown coal monthly, by imports from Bu garia and Hungary on the reparation account.

The production capacity of a few branches of industry was ir creased by the Germans during the war. The Bor copper mines, fc example, were enlarged and worked by forced labor. Pig-iron pro duction was increased to about 250,000 tons annually. Crude-o production, which before the war was negligible, was forced; b April, 1946, it supplied 15–20 per cent of the prewar crude-oil need Chromium-ore mining was stepped up, as Yugoslavia was one c the most important sources of chromite for Germany. Finally, th Germans started the processing of molybdenum ore in the Maka nica mine in Serbia.

During the war Yugoslavia was subjected to two waves of plur der of stocks of food and other commodities: after the invasion i 1941 and again during the German withdrawal in 1944 and 194 There are no exact data regarding the first instance, but fightin lasted only two weeks and the old Yugoslav army did not exer itself in the destruction of food, clothing, and fuel reserves. In th autumn of 1944 war operations prevented the harvesting of cor and sugar beets in the Vojvodina. There was extensive destructio of livestock, transport, and industrial facilities during the Germa withdrawal. According to the State Commission for War Damage the enemy took from the reserves of the National Bank of Yug slavia 10,425 kg. of gold and 82,133 kg. of silver, valued at approx mately $12,000,000. The bulk of the country's gold reserve, abou $60,000,000, was deposited in the United States (part of it was late transferred to Brazil) and Great Britain before the outbreak of wa

The war resulted in total disintegration of business organizatio and great reduction in the number of skilled managerial staf This is partly a result of the fact that in prewar days many busine men were nationals of various central European states and left th country, partly the result of the extermination of the Jewish con munity, and partly the result of the removal of those who wei considered collaborationists. It will take many years to develo skilled personnel and, above all, to reëstablish the necessary co tacts, especially in foreign trade.

During the war, Yugoslavia underwent a hyperinflation. It di ered in degree from area to area and was worst in the puppet state of Croatia. While the bank-note circulation on March 31, 1941, amounted to D. 14,300,000,000, the following amounts of wartime and occupation currencies were presented in 1945 for exchange into the new dinar currency: Croatian kunas, 241,000,000,000; Serbian dinars, 43,400,000,000; Bulgarian levas, 3,400,000,000; Italian lire, 1,860,000,000; Albanian francs, 18,800,000; Partisan promissory notes in Slovenia, 104,000,000; Rupnik's (Slovenian fascists) promissory notes, 156,000,000; Bulgarian promissory notes, 687,000,000; German marks, 428,000,000; Reichskreditscheine, 9,400,000; Hungarian pengös, 490,000,000; old Yugoslav suspect 1,000-dinar notes, 36,000,000.[1] Both during the war and in the first phases after the liberation the Yugoslav economy reverted, for the most part, to a barter system.

Faced with these great losses and disorganization in agriculture, transport, and industry and with the need to start the economy going as fast as possible, the Yugoslavs began repair and reconstruction work immediately after the liberation of various areas. According to eyewitness reports, they were remarkably successful. But many, if not most, of these repairs were of a makeshift nature. The repairs thus far made, however, serve the purpose of reëstablishing essential services.

As of December, 1945, the total number of industrial workers was 50–60 per cent of the 1939 figure, but the level of employment differed greatly from branch to branch, depending on the rate of wartime destruction and the availability of fuel and raw materials. Productivity per worker was about 30 per cent lower than before the war because of the loss of skilled labor, the use of worn-out machinery, and makeshift repairs. Compared with the industrial production (100) of 1939, the December, 1945, indices were as follows: timber, 25; building industry, 30–35; textiles, 30–40; leather footwear, 35–40; leather tanning, 10–15; food processing, 40–50; chemicals, 35–40; metallurgy, 15–20; engineering and repairs, 50–60; paper, 65–70; cement, 70–90. The general index of industrial production was 30–35.

While the damage to such industries as lumber, heavy chemicals, and the mining and processing of nonferrous minerals will impede

---

[1] For notes to chapter xxi see pages 527–528.

exports, damages sustained by the textile, steel, and engineerin
industries will force the country to increase imports or to impo
relatively more finished or semifinished products instead of ra
materials. Since Yugoslav industry was developed entirely wit
imported machinery, its rehabilitation will cause a great and pr
longed strain both on financial resources and on balance of pa
ments. As in population, so in agriculture, transportation, an
industry, wartime losses in Yugoslavia were among the heaviest i
the world. The war has left a physically exhausted population an
a crippled and impoverished economy. The Yugoslavs seem to lac
everything except one asset—the determination to master their ec
nomic difficulties.

*Postwar political changes in Europe.*—Postwar political chang
in Europe will exert great influence on economic relations and wi
require adjustments. It is hardly possible, in the international si
uation at this time, to assess properly the situation of Yugoslavi
and other small countries which are completely influenced by, bu
cannot materially influence, the relations among the Great Powe
and thus the course of world developments. But there is one unde
lying premise which is beyond doubt: the peoples of Yugoslav
need a just and durable peace as much as they need their dai
bread. In fact, without peace they cannot all have bread. A pr
carious peace resulting from the existence of a western and a
eastern bloc would have unbearable consequences for the peopl
of Yugoslavia. Living at the fringe of what would be the easter
bloc, controlled essentially by Communist principles, their positio
would be that of an armed outpost.

Notwithstanding the mechanized nature of the Second Worl
War and the atomic and biological nature of any future world wa
for the prosecution of which its size and economic strength a
unsuited, Yugoslavia would be forced to maintain large arme
forces and to develop war industries and military communication
This would sap its economic strength even more than in the inte
war period and would prevent an improvement in the standard
living. In such a situation civilian economy would have to be deve
oped within the framework of domestic economic and financi
resources, possibly with some help from the other members of t
bloc, and most probably under an overriding system of prioriti

of the bloc as a whole. Thus a favorable political climate in the world, characterized by friendly relations among the Great Powers, primarily between the United States and Great Britain with Soviet Russia, a general feeling of security, and an intensive economic intercourse among the nations of the world are vital necessities for Yugoslavia.

But even assuming the existence of a durable peace and intensive international trade, including a heavy flow of long-term capital from industrial into underdeveloped countries, the position of Yugoslavia would still be difficult. A far-reaching reorientation of its foreign trade seems to be inevitable. One of the basic factors which will necessitate this reorientation is the changed economic position of Germany and Italy, the two most important trade partners of Yugoslavia in the interwar period. Although their new economic status, especially that of Germany, is uncertain, it seems safe to assume that the effective demand of both Germany and Italy for Yugoslav products will be much lower than in the interwar period and that their ability to supply many commodities previously exported to Yugoslavia will be greatly reduced. The same may be true of Austria. At least in the period of transition, many other European countries will be affected by the loss of markets in Germany and Italy, and will, of necessity, buy less from Yugoslavia.

Yugoslavia will probably try hard to compensate for the loss of markets and sources of supply in central Europe and Italy by intensifying trade relations with its neighbors and with Soviet Russia, with which close political relations are maintained and within whose sphere of influence it falls. Before valid judgments can be made regarding the success of this reorientation, it will be necessary to observe Yugoslav foreign trade for several years. Undoubtedly, a substantial volume of trade will be carried on with Soviet Russia. The Yugoslav position with respect to trade with the U.S.S.R. is, however, quite different from that of Czechoslovakia and Poland. These two states have large consumer-goods industries (e.g., textiles and footwear) for the products of which Russia is virtually an unlimited market. Czechoslovakia and, to a lesser extent, Poland are also large producers of capital goods. But Yugoslavia does not have such industries capable of producing an export surplus. Its exports to Russia must consist of fruits, wines, tobacco, nonferrous metals,

and possibly cement and a few other products. Russia does not nee
timber and will not need many food products when they becom
available in Yugoslavia for export. Russia could supply Yugoslavi
with petroleum, coke, armaments, cotton, and possibly later witl
agricultural machinery and vehicles.

Intensive trade relations with Czechoslovakia will simply mea
the reëstablishment of interwar conditions, but competition for th
export of capital goods from Czechoslovakia among Soviet Russi
and the other neighboring countries may become severe. Trad
with Poland, Hungary, Rumania, Bulgaria, and Albania will prol
ably be intensified, but the difficulties which kept the trade wit
these countries at a low level in the interwar period, namely, lac
of economic complementarity, will continue to exist. Howevei
should planned economic development in all these countries b
undertaken on a regional basis, so that each develops the industrie
for which it has the most advantageous natural conditions, an ever
tual intensification of trade among them would be quite feasible

In the Mediterranean markets and in the overseas markets t
which Yugoslavia used to export timber, cement, heavy chemical
and livestock, it seems likely that the former trade position will b
reëstablished. But it may be imperative to improve this positio
markedly in order to compensate for the loss of markets in centra
Europe.

Economic relations with France, Switzerland, Belgium, the Netl
erlands, and Sweden will probably be strengthened. Some of thes
countries may even become important sources of long-term credit
for the financing of Yugoslav economic development. It woul
seem to the author, however, that economic intercourse with thes
countries could only supplement the fundamentally necessary ir
tensive economic intercourse with Great Britain and the Unite
States.

There are two basic reasons why Yugoslavia should concentrat
on establishing and strengthening economic relations with Grea
Britain, and especially with the United States. It is from these tw
countries that Yugoslavia must import much of the machinery
tools, rolling stock, automotive equipment, electric appliances, ir
struments, and other commodities needed for economic develoj
ment. Moreover, the United States and, to a lesser degree, th

United Kingdom and Canada could serve as principal sources of the long-term credits needed for economic development. Whether or not the Anglo-Saxon countries become important sources of new credits, their markets are of basic importance for Yugoslavia to obtain, through exports, the necessary funds for the payment of imports. One factor will force Yugoslavia to seek buyers in the United States and Great Britain in the near future: the need to finance the import of spare parts and accessories to maintain the vehicles, locomotives, and machinery brought into the country by the U.N.R.R.A. Emigrants' remittances, especially from the United States, which in the interwar period were an extremely important source of foreign exchange, now yield only a fraction of what they yielded in the early 1920's.

Because of the tremendous potential economic importance of the United States and Great Britain for Yugoslavia, it seems logical for the latter to develop friendly political and cultural relations with them. Otherwise there is little hope for intensive and mutually advantageous economic relations. The United States and Great Britain may possibly take a somewhat broader view of developments in Yugoslavia; these have much deeper historical, social, and economic reasons than the fact that the country is run by the Communist party. Moreover, it should not be forgotten that the new state had a difficult birth, that it fell heir to an unenviable inheritance, and that, like every new and revolutionary state, it suffers from all sorts of childhood afflictions. Of course, as things now stand, the relations between the United States and Great Britain, on one hand, and Yugoslavia, on the other, are only a minor aspect of the basic complex of the relations between the Western democracies and Soviet Russia.

The postwar activity of the Yugoslav government has been dictated by the exigencies of the moment. Internal and foreign political problems were in the foreground. As with all revolutionary governments, the first preoccupation of the regime was to establish and secure itself in power. To do this it had to create an administrative apparatus, which, considering the conditions in 1945, was a difficult task. A country which for more than four years had been split into several states and administrative units, which had been occupied by troops of several nations, and which had been ravaged by war and internal struggle had to be welded into one again. The tremendous expansion of state managerial activities, the lack of skilled administrative personnel, and the administrative reorganization of the country on a federal basis made the task still harder.

The government encountered great difficulties in securing full recognition by the United States and Great Britain and was from the beginning at loggerheads with these two Powers regarding the border with Italy, the extradition of Yugoslav war criminals, prewar treaty obligations toward these countries, their capital investments in Yugoslavia, reparations, Yugoslav gold deposited in these countries, and the return of property removed during the war by the Axis Powers.

In the economic field the government was faced by a host of staggering problems: feeding and clothing of population in the western and southwestern areas, establishment of internal transport, rehabilitation of agriculture and industry, withdrawal of wartime and occupation currencies, establishment of fiscal administration, management of the state enterprises which were steadily increasing in number, and prevention of epidemics.

*U.N.R.R.A.'s assistance in 1945 and 1946.*—Yugoslavia was one of the leading beneficiaries of relief extended through the United Nations Relief and Rehabilitation Administration,[2] which in 1945 and 1946 represented the only significant economic link between Yugoslavia and the outside world. The activity of the U.N.R.R.A. was important in the repatriation of displaced persons, the administration of refugee camps, the prevention of epidemics, and the furnishing of technical specialists in public health, sanitation, social welfare, agriculture, transport, and industry. Its chief function however, was to provide relief and rehabilitation supplies.[3] The allocation of commodities was determined by and large according to the respective needs of the countries receiving U.N.R.R.A. assistance.

Throughout the span of its operations, which were virtually concluded by the end of June, 1947, the total financial resources of the U.N.R.R.A. amounted to about $3,700,000,000. Of this amount about $2,972,000,000 was spent on supplies, excluding shipping costs. Yugoslavia's share in the supply budget was $424,800,000, or 14.4 per cent of the total. As of the end of December, 1946, this amount was apportioned as follows among the various commodity groups: food, $136,338,000; textiles, clothing, and footwear, $83,149,000; medical and sanitation supplies, $19,904,000; agricultural rehabilitation supplies, $37,188,000; industrial rehabilitation supplies, $109,249,000. An amount of $4,248,000 was still awaiting specifications. A part of the supplies valued at $34,724,000—mostly food and clothing—was bought from the Allied military authorities by the U.N.R.R.A. during the initial stages of its operations in Yugoslavia. By the end of December, 1946, a total of 2,515,000 gross long tons of supplies, valued at approximately $362,551,000, or 85 per cent of the entire program dollarwise, was shipped to that country. By the end of June, 1947, only small quantities of industrial supplies remained to be delivered.

Chief among the supplies delivered up to the end of 1946 were the following, in tons: bread grains, 697,000; dairy products, 55,000; sugar, 47,000; fats, oils, and soap, 51,400; meat products, 28,700; fish, 13,400; quartermaster food, 119,300; pulses, 24,200; raw cotton, 41,500; raw wool, 12,700; clothing and textiles, 11,400; leather and hides, 2,800; finished footwear, 7,800; medical and sanitation supplies, 12,000; fertilizers, 95,000; insecticides, 10,000; seeds, 14,300; animal feed, 21,300; fuels and lubricants, 587,000; various materials, chemicals, and engineering stores, 286,000; farm machinery, 21,500; and repair equipment, 24,800. There were 30,000 head of livestock, 3,500 tractors, 12,000 trucks, 30 switching locomotives, 30 narrow-gauge locomotives for industry, about 120 standard-gauge locomotives, and 780 standard-gauge freight cars.

To what extent did the U.N.R.R.A. satisfy the relief and rehabilitation needs of Yugoslavia? How did its deliveries measure up to the legitimate requirements according to "bases" (a set of rules governing allocation of food and clothing)? On the whole, relief requirements were met more satisfactorily than rehabilitation requirements—which is understandable. Moreover, most of the agricultural and industrial supplies, with the exception of trucks and tractors, were delivered in the second half of U.N.R.R.A. operations. Thus their contribution toward immediate postwar rehabilitation was somewhat smaller than it would otherwise have been.

The rate at which requirements were met depended on the stocks available in the contributing countries and the priorities placed on various supplies by the recipient governments. Grain requirements were met by about 60 per cent, fats by about 25–30 per cent, raw cotton and raw wool 100 per cent. Finished clothing was delivered in greater quantities than requested. Only a small fraction of hide requirements was covered. The full quota of trucks and tractors was supplied, and gasoline and lubricants to keep them in operation, but there were difficulties in getting spare parts. All countries receiving U.N.R.R.A. assistance were adversely affected by the rise in prices in the contributing countries, especially in the chief contributor, the United States, as the increase in prices correspondingly reduced the value of relief programs in terms of commodities.

In spite of the fact that the Administration did not (because it could not) satisfy all the relief and rehabilitation requirements of the country, the significance of its operations for Yugoslavia was tremendous. Between October, 1945, and June, 1946, from 3,000,000 to 5,000,000 people in Montenegro, Dalmatia, Bosnia, Hercegovina, Croatia, and Slovenia were fed almost exclusively by U.N.R.R.A. supplies. Another 3,000,000 received part of their food from the Administration. Except for a small contribution by Soviet Russia of 2,000 tons of cotton and 200 tons of wool, the U.N.R.R.A. was virtually the sole source of civilian clothing and footwear in 1945 and 1946. It was almost the only source of medical and sanitation supplies and thus helped to prevent epidemics.

Through supplies of tractors and draft animals about 8 per cent of the losses in draft-power units in agriculture was replaced. This, in turn, helped to put an estimated 90 per cent of prewar acreage under crops in 1945–1946. The supplies of liquid fuel, plows, and other farm machinery and implements contributed to the same end. Trucks were one of the essential contributions of the Administration, for they distributed imported supplies and helped to use domestic produce more efficiently. Shipment of 120,000 tons of wheat and delivery of 5,700 trucks across the Yugoslav border in September, 1945, convinced even the worst skeptics among the Yugoslavs—and there were plenty of them—that the U.N.R.R.A. meant business. This contributed greatly to the improvement of relations between the government and the Administration and increased the prestige of the latter both among the population and among the officials of the country. All U.N.R.R.A. vehicles and tractors were run on oil, gasoline, and lubricants imported by the Administration, for it was the only source of petroleum products for civilian use. The supply of locomotives aided the improvement of railroad transport; and the supply of industrial machinery, spare parts, belting, and raw materials was an important factor in the improvement of industry and mining.

The per-capita value of U.N.R.R.A. deliveries to Yugoslavia during its operations amounted to about $28. In terms of dinars on the basis of the present exchange rate, the value of such deliveries, without shipping costs, amounted to about D. 21,200,000,000. On an annual basis this corresponded to 23 per cent of the Yugoslav national income in 1938, or to 132 per cent of the average tax revenue of the Yugoslav state between 1936 and 1939. In terms of goods, U.N.R.R.A. supplies represented roughly 50–60 per cent of all Yugoslav imports from 1934 to 1938. These supplies were made available to Yugoslavia without payment or obligation for payment at a later date. Distribution of U.N.R.R.A. supplies in Yugoslavia has been equitable and in agreement with the principles of the U.N.R.R.A. Charter.

Except for those who could not pay, Administration supplies were sold to the population; the proceeds were amassed in a special fund—the Reconstruction Fund. The revenues of the fund were used to finance the relief and rehabilitation activities of the government. By the end of December, 1946, the fund had accumulated, and probably largely spent, a sum corresponding to about $200,000,000. The greater part of the fund was earmarked for rehabilitation of railways, roads, and harbors, and building and repair of hospitals and schools. To the extent that reconstruction outlays are financed from the proceeds of U.N.R.R.A. supplies, tax revenue and current borrowing of the state are free to be used for other government needs. In this fact lies the purely financial importance of the Administration for all states receiving its assistance.

U.N.R.R.A. supplies were undoubtedly the basic factor in re-establishing the flow of agricultural produce from the country to urban areas and in the steady reduction of prices in Yugoslavia in 1945 and 1946. They helped to maintain an extremely frugal salary and wage policy as their purchasing power steadily rose. Without these supplies it would have been impossible to maintain price control and rationing and especially to crush the black market. As in all countries receiving U.N.R.R.A. assistance, its supplies helped to strengthen the regime in power.

Without help from the U.N.R.R.A., Yugoslavia could not have imported in 1945 and 1946 even a fraction of what the Administration supplied. It had no foreign exchange to pay for such imports. Sizable credits from the United States and Great Britain were available only to certain countries, and Yugoslavia was not among them. Without the Administration, most of the recipient countries would have been forced to carry the whole load of relief and rehabilitation. This work would have been limited, and economic revival of these countries would have been delayed for several years.

Yugoslavia and other countries receiving U.N.R.R.A. help pleaded at the fifth session of the U.N.R.R.A. Council at Geneva, in August, 1946, that the Administration's relief and rehabilitation activities be continued: the import needs of the recipients for 1947 far exceeded the amount of foreign exchange which they would probably have at their disposal for the financing of essential imports. The chief contributing countries, especially the United States and Great Britain, were of the opinion that a general international scheme for continued assistance to the beneficiaries of the U.N.R.R.A. program was not necessary and that future relief would have to be arranged on a bilateral basis. Some of the functions of the Administration (e.g., in the field of displaced persons and in public health) are being continued under the auspices of the United Nations.

Although the bulk of U.N.R.R.A. deliveries to Yugoslavia had been completed by the end of 1946, the economic effect, especially of rehabilitation supplies, will continue. Since no other international relief organization has been established which would take over even part of the Administration's supply functions, and since the Yugoslav export trade is still in the early phases of rehabilitation, the country will undoubtedly be faced with grave problems in 1948 resulting from inability to finance the essential imports.

The transition between the termination of U.N.R.R.A. activities and the time when Yugoslavia succeeds in establishing a fair volume of international trade represents a crucial phase in its economy. This is true of all countries which have been receiving large supplies from the Administration. Some countries, however, such as Greece, Italy, and Austria, will continue to receive relief from the United States and possibly from the United Kingdom and Canada, on the basis of bilateral agreements. But Yugoslavia was not eligible for such assistance, partly for economic reasons, as it has made better progress in rehabilitating its economy than the aforementioned countries, but essentially for political reasons. Together with other countries in the Soviet sphere of influence, Yugoslavia did not take part in the Paris Conference of July–September, 1947, on European economic reconstruction following the suggestion of Secretary Marshall, and therefore it cannot participate in or profit from the European Recovery Program sponsored and financed by the United States.

Neither the International Monetary Fund nor the International Bank for Reconstruction and Development could help Yugoslavia in financing its imports of direct consumption goods, for this is not within their range of activity. The Bank could become a source of credit for developmental purposes, but it may take time for the Bank's activities to get fully under way.

The central issue of Yugoslav foreign economic relations is the development of the balance of payments. Import requirements in 1947 were substantially lower than the sum of $420,000,000 stated by the Yugoslav delegate at the fifth session of the U.N.R.R.A Council held at Geneva in August, 1946 (food, $95,000,000; textiles and leather, $105,000,000; medical and sanitation supplies, $48,000,000; agricultural supplies, $60,000,000; industrial supplies, $112,000,000). Nor could exports in 1947 have amounted to $120,000,000, as expected on the same occasion. Poor harvests in 1946 made it impossible to export grains, except for some gifts of grain to Albania and Rumania. No exportable surpluses of livestock or livestock products can be expected for several years. The lumber industry, which used to play an important role in export trade, will have only small exportable surpluses. Thus few items besides nonferrous metals, cement, hemp, fruits, and medicinal herbs will be available for export.

The absence of relief imports and the fact that Yugoslavia has not thus far obtained substantial credits to finance its imports will induce the country to force its exports to the maximum and, in turn, will hold the value of imports near the value of exports. The difficulty of financing essential imports will also force the country to formulate a policy on foreign borrowing.

An extremely important consequence of the cessation of relief imports was a sharp decline in public revenue. Proceeds from the sale of U.N.R.R.A. supplies have provided the funds for virtually all rehabilitation expenditures by the state since the middle of 1945. This source of revenue lasted through most of 1947. Many of the investments financed by the Reconstruction Fund are revenue-producing, but the cessation of new revenue from the sale of relief supplies greatly affected the financial position of the country. In future the government will have to rely exclusively on taxes, profits from its enterprises, and borrowing to defray its outlays.

*New foreign-trade institutions and policies.*—The institutional framework within which Yugoslav foreign trade will work has been completely changed since the interwar period. Foreign trade is under the strict control of the state (decree of March 20, 1945, and ordinance of October 31, 1945). This control is exercised by the Ministry of Foreign Trade through registration of importers and exporters, licensing, price controls, administrative regulation of marketing of essential commodities, and, in conjunction with the Ministry of Finance and the National Bank, exchange controls. To cover the costs of foreign-trade control a tax of 0.5 per cent of the value of all exports and imports is collected. The Ministry must approve the so-called compensation contracts where goods are bartered. The 1925 tariff, increased by a premium of 1,400 per cent, is still in force, but the extent and nature of the administrative controls of foreign trade have greatly reduced its significance.

The system of state corporations for export and import of essential commodities amounts to a virtual state monopoly on foreign trade. The most important pertain to chemicals, mining equipment, transport and forwarding, petroleum, agricultural machinery and tools and implements, timber and tanning materials, leather and textiles, moving pictures, and medical supplies. The General State Trading Corporation (formerly the Chartered State Corporation for the Export of Agricultural Products, or Prizad) is also meant to be a state holding company. Besides, the state owns several corporations for internal trade and some department stores.

The state wishes to control foreign trade in order to adjust it to a general policy of enforced frugality and planned economic development. By concentrating most imports and exports in its own hands it hopes to obtain better terms and achieve greater standardization in exports and imports. Moreover, the state was forced to establish many state corporations for foreign trade for the simple reason that Yugoslav trade before 1941 was controlled mainly by foreigners—Austrians, Germans, and Czechs—who have left the country. The Jewish community of about 80,000, which had been an important factor in the prewar Yugoslav economy, especially in foreign trade, was reduced to only 11,000 by the Germans and the domestic quislings. And, finally, a part of the trading community is considered by the government to be tainted by collaboration.

Yugoslavia introduced an extremely severe control of foreign exchange (law of September 2, 1945, and ordinance of September 21, 1945), which forms an essential link in the control of foreign economic relations. All foreign exchange must be offered to the National Bank, which may or may not—but more probably does—take the whole amount at official rates. No foreign payment can be made without a license from the National Bank. As in prewar days, payments to foreign countries can be made only through duly licensed banks. In view of the stringency in supply of foreign exchange in relation to existing needs, such a foreign-exchange control is unavoidable.

An ordinance of January 18, 1946, prescribed the official rates of the chief foreign currencies, which, in the main, correspond to the rates existing before 1938. The rate of the American dollar was set at D. 50.06, the pound sterling at D. 200, the Swiss franc at D. 10.72. Undoubtedly, these rates do not correspond to the real value of the dinar. The black market in foreign exchange was, however, reduced to a minimum through drastic measures. It is reported that the black-market rate for the dollar fell from D. 300 in December, 1945, to D. 100 in July, 1946.

The overvaluation of the dinar will prove somewhat of an impediment to the export trade. But in a fully controlled economy, in which, moreover, the bulk of exportable goods will come from state-owned enterprises, this situation does not represent the difficulty it would cause in a private-enterprise economy. Losses in export trade can be balanced by profits in import trade. However, intensification of foreign trade will probably necessitate a more realistic adjustment of foreign-exchange rates.

One factor which is already working in this direction is the government's policy of deflation, which, in connection with an increasing supply of goods, has been steadily, if slowly, raising the purchasing power of the dinar. The degree of deflation enforced by the government is perhaps best shown by the fact that the wage level was fixed so low that at the beginning of August, 1945, real wages were only 56 per cent of real wages received at the beginning of August, 1938. Only if one remembers the low prewar wage level in Yugoslavia can one fully appreciate the initial sacrifices involved in this policy.

But the government persisted in a policy of raising real wages by lowering prices rather than by increasing the money wage. Between August, 1945, and August, 1946, the index of real wages rose from 56 to 58, or by about 4 per cent. The index of the cost of living, measured in official prices (August 1, 1938＝100), which stood in August, 1945, at 179, fell to 173 by August, 1946. Measured in free market prices, it fell from 301 in August, 1945, to 189 in August, 1946, which means that the black market was virtually eliminated. One important reason why the cost of living did not increase more in relation to 1938 was the drastic reduction in rents, which in prewar years absorbed 30–50 per cent of the income of large numbers of the urban population. The virtual disappearance of the black market is attributable mainly to its ruthless suppression by government action, the increasing supply of commodities on the market, and the reduced supply of money in the hands of consumers so that there was little demand for goods at prices much higher than those in the controlled markets.

Effective suppression of the black market and the steady rise in the purchasing power of the dinar are two achievements in economic administration of which the Yugoslav government may well be proud. The deflationary pressure has already gone so far, however, that it is beginning to affect unfavorably the part of the country's production which is not directly controlled by the government, namely, a large part of agriculture. The government will have to avoid all monetary and other policies which hamper production.

Adequate discussion of postwar Yugoslav foreign trade is impossible, because no data on the volume, composition, value, and regional distribution of exports and imports have been published. The only available data refer to the period January–September, 1945, and these give only over-all figures on value and tonnages of exports and imports. In this period Yugoslav exports amounted to only 16,000 tons, with a value, at the official rate of exchange, of $4,380,000. In the same period, imports (except those furnished by the Allied military authorities and the U.N.R.R.A.) amounted to 120,770 tons, valued at $12,660,000.

As long as the U.N.R.R.A. operated on a large scale, the country apparently paid little attention to other imports, for it was receiving free from the Administration virtually everything from needles to locomotives. Even less attention was paid to exports, for there were few exportable surpluses during 1945 and 1946. But when it became evident, in the autumn of 1946, that no relief supplies would be forthcoming after the termination of the U.N.R.R.A., Yugoslavia concentrated on its foreign trade.

Foreign commercial efforts of Yugoslavia since the beginning of 1947 have been dictated by one basic consideration: to insure the production targets set forth in the Five-Year Plan. To obtain the necessary imports, especially of machinery and raw materials, trade agreements, based on barter, were concluded with a number of countries. Some are new; others supersede agreements of much narrower scope which were negotiated in 1945 and 1946. The most important of the agreements were made with Russia, Czechoslovakia, Poland, France, Switzerland, Hungary, Egypt, the Netherlands, Finland, Rumania, Bulgaria, Sweden, Italy, and, in August, 1947, with the American-British zone of occupation in Germany. Most of them provide for the import of industrial equipment and raw materials lacking in the country, in exchange for nonferrous ores and metals, iron ore, pyrites, timber, hemp, medicinal herbs, certain chemicals, and some foods, especially fruits. Occasionally, supplementary arrangements are made on an individual commodity, as, for example, with Egypt on cotton and with Hungary on bauxite and aluminum. The elaborate agreement with Sweden includes indemnification for Swedish properties which were nationalized in Yugoslavia.

Thus far, only the agreement with Russia provides for credits to Yugoslavia for purchases in Russia of oil-drilling, chemical, and woodworking machinery, but the amount and other conditions of this credit are not known. The agreement with the American-British zone of occupation in Germany provides for the exchange of goods in the amount of $100,000,000 over a period of four years. Western Germany is to provide machinery in exchange for non-ferrous metals, pyrites, and timber products. This agreement falls in the category of the so-called "offset" agreements concluded between that zone and several other countries, under which outstanding balances for deliveries or services rendered become payable in dollars or pounds sterling after a certain period of time. The first settlement of accounts will be made at the end of one year, and thereafter every three months.

The trade agreements with Russia and those countries within the Russian sphere of influence, which all have developed long-term plans of economic reconstruction or development, are intended to assist the partners in the fulfillment of their respective economic plans.

Some conversations with Great Britain in 1946 in respect to the exchange of goods were without result. The negotiations inaugurated in August, 1947, with special regard to potential exports of food and raw materials from Yugoslavia to England in exchange for industrial equipment, have not yet been concluded. No trade negotiations between the United States and Yugoslavia have been started, and Yugoslavia did not take part in the American-sponsored conference on the International Trade Organization and multilateral reciprocal trade agreements which was held at Geneva in 1947.

Yugoslavia has been engaged during the past year in negotiating a very different type of economic agreement. In December, 1946, the Yugoslav legislature ratified a thirty-year convention on "coördination of economic plans, customs union, and unification of currencies" with Albania. According to an agreement of early August, 1947, a similar arrangement is being prepared with Bulgaria. It will probably be followed by similar agreements with other countries in the Danubian basin. This development seems to have been speeded up since the announcement of the Marshall

Plan, perhaps, in point of timing, as an answer to it on the part of Russia and its neighbors. A gradual political and economic federation of southeastern, eastern, and some central European countries seems to be under way. Such a federation has been advocated many times, but never before did it have favorable political prerequisites and never before was it thought to be guided by the political and economic principles which now animate the governments of these countries.

*Long-term economic development.*—The central economic problem of Yugoslavia for the next two or three decades will be the development of its productive resources in order to improve the standard of living. This problem consists in raising the average productivity per man, per unit of farmland, and per head of livestock. A program of economic development will influence the structure, intensity, and methods of economic relations with the outside world. The government will try to mold its foreign economic policies to make the maximum contribution to the country's economic development. This will be of particular importance for the composition of imports and for the means and methods of stimulating exports so as to provide foreign exchange to pay for the necessary imports. Affected will be price policies in export trade, foreign-exchange rates and controls, the nature of trade agreements, policies on foreign loans, and the hiring of foreign technicians. Moreover, Yugoslav foreign economic relations must operate within the framework of the political and economic situation in the world, and particularly in the countries with which Yugoslavia will maintain intensive trade relations. Thus economic policies will be a compromise between internal and external factors.

Yugoslavia is forced to embark on a program of accelerated economic development because of steadily increasing agrarian overpopulation. How staggering the problem is, can best be seen from the following: if the Yugoslavs want to assure every peasant family (averaging five or six members) of a farm of five hectares of arable land, or one hectare per person, which would enable them to make a decent living, it would be necessary to transfer 3,000,000 to 3,500,000 people, or almost every fourth person, from agriculture to other occupations. Virtually the whole increase in population of about 200,000 annually would have to be absorbed outside agriculture. Since emigration is impossible and birth control could hardly be expected to become a national policy, the solution to the problem of agrarian overpopulation must be found in the country itself, through increased productivity by modernization of agriculture and industrialization.

Even to maintain the standard of living at its prewar level, the national income would have to rise above its prewar volume at an annual rate of 1.3 to 1.5 per cent to balance the rate of population increase. The more-even distribution of national income recently achieved cannot improve the average standard of living, for the basic difficulty lies in the smallness of national income in relation to the size of the population. If current savings and investments are not maximized to provide for growth, a more-even distribution of national income would lead to an increased current consumption and eventually to a lower standard of living.

The rate at which the Yugoslavs will be able to develop their economy will depend on their ability to invest. This, in turn, will depend on their capacity to produce and the volume of current consumption they permit.

Considering the number and the urgency of economic and social problems during the first two postwar years, and the primacy of political issues, it is no wonder that the government was unable to prepare a long-range economic plan until April, 1947. Up to the end of September, 1945, the government put into operation several special programs: sowing and harvesting of crops, repair of transportation facilities, housing repair, and partial rehabilitation of various industrial enterprises. For the fourth quarter of 1945 and for 1946, general industrial production plans were prepared, which were the first attempts at economic planning in Yugoslavia, and which, with the industrial census of 1945, can be taken both as preparatory work and as trials for the launching of the first Five-Year Plan. Moreover, the government created the legal and administrative machinery for a long-term economic plan by establishing a state planning commission under a chairman with the rank of a cabinet member, and by enacting a law on economic planning.

The first inkling of what was to be expected in the coming long-term economic plan in Yugoslavia was given in March, 1946, in the speeches of several cabinet members on the budget for 1946. According to their statements, the country was to modernize its agriculture by increasing the use of machinery, fertilizers, and selected seed, and by improving its animal husbandry. Industrialization was to be pressed by enlarging the raw-material and power basis of the economy by greatly increasing the production of coal, electricity, and oil. Heavy industry was to be especially favored in order to insure further development of the country.

In the words of the chairman of the Federal Planning Commission, A. Hebrang, the Five-Year Plan, as announced in April, 1947, is intended to abolish the economic and technological backwardness of the country, to improve its economic and defensive strength, to enlarge and reinforce the state or socialist sector of the economy, and, finally, to raise the standard of living of the working people. These are the slogans under which the government and its political organizations are mobilizing material and human resources for the fulfillment of the Plan.

The Plan provides for an investment of D. 278,300,000,000 over a period of five years. According to the official dollar-dinar parity, it should be worth $5,500,000,000; but since the purchasing power of the new dinar is internationally much below 2 cents and internally much below its 1939 level, the actual value of this amount is far below its nominal level. Information on the Plan is extremely scanty, but allows some discussion of two basic problems: first, the distribution of the proposed investments among the various branches of the economy, and, second, the targets for increases in the volume of production.

The Plan calls for the following main outlays: D. 30,000,000,000 for electrification; D. 30,000,000,000 for mining and metallurgy; D. 24,000,000,000 for light and food industries; D. 4,500,000,000 for building-material industry; D. 13,400,000,000 for industries furnishing supplies for agriculture, such as fertilizers and machinery; D. 72,600,000,000 for railway, highway, harbor, and other transportation facilities and equipment; D. 37,000,000,000 for housing and urban construction; D. 7,000,000,000 for city improvements; D. 19,400,000,000 for direct investment in agriculture; and the remainder for enlargement and improvement of health, education, and research services.

The preponderance given to industrial investment is striking, especially in electrification and heavy industry. The problem is made far more difficult by the necessity of importing virtually all machinery for the development of these industries. In transportation facilities, rural housing, city improvements, and land reclamation, a preponderance of the investment consists simply of labor, a considerable part of which will be voluntary.

The proposed investment in agriculture is extremely low, but it is explained partly by the fact that the regime puts a much higher priority on industrialization; partly by the fact that investment in agriculture, which is privately owned,[4] cannot be pressed by government action at the same rate as in industry and public utilities; and partly by the fact that basic improvements in agriculture take longer to achieve.

No mention has been made of what portion of the investment proposed by the Plan is to be devoted to military purposes, but it is stated that the Plan, and especially the heavy industry which it aims to develop, will raise the defensive strength of the country.

More revealing than the investment figures mentioned above are the targets for greater physical volume of production. The Plan calls for an increase in production by 1951 over 1939 of coal and coke by 2.5 times, crude oil by 450 times (this would be only perhaps 3 times the top wartime production reportedly achieved by the Germans in Croatia), iron ore 2.5 times, pig iron 5.5 times, steel 3 times, machinery and tools 7 times, electrical appliances 10 times, electric power 4 times, building materials 8 times, chemicals 9 times. The value of handicraft production of goods and services is to be increased by 1.5 times over 1939. The Plan contemplates the construction of 1,800 kilometers of railways, large increases in rolling stock, a merchant marine of 600,000 gross registered tons, and a network of modern highways.

In consumer-goods industries the per-capita production in 1951 is planned to surpass the 1939 production: in sugar by 2 times, lard 1.5 times, edible oil 3 times, processed meat 9 times, pastes (spaghetti and the like) 17 times, canned fish 5.5 times, textiles 2 times, footwear 2.5 times, furniture 4 times. It is implied but not explicitly stated that increased production of consumer goods will be channeled into the domestic consumption, but it should not be forgotten that the country will be forced to increase its exports to the maximum and that part of the exports will consist of protective foods, as it always did, for the simple reason that the domestic population is unable to afford large consumption of such products.

The basic addition in agriculture is the proposed reclamation of about 988,000 acres and the irrigation of another 988,000 acres. The goal set for 1951 is to raise the yield of small grains by 15 per cent, of corn by 20 per cent, and of various industrial crops by 8–30 per cent over those of 1939. Improvements are planned in animal husbandry also. The objective of the Plan is to increase the value of agricultural and livestock production in 1951 by about 52 per cent over 1939. But only 20 per cent of the increase is supposed to result from greater production; the rest is expected to come through improved quality.

In view of the existing difficulties, however, there is little probability that the quality of agricultural and livestock products can be greatly improved within the next five years. Those who are familiar with agricultural technology in Yugoslavia, or, for that matter, in any country of peasant agriculture, know that such improvements require a long time and could result only from large-scale diffusion and application of scientific research, as well as economic incentives to use modern techniques. But in many parts of Yugoslavia the natural conditions are not suitable for revolutionary technical improvements. Moreover, the unsatisfactory ratio between land and the peasant population, which is the basic cause of agricultural backwardness in Yugoslavia, is a factor to be reckoned with, not only at this time but for several decades to come. This precludes marked improvement in the quality of livestock, as competition between the population and livestock for food will remain adverse to livestock.

There is no doubt that the peasantry, owing to sheer preponderance of numbers, will bear the brunt of the burden of planned industrialization, but eventually they will profit thereby, because only through industrialization can the surplus population in agriculture be absorbed into other walks of life and the chief cause of backwardness and poverty be removed.

What are the prospects for the success of the Five-Year Plan? It is obvious that both its general purposes and its specific objectives have been set too high. There is no short cut to an advanced industrial economy combined with a high standard of living. In view of the well-known shortcomings of statistical services in Yugoslavia, the rather scanty knowledge of its economic structure, and the lack of economic planning staffs and managerial experts, many of its goals, and especially their assumed interrelationships, may prove erroneous and require revision. It may be necessary to undertake several five-year plans before the aims set forth in the present one are achieved. At best, it can only lay the foundation for further development. But the current Plan, operating on the trial-and-error method, provides a start in the right direction. It is reported, however, that the first Five-Year Plan has already undergone a major revision because the first half-year targets in certain consumer-goods industries have been overfulfilled, whereas those in some essential producer-goods industries have not been reached.

*Financing of economic development.*—The crux of the problem of economic development in Yugoslavia, as in all undeveloped countries, lies in its financing. Because of the structural undersaving which is characteristic of its economy, domestic savings alone, whatever the degree of frugality imposed by the government, will not suffice to insure the rapid development of productive resources. It is therefore to be hoped that in future the people of Yugoslavia will have the assistance of foreign capital, also, on a mutually advantageous basis. Another source of capital goods from abroad is reparations, although these are intended primarily to help rebuild what was destroyed during the war.

Lack of space permits only a passing reference to the problem of financing the economic development of the country through its own resources. Domestic savings are, of course, the most important and the only definite recurring source of capital on which it can rely with certainty. According to Section IV of the Constitution of the Federal Peoples Republic, of January 31, 1946, Yugoslav economy consists of a state-owned or socialist sector, a coöperative sector tied closely to the state sector, and a private-enterprise sector under the control of the state.

The state-owned sector was greatly enlarged in 1945 and 1946 as the result of expropriation of the property of collaborators and former enemies, and of the policy of taxing war profits which often resulted in the state's participation in taxpayers' property. The process of socialization of industry was completed by the Nationalization Act of December 5, 1946, which brought into government ownership virtually all enterprises in forty-two specified branches of industry, wholesale trade, banking, and transportation. The Act covers foreign-owned firms also. The law stipulates that former owners are to be indemnified in government bonds or, in certain instances, in cash. Although it is not expressly stated, the latter procedure may perhaps be intended for foreign-owned enterprises.

It should be pointed out, however, that public ownership in Yugoslavia was already widespread before 1941, and that socialization only continued a trend of long standing, though under totally different guiding principles. In 1940 the Yugoslav state owned the following production and service facilities: the railroads (a few privately owned lines were leased to and operated by the state), all telegraph and telephone lines and radio stations, the canals, a large share of river shipping and storage facilities, and all processing and wholesale trade facilities for tobacco, cigarette paper, matches, and salt. It owned large stretches of forests and some leading lumber mills, the single existing cellulose factory, several large farms, the chief pig-iron and steel-producing plants in the country, a large number of coal mines, all the arsenals, most of the aircraft assembly and producing plants, several sugar factories, and a few hotels; it had a part interest in several shipyards, a zinc factory, and a chrome-ore mine. It owned and operated some large publishing enterprises, the only news agency of the country, almost all the stage theaters and opera companies, and most of the hospitals. Virtually all schools were state schools. Moreover, the state owned and operated a large part of the country's banking. To this property owned by the central government should be added property owned and operated by local governments, especially municipalities, which included urban transport, waterworks, and most of the gas and power plants. Savings banks of local governments and municipalities were an important segment in banking.

The basic reason for widespread public ownership was the prevailing scarcity of capital. The state alone was capable of obtaining large-scale credits for investment in fields where prospective profits were low and thus unattractive to both domestic and foreign investors, or where investments were not self-sustaining and had to be continually subsidized from the general revenue of the state. Insufficiency of entrepreneurial spirit and lack of managerial experience contributed also to this development.

In the Yugoslav economy as it is now constituted, the rate of savings and investment from a given national income will depend on state decisions, for the state owns virtually all production, trade, and banking facilities except agriculture, and closely controls that part of the economy which it does not own. Private capital formation is almost wholly excluded, except on a negligible scale in handicrafts and agriculture. In agriculture, savings will depend on taxation policies regarding agricultural income and price policies regarding products which farmers sell and buy. Taxation and price policies are to form an organic unity. The backbone of the tax system and the chief instrument of capital formation in government hands will be, to an increasingly greater degree, the general turnover tax collected as part of the price of goods and services (a turnover tax was introduced in Yugoslavia for the first time in 1922).

To coördinate and centralize credit functions and to make them an integral part of the economic developmental effort, the banking system was reorganized in September, 1946, grouped around two chief government banks: the National Bank of Yugoslavia, which is the bank of issue and the source of short-term credit, and the State Investment Bank, the chief source of long-term credit. The nationalization of banking was completed through the Nationalization Act of December, 1946.

For a number of years, at least, the state will probably push the rate of savings and investments as far as it considers politically workable, with little consideration of the immediate economic and social sacrifices imposed on the population. This conclusion is borne out by the Five-Year Plan announced in April, 1947. One thing, however, should be kept in mind. If an accelerated development of the economy is to be achieved, there is no escape from the fact that, even with ample help from abroad, the utmost frugality must remain the cornerstone of economic policy for a long time to come. Only thus could the increase in productive capacity outstrip the increase in population and insure an eventual rise in the standard of living. The principle of frugality should be applied especially with regard to unproductive state outlays. The most important of these are for military purposes, and construction for display, including luxury urban residential construction.

It seems to the author that the present regime in Yugoslavia should be able, because of the changed political and institutional framework of capital formation, to apply an appreciably higher portion of a given national income to investment than was possible before the war. But equally important is the fact that domestic capital formation, if the state so decides, could be directed so as to insure the optimum contribution to economic growth.

*Reparations.*—In view of the great plundering and destruction during the war, Yugoslavia submitted large restitution and reparation claims against the Axis Powers and their satellites. Except for Germany, the amounts of reparations to be paid by former enemy countries of Europe were agreed upon. Hungary is to pay a total of $300,000,000 over a period of eight years, of which $70,000,000 will go to Yugoslavia. Deliveries of petroleum products and coal started in 1946.

Article IX of the Bulgarian armistice agreement provided that the Bulgarian government would restore to Yugoslavia (as to the other Allies) all property taken during the war, and would make such reparation for losses and damages "as may be determined later." The protocol provided that some deliveries of foodstuffs on account of reparations would have to be made immediately to Yugoslavia and Greece for relief purposes. Bulgaria delivered some coal to Yugoslavia in 1945 and 1946. The peace treaty with Bulgaria provides for that country to pay for reparations a total of $70,000,000, in kind, over a period of eight years. The Yugoslav share amounts to $25,000,000, but according to a special Yugoslav-Bulgarian agreement of early August, 1947, Yugoslavia renounced its share of Bulgarian reparations.

Yugoslavia submitted to the Peace Conference in Paris a reparation claim of $1,300,000,000 from Italy, but obtained only $125,000,000 of Italy's reparation obligation of $360,000,000. Italy must pay this debt over a seven-year period, beginning two years after the conclusion of the peace treaty.

The greatest reparation claims were made by Yugoslavia against

Germany, amounting to $11,000,000,000. The Interallied Reparation Agency in Brussels allocated to Yugoslavia 9.6 per cent of all reparation payments from Category B, which refers to capital equipment, including merchant ships and means of inland water transport, to be removed from Germany. Moreover, Yugoslavia is to receive 6.6 per cent from German payments out of Category A, German assets abroad. Yugoslavia asked, however, that a part of the reparation bill presented against Germany be paid by Austria.

As was the situation in the 1920's, the Yugoslavs are interested almost exclusively in capital goods and industrial raw materials as reparation payments. They count heavily on reparation deliveries for their economic reconstruction, and there is no doubt that reparation receipts could again play an important role in that respect.

*Import of foreign capital.*—The problem of new foreign loans for Yugoslavia is an important and extremely complicated one. The present government has accepted in principle all the obligations of the old state. The pre-1941 public debts will probably have to be adjusted to the actual capacity to pay and to transfer interest and amortization. Even before the war it was clear that current interest and amortization on the foreign public debt were too high in relation to the country's ability to pay and to transfer the service funds. Since 1932 Yugoslavia has discharged only a small part of its foreign obligations. Some of the foreign-owned government bonds—those payable in dinars—had to be registered by the end of June, 1947, with the Yugoslav Ministry of Finance for conversion into 3 per cent thirty-year bonds on the basis of ten prewar dinars for one present dinar. But foreign-held bonds represent only a small share of the total Yugoslav foreign debt, and conversion will not contribute much toward easing the burden.

Direct foreign investments in mining, industry, transportation, and banking present an altogether different issue. Some have been expropriated by the government as enemy property, with occasional disputes (e.g., the Bor copper mines) arising from the definition of "enemy property." Conversations were held in 1945 and 1946 between representatives of the Yugoslav government and some of the leading foreign-owned enterprises regarding their future status. The Nationalization Act of December, 1946, affecting virtually all foreign-owned enterprises in the country, will probably make it impossible to delay much longer the solution of such problems. But only the indemnity for formerly Swedish-owned property has thus far been agreed upon. Negotiations with the British concerning their properties in Yugoslavia, including the Trepča mines, were renewed in the spring of 1947, but the outcome is not known.

The problem of American property in Yugoslavia is on the agenda of formal negotiations which opened between representatives of the two governments in Washington, D.C., on May 19, 1947. The negotiations include other outstanding financial questions between the two countries, especially the lend-lease settlement and the release of Yugoslav gold holdings, amounting to about $47,000,000, in the United States.

In 1946 the Yugoslav government explored informally the possibilities of obtaining loans for developmental purposes from private firms in the United States and probably in some other countries. It is not surprising that no formal loan negotiations have yet been undertaken. Even if the political relations between Yugoslavia and its most important potential creditors were cordial (which is not the case), prospects for new loans on purely business bases are slight indeed, so long as the fate of the old foreign investments in the country remains unsettled. It is clear that the Yugoslavs need the assistance of foreign capital, but the present regime shows, publicly, no concern about foreign loans. On the contrary, the chief spokesmen on the Five-Year Plan scoffed at those who consider the execution of the Plan impossible without the assistance of foreign capital, but added that the country may encounter difficulty in obtaining the necessary machinery from abroad.

Before the passage of the Nationalization Act, opinions among some Yugoslavs about foreign loans, if and when available, were somewhat as follows:

1. No concessions of the prewar type would be granted to foreign investors in mining, industry, or other fields of economic activity.

2. In view of the fact that the state owns all natural resources suitable for development by foreign capital (minerals, forests, water power), and facilities in such basic services as transportation and public utilities, the loans would have to be taken either by the

government or by state enterprises. Enterprises of the "fifty-fifty" type are not regarded with favor.

3. Foreign capital would not be allowed to develop the production of raw materials only, as was usually true before 1941, but would also be pressed into developing enterprises producing semi-finished and finished products.

4. It was considered essential that a large part of the production of most enterprises financed by foreign capital be exported, preferably to creditor countries, in order to insure outlets for the production of these enterprises and service on borrowed capital.

5. Finally, investments financed by foreign capital would have to form an organic part of the general plan for economic development of the country.

The question of potential foreign loans for Yugoslavia is, under present conditions, more of a political than an economic issue. Only the United States and a few European countries (e.g., Switzerland and Sweden) are now in a position to export capital, and it may take several years before political conditions become propitious for extensive loan operations. Soviet Russia granted a loan to Yugoslavia in 1946, but exclusively for military purposes. The Russian-Yugoslav trade agreement of July, 1947, regulating the exchange of goods between the two countries for the next two years, provides for Russian credits to Yugoslavia for the purchase of machinery for the metal, oil, chemical, and timber industries. No details on the amount and condition of these credits are known. The International Bank for Reconstruction and Development, which would be a logical source of developmental loans for Yugoslavia, is getting under way very slowly. On January 7, 1948, Yugoslavia applied for a loan of $500,000,000 from the Bank, but was asked to submit additional information before the application could be considered.

*Skilled labor.*—Besides lack of capital, there is another bottleneck in Yugoslavia's economic development which may prove extremely difficult and expensive to overcome, namely, the scarcity of planning and managerial technicians and of skilled labor. The Five-Year Plan calls for an increase in the number of industrial workers by about 170,000, which is double the 1947 industrial labor force; 60,000 skilled technicians, or seven times as many as in 1947; and an additional 20,000 skilled technicians and managers with college education. The government considers the procurement of this labor force, rather than the financing or even the import of the necessary machinery, as the chief hurdle in the execution of the Plan. To develop skilled technicians and workers will take years. The cost of the trial-and-error method which is now being applied, and which will have to be continued for some time, is proving very high. The Yugoslavs may therefore seek to employ some foreign technicians. But again, as in capital goods, the supply of many types of specialists is scarce in the countries with which Yugoslavia maintains its closest political and economic relations.

One factor to which the government pays great attention is the psychological mobilization and exhortation of workers to attain the maximum production. In this, as in most other respects, it follows the example of the Soviet Union.

This chapter covers the Yugoslav economic developments and foreign economic problems since 1941 on the basis of the available data. But the data, especially on foreign trade, are lacking and the reliability of much of the other information is limited. Yugoslavia is now known as a country divulging less economic and statistical information than perhaps any other in Europe. Doubtless it is trying feverishly to master its short and long-run economic problems, and has developed a tremendous *élan* for work. Of course, part of the population is mobilized for work under political and social pressure.

In the treatment of economic problems the country follows a well-known Yugoslav folk proverb—"A bad wound requires drastic surgery." It has the distinction of maintaining perhaps the strictest money, wages, and price controls in Europe and the strictest punishments for their infraction. But speaking economically, this policy seems to have paid good dividends so far.

Needless to say, several years must elapse before valid judgments can be made on the wisdom and success of many current economic policies. Their proof, from the economic point of view, will be in their effect on the standard of living of the great majority of the Yugoslav population. It must be repeatedly stressed, however, that the basic prerequisite for the success of all long-term economic policies in Yugoslavia is the maintenance of a durable and wholesome peace, with intensive and mutually advantageous international economic relations, so that the country may concentrate all its potential energies on the task of economic and cultural development. In the true Biblical sense, bread is the staff of life in Yugoslavia, and, without peace, not all its people can have bread.

## Part Eight

# EPILOGUE

# CHAPTER XXII

# *Epilogue*

## BY ROBERT J. KERNER

YUGOSLAVIA was the scene of much desperate fighting and very extensive devastation during the Second World War. As a people, the Yugoslavs suffered serious losses at the hands of their German, Italian, Hungarian, and Bulgarian invaders, who unscrupulously incited Slovenes, Croats, and Serbs; Catholics, Orthodox, and Mohammedans; Ustaši, Četnici, and Partisans; and bourgeois and common man against each other. In the midst of it all, the Communists initiated a social revolution producing further chaos and class and religious difficulties in postwar Yugoslavia.

From 1944, when Great Britain and the United States decided to assist Marshal Tito's Partisans and then withdrew their support from General Mihailović's Četnici, to the promulgation of the Constitution of the Federal Peoples Republic of Yugoslavia (January 31, 1946), the policy of the Communist party became dominant in the country step by step.

It was in this period that the monarchy was abolished and the republic proclaimed, and that one by one prominent non-Communists from abroad, who had joined the Communist leaders in the national liberation of their people, or who had remained at home, were politically eliminated. The original basis of the previous political framework—that of the three ethnic groups, Serb, Croat, and Slovene—had been abandoned, and a new combination was arranged, consisting of six units: Croatia, Serbia, Slovenia, Bosnia and Hercegovina, Montenegro, and Macedonia. The Serbian nationalists charged that the purpose of the territorial arrangement was to deprive the Serbs of their rightful place in Yugoslav politics in view of their greater numbers and to give the political preponderance to the Croats. The continuing role of the secret police (O.Z.N.A.), and the legislation which had been enacted, made it obvious that Yugoslavia's political administration and internal economy had taken the road toward that evolved in the Soviet Union. The adoption of the Five-Year Plan by the National Assembly, on April 28, 1947, was a concrete indication of this trend. It called for an investment of $5,500,000,000, and its objective was announced by Marshal Tito as the attainment of economic independence on a socialistic basis.

In the same period a series of alliances with the Soviet Union, Poland, Czechoslovakia, Bulgaria, and Albania marked the formal inclusion of Yugoslavia in the orbit of the Soviet Union. A recent manifestation was to be seen in the renewed discussions and agreements which envisage the preliminary outlines of a Balkan or southeast European federation under the aegis of the Soviet Union. These discussions took it for granted that the bases of the federation will be Yugoslavia and Bulgaria. Marshal Tito and Premier Dimitrov of Bulgaria, long prominent in the direction of the Third International, were expected to play leading roles in these developments when Moscow finally gave the signal.

These trends, so long and clearly discernible, could not but cause disappointment in British and American circles. The policies of Britain and of the United States were necessarily and decisively affected. Primarily, however, their policies toward Yugoslavia were determined by what the Soviet Union did in world politics and world economics, because it played the dominant role in Yugoslav internal and foreign policy. This is the cardinal fact in any analysis of the events which characterized the making of peace and hence of boundaries for Yugoslavia after the Second World War.

The future historian will someday be able, it is hoped, to write in copious detail an impartial and adequate account of Soviet foreign policy. Until the necessary materials from all sides are available, only obviously pertinent observations on major trends are possible.

Assuredly there were elements in Soviet policy which stressed security of national and vital interests. They involved more secure frontiers and friendly states as neighbors. These prerequisites to peace both Britain and the United States indicated they were willing to underwrite and, in fact, did so in large measure. In time, however, it became evident that the policy of the Soviet Union and actions of Communist parties abroad had begun to evolve beyond the agreements at Yalta and later conferences, and beyond the obvious and normal requirements of Russian security based on national and vital interests. In the face of this developing situation, the policies of Britain and the United States stiffened in order to prevent the abuse of their former willingness to build peace on the basis indicated, for there could be no peace if one of the Great Powers used as its basis a policy of world revolution or one which was calculated to bring it about openly or under cover. Yugoslavia's claims to boundary changes and reparations from Italy and Austria aroused increasing anxiety on the part of the other Great Powers in regard to the aims of the Soviet Union's foreign policy, particularly in the Balkans, the Near and Middle East, and the eastern Mediterranean, the point of stress being the Turkish Straits.

Regardless of their form of government, whether monarchical or republican, bourgeois or communist, the Yugoslav people would have claimed Trieste from Italy, for that port on the Adriatic was the only harbor easily accessible from the greater part of Yugoslavia. It is, in fact, the culmination of the Yugoslav urge to the sea. Behind it lie centuries of yearning and decades of arrested economic development of the hinterland.

In Italy's possession (1918–1944), Trieste was actually a white elephant from an economic and financial point of view. For the Yugoslavs it was the symbol of their oppression at the hands of Italians before and under Mussolini. In the possession of the Yugoslavs, with free port privileges to hinterland states, and special arrangements for the Italian population, it would lead to extensive economic development for their country and for other states whose commerce naturally would flow through Trieste into the Mediterranean. There is every reason to believe that, with the normal development which has taken place elsewhere in the world around seaports, the people from the countryside (in the case of Trieste overwhelmingly Yugoslav) would have made it a predominantly Yugoslav city within a generation or two, if unhindered by treaty restrictions and foreign rule. The attempt to solve the problem of

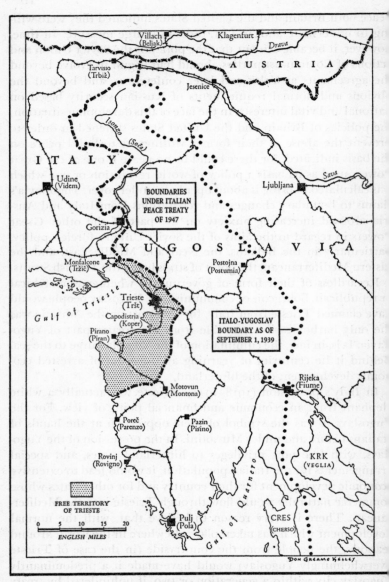

**Italo-Yugoslav Boundaries**

Within the map:

AUSTRIA

Villach (Beljak)

Klagenfurt

Drava

Tarvisio (Trbiž)

Jesenice

I T A L Y

Isonzo (Soča)

Sava

Udine (Videm)

**BOUNDARIES UNDER ITALIAN PEACE TREATY OF 1947**

Ljubljana

Gorizia

Y U G O S L A V I A

Monfalcone (Tržič)

Postojna (Postumia)

Gulf of Trieste

Trieste (Trst)

Capodistria (Koper)

**ITALO-YUGOSLAV BOUNDARY AS OF SEPTEMBER 1, 1939**

Pirano (Piran)

Motovun (Montona)

Poreč (Parenzo)

Pazin (Pisino)

Rovinj (Rovigno)

Rijeka (Fiume)

KRK (VEGLIA)

FREE TERRITORY OF TRIESTE

0  5  10  15  20
ENGLISH MILES

Pulj (Pola)

CRES (CHERSO)

Gulf of Quarnero

DON GREAME KELLEY

Fiume in a somewhat similar fashion in 1919–1924 failed. The loud voices raised in that period in behalf of the temporary Italian plurality in Fiume have been forgotten. Fiume is now wholly within the Yugoslav state, as it should have been in 1919.

There is reason, also, to believe that Trieste was tentatively promised by the British to the Royal Yugoslav Government in 1941, before the rise of the Communists in Yugoslavia. In the long and acrimonious negotiations among the United States, Britain, and the Soviet Union, joined later by France, Communist-controlled Yugoslavia was denied Trieste.

It was decided at the Conference of Paris on September 28, 1946, to create the International Free Territory of Trieste under the United Nations on the basis of a line proposed by the French, a compromise between the British and American lines to the east and the Soviet and Yugoslav lines to the west (which would have given Trieste to Yugoslavia and free port privileges to hinterland states). The drawing of the frontier between Italy and Yugoslavia farther to the north, until it reached the one between Austria and Yugoslavia, was along lines more favorable to Italy than to Yugoslavia, if ethnic and economic (and even geographic) factors are taken into account. Because the Moscow Conference of Foreign Ministers, held in March–April, 1947, was unable to make progress on the German and Austrian peace treaties, the final frontier between Austria and Yugoslavia was left undetermined.

In the midst of the tension leading to the decision on Trieste occurred the tragic and unnecessary attack (August 19, 1946) by Yugoslav airmen upon an American airplane. Five American lives were lost when the plane was shot down. The incident resulted in an ultimatum to the government of Yugoslavia, which agreed to comply with the terms of the ultimatum and to pay indemnities. This grossly impolitic act, carried out under the responsibility of the Yugoslav government, alienated public opinion in other countries and especially in the United States.

The Balkan Inquiry Commission of the United Nations reported on May 23, 1947, that Yugoslavia, and to a lesser degree Bulgaria and Albania, supported the guerrilla uprising against the Greek government. This activity had been one of the reasons for the promulgation of the Truman Doctrine on March 12.

After the consideration of the Marshall Plan was initiated in the summer of 1947, the Cominform was organized under the auspices of the Russian Communist party, and Belgrade was designated the headquarters for its bureau. The immediate objectives of this organization were to block the European Recovery Program and to win Italy and France for the Communists.

After Yugoslav and Italian Communists had negotiated fruitlessly behind the scenes in regard to Trieste in 1947, and it was rumored that the Soviet Union would advocate placing the Free Territory of Trieste under the sovereignty of Italy, the governments of the United States, Great Britain, and France, on March 20, 1948, publicly notified the Soviet Union that they favored this arrangement. Thus the three Powers sought to obtain an advantage for Italian nationalist parties over the Communists in the critical Italian elections scheduled for April 18. The parties opposed to the Communists won.

On June 28 came the publication of the Cominform Resolution condemning the leadership of the Yugoslav Communist party and calling upon "sound elements" within it "to force their present party leaders to confess their faults openly and honestly and correct them . . . or, if unable to do this task, to change them." This sensational turn of events was initiated by the Central Committee of the Russian (All-Union) Communist Party (Bolshevik) in a letter, dated March 20, to the Yugoslav Communist party, and other letters to the central committees of the seven other Communist parties in the Cominform. The latter were not sent to that of Yugoslavia. The substance of the correspondence was obviously a command from the Moscow Politburo to the other politburos to join in demanding that Marshal Tito, Vice-Premier Edvard Kardelj Propaganda Chief Milovan Djilas, and Minister of Interior Colonel General Aleksandar Ranković of Yugoslavia recant or resign

Numerous reasons were stated for this extraordinary action which revealed the character of the imperialistic and world revolutionary policy of the Kremlin toward its satellites. Here only the most important among them can be given. The leadership of the Yugoslav Communist party practiced "a hateful policy in relation to the Soviet Union" and to the Russian Communist party and identified "the foreign policy of Soviet Russia with that of the im perialistic Powers." It conducted a "slanderous propaganda, borrowed from the arsenals of counter-revolutionary Trotskyism about the degeneration" of the Russian Communist party and of the Soviet Union. It had slipped off the "Marx-Lenin path" of the theory of class and class struggle "to the nationalist, kulak road in the question [of the role] of the working class, because they believed that peasants are the firmest basis of the Yugoslav state," whereas the working class should lead the revolution. It subordinated the Yugoslav Communist party to the People's (or National) Front with its bourgeois elements, when it should be the "leading basic power." The Resolution accused the leaders of "a shameful, purely Turkish terroristic regime" within the party and charged that they were "affected by exaggerated ambition, megalomania, and conceit" in declining to accept criticism and to correct their faults. Refusing to imitate the radical steps taken by Soviet Russia thoroughly to uproot the individual economy of Yugoslavia which must inevitably give "birth to capitalism," they suddenly made pretense of doing so. This was "adventurous and non-Marxist." "The experiences of the Russian Communist party prove that only on the basis of mass collectivization of agriculture is the liquidation of the last and most numerous exploiting class, the kulaks, possible and that the liquidation of the kulak as a class is an integral part of the collectivization of agriculture." To do this successfully, the party must carry out carefully prepared preliminary work so as to achieve the transition from restrictions on the capitalist elements to their liquidation.

The Cominform was operated "on the incontestable principle that every party had to settle accounts of its activity before the Information Bureau and that every party had the right to criticize other parties." The Yugoslav Communist party violated this principle of equal right by criticizing other parties, while refusing to allow itself to be criticized. They, therefore, "passed to secession from a united socialistic front against imperialism and took the way of betrayal of the international solidarity of the working masses" toward nationalism. The Yugoslav leaders thought that a series of concessions to imperialistic states whom they feared would save the independence of Yugoslavia and orient it toward capitalism, considering them less dangerous than the Soviet Union.

It is obvious from this that the Communist rulers of Yugoslavia had not obeyed the commands emanating from Moscow on foreign and internal policy. Besides what has already been made public, Moscow and Belgrade probably did not see eye to eye on the Austro-Yugoslav boundary, Trieste, Albania, Macedonia, Salonika, and the Greek problem.

Instead of recanting or resigning, the Yugoslav rulers issued on June 29 a scorching rebuttal of the Cominform Resolution. Their communiqué denied all the charges and made some accusations on its own account, not sparing the Russian Communist party or the Soviet Union along with the others. It pointed out that the Cominform gave no proof for its accusations and took no trouble to verify the facts. It charged that "the Soviet intelligence service ruthlessly tried to enlist [Yugoslavs]" in a country ruled by Communists marching toward socialism and called this "an impermissible relationship, [which] leads to the demoralization of the citizens of Yugoslavia. It weakens and undermines state and party executives." Using such words as "insults," "monstrous," "ridiculous," "unworthy," "absurd," "serious slanders" in reply to the accusations of the Cominform, the Yugoslav leaders declared that "their party, their working class, and working masses of the Yugoslav peoples in general, as well as their selfless and heroic struggle, had been dealt the grossest historical injustice." "The Information Bureau," it asserted, "not only presses the leaders of the Communist party in Yugoslavia to confess mistakes which they did not make, but invites members of the party to revolt in the party to break up the party's unity."

One by one the central committees of the Communist parties of the Cominform led by the Russians and many others, including those of the United States, Great Britain, China, Albania, and Austria, supported the Cominform Resolution against the Yugoslav Communist party's rebuttal. On July 2 an appeal went forth from Belgrade to Premier Joseph Stalin to "do all to remove the unjust accusations flung at our party, our country, and our Central Committee." Proclaiming "the unshatterable brotherhood between the Soviet Union and Yugoslavia," it ended with the words: "Long live your teacher of love toward the Soviet Union, Comrade Tito! And long live our great friend, Stalin!"

Milovan Djilas, in a defense of the position of the Yugoslav Communist party leadership on July 5, argued that "as far as the isolation of Yugoslavia is considered, that question does not depend upon the position taken by the Cominform or on the propaganda of other Communist parties against the Yugoslav Communist party," but "on Yugoslavia herself. . . . We do not feel isolated because we are convinced that the Soviet Union will not and cannot abandon Yugoslavia in her relations with the imperialists." A common fate bound all the "socialist countries" and "it would be strange if the other socialist countries were to force Yugoslavia to prove that she can or cannot build socialism herself." Comparing the Yugoslav with other Communist parties, he asserted, "Any other party except the [Russian] Bolshevik party would have disintegrated in every struggle forced upon our party." He stressed in substance a basis of agreement among the members of the Cominform when he argued for coöperation that (1) took into account the particular conditions and traditions of each participating country; (2) based itself on voluntary agreements and mutual confidence; and (3) was achieved through discussion. The implication is clear. The Yugoslav Communists rejected the principle of compulsion apparently resorted to by the Cominform.*

The Yugoslav intimation to Bulgaria and Albania for the creation of a Balkan bloc fell on deaf ears and the relations of these Soviet satellites with Yugoslavia became strained. The Yugoslav Communist party invited all Communist parties to attend its fifth Party Congress at Belgrade on July 21. This invitation was declined by the Communist parties. It became evident that the Yugoslav Communist party had been read out of the circle of Communist parties, although its leaders loudly proclaimed they remained loyal Communists. It had been isolated. On the other hand, for the time being at least, the relations between the governments of the states concerned, with the exception of Albania, remained normal on the surface.

For better or for worse, the Yugoslav people, willingly or unwillingly, have embarked under Communist control on a road that is new both to themselves and to their neighbors on the west.

---

* This account terminates on July 14, 1948, when the volume was sent to the press.

Whether they will arrive at peace and prosperity in this direction remains to be seen. On their side they have youth, vigor, and hardihood, and a country with considerable resources. As a people they have cultural potentialities of a high order in art and literature, in science and technology. Only the future will reveal how well they recovered from the holocaust of the Second World War and survived the ordeal of building a new society.

## Part Nine

# CHRONOLOGY

# Historical Evolution: A Chronology

## BY HARRY N. HOWARD

### I. THE BEGINNINGS OF THE SOUTH SLAVS

| | |
|---|---|
| A.D. 330 . . . . . | Dedication of Constantinople (Tsarigrad) by the Emperor Constantine. |
| 500 ff. (518–527) . . | First historical record of crossing of Danube by Slavs. |
| 584–642 . . . . . | Kurt (Kubrat), first authenticated ruler of Bulgarians, who were first mentioned by name in 482. |
| 610–650 ff. . . . . | Serbs begin to appear in Balkan Peninsula. Part of Slavs go as far as Carniola and Carinthia. Slovenes, conquered early in ninth century by Franks, become part of German Empire. |
| 818 . . . . . . | Croats, conquered by Franks, revolt and are subdued. |
| 852–889 . . . . . | Boris I of the Bulgars. Suffers defeat from Serbs in 860. |
| 863–885 . . . . . | Missionary activity of St. Cyril and St. Methodius, apostles to the Slavs. In 885 the Slavonic liturgy is introduced among Bulgarian Slavs and thence over the peninsula. |
| 867–886 . . . . . | Reign of Basil of Macedon and beginning of Macedonian dynasty in eastern empire. |
| 924 . . . . . . | Tomislav, crowned by Pope John X, becomes King of Croatia. Reigns over Croatia south to Montenegro. |
| 925 . . . . . . | Tsar Simeon of Bulgaria proclaims himself Tsar of Romans and Bulgars. |
| 926 . . . . . . | Tsar Simeon conquers and devastates Serbia. |
| 960 . . . . . . | Death of Časlav, who made first attempt to unify Serbs. |
| 976–1014 . . . . | Tsar Samuel of Bulgaria. Expansion of domain to Sofia and reëstablishment of patriarchate at Ohrid, center of new state. |
| 976–1025 . . . . | Reign of Basil II the Bulgar-Slayer, direct descendant of Basil of Macedon. |
| 976–1025 . . . . | Reign of Tsar Samuel over Bulgars. |
| 1018 . . . . . . | Basil II destroys Bulgarian kingdom. |
| 1077 . . . . . . | Michael of Serbia crowned by papal legate of Gregory VII. |

1081–1101  . . . .  Serbian state established in the Zeta (Montenegro) by Bodin.

1102  . . . . . .  After defeat of King Peter by King Ladislas of Hungary, Croatia chooses King Koloman of Hungary as sovereign. He swears to maintain autonomous political institutions of Croatia and governs country through a ban.

1168–1196  . . . .  Stephen Nemanja, founder of the dynasty in Serbia proper, or Rascia, as Grand Župan adopts Greek Orthodox faith, establishes independence from Constantinople, and conquers lands in south. Retires to Mount Athos as a monk in 1196.

1196–1223  . . . .  Stephen II Nemanja the First-Crowned, son of founder. Conflict with brother Vukan of Montenegro. Becomes ruler of Serbia proper, crowned in 1217 by papal legate of Pope Honorius III, but in 1222 is recrowned with a crown from Nicaea by St. Sava, who was recognized as Archbishop of Serbia in 1219.

1204  . . . . . .  Constantinople taken in Fourth Crusade.

1223–1234  . . . .  Reign of Radoslav, son of Stephen.

1234–1242  . . . .  Reign of Vladislav, who deposes his brother Radoslav; marries daughter of Tsar John Asen of Bulgaria. Much of Serbia under powerful Bulgarian influence.

1242–1276  . . . .  Reign of Uroš I, third son of Stephen the First-Crowned, marries daughter of Baldwin II, deposes emperor of Constantinople, enters alliance with Charles of Anjou, Latin claimant to Constantinople.

1254  . . . . . .  Magyars establish sovereignty over Bosnia and Hercegovina.

1261  . . . . . .  Constantinople retaken by Michael VIII (Palaeologus).

1276–1282  . . . .  Reign of Dragutin, elder son of Uroš.

1282–1321  . . . .  Reign of Milutin (Stephen II Uroš), younger son of Uroš, extends rule into Macedonia, to Adriatic, and toward Danube and Sava rivers.

1321–1331  . . . .  Reign of Milutin's son, Stephen III Uroš (Stephen Dečanski), is marked by victory over Greeks and Bulgars near Küstendil, 1330. Serbs control most of Vardar River Valley.

1331–1355  . . . .  Reign of Stephen Dušan the Mighty, Stephen IV Uroš, greatest of medieval Serbian rulers. By 1344 Dušan has conquered Macedonia, Albania, Thessaly, and Epirus. Bulgaria under Serbian domination.

1346  . . . . . .  Dušan sets up capital at Skoplje and proclaims himself Emperor of Serbs, Greeks, Bulgars, and Albanians. Serbian patriarchate established at Ipek (Peć).

1349–1354 . . . . Dušan formulates the famous *Zakonik* (Code of Laws), comparable to great codes of West. Attack on Bosnia in 1349 not completed.

1353 . . . . . . Louis of Hungary defeated; Serbs acquire Belgrade, later to become capital.

1355 . . . . . . Death of Dušan, at age of forty-six, on way to Constantinople.

1355–1371 . . . . Reign of Stephen V Uroš, last of House of Nemanja.

1358 . . . . . . Hungary defeats Venice, seizes most of Dalmatian coast; Ragusa becomes Hungarian protectorate.

1371 . . . . . . Battle of the Maritsa. Turkish victory over Serbs.

1371–1389 . . . . Reign of Lazar I (Hrebeljanović family) .

1371–1421 . . . . Montenegro becomes principality under Balša family.

1375 . . . . . . Greek patriarch at Constantinople recognizes Serbian patriarchate of Ipek (Peć).

1376 . . . . . . Tvrtko I (1353–1391) of Bosnia proclaims himself King of Serbia and Bosnia, takes portions of western Serbia, controls most of Adriatic littoral except Zara and Ragusa.

1389 June 20 . . Battle of Kosovo Polje (Field of the Blackbirds). Serbs and others under Lazar are defeated by Turks under Sultan Murad I. Serbs become vassals of Ottoman Empire. "And our souls shall be cleansed of sin, and our land of the stranger, and a king shall rule once more on the throne of Dušan, and Serbia's sun, that hath gone down in darkness, shall rise again, flooding the heavens and earth with golden light! Dear God, send swiftly thy long-promised day!" Ida Zeitlin and Theodore Nadejen, *King's Pleasure* (New York, 1929), p. 227.

1389–1427 . . . . Stephen Lazarević, son of Lazar I, is recognized as Despot of Serbia because of services to Turks.

1392 . . . . . . Durazzo passes into Venetian hands, as does Scutari in 1396 and Cattaro (Kotor) in 1420.

1393 . . . . . . Hungary recovers Croatia and Dalmatian region from disintegrating Bosnian kingdom.

1427–1456 . . . . George Branković is Despot of Serbia.

1456–1458 . . . . Lazar III, son of George Branković, is Despot.

1458–1459 . . . . Stephen Tomašević, heir to Bosnian throne. As a Roman Catholic, is disliked by Orthodox Serbs.

1459 . . . . . . Serbia is completely conquered by Turks and taken into Ottoman Empire.

1463 . . . . . . Bosnia is conquered by Turks.

1483 . . . . . . Hercegovina is conquered by Turks.

1499 . . . . . . Montenegro is conquered by Turks.

## II. The South Slavs under the Ottomans and the Habsburgs

1450–1524 . . . . Marko Marulić, Serb nobleman of Spalato (Split). First to write language spoken by the people.

1480–1525 . . . . Hannibal Lučić, writer of lyrics and the play *Robinja* (The Slave), oldest drama in Serb literature.

1487–1572 . . . . Petar Hektorović, Dalmatian poet. Used Serbian language.

1492 . . . . . . First South Slav printing press founded by Djordje Crnojević, Vojvod of the Zeta (Montenegro).

1520–1566 . . . . Reign of Sultan Suleiman the Magnificent.

1521 . . . . . . Capture of Belgrade by Turks.

1589–1638 . . . . Ivan Gundulić, poet and dramatist of Dalmatia.

1607 . . . . . . Faculty of Theology established at Zagreb by the Jesuits.

1662 . . . . . . Jesuits establish Faculty of Philosophy at Zagreb.

1678 . . . . . . First printing press at Ljubljana, Slovenia.

1688 . . . . . . Austrians take Belgrade; later Vidin (1689).

1690 . . . . . . Ottoman forces drive Austrians out of Belgrade, Serbia, and Transylvania. Many Serbs flee into the Vojvodina.

1699 Jan. 26 . . Treaty of Karlowitz (Karlovac). Among other things, Austria receives Hungary (except the Banat of Temišvar), Transylvania, Croatia, and Slavonia. Venice obtains Morea and most of Dalmatian coast. Peter the Great postpones Balkan liberation.

Ca. 1702–1760 . . Andrija Kačić-Miošić, philosopher, historian, and poet. In 1756 he publishes, in Venice, *Razgovor ugodni naroda slovinskoga* (Pleasant Chat about the Slavic People), a collection of 261 folk songs of Serbs, Croats, and Bulgars.

1711–1787 . . . . Rudjer Josip Bošković, author of seventy works in Latin and Italian on physics, mathematics, meteorology, philosophy.

1716 Aug. 5 . . . Eugene of Savoy wins victory of Peterwardein (Petrovaradin), capturing Belgrade in 1717.

1718 July 21 . . . Treaty of Passarowitz (Požarevac). Turks lose the Banat of Temišvar, northern Serbia, and Little Walachia, but retain the Morea.

1726–1801 . . . . Jovan Rajić, author of *History of the Bulgars, Croats, and Serbs* (1794).

1739 Sept. 18 . . Treaty of Belgrade. Austria surrenders northern Serbia, with Belgrade.

Ca. 1742–1811 . . Dositej Obradović, priest, born at Čakovo in the Banat. Studies at Halle and Leipzig, visits in Paris and London. Philosopher, scientist, and educator, most learned Serb of day. First Minister of Education, 1809; founder of first *velika škola* (high school) in Belgrade.

1747–1819 . . . . Baron Žiga Zois. Introduced rationalism into Slovenia.

1768 . . . . . . *Slaveno-Serpski Magazin* founded by Zaharija Orfelin in Venice.

1776 . . . . . . Royal Academy of Sciences (Regia Academia Scientiarum), with faculties of theology, jurisprudence, and philosophy, is founded at Zagreb. (See 1607, 1622.) Separation of Faculty of Theology from Academy in 1784.

1780–1841 . . . . Jernej Kopitar, distinguished Slovene philologist and folklorist, collaborator with Karadžić in Vienna.

1782–1830 . . . . Peter I, Vladika, or Prince-Bishop, of Montenegro, ally of Russia against Turks.

1787–1864 . . . . Vuk Stefanović Karadžić, born at Tršić, western Serbia. Distinguished philologist and forklorist, collector of songs, dictionaries, grammars, laws. In 1814 publishes *Slaveno Serpska pjesnarica* (National Serbian Book of Songs); followed by *Ženske pjesme* (Women's Songs), *Junačke pjesme* (Songs of Heroes); and *Pismenica Serpskago jezika* (Vienna), first Serbian grammar; in 1818, *Lexicon serbico-germanico-latinum* (Vienna), first Serbian dictionary. He reforms the alphabet, his ideal being to "write as you speak, speak as you write." Karadžić later helps to codify Serbian laws.

1789 . . . . . . Austrians retake Belgrade from Turks.

1789 June 3 . . . Publication of *Kroatischer Korrespondent*.

1790 . . . . . . Professors' council of Royal Academy of Sciences at Zagreb requests Faculty of Medicine; petitions that Academy be raised to level of a university for all Yugoslavs, thus developing idea of Yugoslav national union. (See 1874.)

1791 March 3 . . Markides Pulja, Greek patriot, publisher of *Efemeris*, publishes *Serpskija Povsednevnija Novini*, a newspaper.

Aug. 4 . . . Under pressure from Prussia, Austria makes Treaty of Sistova (Svištov), returning Belgrade to Turkey, retaining northern Bosnia.

1792 Dec. 30 . . . Stevan Novaković publishes *Slaveno-Serpskija Vjedomosti*.

1799 . . . . . . Sultan Selim III recognizes independence of Montenegro.

1804 Feb. . . . . Serbian revolt against Turks is led by George Petrović, or Karageorge Petrović (supreme chief, 1804–1813). Janizaries ousted in December, 1806; supreme command of forces made hereditary in Karageorgević family in 1808.

1805  Dec. 26  . . .  Treaty of Pressburg (Bratislava). Among other things, Austria recognizes Napoleon as King of Italy and cedes Venetian Istria and Dalmatia to Italy.

1806–1856  . . . .  Jovan Popović, poet and dramatist.

1808  . . . . . .  Founding of school at Belgrade; *velika škola,* 1810.

1809  Oct. 14  . . .  Treaty of Schönbrunn. Austria cedes to France all lands beyond Sava River (Villach, Istria, Hungarian Dalmatia, and Ragusa), which, together with Ionian Islands, Napoleon organizes into Illyrian Provinces under General Marmont, Duke of Ragusa.

1809–1872  . . . .  Ljudevit Gaj, founder of Illyrian movement. First to give thought of national unity a solid basis with a program and a journal. Prepares system of Croat-Slav orthography (1830); publishes the review *Danica* (1836).

1810  . . . . . .  Lycée of Ljubljana, central school, out of which university later grew. Founding of Societas Slovenica (Graz).

1811–1870  . . . .  Dimitrije Demetar, Croatian poet and dramatist.

1812  . . . . . .  Teachers College, St. Andre, in the Vojvodina, transferred to Sombor; gymnasium at Novi Sad, 1816; seminary at Vršac, 1820.

1813  . . . . . .  Turks defeat army of Karageorge Petrović, who takes refuge in Hungary.

1813  . . . . . .  *Novine Srpske* founded by Dimitrije Davidović, Vienna. Ceased publication in 1822.

1813–1851  . . . .  Petar Petrović Njegoš, born at Njeguši, Montenegro. Last Prince-Bishop of Montenegro (1830–1851); distinguished poet and philosopher whose most remarkable work is *Gorski vijenac* (Mountain Wreath).

1815–1817  . . . .  Second revolt of Serbs against Turks under leadership of Miloš Obrenović. On his return in 1817 Karageorge Petrović is murdered, beginning the Obrenović-Karageorgević feud.

1815–1905  . . . .  Joseph George Strossmayer, distinguished Croatian bishop. Founder of South Slavic Academy at Zagreb 1867, and of University of Zagreb, 1874. Foe of doctrine of papal infallibility.

1817  . . . . . .  Miloš Obrenović becomes hereditary Prince of Serbia; pashalik of Belgrade attains measure of autonomy.

1818–1872  . . . .  Petar Preradović. Gave Yugoslav and Pan-Slav ideas their most powerful expression.

1821–1830  . . . .  Greek revolt against Ottoman Empire.

1824–1853  . . . .  Branko Radičević, romantic poet of the Vojvodina.

1825  . . . . . .  *Letopis Matice Srpske,* Budapest and Novi Sad.

1829  Sept. 14  . .  Treaty of Adrianople. Serbia is promised autonomy, with religious liberty.

1830 . . . . . . Beginnings of public instruction, Belgrade. Gymnasium, 1831; seminary, 1836; lycée, 1844; superior school, 1863.

1830 Aug. 3 . . . Miloš Obrenović invested by Sultan Mahmud as heredi-tary Prince of Serbia; entire internal administration entrusted to him; Turkish landlords to sell holdings; Turkish troops confined to a few garrisons.

1830–1851 . . . . Peter II (Petar Petrović Njegoš), Prince-Bishop of Monte-negro.

1831 . . . . . . National press founded at Belgrade.

1833–1904 . . . . Jovan Jovanović Zmaj, director of review *Javor*, distin-guished poet and writer.

1834 Jan. 5 . . . *Novine Srpske* published in Serbia by Davidović. On January 22, 1882, it becomes official journal; after 1919, official journal of Kingdom of Serbs, Croats, and Slo-venes; after October 3, 1929, official journal of King-dom of Yugoslavia.

1835 . . . . . . Ljudevit Gaj founds *Novine Hrvatske;* in 1839, *Danica Hrvatska, Slavonska i Dalmatinska,* which at first took title of *Ilirske Narodne Novine* and later (1836), *Danica Ilirska. Novine Hrvatske* becomes *Narodne Novine* in 1857.

Gaj founds a theater at Zagreb.

Todor Pavlović begins publication at Budapest of *Srpske Narodne Novine,* which becomes principal organ of Serbs under Hungarian domination. Ceased publica-tion in 1849.

1835 Feb. 2 . . . Miloš Obrenović opens Skupština, promising constitu-tion with Bill of Rights insuring personal liberty and property rights of Serbs.

1838 . . . . . . With support of Imperial Russia, sultan forces annul-ment of Constitution of 1835; grants charter providing for appointment of Soviet, or Senate, of Notables and limits powers of prince.

Serb theater founded at Kragujevac under patronage of Prince Miloš.

Theater established at Novi Sad; closed in 1848.

Lyceum opened at Kragujevac. Later moved to Belgrade, where, in 1863, it became high school (*velika škola*) and, in 1905, University of Belgrade.

1839 June 13 . . . Abdication of Prince Miloš.

Ascent to throne of Prince Milan (son of Miloš), who dies a few weeks later.

1839–1842 . . . . Reign of Prince Michael Obrenović, son of Miloš. In-trigues with Karageorgević family demand calling of Skupština. Michael is forced to leave in 1842.

1840 . . . . . . Theaters founded at Zagreb, Karlovac, Varaždin, Sisak.

1841 . . . . . . Jovan Sterija-Popović founds theater at Belgrade which becomes permanent in 1860; founds Society of Serbian Letters, origin of future Academy of Sciences.

1842 . . . . . . Illyrian Hive, Zagreb.

1842–1858 . . . . Reign of Alexander Karageorgević, elected by Skupština. Spread of Western ideas, growth of commerce, development of education.

1843 . . . . . . Founding of *Novice*, Ljubljana, under direction of Vitez Bleiweiss. Ceased publication in 1903.

1844 . . . . . . Founding of Zora Dalmatinska at Zara.
Beginnings of University of Belgrade.
Ilija Garašanin, Serbian Minister of Foreign Affairs, presents his *Načertanije*, demanding Serbian policy free from Austria and Russia, based on unity of Serbs, Croats, and Bulgarians.

1845–1926 . . . . Nikola Pašić, Serbian statesman. Elected to Skupština, 1878; exile, 1883–1889; mayor of Belgrade, 1889; Premier of Serbia, 1891; Minister to St. Petersburg, 1893; sentenced to nine months' imprisonment for *lèse-majesté;* Minister of Foreign Affairs in Grujić cabinet, 1904; Premier, 1904–1905, 1906–1908; Minister of Public Works in Novaković cabinet, 1909; Premier, 1910–1911, 1912–1918; president of delegation of Serb-Croat-Slovene state at Paris Peace Conference, 1919; Premier of Yugoslavia, 1921–1926.

1847 . . . . . . Founding of press at Novi Sad under Danilo Medaković.

1848   March 15 . . Croats organize National Committee seeking separation from Hungary and autonomy.

       May 13 . . . Croat National Assembly meets at Karlovac.

1848–1850 . . . . Revolutions in central Europe, Austrian Empire, and the Germanies.
Founding of Zagreb *Slovenski Jug, Südslawische Zeitung, Agramer Zeitung.*

1849 . . . . . . Founding of *Pravi Slovenec,* Ljubljana. Ceased publication in 1869.

1850 . . . . . . Founding of *Katolički List,* Zagreb. Ceased publication in 1860.

1851–1860 . . . . Danilo I of Montenegro. Abolishes office of prince-bishop, becomes first secular ruler. Murdered on August 12, 1860, because of opposition to policy of secularization.

1852–1853 . . . . Turkish invasion of Montenegro under Omer Pasha; forced to withdraw, February, 1853, because of Austrian opposition.

1856   March 30 . . Treaty of Paris ends Crimean War (1853–1856). Principality of Serbia is placed under guaranty of European Powers.

1858   Dec. 23 . . . Alexander Karageorgević expelled by opposition, which was supported by Obrenović family and Ottoman and Russian governments.

1858–1860 . . . . Reign of Miloš Obrenović, who is restored to throne. Dies in 1860.

1860[–1868] . . . Return to throne of Michael Obrenović, son of Miloš. An intelligent statesman, Michael aims at uniting Balkans against Turks. Series of treaties (1867–1868) among Serbia, Montenegro, Rumania, Bulgaria, and Greece, known as "Program of Political Relations of the Serbo-Bulgars, or Bulgar-Serbs, or Their Entente Cordiale," envisages reconstructed Serbo-Bulgarian, or Yugoslav, state in alliance with other Balkan countries.

1860–1918 . . . . Nicholas I, Prince and King of Montenegro, modernizes state.

1860 . . . . . . Beginning of national schools in Dalmatia.

1861 . . . . . . Following revolt in Hercegovina, Omer Pasha invades Montenegro, compels recognition of Turkish influence.

1861 . . . . . . Founding of Serbian journal *Vidovdan* under Prince Michael. Ceased publication in 1876.

1862   June 15 . . After Turkish bombardment of Belgrade, sultan is required to reduce forces to three or four Serbian localities.

1866 . . . . . . Founding of Dalmatian Hive at Zara.

Founding of journal *Zastava*, Budapest; moved to Novi Sad, 1867; calls for union and equality of South Slavs.

Sept. 23 . . Serbo-Montenegrin secret alliance against Turks.

1867 . . . . . . Prince Michael requests withdrawal of all Turkish troops; Sultan Abdul-Aziz accedes in April.

May 26 . . . Serbo-Rumanian secret understanding with view to mutual independence from Ottoman rule.

Aug. 26 . . . Serbo-Greek alliance: Serbia to obtain Bosnia and Hercegovina, Greece to have Thessaly and Epirus. War with Turkey to follow in 1868. Final aim is some sort of Balkan federation.

Founding of South Slavic Academy at Zagreb by Bishop Strossmayer (July 28). Franjo Rački is first president.

Founding of Omladina (United Serbian Youth); advocates union and independence of South Slavs.

Founding of *Slovenski Gospodar* at Maribor.

Instruction in Slovenian permitted in primary schools.

1868  June 10   . .   Assassination of Prince Michael by elements aiming at
                      Karageorgević restoration. Temporary elimination of
                      dream of Balkan federation.

1868–1889  . . . .    Reign of Milan Obrenović begins with more or less lib-
                      eral revision of constitution in 1869. Constitution only
                      thinly veiled autocracy; remains in effect until 1889.

1872  Aug. 22   . .   Milan Obrenović becomes of age, assumes control of
                      government.

1874  Jan. 5  . . .   University of Zagreb founded. It was proposed to Sabor
                      by Bishop Strossmayer in 1861 and by Sabor in 1869
                      to Francis Joseph, who agreed to proposal. Delay
                      brought another appeal by Sabor in 1873.

1875–1878  . . . .    Balkan and Near Eastern crisis, beginning in July, 1875;
                      revolt in Bosnia spreads to Bulgaria, involves Monte-
                      negro and Serbia, brings Russia into war with Otto-
                      man Empire (1877–1878).

1876  July 1  . . .   Prince Milan of Serbia declares war on Turkey, followed
                      on July 2 by Montenegro. Serbs are soon defeated by
                      Turks; "peace" is concluded on March 1, 1877.

1876–1877  Dec., 1876–
           Jan., 1877  Conference of Constantinople to initiate reforms within
                      Ottoman Empire. Proclamation of Ottoman constitu-
                      tion, December 23, 1876.

1877  April 24  . .   Beginning of Russo-Turkish War.
      Dec. 14   . .   Serbs reënter war against Ottoman Empire as allies of
                      Russia.

1878  March 3   . .   Treaty of San Stefano between Russia and Turkey gives
                      independence to Serbia, Montenegro, and Rumania.
                      Serbia is given considerable territory, including Niš
                      and Little Zvornik. Southwestern frontier is so drawn
                      that it almost touches eastern boundary of Monte-
                      negro. Montenegro is more than trebled in size and
                      doubled in population, receiving Nikšić, Bileća, Gacko,
                      in Hercegovina; Spizza (Spič), Antivari (Bar), Dulcigno
                      (Ulcinj), on the Adriatic; Spuž; Podgorica; Plav; Gu-
                      sinje; the medieval Montenegrin capital of Žabljak;
                      and Prijepolje, in the Sanjak of Novi Pazar.

      July 13  . . .   Treaty of Berlin revises Treaty of San Stefano. Serbian
                      independence recognized completely by European
                      Powers, though Article 25 gives Bosnia-Hercegovina
                      and military occupation of Sanjak of Novi Pazar to
                      Austria-Hungary. Bulgaria is given autonomy under
                      sultan and divided into Eastern Rumelia and Bulgaria
                      proper.

1879  Oct. 7  . . .   Austro-German alliance designed especially against Rus-
                      sia and France.

### III. The Period of Serbian Independence

1880   June–Nov.   .   Montenegro attempts unsuccessfully to take over Albanian territory granted by Treaty of Berlin. Montenegro subsequently given Dulcigno (Ulcinj).

1881   June 18   . .   Alliance of Three Emperors (*Dreikaiserbund*), composed of Austria, Germany, and Russia. Among other things, Austria-Hungary reserves right to annex Bosnia-Hercegovina at fitting moment; eventual union of Bulgaria and Eastern Rumelia not to be opposed.

      June 28   . .   Austro-Serbian agreement makes Serbia virtual protectorate of Austria. Serbia not to permit anti-Austrian intrigues, and to enter no political agreement without Austrian consent. Austria to support Serbian aspirations to the south (i.e., in Macedonia), and to recognize Milan as king. Grave protests from Serbian patriots against policy of King Milan.

1882   March 6   . .   Milan of Serbia proclaims himself King of Serbia.

      May 20   . . .   Formation of Triple Alliance, with Italy joining Austria-Hungary and Germany.

1883   Oct. 30   . . .   Rumania enters alliance with Austria.

      Nov.     . . .   Nikola Pašić, leader of Serbian Radical party, in revolt against King Milan's government. (See 1845.)

1883–1889  . . . .   Nikola Pašić in exile.

1885   Sept. 18   . .   Revolt in Eastern Rumelia looking toward union with Bulgaria.

      Nov. 13   . .   Serbian declaration of war on Bulgaria.

      Nov. 17   . .   Terrible defeat of Serbs at Battle of Slivnica.

      Nov. 27   . .   Another defeat of Serbs at Pirot and invasion of Serbia is ended by intervention of Austria-Hungary.

1886   March 3   . .   Treaty of Bucharest between Serbia and Bulgaria restores peace on basis of *status quo ante bellum*.

1887   Feb. 12   . . .   Mediterranean agreement between Great Britain and Italy, to which Austria-Hungary adheres on March 24 and Spain on May 4, looking toward preservation of *status quo* in Mediterranean, Adriatic, Aegean, and Black seas.

      Feb. 20   . . .   Renewal of Triple Alliance among Germany, Austria-Hungary, and Italy. Austro-Hungarian–Italian arrangement stipulates *status quo* in East, but if upset, principle of compensation to apply, though not to possible Austrian annexation of Bosnia-Hercegovina.

      June 18   . .   Russo-German Treaty of Reinsurance, lasting until 1890. Two Powers to observe *status quo* in Balkans, with Russia's influence in Bulgaria recognized. Principle of closure of Straits to warships is upheld.

1887 Dec. 12 . . . Second Mediterranean agreement of Great Britain, Austria-Hungary, and Italy.

1888 Aug. . . . King Milan of Serbia divorces Natalia, Russian wife. Growing antagonism between pro-Russian and pro-Austrian elements in Serbia.

Dec. 16 . . . Serbian Radical party (Pašić) wins victory in national elections.

1889 Jan. 3 . . . Serbian Skupština enacts more liberal revision of Serbian constitution.

March 6 . . King Milan is forced to abdicate throne of Serbia.

1889–1903 . . . . Reign of Alexander I Obrenović, son of King Milan. Ascends throne at age of thirteen. Establishment of regency under Jovan Ristić.

1891–1894 . . . . Foundations of Franco-Russian alliance; finally concluded in diplomatic exchanges of December 27, 1893, and January 4, 1894.

1893 April 14 . . Abolition of regency of Jovan Ristić through *coup d'état* of King Alexander.

1894 May 21 . . . Constitution of 1869 is restored to Serbia.

1897 April 17 . . Outbreak of Greco-Turkish War.

May . . . . Austro-Russian "agreement" on *status quo* in Balkans.

1899 Aug. 5 . . . Marriage of King Alexander to Draga Mashin, which, together with pro-Austrian policy and persecution of Radical party, leads to opposition.

1901 Feb. 11 . . . Death of former King Milan of Serbia.

1903 Feb. . . . . Austro-Russian reform program for Macedonia calls for mixed Christian-Moslem gendarmerie, foreign officers, reorganization of financial and tax systems.

June 10 . . Assassination of King Alexander, Queen Draga, and their entourage.

June 15 . . Skupština selects Peter Karageorgević as King of Serbia, restores Constitution of 1889.

Oct. 2 . . . Mürzsteg program for Macedonian reform.

1903–1921 . . . . Reign of Peter I.

1904 April 8 . . . Anglo-French Entente Cordiale.

1904–1905 Dec., 1904– May, 1905 Cabinet of Nikola Pašić, anti-Austrian, pro-Russian.

1905 . . . . . . *Velika škola* becomes University of Belgrade.

Dec.19 . . . Prince Nicholas of Montenegro grants constitution, with Assembly elected by general suffrage.

1905–1907 . . . . Bitter tariff war with Austria-Hungary, sometimes known as "pig war."

1906–1908 May, 1906– July, 1908 Cabinet of Nikola Pašić.

1907 Aug. 31 . . Anglo-Russian understanding.

1908 Oct. 5 . . . Bulgarian declaration of independence.

1908   Oct. 6   . . .   Bosnian crisis is produced by Autro-Hungarian annexation of Bosnia-Hercegovina.

1909   March 21   . .   Germany demands that Russia abandon support of Serbs and recognize abolition of Article 25 of Treaty of Berlin, with annexation of Bosnia-Hercegovina.

       March 31   . .   Serbian recognition of Austrian annexation of Bosnia-Hercegovina.

1910   March 3   . .   Beginning of famous Agram (Zagreb) treason trial in Croatia.

       Aug. 28   . .   Prince Nicholas of Montenegro becomes king.

       Dec. 9   . . .   Beginning of trial of Heinrich Friedjung, an outgrowth of Agram treason trial.

1910–1911   . . . .   Cabinet of Nikola Pašić.

1911   Sept. 29   . .   Italy declares war on Turkey.

1911–1912   . . . .   Turko-Italian War.

1912   March 13   . .   Treaty of alliance between Bulgaria and Serbia guarantees independence and integrity. Macedonia to be partitioned between them.

       May 29   . . .   Alliance between Bulgaria and Greece.

       Oct. 17   . . .   Outbreak of First Balkan War.

       Dec. 17   . .   Opening of London Conference to attempt settlement of Balkan War.

1912–1918   . . . .   Nikola Pašić is Premier of Serbia.

1913   Jan. 6   . . .   Breakdown of London Conference.

       Feb. 3   . . .   Continuation of hostilities.

       April 10   . .   Blockade of Montenegrin coast at Scutari.

       April 22   . .   Capture of Scutari by Montenegrins.

       May 3   . . .   Montenegro gives up Scutari under threat of war by Austria.

       May 5   . . .   Serbs give up port of Durazzo.

       May 30   . . .   Treaty of London ends First Balkan War.

       June 1   . . .   Serbo-Greek treaty of alliance against Bulgaria.

       June 29   . .   Outbreak of Second Balkan War as result of Bulgarian attack on Serbo-Greek forces in Macedonia.

       July 10   . . .   Rumanian declaration of war on Bulgaria.

       Aug. 10   . .   Treaty of Bucharest. Serbia and Greece divide Macedonia. Bulgaria loses Monastir (Bitolj) and Ohrid to Serbia, Salonika and Kavalla to Greece.

       Sept. 23   . .   Serbian invasion of Albania.

       Oct. 18   . . .   Austrian ultimatum to Serbia demands evacuation of Albania in eight days. Serbs surrender.

1914   March 15   . .   Memorandum prepared by Count Stephen Tisza, Hungarian Premier, urges support of Balkan union of Rumania, Bulgaria, Greece, and Turkey to eliminate Serbia as political factor in Balkans.

1914 June 24 . . This memorandum, known as May Memorandum, no
revised by Austrian Foreign Office.

Prince Alexander, heir to Serbian throne, is made reger
of kingdom.

June 28 . . Assassination of Archduke Francis Ferdinand at Sarajev

July 5 . . . Germany offers "blank check" to Austria against Serbi

July 7 . . . Crown Council in Vienna; majority favors war on Serbi

July 13 . . . Baron von Wiesner unable to find evidence of Serbia
official complicity in assassination. Participation
Black Hand evident.

July 14 . . . Crown Council in Vienna decides for war, Tisza appro
ing if no Serbian territory is annexed.

July 23 . . . Austrian ultimatum to Serbia, with forty-eight-hou
time limit.

July 25 . . . Serbian reply to ultimatum accepts most demands b
rejects Austrian participation in investigation and tri
of accused on Serbian soil. Offer to arbitrate befor
Hague Tribunal.

July 28 . . . Austrian declaration of war on Serbia. Outbreak of wa

## IV. SERBIA IN THE WORLD WAR (1914–1918): THE MOVEMENT TOWARD SOUTH SLAVIC UNITY

1914 July 29 . . . Austrian bombardment of Belgrade.

Aug. 5 . . . Montenegro declares war on Austria.

Dec. 2 . . . . Austrians take Belgrade.

Dec. 7 . . . Declaration of Serbian government to Serbian Nation
Assembly at Niš: "Firmly convinced of the resolutio
of the entire Serbian nation to persevere in the hol
war for the defense of its sacred soil and liberty, th
Royal Government, in these painful moments, co
siders as its principal and sole task to assure the fin
success of this great struggle, which, from its begir
ning, has assumed the exclusive character of a war fc
the liberation and union of all our Serbian, Croatia
and Slovene brothers enslaved by foreign domination.

1915 May 7 . . . Allied Powers give Serbia conditional promise of acquis
tion of Bosnia-Hercegovina and access to Adriatic,
concessions are made to Bulgaria in Macedonia.

May 15 . . . Yugoslav Committee declares to French government th
"the Serbs, Croats, and Slovenes are one and the sam
people and are fulfilling all the conditions demande
for the constitution of an independent state."

Sept. 6 . . . Bulgaria makes secret alliance with Germany an
Austria-Hungary to attack Serbia within thirty day

Oct. 6 . . . Beginning of Austro-German drive against Serbia.

1915  Oct. 9 . . .  Bulgaria begins invasion of Serbia. Belgrade falls October 9; Skoplje, October 28; Niš, November 5. Serbian army retreats through Albania; finds refuge at Corfu.

1916  Aug. 2–21 . .  Battle of Dojran. Beginning of Allied offensive against Bulgaria on Salonika front.

Aug. 30 . .  Venizelist revolt against Greek government.

Oct. 5–Dec. 11  Allied offensive under General Sarrail toward Monastir and Lake Ohrid.

1917  March 11–19 .  Second Battle of Monastir.

May 5–19 . .  Battle of the Vardar.

May 30 . . .  Yugoslav group in Austrian parliament makes declaration favoring freedom and union, formulated by Anton Korošec (Slovene leader), and Laginja (Croat leader).

June 5 . . .  Croat Peasant party in Croatian Diet pronounces in favor of independence and unity of South Slavs.

July 20 . . .  Pact of Corfu. Representatives of Serbian kingdom, Yugoslav Committee of London, Croats, Slovenes, and Montenegrins pronounce themselves one nation under scepter of Karageorgević dynasty.

1918  Jan. 8 . . .  Fourteen Points address of President Wilson. Point 10 calls for "the freest opportunity of autonomous development" of the peoples of Austria-Hungary. Point 11: "Rumania, Serbia, and Montenegro should be evacuated, occupied territories restored, Serbia accorded free and secure access to the sea, and the relations of the several Balkan States to one another determined by friendly counsel along historically established lines of allegiance and nationality, and international guaranties of the political and economic independence and territorial integrity of the several Balkan States should be entered into."

April 10 . .  Congress of Oppressed Nationalities at Rome, composed of Italians, Poles, Rumanians, Czechoslovaks, and Yugoslavs, agrees: (1) Each people proclaims right to set up its own national state; (2) each recognizes Austro-Hungarian Empire as agency of German domination and as obstacle to realization of national rights; (3) Congress recognizes necessity of common struggle until each people has attained liberation and national unity; (4) Yugoslav nation is recognized as of vital interest to Italy and vice versa; (5) liberation of Adriatic Sea and defense are of vital concern to Yugoslavs and Italians; (6) Italians and Yugoslavs to settle frontier problems in friendly manner on basis of nationality; (7) mutual toleration and full rights promised to minorities.

1918 April 21 . . Italian recognition of Czechoslovak National Council as *de facto* government.

May 29 . . . American expression of sympathy for Czechoslovak and Yugoslav people in their struggle for independence.

June 3 . . . Allied declarations support national aims of Yugoslavs, together with Poles and Czechoslovaks.

Sept. 30 . . Bulgarian forces surrender; armistice is signed.

Oct. 29 . . . Yugoslav National Council at Zagreb (Agram) proclaims independence and union of Yugoslavs.

Nov. 1 . . . Serbian troops enter Belgrade.

Nov. 3 . . . Armistice with Austria-Hungary.

Nov. 7 . . . Yugoslav conference at Geneva declares for union of Croatia and Slovenia with Serbia and Montenegro.

Nov. 9 . . . Publication of Geneva Declaration by representatives of Kingdom of Serbia, political groups of Skupština, Yugoslav Committee of London, National Council of Zagreb, proclaiming their resolution on unification of Serbs, Croats, and Slovenes.

Nov. 11 . . Armistice with Germany.

Nov. 24 . . Formal proclamation of Kingdom of Serbs, Croats, and Slovenes at Zagreb, with King Peter as sovereign, Prince Alexander as regent.

Nov. 26 . . Montenegrin National Assembly at Podgorica proclaims union of Montenegro with Serbia and other branches of Yugoslav people.

Dec. 1 . . . Deposition of King Nicholas of Montenegro.
Prince Alexander accepts regency of Kingdom of Serbs, Croats, and Slovenes.

Dec. 4 . . . Kingdom of Serbs, Croats, and Slovenes comes formally into being.

## V. THE KINGDOM OF THE SERBS, CROATS, AND SLOVENES (1918–1929)

1919 Feb. . . . . Controversy with Italy over Fiume and Dalmatian coast.

June 13 . . Decision of Peace Conference divides Banat of Temišvar between Rumania and Kingdom of Serbs, Croats, and Slovenes.

June 28 . . Signing of Treaty of Versailles with Germany.

Sept. 10 . . Treaty of St. Germain with Austria recognizes independence of Czechoslovakia, Poland, Hungary, and Yugoslavia.

Sept. 12 . . D'Annunzio expedition into Fiume.

Nov. 27 . . . Treaty of Neuilly with Bulgaria recognizes independence of Yugoslavia.

1920   June 4 . . .   Treaty of Trianon with Hungary recognizes independence of Yugoslavia and cedes Croatia-Slavonia and part of Banat of Temišvar to Yugoslavia.

     Aug. 14 . .   Convention of alliance between Kingdom of Serbs, Croats, and Slovenes and Czechoslovak Republic at Belgrade. Beginnings of Little Entente.

     Oct. 10 . . .   Austro-Yugoslav plebiscite in Klagenfurt area decided in favor of Austria.

     Nov. 12 . .   Italo-Yugoslav Treaty of Rapallo concerning problem of Fiume.

     Nov. 28 . .   Constituent Assembly elections. Croatian delegates, under Stjepan Radić, reject participation, demand federal structure. Pašić Radical party dominates Assembly.

1921   Jan. 1 . . .   Vidovdan Constitution is formulated; proclamation on June 28, 1921. Provides for centralized, unitary, constitutional monarchy under House of Karageorgević.

     April 23 . .   Rumania and Czechoslovakia sign alliance.

     June 7 . . .   Rumania and Yugoslavia sign alliance providing for cooperation in upholding treaties of Trianon and Neuilly against Hungary and Bulgaria, and resistance to unprovoked aggression.

     Aug. 16 . .   Death of King Peter; ascent of King Alexander to throne.

1921–1934 . . .   Reign of King Alexander I Karageorgević.

1922   Aug. 31 . .   Five-year treaty of alliance between Czechoslovakia and Rumania.

1923   March 18 . .   National elections. Croat deputies under Radić in opposition, refusing to take part in Skupština.

     Sept. 6 . . .   Birth of Prince Peter, who, on October 9, 1934, becomes King Peter II.

1924   Jan. 25 . . .   Franco-Czechoslovak treaty of alliance. Mutual consultation on problems of postwar European settlement; common action against Habsburg restoration; common action to maintain Austrian independence.

     June 27 . .   Italo-Yugoslav five-year treaty of friendship after "settlement" of Fiume question.

     July 18 . . .   Resignation of Nikola Pašić cabinet following resumption of parliamentary activity of Croats under Stjepan Radić. Reconstruction of Pašić cabinet.

     Dec. 24 . . .   Outlawry of Croatian Peasant party; Radić imprisoned.

1925   July 18 . . .   Radić freed from prison, enters cabinet as Minister of Education.

     Oct. 16 . . .   Arbitration treaties between Germany and Poland, Germany and Czechoslovakia, at Locarno.

1926   April 1 . . .   Resignation of Radić and Croatian Peasant group from cabinet.

1926  June 13  . . .  Czechoslovakia and Rumania renew treaty of alliance within Little Entente.

      Aug. 17   . .  Greco-Yugoslav treaty solves problem of free zone for Yugoslavia at Salonika.

      Dec. 1  . . .  Death of Nikola Pašić.

1927  June    . . .  Breaking of relations between Albania and Yugoslavia after frontier incidents. Relations restored in July.

      Nov. 11   . .  Franco-Yugoslav treaty of friendship outlines support of European postwar system. Mutual support is promised in case of attack. Follows models of Franco-Czechoslovak treaty of January 25, 1924; Franco-Rumanian treaty of June 10, 1926; Italo-Albanian agreement of November 27, 1926.

1928  June 20   . .  Riot in Belgrade Skupština; Stjepan Radić is shot by Radical deputy, dies August 8. Withdrawal of Croatian Peasant party deputies from Skupština.

      Aug. 1  . . .  Demand of Croatian Peasant party for federal constitutional structure. Establishment of a Croat "parliament" at Zagreb.

      Aug. 27   . .  Signature of Kellogg-Briand Pact at Paris by various governments, including that of Kingdom of Serbs, Croats, and Slovenes.

1929  Jan. 6  . . .  King Alexander proclaims royal dictatorship and new constitution. Skupština dissolved, government control centralized under personal rule of king.

      Jan. 21  . . .  Dissolution of all political parties.

      Feb. 17  . . .  Establishment of National Legislative Council with advisory powers to replace Skupština.

      March 27  . .  Treaty of amity with Greece.

      May 22  . . .  Arrest of Vladimir Maček, leader of Croatian Peasant party, following murder of Radić.

      June    . . .  Frontier incidents on Bulgaro-Yugoslav border in Macedonia carried on by Macedonian Revolutionary Organization (I.M.R.O.).


## VI. The Kingdom of Yugoslavia (1929–1939)

1929  Oct. 3   . . .  Name of Kingdom of Serbs, Croats, and Slovenes becomes officially Kingdom of Yugoslavia. Nine new districts (banovine) are established in place of old historic divisions: (1) Drava (capital, Ljubljana); (2) Drina (Sarajevo); (3) Dunav, or Danube (Novi Sad); (4) Morava (Niš); (5) Primorje (Split); (6) Sava (Zagreb); (7) Vardar (Skoplje); (8) Vrbas (Banjaluka); (9) Zeta (Cetinje); and the prefecture of Belgrade.

1930   Oct. 5–12   .   .   First Balkan Conference, Athens, attended by unofficial delegations from Albania, Yugoslavia, Bulgaria, Rumania, Greece, and Turkey.

1931   Sept. 3   .   .   .   King Alexander announces end of royal dictatorship, proclaims new constitution concentrating executive power in person of king, exercised through ministers; premier named by king. Legislative power placed in bicameral legislature composed of Senate and Chamber of Deputies; king has power to name number of senators equal to those elected, forty-six each. Judicial power independent of executive or legislative power; life tenure for judges. Yugoslav citizens are granted rights of individual liberty, freedom of conscience, equality before law, private property, civil and political rights.

      Oct. 20–26   .   .   Second Balkan Conference meets at Istanbul and Ankara.

      Nov. 9   .   .   .   Government candidates control national elections.

1932   Oct. 22–28   .   .   Meeting of Third Balkan Conference at Bucharest. Conference adopts draft Balkan Pact of Union among Balkan states.

      Nov. 14   .   .   .   Croatian Peasant party under Vladimir Maček denounces King Alexander's personal rule, demands Croatian autonomy in federal structure for kingdom.

1933   Jan. 30   .   .   .   Adolf Hitler becomes Chancellor of Germany.

      Feb. 16   .   .   .   Statute of Little Entente completed. Czechoslovakia, Rumania, and Yugoslavia form diplomatic federation; Permanent Council, Economic Council, and Permanent Secretariat established.

      April 29   .   .   Croatian Peasant leader Maček imprisoned for treasonable activities against state.

      July 4   .   .   .   Soviet Russia and members of Little Entente (Czechoslovakia, Rumania, and Yugoslavia) conclude nonaggression pact.

      Sept. 18   .   .   King Alexander of Yugoslavia and Tsar Boris of Bulgaria meet at Belgrade. Beginning of Bulgaro-Yugoslav *rapprochement*.

      Oct. 3–6   .   .   Trip of King Alexander to Varna, Bulgaria, to meet King Boris; to Istanbul to meet President Kemal Atatürk; to Greece.

      Oct. 30   .   .   .   King Alexander and King Carol of Rumania meet on Danube.

      Nov. 6–11   .   .   Fourth Balkan Conference at Salonika.

      Dec. 10–12   .   King Boris and Queen Ioanna pay official visit to Belgrade.

1934   Jan. 22   .   .   .   King Boris and Queen Ioanna pay official visit to Bucharest.

1934 Feb. 9 . . . Signing of Balkan Pact by Yugoslavia, Rumania, Greece, and Turkey. Pledge mutual defense of independence and integrity against any attack on a member by another Balkan state.

June 1 . . . Yugoslav-German commercial accord.

June 25 . . Visit of Louis Barthou, French Foreign Minister, to Belgrade to preserve pro-French orientation of Yugoslav foreign policy.

Sept. 23 . . Visit of King Alexander to Sofia to promote Yugoslav-Bulgar friendship.

Oct. 9 . . . Assassination at Marseille of King Alexander and Louis Barthou by Vlada the Chauffeur, who worked in collaboration with Macedonian revolutionaries and Ustaši, a Croatian terrorist organization led by Ante Pavelić. Pavelić, operating from Rome, was under direction of Count Galeazzo Ciano. The terrorists were trained at Janka Pushta, Hungary.

Peter II, son of Alexander I, becomes King of Yugoslavia; Prince Paul Karageorgević, cousin of King Alexander, is chief regent of kingdom.

Nov. 15 . . . Croatian Peasant party offers coöperation with government.

Dec. 19 . . . Vladimir Maček is pardoned.

1935 May 2 . . . Franco-Soviet treaty of mutual assistance is signed.

May 5 . . . Serbian Peasant party, in coalition with Croatian Peasant party, wins two-fifths of votes.

May 16 . . . Czechoslovak-Soviet treaty of mutual assistance is signed.

June 3 . . . Continuation of Croatian parliamentary boycott.

June 20 . . Milan Stojadinović forms cabinet, beginning with "liquidation" of "dictatorship" and possible collaboration with Croats.

Aug. 19 . . Stojadinović forms so-called Radical Union, composed of Serbian Radicals, Slovene Clerical party, and Bosnian Moslems led by Stojadinović, Korošeć, and Spaho.

1936 April 1 . . . Austria repudiates military restrictions of Treaty of St. Germain and institutes general military service.

May . . . Signature of Yugoslav-German barter agreement.

July 20 . . . Signature of Montreux Straits Convention, in which, among others, Yugoslavia takes part.

1937 Jan. 24 . . . Yugoslav-Bulgarian treaty of perpetual peace and friendship.

March 25 . . Yugoslav-Italian treaty of friendship and nonaggression; parties pledge to respect land and sea frontiers and to refrain from supporting any aggressor if either is attacked by a third Power.

1937   July 23 . . .   Yugoslav-Vatican concordat granting wider privileges to Roman Catholics is ratified by Skupština. Attempt to apply it causes serious disturbances in Belgrade and throughout Serbia.

      Oct. 6 . . .   Formation of Agrarian-Democratic coalition of democrats from Serbia and Croatia in opposition to Stojadinović regime.

      Oct. 12 . . .   Renewal of Franco-Yugoslav treaty of alliance of November 11, 1927, for another five-year term.

1938   March 11–14 .   Liquidation of independent Austria and its occupation by forces of Nazi Germany.

      May 5 . . .   Official communiqué of Little Entente Conference stresses unanimity of members on all questions of interest to alliance, and determination to continue collaboration in efforts for peace and understanding, especially for neighborly relations in Danubian area.

      July 31 . . .   Members of Balkan Entente (Yugoslavia, Rumania, Greece, and Turkey) sign agreement with Bulgaria: military and naval clauses of Treaty of Neuilly are renounced; Bulgaria promises pacific attitude.

      Aug. 21 . .   Permanent Council of Little Entente, meeting at Bled, Yugoslavia, affirms unity. Agreement on rearmament with Hungary, but no nonaggression pact.

      Sept. 24 . .   Yugoslavia and Rumania, as members of Little Entente, thanks to popular pressure, promise assistance to Czechoslovakia in its difficulties with Nazi Germany, leading to Munich crisis.

      Sept. 29–30 .   Munich "Conference." Chamberlain, Daladier, Hitler, and Mussolini "confer" on terms of settlement of Czechoslovak-German problem. Beginning of annihilation of Republic of Czechoslovakia.

      Dec. 11 . . .   National elections in Yugoslavia are managed by Stojadinović government. Vladimir Maček's Croatian Peasant party wins overwhelming vote in Croatia.

1939   Feb. 4 . . .   Resignation of Milan Stojadinović as Premier of Yugoslavia.

      Feb. 5 . . .   Dragiša Cvetković becomes Premier of Yugoslavia.

      Feb. 20–22 . .   Meeting of Council of Balkan Entente at Bucharest.

      April 27 . .   *Sporazum,* basic agreement between Cvetković government and Croatian Peasant party, looking toward autonomy of Croatia under federal structure.

      June 1 . . .   Visit of Prince Paul of Yugoslavia to Berlin. Hitler assures him of inviolability of Yugoslav borders and declares that Yugoslav-German borders have been "established for all time."

1939 Aug. 24   .  .    Serbo-Croatian agreement approved by regency of Yugoslavia; Cvetković government resigns.

        Aug. 26   .  .    Yugoslav dictatorship is abolished and a more democratic regime established. Premier Cvetković forms new cabinet; Vladimir Maček is Vice-Premier. Croatia receives complete autonomy in all cultural and economic matters; beginnings of federal structure seem evident.

## VII. Yugoslavia in the World Struggle

1939 Sept. 1  .  .  .   Adolf Hitler begins Second World War by "counter-attack" on Poland.

        Sept. 3  .  .  .   British and French declarations of war against Germany.

1940 Jan. 12  .  .  .   King Carol of Rumania and Prince Regent Paul of Yugoslavia confer secretly on Balkan problems.

        Feb. 2–4   .  .    Last meeting of Council of Balkan Entente, at Belgrade.

        April 19   .  .    Discovery of Nazi conspiracy to overthrow Yugoslav government leads to arrest of former Premier Stojadinović.

        June 22–23  .    France signs "armistice" with Germany and Italy.

        June 27   .  .    Rumania cedes Bessarabia and northern Bukovina to Soviet Union.

        Sept. 6  .  .  .   King Carol of Rumania abdicates in favor of his son Michael.

        Sept. 7  .  .  .   Rumania signs agreement with Bulgaria ceding southern Dobrudja to Bulgaria.

        Sept. 20   .  .    Yugoslavia restricts Jewish participation in economic life for first time in Yugoslav history.

        Oct. 4  .  .  .   Yugoslav government disbands pro-Slovene Association of Yugoslav Immigrants, which had carried on anti-Italian propaganda.

        Oct. 19  .  .  .   Yugoslav-German commercial agreement is signed.

        Oct. 28  .  .  .   Italian forces invade Greece.

        Nov. 1  .  .  .   Yugoslav government expresses friendship for both Italy and Greece, declares its neutrality in Italo-Greek struggle.

        Nov. 4  .  .  .   Belgrade police raid and close headquarters of fascist Zbor political movement.

        Nov. 6  .  .  .   Yugoslav War Minister, General Nedić, resigns post after Italian bombings in southern Serbia on November 5.

        Nov. 17   .  .    King Boris of Bulgaria visits Hitler in Berlin.

        Nov. 20   .  .    Hungary signs German-Italian-Japanese pact of September 27, 1940.

        Dec. 11  .  .  .   Yugoslavia and Hungary sign pact of perpetual friendship and peace.

1941 Jan. 1 . . . Premier Bogdan Filov of Bulgaria leaves Sofia for Vienna.

Jan. 4 . . . King Boris of Bulgaria is reported to have gone to Berlin.

Jan. 5 . . . Soviet Russia is reported to have recalled its ministers to Hungary, Yugoslavia, and Bulgaria for consultation.

Jan. 12 . . . Soviet Russia denies consenting to German troop movements to Bulgaria. Premier Filov declares Bulgaria will remain neutral.

Jan. 23 . . . Colonel Donovan confers with government officials in Belgrade.

Feb. 8 . . . Conference between Field Marshal List and representatives of Bulgarian General Staff, planning attack on Greece and Yugoslavia.

Feb. 14 . . . Yugoslav Premier Dragiša Cvetković and Foreign Minister Dimitrije Cincar-Marković are summoned to Berchtesgaden to confer with Hitler.

Feb. 20 . . . Turkey declares that its pact with Bulgaria will be repudiated if German forces attack Greece through Bulgaria.

March 1 . . Bulgarian government signs Axis agreement; German forces move into Bulgaria.

March 2 . . Premier Filov declares that signature of Axis pact does not alter Bulgaria's diplomatic position.

Prince Paul confers with German minister at Belgrade.

March 6 . . Great Britain demands decision of Yugoslavia in Balkan crisis.

March 20 . . Belgrade reports indicate British are landing at Salonika.

March 21 . . Three members of Yugoslav cabinet resign because of Nazi demands.

March 22 . . Former Premier Milan Stojadinović is turned over to British in Greece for safekeeping.

March 24 . . Greece declares that Yugoslav acceptance of German demands will be considered a hostile act.

Soviet Russia and Turkish Republic sign agreement on neutrality policy, extending treaty of December 17, 1929.

March 25 . . Cvetković government in Yugoslavia signs Tripartite (German-Italian-Japanese) Pact of September 27, 1940. Germany guarantees "independence" of Yugoslavia, promising to make no demand for troop transit through Yugoslav territory.

March 27 . . Army overthrows Cvetković government and, with popular backing, replaces regency of Prince Paul, declares King Peter II of age, and installs General Dušan Simović as Premier.

1941  March 27 . .  President Roosevelt promises material American aid to
                    new Yugoslav government.

                    In conference of Hitler and German High Command on
                    situation in Yugoslavia, the Führer declares determi-
                    nation to destroy Yugoslavia militarily and as a na-
                    tional unit, after Belgrade *coup d'état.*

      March 28 . .  President Roosevelt and King George of England con-
                    gratulate King Peter II of Yugoslavia on Yugoslav
                    resistance to Nazi Germany.

                    Premier Simović assures Germany that Yugoslavia will
                    respect "all outstanding agreements" with Germany
                    but will not surrender independence.

      April 3 . . .  Croats, under Vladimir Maček, join Serbs in supporting
                    general mobilization of army.

      April 4 . . .  Belgrade, Zagreb, and Ljubljana are declared open cities.

      April 5 . . .  Yugoslav cabinet adopts policy of firmness but is willing
                    to enter into honorable relations with Nazi Germany.

                    Soviet Russia and Yugoslavia sign treaty of friendship
                    and nonaggression.

      April 6 . . .  Hitler issues declaration of war on Yugoslavia. German
                    forces begin invasion of Greece and Yugoslavia.

                    Italian planes attack Yugoslav ports on Adriatic. Bel-
                    grade is bombed.

      April 8 . . .  President Roosevelt reiterates promise of material Amer-
                    ican aid to Yugoslavia.

      April 9 . . .  Germans capture Skoplje.

                    Germans take Niš and Salonika.

      April 10 . .  Germans enter Zagreb.

      April 11 . .  German forces enter through Monastir (Bitolj) Gap;
                    Hungarians march into the Vojvodina.

      April 13 . .  Belgrade, with 6,000 massacred by Stuka dive bombers,
                    is a city of the dead after four days of bombing.

      April 15 . .  Bulgaria severs relations with Yugoslavia; ready to march
                    into Macedonian region.

                    Fascist Italy and Nazi Germany accord unconditional
                    recognition to state of "Free Croatia," organized under
                    Ante Pavelić, Croatian terrorist leader who planned
                    the assassination of King Alexander (see Oct. 9, 1934).
                    On April 8 Pavelić had asked Mussolini's assistance in
                    forming state, in collaboration with General Kva-
                    ternik.

      April 17 . .  German forces occupy destroyed city of Sarajevo.

      April 19 . .  German forces announce that "at noon firing ceased in
                    the Serbian theater of war."

      May 5 . . .  Yugoslav forces are reported carrying on guerrilla war-
                    fare in Serbian mountains.

| 1941 | May 9 . . . | Soviet Union withdraws recognition from Yugoslavia barely one month after treaty of friendship. |
|---|---|---|
| | May 10 . . . | Report that Italy might be rewarded with territory along Dalmatian coast of Yugoslavia, together with Montenegro. Italy to receive region of Ljubljana also. German plans reported to crush Serbian resistance. |
| | May 12 . . . | Konstantin Fotić, Yugoslav Minister to the United States, protests creation of "Free Croatia." |
| | May 17 . . . | Croat delegation, headed by Ante Pavelić, goes to Rome to offer throne of "Free Croatia" to Duke of Spoleto, cousin of King Victor Emmanuel of Italy. |
| | May 18 . . . | Duke of Spoleto accepts "throne," to become Tomislav II of Croatia. Croatia to be dependent on Italy and Germany in foreign policy, armament, economic life, and fascist political institutions. |
| | | Italy to receive Dalmatian coast from Zara to Split, with all ports, including Cattaro (Kotor) and Adriatic islands. |
| | | Report that Axis Powers are stripping Croatia of food, cattle, timber, and raw materials. |
| | May 19 . . . | Fascist regime is established for "Free Croatia." |
| | May 24 . . . | Yugoslav government protests to United States against Axis dismemberment of Yugoslavia. |
| | June 3 . . . | Yugoslav government-in-exile, with General Simović as Premier, pledges resistance to Axis "until the restoration of our territorial integrity and the independence of our state, as well as the complete liberation of the Serbs, Croats, and Slovenes." |
| | June 4 . . . | Soviet Union dismisses Yugoslav Minister at Moscow, Milan Gavrilović, who departs for Ankara. |
| | | United States government denounces "the invasion and mutilation of Yugoslavia by various member states of the Tripartite Pact." |
| | June 5–6 . . | A blast at fort of Smederevo on junction of Sava and Danube rivers kills about 800 Germans. |
| | June 12 . . | Representatives of British and Dominion governments, provisional government of Czechoslovakia, governments of Greece, Yugoslavia, Free France, Luxemburg, Belgium, the Netherlands, Norway, and Poland, meeting at London, agree that: (1) they will continue the struggle to victory and will assist each other; (2) there can be no settled peace and prosperity as long as free peoples submit to Nazi Germany and its associates; and (3) the only true foundation for peace is the collaboration of free peoples. |
| | June 14 . . | Croatia formally joins Axis. |

1941  June 20 . . General Kvaternik announces, in Zagreb, intention of establishing complete fascist system.

June 21 . . King Peter II of Yugoslavia, with General Simović, arrives in England to take up residence as head of Yugoslav government. Momčilo Ninčić, Minister of Foreign Affairs; Knežević, Minister at court.

July 11 . . . Declaration of support of Soviet Union in war against Axis.

Sept. 20 . . Reports that hundreds of Italian soldiers have been killed by guerrillas in Hercegovina.

Oct. 11 . . . Croatian revolutionary Ustaši have killed between 300,000 and 340,000 Serbs and pro-Yugoslav Croats since May, 1941, with help of German S.S. units, Gestapo, and regular German army officers and Italians in western Croatia, according to reports.

Nov. 11 . . General Nedić, puppet Prime Minister of Serbia, attempts to make peace with Colonel Draža Mihailović.

1942  Jan. 1 . . . Yugoslavia is among the twenty-six governments which are original signatories to Declaration by United Nations in Washington, D. C.

Jan. 2 . . . Reconstruction of government: Slobodan Jovanović succeeds General Simović as Prime Minister; General Draža Mihailović, leader of guerrilla forces in Yugoslavia, is appointed War Minister.

Jan. 15 . . . Agreement is signed with Greece providing for political, economic, and military coöperation, and outlining constitution for future Balkan union.

March 27 . . King Peter urges Yugoslavia to organize under leadership of Draža Mihailović.

June 21 . . King Peter arrives in United States for extended visit.

July 24 . . . Mutual-aid agreement signed with United States.

Nov. 3 . . . Anthony J. Drexel Biddle, Jr., United States envoy to exiled governments of Nazi-dominated Europe, presents his credentials to King Peter as Ambassador to Yugoslavia.

Dec. 15 . . . Yugoslav government-in-exile defends Draža Mihailović against criticism.

Dec. 30 . . . Resignation of Jovanović government.

1943  Jan. 2 . . . Formation of new Yugoslav cabinet: Premier Jovanović takes over duties of Foreign Minister in place of Dr. Momčilo Ninčić; General Draža Mihailović continues as War Minister.

April 20 . . General Draža Mihailović, in message from secret mountain headquarters in Yugoslavia, says he has rejected "with disgust" many attempts of Germans and Italians to have him surrender.

1943 May 1 . . . According to reports from Yugoslav National Army of Liberation (Partisans), after a four-week offensive nearly 4,000 square miles of Yugoslav territory have been cleared of Axis and quisling troops.

June 10 . . Yugoslavia becomes member of U.N.R.R.A.

June 26 . . After a week-long crisis, King Peter announces formation of new cabinet headed by Miloš Trifunović, deputy leader of Serbian Radical party. Membership of cabinet: Premier and Minister of Interior, Miloš Trifunović; Vice-Premiers, Slobodan Jovanović, Juraj Krnjević, and Miha Krek; Foreign Affairs, Milan Grol; War, General Draža Mihailović; Acting Minister of War, General Petar Živković; Transport, Miloš Bobić; Mining, Jovan Banjanin; Education, Boris Furlan; Finance, Juraj Šutej; Justice, Milan Gavrilović; Social Welfare, Božidar Vlajić.

June 28 . . King Peter, in radio address to his countrymen, declares that Yugoslavia will be restored and Yugoslav peoples will again be free to settle their own fate in accordance with principles of true democracy.

Aug. 10 . . A new Yugoslav government is formed, headed by Božidar Purić as Prime Minister, who also assumes portfolios of Minister of Foreign Affairs and Acting Minister of War. Crisis is provoked by demands of cabinet members that agreement be reached on constitutional structure of Yugoslavia.

Aug. 31 . . Prime Minister Churchill, in address broadcast from Quebec, declares: "I look forward with confidence to the day when Yugoslavia and Greece will once again be free, free to live their own lives and decide their own destiny. I take this opportunity to send a message of encouragement to these peoples and their governments, and to the kings of Greece and Yugoslavia, who have never faltered for one moment in their duty, and whom we hope to see restored to their thrones by the free choice of their liberated peoples."

Sept. 28 . . King Peter and government-in-exile arrive at Cairo, transferring seat of government from London to Cairo.

Oct. 16 . . . King Peter announces admission of underground Yugoslav leaders (Nenad Grizogno and Ivo Čičin-Šain, Croat leaders; Jurij Koče, Slovene leader) into cabinet at Cairo.

Oct. 21 . . . According to communiqué of Yugoslav National Army of Liberation, Partisan forces have extended offensive operations in widely scattered sections of Bosnia, Hercegovina, and Montenegro.

1943  Nov. 8  . . .  General Sir Henry Maitland Wilson, British commander in chief of Mediterranean Theater of Operations, warns Yugoslav guerrilla groups—which, he says, are "helping the Germans in their vain attempts to subdue the forces of liberation"—that they will be regarded as traitors to their own people and as enemies of the United Nations.

Nov. 24  . .  General Draža Mihailović, Yugoslav War Minister and guerrilla leader, announces that Četnici have gained control over entire country of Montenegro and adjacent Adriatic coastal area exclusive of fortress region, and that his forces have hemmed in the Germans and pinned them to tenuous communications in port of Cattaro (Kotor).

Dec. 4  . . .  Yugoslav Partisans announce that provisional government has been established and that 140 delegates have created parliament and governing body for territory already wrested from Germans. Government is headed by Ivan Ribar; General Josip Broz (Tito) is elevated to rank of field marshal and made chairman of new committee for national defense.

Dec. 5  . . .  King Peter II of Yugoslavia protests against formation of government by Partisans, denouncing it as "a movement of terroristic violence."

Announced program of Partisan government in Yugoslavia calls for liberation of country and full democratic rights for all peoples of Yugoslavia; inviolability of private property; no radical changes in social life of people; renunciation of lawlessness.

Dec. 8  . . .  Although it continues to recognize Yugoslav government-in-exile in Cairo, British government announces its policy of supporting all forces in Yugoslavia which are resisting Germans. "As things are, we are supporting the Partisan forces, giving them more support than we are giving to General Mihailović, for the simple reason that the resistance of the Partisan forces to the Germans is very much greater."

Dec. 9  . . .  United States government announces that it will aid Partisan forces in Yugoslavia.

Dec. 14  . . .  Soviet government announces that it has decided to send military mission to Yugoslavia to be with Partisan forces.

Dec. 23  . . .  King Peter denounces Yugoslav Partisans and reaffirms determination of forces of General Mihailović to fight at side of Allies until end of war.

1944 Jan. 4 . . . Yugoslav government-in-exile announces receipt of New Year's greeting from Premier Stalin.

Jan. 31 . . . Soviet Russia is reported to have rejected suggestion of Yugoslav government-in-exile for alliance.

Feb. 9 . . . Marshal Tito's headquarters announces capture of documents proving that General Mihailović is collaborating with Germans.

March 11 . . King Peter and Prime Minister and Home Minister of Yugoslavia arrive at London.

April 12 . . Marshal Tito's military representative, General Terzić, arrives at Moscow from Teheran at head of military mission of Yugoslav Committee for National Liberation.

April 20 . . King Peter, returned to London from Cairo, in address before Anglo-American Press Association, declares Yugoslavia's friendship for the U.S.S.R., Great Britain, and the United States, declaring Yugoslavia could be a link connecting and harmonizing common interests of Great Powers in southeastern Europe.

June 1 . . . King Peter issues declaration to Serbs, Croats, and Slovenes urging unity until war is won.

Ivan Šubašić is new Premier of Yugoslav government-in-exile.

June 16 . . Agreement is signed on Yugoslav territory by Premier Šubašić and Marshal Tito; government is formed to unite conflicting elements.

July 9 . . . Šubašić assures "united" Yugoslavia that Stalin, Roosevelt, and Churchill have followed Yugoslav struggle and will do all in their power to restore independence and freedom to Yugoslav people.

Aug. 2 . . . Prime Minister Churchill advises House of Commons that prospects of bringing unity to Yugoslavia are good.

Aug. 8 . . . Yugoslav government in London issues statement indicating it is seeking to unify all democratic forces within Yugoslavia to bring about speedy deliverance from enemy; will devote energies to development of democratic and federal Yugoslavia "organized by the free will of the Yugoslav peoples."

Aug. 12–13 . Conferences in Italy among Marshal Tito and Prime Minister Churchill, Under Secretary of War Patterson, Lieutenant General B. B. Somervell, and Premier Ivan Šubašić.

Aug. 17 . . Marshal Tito issues statement stressing agreement of June 16 with Yugoslav government in London.

1944   Aug. 26   .   .   General Draža Mihailović loses command in Yugoslavia by royal decree.

Sept. 7   .   .   .   Soviet forces in Balkans reach eastern frontiers of Yugoslavia.

Sept. 16   .   .   Marshal Tito's territorial demands on Italy, including Istria and Trieste, cause dismay among Italians.

Oct. 9–18   .   .   Prime Minister Churchill and Foreign Minister Eden consult with Marshal Stalin in Moscow about Yugoslav problem, reaching agreement "to pursue a joint policy in Yugoslavia designed to concentrate all energies against the retreating Germans and bring about a solution of Yugoslav internal difficulties by a union between the Royal Yugoslav Government and the National Liberation Movement." Meeting takes place with knowledge and approval of the United States.

Oct. 14   .   .   .   Soviet and Yugoslav forces storm into Belgrade; hand to-hand battles rage in center of city.

Nov. 22   .   .   Premier Stalin is publicly quoted as favoring postwar alliance of "equal Slav states."

Nov. 23   .   .   Marshal Tito declares that federal, democratic government will be established and will use all its powers to bring about "the closest collaboration and *rapprochement* with its Balkan neighbors," especially Bulgaria.

Nov. 30   .   .   Premier Enver Hoxha of Albania declares that Albania is seeking close alliance with Yugoslavia.

1945   Jan. 18   .   .   .   Prime Minister Churchill announces in House of Commons that he believes Tito-Šubašić agreement was best which could be made for immediate future of Yugoslavia, since it preserves form of monarchy pending plebiscite.

Feb. 11   .   .   .   Report of Yalta Conference, with recommendation to Tito and Šubašić that "the agreement between them should be put into effect immediately and a new government should be formed on the basis of that agreement."

April 6   .   .   .   Yugoslav government accepts invitation to participate in United Nations Conference at San Francisco.

April 11   .   .   Yugoslavia signs treaty of friendship, mutual assistance, and postwar coöperation with Soviet Union.

Sept. 12   .   .   Marshal Tito expresses sentiment favoring establishment of "cordial fraternal relations and coöperation with our neighbors, Albania, Bulgaria, and Rumania."

Oct. 19   .   .   .   Yugoslavia ratifies United Nations Charter.

Nov. 11   .   .   Plebiscite held in Yugoslavia, Marshal Tito's National Front winning 85 per cent of votes.

| | | |
|---|---|---|
| 1945 | Dec. 22 . . . | Department of State of the United States publishes official notes on American recognition of Federal Peoples Republic of Yugoslavia, noting changes in its constitutional structure and indicating opinion on limitations of basic freedoms. British government also recognizes Yugoslav government, indicating that change of regime will not affect rights and interests of British subjects in Yugoslavia. |
| | Dec. 31 . . . | Recognition of Yugoslav government by France. |
| 1946 | Feb. 6 . . . | General Nedić commits suicide while awaiting trial. |
| | Feb. 16 . . . | Yugoslav government asks Soviet Union to place before Security Council of United Nations a memorandum on Polish troops in Italy, alleging threat to security of Yugoslavia. |
| | March 18 . . | Treaty of mutual assistance between Yugoslavia and Poland is signed. |
| | March 24 . . | Belgrade radio reports that General Draža Mihailović has come into custody of Yugoslav government. |
| | April 1 . . . | Addressing Yugoslav parliament, Marshal Tito says that basis of Yugoslav foreign policy is "to make every effort that Yugoslavia gets her rights and regains her rightful territories, including Istria, the Slovene littoral, and Slav Carinthia, and to improve political, cultural, and economic relations with others, and in the first place with our Slav brother nations." |
| | April 2 . . . | Publication of note from the United States to Yugoslav government (March 30) asking that certain Americans be allowed to testify in trial of General Draža Mihailović. |
| | April 3 . . . | Foreign Minister Bevin of Great Britain announces in House of Commons that Great Britain was convinced by end of 1943 that General Draža Mihailović was no longer fighting against Germans, but some Četnik units were coöperating with them against Partisans. It depends on charges whether Great Britain is involved or concerned with trial. |
| | April 5 . . . | Yugoslav government refuses United States request for officers to give evidence in trial of General Draža Mihailović. |
| | April 18 . . | Formal recognition of Yugoslav government by the United States, Yugoslavia having given formal assurance to observe existing treaties and agreements with the United States. |
| | April 20 . . | Marshal Tito is reported to have presented claim to Allies for $9,900,000,000 reparations from Italy for damage and losses incurred between 1941 and 1943. |

1946   May 9   . . .   Signature of Yugoslav-Czechoslovak treaty of friendship and mutual assistance.

      May 12   . . .   At Zagreb, Marshal Tito declares Yugoslavia has presented claim for incorporation of Trieste and Venezia Giulia on ethnic, economic, and national grounds. "We cannot yield in our demands."

      May 27   . . .   Marshal Tito visits in Moscow, returning June 10. Reports U.S.S.R. is to supply Yugoslav army with munitions and equipment under agreement ratified June 8.

      June 5   . . .   Yugoslavia refuses to participate in victory celebrations in London on ground that British policy has been unfriendly since end of war.

      June 27   . .   Marshal Tito reaffirms position on Trieste and Julian March.

      July 7   . . .   Vice-premier tells press that Yugoslavia cannot accept Paris decision on internationalization of port of Trieste.

      July 9   . . .   Yugoslavia and Albania sign alliance.

      July 15   . . .   Supreme Military Tribunal of Yugoslavia sentences General Draža Mihailović to death for collaboration with Germans and Italians and for war crimes. Sentence executed on July 17.

      July 17   . . .   Ratification of Yugoslav-Czechoslovak treaty of friendship and mutual assistance.

      Aug. 9   . . .   American C-47 transport carrying seven Americans, a Turk, and a Swiss strays from its course near Bled, Yugoslavia, is fired on by two Yugoslav fighter planes, and is forced down near Ljubljana.

      Aug. 19   . .   Another C-47 radios Udine that it is over Klagenfurt. It is not heard from again. Reports indicate it was attacked by Yugoslav fighters and sent down in flames.

      Aug. 20   . .   State Department, in firm note, asks Yugoslav government for information about incidents of August 9 and 19. In reply Yugoslav government charges territorial violations.

      Aug. 21   . .   Acting Secretary of State Dean Acheson, in note to Yugoslav chargé, calls attention to "these outrageous acts" and declares: "If within forty-eight hours . . . these demands are not complied with, the United States government will call upon the Security Council of the United Nations to meet promptly to take appropriate action."

      Aug. 23   . .   Yugoslav note indicates no survivors of August 19 crash. Belgrade government declines to acknowledge latest American note because contents have become irrelevant.

1946 Aug. 24 . . State Department announces that Yugoslavia has apparently complied with United States demands as to airplane incidents.

Aug. 25 . . Yugoslav government charges violation of territory by United States planes, but agrees to pay military honors to American dead. Denounces campaign of calumny.

Aug. 26 . . It is announced that United States transports flying the Austria-to-Italy route are now armed and protected.

Aug. 30 . . Yugoslav note to the United States asks for investigation of flights of United States aircraft over Yugoslav territory and complains that no satisfactory reply to previous notes has been received. Disclaimer of responsibility for loss of plane crew shot down August 9.

Aug. 31 . . Yugoslav note to the United States expresses regret over killing of plane crew, gives assurances that no United States transport plane will be fired at, even if flying without prior notice over Yugoslav territory.

Sept. 3 . . . United States note to Yugoslavia denies allegations that 228 American flights took place over Yugoslav territory between July 16 and August 29. Confidence is expressed that Yugoslav government will offer compensation to families of American dead and to the United States for loss of aircraft.

In Italian Political Commission, Paris Conference, Yugoslav delegate accepts internationalization of Trieste but presses for different frontier than "French" line—a line running east of line originally claimed by Yugoslav government.

Sept. 6 . . . Yugoslav delegation at Paris Peace Conference expresses view that "the Balkan peoples are torn among themselves in the matter of dismembering Macedonia, which has become a principal cause of Balkan quarrels that make for hell for the Macedonians themselves. It is high time to end the tragedy of this valiant people; it is high time that peoples are to resolve this sad question in a manner that will permit this people to unite, and to play a part in an ethnic ensemble, as they now play a part today in the Peoples Republic of Macedonia in the Federation of Yugoslavia." Yugoslav delegation also supports principle of Bulgarian acquisition of western Thrace at expense of Greece.

Sept. 9 . . . Yugoslav delegation begins filibustering tactics concerning issue of Trieste. Reiteration of Yugoslav position that Yugoslavia will not sign treaty unless satisfied as to situation in Trieste.

1946 Sept. 12   . .   The United States rejects ban on U.N.R.R.A. relief to Yugoslavia in spite of current difficulties.

Sept. 13   . .   In Italian Political Commission, large measure of agreement on statute for Free Territory of Trieste. Soviet and Yugoslav drafts differ from those of the United States, France, and Great Britain in authority given to Security Council.

Sept. 15   . .   Yugoslav government gives note to the United States protesting against "harsh and irresponsible behavior" of American occupation authorities toward six Yugoslav soldiers arrested after explosion in Trieste on September 9. Anti-American press campaign continues in Belgrade.

Sept. 16   . .   Senator Connally, United States delegate at Paris, firmly maintains position of the United States on Trieste.

Yugoslav delegate at Paris states that as Western Powers fear Communist domination of Trieste, Yugoslavs fear that statute providing for governor with strong executive powers will be abused by Trieste middle class.

Sept. 18   . .   Stepinac, Archbishop of Zagreb, is arrested and charged with war crimes.

Sept. 20   . .   The United States rejects protests from Yugoslavia concerning incidents in Trieste and sends protest to Belgrade, placing blame on Yugoslavia. United States note cites instances of anti-Tito Yugoslavs in American zone being shot or kidnaped by Yugoslavs. British government publishes note to Yugoslavia repudiating charges that attacks on Yugoslavs in Zone A have been condoned by Allied military authorities.

Sept. 23   . .   Yugoslav delegate at Paris indicates failure of attempt to reach agreement with Italy on Venezia Giulia.

Sept. 26   . .   United States Embassy in Belgrade closes American reading room and library and terminates all functions of United States Information Service on receipt of note from Foreign Ministry requesting suspension of activities without delay.

Sept. 28   . .   Italian Political Commission, Paris Conference, by 12 votes to 5, accepts "French" line as frontier of Italy and Yugoslavia.

Oct. 1   . . .   In Italian Political Commission, Kardelj, Yugoslav delegate, says that treaty should come into force only after Yugoslavia, as well as Big Four, have ratified it, but this is rejected by 13 votes to 5, Greece and the Netherlands abstaining.

Oct. 7   . . .   Kardelj, at Paris Conference, says Yugoslavia will not sign treaty with Italy which embodies "French" frontier line.

1946  Oct. 9 . . . Molotov, at Paris Conference, reaffirms Soviet position on Trieste, stating that even Italian democrats will accept Soviet view.

The United States receives Yugoslav note, stating that decision to pay indemnity for American lives lost on August 19 was inspired by "human" feeling, responsibility for incident being disclaimed.

Oct. 10 . . . Yugoslav delegate at Paris, replying to the United States position as to "freedom of Danube," states that half of Danube system is within Yugoslav territory, denies right of Conference to impose terms on Allied countries, and maintains that navigation should be controlled solely by riparian states. Molotov takes similar view, referring to status of Panama and Suez canals.

Oct. 11 . . . Archbishop of Zagreb is sentenced to sixteen years at hard labor for crimes against state, with loss of civic rights for five years.

Oct. 12 . . . Yugoslav delegate at Paris affirms that Yugoslavia will not accept decision in treaties which do not have Yugoslav consent. Conference adopts new frontiers laid down in treaty, but Yugoslavia does not vote.

Oct. 14 . . . Marshal Tito tells British press representative that he objects in principle to free state for Trieste area, but maintains that two points should be conceded to Yugoslavia: (1) territory around port inhabited by Slavs must go to Yugoslavia; (2) Yugoslavia should be met on question of constitution of the free state. He also denies any quarrel with Greece and states it is untrue that Yugoslavia is arming bands operating on borders. Tito is excommunicated.

Oct. 15 . . . Yugoslav delegation is absent from final session at Paris Conference. In letter to secretary general it is charged that decisions concerning questions in Italian treaty are of such nature that they make it impossible for Yugoslav government to sign treaty if main provisions affecting vital interests of Yugoslavia are not changed.

Oct. 16 . . . Yugoslav government issues statement through embassies in London and elsewhere pointing out that Archbishop Stepinac is indictable on four counts: (1) collaboration with Pavelić from beginning of "independent" Croatia; (2) failure to stop massacres of Orthodox Serbs by Ustaši; (3) fact that his attitude led many Catholic clergy to fight with Ustaši and Germans against National Army of Liberation; (4) postwar continuance of contacts with remnants of Ustaši units, and instigation of clergy to do likewise.

1946   Oct. 16 . . .   In reply to questions from American correspondents, Marshal Tito says question of Trieste is unsolved, and expresses view that attitude of the United States, unlike that of Yugoslavia, does not show desire to improve relations, which is to be seen in Trieste issue, reparations, question of Yugoslavia's Danube ships, etc.

Nov. 1 . . .   Secretary-General Trygvie Lie makes public Yugoslav communication stating that Yuogslavia will not be represented at any international conference on Danube at which nonriparian states are represented.

Nov. 6 . . .   Foreign Minister Stanoje Simić of Yugoslavia tells Council of Foreign Ministers that, although Yugoslavia accepts principle of internationalization for Trieste, it rejects principle of "dictatorial" powers for governor of Trieste. He reiterates Yugoslavia's opposition to so-called "French" line.

Nov. 7 . . .   It is reported from Rome that Marshal Tito has offered to trade Trieste for Gorizia, according to Palmiro Togliatti, head of Italian Communist party. Only condition is that Trieste, while remaining under Italian sovereignty, is to have autonomous status sufficient to guarantee a democratic government.

Nov. 11 . .   Secretary of State Byrnes declares that the United States has instructed Lieutenant General Lucius D. Clay, deputy military governor in Germany, to order return to Danubian states of barges and other vessels held by American forces since their occupation of upper Danube region.

Nov. 12 . .   Yugoslavia demands $6,750,000 as compensation for American detention of its Danube shipping.

Nov. 28 . .   Substantial agreement concerning Trieste is announced in Council of Foreign Ministers: (1) definite arrangement for withdrawal of forces from Trieste; (2) an accord for reduction of occupation forces when governor takes control; (3) an accord that governor will assume direction of forces and decide date of withdrawal; (4) provision for elections after governor has held office four months.

Dec. 2 . . .   Premier Tsaldaris of Greece, in Paris en route to New York to present Greek charges to United Nations, charges that "hostile elements" on Greek-Yugoslav and Greek-Bulgarian frontiers are inciting antigovernment violence in Greece in effort to win support for proposed Macedonian independence movement.

1946 Dec. 2 . . . In memorandum formally submitted to United Nations General Assembly, Yugoslav delegation formally charges that Axis fifth column which operated within Yugoslavia during war still exists in form of subversive organizations in refugee camps under Allied control in Italy, Austria, and Germany.

Dec. 19 . . . U.N. Security Council establishes Commission of Investigation Concerning Greek Frontier Incidents.

Dec. 29 . . . Text of economic treaty with Albania is published. Treaty for period of thirty years, with automatic ten-year extensions. Provides for formation of common tariff and customs territory, unification of state planning in both countries, and monetary equality.

1947 Jan. 6 . . . Supreme Court passes death sentences on a former army officer, a journalist, and a former employee of American Embassy in Belgrade for disclosing military and state secrets. Former prime minister of government in London (1943) is sentenced to eight years' imprisonment, two others to eight years, one to seven years, and prime minister's son-in-law to four years.

Jan. 10 . . . Foreign Ministry receives note from the United States rejecting charges that Embassy employees have engaged in espionage or supported opponents of government.

Jan. 16 . . . Government publishes territorial claims on Austria, claiming "Slovene Carinthia," 2,470 sq. km. (953.42 sq. mi.) in area, with population of 180,000; and 130 sq. km. (50.18 sq. mi.) of frontier areas in Styria, with population of 10,000.

Jan. 21 . . . Court at Sisak sentences an American and four Yugoslavs to death for espionage.

Feb. 10 . . . On signature of treaty of peace with Italy, Yugoslav representative indicates Yugoslavia has not abandoned right to territories not assigned to it by treaty, and will maintain right to these territories.

Feb. 11 . . . Yugoslav representative on U.N. Balkan Commission states that cause of Greek difficulties is internal, and urges investigation of domestic problems in Greece.

Feb. 16 . . . General Löhr, who ordered bombing of Belgrade in April, 1941, is sentenced to death in Belgrade, together with six other generals.

March 8 . . Presidium of National Assembly publishes decree by which King Peter and his close relatives are deprived of nationality and their property is confiscated.

March 12 . . Truman Doctrine promulgated.

1947 March 14 · · Marshal Tito sends urgent appeal to the United States for immediate food relief, supported by U.N.R.R.A. officials in Yugoslavia, who are winding up affairs.

March 17 · · Diplomatic relations with Italy are resumed.

March 26 · · In further appeal for grain, Yugoslav Ambassador Sava Kosanović advises U.S. Department of State that food situation in Yugoslavia is much worse than in Germany, and that 200,000 tons of corn and 50,000 tons of potatoes are needed before next harvest.

March 27 · · It is announced in London that two requests for food supplies have been received from Belgrade.

March 31 · · Marshal Tito, at joint session of National Assembly, declares that, because of American intervention, Greece has become base for imperialist plans that may threaten world peace. Denying that Yugoslavia is satellite of U.S.S.R., Tito declares, "We work with the U.S.S.R. because it is the only country that does not threaten our independence."

April 15 · · Notes are sent to Great Britain, the United States, and Council of Foreign Ministers in Moscow, alleging that British troops in southern Carinthia are terrorizing Slovene minority and violating freedom of expression.

April 26 · · Marshal Tito, at joint session of two Councils of National Assembly, declares that government is submitting Five-Year Plan for industrialization and electrification of country, to cost about $6,000,000,000. Planned economy now possible because mines, industry, and natural wealth are in hands of people. Reactionaries were hoping for change of authority in country, but their dreams would be disappointed.

May 23 · · · U.N. Commission of Investigation Concerning Greek Frontier Incidents, by majority of 8 out of 11 delegations, finds that Yugoslavia, and, to a lesser extent, Albania and Bulgaria, "have supported guerrilla warfare in Greece."

June 4 · · · Marshal Tito declares that chances are small for Yugoslavia to get as much of Carinthia as it demands, though whatever is decided must be accepted because Yugoslavia is member of United Nations.

June 28 · · Yugoslavia refuses permission to Subsidiary Group of U.N. Commission of Investigation Concerning Greek Frontier Incidents to enter Yugoslavia to investigate Kouka-Palaion-Triethnes incidents of March and April, on ground that their own official investigation disclosed no incident had taken place.

1947 July 7 . . . Yugoslavia decides to withdraw from I.L.O. because that body's constitutional structure is incompatible with economic and social conditions of Yugoslavia.

July 10 . . . Government declines to participate in Paris Conference concerning Marshall Plan, on ground that such action is incompatible with principle of national sovereignty.

July 27 . . . Yugoslavia refuses permission to Subsidiary Group of U.N. Commission of Investigation Concerning Greek Frontier Incidents to enter Yugoslavia to investigate Beles-Prokhoma incidents of July 5–6.

Aug. 2 . . . On visit of Premier Dimitrov of Bulgaria, Bulgarian-Yugoslav agreement is signed at Bled, providing for close economic, political, and cultural coöperation. All properties along frontier to be jointly owned and visas to be abolished. Yugoslavia and Bulgaria undertake to keep close contact on "frequent frontier provocations by Greek government" and other international problems, especially regime of Danube River. Tito describes agreement as "death blow" to attempt of imperialists and reactionaries to turn Balkans again into a "powder keg." It is stated that this is not creation of a "bloc," but insurance of peaceful life, "regardless of what reactionaries say in the West."

Aug. 7 . . . Marshal Tito declares that the United States is building "a kind of economic blockade" around Yugoslavia. Yugoslavia has rejected participation in Marshall Plan because "it would merely have imposed on us new obligations."

Aug. 12 . . Supreme Court at Ljubljana sentences three of fifteen intellectuals to death, the rest being given prison terms, for alleged espionage.

Aug. 13 . . U.S. Department of State denies Tito's charges of August 7 that the United States is trying to isolate Yugoslavia by economic blockade.

Sept. 11 . . The United States protests to Yugoslavia against unwarranted detention and maltreatment of Allied troops, and demands immediate release of two Americans and seven British soldiers.

Sept. 14 . . U.S. Department of State issues White Paper on the United Nations and the Problem of Greece, declaring that Yugoslavia, Albania, and Bulgaria have delayed, sabotaged, and obstructed investigations of U.N. Commission of Investigation Concerning Greek Frontier Incidents, and have given assistance to Greek guerrillas.

1947 Sept. 29 . . Former Secretary of State Byrnes rejects invitation of Marshal Tito to visit Yugoslavia and frontier areas, together with five other eminent Americans. Mr. Harold Stassen also rejects invitation.

Oct. 7 . . . Dr. Aleš Bebler, Yugoslav representative on Political and Security Committee of U.N. General Assembly, declares that Yugoslavia did not provoke civil war in Greece, that all charges against Yugoslavia are false, and that the United States and Great Britain "provoked the war in Greece."

Oct. 9 . . . Dr. Bebler declares that establishment of special Balkan committee of General Assembly would be hostile act against Yugoslavia. Soviet representative, Andrei Gromyko, announces that Soviet Union will not participate in work of committee.

Oct. 21 . . . General Assembly, by vote of 40 to 6, with 11 abstentions, approves resolution establishing U.N. Special Committee on Balkans (U.N.S.C.O.B.) with headquarters at Salonika, to carry on investigations and attempt to find solutions of problems involving Greece and its neighbors, Albania, Bulgaria, and Yugoslavia.

Nov. 27 . . Yugoslavia and Bulgaria sign treaty of alliance with broad clause as to collaboration in event of attack by any third Power. Joint communiqué rejects any coöperation with U.N.S.C.O.B. Greek government is denounced.

Nov. 28–Dec. 8 Yugoslavia formally refuses all coöperation with U.N.S.C.O.B.

Dec. 8 . . . Yugoslavia and Hungary sign treaty of alliance.

Dec. 16 . . . Bulgaria and Albania sign treaty of alliance, reject coöperation with U.N.S.C.O.B., and denounce Greek government, expressing sympathy for "Greek people."

Dec. 19 . . . Yugoslavia and Rumania sign treaty of alliance.

Dec. 29 . . . U.N.S.C.O.B. unanimously approves resolution that any recognition of "Free Greek Government," proclaimed on December 24, 1947, by Markos Vafiadies, Greek guerrilla chieftain, even *de facto*, would be contrary to General Assembly resolution of October 21, 1947, and a threat to international peace and security.

Dec. 30 . . . Under Secretary of State Lovett announces that any recognition of "Free Greek Government" would have "serious implications."

1948 Jan. 2 . . . Albania formally refuses to coöperate with U.N.S.C.O.B.

Jan. 7 . . . U.S. Department of State announces that Bulgaria and Yugoslavia have been advised against recognition of "Free Greek Government" of Greek guerrillas.

1948    Jan. 13 . . .   Bulgaria formally announces refusal to coöperate with U.N.S.C.O.B.

Jan. 16 . . .   Bulgaria and Rumania sign an alliance. Dimitrov, Bulgarian Premier, forecasts eastern European federation.

Jan. 24 . . .   Rumania and Hungary sign an alliance.

Jan. 28 . . .   Moscow *Pravda* denounces any scheme for federation in eastern Europe, insisting that "security" is important matter.

Feb. 4 . . .   U.S.S.R. and Rumania sign treaty of alliance.

Feb. 12 . .   U.N.S.C.O.B. approves communications to Albania, Bulgaria, Yugoslavia, and Greece looking toward conciliation. Communication sent by U.N. Secretary-General on February 23 to Albania, Bulgaria, and Yugoslavia. No replies.

Feb. 24 . . .   U.S.S.R. and Hungary sign treaty of alliance.

March 18 . .   U.S.S.R. and Bulgaria sign treaty of alliance.

March 20 . .   The United States, Great Britain, and France notify Soviet Russia that they favor placing Free Territory of Trieste under sovereignty of Italy.

# APPENDIX

APPENDIX

# *Statistics*

## CENSUS STATISTICS AND ESTIMATES OF POPULATION OF YUGOSLAVIA

Census of 1921 . . . . . . . . . 11,984,910
Census of 1931 . . . . . . . . . 13,934,038

### ESTIMATES*

| | | | |
|---|---|---|---|
| 1932 . . . . . 14,300,000 | 1937 . . . . . 15,400,000 |
| 1933 . . . . . 14,513,700 | 1938 . . . . . 15,630,000 |
| 1934 . . . . . 14,730,400 | 1939 . . . . . 15,703,000 |
| 1935 . . . . . 14,950,300 | 1940 . . . . . 15,919,000 |
| 1936 . . . . . 15,173,600 | 1948 . . . . . 14,323,000 |

### POPULATION ACCORDING TO RELIGIOUS AFFILIATION
#### (Estimated on basis of Census of 1931)

| | *Number* | *Percentage* |
|---|---|---|
| Serbian Orthodox . . . . | 6,785,501 | 48.70 |
| Roman Catholic . . . . | 5,217,910 | 37.45 |
| Moslems . . . . . . . | 1,561,166 | 11.20 |
| Protestants . . . . . | 236,981 | 1.70 |
| Others . . . . . . . | 132,543 | 0.95 |
| Total . . . . . . . | 13,934,101 | |

### ESTIMATES OF SLAVIC POPULATION FOR 1948

| | |
|---|---|
| Serbs . . . . . . . . . . . . . | 6,750,000 |
| Bosnian Moslems . . . . . . . | 800,000 |
| Croats . . . . . . . . . . . | 4,250,000 |
| Slovenes . . . . . . . . . . | 1,400,000 |
| Macedonian Slavs . . . . . . . | 700,000 |
| Total . . . . . . . . . . | 13,900,000 |

* Estimates for the years 1932–1938 are from *Annuaire statistique, 1937*, **Vol.** III (Belgrade, 1938). Those for 1939 and 1940 are from *Statesman's Year-Book*.

OFFICIAL ESTIMATE OF POPULATION OF THE SIX
REPUBLICS IN 1948
(Based on Census of 1931)

| | |
|---|---:|
| Serbia . . . . . . . . . . . . | 5,742,000 |
| Croatia . . . . . . . . . . . | 3,564,000 |
| Macedonia . . . . . . . . . | 1,120,000 |
| Montenegro . . . . . . . . | 371,000 |
| Bosnia-Hercegovina . . . . . | 2,398,000 |
| Slovenia . . . . , . . . . . | 1,128,000 |
| Total . . . . . . . . . . | 14,323,000 |

# CONSTITUTION OF THE FEDERAL PEOPLES REPUBLIC OF YUGOSLAVIA, 1946

## PART ONE

### FUNDAMENTAL PRINCIPLES

#### CHAPTER I
#### THE FEDERAL PEOPLES REPUBLIC OF YUGOSLAVIA

##### Article 1

The Federal Peoples Republic of Yugoslavia is a federal peoples state, republican in form, a community of peoples equal in rights who, on the basis of the right to self-determination, including the right of separation, have expressed their will to live together in a federative state.

##### Article 2

The Federal Peoples Republic of Yugoslavia is composed of the Peoples Republic of Serbia, the Peoples Republic of Croatia, the Peoples Republic of Slovenia, the Peoples Republic of Bosnia and Hercegovina, the Peoples Republic of Macedonia, and the Peoples Republic of Montenegro.

The Peoples Republic of Serbia includes the autonomous province of the Vojvodina and the autonomous Kosovo-Metohijan region.

##### Article 3

The state coat of arms of the Federal Peoples Republic of Yugoslavia represents a field encircled by ears of corn. At the base the ears are tied with a ribbon on which is inscribed the date 29-XI-1943. Between the tops of the ears is a five-pointed star. In the center of the field five torches are laid obliquely, their several flames merging into one single flame.

##### Article 4

The state flag of the Federal Peoples Republic of Yugoslavia consists of three colors: blue, white, and red, with a red five-pointed star in the middle. The ratio of the width to the length of the flag is as one to two. The colors of the flag are placed horizontally in the following order from above: blue, white, and red. Each color covers one-third of the flag's width. The star has a regular five-pointed shape and a gold (yellow) border. The central point of the star coincides with the intersection point of the diagonals of the flag. The topmost point of the star reaches halfway up the blue field of the flag, so that the lower points of the star occupy corresponding positions in the red field of the flag.

##### Article 5

The principal town of the Federal Peoples Republic of Yugoslavia is Belgrade.

## CHAPTER II

## THE PEOPLES AUTHORITY

### Article 6

All authority in the Federal Peoples Republic of Yugoslavia derives from the people and belongs to the people.

The people exercise their authority through freely elected representative organs of state authority, the peoples committees, which, from local peoples committees up to the assemblies of the peoples republics and the Peoples Assembly of the FPRY, originated and developed during the struggle for national liberation against fascism and reaction, and are the fundamental achievement of that struggle.

### Article 7

All the representative organs of state authority are elected by the citizens on the basis of universal, equal, and direct suffrage by secret ballot.

The peoples representatives in all organs of state authority are responsible to their electors. It will be determined by law in which cases, under what conditions, and in what way the electors may recall their representatives even before the end of the period for which they were elected.

### Article 8

The organs of state authority exercise their power on the basis of the Constitution of the FPRY, the constitutions of the peoples republics, the laws of the FPRY, the laws of the peoples republics, and the general regulations issued by the higher organs of state authority.

All acts of the state administration and judiciary organs must be founded on law.

## CHAPTER III

## FUNDAMENTAL RIGHTS OF THE PEOPLES AND THE PEOPLES REPUBLICS

### Article 9

The sovereignty of the peoples republics composing the FPRY is limited only by the rights which by this Constitution are given to the FPRY.

The FPRY protects and defends the sovereign rights of the peoples republics.

The FPRY protects the security and the social and political order of the peoples republics.

### Article 10

Any act directed against the sovereignty, equality, and national freedom of the peoples of the FPRY and their peoples republics is contrary to the Constitution.

### Article 11

Each peoples republic has its own Constitution.

The peoples republic makes its Constitution independently.

The Constitution of the peoples republic reflects the special characteristics of the republic and must be in conformity with the Constitution of the FPRY.

### Article 12

The Peoples Assembly of the FPRY determines the boundaries between the peoples republics.

The boundaries of a peoples republic cannot be altered without its consent.

### Article 13

National minorities in the FPRY enjoy the right to and protection of their own cultural development and the free use of their own language.

## CHAPTER IV

### SOCIAL-ECONOMIC ORGANIZATION

### Article 14

Means of production in the Federal Peoples Republic of Yugoslavia are either the property of the entire people, i.e., property in the hands of the state, or the property of the peoples coöperative organizations, or else the property of private persons or legal entities.

All mineral and other wealth underground, the waters, including mineral and medicinal waters, the sources of natural power, the means of rail and air transport, the posts, telegraphs, telephones, and broadcasting are national property.

The means of production in the hands of the state are exploited by the state itself or given to others for exploitation.

Foreign trade is under the control of the state.

### Article 15

In order to protect the vital interests of the people, to further the prosperity of the people and the right use of all economic potentialities and forces, the state directs the economic life and development of the country in accordance with a general economic plan, relying on the state and coöperative economic sectors, while achieving a general control over the private economic sector.

In carrying out the general economic plan and economic control, the state relies on the coöperation of syndicalist organizations of workmen and employees and other organizations of the working people.

### Article 16

The property of the entire people is the mainstay of the state in the development of the national economy.

The property of the entire people is under the special protection of the state.

The administration and disposal of the property of the entire people are determined by law.

## Article 17

The state devotes special attention to the peoples coöperative organizations and offers them assistance and facilities.

## Article 18

Private property and private initiative in the economy are guaranteed.

The inheritance of private property is guaranteed. The right of inheritance is regulated by law.

No person is permitted to use the right of private property to the detriment of the peoples community.

The existence of private monopolist organizations, such as cartels, syndicates, trusts, and similar organizations created for the purpose of dictating prices, monopolizing the market, and damaging the interests of the national economy, is forbidden.

Private property may be limited or expropriated if the common interest requires it, but only in accordance with the law. It will be determined by law in which cases and to what extent the owner shall be compensated.

Under the same conditions, individual branches of the national economy or single enterprises may be nationalized by law if the common interest requires it.

## Article 19

The land belongs to those who cultivate it.

The law determines whether and how much land may be owned by an institution or a person who is not a cultivator.

There can be no large landholdings in private hands on any basis whatsoever. The maximum size of private landholdings will be determined by law.

The state particularly protects and assists poor peasants and peasants with medium-sized holdings by its general economic policy, its low rates of credit, and its tax system.

## Article 20

By economic and other measures the state assists the working people to associate and organize themselves for protection against economic exploitation.

The state protects persons who are engaged as workers or employees especially by assuring them the right of association, by limiting the working day, by insuring the right to paid annual holidays, by controlling working conditions, by devoting attention to housing conditions and social insurance.

Minors in employment enjoy the special protection of the state.

## CHAPTER V
## RIGHTS AND DUTIES OF CITIZENS
### Article 21

All citizens of the Federal Peoples Republic of Yugoslavia are equal before the law and enjoy equal rights regardless of nationality, race, and creed.

No privileges on account of birth, position, property status, or degree of education are recognized.

Any act granting privileges to citizens or limiting their rights on grounds of difference of nationality, race, and creed, and any propagation of national, racial, and religious hatred and discord are contrary to the Constitution and punishable.

## Article 22

The citizens of the FPRY are bound to comply with the Constitution and laws.

## Article 23

All citizens, regardless of sex, nationality, race, creed, degree of education, or place of residence, who are over 18 years of age have the right to elect and be elected to all organs of state authority.

Citizens in the ranks of the Yugoslav Army have the same right to elect and be elected as other citizens.

The suffrage is universal, equal, and direct, and is carried out by secret ballot.

The suffrage is not enjoyed by persons under guardianship, persons deprived of electoral rights by sentence of a court of law for the duration of the sentence, and persons who have lost their electoral rights in accordance with federal law.

## Article 24

Women have equal rights with men in all fields of state, economic, and social-political life.

Women have the right to the same pay as that received by men for the same work, and as workers or employees they enjoy special protection.

The state especially protects the interests of mothers and children by the establishment of maternity hospitals, children's homes, and day nurseries, and by the right of mothers to a leave with pay before and after childbirth.

## Article 25

Freedom of conscience and freedom of religion are guaranteed to citizens.

The Church is separate from the state.

Religious communities whose teaching is not contrary to the Constitution are free in their religious affairs and in the performance of religious ceremonies. Religious schools for the education of priests are free and are under the general supervision of the state.

The abuse of the Church and of religion for political purposes and the existence of political organizations on a religious basis are forbidden.

The state may extend material assistance to religious communities.

## Article 26

Matrimony and the family are under the protection of the state. The state regulates by law the legal relations of marriage and the family.

Marriage is valid only if concluded before the competent state organs. After the marriage, citizens may go through a religious wedding ceremony.

All matrimonial disputes come within the competence of the peoples courts.

The registration of births, marriages, and deaths is conducted by the state.

Parents have the same obligations and duties to children born out of wedlock as to those born in wedlock. The position of children born out of wedlock is regulated by law.

Minors are under the special protection of the state.

### Article 27

Citizens are guaranteed freedom of the press, freedom of speech, freedom of association, freedom of assembly, and freedom to hold public meetings and demonstrations.

### Article 28

Citizens are guaranteed inviolability of person.

No person may be detained under arrest for longer than three days without the written and motivated decision of a court of law or of a public prosecutor. The maximum period of detention is determined by law.

No person may be punished for a criminal act except by sentence of a competent court on the basis of the law establishing the competence of the court and defining the offense.

Punishments may be determined and pronounced only on the basis of the law.

No person, if within the reach of the state authorities, may be tried without being given a lawful hearing and duly invited to defend himself.

Punishments for infringements of legal prescriptions may be pronounced by the organs of the state administration only within the limits set by law.

No citizen of the FPRY may be banished from the country.

Only in cases defined by law may a citizen be expelled from his place of residence.

Federal law determines in which cases and in what manner citizens of the FPRY may be deprived of their citizenship.

Citizens of the FPRY in foreign countries enjoy the protection of the FPRY.

### Article 29

The dwelling is inviolable.

Nobody may enter another person's dwelling or premises or search them against the occupant's will without a legal search warrant.

A search may be made only in the presence of two witnesses. The occupant of the premises has the right to be present during the search of his dwelling or premises.

### Article 30

The privacy of letters and other means of communication is inviolable except in cases of criminal inquiry, mobilization, or war.

### Article 31

Foreign citizens persecuted on account of their struggle for the principles of democracy, for national liberation, the rights of the working people, or the freedom of scientific and cultural work enjoy the right of asylum in the FPRY.

### Article 32

It is the duty of every citizen to work according to his abilities; he who does not contribute to the community cannot receive from it.

### Article 33

All public offices are equally accessible to all citizens in accordance with the conditions of the law.

It is the duty of citizens to perform conscientiously the public duties to which they have been elected or which are entrusted to them.

### Article 34

The defense of the fatherland is the supreme duty and honor of every citizen.

High treason is the greatest crime toward the people.

Military service is universal for all citizens.

### Article 35

The state insures disabled ex-servicemen a decent living and free occupational training.

The children of fallen soldiers and of war victims are under the special care of the state.

### Article 36

The state promotes the improvement of public health by organizing and controlling health services, hospitals, pharmacies, sanatoria, nursing and convalescent homes, and other health institutions.

The state extends its care to the physical education of the people, especially of young people, in order to increase the health and the working capacity of the people and the power of defense of the state.

### Article 37

The freedom of scientific and artistic work is assured.

The state assists science and art with a view to developing the culture and prosperity of the people.

Copyright is protected by law.

### Article 38

In order to raise the general cultural standard of the people, the state insures the accessibility of schools and other educational and cultural institutions to all classes of the people.

The state pays special attention to the young and protects their education.

Schools are state-owned. The founding of private schools may be permitted only by law and their work is controlled by the state.

Elementary education is compulsory and free.

The school is separate from the Church.

### Article 39

Citizens have the right to address requests and petitions to the organs of the state authorities.

Citizens have the right of appeal against the decisions of the organs of the state administration and the irregular proceedings of official persons. The procedure for lodging an appeal will be prescribed by law.

### Article 40

Every citizen has the right to file a suit against official persons before a competent tribunal on account of criminal acts committed by them in their official work.

### Article 41

Subject to conditions prescribed by law, citizens have the right to seek indemnity from the state and from official persons for damage resulting from the illegal or irregular discharge of official functions.

### Article 42

All citizens shall pay taxes in proportion to their economic capacity.

Public taxes and duties and exemptions from them are established only by law.

### Article 43

With a view to safeguarding the civil liberties and democratic organization of the FPRY established by this Constitution, it is declared illegal and punishable to make use of civil rights in order to change or undermine the constitutional order for antidemocratic purposes.


# PART TWO

## ORGANIZATION OF THE STATE


### CHAPTER VI

### THE FEDERAL PEOPLES REPUBLIC OF YUGOSLAVIA AND THE PEOPLES REPUBLICS

### Article 44

The Federal Peoples Republic of Yugoslavia exercises all the rights vested in it by the Constitution.

Under the jurisdiction of the FPRY as represented by the highest federal organs of state authority and the organs of state administration are included:

1) Amendments to the Constitution of the FPRY, control over the observance of the Constitution, and the insuring of the conformity of the constitutions of the peoples republics with the Constitution of the FPRY;

2) the admission of new republics and approval of the foundation of new autonomous provinces and autonomous regions;

3) the delimitation of boundaries between the republics;

4) the representation of the FPRY in international relations; international treaties;

5) questions of war and peace;

6) the general direction and control of commercial relations with foreign countries;

7) national defense and the security of the state;

8) traffic by rail, air, river, and sea and navigational affairs of national importance;

9) posts, telegraphs, telephones, and wireless;

10) federal citizenship;

11) matters connected with emigration and immigration; the legal status of foreigners;

12) the general economic plan of the state; statistics;

13) the federal budget; the passing of the general state budget and of final accounts; supreme control over the administration of the general state budget;

14) the monetary and credit system; federal loans; foreign exchange and currency transactions; insurance; customs; state monopolies;

15) patents, trade-marks, models, samples, measures, weights, precious metals;

16) care for disabled ex-servicemen;

17) amnesty and pardon in cases of acts violating federal laws;

18) financial, industrial, mining, building, commercial, forestry, and agricultural concerns of national importance;

19) roads, rivers, canals, and ports of national importance;

20) control over the carrying out of federal laws;

21) legislation concerning the distribution of revenues to the federal budget, the budgets of the republics and those of autonomous and administrative territorial units; legislation concerning public loans and taxes;

22) legislation concerning the organization of the law courts, public prosecution, advocateship; criminal law; commercial, exchange, and cheque law; maritime law; legislation concerning civil procedure, litigious and nonlitigious; executive, bankruptcy, criminal, and general administrative procedure; the personal status of citizens;

23) basic legislation concerning labor, enterprises, and social insurance; coöperative societies; civil rights;

24) the establishment of general principles for the legislation and administration of the republics in the domains of agriculture, mining, forestry, hunting, water power; building; economic administration; regulation of prices; health and physical culture; education; social welfare and the organization of state authority. The republics may issue their own prescriptions in these matters until general principles are laid down by the FPRY.

Outside these matters the peoples republics exercise their authority independently.

## Article 45

The territory of the FPRY consists of the territories of its republics and forms a single state and economic area.

### Article 46

Federal laws are valid throughout the territory of the FPRY.

In case of discrepancy between federal laws and the laws of the republics, federal law shall be applied.

### Article 47

The traffic of goods between republics is free and cannot be restricted by the laws of any republic.

Acts and documents issued by organs of state administration and organs of justice of one republic have the same validity in every republic.

### Article 48

A single federal citizenship is established for the citizens of the FPRY. Every citizen of a peoples republic is at the same time a citizen of the FPRY.

Every citizen of a republic enjoys in every republic the same rights as the citizens of that republic.

## CHAPTER VII

### SUPREME FEDERAL ORGANS OF STATE AUTHORITY

*a)* The Peoples Assembly of the Federal Peoples Republic of Yugoslavia

### Article 49

The Peoples Assembly of the FPRY is the representative of the sovereignty of the people of the FPRY.

### Article 50

The Peoples Assembly is the supreme organ of state authority of the FPRY and exercises all those rights belonging to the FPRY which are not transferred by the Constitution to the jurisdiction of other federal organs of state authority and state administration.

### Article 51

The Peoples Assembly of the FPRY exercises exclusively the power of legislation in all matters within the jurisdiction of the FPRY.

### Article 52

The Peoples Assembly of the FPRY consists of two Houses—the Federal Council and the Council of Nationalities.

### Article 53

The Federal Council is elected by all citizens of the FPRY. For every 50,000 inhabitants one deputy is elected.

### Article 54

The Council of Nationalities is elected in the republics, autonomous provinces, and autonomous regions. The citizens of each republic elect 30, the autonomous provinces 20, and the autonomous regions 15, representatives.

### Article 55

No person can be a deputy in both Houses of the Peoples Assembly of the FPRY at the same time.

### Article 56

The Peoples Assembly of the FPRY is elected for a term of four years.

### Article 57

Both Houses of the Peoples Assembly of the FPRY have equal rights.

### Article 58

The Houses of the Peoples Assembly of the FPRY as a rule sit separately.

The sessions of the Federal Council and the Council of Nationalities open and close simultaneously.

### Article 59

The Federal Council elects a president, two vice-presidents, and three secretaries.

The Council of Nationalities elects a president, two vice-presidents, and three secretaries.

The presidents conduct the meetings of the Houses and their work according to the rules of procedure.

### Article 60

The sessions of the Peoples Assembly of the FPRY are regular or extraordinary and are convened by a decree of the Presidium of the Peoples Assembly of the FPRY.

Regular sessions are convened twice a year: on April 15 and on October 15. If the Peoples Assembly is not convened on these dates, it can meet even without the decree of the Presidium.

Extraordinary sessions are convened whenever the Presidium of the Peoples Assembly of the FPRY considers it necessary, whenever one of the republics requests it through its supreme organ of state authority, or if one-third of the deputies of one House request it.

### Article 61

Both Houses of the Peoples Assembly of the FPRY sit in joint meeting only when this Constitution expressly provides for it or when both Houses so decide.

Joint meetings of the Peoples Assembly of the FPRY are presided over alternately by the presidents of the Houses.

At a joint meeting of the Peoples Assembly of the FPRY, resolutions are carried by a majority of votes. For the passing of resolutions, the presence of the majority of the deputies of each House is required.

### Article 62

Each House prescribes its own rule of order and the Peoples Assembly of the FPRY prescribes the rule of procedure for joint meetings.

### Article 63

The government of the FPRY, the members of the government of the FPRY, and the deputies of both Houses have the right to introduce bills.

A bill may be introduced in either House of the Peoples Assembly of the FPRY.

No bill may become law unless it receives a majority of votes in both Houses during a meeting at which a majority of the deputies of each House is present.

### Article 64

Each House of the Peoples Assembly of the FPRY has the right to propose amendments to a bill already accepted in one House. Thus amended, the bill is returned for confirmation to the House in which it originated.

If agreement is not reached, the matter is submitted to a coördinating committee of the Peoples Assembly of the FPRY, which comprises an equal number of members of both Houses.

If the coördinating committee does not reach an agreement or if one of the Houses rejects the solution proposed by the coördinating committee, the Houses will reconsider the whole matter.

If again no agreement is reached, the Peoples Assembly of the FPRY shall be dissolved.

The dissolution decree shall also embody the order for holding new elections.

### Article 65

Laws and other general prescriptions of the FPRY are published in the languages of the peoples republics.

### Article 66

A law comes into force on the eighth day after its publication in the *Official Gazette* of the FPRY, unless the law itself provides otherwise.

### Article 67

Each House elects committees to which it entrusts specific matters.

Each House at its first meeting elects a verification committee which examines the deputies' mandates.

On the proposal of its committee each House confirms or annuls the deputies' mandates.

### Article 68

The Peoples Assembly of the FPRY and each of its Houses may, through their inquiry committees, carry out inquiries on any matter of general significance.

It is the duty of all state organs to comply with the demands of inquiry committees for the establishment of facts and collection of evidence.

### Article 69

Deputies of the Peoples Assembly of the FPRY enjoy rights of immunity. Deputies may not be arrested nor may criminal proceedings be instituted against them without the approval of the House to which they belong or of the Presidium of the Peoples Assembly of the FPRY, unless taken in the act of committing an offense, in which case the Presidium of the Peoples Assembly must immediately be informed.

### Article 70

In case of war or similar extraordinary circumstances, the Peoples Assembly of the FPRY may prolong the duration of its mandate as long as such circumstances exist.

The Peoples Assembly of the FPRY may decide to dissolve even before the end of the period for which it was elected.

### Article 71

Elections for a new Peoples Assembly of the FPRY must be announced before the expiry of the last day of the period for which the outgoing Peoples Assembly was elected.

Not less than two and not more than three months shall elapse between the date of dissolution of the Peoples Assembly of the FPRY and the date of elections for a new Peoples Assembly of the FPRY.

### Article 72

The Peoples Assembly of the FPRY passes amendments to the Constitution.

A proposal to amend the Constitution may be submitted by the Presidium of the Peoples Assembly of the FPRY, by the government of the FPRY, or by one-third of the deputies of one of the Houses.

A proposed amendment to the Constitution must be approved by a majority of votes in each House.

The proposed amendment to the Constitution is adopted if an absolute majority of the total number of deputies in each House votes in its favor.

An adopted amendment to the Constitution is promulgated by the Peoples Assembly of the FPRY at a joint meeting of both Houses.

### b) Presidium of the Peoples Assembly of the Federal Peoples Republic of Yugoslavia

### Article 73

The Peoples Assembly of the FPRY elects the Presidium of the Peoples Assembly of the FPRY at a joint meeting of both Houses.

The Presidium of the Peoples Assembly of the FPRY consists of a president, six vice-presidents, a secretary, and not more than thirty members.

### Article 74

The Presidium of the Peoples Assembly of the FPRY performs the following functions:

1) convenes the sessions of the Peoples Assembly of the FPRY;

2) dissolves the Peoples Assembly of the FPRY in the event of disagreement of the Houses over a bill;

3) orders elections for the Peoples Assembly of the FPRY;

4) gives the ruling as to whether a law of the republics is in conformity with the Constitution of the FPRY and with the federal laws, subject to the ratification of the Peoples Assembly of the FPRY, at the request of the government of the FPRY, the Presidium of the peoples assemblies of the republics, the Supreme Court of the FPRY, the public prosecutor of the FPRY, or on its own initiative;

5) gives obligatory interpretations of federal laws;

6) proclaims laws which have been passed; issues decrees;

7) exercises the right of pardon according to the provisions of the law;

8) awards decorations and confers honorary titles of the FPRY according to the provisions of the federal law;

9) ratifies international treaties;

10) appoints and recalls ambassadors, envoys extraordinary, and ministers plenipotentiary to foreign countries on the proposal of the government of the FPRY;

11) receives the credentials and letters of recall of diplomatic representatives accredited to it by foreign countries;

12) declares general mobilization and state of war in the event of an armed attack against the FPRY, or in case of necessity for the immediate fulfillment of international obligations of the FPRY toward the international peace organization or toward an allied country;

13) on the proposal of the president of the government of the FPRY and subject to ratification by the Peoples Assembly of the FPRY, appoints and relieves of their office individual members of the government during the period between two sessions of the Peoples Assembly of the FPRY;

14) appoints the deputies of members of the government on the proposal of the president of the government of the FPRY;

15) modifies, unites, and abolishes existing ministries and commissions on the proposal of the president of the government of the FPRY, during the period between sessions of the Peoples Assembly of the FPRY, and subject to ratification by the latter;

16) determines, upon the proposal of the government of the FPRY, what enterprises and institutions are of national significance and come under the direct administration of the federal government;

17) orders a peoples referendum on matters within the jurisdiction of the FPRY on the basis of a resolution of the Peoples Assembly of the FPRY or on the proposal of the government of the FPRY.

The decrees of the Presidium of the Peoples Assembly of the FPRY are signed by the president and the secretary.

## Article 75

The Presidium of the Peoples Assembly of the FPRY is responsible for its work to the Peoples Assembly of the FPRY. The Peoples Assembly of the FPRY may recall the Presidium and elect a new one, and also relieve individual members of their functions and elect new ones even before the end of the term for which they have been elected.

### Article 76

When the Peoples Assembly of the FPRY is dissolved, the Presidium carries out its duty until the Presidium of the new Peoples Assembly of the FPRY is elected.

The newly elected Peoples Assembly of the FPRY shall meet within one month of the conclusion of the elections.

## CHAPTER VIII
## FEDERAL ORGANS OF STATE ADMINISTRATION

### Article 77

The highest executive and administrative organ of state authority of the Federal Peoples Republic of Yugoslavia is the government of the FPRY.

The government of the FPRY is appointed and relieved of its functions by the Peoples Assembly of the FPRY at a joint meeting of both Houses.

The government of the FPRY is responsible to and accountable for its work to the Peoples Assembly of the FPRY. In the interval between two sessions of the Peoples Assembly of the FPRY the government is responsible to and accountable for its work to the Presidium of the Peoples Assembly of the FPRY.

### Article 78

The government of the FPRY acts on the basis of the Constitution and federal laws.

The government of the FPRY issues regulations for the application of laws and regulations on the basis of legal authorization, as well as instructions and orders for the execution of federal laws. The government of the FPRY sees to the execution of federal laws and supervises their application.

Regulations, instructions, orders, and decisions of the government of the FPRY are signed by the president of the government and by the responsible minister.

### Article 79

Regulations, instructions, orders, and decisions of the government of the FPRY are binding throughout the territory of the FPRY.

### Article 80

The government of the FPRY directs and coördinates the work of its ministries, commissions, and committees.

The government of the FPRY sees to the preparing and carrying out of the national economic plan and budget; draws up and carries out the annual economic plans; controls the credit and monetary system; undertakes all necessary measures for the safeguarding and protection of the constitutional order and of the rights of citizens; directs the general organization of the Yugoslav Army; directs the maintenance of relations with foreign states; sees to the carrying out of international treaties and obligations; decides upon bills presented by individual members of the government to the Peoples Assembly of the FPRY; prescribes the internal organization of ministries and of subordinate institutions; appoints committees, commissions, and institutions for the carrying out of economic, defensive, and cultural measures.

### Article 81

The government of the FPRY consists of the president, vice-presidents, ministers, the chairman of the Federal Planning Commission, and the chairman of the Federal Control Commission.

The government of the FPRY may also include ministers without portfolio.

### Article 82

The members of the government of the FPRY, before taking up their duties, take the oath before the Presidium of the Peoples Assembly of the FPRY.

### Article 83

The president of the government of the FPRY represents the government, presides over the meetings, and directs the work of the government.

### Article 84

Members of the government of the FPRY are responsible under criminal law if, in the execution of their official duties, they trespass against the Constitution and laws.

They are responsible for any damage which they cause to the state by illegal acts.

More explicit provisions concerning the responsibility of members of the government of the FPRY are laid down by federal law.

### Article 85

The ministers of the government of the FPRY direct the branches of the state administration which come within the competence of the FPRY.

The ministers of the federal government, the chairman of the Federal Planning Commission, and the chairman of the Federal Control Commission issue rules, instructions, and orders on the basis of and for the application of federal laws, regulations, instructions, and orders of the federal government.

The ministers see to the proper execution of the federal laws, regulations, instructions, and orders of the federal government and are responsible for their application within the branch of state administration under their direction.

### Article 86

The ministries of the government of the FPRY are either federal or federal-republican.

Federal ministries are: the Ministry of Foreign Affairs; the Ministry of National Defense; the Ministry of Communications; the Ministry of Shipping; the Ministry of Posts; the Ministry of Foreign Trade.

Federal-republican ministries are: the Ministry of Finance; the Ministry of the Interior; the Ministry of Justice; the Ministry of Industry; the Ministry of

Mines; the Ministry of Commerce and Supplies; the Ministry of Agriculture and Forestry; the Ministry of Labor; the Ministry of Public Works.

### Article 87

The federal ministries administer, as a rule directly through their own organs, a given branch of state administration throughout the territory of the FPRY.

The federal ministries, in order to carry out those affairs for which they are responsible, may appoint their representatives to the governments of the republics and set up departments and sections attached to the peoples committees.

### Article 88

The federal-republican ministries direct a determined branch of state administration indirectly through the corresponding ministries of the peoples republics, and can administer directly only specified affairs, enterprises, and institutions of national significance.

### Article 89

The government of the FPRY includes committees concerned with education and culture, public health, and social welfare and appointed for the general direction of these branches of state administration.

Such committees may be formed for other affairs of state administration.

## CHAPTER IX

## SUPREME ORGANS OF STATE AUTHORITY OF THE PEOPLES REPUBLICS

### Article 90

The supreme organ of state authority of a peoples republic is the Peoples Assembly of the republic.

The Peoples Assembly of a republic is elected by the citizens of the republic for a period of four years according to the terms of the Constitution and the laws of the republic.

### Article 91

The Peoples Assembly of a republic exercises the sovereign rights of the republic in the name of the people on the basis of the Constitution of the republic and in conformity with the Constitution of the FPRY. It deals with all matters within the jurisdiction of the republic so far as they are not transferred by the Constitution of the republic to the competence of the Presidium of the Peoples Assembly of the republic or to the government of the republic.

### Article 92

Legislative power in the republic is exercised exclusively by the Peoples Assembly of the republic.

## Article 93

The Peoples Assembly of the republic elects a president, a vice-president, and secretaries to conduct its sessions.

## Article 94

The Peoples Assembly elects the Presidium of the Peoples Assembly of the republic, consisting of a president, one or more vice-presidents, a secretary, and members, whose number is determined by the Constitution of the republic.

The competence of the Presidium of the Peoples Assembly of the republic is determined by the Constitution of the republic.

## Article 95

The Peoples Assembly of the republic appoints the government of the republic and relieves it of its functions.

## CHAPTER X

### ORGANS OF STATE ADMINISTRATION OF THE PEOPLES REPUBLICS

## Article 96

The highest executive and administrative organ of state authority of a peoples republic is the government of the peoples republic.

The government of a peoples republic is responsible to the Peoples Assembly of the republic, to which it gives account for its work. In the interval between two sessions of the Peoples Assembly, the government of the republic is responsible and accountable for its work to the Presidium of the Peoples Assembly of the republic.

## Article 97

The government of a republic acts on the basis of the Constitution of the FPRY, the Constitution of the republic, the federal laws, the laws of the republic, and the regulations, instructions, and orders of the federal government.

The government of a republic issues regulations for the application of the federal laws, the laws of the republic, the regulations, instructions, and orders of the federal government; it issues regulations on the basis of legal authorization and also instructions and orders for the application of federal laws and the laws of the republic, and controls their application.

## Article 98

The ministers of a republic have the right to issue rules, orders, and instructions on the basis of and for the execution of the federal laws, the laws of the republic, and the regulations, instructions, and orders of the federal government and the government of the republic.

The ministers of the republic supervise the proper execution of the federal laws, the laws of the republic, and the regulations, instructions, and orders of the federal government and the government of the republic.

### Article 99

The ministries of a republic are federal-republican or republican.

### Article 100

Federal-republican ministries in a peoples republic direct specified branches of state administration and, in addition to matters within their own competence, deal with matters in the competence of the federal-republican ministries of the federal government, on the basis of their rules, instructions, orders, and decisions.

### Article 101

The republican ministries direct independently certain specified branches of state administration which come within the competence of the peoples republic concerned.

### Article 102

The ministries of a republic are determined by the Constitution of the republic in conformity with the Constitution of the FPRY.

The Presidium of the Peoples Assembly of a republic may change, unite, or abolish the existing ministries in conformity with the Constitution of the FPRY, the Constitution of the republic, the federal laws, and the decisions of the Presidium of the Peoples Assembly of the FPRY.

## CHAPTER XI

## ORGANS OF STATE AUTHORITY OF AUTONOMOUS PROVINCES AND AUTONOMOUS REGIONS

### Article 103

The rights and the scope of the autonomy of autonomous provinces and autonomous regions are determined by the Constitution of the republic.

### Article 104

The statute of an autonomous province or of an autonomous region is drawn up in conformity with the Constitution of the FPRY and the Constitution of the republic by the highest organ of state authority of the autonomous province or autonomous region, and is confirmed by the Peoples Assembly of the republic.

### Article 105

The highest organ of state authority of an autonomous province is the Peoples Assembly of the autonomous province, which is elected by the citizens of the autonomous province for a period of three years and meets in accordance with the provisions of the Constitution of the republic.

The Peoples Assembly of an autonomous province elects the Principal Executive Committee of the autonomous province as its executive and administrative organ.

### Article 106

The highest organ of state authority of an autonomous region is the Regional Peoples Committee, which is elected by the citizens of the autonomous region for a period of three years and holds its assemblies in accordance with the provisions of the Constitution of the republic.

The Regional Peoples Committee elects the Regional Executive Committee as its executive and administrative organ.

## CHAPTER XII

## ORGANS OF STATE AUTHORITY OF ADMINISTRATIVE-TERRITORIAL UNITS

### Article 107

The peoples committees are the organs of state authority in localities (villages, small towns), districts, town-wards, towns, departments, and regions.

The peoples committees of localities are elected by the citizens for a term of two years, and the peoples committees of districts, town-wards, towns, departments, and regions are elected by the citizens for a term of three years.

The peoples committees of districts, town-wards, towns, departments, and regions hold their regular assemblies within terms prescribed by the Constitution of the peoples republic.

### Article 108

The peoples committees direct the work of subordinate organs of administration and economic and cultural development in their sphere of action; they insure the maintenance of public order, the execution of the laws, and the protection of the rights of citizens; they draw up their own budgets.

The peoples committees issue, within the framework of their competence, general rules (decisions) on the basis of the Federal Constitution, the Constitution of the republic, the federal laws, the laws of the republic, and the general rules of higher organs of state authority.

### Article 109

It is the duty of the peoples committees, in the execution of their general and local duties, to rely on the initiative and wide participation of the masses of the people and the workers' organizations.

### Article 110

The executive and administrative organs of the peoples committees, except in smaller villages, are the executive committees. An executive committee consists of a president, vice-president, secretary, and members.

Executive committees are elected by the peoples committees from among their members.

### Article 111

The executive organ of the peoples committee of a smaller village consists of a chairman and a secretary.

### Article 112

The local peoples committee convenes, within the time limits set by law, a local meeting of the electors to whom they are accountable for their work. The rights and duties of the local meeting of electors are determined by law.

### Article 113

The executive and administrative organs of the peoples committees are subordinate both to their own peoples committees and also to executive and administrative organs of state authority of higher rank.

### Article 114

A peoples committee may have, under the control of its executive committee, departments or sections to deal with individual branches of administration. The departments and sections are subordinate in their work to the executive committee and at the same time to the corresponding department of the higher peoples committee and to the competent ministry of the republic.

## CHAPTER XIII

## THE PEOPLES COURTS

### Article 115

The organs of justice in the Federal Peoples Republic of Yugoslavia are: the Supreme Court of the FPRY, the Supreme Courts of the republics and autonomous provinces, the departmental and district courts.

The organization and competence of military tribunals are regulated by federal law.

Special courts for specified categories of disputes may be set up by law.

### Article 116

The law courts are independent in their dispensing of justice and mete out justice according to the law.

The courts are separate from the administration in all instances.

Higher courts have, within the limits of the law, the right of supervision over lower courts.

### Article 117

The law courts dispense justice in the name of the people.

### Article 118

Proceedings in the law courts are as a rule public.

The resolutions of a court may be altered only by a competent higher court.

The accused is guaranteed the right of defense before a court.

### Article 119

All courts as a rule judge in council.

The council of district and departmental courts, when judging in the first instance, consists of judges and judge-jurors, who have equal rights in the court's proceedings.

### Article 120

Judicial proceedings in the courts are conducted in the languages of the republics, autonomous provinces, and autonomous regions where the courts are located. Citizens not speaking the language in which the proceedings are conducted may use their own language. Such citizens are guaranteed the right to acquaint themselves with all the legal material and to follow the proceedings of the court through an interpreter.

### Article 121

Judges of the Supreme Court of the FPRY are elected and released from their functions by the Peoples Assembly of the FPRY at a joint meeting of both Houses.

Judges of the Supreme Court of a republic or autonomous province are elected and released from their functions by the Peoples Assembly of the republic or by the Peoples Assembly of the autonomous province.

Judges and judge-jurors of a departmental court in a department or town are elected and released from their functions by the peoples committee of the department or town.

Judges and judge-jurors of a district court in a district or town are elected and released from their functions by the peoples committee of the district or town.

### Article 122

The Supreme Court of the FPRY is the highest organ of justice of the FPRY.

It is determined by federal law in what cases the Supreme Court of the FPRY shall judge in the first and in what cases in the second instance.

### Article 123

The Supreme Court of the FPRY decides on the legality of the judgments of all courts in the FPRY from the point of view of the application of federal laws.

The Supreme Courts of republics and autonomous provinces ascertain the legality of the judgments of all courts of the republic or autonomous province.

## CHAPTER XIV

### PUBLIC PROSECUTION

### Article 124

The public prosecution is the organ of the Peoples Assembly of the FPRY for supervising the proper application of the law by all ministries and other administrative organs and institutions subordinate to them in the FPRY and in the peoples republics, by public officials and by all citizens.

### Article 125

The public prosecutor of the FPRY and his deputies are elected and released from their functions by the Peoples Assembly of the FPRY at a joint meeting of both Houses.

The public prosecutors of the peoples republics and their deputies are appointed and released from their functions by the public prosecutor of the FPRY.

The public prosecutors of autonomous provinces, autonomous regions, regions, departments, and districts are appointed and released from their functions by the public prosecutor of the republic subject to the confirmation of the public prosecutor of the FPRY.

### Article 126

Public prosecutors are independent in their work and are subordinate only to the public prosecutor of the FPRY.

### Article 127

Public prosecutors have the right to enter appeals and suits, the right of legal intervention in the course of judicial and administrative proceedings, the right to institute criminal proceedings, and the right to file a demand for the defense of legality against valid resolutions of law courts and administrative organs.

### Article 128

The military prosecutor of the Yugoslav Army and other military prosecutors are appointed by the commander in chief of the Yugoslav Army.

The organization and competence of the military prosecution will be determined by federal law.

## CHAPTER XV

## RELATION BETWEEN ORGANS OF STATE AUTHORITY AND ORGANS OF STATE ADMINISTRATION

### Article 129

The Presidium of the Peoples Assembly of the FPRY has the right to annul or abolish the regulations, instructions, orders, and decisions of the federal government if they are not in conformity with the Constitution and federal laws.

The federal government has the right to annul or abolish the rules, orders, instructions, and decisions of members of the federal government if they are not in conformity with the Constitution, the federal laws, and the regulations, instructions, orders, and decisions of the federal government.

### Article 130

The Presidium of the Peoples Assembly of a republic has the right to annul or abolish the regulations, instructions, orders, and decisions of the government of the republic if they are not in conformity with the Constitution of the FPRY, the Constitution of the republic, the federal laws, and the laws of the republic.

The government of the republic has the right to annul or abolish the rules, orders, instructions, and decisions of the ministers of the republic if they are not in conformity with the Federal Constitution, the Constitution of the Republic, the federal laws, the laws of the republic, and the regulations, instructions, orders, and decisions of the government of the republic.

### Article 131

In matters within federal competence, the federal government has the right to suspend the acts of the government of a republic and abolish the acts of the ministers of a republic if they are not in conformity with the Federal Constitution, the Constitution of the republic, the federal laws, the laws of the republic, the regulations, instructions, and orders of the federal government, or the rules, orders, and instructions of a member of the federal government.

Under the same conditions, the members of the federal government have the right to suspend the acts of the ministers of the republic.

### Article 132

The Presidium of the Peoples Assembly of a republic or the Peoples Assembly of an autonomous province and the peoples committees of higher rank have the right to annul or abolish illegal and irregular acts of peoples committees of lower rank.

The government of a republic, its individual ministers, and the Principal Executive Committee of an autonomous province have the right, within the limits of their competence, to annul or abolish the illegal or irregular acts of executive committees. The executive committees of peoples committees of higher rank have the same rights toward executive committees of lower rank.

A peoples committee has the right to annul or abolish illegal and irregular acts of its executive committee.

The executive committee of a peoples committee of higher rank or the Principal Executive Committee of an autonomous province and the government of a republic have the right to suspend the execution of illegal and irregular acts of a peoples committee of lower rank and to propose to its own peoples committee or to the Peoples Assembly of the autonomous province or to the Presidium of the Peoples Assembly of the republic, respectively, to annul or abolish them.

### Article 133

A peoples committee of higher rank, the Peoples Assembly of an autonomous province, or the Presidium of the Peoples Assembly of a republic has the right to dissolve any peoples committee of lower rank and to order elections for a new peoples committee to be held. A peoples committee of higher rank, the Peoples Assembly of an autonomous province, or the Presidium of the Peoples Assembly of a republic has the right to release from its functions the executive committee of any peoples committee of lower rank and to order elections for a new executive committee to be held.

## CHAPTER XVI

### THE YUGOSLAV ARMY

### Article 134

The Yugoslav Army is the armed force of the Federal Peoples Republic of Yugoslavia. Its duty is to safeguard and defend the independence of the state and the freedom of the people. It is the guardian of the inviolability of the state frontiers and serves the maintenance of peace and security.

### Article 135

The commander in chief of the Yugoslav Army is appointed by the Peoples Assembly of the FPRY at a joint meeting of both Houses. The commander in chief directs the entire military and armed forces of the FPRY.

## PART THREE

### TRANSITIONAL AND CONCLUDING PROVISIONS

### Article 136

On the day when the Constitution comes into force, all laws and other legal dispositions contrary to the Constitution are abolished.

Resolutions, laws, and regulations confirmed by the decision of the Constituent Assembly of December 1, 1945, remain in force until a final resolution with regard to them is made.

The legislative committees of both Houses of the Peoples Assembly of the FPRY are authorized, within a period of six months from the day when the Constitution comes into force, to examine all resolutions, laws, and regulations confirmed by the decision of the Constituent Assembly of December 1, 1945, to bring them into conformity with the Constitution and to issue laws deciding which of those resolutions, laws, and regulations shall remain in force without modification or to issue laws for the modification and amplification of those resolutions, laws, and regulations. These laws, issued by the legislative committees of both Houses of the Peoples Assembly of the FPRY, are promulgated by a decree of the Presidium of the Peoples Assembly of the FPRY and are submitted for confirmation to the Peoples Assembly of the FPRY at its first subsequent session. The proposals of resolutions, laws, and regulations shall, in order to be brought into conformity with the Constitution, be transmitted by the president of the government of the FPRY to the legislative committees.

### Article 137

All persons under the age of eighteen who have been entered in the lists of electors for the Constituent Assembly shall retain the electoral right thus acquired.

### Article 138

Existing ministries which are not provided for by the Constitution in the composition of the government of the FPRY may remain in the composition of the government until a resolution with regard to them is passed in accordance with Article 74, §15, of the Constitution.

## Article 139

The Constitution comes into force by promulgation at a joint meeting of both Houses of the Constituent Assembly.

Given at Belgrade, the principal town of the Federal Peoples Republic of Yugoslavia, January 31, 1946

PRESIDIUM OF THE CONSTITUENT ASSEMBLY OF THE
FEDERAL PEOPLES REPUBLIC OF YUGOSLAVIA

*Secretary*, Mile Peruničić                                  *President*, Ivan Ribar

*Vice-Presidents*

| | | |
|---|---|---|
| Moša Pijade | Dimitar Vlahov | Djuro Pucar |
| Josip Rus | Filip Lakuš | Marko Vujačić |

*Members*

| | | |
|---|---|---|
| Josip Broz—Tito | Vlada Zečević | Aleksandar Ranković |
| Bane Andrejev | Stevan Jakovljević | Zlatan Sremec |
| Vlado Bakarić | Blažo Jovanović | Dobrosav Tomašević |
| Dušan Brkić | Dragoljub Jovanović | Frane Frol |
| Josip Vidmar | Boris Kidrić | Andrija Hebrang |
| Milovan Djilas | Sava Kosanović | Avdo Humo |
| Edvard Kardelj | Lazar Kuliševski | Rodoljub Čolaković |
| Sreten Žujović | Blagoje Nešković | Vlado Šegrt |
| Siniša Stanković | Jaša Prodanović | |

# NOTES AND
# REFERENCES

# Notes and References

## NOTES TO CHAPTER I
### The Geographical Scene

[1] Jovan Cvijić, *La Péninsule balkanique* (Paris, 1918), is a standard work on the early history and sociology of Yugoslavia.

[2] Chataigneau, "Pays balkaniques," in *Géographie universelle* (Paris, 1934), Vol. VII, Part II.

[3] See the section on Yugoslavia in *South-Eastern Europe: A Political and Economic Survey*, Royal Institute of International Affairs (London and New York, 1939); also the valuable article by M. R. Shackleton, "Economic Resources of Jugoslavia," in *Scottish Geographical Magazine* (1925).

## NOTES TO CHAPTER II
### Racial History

[1] The evidence is given at greater length in Carleton Stevens Coon, *The Races of Europe* (New York, 1939), where the reader will find also a complete bibliography.

[2] N. Županić, *Revue Anthropologique*, Vol. 29 (1919), p. 28.

## NOTES TO CHAPTER V
### Serbia in the First World War

[1] Fernand Feyler, *Les Campagnes de Serbie* (Paris, 1926), pp. 1, 2; M. D. Lazarević, *Naši ratovi za oslobodjenje i ujedinjenje* ... (Belgrade, 1929–1934), I, 16–19. In 4 vols.

[2] A title bestowed only on a general who had won a victory in the field.

[3] The treaties are given in Vasil Radoslawoff (Radoslavov), *Bulgarien und die Weltkrise* (Berlin, 1923), pp. 172, 188–193; *Oesterreich-Ungarns letzter Krieg* (Oest. Bundesministerium für Heereswesen und vom Kriegsarchiv; Vienna, 1931–1936), III, 10, 11. In 6 vols.

[4] *Oesterreich-Ungarns letzter Krieg*, III², 29–34; Erich von Falkenhayn, *The German General Staff and Its Decisions, 1914–1916* (English trans.; New York, 1920), pp. 183–184.

[5] London *Times*, September 29, 1915.

[6] The treaty and military convention are printed in the Greek White Book (New York, 1917).

[7] *Le Temps*, October 4, 1915; March 6, 1916. See also John Mavrogordato, *Modern Greece: A Chronicle and a Survey, 1800–1931* (London, 1931), p. 109.

[8] *Military Operations, Macedonia* (comp. by Cyril Falls, with maps comp. by A. F. Becke; London, 1933–1935), I, 41. In 2 vols.

[9] Milan Dj. Nedić, *Srpska vojska na Albanskoj golgoti* (Belgrade, 1937), pp. 10, 11.

[10] *Ibid.*, p. 118.

[11] The narrative of the retreat has been drawn mainly from Nedić. The number of survivors has been variously estimated. These estimates are usually too low. The Italians, in particular, tried to convince their allies that no more than 50,000 men had gotten through, apparently hoping that they would not be expected to help so negligible a remnant. The approximate accuracy of this figure may be inferred from the fact that in June, 1916, the Serbian effectives at the Salonika front numbered 120,000 men, 25,000 remained in Corfu or in Africa, and thousands more had died after leaving Albania. See *Military Operations, Macedonia*, I, 120.

[12] Milosh Boghitchévitch (Miloš Bogićević), *Le Procès de Salonique* (Paris, 1927), *passim;* I. Gojković, "Radikali i vojska," in *Nova Evropa*, November 26, 1928, pp. 323–337.

[13] Ferdinand Šišić, *Jugoslavenska misao* (Belgrade, 1937), p. 268.

[14] *Ibid.*, pp. 268–269.

[15] "The Yugoslav Movement," in *Handbook* No. 14, British Foreign Office (London, 1920), p. 24.

[16] For the text of the Pact of Corfu see *ibid.*, pp. 35–38.

[17] *Military Operations, Macedonia*, II, 297.

[18] *Ibid.*, p. 150.

## NOTES TO CHAPTER VII

### CONSTITUTIONAL DEVELOPMENT TO 1914

[1] For the provisions of the Treaty of Bucharest of 1812, see Edward Hertslet, *The Map of Europe by Treaty* (London, 1875–1891), III, 2031–2032. In 4 vols.

[2] *Ibid.*, I, 747–748, 758–759; *British and Foreign State Papers*, XIII, 907.

[3] Hertslet, *op. cit.*, II, 832–834.

[4] *Ibid.*, pp. 842–847.

[5] Emile Haumant trenchantly describes the nuclear Serbian government in the last days of Miloš Obrenović, just before the proclamation of the Constitution of 1838: "The whole government was lodged in the Palace . . . for it was, in the last analysis, Miloš who decided everything, even in judicial matters, for was not every pasha at once judge, administrator, and general? Nevertheless, in this chaos a gradual division of powers took place. There were, in Belgrade, a chancellery—surviving debris of the Senate under Karageorge—a court, one or two police, the bureau of customs or monopolies, one, then two schools. . . . In short, beneath the skeleton apparatus of the Serbian state, the Turkish order persisted." Emile Haumant, *La Formation de la Yougoslavie* (Paris, 1930), p. 269.

[6] Hertslet, *op. cit.*, II, 968–978.

[7] "Russia did not want in Serbia a constitution of European style; its system was always, at this time under the Karageorgević, to surround the prince with councilors independent of him, and when there was disagreement—as in Mol-

davia and Walachia—to employ the Russian consul as arbiter. . . . The *firman* of December 24, 1838, dictated by Buteinev [the Russian consul] but drawn up by Serbian malcontents, was very long, very confused, but very definite on the irremovability of the senators and their right to intervene in every matter." Haumant, *op. cit.*, pp. 272–273.

8 For the text of the Constitution of Kragujevac see *British and Foreign State Papers*, Vol. 61, pp. 1070–1087. The constitution was a lengthy document containing 133 articles. Apart from the transitional and concluding articles, it included nine titles, dealing, respectively, with the dynasty; the bill of rights and duties; national representation; the Council of State; state domains, the private domain, and the civil list; state services; the courts; public worship, schools, and benevolent institutions; and communal government. Otherwise the constitution barely sketched in the administrative and judicial functions, leaving untouched much of the executive domain. The persistence of the regime thus created is proof of Jovan Ristić's shrewd understanding of the political mentality of his countrymen.

9 "Its author, Ristić, was no more convinced than Michael had been of the political maturity of the Serbian people; his liberalism, therefore, did not go far. The Senate, still further reduced, became a sort of prefectural council, while the Skupština continued to be deprived both of the right of initiative and that of modifying the government bills, which were to be accepted or rejected en bloc. In the latter case the government could legislate provisionally without the Skupština and could even promulgate the budget by decree." Haumant, *op. cit.*, p. 372.

10 On the growth of political parties in this period see *ibid.*, pp. 371–384.

11 The text of the constitution and the Speech from the Throne are given in *British and Foreign State Papers*, Vol. 81, pp. 508–540 and 541 ff.

12 The direct intervention of the reigning sovereign is not confined to Balkan history. The conception of the moderative power of the sovereign, who, although normally above partisan strife, may, in an emergency, directly interfere, decide, and govern without leaving his constitutional role, has been part of the public law of the Iberian Peninsula since the days of Alfonso the Wise. In the history of the Yugoslavs, Alexander Obrenović seems to have established a far-reaching constitutional precedent followed later by Alexander Karageorgević and Peter II. It is hardly a coincidence that all three instances of royal assumption of power were used to break the impasse between the people and the monarch on the one side and the legislative body on the other. In the first and third instances the intervention was undertaken by a sovereign still in his minority but seeking to alter the policy pursued by a politically manipulable Regency Council.

Alexander Obrenović's action, justified by a proclamation on April 1, 1893 (*British and Foreign State Papers*, Vol. 86, p. 983), announcing to his people that in response to their wishes he had assumed the royal power and that thenceforth the constitution and laws again entered into full force, is the archetypal juridical formula for what I have elsewhere called direct royal dictatorship. In later rescripts and messages to the Skupština, Alexander elaborated his convictions that "only the regime founded on . . . complete harmony between the King and the Nation" could be successful and that "the mutual confidence which unites the King and People" was the surest guaranty for the future of the country. *Loc. cit.*

13 In a proclamation from Belgrade on May 9, 1894, King Alexander declared to his subjects: "In time I will call upon you, on the basis of acquired experience, to draw up a new Constitution for the country. In the present, I have determined that the Constitution of 1888 in all its terms do cease to exist, and that the Constitution of 1869 be provisionally restored in all its fullness." *British and Foreign State Papers*, Vol. 86, pp. 987–988.

14 The text of the Constitution of 1901 is given in *ibid.*, Vol. 94, pp. 199–229.

15 Haumant, *op. cit.*, p. 395.

16 Early in his reign King Peter epitomized the essential support of his regime by stating: "I consider it a pleasurable duty to declare to the elect of the nation my homage as sovereign to the [outgoing] government for *having, in a critical moment, taken the royal power in hand with devotion, and, relying on the patriotism of the army and of the citizenry, preserved the country from possible disruption.*" *British and Foreign State Papers*, Vol. 96, pp. 252–256.

## NOTES TO CHAPTER VIII

### Constitutional Development, 1914–1941

1 In keeping with the political fragmentation of a postwar Europe in the throes of self-determination, every recalcitrant minority turned to the Helvetic Confederation for a constitutional model, endowing it with a nonexistent aura, and little understanding how the federal structure of the Swiss cantons had undergone a vast transformation under the impacts of war and had erected a complex structure of unitary administration in many fields formerly within the jealously guarded domain of the cantons.

2 Although generally thought of as a diplomatic document—the product of Serbian negotiations with an inchoate grouping and thus, internationally speaking, a step in the successful rounding out of the Yugoslav state—the Declaration of Corfu is also a constitutional document of the first order. "Because there are authors who consider the Yugoslav state as dating from the Declaration of Corfu," declared a Yugoslav scholar nearly a quarter of a century later, it must be viewed "as an act passed between the Serbian government and the Yugoslav Committee, drawn up in the form of a state charter and laying down the bases of the Yugoslav state." Déyan Loutzitch (Dejan Lucić), *La Constitution du royaume de Yougoslavie . . .* (Paris, 1933), p. 11.

3 At the time of the Paris Peace Conference it was not commonly realized that in the hour of the Dual Monarchy's dissolution the Austro-Hungarian Yugoslavs first sought a constitutional compromise which would artifically equilibrate Croatia and the Yugoslav lands of the Habsburg Crown with Serbia and thus, notwithstanding the unitarist postulates of the Declaration of Corfu, permit the survival of dualism. Failing to attain their objectives before the matter passed from a domestic to an international question, the Austrian Yugoslavs, particularly Trumbić, held out for separate diplomatic representation at the Peace Conference in order to gain by international action what they could no longer obtain by constitutional means. Their plans seem to have envisaged for the Yugoslav lands a formal, personal, or real union not unlike that created in 1814 between Norway and Sweden, which was guaranteed by the Powers against internal disequilibration. This would have frozen the relations between the two states on a basis of formal parity and given them the benediction of the Paris Conference.

But the naïve hopes of the Yugoslavs of the Habsburg Monarchy were destined to give way before the cumulative pressure of Poles, Czechs, and the Principal Allied Powers. The Yugoslav Committee was forced to come to an understanding with Serbia; the military pressure of the Italian Occupying Authorities revealed how desperate was the necessity of facing the Allies with a single, not a dual, delegation. Whereas at the opening session of the Peace Conference only Serbia was represented, by the time the draft of the Treaty of Versailles was presented to the Germans, the Kingdom of the Serbs, Croats, and Slovenes was fully recognized as a new entity. Thus a separate Yugoslav delegation was never officially admitted to the deliberations of the Peace Conference.

4 The records of the Constituent Skupština are hardly comparable to those of the Framers' Convention. The psychological climates of Belgrade and Phila-

delphia were very different. For one thing, the Framers' Convention came eleven years, not two, after the proclamation of independence, whereas the scant margin of common historical experience offered at Belgrade little of the atmosphere of compromise that eventually pervaded Constitution Hall. Moreover, the patterns for government offered to the Framers' Convention were presented only by those of agreed views and not by *ci-devant* loyalists. Finally, though there were some abstentions and withdrawals from the Convention, there was no comparable mass exodus. At Belgrade, on the other hand, the Constituent Assembly had to count, as did the contemporary British Parliament, on the absence of an appreciable body of representatives who sought, by abstention, to deny the competence and frustrate the action of the Constituent body. No one would pretend, however, that the acts of the British Parliament passed in a "thin" house, after the withdrawal of the Irish members from Westminster, were invalid. It is therefore difficult to consider invalid the acts of the Constituent Skupština passed in the absence of the Croats who boycotted it.

5 The contemporary experience of republican Austria, compelled to beseech the provinces to extend minimal compliance with the wishes of Vienna, did not convince Belgrade, surrounded by hostile states, of its utility for swift national reconstruction. See Malbone W. Graham, *New Governments of Central Europe* (New York, 1924), pp. 157–166. What was true of Protić's proposal is, *a fortiori*, true of the simulated federalism of the Croatian projects.

6 Dr. Charles A. Beard, in his excellent chapter on "The Formation of the Constitution," in Charles A. Beard and George Radin, *The Balkan Pivot: Yugoslavia* (New York, 1929), pp. 30–56, notes an additional plan, sponsored by Dr. Smodlaka, a Dalmatian Croat, which would have broken up the administrative entity of both Serbia and Croatia and divided the country into a dozen provinces. This savors of the attempt made at Weimar in 1919 to destroy Prussia by carving it up into independent provinces. Small wonder that the plan, which seems to have been drafted in partial imitation of the Weimar Constitution, hardly commended itself as conducive to national unity or strength.

7 For a complete account of the origins of the chapter on the Vidovdan Constitution see Beard and Radin, *loc. cit.* On the constitution in the making see also Howard L. McBain and Lindsay Rogers, *The New Constitutions of Europe* (New York, 1922).

8 A detailed analysis of the Constitution of 1921 from the perspective of 1922 is given in Graham, *op. cit.*, pp. 360–381. See also Howard Webster Wolfe and Arthur Irving Andrews, "The Jugoslav Constitution," in *Current History*, February, 1922, pp. 832–847; and Albert Mousset, "La Constitution yougoslave," in *L'Europe Nouvelle*, July 30, 1921. Texts of the documents may be found in English in McBain and Rogers, *op. cit.*, pp. 348–378.

9 That even the transitory provisional regime possessed this extraordinary power is admitted by Charles Beard and George Radin: "To clinch matters, the law calling the elections for the constitutional convention provided that the King might dismiss the Assembly and direct its work by decree." Beard and Radin, "The Crown," *op. cit.*, p. 63.

10 For the French text of the proclamation and its accompanying documents see *L'Europe Nouvelle*, January 12, 1929, pp. 49–50. "The hour has come," declared King Alexander, "when, between the people and the king there cannot be and ought not to be an intermediary.... My expectations, as well as those of the people, that the evolution of our internal political life would bring order into the country's affairs, have not been realized.... Far from developing and reinforcing the spirit of national union and of the state, parliamentarism, such as it is, began to arouse spiritual disorganization and national disunion. *My sacred duty is to safeguard by all means the national union and the state. I have decided to fulfill this duty to the end unhesitatingly. To maintain the union of my people and safeguard the unity of the state, the highest ideal of my reign,*

*are equally to be the most imperious law for me and for all. This is imposed on me by my responsibility before the people and before history....* I am convinced that in this grave moment all—Serbs, Croats, and Slovenes—will ... be my most faithful helpers in the course of my future efforts, which tend solely to arrive, as quickly as possible, at the realization of the establishing of a state administration and organization which will best respond to the general needs of the people and the interests of the state." The king also admonished his advisers *"never to lose sight of the fact that the safety of the state is the supreme law* and to serve the people the most sacred of duties." See also M. W. Graham, "The 'Dictatorship' in Jugoslavia," in *American Political Science Review,* Vol. XXIII, No. 2, pp. 456–459.

11 How near to dissolution the Yugoslav state came at that time is indicated by a communiqué published by the outgoing cabinet. It stated that Croats and Democrats, acting as a Peasant-Democratic coalition, had proposed to the monarch that "a complete revision of the constitution take place, *with a view to the restoration of the historic regions,* with their legislatures and executives. To this end, a neutral government would be the form which would enjoy the confidence of the sovereign and which, by its composition, would guarantee that the aforesaid matters would be acted upon." What the Peasant-Democratic coalition proposed was, in reality, a ministry of liquidation not unlike that which functioned briefly under the mild, clerical Dr. Heinrich Lammasch in the days of Austria's death agony. Clearly, such proposals were highly unacceptable to the King of the Serbs, Croats, and Slovenes.

12 On the period of the interim regime see Loutzitch, *La Constitution du royaume de Yougoslavie,* pp. 45–47; Jacques Chastenet, "Le Coup d'état royal en Yougoslavie," in *Revue Politique et Parlementaire,* February 10, 1929, pp. 298–301; Albert Mousset, "Les Evénements de Belgrade: une nouvelle ère politique en Yougoslavie," in *L'Europe Nouvelle,* January 12, 1929, pp. 47–49; and Graham, *American Political Science Review, loc. cit.*

13 On the reforms of 1929 the best authority is Miloutine Yovanovitch (Milutin Jovanović), *La Réforme administrative en Yougoslavie* (Paris, 1932).

14 A full description of this unique piece of legislation and its operation is given in Loutzitch, *op. cit.,* pp. 66–91; the method of selecting the Senate is treated in detail on pp. 91–103.

15 Articles 41–49 of the constitution. See Loutzitch, *ibid.,* pp. 142–159, 269–270.

16 Jovan Djordjević, "L'Evolution politique de la Yougoslavie après la Grande Guerre," in *Central European Studies, 1937* (Czechoslovak League of Nations Association, Prague, 1937), pp. 69–95 at p. 93.

17 A veteran French journalist, long an unofficial observer both in Spain and in Yugoslavia, drew this interesting comparison from first-hand impressions in Belgrade. Albert Mousset, "Le Retour au régime constitutionnel en Yougoslavie," in *L'Europe Nouvelle,* September, 1931.

18 "The principle which is at the base of this program elicits only sympathy ... but the procedure proposed to make the principle victorious seems rather hazardous. To return, in the present crisis in Europe, to the situation of 1919, and put in question the very bases of the Yugoslav state in causing the constitution to be voted by tribes and not by the absolute majority of the Assembly, is somewhat appalling." Albert Mousset, "Le Voyage de M. Stoyadinović à Paris et à Londres," *ibid.,* October 23, 1937, pp. 1025–1026.

19 It placed the Regency Council in the embarrassing position of having to violate its oath to support the constitution in order to grant Croat demands.

20 See the anonymous article, "Les Causes du changement politique en Yougoslavie," *ibid.,* February 11, 1939, pp. 144–146.

21 Consult Dinko Tomasić, "Les Negotiations entre le docteur Matchek et le gouvernement de Belgrade," *ibid.*, July 5, 1939, pp. 856–857; and André Pierre, "A Belgrade changement de tableau," *ibid.*, September 2, 1939, pp. 961–962.

## NOTES TO CHAPTER XI

### FOREIGN ECONOMIC RELATIONS, 1918–1941

1 In the 1934–1938 period the exports of meat amounted to 16 per cent, of lard to 24 per cent, and of eggs to 31 per cent of the estimated average annual production.

2 In 1937 Yugoslavia produced 2,724 kg. of gold and 69,800 kg. of silver as by-products of copper and lead production, respectively. Thus it was the second most important producer of silver and third in the production of gold in Europe, excluding Russia.

3 J. N. Dunda, "Značenje iseljeničkih uštednji za našu plaćevnu bilancu" (The Role of Emigrants' Remittances in the Yugoslav Balance of Payments), in *Ekonomist* (Zagreb), April–May, 1940, p. 143.

4 S. D. Obradović, *La Politique commerciale de la Yougoslavie* (Belgrade, 1939), Appendix.

5 A detailed discussion of Yugoslav public debts up to 1933 may be found in Jozo Tomašević, *Die Staatsschulden Jugoslaviens* (Zagreb, 1934).

6 Estimates are based on a study by V. V. Rozenberg and J. Lj. Kostić, *Ko finansira Jugoslovensku privredu?* (Who Is Financing the Yugoslav Economy?) (Belgrade, 1940). Rozenberg and Kostić were for many years officials of the Yugoslav Ministry of Commerce and Industry and had at their disposal all its files; so the figures can be taken as official estimates. For the problem of foreign investments in Yugoslavia see also: Slobodan Ćurčin, *Pénétration économique et financière des capitaux étrangers en Yougoslavie* (Paris, 1935); and M. Lamer, "Die Wandlungen der ausländischen Kapitalanlagen auf dem Balkan," in *Weltwirtschaftliches Archiv* (Jena), November, 1938, pp. 470–524.

7 *Annuaire Desfossés, 1938* (Paris, 1938), p. 1285.

8 *Ibid.*, pp. 1201–1202.

9 Obradović, *op. cit.*, Appendix.

10 M. B. Tošić, A. Vegner, P. J. Rudčenko, and G. Strekačev, *The Balance of Payment of the Kingdom of Serbs, Croats and Slovenes in 1926* (Belgrade, 1928), p. 10.

11 S. M. Kukoleča, *Industrija Jugoslavije, 1918–1938* (Belgrade, 1941), pp. 491–522.

12 While the number of industrial workers increased from about 200,000 in 1919 to 385,000 in 1938, the population of Yugoslavia increased in the same period from 11,600,000 to 15,600,000, or by 4,000,000, of whom about one-half were of working age.

13 Kukoleča, *op. cit.*, pp. 182–183.

14 The average monthly rate of the dinar in Zurich fell from 20.41 Swiss francs for D.100 in October, 1920, to 8.77 in October, 1922, and to 5.82 in August, 1923, to rise again to 7.44 in October, 1924, and 9.23 in August, 1925. The dinar was *de facto* stabilized at 9.13.

15 The French-Yugoslav trade agreement of February, 1939, which substantially increased Yugoslav export quotas of agricultural products to France and was devised to keep exports to and imports from France in a 10:6 ratio, came too late to be of any help.

## NOTES TO CHAPTER XIV
### MODERN ECCLESIASTICAL DEVELOPMENT

[1] *Echos d'Orient*, XXXVII (1938), 190 ff.
[2] The text is published in *Spomenik Srpske Kraljevske Akademije*, XLIX, 9 ff.
[3] M. P. Cheltsov, *Tserkov korolevstva Serbskago (1879–1896)* (St. Petersburg, 1899), p. 3.
[4] *Ibid.*, p. 26.
[5] For Arsenije's address to Emperor Leopold, see *Letopis Matice Srpske* (Novi Sad, 1904), pp. 203 ff.
[6] G. A. Voskresensky, *Pravoslavnye Slavyane v Avstro-Vengrii* (St. Petersburg, 1913), pp. 171–173.
[7] S. V. Troitsky, *Pravoslavie, Uniya i Katolichevstvo* (Petrograd, 1914), p. 25.
[8] E. E. Golubinsky, *Kratky ocherk istorii Pravoslavnikh Tserkvei, Bolgarskoi, Serbskoi, i Ruminskoi* ... (Moscow, 1871), p. 600.
[9] See article, "Serbian Patriarchate," in *Narodna Enciklopedija*, IV (1929).
[10] *Echos d'Orient*, XXXIII (1930), 361.
[11] *Ibid.*, XXXVII (1938), 199 ff.
[12] M. Searle Bates, *Religious Liberty: An Inquiry* (New York and London, 1945), p. 40.
[13] New York *Times*, August 30, 1945.
[14] *Echos d'Orient*, XXXVII (1938), 190 ff.
[15] *Ibid.*, p. 192.
[16] New York *Times*, October 27, 1945.
[17] Matthew Spinka, *A History of Christianity in the Balkans* (Chicago, 1933), p. 182.

## NOTES TO CHAPTER XV
### YUGOSLAVS OF THE MOSLEM FAITH

[1] Safvet Beg Bašagić, Osman Nuri Hadžić, Edhem Mulabdić, Osman Djikić, Rizabeg Kapetanović, the two Avdo Karabegovići, Ćazim Musa Ćatić, and Hifzi Bjelevac were some of the prominent writers whose work appeared in *Behar*.

[2] Osman Kulenović became Vice-Premier in Pavelić's first government. In November, 1941, he was replaced by his brother Džafer, the former Yugoslav Minister of Forests and Mines. Eng. Himlija Bešlagić served as Minister of Transport; Professor Hakija Hadžić was given a post in the Foreign Ministry with the rank of Minister; Dr. Halimbeg Hrastica was given a diplomatic post.

[3] First Deputy Premier, Dr. Zaim Šarac; Minister of Justice, Dr. Hamdija Ćerlić; Minister of Finance, Hasan Brkić; Minister of Trade, Pasaga Mandžić-Hadži Murat; Minister of Industry, Ćazim Ugljen.

[4] Second Deputy Premier, Abdurman Mehmed; Minister of Social Welfare, Nedjad Agoli.

[5] Muhamed Hadžimsmailagić.

[6] In regard to health, however, the condition of Moslems was worse than that of other Yugoslavs. The responsibility for this did not rest with the government, but was due in major part to the peculiar religious and social codes which governed Moslem life. In some villages of eastern Bosnia, venereal diseases have reached high proportions.

[7] A decree by which the government pledged to give the landowners full indemnity for the land they were required to surrender. Payments began in 1921. The Skupština granted D. 255,000,000 for this purpose.

## NOTES TO CHAPTER XVI

### THE SERBO-CROATIAN LANGUAGE

[1] The parallel is not exact, since English and Spanish are at least distant cousins, whereas Serbo-Croatian and Hungarian are unrelated. But the essential point is that in both instances two mutually unintelligible languages have been made to live side by side, with a sharply defined boundary between them.

[2] It is improbable that the speech of the Slavic invaders was ever an absolute unit, but I do not think that this consideration seriously affects the statements in my text.

[3] In describing my traveler's wanderings, I of course omit from consideration all Albanian and other enclaves in the South Slavic territory.

[4] The statements concerning the boundaries of the Serbo-Croatian language and of its dialects follow those given by A. Leskien in his *Grammatik der serbo-kroatischen Sprache* (Heidelberg, 1914), pp. xx–xxviii. The topic is highly controversial; blood as well as ink has been spilled in discussion of the boundaries between the Serbian and the Bulgarian dialects. The map shows the general situation; it is supplemented by reference to the map in an article by Belić in *Rocznik Slawistyczny* (Cracow), III (1910), 82–103.

## NOTE TO CHAPTER XVII

### THE LITERATURE OF THE SOUTH SLAVS

[1] Louis Adamic writes wittily of his return to his native country in 1932: "Gradually, I realized what I had dimly known in my boyhood, that, next to agriculture, Slovenia's leading industry was Culture. It was an intrinsic part of the place. In Lublyana [Ljubljana: a city of 75,000 inhabitants] were seven large bookshops . . . two of them more than a hundred years old." *The Native's Return* (New York and London, 1934), p. 29.

## NOTES TO CHAPTER XVIII

### YUGOSLAVIA, THE LITTLE ENTENTE, AND THE BALKAN PACT

[1] R. J. Kerner and H. N. Howard, *The Balkan Conferences and the Balkan Entente, 1930–1935: A Study in the Recent History of the Balkan and Near Eastern Peoples* (Berkeley, 1936), chap. i; H. N. Howard, "The Little Entente and the Balkan Entente," in *Czechoslovakia* (Berkeley, 1940, 1945), chap. xx; Theodore I. Geshkoff, *Balkan Union: A Road to Peace in Southeastern Europe* (New York, 1940), Part I.

[2] Carlo Sforza, *Fifty Years of War and Diplomacy in the Balkans: Pashich and the Union of the Yugoslavs* (New York, 1940), chaps. i–iii.

[3] Kerner and Howard, *op. cit.*, chap. i; Melitta Pivec-Stelè, *La Vie économique des provinces illyriennes (1809–1813)*, (Paris, 1930); Constantin H. Rindov, *Les Etats-unis des Balkans* (Paris, 1930); N. Iorga, *Le Caractère commun des institutions dans le sud-est de l'Europe* (Paris, 1929), *passim*.

[4] Oscar Jászi, *The Dissolution of the Habsburg Monarchy* (Chicago, 1929), *passim;* T. G. Djuvara, *Cents Projets de partage de la Turquie (1281–1913)* (Paris, 1914), *passim;* L. S. Stavrianos, . . . *Balkan Federation: A History of the Movement toward Balkan Unity in Modern Times* (Northampton, Mass., 1944).

[5] Ernst C. Helmreich, *The Diplomacy of the Balkan Wars, 1912–1913* (Cambridge, Mass., and London, 1938); H. N. Howard, *The Partition of Turkey: A Diplomatic History, 1913–1923* (Norman, Okla., 1931), chap. i.

6 Howard, *The Partition of Turkey*, chap. v.

7 Sforza, *op. cit.*, chap. xiii.

8 Thomas G. Masaryk, *The Making of a State* (London, 1927), p. 330. See also Eduard Beneš, *My War Memoirs* (London, 1928), p. 316, and chap. xiv.

9 The sources on the Little Entente are in the so-called Czechoslovak White Books: *Documents diplomatiques concernant les tentatives de restauration des Habsbourgs sur le trône de Hongrie* (Prague, République Tchécoslovaque, Ministère des Affaires Etrangères, 1922); *Documents diplomatiques relatives aux conventions d'alliance conclus par la république tchécoslovaque avec le royaume des Serbes, Croates et Slovènes et le royaume de Roumanie* (Prague, République Tchécoslovaque, Ministère des Affaires Etrangères), *Recueil des Documents*, No. 2, 1923. The texts of the treaties are in League of Nations, *Treaty Series*, VI, 209, 215; A. B. Keith, *Speeches and Documents on International Affairs, 1918-1937* (London, 1938), I, 63-66. In 2 vols. The Czechoslovak-Rumanian military agreement was signed on July 2, 1921; the Czechoslovak-Yugoslav, on August 1, 1921; and the Yugoslav-Rumanian, on January 23, 1922.

10 Stephen Graham, *Alexander of Yugoslavia: The Story of the King Who Was Murdered at Marseilles* (New Haven, Conn., 1939), chap. xi.

11 For the development of the Little Entente see John O. Crane, *The Little Entente* (New York, 1931); Robert Machray, *The Little Entente* (London, 1929), and *The Struggle for the Danube and the Little Entente, 1929-1938* (London, 1938); Florin Codresco, *La Petite Entente* (Paris, 1931), in 2 vols.; V. M. Radovanovitch, *La Petite Entente: étude historico-juridique* (Paris, 1923). Communiqués of the Little Entente are in Secrétariat du Conseil Permanent de la Petite Entente, *Communiqués des conférences des ministres des affaires étrangères des états de la Petite Entente et des sessions du Conseil permanent.*

12 Secrétariat du Conseil Permanent de la Petite Entente, *Communiqués . . .*, pp. 27-31. The decision, in principle, had been taken December 18-19, 1932, at Belgrade, when the Council declared that "it is necessary that the organization of the Little Entente adapt itself to present-day exigencies." It was decided "to perfect the organization of the Little Entente, completing its present statute. A Council of the Little Entente, composed of the three Ministers of Foreign Affairs and created as a permanent organ of the interests of the three respective countries, will meet regularly at least three times a year to examine current questions of foreign policy, as well as questions of particular interest to the three countries, in their mutual relations." *Ibid.*, pp. 25-27.

13 Eduard Beneš, *Le Pacte d'organisation de la Petite Entente et l'état actuel de la politique internationale: exposé du ministre des affaires étrangères fait devant les commissions des affaires étrangères de la Chambre des Députés et du Sénat le 1er mars 1933* (Prague, 1933). The text of the treaty is on pages 59-64. See also Miloslav Niederle, *L'Evolution et l'état actuel de la collaboration économique dans le bassin du Danube* (Prague, 1938).

14 Secrétariat du Conseil Permanent de la Petite Entente, *Communiqués . . .*, pp. 31-47.

15 For texts of documents consult *L'Esprit International*, No. 27, 1933, pp. 477-484.

16 For the Balkan Conferences see Kerner and Howard, *op. cit.;* Norman J. Padelford, *Peace in the Balkans: The Movement towards International Organization in the Balkans* (New York, 1935); Geshkoff, *op. cit.*

17 For text see Kerner and Howard, *op. cit.*, Doc. XIII, p. 231.

18 Graham, *op. cit.*, chap. xi.

19 For text see Kerner and Howard, *op. cit.*, Doc. XIV, pp. 232-233.

20 Graham, *op. cit.*, chaps. i-iv, viii, xiii-xviii.

21 The communiqués of the Little Entente and the Balkan Entente are in *Les Balkans*, VI (October–November, 1934), 625–626. For the December, 1934, meeting of the Council of the League of Nations see League of Nations, *Official Journal*, 15th Year, No. 12, Part II, December, 1934, *Minutes of the Eighty-third (Extraordinary) Session of the Council*, December 5–11.

22 *Actes de la conférence de Montreux concernant le régime des Détroits. 12 juin–20 juillet 1936. Compte rendu des séances plénières et procès-verbal des débats du comité technique* (Paris, 1936).

23 Florin Codresco, "La VIIᵉ Réunion du Conseil permanent de l'Entente balkanique à Bucharest," in *Affaires Danubiennes*, No. 3, March, 1939, pp. 69–73.

24 *Ethiopia*, No. 2, 1936. *Dispute between Ethiopia and Italy. Correspondence in Connection with the Application of Article 16 of the Covenant of the League of Nations*, January, 1936, Cmd. 5072.

25 Letter to the New York *Times*, April 20, 1941.

26 *Miscellaneous*, No. 3, 1936. *Correspondence Showing the Course of Certain Diplomatic Discussions Directed towards Securing an European Settlement*, June, 1934, to March, 1936, Cmd. 5143.

27 *Les Balkans*, IX (May, 1937), 95–97.

28 Note Dr. Kamil Krofta's fears in *Czechoslovakia and the International Situation at the Beginning of 1937* (Prague, 1937).

29 Secrétariat du Conseil Permanent de la Petite Entente, *Communiqués . . .*, pp. 74–77. At the Bratislava meeting, September 14, 1936, for instance, it was agreed that, although their common policy was to be pursued, the members of the Little Entente could continue "the relations of vital and direct coöperation with other countries which each of them has succeeded in establishing."

30 Text of the communiqué is in *Les Balkans*, X (1938), 348–349.

31 *L'Europe Centrale*, October 1, 1938, p. 639, dates the warning on September 26. The New York *Times*, September 25, 1939, dates it on September 24.

32 *L'Entente balkanique du 9 février 1939 au 8 février 1940* (Bucharest, 1940), pp. 25–27.

33 *Ibid.*, pp. 33–35.

34 *Ibid.*, pp. 39–51.

35 *Ibid.*, pp. 81–109.

36 C. L. Sulzberger, New York *Times*, January 31, 1940.

37 *L'Entente balkanique . . .*, pp. 81–85.

## NOTES TO CHAPTER XIX

### FOREIGN POLICY IN THE SECOND WORLD WAR (1939–1946)

1 Stephen Heald, *Documents on International Affairs, 1937* (Royal Institute of International Affairs, London, 1939), pp. 207–209, 399–401; Germany, Auswärtigesamt, *Dokumente zum Konflikt mit Yugoslawien und Griechenland* (Berlin, 1941), *passim*. Hereafter cited as *GD*.

2 *GD*, Nos. 35–36; German Library of Information, *Documents on the Events Preceding the Outbreak of the War* (New York, 1940), Nos. 272, 317, 318.

3 *L'Entente balkanique du 9 février 1939 au 8 février 1940* (Bucharest, 1940).

4 Royal Ministry of Foreign Affairs, Greek White Book: *Diplomatic Documents Relating to Italy's Aggression against Greece* (London, 1942).

5 *GD*, *passim*. Also S. Shepard Jones and Denys P. Myers, *Documents on American Foreign Relations*, III (1940–1941), 324–334.

6 Grégoire Gafenco (Grigore Gafencu), *Préliminaires de la guerre à l'Est* (Fribourg, 1944), esp. chap. vi.

7 See Nicholas Mirković, "Jugoslavia's Choice," in *Foreign Affairs*, October, 1941. *The Ciano Diaries* indicates that Mussolini was anxious to attack Yugoslavia much earlier and had marked June 1, 1940, as the proper time for an attack, noting that "we must act quickly in Yugoslavia." Later (May 13, 1940) Mussolini changed his mind, announced his intention to attack France and Great Britain, believing that to attack Yugoslavia "would be a humiliating sideline" for Italy. See *The Ciano Diaries, 1939–1943: The Complete Unabridged Diaries of Count Galeazzo Ciano, Italian Minister for Foreign Affairs, 1936–1943* (ed. by Hugh Gibson, intro. by Sumner Welles; New York, 1946).

8 Raphaël Lemkin, *Axis Rule in Occupied Europe* (Washington, D.C., 1944), pp. 248–251, 591–602.

9 *Inter-Allied Review*, June 15, 1941, p. 6.

10 *Ibid.*, September 15, 1941, pp. 6–7.

11 *Ibid.*, February 15, 1942, pp. 25–26.

12 *Ibid.*

13 *Ibid.*, August 15, 1942, p. 195.

14 Boris Furlan, *Fighting Jugoslavia: The Struggle of the Slovenes* (New York, 1942); Winifred N. Hadsel, "The Struggle for Yugoslavia," in *Foreign Policy Reports*, March 1, 1944, pp. 314–328.

15 For text of resolutions see *The Re-creation of Yugoslavia* (United Committee of South-Slavic Americans, New York, 1944).

16 *United Nations Review*, May 15, 1944, pp. 117–118.

17 For convenient translation of texts see United Committee of South-Slavic Americans, *Bulletin*, September 15, 1944. See also *United Nations Review*, September 15, 1944, pp. 240–242.

18 New York *Times*, November 24, 1944.

19 Department of State, *Toward the Peace: Documents* (Washington, D.C., 1945), p. 35.

20 *United Nations Review*, May 15, 1945, pp. 139–140.

21 For a general survey of Yugoslav foreign policy see Josip Broz Tito, *Yugoslavia's Foreign Policy* (United Committee of South-Slavic Americans, New York, 1946), address of March 1, 1946. For the Trieste issue see *La Marche julienne: étude de géographie politique* (Institut Adriatique, Sušak, 1945); Lavo Čermelj, *Life-and-Death Struggle of a National Minority* (2d ed., Ljubljana, 1945); Francis Gabrovšek, *Jugoslavia's Frontiers with Italy: Trieste and Its Hinterland* (New York, 1943?).

## NOTES TO CHAPTER XX

### The Second World War and Beyond

1 When Pope Pius XII received Ante Pavelić in private audience and thus gave his blessing to the new Croat fascist state, his gesture had a profound effect on the great majority of the Yugoslavs, and affected the Catholic Church in Yugoslavia adversely.

2 At the Belgrade trial of Draža Mihailović in June, 1946, an attempt was made to prove that during the German occupation he had established contact with the Agrarian, Mihail Genovski, and the Zvenar, Damian Velčev, with the intention of establishing a Bulgarian-Serbian common anti-Communist front. Both enjoyed high positions in the postwar Bulgarian Fatherland Front governments. Since the trial of Mihailović, the Communists, already dissatisfied with

Velčev's intransigence, lost all confidence in him. Eventually he was expelled from the government and assigned to an innocuous ministerial post in Switzerland.

³ This program actually had the sympathetic support of a number of prominent British officials, who felt that a strong Serbian state would be the best guaranty for peace in the Balkans: the Serbs were the backbone of the Balkans, had twice been allies of the British, and were solely responsible for the coup of 1941 which overthrew the pro-Axis government. Only after intensive study of the Yugoslav situation, during which Winston Churchill, through the British liaison officer at Četnik headquarters, had given Mihailović ample chance to rehabilitate himself, did His Majesty's Government decide to drop Mihailović and adopt Tito.

⁴ It is worth while to note that later, in 1944–1945, the American army officers at Mihailović's headquarters encouraged him in this hope. They were then in no position to know that the fate of Yugoslavia had already been decided by the Big Three and that Yugoslavia had been designated as the Soviet military sphere.

⁵ The first meeting between Tito and Mihailović and their advisers took place in September, 1941, at Strugonik. In their second meeting, held in October at Brajica, the two leaders reached an agreement which called for joint action against the enemy and sharing of the ammunition produced by the Užice plant, which the Partisans had captured. Friendly relations soon ceased because of mutual suspicion and distrust. Tito proposed another meeting, and the representatives of the two groups met at Čačak on November 21 and 28, but no positive results were achieved.

⁶ *Parliamentary Debates* (Hansard), Vol. 397 (1943–1944), cols. 691–695.

⁷ For the full text of the constitution see pages 487–512.

## NOTES TO CHAPTER XXI
### Postwar Foreign Economic Relations

¹ Yugoslavia, Ministry of Information, *The Debate on the Budget for 1946* (Belgrade), April, 1946, p. 59.

² To enhance the morale of the suffering peoples under enemy occupation and to be prepared for the great postwar relief task, the United Nations established, through the Charter of November, 1943, the United Nations Relief and Rehabilitation Administration. The organization was launched at the beginning of 1944 with the objective of rendering speedy relief to the suffering populations immediately upon liberation and to aid in the rehabilitation of essential economic activities of the liberated countries. Although in the beginning the work of the Administration was beset by great difficulties, its operations represent the greatest life-saving undertaking ever made. Millions of people in China, White Russia, the Ukraine, Poland, Czechoslovakia, Yugoslavia, Greece, and Italy are living witnesses of this fact. Without the U.N.R.R.A. millions would have starved or otherwise perished. The contributing countries, namely, those of the United Nations whose territory was not invaded by the enemy, obligated themselves originally to make a contribution to the U.N.R.R.A. for its operations in the amount of 1 per cent of their 1941 national income. Later another contribution of the same magnitude was pledged and fulfilled. The contribution of the United States to the total financial resources of the U.N.R.R.A. amounted to about 72 per cent. All members of the U.N.R.R.A. contributed their share to defray its administrative expenses.

³ Before the signing of the agreement between the U.N.R.R.A. and Yugoslavia on March 24, 1945, and the assumption of U.N.R.R.A. work in Yugoslavia on April 15, 1945, the combined Anglo-American military authorities delivered to

Yugoslavia, between January 1 and April 15, 1945, about 60,000 tons of relief supplies. These deliveries were based on a special agreement with Yugoslavia on January 19, 1945, but financial settlement was left for a later agreement. The United States Typhus Commission, in the winter of 1944–1945, provided supplies and specialists for preventive work against typhus epidemics in Yugoslavia.

4 Government spokesmen on the Plan stressed repeatedly that it does not touch private ownership in agriculture. The problem of land tenure in Yugoslavia, it must be remembered, lies in too-small peasant holdings rather than in large holdings. The oversplitting of farm property is a consequence of the rapid increase in rural population, and the inability of other parts of the economy to absorb and employ the surplus population. The process was intensified, but definitely not caused, by radical agrarian reform after the First World War. According to the agricultural census of 1931, there were only 1,801 farms (in a total of 1,985,725) with holdings of more than 250 acres owning only 6.5 per cent of the 26,200,000 acres of farm land. The new regime carried the agrarian reform somewhat further by breaking up the few remaining large estates, including those belonging to the church; by prohibiting ownership of more than a standard-size farm; and by making it virtually impossible for the nonrural population to own farm land. It also wiped out the prewar peasant debts.

The problem of land tenure as an eminently political issue is apparently in abeyance. Owing to the long tradition of individual property in land, which is deeply ingrained in the Yugoslav peasantry, a policy of collectivization of agriculture, if attempted, would meet insurmountable difficulties. The government seems to be fully aware of this fact and is not raising the issue. It is, however, trying to induce the peasants to organize agricultural coöperatives. But according to a statement of the Yugoslav Under Secretary of Agriculture, in May, 1947, there were only 509 such coöperatives, 281 of which were in the Vojvodina. They included only 25,000 families and owned only 370,000 acres of coöperative land and 39,500 acres of private land. It seems that the government still has some land in the so-called land fund, especially in the Vojvodina, from which farms are allotted to settlers from overpopulated areas. Agriculture is, of course, under the strict control of the government, which owns agricultural-machinery stations and controls the channels supplying the peasantry with consumer and other goods. The peasantry is required to sell the bulk of its produce to state enterprises and coöperatives.

# A SELECTED
# BIBLIOGRAPHY

# A Selected Bibliography

## CHAPTER I
### THE GEOGRAPHICAL SCENE
See the notes to chapter 1, p. 515.

## CHAPTER II
### RACIAL HISTORY
See the notes to chapter ii, p. 515.

## CHAPTER III
### THE YUGOSLAV MOVEMENT

"The Jugo-Slav Movement," in *The Russian Revolution: The Jugo-Slav Movement* (Cambridge, Mass., 1918), pp. 81–109, by the author of this chapter, was one of the first and most complete surveys of this subject. It was based on the author's paper delivered before the American Historical Association in 1917. Its fundamental conclusions, unchanged by later researches, have been reëmphasized here, with thanks to Harvard University Press. Its bibliography extends to the year 1917 and the reader is referred to it in order that repetition may be avoided. See also "The Yugoslav Movement," in *Handbooks*, Historical Section, British Foreign Office (London, 1920).

The outstanding work written on the subject since 1918 is by the noted Croat historian Ferdinand Šišić: *Jugoslavenska misao* (Belgrade, 1937), 277 pp. He stresses particularly the period since 1790, treading somewhat lightly when he comes to Magyar-Croat relations. Šišić's work may be supplemented by Professor Vladimir Ćorović's excellent *Istorija Jugoslavije* (Belgrade, 1933, 1939). Whereas Šišić's conception is thoroughly Yugoslav, that of L. von Südland (Ivo Pilar) is Great Croat and anti-Serb in point of view: *Die südslawische Frage und der Weltkrieg* (Vienna, 1918; Zagreb, 1944), 828 pp.

A good work in German is: Hermann Wendel, *Der Kampf der Südslawen um Freiheit und Einheit* (Frankfort on the Main, 1925).

Various items concerning Slovene history may be found in the following: Bučar, Vekoslav. *Politička istorija Slovenačke* (Biblioteka Politika, Belgrade, 1939), 119 pp.

Lončar, Dragotin. *The Slovenes: A Social History* (trans. by A. J. Klančar; Cleveland, American Jugoslav Printing and Publishing Co., 1939), 77 pp.

Prijatelj, Ivan. *Kulturna in politična zgodovina Slovencev, 1848–1895* (ed. by Anton Ocvirk; Ljubljana, 1938–1939), in 4 vols.

Croat history is at its best in Ferdinand Šišić: *Hrvatska povijest od najstarijih dana do potkraj 1918* (Zagreb, 1925–), Vol. I. Under his editorship appeared *Josip Juraj Strossmayer, dokumenti i korespondencija* ... (Zagreb, 1933–). Three brief, useful accounts published by the Biblioteka Politika (Belgrade, 1939) are: Vaso Čubrilović, *Politička prošlost Hrvata*, 128 pp.; Milan Vladisavljević, *Hrvatska autonomija pod Austro-Ugarskom*, 107 pp.; and Josip Horvat, *Stranke kod Hrvata i njihove ideologije*, 104 pp.

For Serbian history, particularly in the nineteenth century, one may usefully consult the series edited by Stanoje Stanojević, *Srpski narod u xix veku* (Belgrade, 1935–), and such numbers in the Biblioteka Politika (Belgrade, 1939) as: Nikola Stojanović, *Srbija i Jugoslovensko ujedinjenje*, 80 pp.; Živan Mitrović, *Srpske političke stranke*, 115 pp.; Ilija A. Pržić, *Spoljašnja politika Srbije*, 164 pp.; Vladimir Ćorović, *Političke prilike u Bosni i Hercegovini*, 74 pp.; Nikola Djonović, *Crna Gora pre i posle ujedinjenja*, 113 pp. For the Vojvodina see Dušan J. Popović, *Vojvodina* ... (Novi Sad, 1939), Vol. I. Slobodan Jovanović, *Političke i pravne rasprave* (Belgrade, 1932–1933), in 3 vols., is a collection of essays on such noted leaders as Joseph George Strossmayer, Ilija Garašanin, and Svetožar Marković.

## CHAPTER V
### SERBIA IN THE FIRST WORLD WAR

#### I. DOCUMENTS

Greek White Book (New York, 1917).

Marchand, René (ed.). *Un Livre noir, diplomatie d'avant-guerre, d'après les documents des archives russes* (Paris, 1922–).

Nedić, Milan Dj. *Srpska vojska i solunska ofanziva* (Belgrade, 1932); *Srpska vojska na Albanskoj golgoti* (Belgrade, 1937).

 Both books contain many documents from Serbian archives and are, in part, eyewitness accounts.

Notovich, F. (ed.). "Razgrom Serbii v 1915 g. 1 'pomoshch' soiuznikov," in *Krasny Arkhiv* (Moscow, 1934), Vols. 65, 66.

#### II. DIARIES AND MEMOIRS

Boppe, Auguste. *A la Suite du gouvernement serbe, de Nich à Corfou* (Paris, 1917).

 M. Boppe was the French Minister to Serbia at the time of the invasion in 1915.

Cadorna, Luigi. *Altre pagine sulla grande guerra* (Milan, 1925)

 As chief of the Italian General Staff in 1915, Cadorna opposed his government's policy in Albania.

Conrad von Hötzendorf, Franz. *Aus meiner Dienstzeit, 1906–1918* (Vienna, 1921–1925), in 5 vols.

Falkenhayn, Erich von. *The German General Staff and Its Decisions, 1914–1916* (New York, 1920).

Gallwitz, Max von. *Meine Führertätigkeit im Weltkriege* (Berlin, 1929).
   General Gallwitz commanded the German Eleventh Army in 1915.

Labry, Raoul. *Avec l'Armée serbe en retraite à travers l'Albanie et le Montenegro* (Paris, 1916).
   A young medical volunteer at the time, Labry later became a professor of Slavonic history at the University of Paris. The author of this chapter talked with him in 1938.

Radoslawoff (Radoslavov), Vasil. *Bulgarien und die Weltkrise* (Berlin, 1923).

Sarrail, Maurice. *Mon Commandement en Orient (1916–1918)* (Paris, 1920).

Zheraich (Žerajić), M. "Otstuplenie Serbskoi armii cherez Albaniyu," in *Istoricheskii Vestnik* (Petrograd, 1917), Vol. 147.

### III. OFFICIAL HISTORIES

*Military Operations, Macedonia* (comp. by Cyril Falls and A. F. Becke; London, 1933–1935), in 2 vols.

*Oesterreich-Ungarns letzter Krieg* (Oest. Bundesministerium für Heereswesen und Kriegsarchiv; Vienna, 1931–1936), in 6 vols.

### IV. SECONDARY WORKS

Adams, John Clinton. *Flight in Winter* (Princeton, N. J., 1942).
   A history of the Serbian campaigns of 1914–1915 and the Serbian retreat.

Desmazes, René, and Naoumovitch. *Les Victoires serbes en 1914* (Paris, 1928).

Feyler, Fernand. *Les Campagnes de Serbie* (Paris, 1926).

Jakovljević, Stevan J. *Srpska trilogija: devet sto četrnaesta; pod krstom; kapija slobode* (Belgrade, 1938), 3 vols. in 2.
   A novel which is more historical than fictional.

Lazarević, Milutin D. *Naši ratovi za oslobodjenje i ujedinjenje: Srpsko-Turski rat, 1912 godine* (Belgrade, 1929–1934), in 4 vols.

Madol, Hans Roger. *Ferdinand of Bulgaria* (trans. by Kenneth Kirkness; London, 1933).

Mavrogordato, John. *Modern Greece* (London, 1931).

Šišić, Ferdinand. *Jugoslavenska misao* (Belgrade, 1937).

"The Yugoslav Movement," in *Handbook* No. 14, British Foreign Office (London, 1920).

## CHAPTER VI

### YUGOSLAVIA AND THE PEACE CONFERENCE

Of the histories of the Peace Conference, that of H. W. V. Temperley (ed.), *A History of the Peace Conference of Paris* (London, 1920–), Vols. IV–V, is the most extensive and best for the Conference as a whole; that of Paul Birdsall, *Versailles Twenty Years After* (New York, 1941), is the most recent and best single-volume account; the lectures by Charles H. Haskins and Robert H. Lord, *Some Problems of the Peace Conference* (Cambridge, Mass., 1920), and the chapters by D. W. Johnson and Isaiah Bowman, in Edward M. House and Charles Seymour, *What Really Happened at Paris* (New York, 1921), are still very suggestive. The work by René Albrecht-Carrié, *Italy at the Paris Peace Conference* (New York, 1938), is full and thorough and, on the whole, objective. See also his article in the *Journal of Modern History*, December, 1941.

For views of the American delegation see: *Papers Relating to the Foreign Relations of the United States: The Paris Peace Conference, 1919* (Washington, D.C.), Vols. II (1942) and XII (1947).

On the Yugoslav side are the accounts by Ferdinand Šišić, *Abridged Political History of Rieka* [Fiume] (Paris, 1919), and *Jadransko pitanje na konferenciji mira u Parizu, zbirka akata i dokumenata* (Zagreb, 1920); and that of Edward J. and Chase G. Woodhouse, *Italy and the Jugoslavs* (Boston, 1920). Nina Almond and R. H. Lutz (eds.), *The Treaty of St. Germain: A Documentary History of Its Territorial and Political Clauses* (Stanford, 1935), contains many important documents. Reactions of Hungarians and Bulgarians may be glimpsed in: István (Stephen) Bethlen, *The Treaty of Trianon and European Peace* (London and New York, 1934), and G. P. Genov, *Bulgaria and the Treaty of Neuilly* (Sofia, 1935). Further bibliographical items, of which there are many, may be found in the publications by Albrecht-Carrié.

## CHAPTERS VII AND VIII
### Constitutional Development

See the notes to the chapters, pp. 516–521.

## CHAPTER IX
### Yugoslavs in America

Adamic, Louis. *Laughing in the Jungle* (New York, 1932); *The Native's Return* (New York, 1934); *A Nation of Nations* (New York, 1945).

Angelinović, B., and I. Mladineo. *Jugosloveni u Ujedinjenim Državama Amerike* (New York, 1931).

Beard, A. E. S. "An Electrical Wizard—Nikola Tesla," pp. 284–288, and "A Serbian-American Scientist—Michael Pupin," pp. 202–207, in *Our Foreign-Born Citizens* . . . (New York, 1922; 3d ed., 1939).

Bercovici, Konrad. *On New Shores* (New York and London, 1925).

"Jugoslav Farmers in the United States," pp. 134–150, is a colorful sketch of a Yugoslav agricultural community in Ohio.

Bjankini, J. "Yugoslavs in the United States," in *First All-Slavic Singing Festival* (ed. by A. W. Vanek and J. E. S. Vojan; Chicago), pp. 95–99.

Bokšan, Slavko. *Nikola Tesla und sein Werk* (Vienna and New York, 1932).

Fritchey, Clayton. "Cleveland's New Mayor," in *Common Ground*, Winter, 1942, pp. 13–18.

"Jugoslavs in America," in Chicago *Tribune*, June, 1930 (special issue, "The Kingdom of Yugoslavia"), pp. 10–11.

*The Jugoslavs in the United States of America* (New York, 1921).

Kosier, Ljubomir St. *Les Serbes, Croates et Slovènes en Amérique* (Zagreb, 1938).

Ledbetter, Eleanor. *The Slovaks of Cleveland* (Cleveland, 1918).

Maroevich, Ivan N. "Our 100,000 Yugoslavs on the West Coast," in *South Slav Herald*, March 10, 1934, p. 4.

Milošević, Božo N. (ed.). *Slavs, with Special Reference to Americans of Slav Ancestry* (Chicago, 1933).
> See esp. "Jugoslavs in America," pp. 44–47.

Milošević, Božo N. "Yugoslavs of Cleveland," in *Slavia* (New York), Summer, 1934, pp. 61–69.

Mladineo, I. *The American Yugoslavs* (Detroit, 1934), p. 68; "Jugoslavs in America," in *Interpreter*, IV, 3–6; "The Southern Slavs in America," in *Our World*, December, 1923, pp. 91–95.

Niland, Billyanna. "Yugoslavs in San Pedro, California," in *Sociology and Social Research*, September–October, 1941, pp. 36–44.

Pupin, Michael. *From Immigrant to Inventor* (New York, 1934).

Radosavljevich, Paul R. "Slavic Racial Contributions to American Culture."
> Four lectures delivered at New York University, 1935. Mimeographed copies may be secured from the author.

Radosavljevich, Paul R. *Who Are the Slavs? A Contribution to Race Psychology* (Boston, 1919), in 2 vols.

Robinson, M. H. "Dubrovnik—Old Ragusa: The Carcassonne of the Balkans," in *American Srbobran*, November, 1934, p. 3.
> This is the official organ of the Serbian Society, 3414 Fifth Avenue, Pittsburgh, Pennsylvania.

Roucek, J. S. "The Albanian and Yugoslav Immigrants in America," in *Revue Internationale des Etudes Balkaniques* (Belgrade), Vol. II, No. 6 (1938), pp. 499–519; "The Social Character of Yugoslav Politics," in *Social Forces*, IX (1934), 294–305; "Les Yougoslaves d'Amérique," in *Les Balkans* (Athens), X (1938), 5–21; "Yugoslav Americans," in *One America ... Our Racial and National Minorities*, by Francis J. Brown and Joseph S. Roucek (New York, 1945); "The Yugoslav Immigrants in America," in *American Journal of Sociology*, March, 1935, pp. 602–611.

Sestanovich, Stephen N. (ed.). *Slavs in California* (Slavonic Alliance of California, 1937). See esp. "Jugoslavs in Oakland, San Francisco, and Los Angeles," pp. 97–98.

Stanoyevich, M. S. *The Jugoslavs in the United States of America* (New York, 1921).

United States Bureau of the Census. *Religious Bodies: 1926* (Washington, D.C., 1929–1930). See Eastern Orthodox Churches, Consolidated Report, Serbian Orthodox Church, pp. 38–40.

Vlahović, Vlaho S. *Two Hundred 50 Million and One Slavs: An Outline of Slav History* (New York, 1945).

Zavertnik, Joseph. *Ameriški Slovenci* (Slovenska Narodna Podporna Jednota, Chicago, 1925).

## CHAPTER X

### AGRICULTURE

Brewer, Sam Pope. "Control on Trade Tightened by Tito," in New York *Times*, June 29, 1945; "Yugoslavia's Aims and Results Clash," *ibid.*, July 19, 1945.

Calder-Marshall, A. *Watershed* (London, 1947).

Frangeš, Otto von. *Die sozialökonomische Struktur der jugoslawischen Landwirtschaft* (Berlin, 1937).

League of Nations. European Conference on Rural Life, "Yougoslavie," *Monograph* No. 23 (Geneva, 1939).

Michael, Louis G. "Agricultural Survey of Europe: The Danube Basin," Part I, United States Department of Agriculture *Bull.* No. 1234 (Washington, D.C., 1924, 1929); "Agricultural Survey . . . ," Part II, "Rumania, Bulgaria and Yugoslavia," *Technical Bull.* No. 126 (Washington, D.C., 1929), in 2 vols.

Mirkowich (Mirković), Nicholas. "Die Bevölkerungsentwicklung Jugoslawiens und das Problem der agrarischen Uebervölkerung," in *Weltwirtschaftliches Archiv*, Vol. 50, Part I (July, 1939).

Office for Foreign Trade. *Yugoslavia: An Economic Survey* (Belgrade, 1936).

Patton, Kenneth S. "Kingdom of Serbs, Croats and Slovenes (Yugoslavia): A Commercial and Industrial Handbook," *Trade Promotion Series* No. 61, United States Bureau of Foreign and Domestic Commerce (Washington, D. C., 1928).

Royal Institute of International Affairs. *Agrarian Problems from the Baltic to the Aegean* (London, 1944); *South-Eastern Europe: A Political and Economic Survey* (London and New York, 1939).

Stojadinović, Miloslav. *Naše selo* (Belgrade, 1929).

Strauss, Frederick. "Wartime Agricultural Surpluses of the Danube Basin," *Foreign Agriculture*, December, 1940. Issued by the Office of Foreign Agricultural Relations, United States Department of Agriculture.

Warriner, Doreen. *Economics of Peasant Farming* (London and New York, 1939).

## CHAPTER XI

### FOREIGN ECONOMIC RELATIONS, 1918–1941

See the notes to chapter xi, p. 521.

## CHAPTER XII

### SOCIAL STRUCTURE

Materials having a direct bearing on Yugoslav society are fragmentary, but several useful works should be noted. One of the best histories of Yugoslav society is Milan Prelog, *Pregled povijesti Južnih Slavena: Srba, Hrvata i Slovenaca* (Sarajevo, 1922–1926), in 2 vols. The standard work on Serbian history is

Stanoje Stanojević, *Istorija Srpskoga naroda* (Belgrade, 1926). Two recent works on Croatian political history contain information on Croatian society: Josip Horvat, *Politička povijest Hrvatske* (Zagreb, 1936), and Vaso Čubrilović, *Politička prošlost Hrvata* (Belgrade, 1939). Vekoslav Bučar's *Politička istorija Slovenačke* (Biblioteka Politika, Belgrade, 1939), is of value on the subject of Slovenian society.

Material on modern Yugoslav society is to be found chiefly in widely scattered periodical literature. Nicholas Mirković (Mirkowich) has an exhaustive article on population problems: "Die Bevölkerunksentwicklung Jugoslawiens und das Problem der agrarischen Uebervölkerung," in *Weltwirtschaftliches Archiv*, Vol. 50, Part I (July, 1939), 98–144. One of the most informative works on present-day Yugoslav society is the July–August, 1937, number of *Pregled* (Sarajevo). This issue of over 160 pages contains a number of excellent articles dealing with the rural area and the peasantry (*selo i seljaštvo*). They were written by scholars, publicists, and noted political leaders.

On the position of the peasant, the following are invaluable: Maksim Goranović, *Položaj seljaka u Jugoslaviji* (Belgrade, 1938); Jelenko Petrović, *Okućje* (Belgrade, 1930). See also Olive Lodge, *Peasant Life in Jugoslavia* (London, 1942).

Of more general interest are: Louis Adamic, *My Native Land* (New York and London, 1943); Lovett F. Edwards, *Profane Pilgrimage: Wanderings through Yugoslavia* (London, 1938); H. D. Harrison, *The Soul of Yugoslavia* (London, 1941); R. D. Hogg, *Yugoslavia* (London, 1944); Rebecca West, *Black Lamb and Grey Falcon: The Record of a Journey through Yugoslavia in 1937* (London, 1941).

## CHAPTER XIV

### MODERN ECCLESIASTICAL DEVELOPMENT

Bogdanović, David. *Pregled književnosti Hrvatske i Srpske* (Zagreb, 1915).

Branković, Georgiji. *Srpska mitropolija Karlovačka* (Karlovac, 1902).

Cheltsov, M. P. *Tserkov korolevstva Serbskago (1879–1896)* (St. Petersburg, 1899).

Davidović, Svetislav. *Srpska Pravoslavna Crkva u Bosni i Hercegovini (od 960 do 1930 god.)* (Sarajevo, 1931).

Djurić, Kosta. *Crkva i država* (Belgrade, 1923).

French, R. M. *Serbian Church Life* (New York, 1942).

Gavrilović, Andra. *Istorija Srpske Pravoslavne Crkve* (Belgrade, 1927).

Golubinsky, E. E. *Kratky ocherk istorii Pravoslavnikh Tserkvei, Bolgarskoi, Serbskoi, i Ruminskoi* (Moscow, 1871).

Hudal, Alois. *Die serbisch-orthodoxe Nationalkirche* (Graz and Leipzig, 1922).

Janić, Vojislav. *Članci i razprave* (Karlovac, 1921).

Kostić, Petar. *Crkveni život Pravoslavnikh Srba u Prizrenu i njegovoj okolini* (Belgrade, 1928).

Marjanović, Čedomir J. *Istorija Srpske Crkve* (Belgrade, 1929–1930).

Marković, Vasilije. *Pravoslavno monaštvo i manastiri u srednjevekovnoj Srbiji* (Karlovac, 1920).

Milivojevich, Dionisije. *The persecution of the Serbian Orthodox Church in Yugoslavia* (Libertyville, Ill., 1945).

Mousset, Jean. *La Serbie et son église, 1830–1904* (Paris, 1938).

Popović, Jevsevije. *Opća Crkvena istorija* (Karlovac, 1912), in 2 vols.

Spinka, Matthew. *A History of Christianity in the Balkans* (Chicago, 1933).

Stanojević, Stanoje. *Istorija Srpskoga naroda* (Belgrade, 1926).

Strika, Boško. *Srpske zadužbine: Dalmatinski manastiri* (Zagreb, 1930).

Troitsky, S. V. *Pravoslavie, Uniya i Katolichevstvo* (Petrograd, 1914).

Velimirović, Nikolaj. *Živa Crkva* (New York, 1915).

Voskresensky, G. A. *Pravoslavnye Slavyane v Avstro-Vengrii* (St. Petersburg, 1913).

Anglican and Eastern Orthodox Church Union, *Reports*, 1906–1914; Anglican and Eastern Association, *Reports*, 1914–1935; *Christian East*, 1910–1938; *Echos d'Orient; Glasnik Srpske Pravoslavne Patrijaršije* (Karlovac); *Letopis Matice Srpske; Spomenik Srpske Kraljevske Akademije.*

## CHAPTER XV

### YUGOSLAVS OF THE MOSLEM FAITH

A good history of the Yugoslav Moslems is still to be published. Even today one must refer to such classical works on Turkish history as Joseph von Hammer-Purgstall's *Geschichte des Osmanischen Reiches* (1827–1835), in 10 vols. This may be supplemented by many general histories of Yugoslavia and a number of monographs on the Moslems written by Safvet Beg Bašagić. Books and articles by Bašagić are conveniently listed by Hamdija Kreševljaković, in *Narodna Starina*, XXXIII (1937), 89–91.

On the Hercegovinian Moslems there is a short article by Alija Nametak, in *Nova Evropa*, Vol. XXIX, Nos. 7–8 (1936), pp. 254–258. An especially interesting article on the Moslems of Bosnia and Hercegovina is that of M. D. Popović, "Balkanski narodi Muhamedanske vere," *ibid.*, Vol. VII, No. 15 (1923), pp. 447–452. Also valuable are:

Begović, Mehmed. "Muslimani u Bosni i Hercegovini," in *Biblioteka Politika i Društvo*, XIX (1938), 31–32.

A valuable booklet on the social, economic, and political position of the Moslems.

Ćorović, Vladimir. "Muslimani Bosne i Hercegovine," in *Narodna Enciklopedija*, I, 619.

Krcsmárik, János. "Bosnia and Herzegovina," in *Encyclopaedia of Islam*, II, 754–765.

Kulenović, Hakija Š. "Nacionalna svest dinarskih Muslimana," in *Srpski Književni Glasnik*, October–November, 1940, pp. 197 ff.

Kuzmany, N. "Notes on Moslems of Bosnia," in *Moslem World*, XV (1925), 177–181.

Ljubinčić, S. "Muslimani," in *Nova Evropa*, Vol. III, No. 15 (1923), pp. 443–447.

*Nova Evropa*, Vol. VII, No. 15 (1923).

The entire issue of this excellent periodical is devoted to the Yugoslav Moslems, discussing virtually all aspects of Moslem social, economic, and political life.

Radovanović, Mihailo S. "Muslimani Bosne i Hercegovine," in *Srpski Književni Glasnik*, September–October, 1940; "Evolucija etničkih odnosa u Bosni i Hercegovini," *ibid.*, October–November, 1940.

Rebac, Hasan M. "Srbi Muslimanske vere u Bosni i Hercegovini," in *Letopis Matice Srpske*, CCCVI (1925), 110–114.

Vukićević, Milenko M. *Znameniti Srbi Muslimani* (Belgrade, 1906).

A brief account of five notable Moslems.

Much information can be found in the various publications of the Srpski Etnografski Zbornik. These are usually general studies of the Yugoslav inhabitants, but they are interspersed with information on the Moslems.

On the Sporazum and the Moslems see Šukrija Kurtović's article in *Narodna Odbrana*, Vol. XV, No. 5 (1940), pp. 70–72. On the subject of Moslem isolation see Ahmed Muradbegović, in *Nova Evropa*, Vol. III, No. 4 (1921), pp. 111–112. On the art of the Yugoslav Moslems see Hasan M. Rebac, "Umetnička poezija Srba Muslimana u 17, 18 i 19 veku," in *Narodna Odbrana*, Vol. IV, No. 8 (1929), pp. 140–141. On the *sevdalinke* see Ahmed Muradbegović, in *Politika*, December 3, 1940. On Moslem music see Vladimir R. Djordjević, "Turski elementi u našoj muzici," in *Nova Evropa*, Vol. VII, No. 15 (1923), pp. 469–470. On Moslem women see B. Bujić, "Pitanje Muslimanske žene," *ibid.*, pp. 465–469. Also valuable are: *Gazi Husrevbegova spomenica o četiristogodišnjici njegove džamije u Sarajevu, 1530–1930* (Sarajevo, 1932), a collection of some thirty articles written by specialists in the field. The reviewer of the book, in *Narodna Starina*, XXXI (1935), 142–143, gives excellent bibliography on Gazi Husrev Beg. See also Vladimir Ćorović, *Istorija Bosne* (Belgrade, 1940).

Besides the ordinary Yugoslav newspapers and periodicals, the student of Moslem history will find valuable information in Moslem publications such as *Behar* (Sarajevo, 1900), *Biser* (Mostar, begun after the First World War), *Gajret*, and *Muslimanska Biblioteka*. More serious students can find further useful data in various archives, mosques, and libraries (*kjutubhanas*) in Yugoslavia. Yugoslav Orientalists are steadily unearthing new information on Yugoslav Moslems.

## CHAPTER XVI

### THE SERBO-CROATIAN LANGUAGE

In English the best grammar and the best dictionary of Serbo-Croatian are the following: Dragutin Subotić and Nevill Forbes, *Serbian Grammar* (Oxford, Eng., 1918); F. A. Bogadek, *New English-Croatian and Croatian-English Dictionary* (published by the author, 434 Diamond St., Pittsburgh, Pa., 1926; 2d enl. ed., New York, 1944), 2 vols. in 1.

R. H. Ružić, *The Aspects of the Verb in Serbo-Croatian*, Univ. Calif. Publ. Mod. Philol., Vol. 25, No. 2 (Berkeley and Los Angeles, 1943), presents the most characteristic and interesting features of Slavic grammar in the form that it assumes in Serbo-Croatian, and lists the most important Serbo-Croatian grammars and dictionaries.

Most of the literature on the Serbo-Croatian language, however, is either in Serbo-Croatian or in German. A. Leskien, *Grammatik der serbo-kroatischen Sprache*, 1. Teil: *Lautlehre, Stammbildung, Formenlehre* (Heidelberg, 1914), is of fundamental importance and gives ample bibliographic references to the earlier literature of the subject. Unfortunately, the author, a great master of Slavic linguistics, did not live to complete his work by a syntax.

The two excellent small grammars named below are identical, except that one presents the forms of the Ekavština, in the Cyrillic alphabet, and the other those of the Jekavština, in the Latin alphabet: Milan Rešetar, *Elementar-Grammatik der serbischen (kroatischen) Sprache* (2d ed., Zagreb, 1922), and *Elementar-Grammatik der kroatischen (serbischen) Sprache* (Zagreb, 1916).

The following brief grammar is entirely in the Latin alphabet: John D. Prince, *Practical Grammar of the Serbo-Croatian Language* (Belgrade, 1929; New York, 1943), pp. xvi+219.

## CHAPTER XVII

### The Literature of the South Slavs

Six topics have been mentioned in this chapter. No book in English gives an adequate account of any one of them. The book by Murko listed below gives such an account of one of them. There are no comprehensive treatments of the literature of Dubrovnik or of modern Serbian, Croatian, or Slovenian literature outside the Slavic languages; of the Serbo-Croatian oral folk literature there is no such treatment in any language.

Dozon, Auguste. *L'Epopée serbe* (Paris, 1888), lxxx+335 pp. Translations with introduction.

Low, D. H. *The Ballads of Marko Kraljević* (Cambridge, Eng., 1922), xxxix+196 pp. Translations with introduction.

Morison, W. A. *The Revolt of the Serbs against the Turks (1804–1813)*, (Cambridge, Eng., 1942). Translations from the Serbian national ballads of the period with an introduction.

Murko, Matthias. *Geschichte der älteren südslawischen Litteraturen* (Leipzig, 1908), x+248 pp.; "Die südslawischen Litteraturen," in *Die Kultur der Gegenwart*, Teil I, Abt. IX (Berlin and Leipzig, 1908), pp. 194–245.

Noyes, G. R., and L. Bacon. *Heroic Ballads of Servia* (Boston, 1913), vii+275 pp. Translations with brief introduction.

Savkovitch, Miloch (Savković, Miloš). *L'Influence du réalisme français dans le roman serbocroate* (Paris, 1935), 491 pp.

Subotić, Dragutin. *Yugoslav Popular Ballads: Their Origin and Development* (Cambridge, Eng., 1935), xvi+288 pp.

Torbarina, Josip. *Italian Influence on the Poets of the Ragusan Republic* (London, 1931), 243 pp.

Vidmar, Josip. "A Survey of Modern Slovene Literature," in *Slavonic (and East European) Review* (London), VI (1927–1928), 618–634.

Wendel, Hermann. *Aus dem südslawischen Risorgimento* (Gotha, 1921), 199 pp.; *Der Kampf der Südslawen um Freiheit und Einheit* (Frankfort on the Main, 1925), 798 pp.; *Südslawische Silhouetten* (Frankfort on the Main, 1924), 219 pp.

## CHAPTER XVIII

### Yugoslavia, the Little Entente, and the Balkan Pact

See the notes to chapter xviii, pp. 523–525.

## CHAPTER XIX

### Foreign Policy in the Second World War (1939–1946)

See the notes to chapter xix, pp. 525–526. For references on Josip Broz Tito, Draža Mihailović, and the Četniks, see the bibliography for chapter xx.

## CHAPTER XX

### The Second World War and Beyond

The full story of Yugoslavia in the Second World War will not be written until the documents of the British Foreign Office, especially those dealing with Churchill's negotiations with Josip Broz Tito and Draža Mihailović, and the exchange of communications between the Yugoslav and Soviet governments, are published. A large amount of secondary material, however, is available. It includes newspaper and magazine articles, radio bulletins of Mihailović's Četnik organization and the National Liberation Movement, as well as the diaries of Partisan, quisling, and enemy officers and men.

The most useful for this chapter were the following sources: *Ravna Gora*, the organ of the Četnik movement, published in Yugoslavia during the war, 1943–1944; *Borba*, the organ of the Yugoslav Communist party, in existence since 1925, at present published in Belgrade; leaflets and propaganda publications of the Četnik and Partisan movements; publications and daily press digests of the Yugoslav Information Center, New York, 1941–1943; "Free Yugoslavia" radio broadcasts; *Nova Jugoslavija*, a periodical dealing with political and social questions, published by the Partisans in 1944 under enemy occupation; other current and wartime Yugoslav newspapers and periodicals, which, besides daily reporting, have been publishing diaries of the Partisan leaders: e.g., *Politika, Slovenski Poročevalec, Glas,* and *20 Oktobar*. The most useful single source of information is Vladimir Dedijer's *Dnevnik* (Diary), published in Belgrade, of which two of the scheduled three volumes appeared in 1945 and 1946, respectively. Also helpful is Vladimir Nazor, *S Partizanima, 1943–1944* (Belgrade, 1945).

References in English include:

Adamic, Louis (ed.). *Marshal Tito and His Gallant Bands* (New York, 1944); *Liberation* (New York, 1945).

Brown, Alec. *Mihailovitch and Yugoslav Resistance* (London, 1943).

Christowe, Stoyan. "The Balkans Join Up," in *Atlantic Monthly*, July, 1945, pp. 66–70.

Dacie, Anne. *Yugoslav Refugees in Italy* (London, 1945).

Fast, Howard. *The Incredible Tito* (New York, 1944).

Fotić, Constantine. "In Defense of Mihailovich: Reply to R. L. Wolff with Rejoinder," in *Atlantic Monthly*, December, 1946.

Hogg, R. D. *Yugoslavia* (London, 1944).

Huot, Louis. *Guns for Tito* (New York, 1945).

Lehrman, H. A. *Russia's Europe* (New York, 1947).

Markham, R. H. *Tito's Imperial Communism* (Chapel Hill, N.C., 1947).

Martin, David. *Ally Betrayed: The Uncensored Story of Tito and Mihailovich* (New York, 1946).

Melville, Cecil F. *Balkan Racket* (London, 1941).

Mirković, Nicholas. "Jugoslavia's Choice," in *Foreign Affairs*, October, 1941.

Mitchell, Ruth. *Ruth Mitchell, Chetnik, Tells the Facts about the Fighting Serbs, Mihailovich and "Yugoslavia"* (Serbian National Defense Council, Arlington, Va., 1943); *The Serbs Choose War* (New York, 1943).

*A Nation's Fight for Survival: The 1941 Revolution and War in Yugoslavia as Reported by the American Press.*

Padev, Michael. *Escape from the Balkans* (New York, 1943); *Marshal Tito* (London, 1944).

Pavlowitch, K. St. *The Struggle of the Serbs* (London, 1943).

Petrović, S. S. *Free Yugoslavia Calling* (New York, 1941).

Raditsa, Bogdan. "The Plot against Yugoslavia," in *The Nation*, January 29, 1944; "The Fate of the 'Henry Wallace' [Dragoljub Jovanović] of Yugoslavia," in *The New Leader*, June 28, 1947.

Rootham, Jasper. *Miss Fire: The Chronicle of a British Mission to Mihailovich, 1943–1944* (London, 1946).

St. John, Robert. *The Silent People Speak* (New York, 1948).

Sava, George. *The Chetniks* (London, 1942).

Serbian Eastern Orthodox Diocese for the U.S.A. and Canada. *Martyrdom of the Serbs* (Chicago, 1943).

Sudjić, Milovoj J. *Yugoslavia in Arms* (London, 1942).

Tchok (Čok), Ivan M. *First to Resist: Story of the First Underground Movement* (New York, 1945).

*Today & Tomorrow*, 1945–.

*The Trial of Dragoljub-Draža Mihailović* (Belgrade, 1946), 552 pp. Stenographic record and documents from the trial.

Trivanovitch, Vaso. *The Case of Drazha Mikhailovich* (United Committee of South-Slavic Americans, New York).

Union of Slovenian Parishes of America. *Shall Slovenia Be Sovietized? A Rebuttal to Louis Adamic* (Cleveland), 72 pp.

United Committee of South-Slavic Americans. *Bulletin* (New York, 1943–); *Yugoslavia's New Constitution*, 15 pp.

Wolff, Robert Lee. "Mihailovich: A Post-mortem," in *Atlantic Monthly*, October, 1946.

Wolff, Robert Lee, and David Martin. "Was Mihailovich a Collaborator?" (letters pro and con), in *The New Leader*, July 12, 1947.

Yugoslav Embassy Information Office. *Treason of Mihailovitch* (London, 1945).

## CHAPTER XXI

### POSTWAR FOREIGN ECONOMIC RELATIONS

See the notes to chapter xxi, pp. 527–528.

## CHAPTER XXII

### EPILOGUE

In addition to the bibliography indicated in chapter vi, "Yugoslavia and the Peace Conference," the following are among the materials which were available at the time of the Peace Conference negotiations in 1946. Most of them were prepared from the Yugoslav side.

#### GENERAL

*La Marche julienne: étude de géographie politique* (Institut Adriatique, Sušak, 1945), 312 pp.

*Ethnographical and Economic Bases of the Julian March* (maps and charts), 28 pp.

*Documents sur la dénationalisation des Yougoslaves de la Marche julienne* (Belgrade, 1946), 156 pp.

*Memorandum of the Government of the Democratic Federative Yugoslavia Concerning the Question of the Julian March and Other Yugoslav Territories under Italy*, 22 pages+maps.

*Memorandum of the Government of the Federative Peoples Republic of Yugoslavia Concerning the Ethnical Structure of the Julian March*, 6 pp.

*Memorandum of the Regional National Liberation Committee for the Slovene Littoral and Trieste*, 22 pp.

*Report on Italian Crimes against Yugoslavia and Its Peoples* (State Commission for Investigation of War Crimes, Belgrade, 1946), 196 pp.

Salvemini, Gaetano. *The Frontiers of Italy* (reprinted from *Foreign Affairs*, October, 1944), 11 pp. (From a liberal Italian professor.)

#### ON TRIESTE

*L'attività svolta dal Consiglio di Liberazione della città di Trieste* (Trieste, 1945), 102 pp.

Čermelj, Lavo. *The Census in Trieste in 1910* (Yugoslav Institute for International Affairs, Belgrade, 1946), 28 pp.

Melik, Anton. *The Development of the Yugoslav Railways and Their Gravitation toward Trieste* (Belgrade, 1945), 12 pp.

Taylor, A. J. P. *Trieste* (United Committee of South-Slavic Americans, New York), 30 pp.

Vivante, Angelo. *Adriatic Irredentism* (Ljubljana, 1945), 15 pp.

### ON THE SLOVENES

Avšić, Jaka, and Fran Zwitter. *Our First March into the Venetian Slovenia* (Ljubljana, 1946), 24 pp.

Čermelj, Lavo. *Life-and-Death Struggle of a National Minority* (trans. by F. S. Copeland; 2d ed., Ljubljana, 1945), 220 pp.; *La Minorité slave en Italie: Les Slovènes et Croates de la Marche julienne* (2d ed., Ljubljana, 1946), 294 pp.

Grafenauer, Bogo. *The National Development of the Carinthian Slovenes* (Ljubljana, 1946).

Melik, Anton. *Gorica: The Geographical Basis of Its Foundation* (Ljubljana, 1946), 22 pp.

### POSTWAR

Favorable views on postwar Yugoslavia are expressed in the following:

Adamic, Louis (ed.). *Yugoslavia and Italy.* By J. M. Tito, Josip Smodlaka, and Fran Barbalich (United Committee of South-Slavic Americans, New York, 1944), 31 pp.

Ranković, Alexander. *Address* (Embassy of the Federal Peoples Republic of Yugoslavia, Washington, D.C., June, 1946), 16 pp.

Kardelj, Edvard. *Put nove Jugoslavije 1941–1945* (Belgrade, 1946), 568 pp.

Klugman, James; Betty Wallace; Doreen Warriner; and K. Zilliacus. *Yugoslavia Faces the Future* (British-Yugoslav Association, London, 1947), 30 pp.

Warriner, Doreen. "Jugoslavia Rebuilds," *Fabian Research Series* No. 117 (London, 1947).

Pisma CK KPJ i Pisma CK SKP (b), (Belgrade, Štamparija "Borba," 1948). The Yugoslav Communist party's answer to a pamphlet circulated in Yugoslavia from the Soviet side regarding the exchange of letters between the two Communist parties.

An unfavorable view is expressed in:

*The Political Situation in Yugoslavia Today* (Washington, D.C., 1945), 18 pp. (From the point of view of Serbian nationalists.)

# INDEX

# Index

Ackermann, Treaty of, 109

Adams, John Clinton, "Serbia in the First World War," 66–91

Aehrenthal, Alois Lexa, 43–47 *passim*

Agriculture: crops, 13–20 *passim*, 156, 163–164, 165, 167, 173, 174, 175; livestock, 15–20 *passim*, 156, 164, 165, 167, 175, 391–392; forestry, 18–19, 20, 176, 194, 393; area, 19, 161, 163; emphasis on grain production, 19, 162–163, 165; size of holdings, 151–161 *passim*, 223–224, 275, 382, 413, 528; feudalism, 151–153, 220–221; agrarian reform and redistribution of land, 151–158, 224, 274–275, 382, 526; overpopulation, 153, 154, 155, 161, 169, 180, 181, 194, 195, 200, 224, 413–414; processing industries, 155; soil fertility and cultivation, 155, 156, 158–159, 161–162, 180, 415; colonization, 156, 157; coöperatives, 158 ff., 168, 224–225, 528; economic structure and, 165 ff., 169, 202, 205–206; government control, 166, 168, 414; associations, 237; schools, 237–238; peasants permitted to sell, 385; wartime losses, 391–392; U.N.R.R.A. replacements, 403–405; Five-Year Plan, 414–417 *passim;* in Russia, 435

Albania: Serbian invasion, 47; Austro-Hungary demands independence of, 48; Serbian retreat across, in First World War, 81–85; Moslems, 261–262, 263; in Italian Empire, 340, 356; seeks alliances with Tito, 349, 412; slaughter of Serbs, 359; and Russia, 436, 437

Alexander Karageorgević (Karadjordjević), Prince of Serbia, 38, 49, 111

Alexander I Karageorgević: regency, 40, 53, 67; 1916 proclamation, 88; accepts Yugoslav unity, 94; assumes authority, 121, 126; sets aside Vidovdan Constitution, 125, 126; reforms, 126 ff.; Constitution of 1931, 127–129, 130; electoral laws, 129; judiciary, 129–130; Regency Council, 129; death, 130, 328–329; efforts with Vatican, 256; Little Entente, 322; Balkan Pact, 327, 328

Alexander I Obrenović, 41, 87, 115, 517 (n.12, 13)

Anti-Fascist Council for National Liberation (A.V.N.O.J.): endorses federal Yugoslavia, 346; forbids return of Peter, 346, 369; Yalta Conference, 350; first parliament, 366–367; second session, 369; branches, 370; third session, 382

Arsenije III Crnojević, 247, 248, 292

Assembly, National. *See* Skupština

Atlantic Charter. *See* United Nations

Austria-Hungary: and Croatia, 34–35, 38–43 *passim,* 89, 117, 120, 126, 219, 221, 229, 299–300, 310; Habsburg reforms, 36–37; dominates Trieste and Fiume, 37; dualism *vs.* trialism, 38, 39, 40, 43, 55, 119, 121; and Yugoslav unity, 39, 40, 42, 55, 88, 94, 120, 268, 269, 320; *Ausgleich* of 1867, 39, 320; occupation of Bosnia-Hercegovina, 39, 43, 116–117, 118, 248–249, 267, and annexation, 40, 42–51 *passim,* 249, 268, 269; recognizes Peter, 41; commercial treaty of 1893, 41–42; Balkan trade, 41–42, 167, 169–175 *passim;* and Russia, 44–45, 46, 47; and Germany, 45, 63–65; prepares for war with Serbia, 46, 48–49, 60–65; and Albania, 48; declaration

# ACKNOWLEDGMENT

THE GENERAL EDITOR *desires to record his sincere appreciation of the splendid coöperation he has received from the staff of the University of California Press in the editing of the manuscript and the making of this book. In particular he is indebted to Mr. Harold A. Small, the Editor of the Press; to Mr. Amadeo R. Tommasini, Designer and Production Manager; to Miss Genevieve Rogers and Miss Marian B. Harris for editorial assistance; and to Miss Ellen Gordon for accurate typing and secretarial work.*

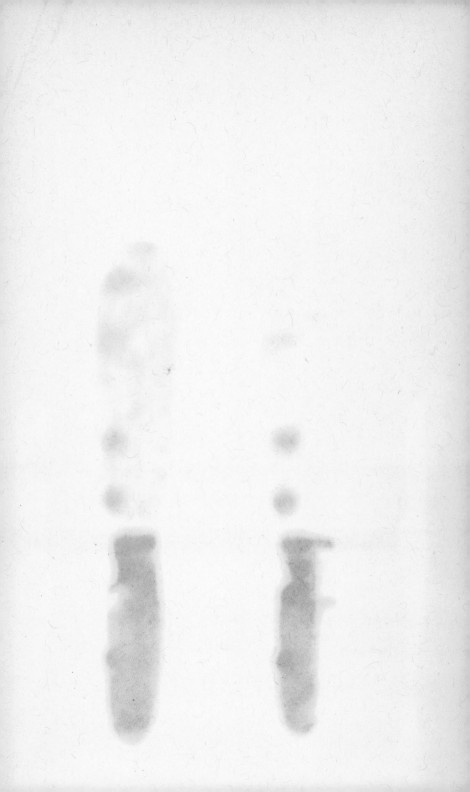

## DATE DUE

| | |
|---|---|
| | |
| | |
| | |
| | |
| | |
| | |
| | |
| | |
| | |
| | |
| | |
| | |
| | |
| | |
| | |

GAYLORD                                       PRINTED IN U.S.A.